J2EE™ AND JAX™:

DEVELOPING WEB

APPLICATIONS AND

WEB SERVICES

ISBN 0-13-047676-5

Hewlett-Packard® Professional Books

HP-UX

Fernandez	Configuring CDE: The Common Desktop Environment
Madell	Disk and File Management Tasks on HP-UX
Olker	Optimizing NFS Performance: Tuning and Troubleshooting NFS on HP-UX Systems
Poniatowski	HP-UX 11i Virtual Partitions
Poniatowski	HP-UX 11i System Administration Handbook and Toolkit
Poniatowski	The HP-UX 11.x System Administration Handbook and Toolkit
Poniatowski	HP-UX 11.x System Administration "How To" Book
Poniatowski	HP-UX 10.x System Administration "How To" Book
Poniatowski	HP-UX System Administration Handbook and Toolkit
Poniatowski	Learning the HP-UX Operating System
Rehman	HP Certified: HP-UX System Administration
Sauers/Weygant	HP-UX Tuning and Performance: Concepts, Tools, and Methods
Weygant	Clusters for High Availability: A Primer of HP-UX Solutions, Second Edition
Wong	HP-UX 11i Security

UNIX, LINUX, WINDOWS, AND MPE I/X

Diercks	MPE i/X System Administration Handbook
Mosberger	IA-64 Linux Kernel
Poniatowski	UNIX User's Handbook, Second Edition
Roberts	UNIX and Windows 2000 Interoperability Guide
Stone/Symons	UNIX Fault Management

COMPUTER ARCHITECTURE

Kane	PA-RISC 2.0 Architecture
Markstein	IA-64 and Elementary Functions

NETWORKING/COMMUNICATIONS

Blommers	Architecting Enterprise Solutions with UNIX Networking
Blommers	OpenView Network Node Manager
Blommers	Practical Planning for Network Growth
Brans	Mobilize Your Enterprise
Cook	Building Enterprise Information Architecture: Reengineering Information Systems
Lucke	Designing and Implementing Computer Workgroups
Lund	Integrating UNIX and PC Network Operating Systems

SECURITY

Bruce	Security in Distributed Computing: Did You Lock the Door?
Pearson et al.	Trusted Computing Platforms: TCPA Technology in Context
Pipkin	Halting the Hacker, Second Edition
Pipkin	Information Security

J2EE AND JAX:

DEVELOPING WEB APPLICATIONS AND WEB SERVICES

Michael Yawn

Hewlett-Packard Company

www.hp.com/hpbooks

Prentice Hall PTR
Upper Saddle River, New Jersey 07458
www.phptr.com

Library of Congress Cataloging-in-Publication Data

Yawn, Mike.
   J2EE and JAX: developing Web applications and Web services / Michael Yawn.
     p. cm.-- (Hewlett-Packard professional books)
   Includes bibliographical references and index.
   ISBN 0-13-047676-5
   1. Java (Computer program language) 2. Web site development. 3. Application
software--Development. I. Title. II. Series.

QA76.73.J38 Y39 2002
005.2'762--dc21

                                    2002029021

Editorial/production supervision: *Vanessa Moore*
Full-service production manager: *Anne R. Garcia*
Cover design director: *Jerry Votta*
Cover design: *Talar Agasyan-Boorujy*
Manufacturing buyer: *Maura Zaldivar*
Executive editor: *Jill Harry*
Editorial assistant: *Kate Wolf*
Marketing manager: *Dan DePasquale*
Manager, Hewlett-Packard retail book publishing: *Patricia Pekary*

© 2003 by Hewlett-Packard Company
Published by Pearson Education, Inc.
Publishing as Prentice Hall PTR
Upper Saddle River, New Jersey 07458

Prentice Hall books are widely used by corporations and government agencies
for training, marketing, and resale.

For information regarding corporate and government
bulk discounts, please contact:
Corporate and Government Sales
Phone: 800-382-3419; E-mail: corpsales@pearsontechgroup.com

Company and product names mentioned herein are the trademarks or registered
trademarks of their respective owners.

Printed in the United States of America
10 9 8 7 6 5 4 3 2 1

ISBN 0-13-047676-5

Pearson Education LTD.
Pearson Education Australia PTY, Limited
Pearson Education Singapore, Pte. Ltd.
Pearson Education North Asia Ltd.
Pearson Education Canada, Ltd.
Pearson Educación de Mexico, S.A. de C.V.
Pearson Education—Japan
Pearson Education Malaysia, Pte. Ltd.

for Debbie

CONTENTS

LIST OF ACRONYMS

ACRONYM	MEANING
API	Application Program Interface
AVK	Application Verification Kit
AWT	Abstract Windowing Toolkit
BMP	Bean-Managed Persistence (for EJB entity beans)
BPSS	Business Process Specification Schema (ebXML component)
CGI	Common Gateway Interface
CMP	Container-Managed Persistence (for EJB entity beans)
CMR	Container-Managed Relationships (for EJB entity beans)
CPA	Collaboration Protocol Agreement (ebXML component)
CPP	Collaboration Protocol Profile (ebXML component)
DOM	Document Object Model
DTD	Document Type Definition
EAI	Enterprise Application Integration
EAR	Enterprise ARchive (for deploying EJBs)
ebXML	Electronic Business XML
ECS	Element Construction Set (Apache software)
EJB	Enterprise JavaBeans
EJB-QL	EJB Query Language
ENC	Environment Naming Context (part of JNDI)

GUI	Graphical User Interface
HTML	Hypertext Markup Language
HTTP	Hypertext Transport Protocol
IDE	Integrated Development Environment
IIOP	Internet Inter-ORB Protocol
ISO	International Organization for Standardization
J2EE	Java 2 Enterprise Edition
J2SE	Java 2 Standard Edition
JAR	Java Archive
JAX	Java API for XML
JAXB	Java API for XML Binding
JAXM	Java API for XML Messaging
JAXP	Java API for XML Processing
JAXR	Java API for XML Registries
JAX-RPC	Java API for XML Remote Procedure Calls
JAX*	Various Java XML APIs
JCP	Java Community Process
JDBC	Java Database Connectivity
JDK	Java Development Kit
JDO	Java Data Objects
JDOM	Java Document Object Model
JFC	Java Foundation Classes
JMS	Java Message Service
JNDI	Java Naming and Directory Interface
JPI	Java Plug-In

JRE	Java Runtime Environment
JSDK	Java Servlet Developer's Kit
JSP	JavaServer Pages
JSPTL	JSP Standard Tag Library (older acronym)
JSTL	JSP Standard Tag Library (see also JSPTL)
JVM	Java Virtual Machine
JWS	Java Web Start
MIME	Multipurpose Internet Mail Extensions
MOM	Message-Oriented Middleware
MSH	Message protocol (ebXML component)
MVC	Model-View-Controller
NFL	National Football League
ORB	Object Request Broker
PKI	Public Key Infrastructure
REGREP	Registry/Repository (ebXML component)
RMI	Remote Method Invocation
RMI/IIOP	Remote Method Invocation over Internet Inter-ORB Protocol
SAML	Security Assertion Markup Language
SAX	Simple API for XML Processing
SDK	Software Development Kit
SGML	Standard Generalized Markup Language
SSL	Secure Sockets Layer
SOAP	Simple Object Access Protocol
TLD	Tag Library Descriptor
UDDI	Uniform Description, Discovery, and Integration

URI	Uniform Resource Identifier
URL	Uniform Resource Locator
W3C	World Wide Web Consortium
WAP	Wireless Application Protocol
WAR	Web ARchive
WLS	WebLogic Server
WML	Wireless Markup Language
WSDL	Web Services Definition Language
XHTML	XML-based HTML
XKMS	XML Key Management Specification
XML	eXtensible Markup Language
XPath	XML Path Language
XSL	eXtensible Stylesheet Language
XSL-FO	XSL Formatting Objects
XSLT	XSL Transformations

PREFACE

When JDK 1.0 was released, it comprised eight packages with a total of 212 classes and interfaces. To be a Java programmer during that time was to know something of all of them. Because four of the eight packages dealt with graphical user interfaces, being a server-side Java programmer (if there had been such a thing then) would probably have meant knowing just about any method call you were likely to use right off the top of your head.

Java 1.3 includes 77 packages with over 2,000 classes and interfaces, but this number understates the explosion of Java APIs. This figure only includes Java 2 Standard Edition; we also have Java 2 Enterprise and Micro Editions, each with many additional APIs. No longer is it possible to expect a Java programmer to be able to put a finger right on the appropriate class needed to solve any problem that arises.

A well-stocked Java bookshelf in the JDK 1.0 timeframe might have had four books. Now, you can't really think in terms of a "one size fits all" selection of Java reference material. There are so many specialized APIs, so many acronyms, that scanning the available titles is likely to provide confusion rather than insight. What topics do you really need to know? JSPs, Jini, JAIN, JAX, JXTA, J-Lo, JFC, JWS—that's just a small selection of the Js (and one of them was probably mis-shelved, but can you really be sure?).

Much of the development being done in Java today is the creation of Web applications. Recently, the mix has shifted to include Web Services as well, which are XML-based interfaces that are commonly used for system-to-system communication in areas such as Enterprise Application Integration (EAI) and Electronic Data Interchange (EDI). There are many things that you need to know in order to create Web applications and Web Services, but frequently half the battle is just figuring out what it is you need to know. While it's easy to find a book on XSLT, or UDDI, or JavaServer Pages, it can be quite a bit harder to figure out which are the right technologies to solve your business problem.

In this book, I'll provide a primer on the current J2EE technologies (J2EE 1.3) that are used to develop Java Web applications, and a look at the coming J2EE technologies (J2EE 1.4) that are used to develop Java Web Services. There is a heavy emphasis on code; for any technology you find useful, you should be able to take the provided example programs as a starting point and just add in your application-specific code. The approach taken has been for breadth of coverage, rather than depth. So if you already have a half-dozen J2EE or Web-Service books on your bookshelf, then this won't add much, if anything, to what you already know. If, on the other hand, you're trying to figure out how to get started with Web applications and Web Services, then this book will get you well on your way. When you need more depth in a particular topic, you'll be directed where to go for further study.

Acknowledgments

There were many people involved in helping bring this book together. Pat Pekary of HP Press provided the initial encouragement that convinced me to write up the proposal that led to this book. At Prentice Hall, executive editor Jill Harry guided the project from inception to completion, and suggested changes in focus and content that improved upon my original proposal in several areas. Production Manager Anne Garcia and Production Editor Vanessa Moore took the book from manuscript to final form.

Mark Klein of DIS International provided technical review and feedback for the entire text and tested many of the example programs. Many other individuals provided valuable feedback on portions of the text, including Jon Diercks (chapter reviews), Arun Gupta of Sun's JAX-RPC team (answered many of my questions on the JAXRPC-INTEREST mailing list, and provided example code on which the Dynamic Invocation Interface example is based), Barry Lemrow of HP Consulting (suggestions for servlets, JSPs, and Struts material), Chris Peltz of HP's Application Development Advanced Technology Center (review of Web-Services material), Nick Sellas of HP Support (chapter reviews), Roxanne Stewart of HP's middleware organization (deployment assistance for EJBs using HP-AS and HP RadPak), Ravi Trivedi of the HP UDDI team (review of registry materials), and Erik Vistica of HP's MPE/iX Java lab (review of several chapters and suggestions for improvements in the original application design). Apologies to anyone I may have omitted from the list.

Finally, thanks to my wife Debbie for her support, patience, and keen editorial eye.

PART 1

Foundations

In this part, I'll provide an overview of the entire book, and then begin our study of Web-application technologies by examining the application that will be used in all of the book's examples. The application will first be introduced in Chapter 2, but then reworked in Chapter 3 wo we can swap out application components as needed to illustrate various technologies throughout the remainder of the book.

## CHAPTER 1

Introduction

I've been watching the evolution of Java technology since the very early JDK 1.0 releases. At that point, much of the excitement about Java had to do with the applet technology, and Java was seen as a serious threat to Microsoft for the desktop. Since then, many other "perfect matches" for Java technology have emerged; many have just as quickly left the scene. But while Java no longer seems likely to displace Microsoft, it has increasingly become the technology of choice for developing server-side applications. The recent emergence of Web-Service technologies has only served to put Java in even better shape on the server side, as a majority of IT managers have indicated they see Java 2 Enterprise Edition (J2EE) technologies as more ready to develop and deploy with than .NET.

Web Services will definitely play a major role in creating future applications; but I believe that role is still secondary to fundamental technologies such as Java servlets that can support both traditional, browser-oriented interfaces as well as newer, XML- and SOAP-based Web Services. For that reason, this book spends a lot of time exploring the foundation technologies that are vital to supporting Web Services, but that are themselves separate from the Web Service.

Web-Service technologies are still immature. Much of the software used to develop the example applications in this book was prerelease, early access, or otherwise not production quality. In many cases, the specifications themselves are still evolving, so the software will change to reflect the final specification. For this reason, anyone starting a Web-Service project today should be budgeting time for rework down the road. In the early chapters of this book, much emphasis is placed on layering software and making good use of object-oriented principles; this will help isolate those portions of your application that will need to be changed to reflect any updates to the underlying technologies.

1.1   Why This Book Was Written

This book came about not because of any burning desire to teach other people J2EE and Web Services, but rather because of a desire to learn more about these topics myself. To learn the new technologies, I did a lot of reading; but the most important activity was creating the sample programs. The same will be true for you; by reading through the text and examples presented herein, you'll be able to get a feel for the technologies that make up J2EE. My goal for each technology covered is to help you understand when it could be used, what the alternative technologies might be, and how to decide which technology is the best fit for the task you're faced with. This level of understanding can be achieved through reading. But once you've decided that a particular technology is something you will use, reading itself will not be sufficient; you'll need to roll up your sleeves and do some programming. I provide exercises in each chapter that can certainly help get you started, but it will be even more important to create your own programs that deal with the kinds of problems you need to solve.

My goals in writing this book are the following:

- Introduce J2EE technologies, explaining each one well enough so that you can determine which ones deserve further study, and which ones aren't a good fit for the job you are trying to do.
- Explain Web Services and show how J2EE technologies can be used to implement them. I believe that Web Services are rarely standalone, but are instead part of larger Web applications. So technologies that are commonly used in Web Services receive extra emphasis, but other Web-application technologies are covered as well, even if they are not directly involved in the delivery of Web Services.
- Provide sample programs for each technology that can be used as a template for how to use the targeted technology.
- Provide only the level of technical detail needed to grasp the capabilities and limitations of each technology. Don't try to examine every single feature or obscure usage. Apply the 80-20 rule.
- Provide exercises that help cement an understanding of each technology.
- Provide references for further study, both printed and online, for those readers who need to gain a more detailed understanding of specific technologies.
- Have fun. Make the examples interesting, and try to avoid dry, boring text.

1.2   Who Needs This Book?

You do. In fact, you probably need several copies; one for home, one for work, maybe one for the car. They make great gifts as well. Tell the guy behind the counter that there aren't nearly enough copies of this book on display, and that they should be up front instead of that Tom Clancy book.

This book won't teach you Java programming (although it provides lots of opinions about good programming practice), so it's intended for readers who already know at least a little about programming in general and Java in particular. It covers many topics, but not in great depth; so if you're looking for the definitive book on servlets, XML, Enterprise JavaBeans (EJB), or any other topic plucked from the table of contents, look for a book focusing on just that topic. This book is more of a sampler. Each of the technologies that make up Java 2 Enterprise Edition are covered in this book, so it can certainly be used as an introduction to J2EE technology. It also introduces the main concepts and technologies used in Web Services. If you're new to both Web Services and J2EE, then everything in the book should interest you. If you know one but not the other, then you'll want to pick and choose particular topics of interest.

Once I help you understand the set of technologies that you need to know, my goal is to provide enough information so that you can be productive with that technology using just the information presented here. If you need more than the basics, I'll try to point you in the direction of more detailed material on the Web and in other books.

1.3   What's This Book About?

There are several complementary things going on in this book. On the one hand, it's an introduction to J2EE technologies, and can serve as a primer for anyone interested in learning about J2EE. The book emphasizes Web Services, so if you are already somewhat familiar with J2EE, but looking to dig more deeply into those technologies that can be used in the development of Web Services, then you should find more information about those topics here than in J2EE books with a different focus. Finally, it's a book about application architecture and design. I'm a strong believer that good software evolves; in fact, Web Services are a perfect example of this. Many companies today are faced with adding Web-Service functionality to existing applications. The degree to which they'll be able to do so easily is directly related to how much flexibility was designed into their applications initially. By using the same application over and over again within this book, deploying it as a standalone application, a servlet, a Web Service, and in other configurations, you'll see how an application can be designed to handle whatever future changes might be required.

Throughout the course of the book, I'll take a simple set of Java classes and evolve them into a number of different architectures. The purpose is twofold. Primarily, you want to gain an understanding about the various architectures that are available. This includes how difficult they are to implement, how well they perform, how well application development tools support the architecture, and similar factors. The secondary goal is to learn what features vary widely between architectures, and what things stay largely the same. By understanding this, we can segregate the architecture-dependent portions of an application so that if we choose, we can change the application architecture at some time in the future in a straightforward manner.

When I speak of changing application architecture, it doesn't mean changing the functionality provided by the application; instead, it means changing the environment in which the application runs. Architectural changes might be changes in the user interface technology used, changes in the way data is stored by the application, or changes in the way the application is distributed across multiple computers and how those distributed components are tied together.

In this book, the initial application will go through lots of changes along the way. Some of those changes will be permanent, as we discover better ways to structure the application to make it more flexible in adapting to different environments. Other changes might be specific to just one architectural model, and not carried forward into later versions; but that doesn't necessarily mean that they represent a dead end.

1.4   Why J2EE and Not Java?

Originally, I set out to cover all possible Java technologies with an emphasis on application architecture and design—which would include JavaBeans, JFC, and Applets, for example, along with the topics presented here such as servlets and Enterprise JavaBeans. The topic was simply too broad, and I could not possibly do justice to the "interesting" architectures simply because of the number of permutations that were to be covered.

Once it became clear that a narrower focus was needed, the Java 2 Enterprise Edition set of technologies became the obvious area on which to focus. The topic was then further refined to include an emphasis on J2EE Web Services. Since the intended audience for this book is programmers who have at least a little prior Java experience, chances are you already have some familiarity with Java 2 Standard Edition (J2SE) features such as JavaBeans and Applets—probably to about the same level that I could have covered in a single chapter. So I decided not to cover those items explicitly. But because some example code had already been developed, you'll probably find some details about these J2SE technologies tucked away in various places.

Java 2 Enterprise Edition is interesting because that's where the action is. While the core Java APIs are relatively (an important qualification) stable, the J2EE APIs are still evolving at a rapid pace, and there is a much greater need for instructional material.

1.5   Architectural Principles

If at every turn we make just the changes required by the architecture at hand, we'll end up reworking the same areas of code repeatedly. To minimize rework and improve the chances of code reuse, it helps to have some guiding principles as we go. As with all object-oriented programming, one important principle to apply is to separate things that change from things that stay the same. We'll also try to introduce some "layering" of the code, and separate out code that deals with areas such as data access, business logic, presentation, and remote access. While this isn't a book on patterns, we'll apply them where appropriate and mention them wherever they're used.

Another guiding principle is the idea of "refactoring"—that is, the idea of making very small incremental changes to code, not for purposes of adding new functionality or fixing errors but merely to improve the design or readability of the code. Not all of the refactoring that took place in the sample application is visible in the finished code, because in most cases you're just looking at the finished product. However, many times there is code that changes just slightly from one version to the next; in some of those cases I'm taking advantage of an opportunity to refactor something in the code along with other changes I may be making. I'll try to point out these refactorings as they happen; I've found looking for such opportunities really improves the quality of the code I produce and I'd like to try to infect you with the habit.

1.6 Organization

Here's what you'll find in this book, chapter by chapter.

1.6.1 Part I: Foundations

- *Chapter 1: Introduction.* The usual introductory fluff. Contains the sentence you are now reading, plus those that immediately precede and follow it.
- *Chapter 2: The Example Application.* Introduces the application that will be used throughout the book. The actual code listings for the application are in the Appendix, to avoid making the chapter too dense. Includes coverage of object design, JavaBeans, and the Strategy and Singleton design patterns.
- *Chapter 3: The Layered Application.* Reworks the example application to make it more suitable for evolving into the various architectural models to be covered. Separates interface from implementation. Creates an Application Layer, a Presentation Layer, and a Persistence Layer within the application. Introduces Model-View-Controller architecture. Covers the Factory pattern and an idiom for handling enumerated types.

1.6.2 Part II: Web Applications

- *Chapter 4: Introduction to Presentation Architecture.* Covers the basic types of presentation typically used: textual interfaces, graphical interfaces, Web-browser interfaces, and Web Services. Provides a brief introduction to HTML, HTTP, and XML as background for the chapters that follow.
- *Chapter 5: Servlets.* Several example servlets are created. Basic servlet APIs are introduced. The example application is altered to behave more dynamically, allowing concurrent access by multiple users. New capabilities are added to the example application. Advanced servlet topics are briefly discussed.
- *Chapter 6: JavaServer Pages.* JSPs are explored as a replacement for servlets. Various methods of embedding Java code in a Web page are examined, including scriptlets, expressions, and declarations. The ugliest ways of writing JSP code are demonstrated for your amusement.
- *Chapter 7: Integrating JavaServer Pages with JavaBeans and Servlets.* Sanity is restored as large chunks of Java code are excised from JSPs and placed in more suitable locations, including JavaBeans and servlets. Making JSPs work well with other code is the focus. Custom Tag Libraries are covered, including the Standard Tag Library and an application-specific tag library that we'll create.
- *Chapter 8: Struts.* The Struts framework is part of the Jakarta project from the Apache Group. The Struts framework is introduced and used to create an example showing servlets, JavaBeans, JSPs, and custom tag libraries all used in a single application. This is the culmination of the discussion of servlets and JavaServer Pages.
- *Chapter 9: Web Presentation via XML and XSLT.* This is the first of several chapters to cover XML topics. The Document Object Model (DOM) and JDOM are used to create

an XML document on the fly. Extensible Stylesheet Language for Transformation (XSLT) is used to convert the XML document to HTML format. The JAXP API is covered. The Apache Xalan and Xerces XML packages are used to parse and transform XML documents.

- *Chapter 10: Using XML with Wireless Clients*. Introduces WML and XHTML, the XML-based languages used for marking up content for wireless devices. Shows how a servlet could detect the client device type and send the appropriately formatted content.

1.6.3   Part III: Distributed Objects and Web Services

- *Chapter 11: Introduction to Distributed Objects and Web Services*. An introduction to technologies used for distributed object applications (RMI and JMS) and Web Services (JAXM and JAX-RPC). Discusses the various models typically used to build distributed applications. Introduces the topic of Web Service security.

- *Chapter 12: The Java Message Service*. Introduces the concept of Message-Oriented Middleware (MOM), and specifically the Java Message Service (JMS). Features of JMS are described along with several deployment scenarios. A new service is created, which sends messages to our example application triggering data updates. The Java Naming and Directory Interface (JNDI) is also introduced, since it is the mechanism by which clients of the JMS locate the JMS server.

- *Chapter 13: XML Messaging: SOAP and JAXM*. The discussion of MOM continues with a look at the SOAP standard for XML-encoded messages. A Java implementation of SOAP, the Java API for XML Messaging (JAXM), is introduced. The JMS examples from the previous chapter are reworked to use SOAP messages via JAXM. These examples provide the best prototype yet of a true Web Service.

- *Chapter 14: Parsing and Manipulating XML*. With a true Web Service now serving XML content, focus turns to XML parsing. Parsing XML messages such as a Web Service returns is demonstrated using DOM, SAX, and JDOM. The new Java API for XML Binding (JAXB), which provides conversion capabilities between XML documents and Java classes, is shown.

- *Chapter 15: Remote Method Invocation (RMI)*. The use of Java RMI to build distributed object applications is demonstrated. New server and client classes are created to work in the remote environment. The ObjectFactory paradigm is extended for creating non-local objects.

- *Chapter 16: Building a Web Service with JAX-RPC*. Just as JMS was followed by XML-based messaging, RMI is followed by XML-based procedure calls. The Java API for XML Remote Procedure Calls (JAX-RPC) is introduced. SOAP-based RPC is shown as an alternative to Java RMI, and the example programs from the previous chapter are adapted accordingly.

- *Chapter 17: Describing, Publishing, and Finding Web Services*. An introduction to Web-Service registries. The Web Services Description Language (WSDL) is introduced and examples based on our Web Service are shown. The functions of registries and repositories are covered, and then UDDI and ebXML are shown as specific examples. Utility software for dealing with WSDL and registries is demonstrated, including HP Service Composer, HP Registry Composer, and BEA's UDDI Explorer.

- *Chapter 18: Clients for JAX-RPC Web Services.* Illustrates the three primary types of clients for JAX-RPC–based Web Services: static clients that access the service via stubs, clients that access the service via dynamic proxies, and clients that use the Dynamic Invocation Interface.

1.6.4 Part IV: Enterprise JavaBeans

- *Chapter 19: Session Beans.* An introduction to Enterprise JavaBeans. The various interfaces supported by EJBs are introduced. Stateless and Stateful session beans are introduced. An example is built using a Stateless Session Bean that replaces the servlet-based implementations used in previous examples. Various options for building and deploying EJBs are covered, including EJB-JAR files and Enterprise ARchive (EAR) files.
- *Chapter 20: Message-Driven Beans.* The new (in EJB 2.0) Message-Driven Bean capability is introduced. An example bean is developed to consume JMS messages from the example server developed in Chapter 12. Using references in the deployment descriptor to assemble an application from multiple beans is demonstrated.
- *Chapter 21: Entity Beans.* Entity Beans are examined as a way of providing persistence for application data. Bean-Managed and Container-Managed Persistence are introduced, and an EJB using Container-Manager Persistence is created. The EJB Query Language (EJB-QL) is used to implement a finder method for the bean.
- *Chapter 22: A Look Back, a Look Ahead.* Includes a brief recap of some of the themes that have emerged through the course of the book. Then, a look at how the standards and APIs are evolving, and what is known and expected for upcoming releases of J2EE and JAX APIs.

1.7 Software Used

Java 2 Standard Edition version 1.3.1 was the basic JDK used to produce all of the example code in this book. On top of this, various portions of J2EE were used. Most of the examples do not require the use of a full-blown application server, so frequently a J2SE SDK and a servlet engine such as Apache Tomcat are all that is needed.

For the J2EE components, J2EE 1.3 was the basis for all examples. Primarily, the servlet 2.3 and JSP 1.2 specifications were used as the foundation for many of the examples in the book. Table 1.1 summarizes the various components included in the J2EE specification for the latest releases.

In the table, I've also included some early information about the forthcoming J2EE 1.4 release. The specification is currently scheduled for final release in the first quarter of 2003;

actual implementations will follow. The specification is not yet in public draft form, and I wasn't able to find any information about some of the components. However, support for Web Services is the major focus of J2EE 1.4, and as it becomes available it will provide the best foundation on which to develop and deploy Web Services. Details about some of the new components are found in various places throughout this book; refer to the index if you just can't wait.

Table 1.1   J2EE Versions and Component Technology Versions

Component	J2EE 1.2 Version	J2EE 1.3 Version	J2EE 1.4 Version
Enterprise JavaBeans	1.1	2.0	2.1
JavaServer Pages	1.1	1.2	1.3
Servlets	2.2	2.3	2.4
JDBC Standard Extension	2.0	2.0	no change?
Java Transaction API	1.0	1.0	no change?
JavaMail	1.1	1.2	no change?
Java Message Service	optional	required	no change?
JAXP	not included	1.1	1.2
J2EE Connector	not included	1.0	1.5
RMI/IIOP	included	Part of J2SE 1.3	Part of J2SE
JNDI	included	Part of J2SE 1.3	Part of J2SE
JAXR	not included	not included	1.0
JAX-RPC	not included	not included	1.0
JAXM	not included	not included	optional
JAXB	not included	not included	1.0?

Examples were tested on various platforms and operating systems, including HP 9000s (HP-UX 11.0 and later operating systems), HP e3000s (MPE/iX 6.0 and later operating systems), HP Vectras (Windows NT 4.0 and Windows 2000), and HP Pavilions (Windows ME).

1.8   Using This Book

In this section, I suggest how, in my opinion, you'll get the most out of this book.

1.8.1   Navigating the Material

I've tried to introduce topics in a logical order, but also to accommodate those readers who will want to skip directly to topics that are of interest. While I'd recommend taking everything in the order presented, you should be able to jump to any chapter, or any major topic within a chapter, and find what you need in that fashion. Within individual topics, you'll find that reading from top to bottom and left to right is absolutely essential for comprehension.

I've tried to make liberal use of tables and boxed material, especially near the beginning of each chapter to call out summary information about the material covered in each chapter.

1.8.2   Exercises

Most chapters have exercises provided at the end of the material. These exercises range from fairly simple to cruelly complicated. The exercises are intended not so much as a review of previous material, but rather as a jumping-off point to explore the material further. In many cases, you'll find that if you attempt the exercises, the material provided in the chapter won't be sufficient. The Further Reading links that are provided conveniently nearby should provide any additional information you need for completing the exercises.

1.8.3   Design Centers

One of the occasional features that will pop up in various chapters is a boxed item called a Design Center. In the Design Centers, I try to summarize the decision criteria that come into play in deciding between two or more technologies that are somewhat similar, where it might be unclear which one is better-suited for a particular task. Some of the Design Centers you'll find include when to use XML Attributes versus XML Elements; when to use DOM, SAX, and JDOM to parse XML documents; and choosing between SOAP Messaging and SOAP RPC models for designing Web Services.

1.8.4   API Reference Material

This book is intended to be instructional in nature. Many of the topics covered here in a single chapter could easily be expanded to full book length. Because of the amount of material covered, it's impossible to provide exhaustive reference material for every API and product that is touched upon.

I've tried to strike an appropriate balance between instructional content and reference material. For the most part, I favored the instructional material, but I also tried to pay close attention to how I do development work. If you're going to always be sitting in front of your computer, then it is simple enough to just open a window to the javadoc API guide for whatever packages you're using. But since I tend to write a lot of code sitting at the kitchen table or

sprawled on the family room floor, I like to have at least enough reference documentation close
at hand to let me scope out the basic flow of each method I develop. I can always dig deeper into
the exact details of an API when I'm actually entering the code back at the computer.

If this isn't your working style, then this is of little interest to you. But if you do something
similar, I've tried to selectively include API documentation for those classes in each package
that you're most likely to need. In servlets, for example, I include full API documentation for the
`HttpServlet`, `HttpServletRequest`, and `HttpServletResponse` classes. I don't include
the various superclasses they extend, or the details of the exception classes, or the stream classes
that they utilize, since these are all pretty much what you'd expect them to be.

I've also placed the API documentation inline in the chapters where they are discussed,
rather than collecting them separately into an appendix. I feel that this is where you're most
likely to want them, and the intent is to optimize the experience you're having as you read the
material sequentially. For coming back later to refer to something, you're either going to be
more likely to grab another book that is more reference-oriented, or be willing to make the extra
stop by the index on the way to your destination.

1.9   On the Web

Errata or clarifications for this book will be posted on the Web at my site, `http://
www.theYawns.com`. There may also be supplemental material or drafts of material for future
publication. If you have feedback, comments, or have found an error, please drop me a note at
`j2eejax-feedback@theYawns.com`.

The Example Application

The example application I've chosen to use throughout this book is a group of classes that are used to compute the standings for teams in the NFL, producing as output listings such as you might find in the sports section of your daily paper. This fairly small set of classes is one of several such "mini-projects" I've undertaken from time to time to give me a chance to explore Java language features while creating something useful or at least entertaining. The package is small enough to be easily understandable, but touches on all the areas we are concerned with when building applications: presentation (user interface), persistence (data storage), and business logic. The package is simple enough to be able to grasp what it does very quickly, but also lends itself to being extended in a number of different ways, which provides us a number of jumping-off points for exploring different technologies without repeating ourselves too frequently.

Depending on your Java programming background, and what you're trying to get out of this book, the material in the following two chapters may or may not be interesting to you. If you want to get right into the APIs and details of how to write Web applications and Web Services, then you should skip right ahead to Chapter 4. In this chapter and the next, I'll introduce the example application and use it to make various points about application design, design patterns, and certain Java idioms that can help improve code quality. If you're already an experienced Java programmer, you may prefer to skip or just quickly browse this material.

The output from the original version of the application is presented in Figure 2.1. It provides two views of the data; one showing division results (the typical format used in newspaper listings), and the other showing conference results (needed only to determine winners of wild-card races and which team will have home-field advantage during playoffs). The output is interrupted occasionally by a "tiebreaker message." When ranking teams, there is a complex set of tiebreakers used to determine the ranking of two teams that have the same win-loss record.

Generally speaking, this information is not presented when team standings are printed, and one
of the features of this particular application is that it always indicates why two or more teams
having identical records are ordered a particular way. These tiebreaker messages are displayed
immediately prior to the output of the division or conference to which the tiebreaker has been
applied.

Figure 2.1   Sample output from the example application.

```
----- AFC East ----
   Team                    W   L   T   PCT   PF   PA   Div   Conf  Streak
   Miami Dolphins          11  5   0   .688  323  226  5-3   9-3   Won 1
   Indianapolis Colts      10  6   0   .625  429  326  5-3   8-4   Won 3
   New York Jets            9  7   0   .562  321  321  6-2   6-6   Lost 3
   Buffalo Bills            8  8   0   .500  315  350  2-6   6-6   Won 1
   New England Patriots     5 11   0   .312  276  338  2-6   5-7   Lost 1

----- AFC Central ----
   Team                    W   L   T   PCT   PF   PA   Div   Conf  Streak
   Tennessee Titans        13  3   0   .812  346  191  8-2   9-3   Won 4
   Baltimore Ravens        12  4   0   .750  333  165  8-2   10-3  Won 7
   Pittsburgh Steelers      9  7   0   .562  321  255  5-5   8-5   Won 2
   Jacksonville Jaguars     7  9   0   .438  367  327  5-5   5-7   Lost 2
   Cincinnati Bengals       4 12   0   .250  185  359  2-8   3-10  Lost 1
   Cleveland Browns         3 13   0   .188  161  419  2-8   3-10  Lost 5

----- AFC West ----
   Team                    W   L   T   PCT   PF   PA   Div   Conf  Streak
   Oakland Raiders         12  4   0   .750  479  299  5-3   8-4   Won 1
   Denver Broncos          11  5   0   .688  485  369  6-2   8-4   Won 1
   Kansas City Chiefs       7  9   0   .438  355  354  5-3   5-7   Lost 1
   Seattle Seahawks         6 10   0   .375  320  405  3-5   4-8   Lost 1
   San Diego Chargers       1 15   0   .062  269  440  1-7   1-11  Lost 4

----- NFC East ----
   Team                    W   L   T   PCT   PF   PA   Div   Conf  Streak
   New York Giants         12  4   0   .750  328  246  7-1   9-3   Won 5
   Philadelphia Eagles     11  5   0   .688  351  245  5-3   8-4   Won 2
   Washington Redskins      8  8   0   .500  281  269  3-5   6-6   Won 1
   Dallas Cowboys           5 11   0   .312  294  361  3-5   4-8   Lost 2
   Arizona Cardinals        3 13   0   .188  210  443  2-6   2-10  Lost 7
```

Packers over Lions based on division record (Tiebreaker 2)
----- NFC Central ----

Team	W	L	T	PCT	PF	PA	Div	Conf	Streak
Minnesota Vikings	11	5	0	.688	397	371	5-3	8-4	Lost 3
Tampa Bay Buccaneers	10	6	0	.625	388	269	4-4	7-5	Lost 1
Green Bay Packers	9	7	0	.562	353	323	5-3	8-4	Won 4
Detroit Lions	9	7	0	.562	307	307	3-5	7-5	Lost 1
Chicago Bears	5	11	0	.312	216	355	3-5	3-9	Won 1

Saints over Rams based on division record (Tiebreaker 2)
----- NFC West ----

Team	W	L	T	PCT	PF	PA	Div	Conf	Streak
New Orleans Saints	10	6	0	.625	354	305	7-1	9-3	Lost 1
St. Louis Rams	10	6	0	.625	540	471	5-3	7-5	Won 1
Carolina Panthers	7	9	0	.438	310	310	4-4	5-7	Lost 1
San Francisco 49ers	6	10	0	.375	388	422	1-7	4-8	Lost 1
Atlanta Falcons	4	12	0	.250	252	413	3-5	3-9	Won 1

Chiefs over Jaguars based on record against common opponents
(Tiebreaker 3)
Steelers over Jets based on head-to-head record (Tiebreaker 1)
Raiders over Ravens because Raiders lead a division
Dolphins over Ravens because Dolphins lead a division

AFC Playoff Seedings

1. Tennessee Titans   Clinched homefield. Clinched AFC Central.
2. Oakland Raiders   Clinched AFC West.
3. Miami Dolphins   Clinched AFC East.
4. Baltimore Ravens   Clinched wildcard.
5. Denver Broncos   Clinched wildcard.
6. Indianapolis Colts   Clinched wildcard.

Cowboys over Bears based on conference record (Tiebreaker 2)
Packers over Lions based on division record (Tiebreaker 2)
Saints over Eagles because Saints lead a division
Buccaneers over Rams based on head-to-head record (Tiebreaker 1)

NFC Playoff Seedings

1. New York Giants   Clinched homefield. Clinched NFC East.
2. Minnesota Vikings   Clinched NFC Central.
3. New Orleans Saints   Clinched NFC West.
4. Philadelphia Eagles   Clinched wildcard.
5. Tampa Bay Buccaneers   Clinched wildcard.
6. St. Louis Rams   Clinched wildcard.

Let's Do the Time Warp Again

When the first examples were created for this book, the 2000 NFL season had just ended. As the book goes to press, it's nearly time for the 2002 season to begin. Although an entire season was played during the development of the examples, I decided to stick with the original data set for consistency throughout all of the example programs.

You are under no such constraints. Included on the CD are data for the 2000 and 2001 seasons, as well as updated Team and Division information to reflect the realignment that will happen for the 2002 season. Here's how you can change out the data to your liking.

Wayback Machine Setting: 2000

This is the way the data is currently set up, so you only need to follow this procedure if you've changed to one of the other data sets and wish to restore the 2000 season data.

- Copy `nfl/persistence/BasicGameDataImpl.2000`
  to `nfl/persistence/BasicGameDataImpl.java`
- Copy `nfl/persistence/BasicTeamDataImpl.2000`
  to `nfl/persistence/BasicTeamDataImpl.java`
  (only necessary if resetting from 2002 data).
- Copy `nfl/application/Division.2000`
  to `nfl/application/Division.java`
  (only necessary if resetting from 2002 data).

Wayback Machine Setting: 2001

Full data for games played during the 2001 season are also on the CD.

- Copy `nfl/persistence/BasicGameDataImpl.2001`
  to `nfl/persistence/BasicGameDataImpl.java`
- Copy `nfl/persistence/BasicTeamDataImpl.2000`
  to `nfl/persistence/BasicTeamDataImpl.java`
  (Team data is the same for 2000 and 2001 seasons. Only necessary if resetting from 2002 data.)
- Copy `nfl/application/Division.2000`
  to `nfl/application/Division.java`
  (Division data is the same for 2000 and 2001 seasons. Only necessary if resetting from 2002 data.)

> **Wayback Machine Setting: 2002**
>
> Game data is not provided, but updated division and team information is.
> - Copy `nfl/persistence/BasicTeamDataImpl.2002`
>   to `nfl/persistence/BasicTeamDataImpl.java`
> - Copy `nfl/application/Division.2002`
>   to `nfl/application/Division.java`
> - Create a new `BasicGameDataImpl.java` file to which 2002 results can be
>   added.

The package was originally designed without any intention of using it for more than personal entertainment, which is probably a blessing. It wasn't thoroughly thought out ahead of time, but instead grew organically during the development process. The less-than-perfect design reflects the reality of any application you're likely to be supporting. We'll find the need for several refactoring exercises along the way to get the code in better order for the types of architectural transformations we intend to make.

In this chapter, we'll look at each of the classes that make up the example application. Full code listings for every class described here can be found in the Appendix. Having the code listings in the chapter proved to be unwieldy; some of them are rather long and it's difficult to find the "good bits" that deserve particular attention. So instead we'll confine ourselves to tables of properties, lists of methods, and just enough code to illustrate particular points of interest.

2.1 Finding the Objects

The first step in the development of any object-oriented program is to identify the objects that will be needed. If you're already an experienced object designer, feel free to skip ahead; for the novices, it's worth spending a little time talking about the set of objects we expect to need for this application.

Look at the output shown in Figure 2.1 and ask yourself what set of objects you think would be required to generate this output. There is no single best answer; if you come up with a different list than the one I chose, chances are you could make a good argument for your choices. I think the most obvious object seen in the output is a `Team` object. All of the columns of information displayed would then be attributes or properties of the `Team` objects, and not objects themselves. There also needs to be an object that represents the entire list and is responsible for the ordering and display of the `Teams`; we'll call this object the `Standings` object.

I've chosen to use `Division` and `Conference` objects to represent the groupings of teams. You could make a very good case that these are merely attributes of the `Team`, and based on the simplicity of the classes we'll develop, I couldn't argue with choosing that design as an alternative.

The next class needed becomes obvious if you look at the various columns of information we display, and ask "Where does this information come from?" It's not our intention to have a user typing in every column of information. Instead, these fields are all calculated based on the results of the games played by each team during the season. So we need a `Game` class that represents the result of each game played.

Our final two classes are collection classes. Since SDK 1.2, Java has provided a very nice set of collection classes, such as `List`, `Map`, and `Stack`. Our collections will be based on the `java.util.List` class. But we'd like to add some application-specific functionality to allow us to subset the data in various ways. So we create a `Games` class to contain all the `Game` objects, and a `Teams` class to contain all the `Team` objects. The need for these classes wasn't obvious to me until coding had started, so extra credit to you if you saw the need for such classes right way. This gives us a total of seven classes, which are summarized in Table 2.1.

Table 2.1   Classes in the `nfl.original` Package

Class Name	Usage
Division	Represents NFL divisions
Conference	Represents NFL conferences
Team	Represents an NFL team; performs calculations
Game	Represents a game
Teams	Collection of all `Team` objects
Games	Collection of all `Game` objects
Standings	Main class; drives calculations and displays results

2.2   The Division and Conference Classes

The `Division` and `Conference` classes are classes that represent enumerated types for the divisions and conferences within the NFL. These classes define numeric constants that will be used to represent the divisions and conferences, and map those constants to the corresponding names. The data is static; although there are occasional changes (such as the realignment occurring in 2002), these changes are infrequent enough that they can be handled by changing the code. (Note that a better way of implementing enumerated types will be shown when we rework these two classes in Chapter 3). Listing 2.1 shows the `Division` class; the `Conference` class is implemented in a very similar way. (Full listings of these and all other classes in this version of the application can be found in the Appendix).

Listing 2.1 The Division Class

```
// Division.java

package nfl.original;

/** This class provides numeric constants for the NFL
  * divisions, and strings for each division name.
  */
public class Division
{
   public static final int AFC_EAST    = 0;
   public static final int AFC_CENTRAL = 1;
   public static final int AFC_WEST    = 2;

   public static final int NFC_EAST    = 3;
   public static final int NFC_CENTRAL = 4;
   public static final int NFC_WEST    = 5;

   /** Return the name associated with a numeric constant.
     */
   public static String getName(int i) {
      if (i == AFC_EAST) return "AFC East";
      else if (i == AFC_CENTRAL) return "AFC Central";
      else if (i == AFC_WEST)    return "AFC West";
      else if (i == NFC_EAST)    return "NFC East";
      else if (i == NFC_CENTRAL) return "NFC Central";
      else if (i == NFC_WEST)    return "NFC West";
      else return "INVALID";
   }
}
```

2.3 The Team Class

The Team class is central to the application. Each team has a small number of invariant attributes, such as the name of the team, its home city, and the Conference and Division to which it belongs. There is then quite a bit of data that is updated throughout the season: games won, lost, and tied; points scored; points allowed; etc. Although our classes aren't fully Java-Beans-compliant (see the following sidebar), we do follow the convention of providing accessor methods to our private data properties. The properties of the Team class are shown in Table 2.2. A full listing of the code is shown in the Appendix.

JavaBeans Coding Style

While we aren't going to spend any time in this book specifically exploring Java-Beans, I've taken some of the design principles of JavaBeans and made them part of my normal Java coding style. Chief among these principles is the idea of using private data attributes (known as properties), with accessor functions to read and write the data value. For example, in the `Team` class, `name` is a property of the class, and `getName()` and `setName()` are the accessor functions.

When using tools such as Integrated Development Environments (IDEs) that support JavaBeans, following this naming convention makes it possible for the tools to immediately see what the properties are of a class, and give the developer a way (typically via a property sheet) to change any that are modifiable (those that provide set methods).

Making data values accessible only through accessor functions helps ensure that encapsulation is not broken. Following the JavaBean naming convention helps improve code readability, since most Java programmers are familiar with this naming style. If we need to convert some of our classes to JavaBeans in the future, the additional changes required are small: Generally, we'll just need to make sure that each class is Serializable and provides a no-argument constructor. The JavaBeans can then be packaged in a JAR file and be ready for use in tools that support JavaBeans.

Table 2.2   Properties of the `Team` Class

Property Name	Type	Get/Set?	Comment
city	String	Y/Y	
conference	int	Y/Y	enumerated type
conferenceLosses	int	Y/N*	
conferenceRecord	int[]	Y/N	wins, losses, ties
conferenceTies	int	Y/N*	
conferenceWins	int	Y/N*	
conferenceWinLossPct	float	Y/N	calculated field
division	int	Y/Y	enumerated type
divisionLosses	int	Y/N*	
divisionRecord	int[]	Y/N	wins, losses, ties
divisionStatus	int	Y/N	enumerated; calculated

Table 2.2 Properties of the `Team` Class (Continued)

Property Name	Type	Get/Set?	Comment
divisionTies	int	Y/N*	
divisionWins	int	Y/N*	
divisionWinLossPct	float	Y/N	calculated field
fullName	String	Y/N	city + name
gamesRemaining	int	Y/N	calculated field
homefieldStatus	int	Y/N	enumerated, calculated
name	String	Y/N	
netOverallPoints	int	Y/N	calculated
netPointsDivisionGames	int	Y/N*	
netPointsConferenceGames	int	Y/N*	
overallRecord	int[]	Y/N	calculated
overallWinLossPct	float	Y/N	calculated
points	int	Y/N	calculated
pointsAllowed	int	Y/N	calculated
streak	int	Y/N	calculated
wins	int	Y/N*	

* While these properties don't provide a "set" method, they do provide an "add" method
used to increment the value.

2.3.1 Methods of the Team Class

Almost of all of the methods in the `Team` class are involved in the calculation of the rankings. These methods are discussed in the sections that follow. That leaves us just two methods to discuss here. The `Team` class has only one constructor, which takes as arguments the team's home city and the name of the team. It also has a `loadGames()` method. This method causes a list of all games played to be obtained from the `Games` class; this list will then be used in the calculations to follow.

Construction and Initialization Methods of the Team Class

```
public Team(String city, String name)
public static void loadGames()
```

2.3.2   Support for Ranking the Teams

The whole purpose of the application is to put the `Team` objects in the sequence shown in Figure 2.1. The `Standings` object is responsible for doing this, but it in turn delegates almost all of the responsibility back to the `Team` objects. The code in the `Standings` class that performs this magic is simply this:

```
Comparator comp = new Team.DivisionComparator();
List divisionList = teams.getDivisionTeams(div);
Collections.sort(divisionList, comp);
```

We use the `sort()` method of the `Collections` class to order a set of teams. The list of teams is obtained from a `Teams` object, which we haven't introduced yet, and the ordering of the teams is done by a class that implements the `Comparator` interface. Let's take a look at how the `Comparator` works.

The Comparator Classes

The `Collections` class (part of the `java.util` package) provides a sort facility. There are two interfaces we could use within our `Team` class to make the team sortable by `Collections`. The `Comparable` interface is the most straightforward. If we implemented `Comparable` in the `Team` class, then we would just need to add a `compare(Object o)` method to the class. This would be invoked by the sorting code to compare the `Team` object to another `Team`. The drawback to `Comparable` is that we can only define a single ordering this way, since there can only be one `compareTo()` method. The `Comparator` interface, on the other hand, can be implemented independently of the class of objects being compared, allowing as many to be created as necessary. We implemented two: a `DivisionComparator` and a `ConferenceComparator` class. They have been made nested classes within the `Team` class, but they just as easily could have been made separate standalone classes. Using a `Comparator` class is more extensible, allowing us to define as many different orderings as we like and then passing the appropriate `Comparator` into the `Collections.sort()` method.

Each `Comparator` class has just a single method, `compare(Object o1, Object o2)`, which returns either a negative, zero, or positive value depending on whether the first object passed is less than, equal to, or greater than the second object.

Our comparator classes make this determination by first checking the win-loss percentage of the two teams. If they are unequal, then the team with the highest percentage is ranked higher, and the result is returned. If the percentages are equal, then the teams are tied, and we have to apply a set of tiebreakers to determine the higher-ranked team. After the application of each tiebreaker, we either return a winner, or continue to the next tiebreaker if the two teams are still tied.

Division Tiebreakers	Conference Tiebreakers
Head-to-head record	Head-to-head record
Division record	Conference record
Conference record	Record against common opponents
Record against common opponents	Net points in conference games
Net points in division games	Net points in all games
Net points in conference games	Strength of schedule
Net points in all games	Net touchdowns
Strength of schedule	Coin toss
Net touchdowns	
Coin toss	

The Strategy Pattern

The `Comparable` and `Comparator` interfaces are examples of the Strategy pattern.[a] They permit various operators (such as sort, min, max, and binarySearch) to be performed on classes that implement the interfaces, without requiring the code that does the ordering to know any of the details about the actual data contained in the classes.

The Strategy pattern allows for a number of different algorithms to be encoded, all exposing the same interface. We could extend this pattern by including other types of teams in our package. For example, an hockey team would implement a `Comparator` that simply ranked teams based on points, while a baseball team would implement a `Comparator` that ranked on win-loss record without any tiebreakers being applied.

Without the Strategy pattern, we would have to write our own sort method for each subclass that used a different algorithm for ordering the teams.

---

a. This and all other design patterns I'll discuss are introduced in the book *Design Patterns* by Gamma et al. See the Bibliography for more details.

Comparison Helper Functions

Because most of the tiebreakers are common to both comparators, it made more sense to implement them outside of the individual comparators so they could be shared. We could have created a common class that was subclassed by both comparators, but instead placed these common methods in the `Team` class.

Comparison Methods of the Team Class

```
private static int compareConferenceRecords(Team t1, Team t2)
private static int compareDivisionRecords(Team t1, Team t2)
private static int compareHeadToHead(Team t1, Team t2)
private static int compareOverallRecords(Team t1, Team t2)
private static int compareNetPointsAllGames(Team t1, Team t2)
private static int compareNetPointsConferenceGames(Team t1, Team t2)
private static int compareNetPointsDivisionGames(Team t1, Team t2)
public static float winLossPct(int[] record)
```

Each one of these methods follows the same basic design: Given two teams, return a negative value if `Team t1` should sort ahead of `Team t2`, return zero if the teams are tied based on this particular comparison, and return a positive value if `Team t2` should sort ahead of `Team t1`. The final method is not actually a comparison itself, but rather a utility function used by several of the other comparison functions to convert a win-loss record to a percentage.

2.3.3   Tracking Status in the Team Class

One of the trickier bits of coding in the standings is figuring out what we know, and when we know it. Once the season is ended, it's pretty obvious (once tiebreakers have been applied) who won. But it's possible to know this ahead of time. For example, if a team is in the lead by four games, with only three games left to play, then they'll be the winner when the season ends no matter what happens in those final three games.

We'd like to note this information wherever possible, so we track the status of three items of interest: division winners, wildcard winners, and teams that earn home-field advantage throughout the playoffs. We use a very simplistic algorithm for determining this—namely, the one just mentioned, where the lead is greater than the games remaining. A more complex algorithm that took the tiebreakers into account would be desirable, but would add a lot of complexity to the code. And let's face it, the subject of the book isn't football (in case you were wondering).

So we have in our `Team` class three properties that track the three items of interest. For each property, there are five possible values. At the beginning of the season, every team is in contention for every race, so we initialize the fields to the IN_CONTENTION value. Over the course of the season, as game results are posted, the status of each team in each race can change to any of the other four legal values.

Listing 2.2 Properties to Track Team Status, and Their Legal Enumerated Values

```
public static final int CLINCHED      = 1;
public static final int CLINCHED_TIE  = 2;
public static final int LEADING       = 3;
public static final int IN_CONTENTION = 4;
public static final int ELIMINATED    = 5;

private int  divisionChampStatus = IN_CONTENTION;
public int getDivisionChampStatus() { return divisionChampStatus; }
public void setDivisionChampStatus(int s) { divisionChampStatus = s; }

private int homeFieldStatus = IN_CONTENTION;
public int getHomeFieldStatus() { return homeFieldStatus; }
public void setHomeFieldStatus(int s) { homeFieldStatus = s; }

private int wildcardStatus = IN_CONTENTION;
public int getWildcardStatus() { return wildcardStatus; }
public void setWildcardStatus(int s) { wildcardStatus = s; }
```

Note that the constants defined in Listing 2.2 represent another use of an enumerated type; as with the enumerated types in the `Conference` and `Division` classes, we'll reimplement this as a class in the next chapter.

2.4 The Game Class

Now that we're finally done with `Team`, we can move on to the `Game` class. The `Game` class represents the result of a game played between two teams. The `Game` class simply consists of four properties that describe a game (see Table 2.3).

    `Game` stores the full name (City + Name) of each team, but for convenience, a partial name can be passed. As long as the name passed is enough to uniquely identify a team, the correct team will be looked up and stored.

Table 2.3 Properties of the `Game` Class

Property Name	Type	Get/Set?	Comment
home	String	Y/Y	fullName of team
score	int[]	Y/Y	visitor score, home score
visitor	String	Y/Y	fullName of team
week	int	Y/Y	week during season

    Methods of the `Game` class, other than the property accessors, are a single constructor that requires values for all properties, and a method to print the `Game`.

Methods of the Game Class

```
public Game(int week, String visitor, int vscore,
                    String home, int hscore)
public String toString()
```

2.5 The Teams and Games Container Classes

As soon as we start trying to process the data in the `Team` and `Game` classes, we will realize that we need to operate on various subsets of the data. We'd like to know what teams are within the NFC West, or which games played by the New York Jets were within its own division. So two new classes, `Teams` and `Games`, were created to be containers for all the `Team` objects and all the `Game` objects, respectively, and to provide methods for answering various queries about the data. The `Games` class includes in its constructor all the data for games played during the 2000 NFL season, which is loaded into an `ArrayList`. There are then methods to return all games, division games played by a team, conference games played by a team, games between two specified teams, games in which the two specified teams faced common opponents, and a method to calculate the win-loss percentage for a team in a specified set of games.

The Singleton Pattern

The Games and Teams classes are both examples of a pattern known as Singleton. The Singleton pattern is used whenever you have a class that needs to be instantiated exactly one time. (If a class needs to be instantiated at most once, you can alter the pattern by using lazy initialization of the Singleton.)

A singleton pattern is implemented in Java by following these rules:

- The Singleton class constructor must be private, so that other classes cannot purposefully or inadvertently create additional instances of the class.
- The Singleton class can instantiate itself statically. Code in a static block is executed exactly once, when the class is first loaded, so by putting the creation code in a static block we can ensure that only one instance is created.
- In most cases, the Singleton class should also be a final class, to prevent a user from instantiating subclasses of the class. In our case, that is an unacceptable restriction on our classes, and we must instead take additional care to ensure that we don't have a class and one of its superclasses or subclasses both instantiated within the same application. Fortunately, the design of our object factory (introduced in the next chapter) will take care of this for us.
- Finally, the Singleton class must provide an accessor to provide access to the single instance. We've used a method named getHandle() in our Singleton classes; getInstance() or just instance() are also commonly used.

Table 2.4   Properties of the Games Class

Property Name	Type	Get/Set?	Comment
gameList	ArrayList	Y/Y	contains Game objects

Methods of the Games class include a private constructor and a static getHandle() method (these two help enforce the Singleton property of our class). There are then five methods used to return as Lists various subsets of the data. Finally, a helper method is provided to compute the win-loss percentage of a team given a list of games that team played (this is used, for example, when determining which team had the better record against common opponents).

Methods of the Games Class

```
private Games()
public  static Games getHandle()
public List getAllGamesFor(String team)
public List getDivisionGamesFor(String team)
public List getConferenceGamesFor(String team)
public List getGamesBetween(String team1, String team2)
public List getCommonGamesFor(String team1, String team2)
public static float computeWinLossPctFor(String team, List games)
```

The `Teams` class is very similar; it contains within its constructor the information needed to construct a `Team` object for every NFL team that played during the 2000 season. There are methods to return all teams, teams for a specified division, and teams for a specified conference; there are also methods to get the conference or division of a specified team, or to return the full name of a team given enough letters of either the team's home city or the team's name to uniquely identify the team.

Table 2.5   Properties of the `Teams` Class

Property Name	Type	Get/Set?	Comment
teamList	List	Y/N	Contains Team objects

Methods of the `Teams` class include the private constructor and `getHandle()` method we expect in our singleton classes. Like the `Games` class, there are also a set of methods to subset the data; in this case only two are needed. The `getConferenceOf()` and `getDivisionOf()` methods return the conference or division of a team for which we have only the name (if we had a `Team` object, we could simply access its corresponding property). Finally, the `findName()` method allows us to get a full name of a team based on just a piece of either the city or team name.

Methods of the Teams Class

```
private Teams()
public  static Teams getHandle()
public List getConferenceTeams(int conf)
public List getDivisionTeams(int div)
public int getConferenceOf(String team)
public int getDivisionOf(String team)
public String findName(String partial)
```

The inclusion of all the data in the constructors was a convenience for getting the application up and running quickly without needing to decide what sort of database or other persistence mechanism would be used to store the application's data. Obviously, this isn't a very useful design for production applications, so we'll be replacing this with more suitable persistence mechanisms as we evolve the application. (You might want to consider using data embedded in a class this way as an easy way to keep test data for a class handy).

2.6   The Standings Class

The last class we'll look at is the `Standings` class, which contains much of the logic of the application. The task of the `Standings` class is to process all the games that have been played, update `Team` data with the results of those games, and then put the teams into order according to their win-loss percentage and (the really interesting part) applying the various NFL tiebreaking procedures used to rank teams having the same win-loss percentage.

The `Standings` class is the main class of the application, insofar as it is the class that makes things happen. Table 2.6 shows the properties of the `Standings` class. Here we see that the `Standings` class contains a `Teams` object, which holds all the teams in the league, as well as a `Games` object which holds the games that have been played. Each of these is also shadowed by a `List`, which we use for sorting and subsetting the data. We also have some properties that control how the `Standings` class behaves. The `verbose` flag causes additional information to be printed when the class runs. The `printConferenceStandings` flag allows us to suppress printing the conference standings (since these aren't typically significant until late in the season when wildcards are being determined). The `printEliminatedTeams` flag is used when printing the conference results to tell us whether we want to see all teams, or just those in playoff contention. The `printTimings` flag allows us to see how long certain things (such as sorting) take to allow us to assess the impact of different algorithms we might be playing with.

Table 2.6   Properties of the `Standings` Class

Property Name	Type	Get/Set?	Comment
games	Games	Y/Y	Handle to the `Games` object
gameList	List	Y/Y	List of `Game` objects
printConferenceStandings	boolean	Y/Y	Prints conference standings
printEliminatedTeams	boolean	Y/Y	Prints all teams in the conference standings, not just teams in contention
printTimings	boolean	Y/Y	Prints timing information
teams	Teams	Y/Y	Handle to the `Teams` object
teamList	List	Y/Y	List of `Team` objects
verbose	boolean	Y/Y	Shows progress when running

Shown next are the methods of the `Standings` class. Again, we have the private constructor along with a `getHandle()` method that tells us this class is a Singleton. Because this is the 'driver' class of our application, it has a `main()` method. The `findTeam()` method simply finds a `Team` object in the `teamList` array based on its name (which could be a full name, or a partial name, using either the team's name or the city). The `loadData()` method does more than the name implies. It first loads the `teamList` and `gameList` arrays by method calls to the `Teams` and `Games` objects, but it then runs through all the games that have been played and updates all the statistics of the `Team` objects accordingly. The two `compute` methods are called to perform the ranking of teams once data has been loaded, and then the two `print` methods are called to display the results.

Methods of the Standings Class
```
public  static Standings getHandle()
private Standings()
public static void main(String[] args)
public int findTeam(String name)
public void loadData()
public List computeDivisionStandings(int div)
public List computeConferenceStandings(int conf)
public void printDivisionStandings(int div, List list)
public void printConferenceStandings(int conf, List list)
```

2.7 Building and Running the Example Application

In each chapter, we'll be covering how to build, deploy (if necessary), and execute the example programs used in the chapter.

2.7.1 The Ant Build Utility

All of the examples in this book include Ant buildfiles that can be used to compile and, when necessary, package the example code. The advantage of Ant is that, because it is written in Java, it is completely portable, being runnable on any platform that provides a Java environment. Ant itself is free, part of the Apache Jakarta project. Ant 1.4.1 is included on the enclosed CD. You can also download Ant from `http://jakarta.apache.org`. Ant 2.0 is expected to introduce incompatible changes in buildfile syntax. So while later 1.x versions of Ant will probably work with all of the buildfiles, Ant 2.x will almost certainly fail.

Ant buildfiles are XML documents. Since we're several chapters away from introducing XML, we won't go into any further details about that just yet. The structure of a buildfile is that it contains a single *project*; this project then has some number of *targets*. The targets specified will vary depending on the project, but here are some that will be frequently seen:

- `compile`: compile sources for this version of the application
- `clean`: remove any generated files, such as .class files
- `test`: test this version of the application

Listing 2.3 shows the build.xml file for the original version of the application. It has the three common targets specified in the preceding list. Each target is made up of *tasks*, which is a series of steps performed to satisfy the target. For example, the <compile> target has a <javac> task that compiles the specified source files. Other tasks shown in this build.xml file are a <delete> task, within the <clean> target, that can delete files or directories; and a <java> task, within the <test> target, that is used to invoke java on our main class.

The <java>, <javac>, and <delete> tasks are built-in tasks, meaning they are part of Ant itself. Ant also allows us to define our own tasks, which we will do in some of the more complex examples later in the book.

The Ant buildfile for the original version of the application is shown in Listing 2.3. This buildfile is located in the nfl/original directory on the CD. In general, the Ant buildfile for any particular version of the application will be located in the same directory that contains the majority of new files introduced with that particular application revision.

Listing 2.3 Ant Buildfile (build.xml) for the Example Application

```
<project name="original" default="compile" basedir=".">

<target name="compile">
  <javac srcdir=".">
    <include name="Conference.java"/>
    <include name="Division.java"/>
    <include name="Game.java"/>
    <include name="Games.java"/>
    <include name="Standings.java"/>
    <include name="Team.java"/>
    <include name="Teams.java"/>
  </javac>
</target>

<target name="clean">
  <delete includeEmptyDirs="true">
    <fileset dir="." includes="*.class" />
  </delete>
</target>

<target name="test">
  <java classname="nfl.original.Standings" />
</target>

</project>
```

2.7.2   Downloading and Installing Ant

The CD included with this book contains Apache Ant version 1.4.1. In the Apache directory of the CD are two subdirectories: UNIX and Windows. The UNIX subdirectory contains a gzipped `.tar` file of Ant; the Windows subdirectory contains a `.zip` file of the same software. You can also download the latest version of Ant from `http://jakarta.apache.org`. Select the version of Ant appropriate to your system and copy the installation file (`.zip` or `.tar`) to your development system.

After copying the file to your development system, unpack the contents into a directory of your choosing. Set your `PATH` environment variable to include the `bin` directory in the Ant hierarchy (e.g., `export  PATH=$PATH:$ANT_HOME/jakarta-ant-1-4-1/bin`). Most of the buildfiles in the book also require that you set your Java CLASSPATH variable to include the directory where the source tree is rooted (i.e., the directory that includes the `nfl` directory).

2.7.3   Invoking Ant

If you invoke Ant with −`help` as an argument, it provides the following usage information:

```
ant [options] [target [target2 [target3] ...]]
Options:
  -help                   print this message
  -projecthelp            print project help information
  -version                print the version information and exit
  -quiet                  be extra quiet
  -verbose                be extra verbose
  -debug                  print debugging information
  -emacs                  produce logging information without adornments
  -logfile <file>         use given file for log
  -logger <classname>     the class which is to perform logging
  -listener <classname>   add an instance of class as a project listener
  -buildfile <file>       use given buildfile
  -D<property>=<value>    use value for given property
  -find <file>            search for buildfile towards the root of the
                          filesystem and use it
```

We won't generally need to specify any options, just the target that we want to build. The project declaration within our `build.xml` file specifies that the `<compile>` target is the default target for this buildfile. This means that if we are in the directory where the buildfile resides, we simply need to type:

```
ant
```

to compile the project. We could also specify the target explicitly by typing:

```
ant compile
```

To test the program, we invoke `java` on the `Standings` class. Java will require that the full package name be used, so the correct command is:

```
java nfl.original.Standings
```

We can do this manually as shown, or use the target defined for us by the buildfile:

```
ant test
```

2.8 Exercises

We haven't introduced any new technologies yet, so there aren't any exercises that are relevant to the book's subject matter that I can suggest at this point. However, if you're interested in using the example application to actually track results, then there are a number of enhancements that could improve the usefulness of the package.

2.1 Three-way comparisons: The NFL rules provide different tiebreaker rules for cases where three or more teams are tied at any point during the tiebreaker procedure. Our package ignores this in favor of being able to leverage the Comparator capability provided by Java, which supports only two-way comparisons. Update the package to properly handle three-way ties.

2.2 Forward-looking clinch/elimination info: Perhaps the most interesting enhancement would be to provide the capability of looking forward, to games remaining to be played, in order to report what a team needs to do to clinch or avoid elimination. In the following chapter, we'll introduce some changes that permit scheduled games to be entered as well as the results of completed games; this information would of course be required for any such calculations.

2.3 Handling playoff games: Our application only deals with regular-season games. Based on the playoff seedings, generate a ladder diagram showing the playoff matchups from the wild-card round through the Super Bowl. (You won't be able to complete the diagram based on just the initial seedings, but rather will have to update the ladder after each round of playoffs).

2.4 Extending to support other sports: If football isn't your sport, consider changing the package to support the National Hockey League, National Basketball Association, Major League Baseball, or whatever other teams you prefer. You could subclass the Team type to provide teams of different sports. A few things (such as the GAMES_IN_SEASON constant) would need to be relocated to the proper subclass, and you'll need to create new Comparators to order the teams properly.

2.9 Further Reading

Information about tiebreakers, playoff rules, game results, and additional information that might be useful in extending the package can be found on the NFL.com Web site:

`http://www.nfl.com`

The Singleton and Strategy patterns are explained in *Design Patterns*; details on implementing these patterns in Java can be found in Bloch's *Effective Java* and Eckel's *Thinking in Java*. See the bibliography for book details.

The home page for the Apache Ant project is:

`http://jakarta.apache.org/ant/index.html.`

The Ant User's Manual is at:

`http://jakarta.apache.org/ant/manual/index.html`

## CHAPTER 3

The Layered Application

The application we introduced in Chapter 2 functions properly, but it wasn't designed with flexibility in mind. Over the course of this book, the plan is to introduce the various APIs that make up the Java 2 Enterprise Edition (J2EE), and show how they can be incorporated into the example application. In order to do this, we'd like the application to be modularized in such a way that we can swap in various pieces of technology without disturbing the rest of the system. Although such flexibility is frequently touted as a benefit of object-oriented systems, in reality flexibility never comes about as an accident, no matter what language or methodology you might be using.

In order to give us this degree of flexibility, we'll make some fairly simple changes to the application design we introduced in Chapter 2. The main changes are:

- Separating the interface from the implementation of nearly all classes.
- Creating layers, or tiers, of application components. In particular, create a presentation layer, an application (business objects) layer, and a persistence (database) layer.

Separating interface from implementation is generally thought to be a "good thing" in object-oriented design. It is also a requirement for any classes using Remote Method Invocation (RMI), which we'll be incorporating into our design beginning in Chapter 15. Enterprise Java-Beans (EJB) functionality, which is covered beginning in Chapter 19, is built on top of RMI and thus also requires this separation of interface from implementation.

The creation of layers will allow our application to be deployed in a multi-tiered fashion, but does not require it to be physically separated. We will have the flexibility to deploy the application in a monolithic, two-tier, or three-tier configuration.

We'll cover the transformation of our example classes in the same order that the classes were originally introduced, beginning with the `Division` and `Conference` classes.

At this point I've created three new subpackages under `nfl`, to represent the three layers of the architecture. These subpackages are `nfl.application`, `nfl.presentation`, and `nfl.persistence`. Table 3.1 identifies all the classes and interfaces that make up the layered version of the application, along with what package they are part of.

Table 3.1   Classes and Interfaces in the Layered Application

Name	Package	Class or Interface	Comment
Conference	nfl.application	Class	Uses new Enumerated Type idiom
Division	nfl.application	Class	Uses new Enumerated Type idiom
ObjectFactory	nfl	Class	Instantiates other classes
VersionInfo	nfl	Abstract class	Data class for ObjectFactory
LayeredVersionInfo	nfl	Class	Concrete subclass of VersionInfo
Team	nfl.application	Interface	
BasicTeamImpl	nfl.application	Class	Implements Team
Team.Status	nfl.application	Class	Uses new Enumerated Type idiom
Messaging	nfl.application	Interface	Creates tiebreaker messages
BasicMessagingImpl	nfl.application	Class	Implements Messaging
Game	nfl.application	Interface	
BasicGameImpl	nfl.application	Class	Implements Game
Games	nfl.application	Interface	
BasicGamesImpl	nfl.application	Class	Implements Games
GameData	nfl.persistence	Interface	
BasicGameDataImpl	nfl.persistence	Class	Implements GameData
Teams	nfl.application	Interface	
BasicTeamsImpl	nfl.application	Class	Implements Teams

Table 3.1   Classes and Interfaces in the Layered Application (Continued)

Name	Package	Class or Interface	Comment
TeamData	nfl.persistence	Interface	
BasicTeamDataImpl	nfl.persistence	Class	Implements TeamData
Standings	nfl.application	Interface	
BasicStandingsImpl	nfl.application	Class	Implements Standings
Console	nfl.presentation	Class	Separated out from Standings

3.1   A Better Design for Handling Enumerated Types

The `Division` and `Conference` classes represent enumerated types. Although the way these classes were developed in Chapter 2 worked well, there is a Java idiom for doing enumerated types that is superior to using integer constants. Listing 3.1 shows how this idiom (described in the following sidebar) has been applied to the `Conference` class; the corresponding changes have also been made to the `Division` class.

The Enumerated Type Idiom

Basic Usage

In our original application, we used static `int` or `String` types to assign constant values to several variables that collectively made up an enumerated type (we did this for `Conferences`, `Divisions`, and for the `Status` fields within the `Team` class). A superior idiom for doing this is described in Joshua Bloch's book *Effective Java Programming Language Guide*, and we'll use it in this and future versions of our example application.

Instead of using `int` values, we create a class to represent the type. By creating a class, we gain the advantage of type-safety; now we can't be passed just any arbitrary integer or `String` value in a method that expects a member of one of these enumerated types.

To prevent users from creating illegal values as members of this class, we make the constructor private, and create a series of static final variables representing all the legal values of the type. This is very similar to the mechanism used for Singletons. The similarity is not accidental; with the Singleton class, we wanted to create exactly one instance of the class; with an enumerated type, we want to create exactly two, or exactly six, or some other precise number of legal values.

> **Using Serializable with the Enumerated Type**
>
> At this point in the evolution of our application, there isn't any need for any class to be `Serializable`. But in future versions, we'll use facilities such as Remote Method Invocation (RMI) and Enterprise JavaBeans (EJB) to make some of our classes accessible remotely. In these two-tier and three-tier architectures, it is sometimes necessary for classes to be passed between the client, middle tier, and server tier portions of the application. Only classes marked `Serializable` can be passed in this way. Rather than create classes that differ from each other only in whether they are serializable or not, we've altered certain classes at this point as a result of knowledge gained from writing the later examples, and made `Serializable` those classes that need it in later iterations.
>
> When we made our enumerated types serializable, the application began to fail in interesting ways. Comparisions of items that should have been equal (such as `team1.getConference() == team2.getConference()`) were in fact not equal. Originally, I patched around this by replacing the `==` comparison with `team1.getName().equals(team2.getName())`, which works and is a perfectly acceptable solution. But it should not have been required, since the equality test should be usable on enumerated types.
>
> The answer was found in Bloch's *Effective Java Programming Language Guide*, where it is shown that any Singleton or Enumerated Type that implements `Serializable` must also implement the `readResolve()` method in order to maintain correct behavior when de-serialized. So our enumerated types now implement the `readResolve()` method and behave as expected even in distributed deployments.

Listing 3.1 The `Conference` Class

```
// Conference.java

package nfl.application;

import java.util.*;  /* Collections, List, Arrays */
import nfl.ObjectFactory;

/** This class provides a typesafe enumeration of the
  * NFL Conferences.
  */
public class Conference implements java.io.Serializable
{
    private final String name;

    private Conference(String name) { this.name = name; }

    public String toString()        { return name; }
```

```
public static final Conference AFC = new Conference("AFC");
public static final Conference NFC = new Conference("NFC");

public final static Conference[] PRIVATE_DATA = { AFC, NFC };
public final static List CONFERENCES =
   Collections.unmodifiableList(Arrays.asList(PRIVATE_DATA));

/** Return the number of divisions in this conference.
  * Assumes all conferences have the same number of
  * divisions; if this is violated another algorithm
  * will be needed.
  */
public int numDivisions() {
   return Division.DIVISIONS.size() /
                CONFERENCES.size();
}

private int teamsInConference = -1;
/** Return the number of teams within the conference.
  * Does by counting; does not assume conferences have
  * equal number of teams.
  */
public int numTeams() {
   Teams teams = (Teams)
        ObjectFactory.getHandle().getInstance("Teams");
   if (teamsInConference == -1) {
      List allteams = teams.getTeamList();
      for (int i=0; i<allteams.size(); i++) {
         if (((Team)allteams.get(i)).getConference() == this)
            teamsInConference++;
      }
   }
   return teamsInConference;
}

// Support for serialization
private static int nextOrdinal = 0;
private final int ordinal = nextOrdinal++;
public Object readResolve() throws ObjectStreamException
{
   return PRIVATE_DATA[ordinal];
}
}
```

Having reworked these classes this far, I then tried to look at ways to create a separate interface for each of these classes. Since a user's interaction with these classes is not really through methods, but rather by use of the defined set of instance classes, there is not a satisfactory way to create a separate interface.

3.2   Using an Object Factory

All Java classes have constructors. If you write code for a class without explicitly supplying one, then a default constructor taking no arguments will be provided for you by the compiler. Invoking the constructor of a class is a straightforward operation when you know the type of object you want to create, but frequently there is the need to write code that has the flexibility to create several different classes of objects. Sometimes the set of possible object types is known in advance, but often software needs to be designed to provide extensibility to handle types that may be created later.

An Object Factory is a common design pattern for handling the need to create objects of types that aren't specified at compile time, but instead at run time. The degree of flexibility required may vary widely; a simple object factory might just provide creation for a small set of predefined classes. A very complex and flexible object factory might conceivably be able to generate instances of any class, using the Reflection APIs to find what classes are available and what constructors could be called for those classes.

The Abstract Factory Pattern

Our `ObjectFactory` is a slightly modified implementation of the Abstract Factory pattern.[a] In the Abstract Factory, the factory is an abstract class or interface, and various subclasses or subpackages are then responsible for creating a concrete subclass that provides the implementation of the factory.

There are two main advantages of using an Object Factory over `new()`. First, a factory isn't required to actually create a new object; it could instead return a pre-created object from a pool, or provide a handle to an existing object. We use this capability to allow our `ObjectFactory` to provide a consistent instantiation mechanism for all classes, so that the user does not have to use different API calls when dealing with Singleton classes.

Secondly, while `new()` will return exactly the class it is told to create, an `ObjectFactory` can return any subclass of the requested class, or in cases where an interface is passed, it can return any class that implements that interface. This is used heavily within our examples to allow us to configure our application out of many interchangeable components.

Since Java's Reflection API gives us enough flexibility to be able to construct an object that isn't predefined to us at compile time, we're able to make an `Object-Factory` that doesn't need to be subclassed or extended, even when the types of objects it may be called upon to create change. This is the main way in which our `ObjectFactory` (which is a concrete class) differs from the design pattern, which describes an abstract class.

---

a. For more information on the Abstract Factory pattern, see *Design Patterns: Elements of Reusable Object-Oriented Software*, mentioned in the Bibliography.

The Object Factory we need falls somewhere between these extremes. We are going to create interfaces that describe the basic functions of each component in our system; for example, a `Team` interface and a `Game` interface. But as the application evolves, there will be several classes developed that implement each of these interfaces. We want to be able to ask our Object Factory to return us a class that implements `Team`, for example, and get the proper object depending on whether we're running as a standalone application, a servlet, or an Enterprise JavaBean. The configuration of the proper set of classes to use in each application can be provided from a source external to the `ObjectFactory`.

Our `ObjectFactory` is shown in its entirety in Listing 3.2. The `getInstance()` methods are the core of the class; everything else in the class is there to support this single critical function. To get an instance of a class implementing the `Team` interface, for example, we would make the following call:

```
ObjectFactory.getHandle().getInstance("Team");
```

The `ObjectFactory` uses a `VersionInfo` subclass to provide it with a mapping between interfaces or classes, and the classes that extend or implement them. This information is initialized just once at the time the `ObjectFactory` class is first loaded, so users must be careful to set the `nfl.versioninfo` property, which provides the name of the `VersionInfo` subclass, before first accessing the `ObjectFactory`. The property can be set via the command line, using the `-Dnfl.versioninfo=classname` syntax, or programmatically via a `setProperty()` call. Both methods are demonstrated in our example programs.

The `ObjectFactory` is a singleton, so we don't need to explicitly instantiate it but rather just get a handle to the single instance. With this handle, we then call `getInstance()` and pass the name of the interface for which we need an instantiating class. There are actually three different `getInstance()` methods, to permit us to create objects whose constructors might require different sets of parameters. If we wanted more flexibility in this class, or if the number of different method signatures in our classes made the overloading of `getInstance()` unwieldy, we could instead create a single `getInstance()` method that took as parameters two arrays: one of type `Class[]` indicating the argument types, and the other of type `Object[]` containing the parameter values. This would force callers to wrapper any primitive types with the corresponding `Class` object, and would also require passing empty arrays when creating a class via its zero-element constructors. These seemed too much of an extra burden to place on users of the `ObjectFactory`, so we've gone with the overloaded `getInstance()` method instead.

The chain of events that is set in motion by a `getInstance()` call is as follows:

1. The `getInstance()` call invokes `getClass()`.
2. `getClass()` looks up the interface name in the `VersionInfo` object, and finds the name of the class we should instantiate. Because the top-level package name (nfl) is not part of the name stored in the `VersionInfo` object, we prepend the package name.

3. We then use the `Class.forName()` method to create an object of type `Class` corresponding to the class we want. If you're unfamiliar with the Reflection data types, it's important to note that a `Class` object is not the same as an `Object` of the requested class; it is instead an object providing access to information about the class (the class metadata).

4. The `Class` is returned to the calling `getInstance()` variant.

5. In the case where there are no arguments to be passed to the constructor, the `Class` object provides a convenient `newInstance()` method; we call this to obtain an instance of our target class and return it.

6. For constructors that require arguments, we call the `getConstructor()` method of the `Class` to return us a `Constructor` object. We pass `getConstructor()` the types (`Class` objects) of the arguments we wish to pass, so that we can obtain the proper constructor in the case where our target class provides multiple constructors. We then call the `newInstance()` method of the `Constructor` object, passing in the appropriate arguments.

There are several ways this could go wrong—if an invalid interface name was passed, for example, or if the parameters passed did not match the expected types. In these cases, we'll return a null object back to the caller. There is one failure, however, that we'd like to recover from gracefully. Some of the classes we will create and use are singleton classes, which means they cannot be instantiated by an external agent such as the Object Factory. Since the job of the Object Factory is to create new instances of classes, it can be argued (quite validly) that we should never call the Object Factory for such a class. But then we've required the caller to know an implementation detail about the class that I really don't think they should have to keep track of; and in fact, it's even possible that a particular class might be a Singleton in some of our implementations, but not in others.

Singleton objects have private constructors; because the Object Factory is not of the same class as the object we're trying to create, this means that the invocation of the constructor via the `newInstance()` call will fail with an `IllegalAccessException`. Because all of our Singleton objects implement a `getHandle()` method, we've added error handling to each of the `getInstance()` calls so that if the invocation of the constructor fails with an `IllegalAccessException`, we instead invoke the target class' `getHandle()` method, and return that to the caller. Now the user of the Object Factory is given a consistent interface to get access to both Singleton and ordinary classes within the application.

Listing 3.2 The `ObjectFactory` Class

```java
// ObjectFactory.java

package nfl;

import java.lang.reflect.Constructor;
import java.lang.reflect.Method;
import java.util.Properties;

/** The ObjectFactory is used to instantiate classes. The
  * getInstance() method is passed the name of an interface;
  * the factory then looks up that interface in the
  * VersionInfo object to determine what class implementing
  * the requested interface should be instantiated and
  * returned. If the class is a Singleton, no new class
  * is instantiated, but a handle to the single instance
  * of the class is returned instead.
  */
public class ObjectFactory {

    /** VersionInfo is the data about which version should
      * be instantiated for each class handled by the
      * ObjectFactory
      */
    private VersionInfo vinfo;

    private static ObjectFactory factory = new ObjectFactory();
    public  static ObjectFactory getHandle() {
        return factory; }

    private final static String defaultVersionInfo =
                          "nfl.LayeredVersionInfo";
    private final static String versionInfoProperty =
                          "nfl.versioninfo";

    private String versionInfoClassName;

    /** The verbose flag can be turned on to debug the ObjectFactory
      */
    private static boolean verbose = false;
    public static void setVerbose()          { verbose = true; }
    public static void setVerbose(boolean b) { verbose = b; }

    /** Constructor for ObjectFactory.
      */
    private ObjectFactory() {
        Properties p = System.getProperties();
```

```
      versionInfoClassName = p.getProperty(
                  versionInfoProperty, defaultVersionInfo);
      if (verbose) {
        System.out.println("Using version info: " +
                            versionInfoClassName);
      }
      try {
        Class vinfoclass = Class.forName(versionInfoClassName);
        vinfo = (VersionInfo) vinfoclass.newInstance();
      } catch (Exception e) {
        e.printStackTrace();
      }
    }


    /** getInstance is called to instantiate the correct
      * version of the class named in the argument.
      */
    public Object getInstance(String interfaceName) {
       Class klass = getClass(interfaceName);
       if (klass == null) return null;
       try {
          return klass.newInstance();
       } catch (IllegalAccessException e) {
          return invokeGetHandleOfTarget(klass);
       } catch (Exception e) {
          System.out.println("Cannot instantiate " + klass.getName());
          e.printStackTrace();
          return null;
       }
    }


    /* A variant of getInstance for objects whose
     * constructor takes two strings as arguments (e.g, Team)
     */
    public Object getInstance(String interfaceName,
                              String arg1, String arg2) {
       Class klass = getClass(interfaceName);
       if (klass == null) return null;
       try {
          Constructor c = klass.getConstructor(
             new Class[] { String.class, String.class } );
          return c.newInstance(
             new Object[] { arg1, arg2 });
       } catch (IllegalAccessException e) {
          return invokeGetHandleOfTarget(klass);
       } catch (Exception e) {
          System.out.println("Cannot instantiate: "
                             + klass.getName());
```

```
         e.printStackTrace();
         return null;
      }
   }

   /* A variant of getInstance for use by Game() */
   public Object getInstance(String interfaceName, int arg1,
                             String arg2, int arg3,
                             String arg4, int arg5) {
      Class klass = getClass(interfaceName);
      if (klass == null) return null;
      try {
         Constructor c = klass.getConstructor(new Class[] {
            int.class, String.class, int.class,
            String.class, int.class } );
         return c.newInstance(new Object[] {
            new Integer(arg1), arg2, new Integer(arg3),
            arg4, new Integer(arg5) } );
      } catch (IllegalAccessException e) {
         return invokeGetHandleOfTarget(klass);
      } catch (Exception e) {
         System.out.println("Cannot instantiate: " +
                            klass.getName());
         e.printStackTrace();
         return null;
      }
   }

   /** Since all three variants of getInstance need to first
     * obtain a Class object, that functionality has been
     * refactored out into this method.
     */
   private Class getClass(String interfaceName) {
      String fqKlassName = "nfl." +
                        vinfo.getVersion(interfaceName);
      if (verbose)
         System.out.println(
            "ObjectFactory: attempting to load " +
                            fqKlassName);
      try {
         Class klass = Class.forName(fqKlassName);
         return klass;
      } catch (ClassNotFoundException e) {
         if (verbose) System.out.println(
                     "Class not found: " + fqKlassName);
         return null;
      }
   }
```

```
      /** For Singleton objects, the invocation of the
        * constructor will fail with an IllegalAccessException
        * (because the constructors of Singletons are private
        * or protected). When that happens, we call this
        * method which will invoke the getHandle() method of
        * the class.
        */
      public Object invokeGetHandleOfTarget(Class klass) {
         if (verbose) System.out.println(
             "Couldn't access constructor, trying getHandle()");
         Method method = null;
         try {
            method = klass.getMethod("getHandle",
                                     new Class[] {});
            return method.invoke(klass, new Object[] {});
         } catch (Exception e) {
            System.out.println("Failed trying to invoke " +
                               method + " of " + klass);
            e.printStackTrace();
            return null;
         }
      }
   }
}
```

The `ObjectFactory` requires data about what classes to return for each requested inter-face; this data is provided by a `VersionInfo` class. The root `VersionInfo` class is shown in Listing 3.3, and then Listing 3.4 shows the subclass created specifically for the current version of the application. `VersionInfo` is essentially just a wrapper around a `Map` used to associate interface names with class names, and provide `getVersion()` and `setVersion()` access methods to those associations.

Listing 3.3 The `VersionInfo` Class

```
// VersionInfo.java

package nfl;

import java.io.Serializable;
import java.util.*; /* Map, HashMap */

/** The VersionInfo object for each revision provides
  * information about which version of each class to use.
  */
public abstract class VersionInfo implements Serializable
{
   private Map versions;
```

```
   public VersionInfo() {
      versions = new HashMap();
   }

   /** setVersion is called by the constructor
     * of each class derived from VersionInfo
     */
   public void setVersion(String interfaceName,
                          String className) {
      versions.put(interfaceName, className);
   }

   /** getVersion is called by the ObjectFactory */
   public String getVersion(String interfaceName) {
      return (String) versions.get(interfaceName);
   }

}
```

Listing 3.4 The LayeredVersionInfo Class

```
// LayeredVersionInfo.java

package nfl;

import java.io.Serializable;

public class LayeredVersionInfo extends VersionInfo
                                implements Serializable
{

   /** The constructor sets versions for all classes
     * that are to be instantiated.
     */
   public LayeredVersionInfo() {
      setVersion("Game",
                 "application.BasicGameImpl");
      setVersion("Games",
                 "application.BasicGamesImpl");
      setVersion("Messaging",
                 "application.BasicMessagingImpl");
      setVersion("Standings",
                 "application.BasicStandingsImpl");
      setVersion("Team",
                 "application.BasicTeamImpl");
      setVersion("Teams",
                 "application.BasicTeamsImpl");
```

```
    setVersion("GameData",
             "persistence.BasicGameDataImpl");
    setVersion("TeamData",
             "persistence.BasicTeamDataImpl");
  }
}
```

3.3   MVC Architecture

The Model-View-Controller (MVC) architecture is one of the most widely used designs in object-oriented software development. Within Java, we can see MVC used at many levels, including:

- JFC components
- The interaction of servlets and JavaServer Pages
- The Apache Struts framework

The "model" encapsulates the application's state and contains the business logic. For our application, we've created the package nfl.application to represent the model. (The nfl.persistence package provides persistent storage for the data in our model, but doesn't really play into the MVC interactions described here.) The model should not have any dependence on how the information will be displayed to the user; for example, by the end of this chapter, our Standings class will simply order teams into a List, but will not have any responsibility for presenting that List to the user.

The "view" is the user interface, or what we've been calling the presentation layer. Frequently, there are multiple views being presented, sometimes simultaneously, of the same model. For example, consider a spreadsheet program that allows data to be plotted on a graph. If you change a cell in the spreadsheet, the graph changes as well. The cell does not update the graph; instead, it updates the data model, and the graph changes to reflect the changed state of the model. The classes in the nfl.presentation package represent various views available for our application.

The "controller" can be thought of as sitting between the model and the view, and updating one to reflect changes in the other. For example, the controller receives requests from the user that are typically generated by interacting with some component of the view (a menu item, a pushbutton, a scrollbar); it then delegates some action to the business logic as necessary to perform the indicated action. The state of the application data may change as a result, in which case the controller is notified of the change and directs the view to update itself accordingly. The controller part of our example application isn't isolated in any particular class or package. In the original application, the main() method of the Standings class was basically the controller for the application. As our application evolves and becomes more dynamic, we'll introduce other components that take on more aspects of the controller role.

3.4   The Team Interface and Implementation

The next class to be transformed is the `Team` class. The first step in the transformation is to extract all of the public methods of the class and place them in an interface, which retains the name `Team`. The original `Team` source file is then renamed `BasicTeamImpl.java`; the `Impl` suffix will be used throughout our examples to indicate implementation classes. The `Basic` prefix indicates that this is the simple, standard "reference implementation," if you will, of a `Team` object. While the interface allows us to create entirely separate implementations, it is expected that instead we will extend the `BasicTeamImpl` class and add or override methods to add new functionality. The `Team` interface is shown in Listings 3.5 and 3.6.

Listing 3.5 The `Team` Interface (Part 1 of 2)

```
// Team.java

package nfl.application;

import java.util.Comparator;

/** An NFL team. Includes various statistics needed to
  * produce the standings.
  */
public interface Team
{
   // Identity
   public  String getName();
   public  void    setName(String n);

   public  String getCity();
   public  void    setCity(String c);
   public  String getFullName();

   public void setConference(Conference c);
   public Conference  getConference();

   public void       setDivision(Division d);
   public Division getDivision();

   public int[] getOverallRecord();
   public int    getWins();
   public int    getLosses();
   public int    getTies();
   public void  addWin();
   public void  addLoss();
   public void  addTie();
```

```
public   int[]  getDivisionRecord();
public   int    getDivisionWins();
public   int    getDivisionLosses();
public   int    getDivisionTies();
public   void   addDivisionWin();
public   void   addDivisionLoss();
public   void   addDivisionTie();

public   int[]  getConferenceRecord();
public   int    getConferenceWins();
public   int    getConferenceLosses();
public   int    getConferenceTies();
public   void   addConferenceWin();
public   void   addConferenceLoss();
public   void   addConferenceTie();

public   int   getPoints();
public   void  addPoints(int p);

public   int   getPointsAllowed();
public   void  addPointsAllowed(int p);

public   int  getGamesRemaining();

public void forceRecalculation();

// Fields calculated at time standings are computed

public   float  getOverallWinLossPct();
public   void   setOverallWinLossPct(float p);

public   float  getDivisionWinLossPct();
public   void   setDivisionWinLossPct(float p);

public   float  getConferenceWinLossPct();
public   void   setConferenceWinLossPct(float p);

public   int   getNetOverallPoints();
public   void  setNetOverallPoints(int p);

public   int   getNetDivisionPoints();
public   void  setNetDivisionPoints(int p);

public   int   getNetConferencePoints();
public   void  setNetConferencePoints(int p);

public   int  getStreak();
```

In our original `Team` class, we had another repetition of the enumerated type pattern, this time with a set of integer values used to represent the status of teams in the division and conference races. Just as we did with the `Division` and `Conference` classes, we've replaced these integer constants with a set of constant classes. A new class, `Status`, has been introduced to represent these values. We've made the `Status` class a nested class of the `Team` interface, simply by placing the class definition inside the `Team` interface definition. In the implementation class that follows, you'll see these constants referenced by their fully qualified names, such as `Team.Status.CLINCHED`. Listing 3.6 shows the remainder of the `Team` interface, including the nested class and the functions that take `Status` as a parameter or return values of type `Status`.

Listing 3.6 The `Status` Nested Class (Part 2 of 2 of `Team`)

```
public class Status implements java.io.Serializable {
    private int value;
    private Status(int value) { this.value = value; }

    public boolean isLeader() {
        return value <= LEADING.value;
    }

    public boolean equals(Status other) {
        return this.value == other.value;
    }

    public String toString() {
        switch(value) {
            case 1: return "Clinched";
            case 2: return "Clinched a tie for";
            case 3: return "Leads race for ";
            case 4: return "In contention for";
            case 5: return "Eliminated from";
            default: return "invalid value";
        }
    }

    public final static Status CLINCHED = new Status(1);
    public final static Status CLINCHED_TIE =
                                    new Status(2);
    public final static Status LEADING = new Status(3);
    public final static Status IN_CONTENTION =
                                    new Status(4);
    public final static Status ELIMINATED = new Status(5);
}

public  Status getDivisionChampStatus();
```

```
    public  void    setDivisionChampStatus(Status s);

    public  Status getHomeFieldStatus();
    public  void    setHomeFieldStatus(Status s);

    public  Status getWildcardStatus();
    public  void    setWildcardStatus(Status s);
}
```

The `BasicTeamImpl` class is almost identical to the `Team` class in the original application (Chapter 2). The differences are as follows:

- The package name is changed to `nfl.application` because of our layering approach.
- We import the `nfl.ObjectFactory` class.
- The `BasicTeamImpl` class implements the `Team` and `Serializable` interfaces.
- The `Conference` and `Division` types are used rather than ints.
- A new interface, `Messaging`, is introduced, to handle messages that were previously handled with `System.out.println()`. More about this later.
- The `Status` class constants are used rather than int constants.
- The `ObjectFactory` is used to create an instance of the `Games` class, rather than using the verb `new()`.

All of these differences can be spotted in Listing 3.7, which shows the first part of the `BasicTeamImpl` class.

Listing 3.7 The `BasicTeamImpl` Class (Part 1 of 2)

```
// BasicTeamImpl.java

package nfl.application;

import java.io.*;
import java.util.*;
import nfl.ObjectFactory;

/** An NFL team. Includes various statistics needed to
  * produce the standings.
  */
public class BasicTeamImpl implements Team,
                                      java.io.Serializable
{
    // Identity
    private String name;
    public  String getName()       { return name; }
    public  void    setName(String n) { name = n; }
```

```
  private String city;
  public  String getCity()        { return city; }
  public  void    setCity(String c) { city = c;   }
  public  String getFullName() {
     return new String(city + " " + name); }

  private Conference conference;
  public void setConference(Conference c) {
     conference = c; }
  public Conference getConference() { return conference; }

  private Division division;
  public void setDivision(Division d) { division = d; }
  public Division getDivision()    { return division; }

  private static Messaging messaging = (Messaging)
       ObjectFactory.getHandle().getInstance("Messaging");
  public static Messaging getMessaging() {
     return messaging; }
  public static void setMessaging(Messaging m) {
     messaging = m; }

... code identical to original version not reproduced ...

  private Status divisionChampStatus =
                          Status.IN_CONTENTION;
  public Status getDivisionChampStatus() {
     return divisionChampStatus; }
  public void setDivisionChampStatus(Status s) {
     divisionChampStatus = s; }

  private Status homeFieldStatus = Status.IN_CONTENTION;
  public Status getHomeFieldStatus() {
     return homeFieldStatus; }
  public void setHomeFieldStatus(Status s) {
     homeFieldStatus = s; }

  private Status wildcardStatus = Status.IN_CONTENTION;
  public Status getWildcardStatus() {
     return wildcardStatus; }
  public void setWildcardStatus(Status s) {
     wildcardStatus = s; }

  // Constructor
  public BasicTeamImpl(String city, String name) {
     this.city = city;
     this.name = name;
     overallRecord   = new int[] { 0,0,0 };
```

```
      divisionRecord   = new int[] { 0,0,0 };
      conferenceRecord = new int[] { 0,0,0 };
      points = 0; pointsAllowed = 0; streak = 0;
   }


   private static void loadGames() {
      games = (Games)
         ObjectFactory.getHandle().getInstance("Games");
   }


   /** The Team and Standings objects both have logic to do
    * lazy calculations; essentially, the original code
    * assumed that processing flow would be such that all
    * results were posted before any results were printed.
    * Once we've completed the initial data load, if we
    * post additional results, they will not be reflected
    * in the totals because the calculation routines will
    * see the values have already been calculated. So, if
    * we update any data after the initial load, we call
    * this routine to reset various fields to their
    * uninitialized state, forcing a recalculation.
    */
   public void forceRecalculation() {
      setOverallWinLossPct(-1.0f);
      setDivisionWinLossPct(-1.0f);
      setConferenceWinLossPct(-1.0f);
      setDivisionChampStatus(Status.IN_CONTENTION);
      setHomeFieldStatus(Status.IN_CONTENTION);
      setWildcardStatus(Status.IN_CONTENTION);
      setNetOverallPoints(-1);
      setNetConferencePoints(-1);
      setNetDivisionPoints(-1);
   }
```

We don't want to duplicate the majority of the code from `BasicTeamImpl` in the listings here, since the code is mostly unchanged. But let's jump ahead to see how the code that prints out messages during the comparison of teams in the sorting process has been changed to use the new `Messaging` facility. In Listing 3.8, we see that the `Messaging.show()` method is being used instead of `System.out.println()`.

Listing 3.8 The `BasicTeamImpl` Class (Part 2 of 2)

```
// Following methods are for use by division and
// conference comparators

   private static List      gameList;
   private static Games     games;
   private static boolean verbose = true;

   private static int compareHeadToHead(Team t1, Team t2) {
      List head2head = games.getGamesBetween(
                       t1.getFullName(), t2.getFullName());
      float h2hpct;
      if (head2head.size() > 0) {
         h2hpct = games.computeWinLossPctFor(
               t1.getFullName(), head2head);
         if (h2hpct > .500) {
            if (verbose)
               messaging.show(t1.getName() + " over " +
                  t2.getName() + " based on head-to-head" +
                  " record (Tiebreaker 1)");
            return -1;
         } else if (h2hpct < .500) {
            if (verbose)
               messaging.show(t2.getName() + " over " +
                  t1.getName() + " based on head-to-head" +
                  " record (Tiebreaker 1)");
            return 1;
         }
      }
      return 0;
   }
```

3.5   Messaging Facility Interface and Implementation

As seen in the `Team` class, we've created a separate `Messaging` interface to handle the messages
we display. Our original application wrote all of its output to the terminal device, so we could do
the same with our messages. But with our layered approach, we don't know in the `Team` class
what sort of user interface we're dealing with; it might be graphical, or Web-based, or conceivably even a voice-based or wireless interface. By creating a `Messaging` interface, we remove
any dependence of the `Team` class on the specifics of the user interface.

Our `Messaging` interface has only a single method, to show a message (which is a string).
You can see the interface in all its radiant glory in Listing 3.9.

Listing 3.9 The `Messaging` Interface

```
// Messaging.java

package nfl.application;

/** Provides a messaging facility. */
public interface Messaging {

   /** Shows the indicated message */
   public void show(String message);

}
```

We will have several implementations of the `Messaging` facility over time (essentially needing one for each different presentation option we provide for the user interface). For now, `System.out.println()` is still sufficient as a way to display our messages to the terminal, so our first implementation of the `Messaging` interface just duplicates what we originally did inline in the code.

Listing 3.10 The `BasicMessagingImpl` Class

```
// BasicMessagingImpl.java

package nfl.application;

import nfl.ObjectFactory;

/** Provides a messaging facility. */
public class BasicMessagingImpl implements Messaging {

   private static Messaging m = new BasicMessagingImpl();
   public  static Messaging getHandle() { return m; }

   private BasicMessagingImpl() {}

   /** Shows the indicated message */
   public void show(String message) {
      System.out.println(message);
   }

}
```

3.6   Continuing the Separation of Interface and Implementation

Most of the changes that are required to separate interface from implementation have now been shown, so we won't belabor the point by showing the same pattern repeated on class after class. All programs are included on the CD, so you can refer to them there if there are particular aspects that haven't been adequately covered in the text. The new classes and interfaces are listed so you can find them easily.

The functionality of the `original.Game` class has been separated into the `application.Game` interface and the `application.BasicGameImpl` implementation. The `original.Team` class has similarly been separated into `application.Team` (the interface) and the implementing class `application.BasicTeamImpl`.

Our `Games` and `Teams` classes—that represent collections of `Game` objects and `Team` objects, respectively—need more work than just the separation of an interface. In order to achieve the layering we desire (in which application logic, persistence, and presentation are independent of each other), we will need a more complex split of the `Games` and `Teams` classes.

3.7   Separating Persistence from Games and Teams

For the `Team` and `Game` classes, we performed very simple modifications by separating the interface from the implementation. For the `Games` and `Teams` classes, we'll perform these same modifications, but also additional changes needed to separate the storage of the application data from the application logic.

Our application doesn't really support persistence as such. As originally envisioned, the application was expected to evolve to show various persistence mechanisms including storing data to flat files, using JDBC, and using the forthcoming Java Data Objects (JDO) interfaces. However, I decided that these permutations would distract from the book's primary subject, rather than contribute to it. Although we will continue to use our hard-coded data for now, we should prepare ourselves for the future by separating the persistence layer from the application layer now. So our original `Games` class will be transformed into two interfaces (`Games` and `GameData`) and two implementation classes (`BasicGamesImpl` and `BasicGameDataImpl`).

In Listing 3.11, there has also been another change made. Our original application was a "batch" application—read in data, compute results, print the standings. In many of the architectures to come, we'll add support for more dynamic behavior. One such dynamic behavior is the ability to enter the results of a game while the application runs, and then have the standings updated to reflect these new results. To facilitate doing so, our `Games` interface (and implementation) should allow `Game` objects to be added to the `gameList` field after the initial data load, and also allow for `Game` objects to be updated after their initial creation. The `addGame()` and `findGame()` methods allow this. (Note that an `updateGame()` method isn't required; once a user finds a game, they can use the methods of that `Game` object to perform updates).

Listing 3.11 The Games Interface

```
// Games.java

package nfl.application;

import java.io.*;
import java.util.*;
import nfl.ObjectFactory;

/** All games that have been played, and summary
  * information about them
  */
public interface Games
{
    public static final int GAMES_IN_SEASON = 16;

    // Accessors for the underlying gameList
    public  List getGameList();
    public  void setGameList(List g);

    // Following 2 methods were not part of original
    // interface. Added to permit updating of game
    // results while the application is running.

    // Add a game to the game list
    public void addGame(Game g);

    // Find a game in the game list
    public Game findGame(int week, String team);

    // Access subsets of the gameList
    public List getAllGamesFor(String team);
    public List getDivisionGamesFor(String team);
    public List getConferenceGamesFor(String team);
    public List getGamesBetween(String team1, String team2);
    public List getCommonGamesFor(String team1,
                                  String team2);

    // This is really a utility method, not tied to any
    // specific instance of the class. But interfaces
    // can't have static methods, so it becomes an instance
    // method.
    public /*static*/ float computeWinLossPctFor(String team,
                                          List games);
}
```

Listing 3.12 shows the class created to implement the Games interface. This class is nearly identical to the original Games class, with the addition of the methods mentioned previously.

Listing 3.12 The `BasicGamesImpl` Class

```
// BasicGamesImpl.java

package nfl.application;

import java.io.*;
import java.util.*;
import nfl.ObjectFactory;
import nfl.persistence.GameData;

/** All games that have been played, and summary information
  * about them
  */
public class BasicGamesImpl implements Games, Serializable
{
    private static Games games = new BasicGamesImpl();
    public  static Games getHandle() { return games; }

    /** The list of games that have been played */
    private List gameList;

    /** Returns all games played as a List */
    public  List getGameList()          { return gameList; }

    /** Sets the list of played games */
    public  void setGameList(List g)  { gameList = g; }

    /** Add a game to the game list */
    public void addGame(Game g) { gameList.add(g); }

    /** Find a game in the game list */
    public Game findGame(int week, String team) {
        String name = teams.findName(team);
        Iterator i = gameList.iterator();
        while (i.hasNext()) {
            Game g = (Game) i.next();
            if ((g.getWeek() == week) &&
                (g.getHome().equals(name) ||
                 g.getVisitor().equals(name))) {
                return g;
            }
        }
        return null;
```

```
      }

      /** A handle to the Teams object is used for determining
        * conference & division membership.
        */
      private Teams teams = (Teams)
            ObjectFactory.getHandle().getInstance("Teams");

      /** Constructor for the Games object. */
      private BasicGamesImpl() {
         ObjectFactory of = ObjectFactory.getHandle();
         GameData data = (GameData) of.getInstance("GameData");
         setGameList(data.getGameList());
      }

// ... skipping over unchanged methods
```

The GameData interface, shown in Listing 3.13, separates a single method from our previous design. This getGameList() method allows the Games class to request that the class' data be read from persistent storage and returned as a List. The implementation of the class is shown in Listing 3.14.

Listing 3.13 The GameData Interface

```
// GameData.java

package nfl.persistence;

import java.util.List;

public interface GameData
{
   /** Returns a List of Game objects */
   public List getGameList();
}
```

Listing 3.14 The BasicGameDataImpl Class

```
// BasicGameDataImpl.java

package nfl.persistence;

import java.io.*;
import java.util.*;
import nfl.application.Game;
import nfl.ObjectFactory;
```

```
public class BasicGameDataImpl implements GameData
{
    private static GameData gamedata = new BasicGameDataImpl();
    public static GameData getHandle() { return gamedata; }

    private List gameList = new ArrayList();
    public  List getGameList()        { return gameList; }

    // Constructor.
    private BasicGameDataImpl() {
        // format is week, visiting team & score,
        //                   home team & score
        ObjectFactory of = ObjectFactory.getHandle();

        // Week 1
        gameList.add(of.getInstance("Game", 1,
                    "San Francisco", 28, "Atlanta", 36));
        gameList.add(of.getInstance("Game", 1,
                    "Jacksonville", 27, "Cleveland", 7));
        gameList.add(of.getInstance("Game", 1,
                    "Colts", 27, "Kansas City", 14));
 // ... many more deleted
    }
}
```

The same pattern is repeated with the `Teams` and `TeamData` interfaces, and the implementing classes `BasicTeamsImpl` and `BasicTeamDataImpl`. Those listings won't be shown because they are basically repetitive.

3.8   Separating Presentation from the Standings Class

The `Standings` class includes both application logic and presentation logic, so it will be split into two parts. The part containing the application logic will continue to be called `Standings`, while the presentation logic will be placed into a class called `Console`, since that is the device it currently supports for output.

The `Standings` class is separated out into interface and implementation just as with all the previous classes. Listing 3.15 shows the `Standings` interface.

Listing 3.15 The `Standings` Interface

```
// Standings.java

package nfl.application;

import java.util.List;
import nfl.ObjectFactory;
```

```
/* Calculates and prints standings for all NFL conferences
 * and divisions
 */
public interface Standings
{
    // Hold all teams
    public  Teams getTeams();
    public  void  setTeams(Teams t);

    public  List getTeamList();
    public  void setTeamList(List t);

    // Holds all games
    public  Games getGames();
    public  void  setGames(Games g);

    public  List getGameList();
    public void  setGameList(List g);

    public  boolean getVerbose();
    public  void     setVerbose(boolean b);

    public  boolean getPrintTimings();
    public  void     setPrintTimings(boolean b);

    public int findTeam(String name);
    public void loadData();

    public List computeDivisionStandings(Division div);
    public List computeConferenceStandings(Conference conf);
}
```

Listing 3.16 shows the BasicStandingsImpl class that implements the Standings interface.

Listing 3.16 The BasicStandingsImpl Class

```
// BasicStandingsImpl.java

package nfl.application;

import java.io.*;
import java.text.DecimalFormat;
import java.util.*;

import nfl.ObjectFactory;
import nfl.VersionInfo;
import nfl.LayeredVersionInfo;
```

```java
/* Calculates and prints standings for all NFL conferences
 * and divisions
 */
public class BasicStandingsImpl implements Standings,
                                           Serializable
{
    // Hold all teams
    private Teams teams = (Teams)
            ObjectFactory.getHandle().getInstance("Teams");
    public  Teams getTeams()        { return teams; }
    public  void  setTeams(Teams t) { teams = t; }

    private List teamList;
    public  List getTeamList()       { return teamList; }
    public  void setTeamList(List t)  { teamList = t; }

    // Holds all games
    private Games games = (Games)
            ObjectFactory.getHandle().getInstance("Games");
    public  Games getGames()        { return games; }
    public  void  setGames(Games g) { games = g; }

    private List gameList;
    public  List getGameList()       { return gameList; }
    public void  setGameList(List g) { gameList = g; }

// ... skipping over unchanged methods

    /* Can't use getInstance() to init standings, because it
     * would just call getHandle()--getting null, since we
     * are in the middle of code to set value of standings
     */
    private static BasicStandingsImpl standings =
            new BasicStandingsImpl();
    public  static Standings getHandle() {
       return standings; }

    // Protected constructor makes subclassable singleton
    protected BasicStandingsImpl() {}

// ... omitting unchanged methods
}
```

3.9 Separating the User Interface: The Console Class

As we mentioned when discussing the `Standings` class, the presentation logic was removed from that class. The presentation logic was in two methods: `printConferenceStandings()` and `printDivisionStandings()`. For this round of refactoring, we've simply separated those methods but otherwise left them intact.

With the separation, `Console` now becomes our main class, rather than `Standings`. If you examine the `main()` method, you'll see that we create both a `Console` object and a `Standings` object, and then alternately invoke methods of the `Standings` object (to perform calculations) and the `Console` object (to display the results).

`Console` doesn't get a separate interface class; this is because `Console` is the "driver" class, and thus doesn't have any methods that we expect to be called from outside of the class (except for `main()`).

Listing 3.17 The `Console` Class

```
// Console.java

package nfl.presentation;

import java.text.DecimalFormat;
import java.util.List;

import nfl.ObjectFactory;
import nfl.application.*;

/** Displays standings on the stdout device */
public class Console
{
    private boolean printConferenceStandings = true;
    public  boolean getPrintConferenceStandings() {
       return printConferenceStandings; }
    public  void     setPrintConferenceStandings(boolean b) {
       printConferenceStandings = b; }

    // only used by Conference standings
    private boolean printEliminatedTeams = false;
    public  boolean getPrintEliminatedTeams() {
       return printEliminatedTeams; }
    public  void     setPrintEliminatedTeams(boolean b) {
       printEliminatedTeams = b; }

    public static void main(String[] args) {

        Standings standings = (Standings)
```

```
      ObjectFactory.getHandle().getInstance("Standings");
    Console console = new Console();

    standings.loadData();

    // Loop through divisions
    List divList = Division.DIVISIONS;
    for (int i=0; i<divList.size(); i++) {
       Division d = (Division) divList.get(i);
       List l = standings.computeDivisionStandings(d);
       console.printDivisionStandings(d, l);
    }

    if (!console.getPrintConferenceStandings()) return;
    // Loop through conferences

    List confList = Conference.CONFERENCES;
    for (int i=0; i<confList.size(); i++) {
       Conference c = (Conference) confList.get(i);
       List l = standings.computeConferenceStandings(c);
       console.printConferenceStandings(c, l);
    }
  }

  public void printDivisionStandings(Division div,
                                     List list) {
// ... method lifted unchanged from original Standings
  }

  public void printConferenceStandings(Conference conf,
                                       List list) {
// ... method lifted unchanged from original Standings
  }
}
```

3.10   Building and Running the Layered Application

The Ant buildfile for the layered application is shown in Listing 3.18. This buildfile is named layered.xml and located in the nfl directory on the CD.

In addition to the <compile>, <clean>, and <test> targets that were present in the original version of the buildfile, we add a new target named <jar>. This target creates a JAR file of all the application classes, which makes it easier to distribute the application. The <test> target has been modified to run the application out of the JAR file.

The <jar> target uses Ant's built-in <jar> task to accomplish its work. The <jar> task has a number of attributes that can be specified; we are using four of the more commonly used in this example. The jarfile attribute is required, and specifies the name of the file to be created.

The `manifest` attribute allows us to specify an optional manifest file for the JAR. We use the manifest to specify the `main-class` attribute of this JAR file, which is what allows us to run the application (in the test target) out of the JAR file without needing to know the precise classname to be invoked. The `basedir` attribute specifies the base directory from which `jar` will operate. With classes that are in packages, it's important that the full package name be stored as directory paths within the JAR. So our main class must be stored as `nfl/application/Stand-ings.class`, which means we must have the JAR file created from the directory above `nfl/`. Finally, the `includes` attribute allows us to JAR only files in the `nfl` directory; files to be JARred will be further restricted by the `fileset` elements that are nested inside the `<jar>` task.

   Three of the tasks in this buildfile—the `<compile>`, `<clean>`, and `<jar>` tasks—feature the use of filesets of one sort or another. Ant has several different ways of representing files and filesets, and many Ant tasks allow `<filesets>` to be specified as operands. In the `<compile>` target, we have nested within the `<javac>` task a set of source paths to be searched, and then the individual files to be compiled using the `include` file specification. In the `<clean>` target, the `<delete>` task uses the `<fileset>` command to match multiple files against the specified patterns, rather than specifying each file individually. And in the `<jar>` target, the `<jar>` task uses `<zipfilesets>`, which are very similar to `<filesets>` but allow the specification of an additional `prefix` attribute that ensures our full package name is stored as part of the class name within the JAR file.

Listing 3.18 The Ant Buildfile (`layered.xml`)

```
<project name="layered" default="jar" basedir=".">

<target name="compile">
  <javac>
    <src path="." />
    <include name="ObjectFactory.java"/>
    <include name="VersionInfo.java"/>
    <include name="LayeredVersionInfo.java"/>
    <src path="application" />
    <include name="Conference.java"/>
    <include name="Division.java"/>
    <include name="Game.java"/>
    <include name="BasicGameImpl.java"/>
    <include name="Games.java"/>
    <include name="BasicGamesImpl.java"/>
    <include name="Messaging.java"/>
    <include name="BasicMessagingImpl.java"/>
    <include name="Standings.java"/>
    <include name="BasicStandingsImpl.java"/>
    <include name="Team.java"/>
    <include name="BasicTeamImpl.java"/>
```

```
      <include name="Teams.java"/>
      <include name="BasicTeamsImpl.java"/>
      <src path="persistence" />
      <include name="GameData.java"/>
      <include name="BasicGameDataImpl.java"/>
      <include name="TeamData.java"/>
      <include name="BasicTeamDataImpl.java"/>
      <src path="presentation" />
      <include name="Console.java"/>
    </javac>
</target>

<target name="clean">
  <delete includeEmptyDirs="true">
    <fileset dir="." includes="*.class, *.jar" />
    <fileset dir="application" includes="*.class" />
    <fileset dir="persistence" includes="*.class" />
    <fileset dir="presentation" includes="*.class" />
  </delete>
</target>

<target name="jar" depends="compile">
   <jar jarfile="layered.jar" manifest="Manifest"
        basedir=".." includes="nfl" >
     <zipfileset dir="." prefix="nfl"
                         includes="*.class"
                         excludes="MakeListing.class" />
     <zipfileset dir="application" prefix="nfl/application"
         includes="Conference.class, Division.class,
            Game.class, Games.class, Messaging.class,
            Standings.class, Team*.class, Basic*.class" />
     <zipfileset dir="persistence" prefix="nfl/persistence"
         includes="*Data.class, Basic*.class" />
     <zipfileset dir="presentation" prefix="nfl/presentation"
         includes="Console.class" />
   </jar>
</target>

<target name="test">
   <java jar="layered.jar" fork="true" />
</target>

</project>
```

3.11   Exercises

3.1 XML-based `ObjectFactory`: Our `ObjectFactory` uses Java classes (`Version-Info` subclasses) to control the configuration. Nearly every Java utility that supports some sort of configuration or preferences file is moving toward XML-formatted files for this purpose. After learning XML syntax later in the book, you might try creating an `Object-Factory` that uses XML files rather than Java classes to choose the specific classes to be instantiated by the `ObjectFactory`.

3.12   Further Reading

The Enumerated Type idiom, used in the `Division`, `Conference`, and `Team.Status` classes, is described in both Bloch's *Effective Java Programming Language Guide* and Eckel's *Thinking in Java*.

The Abstract Factory pattern is described in Gamma et al's *Design Patterns: Elements of Reusable Object-Oriented Software*.

Web Applications

The difference between Web Services and Web applications is primarily one of presentation. Most Web Services will not be built from scratch, but rather bolted on to existing applications as a way to extend the usefulness of the underlying application. Understanding Web-application design thus becomes a prerequisite for being able to design Web Services.

The key technology in this part of the book is servlets. Servlets are perhaps the most important Java server-side technology; the attention given to Enterprise JavaBeans has tended to obscure just how versatile and powerful servlet technology is. If you have no interest in presenting your application via Web pages in addition to as a Web Service, then you can safely ignore the material on JavaServer Pages and Struts, and move directly from the servlets chapter to Part III of the book.

CHAPTER   4

Introduction to Presentation Architecture

I n the next several chapters, we'll be looking at ways to present the user interface of our application. With all the attention given to Web applications and Web Services, it's easy to start thinking that these are some radically new types of applications. In reality, the difference between a legacy application, a Web application, and a Web Service frequently comes down to nothing more than a change to the user interface. Not surprisingly, a great number of the examples in this book boil down to changing out the presentation, or user interface, layer within our example application.

We'll start in this chapter by broadly classifying our user interface choices into four groups: textual, graphical, Web presentation, and Web Services. We'll explain each of these categories in detail, as well as give some overview information about a few of the supporting technologies of which you'll need to have some understanding.

Then, in the remaining chapters of this section, we'll take a more detailed look at several popular options for Web presentation.

4.1 Textual Interfaces

Our example application provided a text-based, character-mode interface that was displayed to the terminal device from which the program was launched. This type of interface is one of the easiest to whip up during development, and also can be of aid in debugging because you can sprinkle `println()`s throughout your code.

Java has had a graphical user interface, in the form of the Abstract Windowing Toolkit (AWT), since JDK 1.0. This user interface was then greatly enhanced and expanded with the introduction of Java Foundation Classes (JFC) in JDK 1.2. But beginning in Java 2 SDK 1.4, Java also supports "headless" implementations of the SDK, which means that vendors that do not typically support graphical interfaces (such as mainframes) are not required to ship AWT and JFC components. So if you desire your application to be truly "Write Once, Run Anywhere," you must make some provision for non-graphical access to the application. A text-based interface is perhaps the simplest, but by no means the only, way to do so.

Since both our original and the layered application included text-based interfaces, we won't spend any additional time exploring this alternative in this section.

4.2 Graphical User Interfaces

Thanks to Windows and the Macintosh, when we think of user interfaces today it's almost always in terms of a window-based, graphical user interface (GUI). The APIs used within Java to create such GUIs are part of the J2SE package, and thus not within the scope of this book. A few good reference books on developing GUIs in Java are listed at the end of this chapter; here we'll just cover some of the basics without getting into the details.

4.2.1 The Abstract Windowing Toolkit

In the original versions of Java (JDK 1.0 and JDK 1.1.x), the Abstract Windowing Toolkit (AWT) was the GUI toolkit for Java. The goal of the AWT was to provide write-once, run-anywhere capability for one of the least portable parts of most applications, the user interface. The AWT didn't meet this objective perfectly (most of the complaints about the write-once, debug-everywhere nature of Java were directed at incompatibilities in AWT between Windows, UNIX, and Mac systems), but it was an important step toward meeting this goal. The AWT also suffered from not being as advanced as the platform-specific toolkits available; there was something of a least-common-denominator flavor to the interfaces created with AWT.

4.2.2 Java Foundation Classes and Swing

In the Java 2 platform (SDK 1.2), the Java Foundation Classes (JFC) were introduced. The JFC are built on top of the AWT framework, but extend it and in many cases replace its functionality. The JFC included an all new set of graphical components known as Swing; these lightweight components provide better performance than the heavyweight AWT components and also provide greater capabilities. Rather than providing just the basic graphical widgets, Swing components provided additional capabilities such as floating, dockable toolbars, tooltips, and tabbed dialogs. The pluggable look-and-feel design of Swing allows the designer (or, if the designer decides to defer to the end-user, the user) to decide whether to give a platform-dependent look-and-feel or a portable look-and-feel to the application. Aside from the Swing components, JFC included features such as greater localizability, accessibility APIs, and drag-and-drop support.

JFC and Swing were largely successful in realizing the promise of write-once, run-anywhere capability across the various clients that were envisioned at the time—PCs, workstations, and Macs—with the code running either as a standalone application or within a browser. However, this success came just as the market was shifting, and suddenly the range of client devices expanded to include PDAs, cellphones, and many other devices with form factors not addressed by Swing's flexible layout managers. We'll see how these new clients are being addressed in the wireless and Web Services chapters.

Although developing a JFC interface for the application isn't covered in this book, I did experiment with creating one. Although the code was never finished, enough was completed to create the screen shot in Figure 4.1 of a prototype JFC user interface.

Figure 4.1   A JFC interface.

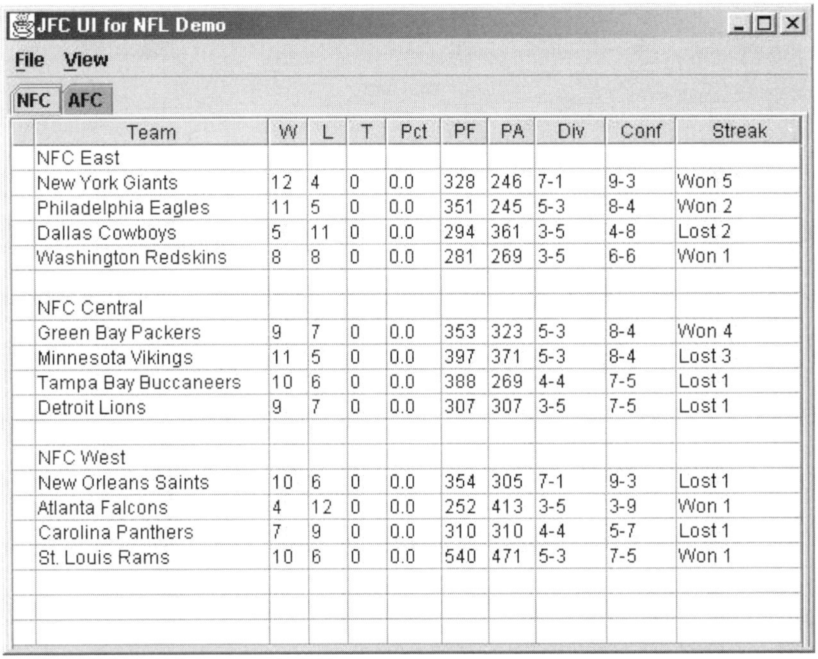

JFC UI for NFL Demo

File   View

NFC | AFC

Team	W	L	T	Pct	PF	PA	Div	Conf	Streak
NFC East									
New York Giants	12	4	0	0.0	328	246	7-1	9-3	Won 5
Philadelphia Eagles	11	5	0	0.0	351	245	5-3	8-4	Won 2
Dallas Cowboys	5	11	0	0.0	294	361	3-5	4-8	Lost 2
Washington Redskins	8	8	0	0.0	281	269	3-5	6-6	Won 1
NFC Central									
Green Bay Packers	9	7	0	0.0	353	323	5-3	8-4	Won 4
Minnesota Vikings	11	5	0	0.0	397	371	5-3	8-4	Lost 3
Tampa Bay Buccaneers	10	6	0	0.0	388	269	4-4	7-5	Lost 1
Detroit Lions	9	7	0	0.0	307	307	3-5	7-5	Lost 1
NFC West									
New Orleans Saints	10	6	0	0.0	354	305	7-1	9-3	Lost 1
Atlanta Falcons	4	12	0	0.0	252	413	3-5	3-9	Won 1
Carolina Panthers	7	9	0	0.0	310	310	4-4	5-7	Lost 1
St. Louis Rams	10	6	0	0.0	540	471	5-3	7-5	Won 1

4.2.3   Applets

Applets are another technology that dates back to the earliest versions of Java. One of the biggest problems with the client-server software model is the distribution of client software. Even in a corporate environment, where all of the clients are theoretically under the control of a central IT staff, updating all clients with new software is difficult and expensive. If your intent is to make your application accessible to anyone, from any device, then software distribution via diskette or CD becomes inconceivable (unless you're AOL) and you must leverage the Internet.

HTML, which will be covered shortly, is an obvious solution, since it doesn't require distributing any software. But the graphical capabilities of HTML fall far short of the capabilities even of the older AWT interfaces.

Java applets address the distribution problem. They are AWT or Swing-based clients that are distributed via the Web. When a user accesses an HTML page containing an applet, that applet is downloaded to the user's system, and is then executed locally under the control of the Web browser. Applets have a very strict security model, since the downloading and execution of code from untrusted sites is potentially a very dangerous thing to do. Although Java-capable browsers are installed on at least as many systems as Microsoft Outlook, applets have not been used as a virus delivery mechanism because of this solid security model.

Applets helped propel the initial explosive growth of Java, but over time other designs have gained greater favor and they are not so widely used today. Applets have several disadvantages that eventually led to this decline in popularity. One disadvantage is the download time required to bring the applet into the browser, especially as applications become more complex. An even bigger disadvantage was the dependency this introduced on the Web browser platform, especially in an environment where the dominant browser vendor is hostile to Java. These shortcomings are at least partially addressed—for example with compressed JAR files to speed downloads, and the Java Plug-In technology to facilitate easy upgrades of the Java capabilities within any major browser. But other technologies, such as servlets, appeared on the scene, and applets will probably continue to fall out of favor.

4.2.4   Java Web Start

Java Web Start (JWS) can be seen as a direct descendent of applet technology. JWS tries to take what was good about applets—the ability to have a client that was far more robust than just HTML, and have it downloaded on demand—and build upon that while avoiding some of the drawbacks of applets. These drawbacks included being tied to the browser, and forcing repeated downloads of the same applet even if it did not change.

With JWS, you access and launch the application via a URL, just as you do with an applet. The first time you access an application via JWS, it will be downloaded to your system. It then runs outside of, and completely independent from, the browser. JWS can also handle downloading the Java Virtual Machine for your system or other components that might be required.

The next time you launch the application (via the browser as before), you won't download any unchanged components; so if the application hasn't changed, you'll have no download time at all.

4.3   Web Browser Interfaces

Perhaps the most in-demand style of interface today is for a browser-accessible Web interface. We'll look at specific technologies for creating a Web-based interface in the next few chapters, but right now we'll lay the foundation by looking at two standards upon which all browser technologies are based: HTTP and HTML.

4.3.1   HTTP: The World Wide Web Protocol

HTTP stands for HyperText Transfer Protocol. Web browsers and Web servers communicate to each other using this protocol. It is usually thought of together with HTML, a standard for marking up documents, which will be covered in the next section. However, HTTP is used today to transfer much more than just simple text documents: video, audio, and all sorts of complex document types are regularly shipped between systems via the HTTP protocol. The reason this is possible is that the protocol itself is just a transport mechanism; it doesn't care what sort of cargo it carries. There's a facility for communicating what type of data is being passed (using an extensible mechanism known as MIME types), but that is just so that the sender and receiver can notify each other of the content type; the transport protocol doesn't care.

HTTP is a request-reply protocol. Requests are sent by the client; the server acts upon the request and sends a reply. HTTP is stateless, meaning that once a reply has been sent, the interaction is considered complete; if another request comes from the same client, it will be as if it's the first time we ever heard from that client. Much smoke and mirrors has been expended upon adding state on top of the stateless protocol, via cookies, hidden fields on forms, URL rewriting, and many other techniques. But the underlying protocol continues to operate on the basis of one request, one response, end of story.

An HTTP request consists of a method name (typically GET or POST), a resource identifier (what we're trying to get), and the client's HTTP protocol version. For example, if we type the following into our browser's navigation bar:

```
http://localhost:8080/nfl/servlet/NFLStandings
```

The browser is going to then format a request and send it to the server. The first line of the request will look like this:

```
GET /nfl/Servlet/NFLStandings HTTP/1.0
```

The protocol, server name, and port number were pieces of information actually used by the browser and by the HTTP protocol itself to get the request routed properly; the request tells the recipient (the server) to retrieve the resource identified by the Uniform Resource Identifier (URI) and send it back, using HTTP 1.0 protocol. A complete HTTP request will contain other lines following this one that specify the document types the browser is able to receive, the browser version, and localization information (language and character set encoding). These elements aren't of interest to us in the context of this discussion; we'll trust the server and browser to get them right.

The server will produce and send back an HTTP response. The response consists of the header, primarily for the use of the browser, and the body, which is the resource that was requested. The first line of the header consists of the HTTP protocol version, a numeric status code, and then a brief textual description of that status. For our request in this example, we might see a response beginning with the following:

```
HTTP/1.0 200 OK
```

The remainder of the header includes timestamps, version information about the server, the content type (from the list of MIME types), and the content length if known. Although there are many MIME types, we're concerned only with the type `text/html`, which is used for all HTML documents.

If the browser couldn't satisfy our request for some reason, we'd get back a different header status, such as the very familiar:

```
HTTP/1.0 404 NOT FOUND
```

The only other method we're concerned with is the POST method, which is used when filling out HTML forms and pressing a button to submit the data. POST is routed to the server exactly like a GET method, with the addition of a request body following the standard headers. The message body contains a set of name=value pairs, joined by ampersands. For example, if we had a form with two fields, firstname and lastname, and entered the name Bob Smith into this form, then the message body when we posted the form would include the following:

```
firstname=Bob&lastname=Smith
```

Because the message body is not saved when you bookmark a URL, and cannot be easily embedded as a link to another page, frequently browsers will choose to use a GET method rather than POST, and encode the parameters as part of the URL. The parameter name-value pairs are appended to the URL, with a question mark used to mark the start of the parameters. When this is done, you'll see something like this in your navigation bar:

```
http://localhost/logon.cgi?firstname=Bob&lastname=Smith
```

That's really about all the HTTP you need to know as a user of Web browsers and Web servers. Let's move on to what's actually in those documents we're serving.

4.3.2   HTML: The Language of Web Presentation

Output designed to be displayed in Web browsers has traditionally been formatted as HyperText Markup Language (HTML). As browsers have become more sophisticated, they have acquired capabilities to display many more types of documents, including those containing audio and video. For the purposes of this book, we'll restrict ourselves to HTML and XML (which will be described in the following section) as Web presentation alternatives.

Many readers will already be familiar with HTML, but for those who haven't had exposure I'll present just enough of a primer here to help you understand the example programs that follow. For more detailed information about HTML, see the references listed at the end of this chapter.

HTML is a markup language. An HTML document is made up of elements; the elements are separated by tags. Most elements have both a start and an end tag, although some tags can be used singly. The tags in an HTML element can be easily identified because they are set between angle brackets (< and >).

An HTML document should begin with the tag <HTML> and end with the tag </HTML>. The slash character is used to indicate that it is an end tag. The document is further divided into a HEAD element and a BODY element. For example, here's about the simplest possible HTML document:

```
<HTML>
  <HEAD>
    <TITLE>This is a sample HTML page</TITLE>
  </HEAD>
  <BODY>
    <B>Hello, World!</B>
  </BODY>
</HTML>
```

In this example, we have an HTML document that includes both a head and a body. The head contains a single element, the title. (The title is the text that will appear in the title bar of the browser window when this document is displayed.) In the body portion, we have the text "Hello, World!" surrounded by tags that indicate formatting style B—which is bold. HTML tags are not case-sensitive; however, XML tags are. Future versions of HTML are becoming XML-specified languages, so using lowercase is actually preferable, although I expect browsers to continue to support uppercase HTML tags for the foreseeable future.

HTML documents can get quite complex; for example, they can include JavaScript programming code (which bears only a passing similarity to Java), forms, tables, links to other documents, and many different types of complex formatting.

The next section covers only a small number of the HTML elements, focusing primarily on those used within the examples in this book.

A Brief Introduction to HTML Elements

Structural Elements. The basic HTML document structure has these elements: HTML, HEAD, and BODY. Elements can also have attributes attached to them. An attribute is additional information in the format name='value' that is placed within the start tag of an element. The quotes can be either single or double quotes. For example,

```
<BODY bgcolor='white' text='black'>
```

is a start tag for the body of an HTML document that sets two attributes: the background color and the text color. This particular example is actually a deprecated usage, as the preferred way to accomplish the same thing is now to use style sheets. The same settings could be specified in a style sheet as follows:

```
<STYLE type='text/css'>
  BODY { background: white; color: black }
</STYLE>
```

Text Formatting. When you enter text in an HTML document, white space and paragraph formatting are ignored when the document is actually formatted. So, for example, just hitting Return a couple of times at the end of a paragraph will not begin a new paragraph. To create a paragraph, use the <P> and </P> tags around your text. If you have something, such as computer output, that needs to be reproduced exactly as you type it in, use the <pre> and </pre> tags around it to indicate that it is pre-formatted and should not be reformatted. Also, you can force a line break at any point you need with the <br> tag, which does not have a matching end tag.

Lists. Frequently you'll need to format a list within an HTML document. There are three basic list styles available. An unordered list is a simple bulleted list of items. The list is delimited by <UL> and </UL> tags, and within the list each item begins with <LI> (List Item) and has no end tag. An ordered list is nearly identical to the unordered list, except that items will be numbered rather than bulleted. The ordered list is delimited by <OL> and </OL> tags, and list items are identified with <LI> start tags just as within the unordered list. The final style is a definition list, useful for producing something like a glossary or index. The definition list is delimited by <DL> and </DL> tags; each entry is made up of a pair of items, the term (marked by <DT> and </DT> tags), and the definition (marked by <DD> and </DD>).

Tables. Tables can be quite complex; the HTML syntax for tables is quite flexible and robust. We only use a small subset of the available functionality in creating our table of standings. The complete table is enclosed in <TABLE> and </TABLE> tags; within those tags are a number of additional elements. For example, a <CAPTION> element can be used to provide a caption for the table. Rows within the table can be grouped, using the <THEAD>, <TBODY>, and <TFOOT> tags along with their matching end tags. Columns can also be grouped using <COLGROUP>. None of these grouping elements are required, so our initial examples don't use them. We instead just provide a series of table rows, delimited by the <TR> tag. Within each row, we have either a series of <TH> cells, in the table header, or <TD> cells in the data portion of the table.

Links. Almost all HTML documents have at least one link to another document. These links are put into the document by the <A>, or anchor, tag. An anchor tag must have an href= attribute that indicates the URL to which the link is attached.

Forms. HTML forms provide a way to collect data from the user for processing. An HTML form is contained within <FORM> and </FORM> tags (did anybody not see that coming?) The <FORM> tag has two important attributes. The action=attribute, which is required, identifies (via URI) the form processing agent, such as a script or servlet, that will handle the form's data. The method=attribute specifies the HTTP method to be used, either GET or POST (defaults to GET). Within the form are various controls, such as checkboxes, radio buttons, textfields, and menus.

The <INPUT> tag is used for any field that allows user input. This comprises several types of controls; the type=attribute in the start tag is used to select which control type is desired. In our examples, we use only type=text, for textfields, and type=submit, to create a pushbutton to submit the data.

The <SELECT> tag is used to create a selection menu, typically rendered as a drop-down selection list. Within the <SELECT> and </SELECT> tags can be any number of <OPTION> tags, which identify the selectable choices.

Producing HTML Output of the Standings

In the following chapter, we'll look at Java servlets, and the servlets we construct there will use HTML as their output format. However, because HTML can be used in many different architectures other than servlets, and because servlets can produce output in formats other than HTML, it seemed best to separate out the discussion of HTML to this more general chapter. Each time we alter the application, we'll summarize the changes and additions in a table such as Table 4.1.

Table 4.1   Components in the HTML via CGI Application

New Components			
Name	**Package**	**Class or Interface**	**Comment**
CgiVersionInfo	nfl.presentation.cgi	Class	`VersionInfo` subclass
NullMessagingImpl	nfl.application	Class	Empty implementation of `Messaging.show()`
HTML	nfl.presentation	Class	Based on `Console` class, with HTML formatted output
Existing Components			
Component	**Description**		
layered.jar	All classes and interfaces of the layered version of the application (as presented in Chapter 2)		

In Listing 4.1, we've taken the `Console` class we developed for the layered application (Chapter 3) and rewritten it to display its output in HTML. For the division standings, we've used HTML tables. For the conference standings, we just use normal text. All of the tags used within this page are described in the HTML section found previously in this chapter.

Listing 4.1 The HTML Class

```
// HTML.java

package nfl.presentation;

import java.io.PrintWriter;
import java.text.DecimalFormat;
import java.util.List;

import nfl.ObjectFactory;
import nfl.application.*;

/** Displays standings with HTML markup */
public class HTML
{
    private boolean printConferenceStandings = true;
    public  boolean getPrintConferenceStandings() {
        return printConferenceStandings; }
    public  void    setPrintConferenceStandings(boolean b) {
        printConferenceStandings = b; }

    // only used by Conference standings
    private boolean printEliminatedTeams = false;
    public  boolean getPrintEliminatedTeams() {
        return printEliminatedTeams; }
    public  void    setPrintEliminatedTeams(boolean b) {
        printEliminatedTeams = b; }

    public static void main(String[] args) {

        HTML html = new HTML();
        PrintWriter out = new PrintWriter(System.out);

        out.println("Content-type: text/html\n");
        html.printHtmlHead(out, "NFL Standings");

        Standings standings =  (Standings)
          ObjectFactory.getHandle().getInstance("Standings");
        standings.loadData();

        // Loop through divisions
        List divList = Division.DIVISIONS;
        for (int i=0; i<divList.size(); i++) {
            Division d = (Division) divList.get(i);
            List l = standings.computeDivisionStandings(d);
            html.printDivisionStandings(d, l, out);
        }
```

```java
      if (!html.getPrintConferenceStandings()) return;
      // Loop through conferences

      List confList = Conference.CONFERENCES;
      for (int i=0; i<confList.size(); i++) {
         Conference c = (Conference) confList.get(i);
         List l = standings.computeConferenceStandings(c);
         html.printConferenceStandings(c, l, out);
      }

      html.printHtmlEnd(out);
   }

   public void printHtmlHead(PrintWriter out,
                             String title) {
      out.println("<!DOCTYPE HTML PUBLIC " +
         "'-//W3C/DTD HTML 4.01 Transitional//EN'" +
         "'http://www.w3.org/TR/html4/loose.dtd'>");
      out.println("<html>");
      out.println("<head>");
      out.println("<title>" + title + "</title>");
      out.println("</head>");
      out.println("<body>");
   }

   public void printHtmlEnd(PrintWriter out) {
      out.println("</body>");
      out.println("</html>");
   }

   public void printDivisionStandings(Division div,
                             List list, PrintWriter out) {
      // Print details
      Team team = (Team) list.get(0);

      out.println("<table border=1>");
      out.println("<TD colspan=10>" +
                  "<H2>" + div  + "</H2></TD><TR>");
      out.println("<TH>Team</TH>    <TH>Wins</TH> " +
                  "<TH>Losses</TH> <TH>Ties</TH>"   +
                  "<TH>PCT</TH>     <TH>PF</TH>"     +
                  "<TH>PA</TH>      <TH>Div</TH>"    +
                  "<TH>Conf</TH>    <TH>Streak</TH>");
      out.println("<TR>");

      for (int i=0; i<list.size(); i++) {
         team = (Team) list.get(i);
```

```
      out.print("<TD>");
      out.print(team.getFullName() + "<TD>");
      out.print(team.getWins()     + "<TD> ");
      out.print(team.getLosses()   + "<TD> ");
      out.print(team.getTies()     + "<TD> ");

      DecimalFormat nf = new DecimalFormat("#.000");
      out.print(nf.format(team.getOverallWinLossPct()) + "<TD> ");

      out.print(team.getPoints()            + "<TD> ");
      out.print(team.getPointsAllowed()     + "<TD> ");
      out.print(team.getDivisionWins()      + "-" +
             team.getDivisionLosses()    + "<TD> ");
      out.print(team.getConferenceWins()    + "-" +
             team.getConferenceLosses()  + "<TD> ");

      if (team.getStreak() > 0) {
         out.println("Won " + team.getStreak());
      } else if (team.getStreak() < 0) {
         out.println("Lost " + (-1 * team.getStreak()));
      } else out.println();
      out.println("<TD><TR>");
   }
   out.println("</TABLE>");
}

public void printConferenceStandings(Conference conf,
                     List list, PrintWriter out) {
   Team t = null;

   out.println("<H2>" + conf +
             " Playoff Seedings</H2>");

   for (int i=0; i<list.size(); i++) {
      t = (Team) list.get(i);

      if (!getPrintEliminatedTeams())
         // Don't print teams that are eliminated from
         // playoff contention
         if (t.getWildcardStatus() ==
                   Team.Status.ELIMINATED) break;

      out.print((i+1) + ". ");

      out.print(t.getFullName() + ": ");

      // Home field advantage
      if (t.getHomeFieldStatus() ==
            Team.Status.CLINCHED) {
```

```
      out.print("Clinched homefield. ");
   } else if (t.getHomeFieldStatus() ==
                     Team.Status.CLINCHED_TIE) {
     out.print("Clinched tie for homefield. ");
   } else if (t.getHomeFieldStatus() ==
                     Team.Status.LEADING) {
     out.print("Leading in homefield. ");
   } else if (t.getHomeFieldStatus() ==
                     Team.Status.IN_CONTENTION) {
     out.print("Contender for homefield. ");
   } /* print nothing for eliminated teams */

   // Division leaders
   if (t.getDivisionChampStatus() ==
                   Team.Status.CLINCHED) {
     out.print("Clinched " + t.getDivision()+ ". ");
   } else if (t.getDivisionChampStatus() ==
                     Team.Status.CLINCHED_TIE) {
     out.print("Clinched at least tie in " +
             t.getDivision() + ". ");
   } else if (t.getDivisionChampStatus() ==
             Team.Status.LEADING) {
     out.print("Leads " + t.getDivision() + ". ");
   } else if (t.getDivisionChampStatus() ==
             Team.Status.IN_CONTENTION) {
     out.print("Contender for " + t.getDivision() +
             ". ");
   } /* print nothing for eliminated teams */

   // Wildcards
   if (t.getWildcardStatus() ==
       Team.Status.CLINCHED) {
     // If division clinched, don't print wildcard
     // clinched also.
     if (!(t.getDivisionChampStatus() ==
                     Team.Status.CLINCHED))
       out.print("Clinched wildcard");
   } else if (t.getWildcardStatus() ==
                     Team.Status.CLINCHED_TIE) {
     if (!(t.getDivisionChampStatus() ==
                     Team.Status.CLINCHED))
       out.print("Clinched tie for wildcard");
   } else if (t.getWildcardStatus() ==
                     Team.Status.LEADING) {
     // We only print something here if not
     // leading division
     if (!t.getDivisionChampStatus().isLeader())
       out.print("In position for wildcard berth");
```

```
        } else if (t.getWildcardStatus() ==
                            Team.Status.IN_CONTENTION) {
            // We only print something here if not in
            // division contention
            if (t.getDivisionChampStatus() ==
                            Team.Status.ELIMINATED)
                out.print("Contender for wildcard");
        } else out.print("Eliminated from playoffs");
        out.println("<br>");
    }
    out.println();
    out.flush();
    }
}
```

There are several things worth noting in the listing of the HTML class. There are new methods, printHtmlHead() and printHtmlEnd(), that take care of the very first and last items on our page. Within the printDivisionStandings() method, we've been able to jettison all the ugly code dealing with column alignment, because the HTML table will take care of this for us. In our main() method, we write out the line Content-type: text/html, which tells the browser that the content that follows is in HTML format.

We have one other trivial class we've added. Since our tiebreaker messages are not properly HTML formatted, it's not a good idea to have them interspersed into the output. We'll look at better solutions later, but for right now we'll just suppress the messages altogether by creating a Messaging class that throws away the messages. This is called the NullMessagingImpl class, and it's shown in Listing 4.2.

Listing 4.2 The NullMessagingImpl Class

```
// NullMessagingImpl.java

package nfl.application;

import nfl.ObjectFactory;

/** Disables the messaging facility. */
public class NullMessagingImpl implements Messaging {

    private static Messaging m = new NullMessagingImpl();
    public  static Messaging getHandle() { return m; }

    private NullMessagingImpl() {}

    /** Discards the message */
    public void show(String message) { }

}
```

Building the Example Code and Executing Using CGI

We'd like a way to test this code and make sure it's correct. We can actually run our HTML class from the command line, just as we did with the Console class on which it is based. But unless you're particularly good at reading embedded HTML tags, you won't really know whether this document is being formatted the way you'd like.

In Listing 4.3, we see an example Ant buildfile for creating an application that allows us to test the new HTML class. This buildfile is located in the nfl/application/cgi directory on the CD. The default <jar> target creates a JAR file that can be deployed on a Web server to be invoked via the CGI facility.

Listing 4.3 Ant Buildfile for Testing HTML Output with CGI

```
<!-- build.xml for HTML & CGI example -->

<project name="cgi" default="jar" basedir="." >

<target name="compile">
   <javac>
      <src path="." />
      <include name="CgiVersionInfo.java" />
      <src path=".." />
      <include name="NullMessagingImpl.java" />
      <src path="../../presentation" />
      <include name="HTML.java" />
   </javac>
</target>

<target name="clean">
   <delete>
      <fileset dir="." includes="*.class,*.jar" />
      <fileset dir=".."
         includes="NullMessagingImpl.class" />
      <fileset dir="../../presentation"
         includes="HTML.class" />
   </delete>
</target>

<target name="jar" depends="compile">
   <jar jarfile="nflcgi.jar">
      <zipfileset dir="../.." prefix="nfl"
            includes="ObjectFactory.class,
                      VersionInfo.class" />
      <zipfileset dir=".." prefix="nfl/application"
            includes="*.class" />
```

```
        <zipfileset dir="." prefix="nfl/application/cgi"
              includes="CgiVersionInfo.class" />
        <zipfileset dir="../../persistence"
                prefix="nfl/persistence"
              includes="*.class" />
        <zipfileset dir="../../presentation"
                prefix="nfl/presentation"
              includes="HTML.class" />
    </jar>
</target>

</project>
```

The oldest method for presenting dynamic content from a Web server is using a facility known as CGI, the Common Gateway Interface. CGI is not particularly well-suited to Java, because it requires starting up a new Java Virtual Machine for every page request that comes in. The architectures we'll examine later for doing dynamic Web content are all better for this type of task than CGI. But you may occasionally need to fall back to CGI if you're dealing with an older Web server that doesn't support servlets or JSPs. We'll use CGI to test out our HTML class simply because we haven't yet covered any other mechanisms.

To invoke our class, we'll need to create a small shell script (or .bat file on Microsoft Windows) and place that class in the appropriate place. For most Web servers, there is a dedicated directory named cgi-bin where such scripts should be placed (on my system, for example, this directory is located at /usr/local/apache/cgi-bin). Web servers can also be configured to treat files in other directories as CGI files if they have an appropriate extension, such as .cgi. For the Apache Web Server, the cgi directory and file extensions that should be considered CGI scripts are configured via the httpd.conf file.

Listing 4.4 shown an example of a script that could be used to invoke our class.

Listing 4.4 The nfl.cgi Script

```
#!/bin/sh
cd /home/myawn
. ./.profile
# needed for uname, basename in java wrapper script
export PATH=/usr/bin:$PATH
cd public_html
java -cp nflcgi.jar nfl.presentation.html
#java -cp nflcgi.jar nfl.presentation.html | \
   tee cgi.out 2>&1
```

The CGI script turned out to be a bigger challenge than I would have guessed. For one thing, Apache clears many of the environment variables when creating son processes to execute CGI scripts, probably for reasons of security. As a result, the script that worked fine when run from a command prompt failed when executed via CGI. Furthermore, the error messages that might have helped identify the problem went into the bit bucket. On the last (commented) line of the script, you can see how I captured all of the output from both `stdout` and `stderr` to a file when testing the script; from here I could find that my `PATH` was not set correctly, and that other elements from my environment were not properly set. With a few added lines to the script to correct for these, the script then functioned, and it no longer needs to capture this information.

After placing the script within the appropriate directory, we just need to point our browser at the script. The resulting output is shown in Figure 4.2.

Figure 4.2 Output of the `HTML` class.

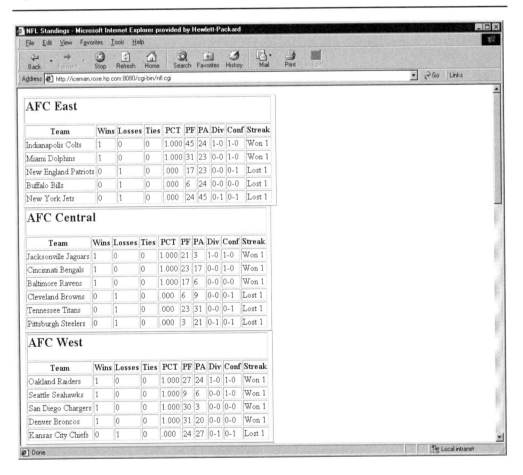

4.4   Web Services

Like the Web-browser interfaces, these are interfaces that are designed to support access via the Internet. But instead of a browser being viewed by a user, in the Web Services arena we think of system-to-system communications where our client is another computer program, rather than a human. Sometimes this client that accesses the service is going to format any data it receives and display it to the user, but in the future it will be more and more common that the data be stored, massaged, consolidated with data from other sources, summarized, and then made available to end-users.

4.4.1   XML: The Language of Web Services

XML is a markup language similar to HTML (in fact, both are derived from the same root, SGML, which is the Simplified General Markup Language). XML stands for eXtensible Markup Language, and it is the extensibility that gives XML its power.

With HTML, there is a predefined set of tags that we are allowed to use. Every HTML document designer has the same set of tags with which to work, even though the tasks they may try to perform might be radically different. With XML, the document author gets to define whatever tags are needed to represent the data they are presenting. For example, let's look at how we might define an XML representation of our Game class. Like HTML tags, XML tags may also contain attributes. There are actually some who argue against the use of attributes, since they are not strictly necessary: Everything that could be put as an attribute value could also be declared as a separate element. To illustrate this, in Listing 4.5 we show a Game represented using as few elements as possible, with attributes on nearly every element. Listing 4.6 shows the same Game represented using only elements. Figure 4.3 is a graphical representation of the XML document shown in Listing 4.6. The important thing to notice is that this document, like all XML documents, is a hierarchical structure having a single top-level element.

Listing 4.5 Game Represented with Elements and Attributes

```
<?xml version="1.0" ?>
<!DOCTYPE game SYSTEM "game-elem-attr.dtd" >
<game week="01" played="yes">
   <home city="Atlanta" name="Falcons" score="14" />
   <visitor city="San Francisco" name="49ers" score="17" />
</game>
```

Listing 4.6 Game Represented Using Only Elements

```xml
<?xml version="1.0" ?>
<!DOCTYPE game SYSTEM "game-elem.dtd">
<game>
    <week>01</week>
    <played>yes</played>
    <home>
        <city>Atlanta</city>
        <name>Falcons</name>
        <score>14</score>
    </home>
    <visitor>
        <city>San Francisco</city>
        <name>49ers</name>
        <score>17</score>
    </visitor>
</game>
```

Figure 4.3 The Game document represented hierarchically.

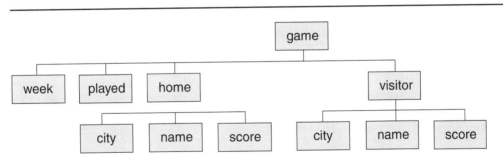

Now if you're thinking about sending one of these documents to a Web browser, it's pretty clear that the Web browser is not going to have any idea what formatting you might want to apply to something tagged with one of these identifiers. And that's because XML isn't describing formatting for a document, but rather the data content. Although the latest browsers can display XML documents, as seen in Figure 4.4, XML should be thought of more as a self-describing file format for passing data between programs.

Figure 4.4   XML displayed in a browser.

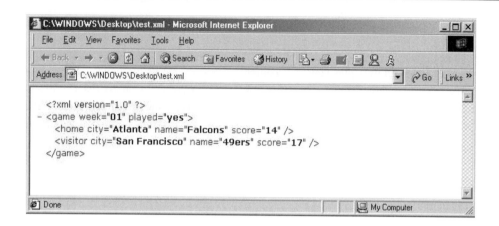

The browser can detect whether our XML document is well-formed. For example, the browser checks whether all start tags have either a matching end tag, or terminate with a slash character indicating that they are complete in and of themselves. But it can't determine that the document is valid—that the elements and attributes we specify are valid subelements for the <game> element. For this, we need to provide a description of the document that tells what tags are available, whether they are required or optional, what attributes they may (or must) have, and so forth. This description can take one of two forms: a Document Type Definition (DTD) or an XML Schema. DTDs use different syntax than XML, and don't have as much flexibility as schemas—for example, you are constrained to use a predefined set of datatypes in DTDs, while you can define your own new ones in a schema. But as of XML 1.0, DTDs are the only way to validate an XML file, so XML schemas are more of an up-and-coming technology that isn't yet fully supported by the many XML tools and utilities you'll be using to create documents and Web Services.

Document Type Definitions (DTDs)

In order to validate an XML document, it must have a DTD, either included inline or as a separate document. Before looking at a sample DTD, I'll briefly cover the types of elements we'll see in the DTDs.

Doctype. The !DOCTYPE element is placed in the XML file, and specifies the element name being defined (game). This is followed by either an embedded DTD or a reference to where the DTD can be found.

Elements. The document is made up of elements; our DTD includes an !ELEMENT declaration for each element that may exist. In Listing 4.7, we define only three elements; game, home, and visitor. Listing 4.8, where we use only elements and no attributes, includes eight elements.

The `!ELEMENT` tag is followed immediately by the element name, and then additional information about the contents of the element. Let's take several examples to show the possible ways we can specify an element's contents.

The `game` element in Listing 4.7 has a content of `(home, visitor)` specified. This indicates that exactly one `home` element is required, followed by exactly one `visitor` element. If either name was followed by a plus sign, (for example, `home+`), that would indicate that one or more occurrences of the item were required. If instead it were followed by an asterisk (for example, `visitor*`), then it would be an optional element with zero or more allowed. Finally, if a question mark were used (for example, `home?`), then either zero or one occurrence would be allowed.

The `home` and `visitor` elements in Listing 4.7 have their content specified as `EMPTY`. This means it is illegal to provide any content for the element. Instead of a start tag, content, and an end tag, there should be only a start tag terminated by a slash. We use empty elements here because everything for these elements is being specified as an attribute, rather than as content.

The `played` element in Listing 4.7 provides an "or" choice; either `yes` or `no` is required as the element content; we further specify that "yes" is the default value if this attribute is not specified in an XML document using this DTD. More choices could be specified; the choices could also include other elements as choices along with the constant values.

Finally, anywhere we expect to see text between a start tag and an end tag we specify the content as `#PCDATA`, which stands for Parsed Character Data. Parsed Character Data may include markup (for example, nested tags). `CDATA`, or Character Data, is used for elements or attributes where only simple character text is permitted.

Another option, but one that isn't used in our example, is to specify `ANY`, which allows any valid content (character data, other elements, or `EMPTY`) to be provided as content for the element.

Attributes. In Listing 4.7, each of our three elements has an attribute list, identified by an `!ATTLIST` element. The `!ATTLIST` tag is followed by the name of the element to which the attribute list applies. Following this are the attributes; each one begins with a name, followed by a type and any additional information that might be needed. Our `game` element, for example, has two attributes: `week` is a `CDATA` field, which is required; `played` is one of either `yes` or `no`, with `yes` being implied if no value is provided.

The `home` and `visitor` elements have identical attribute lists: `city`, `name`, and `score`, all three of which are `CDATA` fields. The `city` and `name` are required; `score` will default to zero if not provided.

Listing 4.7 Game.dtd for the Attribute-Heavy Version of Game.xml

```
<!ELEMENT game (home, visitor)>
<!ATTLIST game
         week CDATA #REQUIRED
         played (yes | no) "yes" >
<!ELEMENT home EMPTY>
<!ATTLIST home
         city CDATA #REQUIRED
         name CDATA #REQUIRED
         score CDATA #REQUIRED>
<!ELEMENT visitor EMPTY>
<!ATTLIST visitor
         city CDATA #REQUIRED
         name CDATA #REQUIRED
         score CDATA #REQUIRED>
```

The DTD and the XML file are associated by the <!DOCTYPE> line in the XML game.xml file, immediately following the <?xml> header:

```
<!DOCTYPE game SYSTEM "game-elem-attr.dtd">
```

Alternately, we could embed the DTD directly into our XML file at the same point; if we did so, then we would add the attribute standalone="yes" to our xml header line. Listing 4.8 presents another DTD, this time for the version of game.xml that uses only elements. Another alternative is to specify a PUBLIC DTD rather than a SYSTEM local DTD; in this case, the local filename would be replaced by a URI that pointed to the DTD somewhere on the Internet.

Listing 4.8 Game.dtd for the Element-Only Version of Game.xml

```
<!ELEMENT game (week, played, home, visitor)>
<!ELEMENT week (#PCDATA)>
<!ELEMENT played (#PCDATA)>
<!ELEMENT home (city, name, score)>
<!ELEMENT visitor (city, name, score)>
<!ELEMENT city (#PCDATA)>
<!ELEMENT name (#PCDATA)>
<!ELEMENT score (#PCDATA)>
```

XML Schemas

XML schemas are a replacement for DTD. There are several advantages of using XML schemas. First of all, there is no new language and syntax to learn; XML schemas are themselves XML documents, so if you know how to author an XML document, you already know enough to author the schema as well.

As with DTDs, XML schemas define the elements and attributes used within the XML document. In Listing 4.9, we've altered the example from Listing 4.4 to reference an XML schema rather than a DTD. This document also introduces XML namespaces, which we'll cover in detail in the section that follows. All of our elements are now prefixed by the string `nfl:`, which identifies them as being part of the `nfl` namespace. In the first element, we reference two namespaces: the `nfl` namespace, which has the schema for the elements within this file, and the `XMLSchema-instance` namespace. We need this latter file so that we can use the `schemaLocation` attribute that it defines. Because our schema is not actually published on the Web anywhere, the `schemaLocation` attribute allows us to associate the URI with a local filename, much as a `DOCTYPE` element with a `SYSTEM` declaration allowed reference to a local file for the DTD.

Listing 4.9 `game.xml` Variant Using XML Schema

```
<?xml version="1.0" ?>
<nfl:game xmlns:nfl="http://nfl.mydomain.com"
    xmlns:xsi="http://www.w3.org/2001/XMLSchema-instance"
    xsi:schemaLocation=
        "http://nfl.mydomain.com file:game.xsd"
    week="01" played="true">
  <nfl:home city="Atlanta" name="Falcons" score="14" />
  <nfl:visitor city="San Francisco" name="49ers" score="17" />
</nfl:game>
```

Listing 4.10 shows the schema that matches this document. This schema is stored in a file named `game.xsd` in the same directory as the XML file, so that the `schemaLocation` attribute in the XML file is able to locate it. XML schemas traditionally use a namespace prefix of `xsd:`, although this is not required. The schema in Listing 4.10 defines the elements and attributes used in the `game.xml` file; although verbose, most of the content is self-explanatory.

Listing 4.10 XML Schema for Game Document

```
<xsd:schema xmlns:xsd="http://www.w3.org/2001/XMLSchema"
        xmlns:nfl="http://nfl.mydomain.com"
        targetNamespace="http://nfl.mydomain.com" >

  <xsd:element name="game">
    <xsd:complexType>
      <xsd:sequence>
        <xsd:element ref="nfl:home" />
        <xsd:element ref="nfl:visitor" />
      </xsd:sequence>
```

```
            <xsd:attribute name="week" use="required"
                    type="xsd:int"/>
            <xsd:attribute name="played" use="optional"
                    type="xsd:boolean" default="true" />
        </xsd:complexType>
    </xsd:element>

    <xsd:element name="home">
        <xsd:complexType>
            <xsd:attribute name="city" use="required"
                    type="xsd:string" />
            <xsd:attribute name="name" use="required"
                    type="xsd:string" />
            <xsd:attribute name="score" use="required"
                    type="xsd:int" />
        </xsd:complexType>
    </xsd:element>

    <xsd:element name="visitor">
        <xsd:complexType>
            <xsd:attribute name="city" use="required"
                    type="xsd:string" />
            <xsd:attribute name="name" use="required"
                    type="xsd:string" />
            <xsd:attribute name="score" use="required"
                    type="xsd:int" />
        </xsd:complexType>
    </xsd:element>
</xsd:schema>
```

Each element can be either a simple (predefined) type, such as a `string` or `int`, or a complex type, which is made up of additional elements and/or attributes. Elements may have constraints on them, such as `minOccurs` and `maxOccurs`. The `use=` restriction may be used to specify `required`, `optional`, or `fixed` (the latter for constant values).

Although you can develop XML schemas by hand (as I originally did with the previous schema), there are also tools available to help you develop them. I was evaluating the HP Service Composer tool for a completely unrelated use (to develop WSDL documents, which we'll get to in Chapter 17) when I found it had a very nice graphical designer for XML schemas. I pointed it at the schema file from Listing 4.10 and got the result shown in Figure 4.5. I could have done the original development of the schema using this tool, just by defining each `<complexType>` and adding elements and attributes to it. Or I could use this tool if I need to make any changes to the schema in the future. We'll look at more capabilities of the HP Service Composer tool later in the book.

Figure 4.5 XML schema displayed in HP Service Composer.

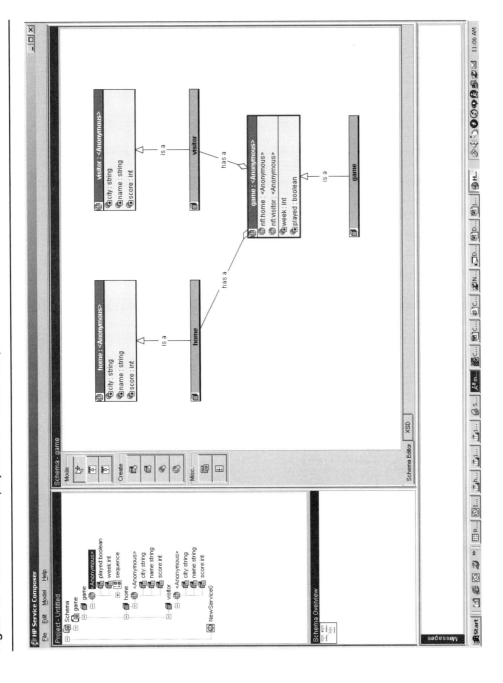

XML Namespaces

As long as we're only working with a single XML document, we can use whatever element names we like and never worry about conflicting uses of the same name. But later on, when we begin doing more complex tasks with XML, there will be times when we want to combine XML fragments from several sources into the same document. In this case, it's entirely possible that we'll find two XML authors who used the same element name, resulting in a conflict.

The solution to this is XML namespaces. XML namespaces are a relatively recent extension, so not all tools fully support namespaces. Each XML document author can designate a namespace for his XML document. When there is a conflict between names, the conflicting element name can be qualified to indicate to which namespace it belongs.

This is analogous to what happens in the Java programming language with package names. For example, I can create a class called `Date`, and use it freely in my own program just calling it by the unqualified class name `Date`. However, if I then import `java.util.Date` into one of my programs—either individually or by importing the whole `java.util.*` package— then I have created a conflict. Any use of `Date` within the program now must be qualified, as either `java.util.Date` or `mypackagename.Date`.

XML namespaces provide the same benefit as Java package names in allowing you to define your own private namespace, within which you can use any names you choose. The XML namespace is declared with the `xmlns` attribute, which can be attached to various elements within an XML document depending on the scope you want to establish for the namespace. The value of the `xmlns` attribute is a URI. This URI doesn't point to anything; it's simply a convention for giving unique names to namespaces, in the same way that the Java package name hierarchy, although based on Internet domain names, does not actually refer to resources anywhere on the internet.

Because namespace strings are URIs and therefore somewhat lengthy, you can assign a short prefix—as short as a single character—that is used as a reference to the namespace when used to qualify element names. Element names within the prefix can be qualified by using the prefix, a colon, and then the element name. This format is called a qualified name, frequently abbreviated to qName. The part after the colon is referred to as the local name. The XML schema examples in Listings 4.9 and 4.10 use a namespace of `nfl` for the game document, and a namespace of `xsd` for the schema.

Design Center: XML Attributes or Elements?

Much of the time, the decision of whether to use XML attributes or XML elements is merely one of personal preference. Some purists maintain that attributes should never be used, because everything can be represented using only XML elements.

There are a few occasions when the decision is made for you, at least insofar as certain things cannot be expressed using only attributes. For example:

- Attributes cannot contain multiple values. If something needs to be repeated, use an element.

> • Attributes cannot be subdivided; if the data is structured, use an element. Even if the data is not currently being broken down, if there is any possibility that you may want to break values down further in the future, best to use an element.
> • Attributes are more difficult to manipulate programmatically. Tools for manipulating XML documents move elements around within the document hierarchy, but attributes usually cannot be manipulated independently of the elements to which they are attached.

4.5   XML Validation

Most XML parsers provide a validation capability. Validation means that beyond just ensuring that the XML is well-formed, the parser will also verify that the XML document conforms to the DTD or XML Schema. Unfortunately, telling a parser whether or not it should use validation is one of the things that is implementation-dependent, so there is no portable way to turn validation on or off.

For the Apache Xerces parser, validation is turned on and off by a `setFeature()` method. For SAX, you can call `setFeature()` on the `org.xml.sax.XMLReader` object (if you're using JAXP, you can obtain a reference to this object by calling the `getXMLReader()` method of the `javax.xml.parsers.SAXParser` object). For DOM, you must call the `set-Feature()` method of the `org.apache.xerces.parsers.DOMParser` object. In both cases, the `setFeature()` call takes two arguments: a feature ID string and a boolean value that enables or disables the feature. There are actually several features dealing with validation. Two that are particularly useful are:

```
http://xml.org/sax/features/validation
```

and

```
http://apache.org/xml/features/validation/dynamic
```

The first feature, when enabled, will force validation on for any XML document. If the document does not reference a DTD against which validation can occur, an error will result. The second feature, when enabled, will perform validation for any XML document that includes a reference to a DTD. Documents that do not refer to a DTD will not be validated, and no error will occur as a result.

Other Xerces features allow validation against XML schemas rather than DTDs, and control whether specific validation checks will be performed or not. See the Xerces documentation for full details.

The XML validation features on the parser allow you to validate a document when you are programmatically parsing it. There are times, however, when you would like to validate XML that you aren't programmatically parsing. For example, you may have created an XML file manually, such as the Ant buildfiles we use throughout the book, or the small XML examples shown earlier in this chapter. We'd like to just do a sanity check on these XML documents to see if they are valid. For this, the Xalan processor includes a sample validator you can invoke directly from the command line. The sample class is called `Validate`, and is in the `xalansamples.jar` file of the Xalan distribution. You can invoke it against either a single file, or a directory. In the latter case, all filenames ending in `.xml` will be validated.

4.6 Exercises

No homework for tonight.

4.7 Further Reading

The Java Foundation Classes (JFC) provide everything needed to build Graphical User Interfaces for Java applications. The home page for JFC is `http://java.sun.com/products/jfc`.

Java Web Start provides an alternative to applets; using JWS, you can use any version of the JVM and the JFC/Swing components needed by your application without having to worry about what is supported in various browsers. JWS provides software distribution for your application and for the Java components on which it depends. More information is available at `http://java.sun.com/products/javawebstart`.

HyperText Transfer Protocol (HTTP) is a World Wide Web Consortium (W3C) standard. The home page at `http://www.w3c.org/Protocols` includes links to the standard and anything else you're likely to need.

The latest version of HTML as of this writing is 4.01. You can find the full specification and useful documentation at `http://www.w3.org/TR/html4/`. The main page at W3C for HTML is `http://www.w3c.org/Markup`.

XML is yet another W3C standard. `http://www.w3.org/XML` is the main page for XML activities at W3C. XML document formats can be described via XML schemas (`http://www.w3.org/XML/Schema`) or Document Type Definitions (DTDs). DTDs are not a W3C standard (not that there's anything wrong with that), but rather part of the ISO SGML standard.

The XML.com Web site (`http://www.xml.com`) provides lots of links to XML-related topics, as does the Web site XML.org (`http://www.xml.org`). The former site is geared more toward instructional and reference materials, while the latter is more news-oriented.

CHAPTER 5

Servlets

The appearance of servlets on the Java scene marked an important transition point in the evolution of Java. In the earliest versions of Java, the promise of write-once, run-any-where as realized through the AWT and applet technology was primarily directed at providing portability on the client side. But despite the hopes that Java would displace, or at least challenge, Microsoft for desktop dominance, it was on the server that the true promise of Java began to be realized.

Discussions of Java on the server frequently focus on the capabilities of Enterprise Java-Beans (EJB), but EJB is often overkill. Servlets are the workhorse of server-side Java. Following in the footsteps of Albert Einstein, who claimed that "Everything should be made as simple as possible—but not simpler," you should always think of server-side Java functionality in terms of simple components and servlets until and unless the specific requirements force you to accept the added complexity of EJB.

And as we'll see, even in cases where EJB is your eventual goal, servlets can be a very useful stop along the way to allow you to prototype, develop, and debug your code in a more lightweight environment.

Software Used In This Chapter

Java Servlet Developer's Kit (JSDK)

Version 2.2, downloaded from `http://java.sun.com/products/servlet`. The only component used is the `servlet.jar` file, which is required to compile the example applications. All servlets shown here are also compatible with the newer servlet 2.3 standard. (Any servlet container, such as Tomcat, will also include any JAR files needed for compiling servlets. The download of the JSDK separately from any container is primarily useful if you plan to develop and compile on a system different than where servlets will be deployed.)

Servlet Containers

You'll need a servlet container in which to deploy servlets. The following three servlet containers are covered in this chapter; there are many others available that should also be compatible with our examples.

- **Tomcat Servlet Container**
  Version 3.2.3, from `http://jakarta.apache.org`. Can be used standalone, or integrated with a Web or application server such as Apache, Enhydra, IIS, or iPlanet. This provides the servlet container into which we deploy our servlets. Servlets were also tested in Tomcat 4.0 releases (4.0.1 and 4.0.3) and an early development version of Tomcat 4.1.
- **BEA WebLogic Server**
  Version 6.1, with Service Pack 2. Downloaded from `http://www.bea.com`. A WebLogic 7.0 beta release was also tested.
- **HP Application Server (HP-AS)**
  Version 8.0, downloaded from `http://www.hpmiddleware.com`.

5.1   What Is a Servlet?

A servlet is a piece of server-side Java that responds to requests coming in from a client. Although servlets can be created for any protocol that is based on requests and responses, by far the overwhelming majority of servlets are built to handle HTTP requests. In this book, we'll only consider HTTP servlets.

Servlets are frequently compared to applets, and considered a server-side replacement for applets. However, in functionality, what they really replace are CGI scripts (see Chapter 4). Servlets don't provide all of the user interface flexibility that applets can provide, and in fact some deployments of servlets use applets as the client-side technology. HTML is the most widely used presentation option, and our servlets will follow this model.

To develop servlets, you will need two things: the servlet APIs, and a servlet container (also sometimes called a servlet engine).

5.1.1   Servlet APIs

The servlet APIs aren't part of the J2SE package, so you'll need to obtain them from somewhere. If you already have a servlet container, such as an application server, then the APIs were probably distributed as part of that package. Otherwise, you can download them from `http://java.sun.com/products/servlet/index.html`. The servlet APIs are packaged in a file called `servlet.jar`. You'll need access to this file both at compile time and at run time, so you'll need to make sure it's along the `CLASSPATH` of your IDE or compiler and of the servlet container.

The servlet APIs are arranged into two packages: `javax.servlet` and `javax.serv-let.http`. The primary components of interest in the `javax.servlet` package are the `servlet` interface and the `GenericServlet` implementation; other classes in the package are primarily to support the use of these. In the `javax.servlet.http` package is the `HttpServ-let` class, the most common starting place for developing a servlet.

In Listing 5.1, we see a simple servlet, the ever-popular `HelloWorld` servlet. There isn't a whole lot to it, which is the real beauty of it. Our `HelloWorldServlet` extends `HttpServlet`, which is the class designed to be extended by servlets that use the HTTP protocol. (Servlets working over any other protocol would instead extend `GenericServlet`.) The `HttpServlet` class takes care of handling incoming requests in its `service()` method. Although you can override the `service()` method, it generally does exactly what we need—it routes the request to the appropriate method based on the request type. For example, HTTP GET requests are routed to the `doGet()` method, and HTTP POST requests are routed to `doPost()`. These are nearly always the only methods you'll need to override.

Each method invoked from `service()` is passed an `HttpServletRequest` object and an `HttpServletResponse` object. The request object can be interrogated to find out information about the incoming request—the exact URL that was used, and parameters that were passed, for example. In the `HelloWorld` case, there isn't anything being passed in to the servlet, so we don't need to invoke any methods of the request object. The response object allows us to dynamically create the response, generally an HTML page. From the response object, we obtain a handle to the `PrintWriter` object that allows us to write HTML back to the client. Prior to writing the first line of output, we use the `response.setContentType()` call to set the appropriate content type, which in most cases will be `text/html`.

Although we expect most requests for this page to come in via the GET method, we also redirect any POST requests that come in to the same page. This protects us from the sometimes unpredictable behavior of the various browsers we may encounter.

Listing 5.1 `HelloWorld` Servlet

```java
// HelloWorldServlet.java

import java.io.IOException;
import java.io.PrintWriter;

import javax.servlet.*;
import javax.servlet.http.*;

public class HelloWorldServlet extends HttpServlet
{
   public void doGet(HttpServletRequest request,
                     HttpServletResponse response)
              throws ServletException, IOException {

      response.setContentType("text/html");
      PrintWriter out = response.getWriter();

      out.println("<html>" +
                  "<head>" +
                  "<title>HelloWorld Servlet</title>" +
                  "</head>" +
                  "<body>" +
                  "Hello, World" +
                  "</body>" +
                  "</html>");

   }

   public void doPost(HttpServletRequest request,
                      HttpServletResponse response)
              throws ServletException, IOException {
      doGet(request, response);
   }
}
```

The methods of the most frequently used servlet classes and interfaces are summarized in the API reference listings API 5.1 through API 5.5 on the following pages.

API 5.1 javax.servlet.http.**HttpServlet**

```
public abstract class HttpServlet extends GenericServlet implements Serializable
    public HttpServlet();
    // Methods inherited from GenericServlet
    public void init() throws ServletException;
    public void log(String msg);
    public void log(String message, Throwable error);
    // Methods from Servlet interface (implemented in GenericServlet)
    public void destroy();
    public ServletConfig getServletConfig();
    public String getServletInfo();
    public void init(ServletConfig config) throws ServletException;
    public void service(ServletRequest request, ServletResponse response)
        throws ServletException, IOException;
    // Methods from ServletConfig interface (implemented in GenericServlet)
    public String getInitParameter(String name);
    public java.util.Enumeration getInitParameterNames();
    public ServletContext getServletContext();
    // Instance Methods
    public void doDelete(ServletRequest request, ServletResponse response)
        throws ServletException, IOException;
    public void doGet(ServletRequest request, ServletResponse response)
        throws ServletException, IOException;
    public void doOptions(ServletRequest request, ServletResponse response)
        throws ServletException, IOException;
    public void doPost(ServletRequest request, ServletResponse response)
        throws ServletException, IOException;
    public void doPut(ServletRequest request, ServletResponse response)
        throws ServletException, IOException;
    public void doTrace(ServletRequest request, ServletResponse response)
        throws ServletException, IOException;
    protected long getLastModified(HttpServletRequest request);
    protected void service(HttpServletRequest request, HttpServletResponse response)
        throws ServletException, IOException;
```

API 5.2 javax.servlet.http.**HttpServletRequest**

```
public interface HttpServletRequest extends ServletRequest
    // Methods inherited from ServletRequest interface
    public Object getAttribute(String name);
    public java.util.Enumeration getAttributeNames();
    public String getCharacterEncoding();
    public int getContentLength();
    public String getContentType();
    public ServletInputStream getInputStream() throws IOException();
    public String getParameter(String name);
    public java.util.Enumeration getParameterNames();
    public String[] getParameterValues();
    public String getProtocol();
    public BufferedReader getReader() throws IOException;
    public String getRemoteAddr();
    public String getRemoteHost();
    public String getScheme();
    public String getServerName();
    public int getServerPort();
    public void setAttribute(String key, Object o);
    // Instance Methods
    public String getAuthType();
    public Cookie[] getCookies();
    public long getDateHeader(String name);
    public String getHeader(String name);
    public java.util.Enumeration getHeaderNames();
    public int getIntHeader(String name);
    public String getMethod();
    public String getPathInfo();
    public String getPathTranslated();
    public String getQueryString();
    public String getRemoteUser();
    public String getRequestedSessionId();
    public String getRequestURI();
    public String getServletPath();
    public HttpSession getSession();
    public HttpSession getSession(boolean create);
    public boolean isRequestedSessionIdFromCookie();
    public boolean isRequestedSessionIdFromURL();
    public boolean isRequestedSessionValid();
```

API 5.3 javax.servlet.http.**HttpServletResponse**

```
public interface HttpServletResponse extends ServletResponse
    // Methods inherited from ServletResponse interface
    public String getCharacterEncoding();
    public ServletOutputStream getOutputStream() throws IOException;
    public PrintWriter getWriter() throws IOException;
    public void setContentLength(int length);
    public void setContentType(String type)
    // Instance Methods
    // NOT SHOWN: constant values representing return status codes
    public void addCookie(Cookie cookie);
    public boolean containsHeader(String name);
    public String encodeRedirectURL(String url);
    public String encodeURL(String url);
    public void sendError(int statuscode) throws IOException;
    public void sendError(int statuscode, String msg) throws IOException;
    public void sendRedirect(String location) throws IOException;
    public void setDateHeader(String name, long date);
    public void setHeader(String name, String value);
    public void setIntHeader(String name, int value);
    public void setStatus(int statuscode);
```

API 5.4 javax.servlet.**ServletConfig**

```
public interface ServletConfig
    public String getInitParameter(String name);
    public Enumeration getInitParameterNames();
    public ServletContext getServletContext();
    public String getServletName();
```

API 5.5 javax.servlet.**ServletContext**

```
public interface ServletContext
    // Note: Deprecated methods not shown
    public Object getAttribute(String name);
    public Enumeration getAttributeNames();
    public ServletContext getContext(String uripath);
    public String getInitParameter(String name);
    public Enumeration getInitParameterNames();
    public int getMajorVersion();
    public String getMimeType(String file);
    public int getMinorVersion();
    public RequestDispatcher getNamedDispatcher(String name);
    public String getRealPath(String path);
    public RequestDispatcher getRequestDispatcher(String path);
```

```
public URL getResource(String path);
public InputStream getResourceAsStream(String path);
public Set getResourcePaths(String path);
public String getServerInfo();
public String getServletContextName();
public void log(String msg);
public void log(String msg, Throwable throwable);
public void removeAttribute(String name);
public void setAttribute(String name, Object object);
```

You'll notice that in all of our servlet examples, we simply embed the HTML tags into the document we create. This is fairly typical practice in servlets, but it is also error-prone. Because the tags we enter are just passed through as part of the output stream, neither the Java compiler nor the servlet engine will catch any errors such as unmatched or misspelled tags, incorrect document formatting, or any other HTML syntax errors.

If the documents you're creating are more complex than the trivial page we're using here, you might want to investigate an HTML generation utility. For example, the Element Construction Set (ECS) from the Apache Jakarta project provides a set of APIs to generate HTML, and helps prevent the occurrence of most common typographical-type errors.

If we used ECS in the servlet from Listing 5.1, this code could be used to generate our page:

```
Document doc = (Document) new Document()
            .appendTitle("HelloWorld Servlet")
            .appendBody("Hello, World!")
out.println(doc.toString());
```

There is quite a bit more possible with ECS; this example is overly trivial because it contains only a single element within the body. Normally, you would build up the body out of many different types of elements, including text, headings, images, links to other pages, and so forth. ECS can also be used to generate XML code. We won't spend a lot of time exploring alternatives for generating HTML within our servlets, because conventional wisdom today is that it is better to put the HTML in a JavaServer Page (see Chapter 6) rather than embedding it within the servlet.

5.1.2   Servlet Containers

Simple Java applications require only a Java Runtime Environment (JRE) to run; there is nothing else needed. However, some architectures require additional components; for example, an applet requires a browser (or appletviewer) in which to run. Servlets require a hosting environment, typically known as either a servlet container or a servlet engine. Some servlet containers are standalone, meaning that their only function is to provide an environment for servlets. Others are part of a larger application server that serves as a container not only for servlets, but for Enterprise JavaBeans and possibly other types of components as well.

The Tomcat Servlet Container

Tomcat is a standalone servlet and JavaServer Pages container. It is maintained by the Apache group and is the reference implementation for the servlet and JavaServer Pages APIs.

Installing Tomcat

Tomcat version 4.0.3 is included on the enclosed CD. You can also download the latest Tomcat from `http://jakarta.apache.org/tomcat`. To install Tomcat, copy the installation file (`.tar` file or `.zip` file) to your target system and unzip it in the location of your choice.

Running Tomcat

Tomcat comes with a number of scripts in the `bin` directory that can be used to run the server in a standalone configuration. For example, `startup.bat` starts the server, and `shutdown.bat` stops it. (These are the Windows versions of the scripts; for UNIX systems, the scripts would be `startup.sh` and `shutdown.sh`). These scripts depend upon the `JAVA_HOME` variable being set to the location where Java is installed (for example, `C:\jdk1.3.1`). You can either set the `JAVA_HOME` variable each time you run Tomcat, or simply edit the scripts to set the variable for you.

Tomcat Directory Structure

Under the Tomcat root directory, the main things of interest are the `conf` directory, where configuration files are found; the `bin` directory, where the scripts are found; and the `webapps` directory, where servlets are installed by default.

Under the `webapps` directory are the directories related to specific servlets. In our case, `<TOMCAT_HOME>/webapps/nfl` is where we will install our servlet. Directly under this directory is a `WEB-INF` directory. Any nontrivial servlet will have a deployment descriptor named `web.xml` in this directory that provides configuration options specific to our servlet. Under `WEB-INF` is a `classes` directory, which is where the servlet's class files go.

Deploying Servlets in .class Files

If you build your servlet simply as one or more class files, then you would deploy your servlet by placing these class files in the `<TOMCAT_HOME>/webapps/<CONTEXT>/WEB-INF/classes` directory. If the servlet is part of a package, then you must reproduce the normal Java directory structure for the package under the classes directory. `<CONTEXT>` can be anything you desire, as long as it is a legal directory name and isn't in use by any other servlet. We use `nfl` as the context name for our example servlets.

Deploying Servlets in .war Files

A better option is to package your class files, and any related files (HTML, JavaServer Pages, images, and so forth) into a Web ARchive (WAR) file. You can then install this WAR file directly under the `webapps` directory. When Tomcat is started, it will unpack the WAR file, creating a directory structure identical to what you would have created manually if deploying the servlets as individual class files in the preceding step. Deploying as a WAR file is the only method specified by the servlets standard, so this is the method that will be the most portable between different servlet containers.

Configuring the server.xml File

In the `conf` directory under the Tomcat root directory is a file called `server.xml`. This XML-format file has all of the configuration options for the Tomcat server. You can run all of the example programs shown herein without having to change anything in the configuration. If you desire, you can add a `Context` entry either for the examples here, or for servlets you develop on your own. For example, here's a sample `Context` entry we could use for our example servlets:

```
<Context path="/nfl"
    docBase=" nfl"
    debug="0"
    reloadable="true" />
```

This `Context` entry essentially just reiterates default values with one useful exception: the `reloadable` flag causes our servlet to be reloaded if it changes, so that we don't have to stop and restart the server after every change during development. In production, this option can slow the performance of the server, so it's best used only during development. We could also use the `Context` to point to a location other than the `webapps` directory if we wanted to install our servlets in a nonstandard location.

5.1.3   Servlet Life Cycle

When a servlet is originally loaded (which may be when the servlet container is first started, or the first time the servlet is accessed, depending on configuration) its `init()` method is executed. The `init()` method can take care of any initialization and resource allocation tasks needed for the servlet, such as opening database connections. In our case, we use the `init()` method to create the initial standings based on all the data available at the time the servlet starts. The `destroy()` method will be called when the servlet is unloaded, so it provides a place to clean up and release the resources allocated in `init()`.

5.2   Using a Servlet for the Standings Class

In order to make our `Standings` class function as a servlet, there are just a few things we need to add to it. The first decision to make is what to base the new servlet on. We could extend our `BasicStandingsImpl` class, creating a new `ServletStandingsImpl` class that added the necessary servlet methods. Because Java doesn't support multiple inheritance, if we decide to subclass `BasicStandingsImpl` then we cannot also subclass one of the servlet classes (`GenericServlet` or `HttpServlet`), which means we would instead have to implement the `Servlet` interface. While this approach would be perfectly valid, we would rather leverage the `service()` method provided in the `HttpServlet` class that already takes care of routing requests to the appropriate doXXX methods (`doGet()` and `doPost()`, primarily).

When inheritance is impossible, aggregation is frequently the answer, and that's what we'll do here. Instead of extending `BasicStandingsImpl`, we'll have our servlet, cleverly named `ServletOneImpl`, include a `Standings` object. By using aggregation, we also get some additional flexibility through the `ObjectFactory`: although our initial application will be using a `BasicStandingsImpl` object, we'll have the option in the future of using any other class that implements the `Standings` interface. The new and reused components of our servlet are shown in Table 5.1.

Table 5.1   Components in the ServletOne Application

New Components			
Name	**Package**	**Class or Interface**	**Comment**
ServletOneImpl	nfl.application.servlet	Class	A simple servlet
ServletOneVersionInfo	nfl.application.servlet	Class	Configures `ObjectFactory`
Existing Components			
Component	**Description**		
layered.jar	All classes and interfaces of the layered version of the application (as presented in Chapter 2).		
nfl.presentation.HTML	HTML-formatted presentation class from Chapter 4.		

5.2.1   Compute Once, Serve Repeatedly

In our initial application, once standings for a particular division or conference were calculated, we immediately printed the results and then reused the same `List` object to compute the next division or conference. In other words, results were thrown away once they were used. In a servlet architecture, we expect the servlet lifetime to extend over many requests; it would be foolish to constantly recalculate the results based on the same data. So our servlet class includes arrays of List objects to provide a place to store the results of the standings once they've been calculated, which we will then serve again and again as requests come in from clients.

The init() method, executed when the servlet is first loaded, performs all of the calculations and stores the results in the List arrays. There are actually two init() methods in the HttpServlet class; it is generally preferable to use the zero-argument init() method for any application-specific initialization your servlet must perform. This version of init() will be invoked by the superclass' init(ServletConfig) method. If you need access to the ServletConfig parameter in your own initialization code, then you can choose to override init(ServletConfig), but should call super.init(ServletConfig) from your init() routine to make sure the superclass is properly initialized.

The doGet() method, executed each time the page is accessed, uses the HTML class developed in Chapter 4 to actually print the standings in HTML format. On the chance that we might get a POST request on our page, we forward any POST requests to the doGet() method as well.

Listing 5.2 The ServletOneImpl Class

```
// ServletOneImpl.java

package nfl.application.servlet;

import java.io.*;
import java.text.DecimalFormat;
import java.util.*;

import javax.servlet.*;
import javax.servlet.http.*;

import nfl.ObjectFactory;
import nfl.VersionInfo;
import nfl.LayeredVersionInfo;
import nfl.application.*;
import nfl.presentation.HTML;

public class ServletOneImpl extends HttpServlet
{
    private Standings standings;
    private HTML      html;

    // Standings in this model aren't just calculated,
    // printed, and discarded; we'll reuse the same
    // standings List for multiple requests
    private List[] divStandings;
    private List[] confStandings;
```

```
public void init() throws ServletException {
   standings = (Standings)
      ObjectFactory.getHandle().getInstance("Standings");
   html       = new HTML();

   standings.loadData();

   // Calculate an initial set of standings.
   divStandings  = new List[Division.DIVISIONS.size()];
   confStandings = new List[
                       Conference.CONFERENCES.size()];

   // Loop through divisions
    List divList = Division.DIVISIONS;
    for (int i=0; i<divList.size(); i++) {
       Division d = (Division) divList.get(i);
       divStandings[i] =
           standings.computeDivisionStandings(d);
    }

    if (!html.getPrintConferenceStandings()) return;
    // Loop through conferences

    List confList = Conference.CONFERENCES;
    for (int i=0; i<confList.size(); i++) {
       Conference c = (Conference) confList.get(i);
       confStandings[i] =
           standings.computeConferenceStandings(c);
    }
}

public void doGet(HttpServletRequest request,
                  HttpServletResponse response)
            throws ServletException, IOException {

   response.setContentType("text/html");
   PrintWriter out = response.getWriter();
   html.printHtmlHead(out, "Servlet One");

   // Loop through divisions
    List divList = Division.DIVISIONS;
    for (int i=0; i<divList.size(); i++) {
       Division d = (Division) divList.get(i);
       html.printDivisionStandings(d, divStandings[i],
                                   out);
    }
```

```
      if (!html.getPrintConferenceStandings()) return;

      // Loop through conferences
      List confList = Conference.CONFERENCES;
      for (int i=0; i<confList.size(); i++) {
         Conference c = (Conference) confList.get(i);
         html.printConferenceStandings(c,
                        confStandings[i], out);
      }

   html.printHtmlEnd(out);
   }

   public void doPost(HttpServletRequest request,
                   HttpServletResponse response)
            throws ServletException, IOException {
      doGet(request, response);
   }
}
```

5.2.2   Building, Packaging, and Deploying the Servlet in Tomcat

Implementing the servlet was straightforward. Now, we need to get it installed in such a way that users interact with our servlet when they visit the URL we've selected. I've chosen to put this servlet under a path of `/nfl`. (`/nfl` is therefore the "context directory" for our servlets.) If I were accessing it on my local system, with a server running on port 8080, the first part of the URL would thus be:

```
http://localhost:8080/nfl
```

What follows in the URL at this point may vary, depending on what servlet engine we are using and how we choose to package and deploy our servlets. So let's look at the alternatives.

For a single file, such as our `HelloWorld` servlet, we could just distribute the `.class` file. However, for servlets such as this one that include several classes, the more common option is to package them in a WAR file. A WAR file is merely a JAR file; it doesn't have any special attributes, manifest entries, or unusual characteristics. It does have a particular directory structure that is expected, as shown here:

```
/nfl   The context directory for the servlet
      any HTML files at this level (directly under context)
      any JSP files at this level (directly under context)
      /WEB-INF                  directory
         web.xml                deployment descriptor
         /classes               directory
              *.class           files
         /lib
              *.jar             jar files
```

You don't need for all HTML and JSP files to be located directly under the context directory; you can create as complex and multileveled a hierarchy as you want for them. It's just that this is where the hierarchy will be rooted. If you are going to have a main page such as index.html, this would be the most logical place to put it; everything else could then be distributed as in a normal HTML application.

The classes directory is where you'd put the class files for your servlet and any additional classes that are part of your application. Here again, these can be spread out in a normal directory structure, and in fact if your servlet is part of a package, then the normal hierarchy of package names must be reproduced beginning at this level. For ServletOne, the actual full path to the class file is <TOMCAT_HOME>/webapps/nfl/WEB-INF/nfl/application/servlet/ServletOneImpl.class.

Listing 5.3 shows the first part of the Ant buildfile for the servlet directory. There are targets in this buildfile to build several servlets; the listing only shows the first part of the file, with the targets associated with ServletOne. There are a few new Ant features being used in this buildfile. First of all, we need to have the servlet.jar file somewhere along our CLASSPATH in order for these classes to compile. We don't want to change this in multiple places, and there are multiple javac tasks in the full buildfile. To isolate the changes, we use the Ant <property> element. We create a property named servlet.jar, and give it a value pointing to the location of the servlet.jar file on my development system. You'll almost certainly need to change this value for your own development system. The property is then referenced in the javac task, where the classpath attribute dereferences the property. Alternately, if you install the servlet.jar file in the Java extensions directory, then it will be searched automatically and doesn't need to be on the explicit CLASSPATH.

The second new feature being introduced in this buildfile is the <war> task. The <war> task is an alternative way of invoking the Java jar command. The <war> task has built-in knowledge of the directory structure utilized within WAR files, and facilitates this by providing <lib>, <classes>, and <webinf> subtasks. Each of these subtasks allows a group of files to be specified, and they will be placed in the corresponding directory (WEB-INF/lib, WEB-INF/classes, and WEB-INF, respectively).

If the files we were adding to the classes directory were not part of a package, we would not need to specify a prefix attribute, but because we need to prepend the package name, we must also include the WEB-INF/classes part of the prefix that would otherwise have been defaulted for us.

Listing 5.3 Ant Buildfile for ServletOne (Part 1 of build.xml)

```
<project name="servlets" default="servlet1" basedir=".">

<property name="servlet.jar" value="../../../servlet.jar" />

<target name="compile-servlet1">
```

```
    <javac srcdir="." classpath="${servlet.jar}">
        <include name="ServletOneImpl.java" />
        <include name="ServletOneVersionInfo.java" />
        <src path="../../presentation" />
        <include name="HTML.java" />
    </javac>
</target>

<target name="servlet1" depends="compile-servlet1">
    <delete file="nfl.war" />
    <war warfile="nfl.war" webxml="servlet1.xml" >
        <lib dir="../.." includes="layered.jar" />
        <classes dir="."
            includes="ServletOne*.class"
              prefix="WEB-INF/classes/nfl/application/servlet"
            />
        <classes dir="../../presentation"
            includes="HTML.class"
              prefix="WEB-INF/classes/nfl/presentation" />
    </war>
</target>

<target name="clean-servlet1">
  <delete>
    <fileset dir="." includes="ServletOne*.class,nfl.war" />
    <fileset dir="../../presentation"
        includes="HTML.class" />
  </delete>
</target>
```

In our deployment descriptor (web.xml) file for ServletOne, we simplify the path by assigning a servlet name, which can be used as shorthand for the full path to the servlet. This particular servlet could be deployed in Tomcat without a web.xml file; in that case, in order to access the servlet, we would need to use a URL such as the following:

`http://localhost:8080/nfl/servlet/nfl.application.servlet.ServletOneImpl`

Let's parse this URL to understand what's going on. The protocol (http), server name (localhost), and port (8080) are standard URL syntax. The next thing (/nfl) is our servlet context, which will map to a directory under the webapps directory. This is followed by a special token, /servlet, that lets the server know to look in /webapps in the first place—otherwise, we would be looking for /nfl under the htdocs directory (or whatever the document root is for the particular server we're running). So in this case, /servlet is a tip-off to the container to look in the root directory for servlets (/webapps) rather than the root directory for HTML files (/htdocs). In a later example, we'll see how we can map URL patterns to servlet contexts, so that we don't have to use the /servlet keyword in the URL. The remainder of the URL in this example is simply the full name of our servlet class, exactly as we would specify it on a command line to the Java interpreter.

In Listing 5.4, we see the web.xml file that could be used to deploy ServletOne. A web.xml file contains a single root element, web-app. Within this, we can specify several types of components; in this example, we have only a single servlet to deploy. Our servlet has three elements specified for it. The `<servlet-class>` is the full class name of the servlet, exactly as we used in our URL. The `<servlet-name>` is any name we choose to give our servlet; it provides a shortcut that can be used in the URL in place of the full class name. Finally, `<load-on-startup>` instructs the servlet container to load our servlet when the container itself is initialized, rather than waiting for a request for the servlet to be processed. The `<load-on-startup>` element contains a numeric value which is a priority; servlets with lower numbers here will be loaded before higher numbered servlets. The web.xml file must have the name web.xml; but in our case, we have code for three different servlets within the same source directory. We have therefore named the files `servlet1.xml`, `servlet2.xml`, and `servlet3.xml`; the Ant build-file is responsible for renaming the appropriate file for the servlet being built to web.xml when creating the WAR file for that servlet. Also, the three files are cumulative, so `servlet3.xml` contains the configuration data for all three servlets. With the web.xml file in place, we can now access the servlet via a simpler URL:

```
http://localhost:8080/nfl/servlet/NFLStandings
```

Listing 5.4 web.xml File for ServletOne (`servlet1.xml`)

```
<?xml version="1.0" encoding="ISO-8859-1"?>

<!DOCTYPE web-app PUBLIC
  "-//Sun Microsystems, Inc.//DTD Web application 2.2//EN"
  "http://java.sun.com/j2ee/dtds/web-app_2_2.dtd">

<web-app>
  <servlet>
    <servlet-name>NFLStandings</servlet-name>
    <servlet-class>
      nfl.application.servlet.ServletOneImpl
    </servlet-class>
    <load-on-startup>1</load-on-startup>
  </servlet>

  <!-- Without servlet-mapping, Tomcat finds servlet OK,
       but BEA WLS and HP-AS will fail -->
  <servlet-mapping>
    <servlet-name>NFLStandings</servlet-name>
    <url-pattern>/</url-pattern>
  </servlet-mapping>
</web-app>
```

5.2.3   Deploying the Servlet in BEA WebLogic

The WAR file we created in the preceding section is not specific to any application server, so we'll be able to take the same packaged application and deploy it in BEA WebLogic and also in the HP Application server (HP-AS). The steps in deploying WAR files are different between these servers. In this section and the one that follows on HP-AS, we'll cover just the differences.

The first change actually is a change that was made to the file contents. When creating the web.xml file for Tomcat, no <servlet-mapping> element was specified. The application deployed fine in Tomcat without the element. However, when I attempted to deploy this same WAR file in WebLogic, it appeared to deploy okay but the servlet could not be reached. Any attempt to reach the servlet received an error status of 403 (Forbidden) or 404 (Not Found). In HP-AS, a status of 404 was always returned.

To deploy the WAR file in WebLogic, you'll install it in the WebLogic equivalent of Tomcat's webapps directory. That directory is $WLS_HOME/wlserver6.1/config/mydomain/ applications/ in WebLogic 6.1, and $WLS_HOME/user_domains/mydomain/applications in the WebLogic 7.0 beta. This is probably correct for a development system, but in a production environment your WLS administrator may have created domains other than the default "mydomain"; in this case, you should substitute the appropriate domain name in the directory path.

If WebLogic is not already running, you can start it by running the startWebLogic.sh script (or .bat file on Windows) located at $WLS_HOME/config/mydomain. WebLogic provides a graphical administration console, which is used to install and deploy applications. You can access the console by pointing your browser to http://<systemname>:7001/console. (7001 is the default port on which WebLogic listens, although this might have been changed at your site). The console screen has a panel on the left in which you select functions from a tree-like structure, and a panel on the right that contains forms appropriate to the selected task. To deploy a WAR file, select the Deployments item on the left side, expanding it if necessary. From the choices under Deployments, select Web Applications. On the right panel, you'll now see a list of already-installed Web applications. At the top, you have choices to "Install a new Web Application" or "Configure a new Web Application." If you haven't already copied the WAR file into the target domain, you can use the install option to search your local hard drive (local meaning the system on which the browser is running, which may be different than the system on which WebLogic is running) for the WAR file, and then upload it to the WebLogic server. The installer screen is shown in Figure 5.1.

Once the WAR file is installed, you can select the Web application by name (nfl) from the directory tree in the left-hand panel. This will bring up a configuration screen for the application in the right-hand panel. The configuration screen contains a tabbed panel, and each tab leads to several configuration items. On the initial screen, the Name of the Web application and the Path to the Context directory are shown.

To complete the deployment of the Web application, you'll need to select the Targets tab, and then select the server name (most likely the default myserver) from the Available selection box on the left. Click the right-facing arrow to move the selected server from the Available box to the Chosen box, then click the Apply button to complete the deployment.

You should now be able to reach the servlet via the following URL:

```
http://<hostname>:7001/nfl/NFLStandings
```

Actually, because of the `<servlet-mapping>` entry we added to the `web.xml` file for this servlet, the `NFLStandings` portion of the URL is unnecessary. Any URL that begins with `nfl` will be routed to the servlet.

Figure 5.1   The BEA WebLogic 7.0 installer screen (from the Beta version).

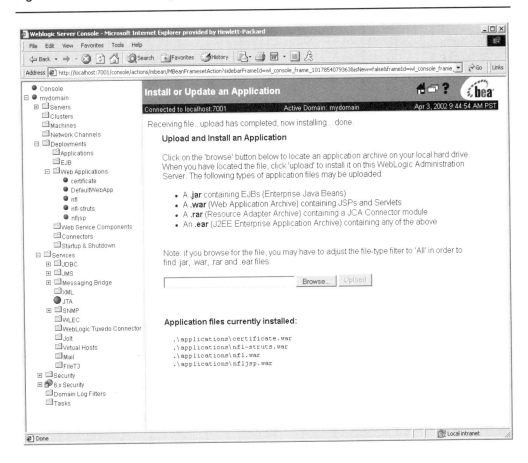

5.2.4   Deploying the Servlet in HP-AS

Like the WebLogic server, the HP-AS includes a graphical administration console that can be used to deploy servlets. HP-AS also comes with a utility known as RADPak that can help with the packaging of the servlet. I've chosen not to show this feature simply because I'd prefer to focus on the similarities between the deployment options, rather than on how they can be different.[1] The console can also be started in a text mode if you prefer a non-graphical interface. On the Windows platform, an option to start the console will be found in the HP-AS menu accessible off the Start menu.

In the console, select the View menu, and the Deployment Window item within that menu. You will then see a two-panel window. The left panel, by default, shows only a single item; the kernel.j2ee-partition. This is the container in which we want to deploy the servlet. On the right panel is a graphical directory tree. Navigate through the tree until you find the `nfl.war` file containing the servlet. You then need to drag the `nfl.war` file onto the left panel and drop it onto the icon representing the container. The HP-AS deployment window is shown in Figure 5.2.

Figure 5.2   The HP-AS deployment window.

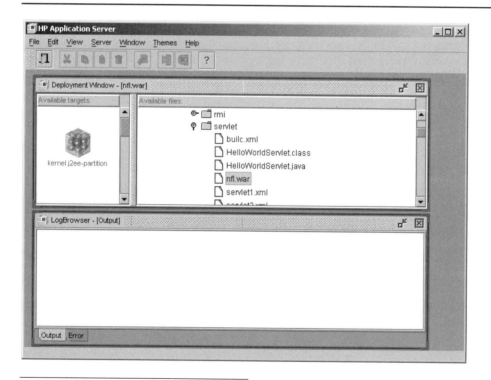

---

1.   RadPak will be shown when we deploy Enterprise JavaBeans in Chapter 19.

You should now be able to reach the servlet via the following URL:

```
http://<hostname>:9090/nfl/NFLStandings
```

5.3 Messaging Implementation for Servlets

If you look at the design of our `Messaging` interface and class, this is one place where, frankly, I blew it. Rather than going back and reimplementing the class as it should have been done, let's use it as a study of how bad assumptions can come back to bite us later.

In the original application, the output was under the control of the `Standings` class, and we chose to just show the messages as they were generated. When we redesigned the application into a layered application, we separated the `Messaging` interface from the `Messaging` implemention, but didn't really give sufficient thought to how this was going to work. Yes, we can now implement the `show()` method to format its output as HTML, or XML, or write it into a textbox in a JFC application, but it is still being driven by when the message is generated, rather than when the user needs to see it. Now consider our dynamic behavior. We might load the servlet and perform all the calculations long before any user actually requests the page. So where do we send the messages in this case? (As it is, they show up on the `stdout` window for the servlet container, where they really aren't doing anybody any good.)

At this point in the development, I wrote two alternate implementations of the `Messaging` class. The `NullMessagingImpl` class simply throws the messages away, which may be fine because they were really additional information and not needed to present the standings. This version was already shown in Chapter 4 as part of the XML output example. The second implementation is called `AsyncMessagingImpl`. This class stores the messages in a `Map` as they are generated. Each message is stored twice, keyed once by the Home team and once by the Visiting team. A new method is introduced, `retrieveMessages(String team)`, which allows the retrieval of all messages generated for that team.

Neither of these classes is in use in our examples at this point, but you're free to use them in your own experimentation if you'd like. To be really useful, this class should be evolved further, which would require changing some of our earlier classes. There should be an extension to the `Messaging` interface to include the new `retrieveMessages()` method. It would also be nice to know whether a message was generated during the division sort or the conference sort; this would actually require quite a few changes in the `Comparator` classes to pass this information along as part of every message.

We aren't showing listings of the new `AsyncMessagingImpl` class here, but the source is included on the CD-ROM in the `nfl/application/` directory.

5.4 Dynamic Behavior in the Standings Application

Up to this point, our example application has behaved in a batch mode. When the application is started, it reads all of the data it needs, performs the necessary calculations, and then displays the results.

Now that we've started to support Web access to the application, we have to ask whether this still makes sense. For one thing, we may get many requests for the data from different users. It would be silly to recalculate the standings each time we get a page request, if the data has not changed. So in ServletOne we began caching the results of our calculations. But let's take that a step further. If the application is going to be up and running for a period of time, rather than just long enough to print the standings once, then the data could change while the application is running.

The logical evolution of the application at this point is to support the ability to change the data while the application runs. So when we start the application, we should read the results of any games already played, but we should also accept the input of the results of games played while the application is up. When we get a request for the standings page, we should recalculate only if new data has been posted since the last time we performed the calculations.

ServletTwo will be the servlet that utilizes these new features. The two main changes between ServletOne and ServletTwo are this dynamic behavior, and the fact that ServletTwo will handle multiple pages (a main page, a page to post game results, and a page to display the standings) whereas ServletOne only handled a single page (the standings). Table 5.2 shows the new components introduced in ServletTwo.

Table 5.2   Components of the ServletTwo Application

New Components			
Name	**Package**	**Class or Interface**	**Comment**
ServletTwoImpl	nfl.application.servlet	Class	A Servlet that handles multiple pages, including GET and POST methods
ServletTwoVersionInfo	nfl.application.servlet	Class	Configures `Object-Factory`
DynamicStandingsImpl	nfl.application	Class	Version of `Standings` which posts games dynamically, rather than only when initialized
AsyncMessagingImpl	nfl.application	Class	Stores messages rather than displaying them

Table 5.2   Components of the ServletTwo Application (Continued)

Existing Components	
Component	**Description**
layered.jar	All classes and interfaces from the layered version of the application.
nfl.presentation.HTML	HTML output formatter from Chapter 4 and ServletOne.
nfl.application.NullMessagingImpl	Bit bucket implementation for tiebreaker messages.

Before jumping into ServletTwo, we must go back and revisit our Standings class to provide the capability to post new game results as they come in. For this, we'll create a new interface, DynamicStandings, and a new implementing class, DynamicStandingsImpl, which extends BasicStandingsImpl. DynamicStandingsImpl is shown in Listing 5.5. In the original implementation, we had a method called loadData() which was called to post the results of all the games that were in the gameList (a List we could access via the Games class). Once loadData() had been called, there was no way to go back and process any additional games. In the dynamic version, we've split the bulk of the logic from the old loadData() method into a new method called postGameData(), whose job it is to post the results of a single game and update the Team statistics accordingly. We still have a loadData(); in this implementation, it loops through all the games that are available to us at startup time, calling postGameData() for each game. In this way, we can process all games that have been played previously during the application startup process; then, while the application runs, we can take new results and invoke postGameData() directly. postGameData() will also add the game result to the list of games played, if it is not already present in the list.

We did add two new behaviors, or features, into the postGameData() method. It's possible that in this dynamic version of the application, we might want to preload some game data. Go ahead and enter the home team and visiting team for the game, but leave the score at zero-zero. We could do this either a week at a time, or for the entire season. (The ability to do this would be needed if we were to ever implement a forward-looking calculation that reported what a team must do to clinch a berth or avoid elimination.) But our original code would see these zero-zero scores and count the game as a tie. So, we added a quick check for unplayed games, and bail out of updating the statistics for any zero-zero game. (A separate gamePlayed boolean would be another way to accomplish the same thing.) The other change is that for each team involved in the Game, we call its forceRecalculation() method (which actually did not enter into the design of the Team class until this point, but I went ahead and included it in Chapter 3 as if I'd known we'd need it all along). The Team class does lazy initialization of many of its fields, such as win-loss percentage. Once it sees a valid value (the fields are initialized to –1) in these fields, it assumes the calculation has already been performed and doesn't need to be repeated. Whenever we post a new game result, we must reset these fields to their initial values in order for them to be recalculated properly.

With the infrastructure in place to handle dynamic calculations, we want to optimize when they are done. Updating each time a result is recorded might result in multiple updates being done even when no client has looked at the results; likewise, updating each time a client asks for the standings could cause multiple updates when no data has changed. The solution is to flag the results as dirty whenever new results are posted, but not actually do the recalculations until a client request for the standings comes in. This leads to the `calcsUpToDate` boolean flag, and the new `update()`, `updateConferences()`, and `updateDivisions()` methods all visible in Listing 5.5. A final change in support of the dynamic model is that the clients no longer call `computeDivisionStandings()` or `computeConferenceStandings()` to get results back; instead, they call `getDivisionStandings()` or `getConferenceStandings()`, and these routines decide whether to perform new calculations or return the cached data.

One additional minor change you might note in the code: In `BasicStandingsImpl`, the `loadData()` method directly sets the `gameList` and `teamList` fields. Because these fields are `private`, we can't touch them directly from the subclass. We could have gone back into the superclass and changed the access to `protected`, but a cleaner way is to instead use the accessor functions, which is what we've done.

Listing 5.5 The `DynamicStandingsImpl` **Class**

```
// DynamicStandingsImpl.java

package nfl.application;

import nfl.ObjectFactory;

import java.io.Serializable;
import java.util.List;
import java.util.Properties;

/** This extension to the Standings allows for additional
  * Game results to be posted after the intial data load
  * and calculations are performed
  */
public class DynamicStandingsImpl
        extends BasicStandingsImpl
        implements DynamicStandings, Serializable {

    private static boolean initialized = false;

    // A more fine-grained indicator would be nice.
    private static boolean calcsUpToDate = false;
```

```
private List[] divStandings;
private List[] confStandings;

private static DynamicStandings standings =
          new DynamicStandingsImpl();
public static Standings getHandle() {
   return standings;
}

protected DynamicStandingsImpl() { }

public void init() {
   if (initialized) return;
   Properties p = System.getProperties();
   if (p.getProperty("nfl.versioninfo") == null) {
      p.setProperty("nfl.versioninfo",
        "nfl.application.DynamicVersionInfo");
   }
   loadData();
   divStandings = new List[Division.DIVISIONS.size()];
   confStandings =
             new List[Conference.CONFERENCES.size()];
   update();
   initialized = true;
}

private void update() {
   if (!calcsUpToDate) {
      updateDivisions();
      updateConferences();
   }
   calcsUpToDate = true;
}

public List[] getDivisionStandings() {
   update();
   return divStandings;
}

public List getDivisionStandings(int i) {
   update();
   return divStandings[i];
}

public List getDivisionStandings(Division d) {
   for (int i=0; i<divStandings.length; i++) {
      Team t = (Team) divStandings[i].get(0);
      if (t.getDivision() == d) {
```

```
           return getDivisionStandings(i);
        }
    }
    return null; /* error! */
}

public List[] getConferenceStandings() {
    update();
    return confStandings;
}

public List getConferenceStandings(int i) {
    update();
    return confStandings[i];
}

public List getConferenceStandings(Conference c) {
    for (int i=0; i<confStandings.length; i++) {
        Team t = (Team) confStandings[i].get(0);
        if (t.getConference() == c)
            return getConferenceStandings(i);
    }
    return null; /* error! */
}

/* loadData has had most of its guts ripped out and moved
 * to postGameData. loadData is still called at startup,
 * but there may be additional calls to postGameData()
 * made after the initial load.
 */
public void loadData() {
    if (initialized) {
        return;
    }
    // equiv to teamList = teams.getTeamList();
    standings.setTeamList(
            standings.getTeams().getTeamList());
    // equiv to gameList = games.getTeamList();
    standings.setGameList(standings.
            getGames().getGameList());

    long starttime = 0;
    if (getPrintTimings()) {
        starttime = System.currentTimeMillis();
    }
    for (int g=0; g<standings.getGameList().size(); g++) {
        Game game = (Game) standings.getGameList().get(g);
        postGameData(game);
```

```
      }
      if (getPrintTimings()) {
         System.out.println(System.currentTimeMillis() -
             starttime +
             " milliseconds loading initial game data");
      }
   }

   private void updateDivisions() {
      // Loop through divisions
      List divList = Division.DIVISIONS;
      for (int i=0; i<divList.size(); i++) {
         Division d = (Division) divList.get(i);
         divStandings[i] =
             standings.computeDivisionStandings(d);
      }
   }

   private void updateConferences() {
      // Loop through conferences
      List confList = Conference.CONFERENCES;
      for (int i=0; i<confList.size(); i++) {
         Conference c = (Conference) confList.get(i);
         confStandings[i] =
             standings.computeConferenceStandings(c);
      }
   }

   public void postGameData(Game game) {
      calcsUpToDate = false;
      if (getVerbose())
         System.out.println("Posting results: "  + game);
      // If not yet in the gamelist, add it
      Game listedGame = standings.getGames().findGame(
                          game.getWeek(), game.getHome());
      if (listedGame == null)
         standings.getGames().addGame(game);
      boolean confgame = false, divgame = false;
      int thindex, tvindex;
      int[] score;
      thindex = standings.findTeam(game.getHome());
      tvindex = standings.findTeam(game.getVisitor());
      Team th = (Team) standings.getTeamList().get(thindex);
      Team tv = (Team) standings.getTeamList().get(tvindex);
      // NEW: Force recalculation of win-loss percentages
      th.forceRecalculation();
      tv.forceRecalculation();
```

```
        if (th.getConference() == tv.getConference())
            confgame = true;
        if (th.getDivision() == tv.getDivision())
            divgame = true;
        score = game.getScore();
        // NEW: bail out for scheduled-but-not-played games;
        // otherwise they'll get counted as ties!
        if (score[0] + score[1] == 0) return;
// ... remainder identical to old loadData
    }
}
```

With an updated version of Standings ready to handle dynamic posting of game results, now we just have to create a servlet that drives it. ServletTwoImpl is spread out across the next seven listings. In the first listing, Listing 5.6, we can see the class level variables we're setting up for access to the Teams, Games, and Standings objects, and the HTML output formatter. We copy the code from ServletOne that allows us to maintain the sorted Lists of standings, so we won't re-sort the results if no new results have been posted. A calcsUpToDate boolean helps us keep track of when that recalculation is required. We have only a single boolean; a more sophisticated implementation might track this on a division level. The code that loops through divisions and conferences has been refactored into a new showStandings() method (see Listing 5.10), which is called from doGet() (see Listing 5.7).

Listing 5.6 The ServletTwoImpl Class (Part 1 of 6)

```java
// ServletTwoImpl.java

package nfl.application.servlet;

import java.io.*;
import java.text.DecimalFormat;
import java.util.*;

import javax.servlet.*;
import javax.servlet.http.*;

import nfl.ObjectFactory;
import nfl.application.*;
import nfl.presentation.HTML;

public class ServletTwoImpl extends HttpServlet
                        implements SingleThreadModel
{
    /* We can't use just any Standings object; it must
     * support the dynamic behavior.
     */
```

```
private DynamicStandings standings = null;
private HTML       html     = null;
private Teams      teams    = null;
private Games      games    = null;
private List       teamList = null;

public void init() throws ServletException {
    Properties p = System.getProperties();
    /* If property set via command line -D option,
     * do not override that setting.
     */
    if (p.getProperty("nfl.versioninfo") == null) {
        p.setProperty("nfl.versioninfo",
            "nfl.application.servlet.ServletTwoVersionInfo");
    }
    standings = (DynamicStandings)
        ObjectFactory.getHandle().getInstance( "DynamicStandings");
    standings.init();
    html       = new HTML();
}

}
```

Listing 5.7 shows the doGet() method, which is the central control point for our servlet, as well as doPost(), which simply forwards requests along to the doGet() method.

In doGet(), we use the getRequestURI() method of the HttpServletRequest object we are passed to see exactly where in the processing we are, and route the request accordingly. This single servlet actually manages three different pages. Two of the pages are display-only HTML, so for the main page and the standings page, we just branch to the code that displays the appropriate page. The third page is the one used to enter game results; in that case, we need to know the HTTP method involved. If it is a GET, then we're doing the initial display of the page; if it is a POST, then the user has submitted the page complete with data. We branch to the appropriate method based on the getMethod() result of the HttpServletRequest object.

Listing 5.7 ServletTwoImpl doGet(), doPost() Methods (Part 2 of 6)

```
public void doGet(HttpServletRequest request,
                  HttpServletResponse response)
        throws ServletException, IOException {

    response.setContentType("text/html");
    PrintWriter out = response.getWriter();

    String uri = request.getRequestURI();
    if (uri.equals("/nfl/servlet2/Main"))
      showMainPage(out);
```

```
    else if (uri.equals("/nfl/servlet2/ShowStandings"))
      showStandings(out);
    else if (uri.equals("/nfl/servlet2/GameResult")) {
      if (request.getMethod().equals("POST"))
        postGameResults(request, out);
      else
        showGameResultForm(out);
    } else
      response.setStatus(response.SC_NOT_FOUND); /* 404 */
  }

  public void doPost(HttpServletRequest request,
                     HttpServletResponse response)
            throws ServletException, IOException {

    doGet(request, response);
  }
```

In the next four listings, we'll see the four possible target methods that the doGet() routine might route us to. Listing 5.8 shows the showMainPage() method; this is our entry point to the application. In this as with the other pages, we take advantage of some convenience methods we created in our HTML class to print the tags at the very beginning and end of the document.

Listing 5.8 ServletTwoImpl showMainPage Method (Part 3 of 6)

```
  private void showMainPage(PrintWriter out) {
    html.printHtmlHead(out, "NFL Standings Main Page");
    out.println("<H1>Select a Function</H1>");
    out.println("<a href=./ShowStandings>" +
                "Show Current Standings</a>");
    out.println("<br>");
    out.println("<a href=./GameResult>" +
                "Post Game Results</a>");
    html.printHtmlEnd(out);
  }
```

Let there be no mistake; designing impressive-looking HTML pages is not one of my strong points. When displayed, the main page looks like Figure 5.3.

Figure 5.3   The ServletTwo main page.

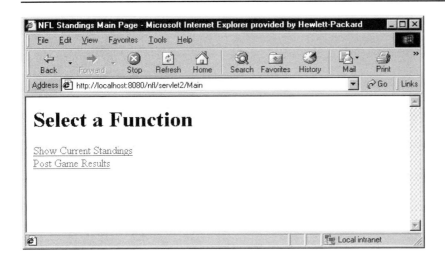

In Listing 5.9, we display a form to allow entry of a game result. The form consists of two drop-down lists for the team names, and three text entry fields for the week number and for the team scores.

Listing 5.9 `ServletTwoImpl showGameResultForm` Method (Part 4 of 6)

```
private void showGameResultForm(PrintWriter out) {

   if (teamList == null) {
      teams = (Teams)
         ObjectFactory.getHandle().getInstance("Teams");
      teamList = teams.getTeamList();
   }

   html.printHtmlHead(out, "Post results of a game");
   out.println("<form method=post " + "action=GameResult>");

   out.println("<H1>Enter Game Results</H1>");

   // Input Week Number
   out.println("Week Number");
   out.println("<INPUT name='week'" + "type=text size=3><br>");

   // Select Visiting Team, enter score
   out.println("Visiting Team");
   out.println("<SELECT name=visitor>");
```

```
        Iterator ti = teamList.iterator();
        while (ti.hasNext()) {
            Team t = (Team) ti.next();
            out.println("<Option>" + t.getFullName());
        }
        out.println("</SELECT>");
        out.println("Score   <INPUT name='vscore' " +
                                "type=text size=3><br>");

        // Select Home Team, enter score
        out.println("Home Team");
        out.println("<SELECT name='home'>");
        ti = teamList.iterator();
        while (ti.hasNext()) {
            Team t = (Team) ti.next();
            out.println("<Option>" + t.getFullName());
        }
        out.println("</SELECT>");
        out.println("Score   <INPUT name='hscore' " +
                                "type=text size=3><br>");

        out.println("<INPUT type=submit " + "value='Post Results'>");

        out.println("</FORM>");
        html.printHtmlEnd(out);
    }
```

Figure 5.4 shows the GameResult page with data entered.

Figure 5.4   The GameResult form.

Listing 5.10 shows the code to display the standings page. This is not much different from the code we used in ServletOne to perform the same task; the only change is that we use the new "get" methods of the dynamic Standings implementation.

Listing 5.10 `ServletTwoImpl showStandings` Method (Part 5 of 6)

```
private void showStandings(PrintWriter out) {
    html.printHtmlHead(out, "NFL Standings");

    // Loop through divisions
    List divList = Division.DIVISIONS;
    for (int i=0; i<divList.size(); i++) {
        Division d = (Division) divList.get(i);
        List l = standings.getDivisionStandings(d);
        html.printDivisionStandings(d, l, out);
    }

    if (!html.getPrintConferenceStandings()) return;

    // Loop through conferences
    List confList = Conference.CONFERENCES;
    for (int i=0; i<confList.size(); i++) {
        Conference c = (Conference) confList.get(i);
        if (html.getPrintConferenceStandings()) {
            List l = standings.getConferenceStandings(c);
            html.printConferenceStandings(c, l, out);
        }
    }
    html.printHtmlEnd(out);
}
```

In Listing 5.11, we see the `postGameResults()` method, which is invoked when the user clicks the Post Results button on the `GameResult` form. The `getParameter()` method of the `HttpServletRequest` object gives us access to all of the field values. They are all returned as strings, so for those we need to make numeric we use the `Integer.parseInt()` method to perform the conversion. We print out a confirmation of what we've done, mainly as a debugging aid if something were to have gone wrong at this stage.

We want to deal with the scenario where a `Game` has already been entered for these teams, in which case we just update the score, as well as the case where we need to create a new `Game` object. The update case is made a little trickier by checking to make sure that once we've looked up a team (we arbitrarily chose the Home team on which to search), we do in fact have the right opponent. Once that checks out, we call the new `postGameData()` method in `DynamicStandingsImpl` to record the result, and set our local `calcsUpToDate` flag false, so that if the standings page is requested again, we'll redo the calculations.

Listing 5.11 `ServletTwoImpl postGameResults` Method (Part 6 of 6)

```java
public void postGameResults(HttpServletRequest request,
                            PrintWriter out) {
   if (games == null) {
      games = (Games)
         ObjectFactory.getHandle().getInstance("Games");
   }


   int    week    = Integer.parseInt(request.
                                getParameter("week"));
   String home    = request.getParameter("home");
   String visitor = request.getParameter("visitor");
   int    hscore  = Integer.parseInt(request.
                                getParameter("hscore"));
   int    vscore  = Integer.parseInt(request.
                                getParameter("vscore"));

   html.printHtmlHead(out, "Game Result Posted");
   out.println("<H1>Posting the following result</H1>");
   out.println("Week " + week);
   out.println("<br>" + visitor + " " + vscore);
   out.println("<br>" + home    + " " + hscore);
   out.println("<br>");
   out.println("<a href=./GameResult>" +
               "Post results for another game</a><br>");
   out.println("<a href=./Main>" +
               "Return to the main page</a>");
   html.printHtmlEnd(out);

   Game g = games.findGame(week, home);

   if (g == null) {
      // Create a new Game
      g = (Game) ObjectFactory.getHandle().getInstance(
         "Game", week, visitor, vscore, home, hscore);
   } else {
      // Update the existing game. It's quite easy
      // to reverse the home & visiting teams, either
      // now or when the scheduled game was entered.
      // Rather than demand perfection, flip the
      // score if necessary to match existing game
      if (g.getHome().equals(home) &&
          g.getVisitor().equals(visitor))
         g.setScore(vscore, hscore);
      else if (g.getHome().equals(visitor) &&
               g.getVisitor().equals(home))
         g.setScore(hscore, vscore);
```

```
            else
                /* trying to record game with different
                 * opponent than scheduled. We're not
                 * gonna take it. */
                out.println("\nERROR: not posted because " +
                "there is already a game recorded for this " +
                "week against a different opponent!<br>" +
                "Home team " + home + "<br>" +
                "Previously entered opponent " +
                    g.getVisitor() + "<br>" +
                "Attempted to add opponent " +
                    visitor + "<br>");
        }

        // Update team statistics and add g to gamelist
        standings.postGameData(g);
    }
}
```

Figure 5.5   This page is displayed after posting the result.

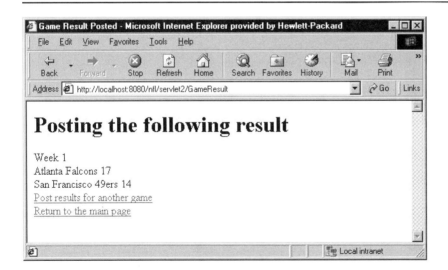

5.4.1   Thread Safety in Servlets

You'll note that our second servlet implements `SingleThreadModel`. This is an interface that signals to the servlet container that we'd like our servlet to be managed in such a way that thread safety is guaranteed to us. This allows us to avoid having to add explicit synchronization into our application, but at a cost of higher resource usage. In a servlet that does not implement `SingleThreadModel`, each request that comes in will cause a new thread to be started, and without explicit synchronization, these threads may see data in an inconsistent state or even cause corruption of data. With `SingleThreadModel`, the servlet engine will either queue all requests to a single instance of the servlet, or more commonly, create a pool of servlet instances, with each instance running only a single thread (handling just one request) at a time.

5.4.2   Building, Packaging, and Deploying ServletTwo

The Ant buildfile for ServletTwo doesn't introduce any new features; it is presented in Listing 5.12. To select this target, simply invoke Ant with a target of `servlet2`. Note that the default target for the buildfile is `servlet1`, so you must specify the target explicitly in order to build this servlet. If you haven't already modified the buildfile for building `servlet1`, you'll need to alter the `servlet.jar` property to point to where you have installed `servlet.jar` on your system.

Listing 5.12 Ant Buildfile for ServletTwo (Part 2 of `build.xml`)

```
<target name="compile-servlet2">
   <javac srcdir="." classpath="${servlet.jar}">
      <include name="ServletTwoImpl.java" />
      <include name="ServletTwoVersionInfo.java" />
      <src path=".." />
      <include name="DynamicStandings.java" />
      <include name="DynamicStandingsImpl.java" />
      <include name="AsyncMessagingImpl.java" />
      <src path="../../presentation" />
      <include name="HTML.java" />
   </javac>
</target>

<target name="servlet2" depends="compile-servlet2">
   <delete file="nfl.war" />
   <war warfile="nfl.war" webxml="servlet2.xml">
      <lib dir="../.." includes="layered.jar" />
      <classes dir="."
          includes="ServletTwo*.class"
            prefix="WEB-INF/classes/nfl/application/servlet"
          />
      <classes dir=".."
          includes="DynamicStandings*.class,
                    AsyncMessagingImpl.class"
            prefix="WEB-INF/classes/nfl/application" />
      <classes dir="../../presentation"
          includes="HTML.class"
            prefix="WEB-INF/classes/nfl/presentation" />
   </war>
</target>
```

```
<target name="clean-servlet2">
  <delete>
    <fileset dir="." includes="ServletTwo*.class,nfl.war" />
    <fileset dir=".." includes="DynamicStandings*.class,
                                AsyncMessagingImpl.class" />
    <fileset dir="../../presentation"
        includes="HTML.class" />
  </delete>
</target>
```

We do introduce one important new feature in the `web.xml` file for ServletTwo. This new feature is the `<servlet-mapping>` element (this element was added to ServletOne later, when redeploying the servlet to containers other than Tomcat). With the `servlet-mapping` element, we can specify a pattern to be matched, and a servlet to be used for any URL request matching that pattern. We specify a pattern of `/servlet2/*`, which means that any URL that we see containing this string will be passed along to the designated servlet, in this case `NFLServlet2`. Also notice that this single `web.xml` file includes both our new servlet and the older ServletOne; you can deploy multiple servlets into the same servlet context in this way.

To reach ServletTwo in Tomcat, we would use thefollowing URL:

```
http://localhost:8080/nfl/servlet2/Main
```

(In WebLogic or HP-AS, the only change we would need to make is to the port number—7001 for WebLogic and 9090 for HP-AS—if each server were running at the default port location.) Note that we still need to specify the context (`/nfl`)—which is obvious if you think about where the `web.xml` file resides; it is part of the `nfl` context, so the `/servlet2` pattern is only being applied to URLs that direct the server to look in our context. If we wanted to match `/servlet2` without having to also specify `/nfl`, then we could instead put the servlet mapping into the `server.xml` file for the servlet container, rather than our local `web.xml`. And if you examine this `server.xml` file, you'll see that in fact that is exactly why any URL containing `/servlet` gets special treatment. There is already a mapping set up to match this pattern in the default configuration. (`server.xml` is a Tomcat-specific file. WebLogic has a `config.xml` file that serves a similar purpose, while the HP-AS has a `j2ee-partition-config.xml` file.)

Listing 5.13 `web.xml` File for ServletTwo (`servlet2.xml`)

```
<?xml version="1.0" encoding="ISO-8859-1"?>

<!DOCTYPE web-app PUBLIC
  "-//Sun Microsystems, Inc.//DTD Web application 2.2//EN"
  "http://java.sun.com/j2ee/dtds/web-app_2_2.dtd">

<web-app>
  <servlet>
    <servlet-name>NFLStandings</servlet-name>
```

```
    <servlet-class>
        nfl.application.servlet.ServletOneImpl
    </servlet-class>
  </servlet>

  <servlet>
    <servlet-name>NFLServlet2</servlet-name>
    <servlet-class>
        nfl.application.servlet.ServletTwoImpl
    </servlet-class>
    <load-on-startup>1</load-on-startup>
  </servlet>

  <servlet-mapping>
     <servlet-name>NFLServlet2</servlet-name>
     <url-pattern>/servlet2/*</url-pattern>
  </servlet-mapping>
</web-app>
```

5.5   Advanced Servlet Topics

There's quite a bit more that you can do with servlets. Although we didn't need these features for our examples, I thought they were important enough to give at least a mention to these servlet capabilities.

5.5.1   Server-Side Includes

Looking at the way a servlet is structured, it is typical to wonder if there's a better separation possible between the behavior of the servlet (the business logic) and the HTML markup embedded in the servlet. One of the first attempts to make a more logical separation of these was support for server-side includes in some Web servers.

In the Apache Web Server, for example, there was an add-on package called JSSI that provided the ability to pull all of the HTML out into a separate file. This file, which was given a .jhtml extension, would then include a SERVLET tag to indicate where the output of the servlet should be placed. For example, our Standings application might look something like this:

```
<HTML>
<HEAD>
<TITLE>NFL Standings</TITLE>
</HEAD>
<BODY>
<SERVLET CODE=nfl.application.ServletOneImpl>
<!--If our servlet accepted any parameters, we would
   include <PARAM NAME=name VALUE="value"> items here
 -->
</SERVLET>
</BODY>
```

The Java Web Server from Sun also provided a server-side include capability that supported the SERVLET tag, although using a different file extension (.shtml). The Apache JSSI module is not compatible with the Tomcat servlet container and the latest versions of the servlet specification (JSDK 2.1), and Sun has discontinued the Java Web Server in favor of the iPlanet server. With the introduction of JSP and the tight integration of servlets and JSPs, it appears server-side includes will disappear from the servlet scene.

5.5.2   Initialization Parameters

Initialization parameters provide a way for you to pass information into the servlet without having to hard-code it into the program. This might be preferences information, or configuration information, or anything else for which you might want to provide run-time values. Initialization parameters are set by values specified in the web.xml file that describes the servlet. Programmatically, the servlet retrieves the value for the parameter by calling the getInitParameter(String name) method of the HttpServletConfig object. Here are some initialization parameters we might choose to set for our servlet (currently, the servlet code doesn't check for any of these values; one of the exercises at the end of this chapter encourages you to enable these settings).

```
<servlet>
. . . existing options omitted . . .
  <init-param>
     <param-name>verbose</param-name>
     <param-value>false</param-value>
  </init-param>
  <init-param>
     <param-name>printConferenceStandings</param-name>
     <param-value>true</param-value>
  </init-param>
  <init-param>
     <param-name>printEliminatedTeams</param-name>
     <param-value>true</param-value>
  </init-param>
</servlet>
```

5.5.3   Session Tracking

As mentioned back in Chapter 4 during our brief discussion of HTTP, connections between a Web server and Web browser are stateless. Because many uses of the Web, especially in the area of e-commerce, require at least the appearance of a stateful connection, mechanisms for tracking state are a part of most Web applications. Servlets provide several different mechanisms that all fall under the general heading of session tracking.

There are some methods of session tracking that are done entirely within HTML; that is, there is no special support required from the servlet APIs or the servlet container to provide the tracking capability. One of these is the use of hidden fields within HTML forms. This capability is certainly usable from within a Java servlet, but given the more sophisticated types of tracking mechanisms, few users will find any need for it. Hidden fields must be placed on every single page the user sees in order for the session data to be maintained, which means that every page must be dynamically generated. Furthermore, the hidden information is sent as part of every request to the server, and part of every page sent back to the browser, so bandwidth is being consumed passing information back and forth that we'd really prefer the server to simply keep track of.

A second HTML-only way of tracking state is via URL rewriting, where the fields are encoded as name/value pairs and passed along as part of the query string with each page request. This is similar to hidden fields in the fact that we're constantly bouncing the data fields back and forth between client and server like some ASCII-encoded hot potato.

Session Tracking via Cookies

One of the more prevalent ways to keep track of state information in modern Web applications is to use cookies. Unlike the previous mechanisms, which just ride along in the data, cookies require some assistance from the Web browser. A cookie is a piece of data that the server sends to the browser, asking that it be kept around and passed back as part of future requests. Cookies are commonly used to save such information as login identity, preferences (at sites that allow some user customization), or data to be used to prefill forms. Cookies incur the same request-side overhead as the previous methods, but the server doesn't need to keep resending the same cookie information as part of every page served. Be aware that many users explicitly disable cookies within their browser, perceiving them as a privacy violation because they are frequently used to track how a user moves around within or between Web sites. For this reason, relying on them for session tracking may not always succeed.

The servlet API provides methods for creating cookies and attaching them to responses, as well as for requesting cookies from requests. However, I don't think most users will choose this route, because the Session Tracking API is more flexible and easier to use.

Servlet Tracking via HttpSession

Finally, we come to the recommended way of providing a session tracking capability within your servlet. Servlets can access an `HttpSession` object to store and retrieve information about a user session.

It's up to the servlet container to decide how to actually implement the session-tracking capability. Usually, the underlying technique is one of those we've already seen, such as cookies or URL rewriting. However, if we're keeping track of 10 items for a particular user, using cookies or URL rewriting would require that we pass all 10 of these items back and forth on each request and response. With servlet tracking via an `HttpSession`, we just pass a session ID that is used to help us locate the user's information in a server-resident data structure.

Finally, a bit of foreshadowing: Much more sophisticated session tracking capabilities are provided by Session Beans, one of the flavors of Enterprise JavaBeans. If you can't find the capability you need within servlets, this might indicate that EJB would better suit at least this part of your application.

Session tracking is accomplished via a new object, the `HttpSession` object. You can access this object as needed by requesting a reference to it via the `getSession()` method of any `HttpServletRequest` object. A session can be thought of as a series of requests and responses coming from the same user. A session can be created at any time, and the typical way we do so is to call `getSession(true)`, with the boolean parameter requesting that a session be started for this user if one is not already in progress.

The `HttpSession` is mainly just a `Map` that allows us to track arbitrary name/value pairs for the session. We do this through the API calls:

```
Object getAttribute(String name);
void setAttribute(String name, Object value);²
```

Other calls we might want to make on the `HttpSession` object include `remove-Attribute(String name)`, for any elements we no longer need to track, and `invalidate()`, to end a session and release any data we're tracking for it. All of the methods available on `HttpSession` objects can be seen in API 5.6.

API 5.6 javax.servlet.http.**HttpSession**

```
public interface HttpSession
    public Object getAttribute(String name);
    public java.util.Enumeration getAttributeNames();
    public long getCreationTime();
    public String getId();
    public long getLastAccessedTime();
    public int getMaxInactiveInterval();
    public ServletContext getServletContext();
    public void invalidate();
    public boolean isNew();
    public void removeAttribute(String name);
    public void setAttribute(String name, Object value);
    public void setMaxInactiveInterval(int interval);
```

5.5.4 Forwarding Requests

In both of the examples we've seen so far, a single servlet provides all of the capabilities we need. In more complex applications, you may have multiple servlets, or you might have a combination of servlets, JavaServer Pages, and static HTML pages. In these more complex configurations, you need to have a mechanism for transferring control from a servlet to another servlet or page. This is done via the `RequestDispatcher` object. The use of the `RequestDis-patcher` is quite simple; a `RequestDispatcher` is created using the URL of the target servlet,

---

2. In the Servlet 2.1 API, these methods were named `getValue()` and `setValue()` instead. The older methods are still present, but deprecated, in Servlet 2.2.

JSP, or HTML page as a parameter, then the `forward()` method of the `RequestDispatcher` is invoked with the `HttpServletRequest` and `HttpServletResponse` objects passed as parameters. For example:

```
URL target = new URL(http://systemname:80/path/to/servlet)
RequestDispatcher dispatcher =
       getServletContext().getRequestDispatcher(url);
dispatcher.forward(request, response)
```

In addition to forwarding requests, the `RequestDispatcher` also provides an `include()` method that can be used to include the contents of the specified URL as part of the output of the current servlet. The `RequestDispatcher` object is used in some of the examples in Chapter 6, when we explore using servlets and JavaServer Pages together. The URL can be a local resource, as we'll show in our examples in Chapter 6, or a remote resource as we've shown here. The remote resource can be used, for example, to have a servlet running on a system outside your firewall take incoming requests, and then pass them to a servlet inside the firewall via a secure connection.

5.6   Exercises

5.1 Selectable output format: We now have two output formatter classes: Console and HTML. Adapt either of the example servlets so that it reads an initialization parameter to determine what output format to use. Based on the setting, set the content type to either `text/plain` or `text/html`, and then use the appropriate class to format the output.

5.2 Pluggable output format: Extend the code from Exercise 5.1 even further. In that exercise, we are able to add additional format options by changing code in the servlet. We'd like to be able to drop in new formatting classes without having to change our servlet at all. Accept as configuration parameters a MIME type string and a formatter class name. In the servlet, set the content type of the `HttpServletResponse` to the MIME type string, and invoke the appropriate print methods of the formatter class. (Hint: You'll either need to create an interface that all the formatter classes implement, or use reflection to be able to invoke the print methods of an arbitrary class.)

5.3 Initialization parameters: In the section on initialization parameters, we show `web.xml` settings for three boolean values that are defined within the `Standings` class, but that provide no mechanism for change other than editing the source and recompiling. Add code to the example servlets to read values from the initialization parameters and set the boolean values accordingly.

5.4 Request forwarding: Break the single ServletTwo servlet into multiple servlets, and use the `RequestDispatcher`'s `forward()` method to pass control between them.

5.5 Team data servlet: Create a new servlet (or extend ServletTwo) to allow entry and updating of Team data, just as the existing servlet allows entry and updating of Game data.

5.6 On-demand messages: Using the AsynchMessagingImpl class to hold messages, make the team names in the HTML output a link that, when clicked, shows any messages generated for the selected team.

5.7 Further Reading

The home page for servlets is http://java.sun.com/products/servlet/index.html. From this page, you can link to tutorials, downloadable binaries, and other technical information.

The Apache Element Construction Set (ECS) provides a way to generate HTML programmatically. See http://jakarta.apache.org/ecs/index.html for details, including documentation and downloadable binaries.

Marty Hall's *Core Servlets and JavaServer Pages* is a valuable reference for moving beyond the examples given in this and the following chapter.

The Tomcat engine, which supports Java servlets and JSP, is located at http://jakarta.apache.org/tomcat/index.html. You can download released and Beta versions of the software from this location.

The BEA WebLogic Application Server is available at http://www.bea.com. You can download a trial version with a 30-day license at no charge.

HP has announced the discontinuation of the HP-AS application server product. As of late July 2002, free downloads are still available from http://www.hpmiddleware.com.

CHAPTER 6

JavaServer Pages

If you felt there was something awkward about the combination of business logic and HTML formatting going on in the early servlet examples, you're not alone. We sidestepped this issue nicely, I think, in our own servlet examples by creating a separate HTML class that handled the responsibility of formatting our output. Certainly a well-designed architecture built upon servlets can enforce a separation of application code and presentation code into different classes just as we have done, but JavaServer Pages (JSPs) have emerged to fill the perceived need for a tool to assist in making this separation. JSPs turns the servlet concept upside down. A servlet can be seen as a program that has HTML embedded in it. A JavaServer Page is an HTML page that has Java code embedded in it (or at least invoked from it). In either the JSP or servlet case, it's possible to cleanly separate the presentation and logic, or to have them hopelessly tangled together. Selecting which technology to use is frequently based on the comfort of the designer (are you primarily a page designer or a programmer?) and the mix of content on the page (primarily static, with a few dynamic items, or primarily dynamic?).

JavaServer Pages provide several design alternatives; used properly, they can improve the quality of your application, but used incorrectly they can make your application slower performing and harder to understand and debug. We'll look at several ways in which JSPs can be used and try to assess the strengths and weaknesses of each model.

JSPs start life looking like an HTML page (with an extension of .jsp rather than .html or .htm), but end up as servlets. The JSP/Servlet container will load your JSP, compile it into a servlet, and then execute the servlet in order to generate the content that is passed back to the requestor. If you haven't already read the servlets chapter, I recommend you do so, as much of the discussion of JSPs is based on understanding the basic parts of a servlet.

Software Used in This Chapter

JavaServer Pages (JSPs)

All examples in this chapter use only JSP 1.1 features. There are no development-time components needed because JSPs are compiled dynamically by the container when they are deployed or accessed. All JSPs shown here are also compatible with the JSP 1.2 standard; because examples in later chapters will require JSP 1.2, software supporting JSP 1.2 is recommended. Any of the following three servlet engines will work.

- **Tomcat Servlet Container**
  Version 3.2.3 with support for JSP 1.1 support, or Version 4.0, which also supports JSP 1.2. Downloadable from `http://jakarta.apache.org`. Can be used standalone, or integrated with a Web or application server such as Apache, Enhydra, IIS, or iPlanet. JSPs will be compiled into servlets and then executed within the Tomcat Servlet Container.
- **HP Application Server (HP-AS)**
  The HP-AS 8.0 version was used (JSP 1.2 support). Freely downloadable from `http://www.hpmiddleware.com`.
- **BEA WebLogic Application Server**
  WebLogic 6.1 was used (JSP 1.2 support). A 30-day trial version is freely downloadable from `http://www.bea.com`. Product can be purchased at the same site.

6.1 JSP Scripting Elements

Perhaps the easiest way to start with JSPs is doing something known as "scriptlets." This is a good way to learn JSP, but a bad way to use JSP. With scriptlets, you embed the Java code directly in your JSP, and the code will be compiled and executed at the time the page is accessed. One obvious problem here is that the initial page load will be slow; just how slow depends upon the complexity of the servlet that needs to be generated and the power of the server.

An even bigger problem is the unwieldy development process. If you write Java code that has errors (not that you ever would), and compile the code with the `javac` compiler, many errors will be caught by the compiler before you even attempt to run the code. With scriptlets, errors that could be caught by the compiler aren't going to be caught until the page is served.

Putting the bulk of your logic in classes (particularly JavaBeans) and just embedding small access functions in the JSP is a far better way to go. We'll come to that design presently, but it seems that the best way to understand just what goes on with a JSP is to start with scripting and then move on to the other alternatives.

There are three types of scripting elements at your disposal as a JSP programmer: expressions, declarations, and scriptlets.

6.1.1   Expressions

A JSP expression is an HTML-like element that has the format `<%= expression %>`. All JSP elements have the beginning and ending elements `<%` and `%>`; the equals sign denotes that this JSP element is an expression. When the JSP page is served, the expression is evaluated and the entire element is replaced by the result. If you look at the HTML source page (using the View Source capability of the browser), you won't see any trace of the expression; it is evaluated on the server side and only the result text is sent to the client. For example, suppose you had the following code in a JSP:

```
<p>The result of adding 2 + 2 is <%= 2 + 2 %></p>
```

Then the HTML sent to the browser would simply be:

```
<p>The result of adding 2 + 2 is 4</p>
```

Now, this doesn't seem particularly exciting, because there is nothing we've done that takes advantage of any of the powerful Java classes or capabilities. But our expression could also include references to methods of Java classes, including classes that we provide as part of our application. So we could write, for example:

```
<p>NFL Standings current as of <%= new java.util.Date() %>:
<br>Team <%= team.getName() %> has won <%= team.getWins() %>
         games and lost <%= team.getLosses() %> games.</p>
```

Note that this snippet of code isn't complete: While the output of the `Date` is complete as written, the output of the team data would require that the variable `team` be declared, which in turn requires that we import portions of our NFL package. We'll cover how to do these things in the sections that follow. We'd probably also want to introduce some sort of a loop construct so that we could print results for more than just one team; we'll see how that is done when we introduce custom JSP tags. Because HTML is text-based, for us to be able to use a method or class in the output, it must either be a `String` or of a type that can be converted to a string without any special effort on our part. With the `Date`, for example, the `Date.toString()` method is actually being called in the servlet to return the object's value as a printable string. The `Team getName()` method returns a `String`, while `getWins()` and `getLosses()` return `int`s, which Java will convert to string representation without requiring any cast or method call.

Because the JSP expression resembles a Java statement, it feels natural to end it with a semi-colon. Don't. The entire expression will be placed inside of a `print()` statement in the generated servlet; any semicolon you might add will end up inside the parentheses and cause compilation errors.

6.1.2   Declarations

We've already shown why we need declarations; in either our expressions or our scriptlets, we may want to refer to some externally defined variables or classes. JSP declarations are HTML elements of the form `<%! declaration %>`. Note that we have the same basic JSP tag format, merely changing the equals sign that denoted an expression to the exclamation point denoting a declaration.

With JSP declarations, we can declare variables that will be used later in the JSP in expressions or scriptlets. Some examples include:

```
<%! Standings s = (Standings)
            ObjectFactory.getInstance("Standings") %>
<%! int counter = 0 %>
```

In addition to variable declarations, the same syntax can be used to declare methods, which are then available for use within expressions or scriptlets on the page. Listing 6.1 (on page 151) includes both variable and method declarations.

6.1.3   Scriptlets

Scriptlets are blocks of Java code that you just plop down in the middle of a JSP. Scriptlets take the form `<% code %>`. The code within your scriptlet will become part of the body of the `service()` method of the generated servlet. It will have access to any variables or methods defined in your JSP declarations, along with some container-provided variables shown Table 6.1.

Table 6.1   Predefined Objects Available on All JSP Pages

Object Name	Class	Usage
request	HttpServletRequest	The servlet request object
response	HttpServletResponse	The servlet response object
session	HttpSession	Information about current session
config	ServletConfig	Access to configuration data
application	ServletContext	Access to application data
pageContext	PageContext	Access to page data
out	PrintWriter	The output stream
page	Object	None

Listings 6.1 through 6.3, which appear at the end of the section on JSP directives, show all of the JSP scripting elements (expressions, declarations, and scriptlets) being used together in a single JSP that enables us to retrieve information about a favorite team from the `Standings` object.

6.1.4 XML-Compatible Formatting of JSP Scripting Elements

You might be generating a document in XML format, rather than HTML. If so, you can still use JSP in your document, although the element format is different. Here are alternate representations of all of the JSP scripting elements that you can use:

```
<jsp:expression>java expression</jsp:expression>
<jsp:declaration>java declaration</jsp:declaration>
<jsp:scriptlet>java code</jsp:scriptlet>
```

All of the tags that use XML format, including all of the JSP action tags, are case-sensitive. Because HTML tags are not case-sensitive, this may be a point of confusion for page designers. Also, attribute values may use either single quotes or double quotes; we've used double quotes in all of our examples, but either is acceptable.

6.1.5 Using Comments in JSP Pages

There are two different comment formats you can include in your JSP pages. You can use normal HTML-formatted comments, such as:

```
<!-- This comment will be included in the HTML page
     that is sent to the client -->
```

As the comment itself notes, comments done in normal HTML fashion will be part of the page generated by the servlet and sent to the client.

An alternate form of comment can be used when you're just documenting something in the JSP that doesn't need to be seen in the HTML:

```
<%-- This comment will not be seen by the client --%>
```

This type of comment serves only as documentation for the JSP itself; it will not appear in the generated servlet or the HTML output created by the servlet.

Also, inside a scriptlet you can use normal Java comments, either C style (`/*` and `*/`), C++ style (`//comment to end of line`), or Javadoc style (`/** doc comment */`).

6.2 JSP Directives

Just as there were three types of JSP scripting elements, there are also three types of JSP directives. The directives are the `page` directive, the `include` directive, and the `taglib` directive. The JSP directive tag format is:

```
<%@ directive attrname="attrvalue" [...] %>
```

Directive names and attribute names are all case-sensitive; all are predominantly lower-case with the occasional infix capitalization for readability. There may be multiple attribute name/value pairs specified. The permitted attributes vary by directive, and are covered in the sections that follow.

6.2.1   The page Directive

The page directive gives you a way to customize the servlet that is being generated in several ways, such as controlling what classes are imported, setting the content type of the response, or even changing what class the servlet extends. An example page directive is:

```
<%@ page import="java.util.*" %>
```

Table 6.2 shows the attributes available for use with the page directive. In our examples, only the import attribute is being used.

Table 6.2   Attributes Available for Use with the page Directive

Attribute Name	Value	Comment
import	Class names	Wildcards OK; multiple imports may be specified, separated by commas.
contentType	MIME type	Default is text/html.
isThreadSafe	true | false	If false, generated servlet implements SingleThreadModel. Default is true.
session	true | false	If true, this JSP participates in a session. Default is true.
buffer	'none' or XXkb	Size in kilobytes. Default is server-specific, but will be at least 8 KB.
autoflush	true | false	If true, flush page when buffer is full. If false, throw exception if buffer fills. Default is true.
extends	Class name	Superclass of generated servlet.
info	String	Descriptive string; can be accessed via getServletInfo().
errorPage	URL	If an uncaught exception is thrown by this page, redirect to given URL.
isErrorPage	true | false	True if this page is an error target. Provides access to exception object.
language	java	Statement of the obvious.

6.2.2   The include Directive

The `include` directive can be used to include a file into the JSP document. The included file might contain static HTML, JSP code, or anything else that would be legal in the JSP document at the point at which it is included. The `include` directive accepts a single attribute, the `file` attribute, which takes as its value a relative URL:

```
<%@ include file="stdnavbar.html" %>
```

If the included file changes, the servlet will not automatically detect the change and be recompiled, so this mechanism is not good for including dynamic content. If the included content may change dynamically, you should instead use the `include()` method of the `Request-Dispatcher`, which we'll cover in the section on using servlets and JSPs together.

There is also an `include` action, described in the section "JSP Actions" on page 163. The difference between an `include` directive and an `include` action is when they are executed. The `include` directive is processed when the JSP is being translated to a servlet; so typically only once during the lifetime of the servlet container. The `include` action is processed at the time the page is being served. This partially solves the problem of dynamic content: If the included file changes, the most recent version of the file will be included. However, because the inclusion is done after the servlet has been generated, files included in this way cannot contain JSP elements because the translation of JSP has already been done. Typically, HTML or plain text files are included via this mechanism.

6.2.3   The taglib Directive

The `taglib` directive is similar to the `import` directive. In both cases, we are making additional Java classes available for use by our JSP. In this case, the classes we are allowing access to are of a special type. Tag libraries are a JSP mechanism to allow the basic actions to be supplemented by additional actions that have been developed by the application author or the author of a tag library. The `taglib` directive takes two attributes: a `prefix` and a `uri`. The URI points to an XML-format file that contains the tag library descriptors (and typically has an extension of `.tld`). The `prefix` is a string that will be used to prefix any actions used from this tag library within the JSP page. When used, the prefix will be separated from the action name by a colon, but you do not specify the colon as part of the prefix in the attribute declaration. The use of prefixes avoids name collisions if multiple tag libraries declare tags having the same name, and also makes it clearer when looking at the JSP what tags are being used from what tag libraries. For example, this directive:

```
<%@ taglib prefix="nfl" uri="/nfltaglib.tld" %>
```

causes the tag library `nfltaglib` to be loaded. Any JSP tag in our document of the form `<%nfl:tagname attributes %>` specifies that `tagname` is not a standard JSP action, but rather one defined in `nfltaglib`. We'll explore tag libraries in more detail in the next chapter.

6.2.4   XML Syntax for JSP Directives

Just as with the scripting elements, the JSP directives also can be specified using an alternate XML-friendly syntax, as shown here:

```
<jsp:directive.page import="nfl.application.*" />
```

In place of `page` you could instead specify `taglib` or `include`, and the attribute (`import` in the example) can be replaced by any attribute legal for that particular directive.

6.2.5   JSP Scripting Example: Favorite Team Info

We're going to add some new functionality to our application now. We do this both for variety (how many more times do you really want to see the loop used to calculate standings?) and because it gives us an example better suited to some of the points I'd like to emphasize.

In the next three listings, we introduce the Favorite Team page, which enables a user to specify a favorite NFL team and receive an update on just that team. The update includes any game results that have been posted since the user last visited the page, and the current ranking of his favorite team in both division and conference standings.

We'll implement this capability in two different ways. First, we'll show it using just the JSP scripting elements we've introduced so far. Then, after our discussion of using JavaBeans with JSPs, we'll look at how the JSP could be reimplemented using JavaBeans.

Table 6.3   Components in the Scriptlet JSP

New Components		
Name	**Component Type**	**Comment**
FavoriteTeamScriptlet.jsp	JSP	JSP with embedded scriptlet
Existing Components		
Component	**Description**	
layered.jar	All classes and interfaces of the layered version of the application (as presented in Chapter 2).	
ServletTwo	JSP is installed on top of fully functioning example servlet.	

In Listing 6.1, we see the first part of the scriptlet version of the Favorite Team JSP. This portion of the code contains just the import directives and the declarations. Note that we declare a number of variables that we wish to use, as well as a few methods that we'll be using later in the page.

Listing 6.1 `FavoriteTeamScriptlet.jsp` (Part 1 of 3)

```
<!DOCTYPE HTML PUBLIC
 "-//W3C//DTD HTML 4.0 Transitional//EN">
<html>
<%-- This .jsp uses embedded scriptlet code. Not
     the recommended way to go!
  --%>

<%@ page import="nfl.ObjectFactory" %>
<%@ page import="nfl.application.*" %>
<%@ page import="java.util.*"     %>

<%-- Variable declarations --%>
<%! DynamicStandings standings = null; %>
<%! Team     team;              %>
<%! Game[]   gameResults;       %>
<%! String[] messages;          %>
<%! int      conferenceRank; %>
<%! int      divisionRank;      %>
<%! int      gameCounter;       %>

<%-- Method declarations --%>

<%! public String intToOrdinal(int rank) {
        switch(rank) {
           case 1: return "1st";
           case 2: return "2nd";
           case 3: return "3rd";
           default: return (rank+"th");
        }
    }
%>

<%! public String divisionStatus() {
        String result = null;
        Team.Status s = team.getDivisionChampStatus();
        if (s == Team.Status.CLINCHED)
           result = "Clinched ";
        else if (s == Team.Status.CLINCHED_TIE)
           result = "Clinched at least tie in ";
        else if (s == Team.Status.LEADING)
           result = "Leads ";
        else if (s == Team.Status.IN_CONTENTION)
           result = "Contender for ";
        else if (s == Team.Status.ELIMINATED)
           result = "Cannot win ";
        return result + team.getDivision();
    }
```

```
public String conferenceStatus() {
   String result = null;
   // homefield
   Team.Status s = team.getHomeFieldStatus();
   if (s == Team.Status.CLINCHED)
      result = "Clinched ";
   else if (s == Team.Status.CLINCHED_TIE)
      result = "Clinched at least tie for ";
   else if (s == Team.Status.LEADING)
      result = "Leads race for ";
   else if (s == Team.Status.IN_CONTENTION)
      result = "Contender for ";
   else if (s == Team.Status.ELIMINATED)
      result = "Cannot win ";
   result = result + " home-field advantage<br>";

   // wildcards
   s = team.getWildcardStatus();
   if (s == Team.Status.CLINCHED)
      result += "Clinched ";
   else if (s == Team.Status.CLINCHED_TIE)
      result += "Clinched at least tie for ";
   else if (s == Team.Status.LEADING)
      result += "Leads race ";
   else if (s == Team.Status.IN_CONTENTION)
      result += "Contender for ";
   else if (s == Team.Status.ELIMINATED)
      result += "Cannot win ";
   return result + "wildcard";
}
%>
```

In the second listing, Listing 6.2, we have a scriptlet that contains all of the business logic for our page. Because the scriptlet declares any variables it needs, you might wonder why we didn't just put all of our variable declarations here. The variables declared here will go out of scope once our scriptlet ends. If you look ahead to the third listing, you'll see that in that code we use the JSP expression syntax to refer to variables that were declared in the declarations section, and then set or modified in the scriptlet section.

Much of the code in the scriptlet is quite similar, or identical, to code in our Standings implementation. One difference is that we interrogate the request object (via the getParameter() method) to find out what team name and week we've been passed. Although a more sophisticated implementation could keep track of when a user last visited our site, and what his favorite team was, in this implementation we require those items to be passed to us. If they are not passed, we assume that the favorite team is the 49ers, and that this is the first visit to the site this season.

Our `Teams` object doesn't give us a way to get the `Team` object for a specific team (bad design, that) so we must instead get the `teamList` and search it ourselves. We can obtain a list of all games played by that team, but must process it ourselves to get those games that meet our selection criteria (played since our last visit). These programmatic actions are arguably not specific to this JSP page, and therefore would be good candidates for being relocated to somewhere other than the JSP page. (This is what your English teacher would call foreshadowing. Or is it irony? I didn't pay much attention.)

Listing 6.2 `FavoriteTeamScriptlet.jsp` (Part 2 of 3)

```
<% // The main body. Becomes part of jspService() method

   // Initialize. Do only once.
   if (standings == null) {
      Properties p = System.getProperties();
      /* Rather than create a new VersionInfo variant,
       * we'll just use the one from ServletTwo
       */
      if (p.getProperty("nfl.versioninfo") == null) {
        p.setProperty("nfl.versioninfo",
           "nfl.application.servlet.ServletTwoVersionInfo");
      }
      standings = (DynamicStandings)
         ObjectFactory.getHandle().getInstance(
                                "DynamicStandings");
      standings.init();
   }

   // Parse arguments from query string
   String favorite = request.getParameter("team");
   if (favorite == null) favorite = "49ers";
   String sVisit = request.getParameter("week");
   int lastVisit;
   if (sVisit == null)
      lastVisit = 0;
   else
      lastVisit = Integer.parseInt(sVisit);

   Teams teams = standings.getTeams();
   Games games = standings.getGames();

   String fullName = teams.findName(favorite);
   team = teams.getTeam(favorite);
   if (team == null) {
     // TODO: route to or generate error page
     System.out.println("BAD TEAM");
   }
```

```
    List gameList = games.getAllGamesFor(team.getFullName());
    gameResults = new Game[16];
    gameCounter = 0;
    for (int i=0; i<gameList.size(); i++) {
       Game g = (Game) gameList.get(i);
       if (g.getWeek() > lastVisit) {
          gameResults[gameCounter++] = g;
       }
     }

    List divStandings = standings.getDivisionStandings(
                             team.getDivision());
    for (int i=0;i<divStandings.size(); i++) {
       Team rankedTeam = (Team) divStandings.get(i);
       if (rankedTeam.getFullName().equals(fullName)) {
          divisionRank = i+1;
          break;
       }
    }
    List confStandings= standings.getConferenceStandings(
                             team.getConference());
    for (int i=0;i<confStandings.size(); i++) {
       Team rankedTeam = (Team) confStandings.get(i);
       if (rankedTeam.getFullName().equals(fullName)) {
          conferenceRank = i+1;
          break;
       }
    }
 }
%>
```

In the third portion of our scriptlet, we have the code that actually formats the output. It is made up of standard HTML tags plus JSP expressions. The expressions are primarily method calls of the Team and Game objects that we selected in Part 2 of the scriptlet.

Listing 6.3 FavoriteTeamScriptlet.jsp (Part 3 of 3)

```
<!-- HTML output using embedded expressions -->
<head>
<title>NFL Standings for <%= team.getFullName() %></title>
</head>

<body>

<H1>Recent Results for <%= team.getFullName() %></H1>

<H2><%= gameCounter %> games played
    since your last visit</H2>
```

```
<!-- loop through newGameResults -->
<% for (int i=0; i<gameCounter; i++) {
   Game g = gameResults[i];
 %>
   Week <%= g.getWeek() %>
     <%= g.getVisitor() + " " + g.getScore()[0] %>
     <%= g.getHome()    + " " + g.getScore()[1] %>
   <br>
<% } %>

<H2>Division Standing</H2>

<%= team.getName() %> are ranked
<%= intToOrdinal(divisionRank) %>
    in the <%= team.getDivision() %>
<br>
<%= divisionStatus() %>

<H2>Conference Standing</H2>
<%= team.getName() %> are ranked
<%= intToOrdinal(conferenceRank) %>
    in the <%= team.getConference() %>
<br>
<%= conferenceStatus() %>

</body>
</html>
```

The good thing about this scriptlet is that it works. The bad thing about it is that it completely misses the point of JSPs: they are targeted at page designers, not at Java programmers. Writing a complete Java program and embedding it inside a JSP will work, as this example proves. But it isn't realistic to expect most Web page designers to be comfortable tossing out code such as we've embedded in this example. And most Java programmers would rather just write the servlet code directly, rather than coding a JSP and then (you know you're going to do it) peeking at, and perhaps even tweaking, the generated servlet code to see how it was generated. In fact, let's go ahead and satisfy our curiosity and see what we have wrought.

6.3   Building, Installing, and Running the Scriptlet

JavaServer Pages are unlike any of the examples we've looked at before in that they aren't compiled until they are deployed. So we don't have a `build.xml` for this example. Our scriptlet does need the various components that went into the layered version of the application, and we'll leverage off the installation of ServletTwo. To test our scriptlet example, do the following:

1. Build and install ServletTwo as described in Chapter 5.
2. Copy the file `FavoriteTeamScriptlet.jsp` into the context directory of the servlet. With Tomcat, for example, this would place the JSP at the path `<TOMCAT_HOME>/webapps/nfl/FavoriteTeamScriptlet.jsp`.
3. Start the servlet container, if it's not already running.
4. Point your Web browser at the JSP.
5. You can specify values for the `team` and `week` parameters by appending them to the end of the URL, for example:

```
http://localhost:8080/nflFavoriteTeamScriptlet.jsp?team=Falcons&week=10
```

If deploying in a different container, the port number is the only thing that should need to change—use 9090 for HP-AS, and 7001 for BEA WebLogic (assuming default configuration of the listening port was retained for each container). These steps assume that the servlet container is unpacking the WAR file, so that the `FavoriteTeamScriptlet.jsp` file can easily be dropped into the correct directory location of the deployed servlet. However, HP-AS and BEA don't unpack the WAR file when it is deployed. In this case, a better deployment option is just to add the JSP file to the original WAR file as follows:

1. Copy the `nfl.war` file from the `nfl/application/servlet` directory to the `nfl/presentation/jsp` directory.
2. Update the WAR file with the following command:
   ```
   jar -uf nfl.war FavoriteTeamScriptlet.jsp
   ```
3. Deploy this updated WAR file instead of the original one.

When the page is accessed, it will be compiled into a servlet at that time. Listing 6.4 shows the servlet that is generated from this JSP.

Listing 6.4 The Generated Servlet

Notice: This listing has been edited for content and formatted to fit your screen.

```
package org.apache.jsp;

import nfl.ObjectFactory;
import nfl.application.*;
import java.util.*;
import javax.servlet.*;
import javax.servlet.http.*;
import javax.servlet.jsp.*;
import org.apache.jasper.runtime.*;
```

```
public class FavoriteTeamScriptlet$jsp extends HttpJspBase {

    Standings standings = null;
    Team     team;
    Game[]   gameResults;
    String[] messages;
    int      conferenceRank;
    int      divisionRank;
    int      gameCounter;
    public String intToOrdinal(int rank) {
        switch(rank) {
            case 1: return "1st";
            case 2: return "2nd";
            case 3: return "3rd";
            default: return (rank+"th");
        }
    }
    public String divisionStatus() {
        String result = null;
        Team.Status s = team.getDivisionChampStatus();
        if (s == Team.Status.CLINCHED)
            result = "Clinched ";
        else if (s == Team.Status.CLINCHED_TIE)
            result = "Clinched at least tie in ";
        else if (s == Team.Status.LEADING)
            result = "Leads ";
        else if (s == Team.Status.IN_CONTENTION)
            result = "Contender for ";
        else if (s == Team.Status.ELIMINATED)
            result = "Cannot win ";
        return result + team.getDivision();
    }

    public String conferenceStatus() {
        String result = null;
        // homefield
        Team.Status s = team.getHomeFieldStatus();
        if (s == Team.Status.CLINCHED)
            result = "Clinched ";
        else if (s == Team.Status.CLINCHED_TIE)
            result = "Clinched at least tie for ";
        else if (s == Team.Status.LEADING)
            result = "Leads race for ";
        else if (s == Team.Status.IN_CONTENTION)
            result = "Contender for ";
        else if (s == Team.Status.ELIMINATED)
            result = "Cannot win ";
        result = result + " home-field advantage<br>";
```

```
            // wildcards
            s = team.getWildcardStatus();
            if (s == Team.Status.CLINCHED)
               result += "Clinched ";
            else if (s == Team.Status.CLINCHED_TIE)
               result += "Clinched at least tie for ";
            else if (s == Team.Status.LEADING)
               result += "Leads race ";
            else if (s == Team.Status.IN_CONTENTION)
               result += "Contender for ";
            else if (s == Team.Status.ELIMINATED)
               result += "Cannot win ";
            return result + "wildcard";
       }

   // end

   static {
   }
   public FavoriteTeamScriptlet$jsp( ) {
   }

   private static boolean _jspx_inited = false;

   public final void _jspx_init()
       throws org.apache.jasper.runtime.JspException {
   }

   public void _jspService(HttpServletRequest request,
                           HttpServletResponse  response)
       throws java.io.IOException, ServletException {

       JspFactory _jspxFactory = null;
       PageContext pageContext = null;
       HttpSession session = null;
       ServletContext application = null;
       ServletConfig config = null;
       JspWriter out = null;
       Object page = this;
       String  _value = null;
       try {

            if (_jspx_inited == false) {
                synchronized (this) {
                    if (_jspx_inited == false) {
                        _jspx_init();
                        _jspx_inited = true;
                    }
```

```
            }
        }
        _jspxFactory = JspFactory.getDefaultFactory();
        response.setContentType(
                "text/html;charset=ISO-8859-1");
        pageContext = _jspxFactory.getPageContext(
            this, request, response, "", true, 8192, true);

        application = pageContext.getServletContext();
        config = pageContext.getServletConfig();
        session = pageContext.getSession();
        out = pageContext.getOut();

            out.write("\r\n<!DOCTYPE HTML PUBLIC\r\n \"-//W3C//DTD
HTML 4.0 Transitional//EN\">\r\n<html>\r\n");
// Many newlines were written to the output stream at this
// point for no apparent reason. Code removed.
    // The main body. Becomes part of jspService() method

        // Initialize. Do only once.
        if (standings == null) {
            Properties p = System.getProperties();
            /* Rather than create a new VersionInfo variant,
             * we'll just use the one from ServletTwo
             */
            if (p.getProperty("nfl.versioninfo") == null) {
                p.setProperty("nfl.versioninfo",
          "nfl.application.servlet.ServletTwoVersionInfo");
            }
            standings = (Standings)
                ObjectFactory.getHandle().getInstance("Standings");
            standings.loadData();
        }

        // Parse arguments from query string
        String favorite  = request.getParameter("team");
        if (favorite == null) favorite = "49ers";
        String sVisit = request.getParameter("week");
        int lastVisit;
        if (sVisit == null)
            lastVisit = 0;
        else
            lastVisit = Integer.parseInt(sVisit);

        Teams teams = standings.getTeams();
        Games games = standings.getGames();
        List teamList = standings.getTeamList();
        String fullName = teams.findName(favorite);
        List gameList = games.getAllGamesFor(fullName);
```

```
// We don't export the Map view of the teamList, or a
// method to retrieve a team by name, which is awkward.
        team = null;
        for (int i=0; i<teamList.size(); i++) {
          Team t = (Team) teamList.get(i);
          if (t.getFullName().equals(fullName)) {
              team = t;
              break;
          }
        }
        if (team == null) {
          // TODO: route to or generate error page
          System.out.println("BAD TEAM");
        }

        gameResults = new Game[16];
        gameCounter = 0;
        for (int i=0; i<gameList.size(); i++) {
            Game g = (Game) gameList.get(i);
            if (g.getWeek() > lastVisit) {
                gameResults[gameCounter++] = g;
            }
         }

        List divStandings = standings.computeDivisionStandings(
                                    team.getDivision());
        for (int i=0;i<divStandings.size(); i++) {
            Team rankedTeam = (Team) divStandings.get(i);
            if (rankedTeam.getFullName().equals(fullName)) {
                divisionRank = i+1;
                break;
            }
        }
        List confStandings=
            standings.computeConferenceStandings(
                                    team.getConference());
        for (int i=0;i<confStandings.size(); i++) {
            Team rankedTeam = (Team) confStandings.get(i);
            if (rankedTeam.getFullName().equals(fullName)) {
                conferenceRank = i+1;
                break;
            }
        }

    out.write("\r\n\r\n");
    out.write("\r\n");
    out.write("\r\n<!-- HTML output using embedded expressions --
        >\r\n<head>\r\n<title>NFL Standings for ");
```

```
      out.print( team.getFullName() );
      out.write("</title>\r\n</head>\r\n\r\n<body>\r\n\r\n<H1>Recent
         Results for ");
      out.print( team.getFullName() );
      out.write("</H1>\r\n\r\n<H2>");
      out.print( gameCounter );
      out.write(" games played \r\n    since your last visit
         </H2>\r\n\r\n<!-- loop through newGameResults -->\r\n");
       for (int i=0; i<gameCounter; i++) {
         Game g = gameResults[i];
      out.write("\r\n    Week ");
      out.print( g.getWeek() );
      out.write(" \r\n       ");
      out.print( g.getVisitor() + " " + g.getScore()[0] );
      out.write("\r\n       ");
      out.print( g.getHome()    + " " + g.getScore()[1] );
      out.write("\r\n    <br>\r\n");
       }
      out.write("\r\n\r\n<H2>Division Standing</H2>\r\n\r\n");
      out.print( team.getName() );
      out.write(" are ranked \r\n");
      out.print( intToOrdinal(divisionRank) );
      out.write(" \r\n    in the ");
      out.print( team.getDivision() );
      out.write("\r\n<br>\r\n");
      out.print( divisionStatus() );
      out.write("\r\n\r\n<H2>Conference Standing</H2>\r\n");
      out.print( team.getName() );
      out.write(" are ranked \r\n");
      out.print( intToOrdinal(conferenceRank) );
      out.write(" \r\n    in the ");
      out.print( team.getConference() );
      out.write("\r\n<br>\r\n");
      out.print( conferenceStatus() );
      out.write("\r\n\r\n</body>\r\n</html>\r\n");
      out.write("\r\n");

 // end

        } catch (Throwable t) {
            if (out != null && out.getBufferSize() != 0)
               out.clearBuffer();
            if (pageContext != null) pageContext.handlePageException(t);
        } finally {
            if (_jspxFactory != null)
_jspxFactory.releasePageContext(pageContext);
        }
    }
}
```

Figure 6.1 shows the `FavoriteTeamScriptlet.jsp` page.

Figure 6.1   `FavoriteTeamScriptlet.jsp` output.

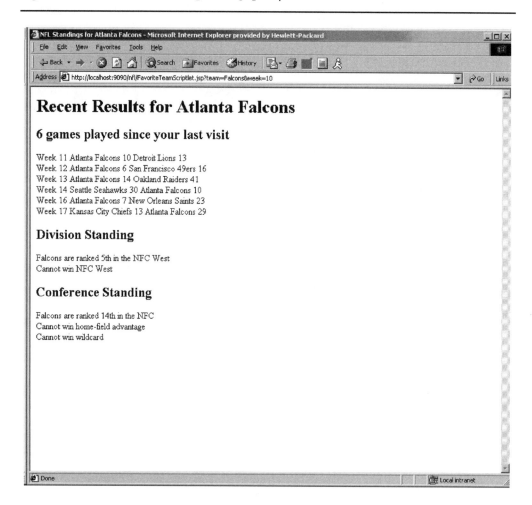

Now that we've seen how not to write a JSP, what is the alternative? The complexity of the task we've undertaken isn't the problem with this JSP. It's quite conceivable that a JSP designer will need to put together pages much more complex than the one we've just seen. So what does JSP provide to permit the page designer to tackle the tough jobs without resorting to program-buried-in-JSP design?

The key is in separation of roles. The page designer needs to focus on the formatting and presentation, but not on the nuts-and-bolts coding. So the third part of our three-part servlet isn't far off the mark, as it deals exclusively with presentation. It just shouldn't be up to the JSP page author to figure out how to get the right `Team` and `Game` objects into the page. After we introduce the JSP Actions, we will revisit this page with a better set of tools at our disposal.

6.4 JSP Actions

You're probably expecting there to be three JSP actions, since there were three scripting elements and three directives. You would be right, for sufficiently large values of three. There are three JSP actions used to support access to JavaBeans, another three used to support applets, and then two that are still searching for a third partner. We'll cover those last two actions first, followed by a brief look at the applet support actions. We'll save the actions related to JavaBeans until the next chapter.

The JSP action syntax resembles the XML-based syntax presented as an option for our previous tags, rather than the ASP-derived brief syntax we presented first.

6.4.1 The <jsp:include> Action

We already mentioned this when we talked about the `include` directive. As a refresher, the difference is that when an `include` directive is specified on a page, the inclusion happens when the servlet is being generated from the JSP. By using the `include` action instead, we cause the inclusion to happen when the page is being served to the client. This could be important if we are including a file that might change while the servlet container is up and running. A limitation of using the action is that because we don't evaluate it until we've already completed the compilation of our JSP, we can't use any JSP elements within files included via the `include` action.

The `include` action takes two attributes. The `page` attribute takes as its value the relative URL of the page to be included. The `flush` attribute takes as its value the boolean value `true`. One must assume that in some future revision of JSP, a value other than `true` might be permitted; otherwise, this is just silly.

```
<jsp:include page="privacy.html" flush="true"/>
```

6.4.2 The <jsp:forward> Action

The `forward` action is used to transfer processing to another page (which could be another JSP page, a servlet, or just a static HTML page). The `forward` action takes a single attribute, the `page` attribute. The `page` attribute has as its value the relative URL of the target page. The value can include a JSP expression, allowing the target to be assigned dynamically during JSP processing.

```
<jsp:forward page="/servlet2/ShowStandings"/>
```

6.4.3   The <jsp:plugin> Action

If you've ever worked with Java applets, then you know that they are embedded within HTML pages using an `<APPLET>` tag. The APPLET tag takes at a minimum a `CODE` attribute, to provide the name of the applet class. It typically also specifies `WIDTH` and `HEIGHT` attributes (in pixels) to properly size the applet on the page.

The APPLET tag is not deprecated, so you can continue to use it to embed applets within your pages. However, applets had several limitations, and the Java Plug-In technology (JPI) was developed to help address many of these shortcomings. Because applets are a client-side technology as well as being part of the Java 2 Standard Edition (J2SE) package, they are really beyond the scope of this book. But in the interest of being complete in our discussion of JSPs, we'll briefly cover the JSP actions related to the Java Plug-In.

With the APPLET tag, you're limited to the capabilities of the Java Virtual Machine (JVM) embedded in the Web browser used by your client. This typically forces applet authors to adopt a least-common-denominator approach and write their code to the JDK 1.1 standard.

Sun developed the Java Plug-In when it became obvious that Microsoft did not want to support Java features in its Internet Explorer browser, and Netscape was having difficulty keeping up with the rapidly evolving Java standards. Even if the browser vendors had been aggressive about keeping up, most browser users would not update their software with any frequency, so the applet author would be faced with the same difficulty. With the plug-in, the version of the Java Runtime Environment (JRE) required to run a particular applet can be specified with the applet, and if the browser doesn't have the required version then it will be downloaded when the page is accessed.

Access to the JPI capability doesn't take the same format for the two leading browsers (Internet Explorer and Netscape Navigator). Fortunately, the `jsp:plugin` syntax frees the page author from having to worry about the differences, because it is the responsibility of the servlet container to generate plug-in directives appropriate for the browser used to access the page.

We won't cover in detail the attributes available with the `plugin` tag. Briefly, there is a `type` attribute, which can have a value of either `applet` or `bean`. There are `code`, `height`, `width`, `codebase`, `align`, `hspace`, `vspace`, `archive`, `name`, and `title` attributes that work the same as the corresponding attributes of the `<APPLET>` tag. There is a `jreversion` tag that specifies the required version of the JRE to run this applet or bean. Finally, `iepluginurl` and `nspluginurl` attributes specify URLs at which the JPI for Internet Explorer and Netscape can be downloaded. These will default to Sun's Web site, but you might want to override these in an intranet environment or other situation where a more appropriate download site is located closer to your users' location.

It's worth reiterating that the tag names and attribute names are all case-sensitive, and must be lowercase. Even if you understand this in general, it might be easy to miss on these particular items because they are otherwise so similar to the APPLET tags, which were not case-sensitive.

6.4.4   The <jsp:params> and <jsp:param> Actions

Between the `<APPLET>` start tag and `</APPLET>` end tag you can embed a number of `<PARAM>` tags to pass parameters to your applet. As you might guess, this functionality has also been replicated for the plug-in. Between the `<jsp:plugin>` start tag and `</jsp:plugin>` end tag, you can include a single `<jsp:params>` start tag, followed by any number of individual `<jsp:param>` parameter elements. The parameter list is closed by the `</jsp:params>` end tag. There are no attributes on the `params` element. Each `param` element has two required attributes: the `name` and the `value`.

That wraps up our brief look at most JSP actions. We still have a few more actions to cover in the next chapter. There, we'll look at how we can use JSPs cooperatively with other objects such as JavaBeans, servlets, and custom tag handlers.

6.5   Exercises

6.1 Login page: Create a login page that allows the user to specify team and week to pass to favorite team page. You may want to wait to see how this is implemented in Chapter 8, "Struts," if you need help getting started.

6.2 Error page: Add error handling to the application. Create a JSP error page and direct any errors to that page.

6.6   Further Reading

See the Bibliography for recommended JSP books, including *JavaServer Pages* and *Core Servlets and JavaServer Pages*.

The JSP home page is `http://java.sun.com/products/jsp`. From there you can reference tutorials, API documentation, and many other resources.

Integrating JavaServer Pages with JavaBeans and Servlets

I n Chapter 6, our JavaServer Pages (JSPs) weren't completely standalone. They interacted with other Java objects, such as the `Team` and `Standings` objects. But whenever they did so, it was by way of familiar Java syntax expressed as a scriptlet or an expression. As we've said, JSPs are targeted at page designers, and this is therefore not a very good model for how we should integrate JSPs with other Java objects.

By "integrating," I don't mean that we're going to load our JSPs onto the system bus and send them off to a different container. Instead, we just want our JSPs to play well with other objects, while still preserving a JSP-like syntax. There are four approaches we'll look at in this chapter. First, we'll look at the JSP actions that allow JSPs to interact with JavaBeans. Second, we'll see how we can use JavaServer Pages and servlets together. Next, we'll look at extending JSP functionality through the use of custom tag libraries. This will include a very brief look at the still-under-development JSP Standard Tag Library (JSPTL), and then development of our own application-specific custom tag library.

Software Used in This Chapter

Servlets

Servlet 2.2, from `http://java.sun.com/products/servlet`, is sufficient for most examples in this chapter. The example using the standard tag library requires Servlet 2.3, available from the same location.

JavaServer Pages

Version 1.1. There are no development-time components needed, because JSPs are compiled dynamically by the container when they are deployed or accessed. All JSPs shown here are also compatible with the newer JSP 1.2 standard.

Tomcat Servlet Container

Version 3.2.3, from `jakarta.apache.org`. Can be used standalone, or integrated with a Web or application server such as Apache, Enhydra, IIS, or iPlanet. Our JSPs will be compiled into servlets and then executed within the Tomcat Servlet Container. Tomcat 4.0.1 was used for examples that utilize the JSP Standard Tag Library (JSPTL).

Java Standard Tag Library (JSPTL)

An early access release (JSPTL EA1.2) was used. You can download the software from `http://jakarta.apache.org/taglibs` (follow the JSPTL link). Additional information is also available at `http://java.sun.com/products/jsp/taglibraries.html#jsptl`.

7.1   Using JavaServer Pages with JavaBeans

JavaServer Pages should be seen as part of the presentation layer of our application. If this is so, then where should the business logic reside? There are two popular answers to this: in a servlet, or in an Enterprise JavaBean (EJB). We'll look at the servlet case coming up very shortly, and at the EJB case later in the book.

In either case, we have a common challenge: How do we share data between the JSP and the component handling the logic? Because the HTTP request and response objects are accessible within both JSPs and servlets, you might guess (correctly) that they will be part of the solution. If we have more than just one or two data items that need to be passed, it is logical and desirable that we lump these together into a single object or small number of objects. The characteristics of JavaBeans make them an ideal mechanism for this transfer of data between our components.

To briefly review, JavaBeans have properties (data members) that can be get and set via accessor methods. That is the only concrete requirement we have for the beans we'll use to transport data for us. A true JavaBean should have a zero-element constructor; this is required for any JavaBean we want the JSP to be able to create on the fly, but we don't have to strictly observe this requirement if we aren't needing the JSP or servlet container to instantiate beans on our behalf. Finally, JavaBeans should implement `Serializable`, but this is also an optional requirement; we need to enforce it only if it is necessary for the state of our beans to be stored at some point by the container.

7.1.1 JSP Actions for Manipulating JavaBeans

There are three JSP actions provided to work with JavaBeans. The `<jsp:useBean>` action defines a bean. If a bean of the given name already exists in the page context at the time the `<jsp:useBean>` is evaluated, then that bean is used; otherwise, a new bean is instantiated. The `<jsp:getProperty>` and `<jsp:setProperty>` actions can then be used to read and write the properties (data) of the bean.

There isn't a general-purpose method call mechanism for accessing beans from JSPs; only the accessor methods are accessible via the JSP action syntax. However, if your bean contains other methods, you could call these methods from within JSP expressions or scriptlets. (You could also just name all your methods so that they have signatures that match the form of accessor functions, but that would be dishonest.)

The <jsp:useBean> Action

Before you can use either of the JSP property-related actions, you must declare the bean by using the `<jsp:useBean>` action. The `useBean` action has two required attributes: the `id` of the bean and the `class` of the bean. The `id` is the name by which you will refer to the bean in other actions, expressions, or scriptlets; the `class` must be the fully qualified (`package.class`) name of the class of the bean. In our next example, we have the following `useBean` action:

```
<jsp:useBean id="team" class="nfl.application.Team"/>
```

This declaration will cause the page context to be examined for an object named "`team`"; if no such object is found, one will be created by instantiating the `nfl.application.Team` class (which would fail, because `Team` doesn't provide a zero-argument constructor. So we better be sure that the team object is found).

There are also two optional attributes which can be specified for a bean. The `scope` attribute will be covered in the section, "JavaBean Scope" on page 171. We'll look at the `type` attribute here. The `type` attribute should be used if in our generated servlet code we want the declaration to use a different type than what we actually instantiate. For example, `Team` is not an instantiable class; it is an interface. If we wanted the `<jsp:useBean>` tag to be able to instantiate this bean, we would first have to provide a zero-element constructor, and then rewrite the tag as follows:

```
<jsp:useBean id="team" type="nfl.application.Team"
            class="nfl.application.BasicTeamImpl"/>
```

This is equivalent to scriptlet code:

```
<% Team team = new BasicTeamImpl(); %>
```

If you're like me, you probably look at these two code examples and think: Hey, the second example is more concise. It's clearer, because it's well-known Java syntax rather than something new and unfamiliar. And if you go look at the generated code, the second form gets dropped exactly as written into the servlet, while the first call gets rewritten into several method calls that do who knows what. So why ever use the first syntax?

You must remember that JSPs weren't created for use by Java programmers; they were created for use by Web page authors familiar with HTML, JavaScript, and perhaps Active Server Pages, and not at all familiar with Java. So the first form, which has the feel of an HTML tag with attributes, is going to be far easier to get used to.

You can also include code between a `<jsp:useBean>` start tag and the end tag. If you do so, the code so enclosed is executed conditionally, only in the case where a new bean is instantiated. This permits you to have some initialization code for the bean, as in this example:

```
<jsp:useBean id="game" type="nfl.application.Game"
          class="nfl.application.BasicGameImpl">
   <%-- initialization, via jsp:setProperty actions --%>
</jsp:useBean>
```

The <jsp:getProperty> Action

Once a bean is declared via `<jsp:useBean>`, we can read any of its properties by using the `<jsp:getProperty>` action. The `getProperty` tag has two parameters: the `id` (which must match the one used in the `useBean` action) and the property `name`. The property name must match a property of the bean. The property name is the same as the name of the accessor method used to read the bean, with the prefix `get` removed and the initial letter shifted to lower-case. (This should match exactly the name of the private data field the accessor function returns, in most cases; but in cases where accessor functions return a calculated value, there may not be a single data field that represents the property.)

The value returned by the `getProperty` call will be inserted into the generated page at the point the action is called. In Listing 7.1, you can see `getProperty` actions being used to retrieve several properties from the `Team` and `Game` objects. One notable limitation of `getProperty` is that it provides no way to retrieve the value of an indexed property. Because our score is such a property (it is an array of two `int`s), we must revert to expression syntax to retrieve these values. For page authors wanting to stay with the more familiar HTML-like syntax, there are many custom tag libraries that provide actions that can access indexed properties; we'll look at one such library before this chapter is done.

The <jsp:setProperty> Action

As you can no doubt guess, the `setProperty` action is the method used to set a property in a bean. It has three attributes: the `id` and property `name` exactly as in the `getProperty` action, plus a property `value` attribute. The following line is from the `PostGameResult.jsp` page shown in Listing 7.5, and sets all properties in the bean based on form input fields:

```
<jsp:setProperty name="game" property="*"/>
```

Although the `id` attribute is normally required, it was not in this specific instance because the `setProperty` action is nested between the start tag and end tag of a `<jsp:useBean>` action. When used in this manner, the bean `id` is obviously the one we are in the process of initializing and does not need to be specified.

7.1.2 JavaBean Scope

All of our examples so far have involved just a single JSP. So the default scope—which is page scope—has been assumed with no ill effects. As you develop more complex applications, you'll need to share beans, either between multiple JSP pages or between JSP pages and servlets. To accomplish this, the `<jsp:useBean>` tag allows you to specify one of four scopes for the bean you are creating or accessing:

- **Application Scope** is the broadest scope, and makes your bean globally accessible. Specifying `scope="application"` for a bean attaches it to the `ServletContext` object, which is available to servlets through the `getServletContext()` call, or to JSPs through the predefined `application` object. Once you have the `ServletContext` object, `getAttribute(String name)` and `setAttribute(String name, Object value)` calls can be made upon the object to access the bean by its name.
- **Session Scope** is the next broadest. Specifying `scope="session"` for a bean attaches it to the `HttpSession` object. Beans at session scope live for as long as the session is active, and are therefore useful to track user-specific information through a series of requests and responses. Beans at session scope are accessed via `getValue(String name)` and `setValue(String name, Object value)` calls on the `HttpSession` object.
- **Request Scope**, specified by `scope="request"`, attaches the bean to an `HttpServletRequest` object. The `HttpServletRequest` object provides `getAttribute(String name)` and `setAttribute(String name, Object value)` methods to access the bean.
- **Page Scope** is the narrowest scope, and the default. Specifying `scope="page"` (or not specifying scope at all) attaches the bean to the `PageContext` object. There doesn't seem to be much practical difference between page and request scope; just the object through which you gain access. Beans at page scope can be accessed via the `<jsp:getProperty>` and `<jsp:setProperty>` actions, or via the `PageContext` `getAttribute(String name)` and `setAttribute(String name, Object value)` methods, while items at request scope are accessed via the `HttpServletRequest` object.

When we talk about the "default scope" for beans, we speak only of beans that are instantiated via the `<useBean>` action. If we have variables that we've declared via the JSP declaration syntax, these are not being attached to any of the objects we've just described that provide mechanisms for sharing beans. To give a concrete example, we declared a variable named `Team` in the variable declarations at the top of our `FavoriteTeamScriptlet` in the previous chapter (see Listing 6.1). Our `FavoriteTeamBean` (Listing 7.4) includes the same declarations at the front; we just haven't shown them again because they are repetitive. In the second part of the original JSP (Listing 6.2), we assign a value to the `team` variable. In our JavaBean-using variant of the JSP code (shown below), we have a `useBean` action with `id="team"` that we would like to pick up the current value of the `team` object we declared at the beginning of the file. But based solely on the declaration, our `<useBean>` tag will not find any such bean and instead try to instantiate a new one. If we want to make the declared team variable visible as a bean, we must explicitly attach it to the appropriate object for whatever scope we want it to have.

Now that we know about the bean actions, we can rewrite our `FavoriteTeamScriptlet` JSP. We'll call the new JSP `FavoriteTeamBean`, because it uses JavaBeans. The first part (corresponding to Listing 6.1) is identical, so it won't be shown again. In the second part (corresponding to Listing 6.2), we simply need to add one line to make our bean accessible at page scope. Here's the updated version of the code; the addition is highlighted in bold :

```
... code prior to this point unchanged ...
   team = teams.getTeam(favorite);
if (team == null) {
   // TODO: route to or generate error page
   System.out.println("BAD TEAM");
}
// Make accessible via useBean
pageContext.setAttribute("team", team);

List gameList = games.getAllGamesFor(team.getFullName());
... code continues as before ...
```

Then we rewrite the third portion, as shown in Listing 7.1, to use the bean properties rather than JSP expressions. Table 7.1 shows the set of components used in this version of the application.

Table 7.1   Components in the JavaBean JSP

New Components		
Name	**Component Type**	**Comment**
FavoriteTeamBean.jsp	JSP	JSP with JavaBean access.
Existing Components		
Component	**Description**	
layered.jar	All classes and interfaces of the layered version of the application (as presented in Chapter 2).	
ServletTwo	JSP is installed on top of fully functioning example servlet.	

Listing 7.1 `FavoriteTeamBean.jsp`

```
<!-- HTML output using JavaBean Properties -->

<jsp:useBean id="team" class="nfl.application.Team"/>

<head>
<title>NFL Standings for
   <jsp:getProperty name="team" property="fullName"/>
</title>
</head>

<body>

<H1>Recent Results for
   <jsp:getProperty name="team" property="fullName"/>
</H1>

<H2><%= gameCounter %> games played
    since your last visit</H2>

<!-- loop through newGameResults -->
<% for (int i=0; i<gameCounter; i++) {
   Game g = gameResults[i];
   // make accessible via useBean at page scope
   pageContext.setAttribute("game", g);
 %>

<jsp:useBean id="game" class="nfl.application.Game"/>

Week <jsp:getProperty name="game" property="week"/>
     <jsp:getProperty name="game" property="visitor"/>
<%-- can't use getProperty to retrieve indexed property --%>
     <%= game.getScore()[0] %>
     <jsp:getProperty name="game" property="home"/>
     <%= game.getScore()[1] %>
<br>
<% } %>

<H2>Division Standing</H2>

<jsp:getProperty name="team" property="name"/>
  are ranked <%= intToOrdinal(divisionRank) %>
  in the <jsp:getProperty name="team" property="division"/>
<br>
<%= divisionStatus() %>

<H2>Conference Standing</H2>
```

```
<jsp:getProperty name="team" property="name"/>
 are ranked <%= intToOrdinal(conferenceRank) %>
 in the <jsp:getProperty name="team" property="conference"/>
<br>
<%= conferenceStatus() %>

</body>
</html>
```

One noteworthy thing in this code is the way the scriptlet code is interleaved with the JSP actions. The beginning and end of the `for` loop has been highlighted to emphasize this. The `for` loop begins in a scriptlet block; that scriptlet is then terminated. `<jsp:useBean>` actions, expressions, and HTML formatting elements are then encountered before we find the one-line scriptlet that provides the closing brace for the `for` loop. Because of the way the code is generated in the servlet, we can do this knowing that everything in the JSP—including HTML elements, expressions, and actions—will be transformed into Java code without any reordering in the generated servlet.

We weren't able to eliminate JSP expression syntax entirely from this example for two reasons. First, we're still accessing several variables and methods that are not beans. Secondly, we have an indexed property (the score) on the `Game` object, and the standard `<jsp:getProperty>` action doesn't give us the ability to access an indexed property. There are a number of tag libraries available that overcome this limitation. As an alternative, later on we'll develop a new implementation of the `Game` class that allows us to access this property without using an index.

7.2   Installing and Running the Bean Example

The installation of this example is identical to the process for the scriptlet example; the JSP page (`FavoriteTeamBean.jsp`) just needs to be installed in the context directory of our ServletTwo servlet example.

1. Build and install ServletTwo as described in Chapter 5.
2. Copy the file `FavoriteTeamBean.jsp` into the context directory of the servlet. With Tomcat, for example, this would place the JSP at the path `<TOMCAT_HOME/webapps/nfl/FavoriteTeamBean.jsp`.
3. Start the servlet container, if it's not already running.
4. Point your Web browser at the JSP.
5. You can specify values for the `team` and `week` parameters by appending them to the end of the URL. For example:
   `http://localhost:8080/nfl/FavoriteTeamBean.jsp?team=Ravens&week=6`

As an alternative to Step #2, you can use the `jar -uf` syntax to add the JSP file to the servlet's WAR file.

7.3   Using Servlets and JSP Together

We've learned how to use both servlets and JavaServer Pages now, and we've seen how we can use JavaBeans as a mechanism to pass data between them. So it's time to pull it all together. ServletThree is essentially ServletTwo with all of the HTML pulled out of it. The logic that was part of the servlet still remains, and the HTML formatting code has been farmed out to an HTML page (for the static main page) and two JSP pages (to enter a game result and to show the standings). Several new components will be introduced to the application in the ServletThree version; these are shown in Table 7.2.

Table 7.2   Components in the JSP/Servlet/JSPTL Example

New Components		
Name	**Component Type**	**Comment**
ServletThreeImpl	Servlet	A new servlet, based on ServletTwo.
PostGameResult.jsp	JSP	JSP to process game result.
BeansGameImpl	Class	Subclass of `BasicGameImpl` that provides zero-arg constructor and access to indexed properties.
EnterGameResult.jsp	JSP	JSP to enter game result. Uses iteration tag from JSPTL library.
Existing Components		
Component	**Description**	
layered.jar	All classes and interfaces of the layered version of the application (as presented in Chapter 2).	

Because much of the servlet is unchanged, we've only included the `doGet()` method in Listing 7.2. The `doGet()` method is not changed much from ServletTwo. The main difference is that for the main page, we create a `RequestDispatcher` object and use that to forward the request to the HTML page (shown in Listing 7.4). For the other pages, we'll be forwarding requests to JSPs, but need to pass some data into those JSPs via JavaBeans. Therefore, we leave the basic servlet structure intact, and make the changes in the various helper methods rather than in the `doGet()` method.

Listing 7.2 `ServletThreeImpl.java` (Part 1 of 2)

```
public void doGet(HttpServletRequest request,
                  HttpServletResponse response)
           throws ServletException, IOException {

    String uri = request.getRequestURI();
    if (uri.endsWith("/servlet3/Main")) {
        String url = "/MainPage.html";
        RequestDispatcher dispatcher =
            request.getRequestDispatcher(url);
        dispatcher.forward(request, response);
    } else if (uri.endsWith("/servlet3/ShowStandings"))
        showStandings(request, response);
    else if (uri.endsWith("/servlet3/GameResult")) {
        if (request.getMethod().equals("POST"))
            postGameResults(request, response);
        else
            showGameResultForm(request, response);
    } else
        response.setStatus(response.SC_NOT_FOUND); /*404*/
}

public void doPost(HttpServletRequest request,
                   HttpServletResponse response)
            throws ServletException, IOException {

    doGet(request, response);
}
```

In Listing 7.3, we see the remainder of ServletThree, which contains the various helper methods invoked from the `doGet()` method. In the first method, `showGameResultForm()`, we get the list of teams and make it available to the JSP by attaching it as an attribute to the `ServletContext` object. (The team list will be used to populate selection boxes in the JSP that allow the user to select the home team and visiting team when entering game results). Once the team list has been made available in this fashion, we then transfer control to the JSP by getting a `RequestDispatcher` object and calling its `forward()` method.

There are two methods of obtaining a `RequestDispatcher` object. The first way is to call the `getRequestDispatcher()` method of the `ServletContext` object. A `RequestDispatcher` obtained in this manner will only be able to accept a context-relative path to the URL, because it has no knowledge about the particular page we are on. Alternately, we can call the `getRequestDispacher()` method of the request object. Because the request object is tied to the particular page we are currently processing, a `RequestDispatcher` obtained this way can take either a context-relative URI (beginning with a slash) or a page-relative URL. Because our context for this application is `/nfl`, the context-relative URL in the `showGameResultForm()`

method below is equivalent to /nfl/EnterGameResult.jsp. It's important that the URL we forward to does not include /servlet3/, otherwise we would just end up forwarding back to our self because the servlet mapping in web.xml causes anything with /servlet3/ in the URL to be processed in the servlet. A page-relative URL would need to begin with the parent directory selector (for example, ../EnterGameResult.jsp) to back us out of the /servlet3 directory.

The Standings page has not been reimplemented for ServletThree. In the showStandings() method, we take our List arrays of the division and conference standings and make them available at application scope, and then forward on to the page. However, the JSP action syntax doesn't really provide any satisfactory syntax for dealing with complex items of this type. Many of the custom tag libraries do provide tags for iterating through collections and handling various complex data types, so by the time you've finished this chapter, you could complete this page using a custom tag library if you desired.

In both the showGameResultForm() and showStandings() methods, the servlet is placing data in the application context and then transferring control to the JSP. The third method shown below, postGameResults(), behaves differently. Here, we use the RequestDispatcher include() method, rather than forward(). This allows us to retain control after the JSP has been executed. The PostGameResult.jsp page, shown in Listing 7.5, will pass a JavaBean back to the servlet. The bean is retrieved by the request.getAttribute() call because it was created with scope="request". In case of an error, we actually get a handle to the PrintWriter object within the servlet and write our error message directly on the page; in this manner, the JSP and servlet are both outputting via the same HTML page. Generally speaking, it would be preferable to create a separate error JSP, but the ability to write servlet output directly in this fashion is frequently helpful during development and debugging.

Listing 7.3 ServletThreeImpl.java (Part 2 of 2)

```
private void showGameResultForm(HttpServletRequest req,
    HttpServletResponse res) throws ServletException,
                                IOException {

  if (teamList == null) {
    teams = (Teams)
      ObjectFactory.getHandle().getInstance("Teams");
    teamList = teams.getTeamList();
    // Make available with application scope
    getServletContext().setAttribute("teamList",
                                teamList);
  }
  String url = "/EnterGameResult.jsp";
  RequestDispatcher dispatcher =
    req.getRequestDispatcher(url);
  dispatcher.forward(req, res);
}
```

```java
    private void showStandings(HttpServletRequest request,
                               HttpServletResponse response)
       throws ServletException, IOException {

       // Make standings available with application scope
       getServletContext().setAttribute("divStandings",
          standings.getDivisionStandings());
       getServletContext().setAttribute("confStandings",
          standings.getConferenceStandings());

       String url = "/ShowStandings.jsp";
       RequestDispatcher dispatcher =
          request.getRequestDispatcher(url);
       dispatcher.forward(request, response);
    }

    public void postGameResults(HttpServletRequest request,
                                HttpServletResponse response)
       throws ServletException, IOException {

       // Display the confirmation page
       String url = "/PostGameResult.jsp";
       RequestDispatcher dispatcher =
          request.getRequestDispatcher(url);
       dispatcher.include(request, response);

       //Retrieve game from request context (placed there by
       //PostGameResult.jsp
       Game g = (Game)request.getAttribute("game");

       if (games == null) {
          games = (Games)
             ObjectFactory.getHandle().getInstance("Games");
       }

       Game prev = games.findGame(g.getWeek(),g.getHome());

       if (prev != null) {
          // Update the existing game. It's quite easy
          // to reverse the home & visiting teams, either
          // now or when the scheduled game was entered.
          // Rather than demand perfection, flip the
          // score if necessary to match existing game
          if (g.getHome().equals(prev.getHome()) &&
              g.getVisitor().equals(prev.getVisitor()))
             prev.setScore(g.getScore()[0], g.getScore()[1]);
          else if (g.getHome().equals(prev.getVisitor()) &&
                   g.getVisitor().equals(prev.getHome()))
             prev.setScore(g.getScore()[1],g.getScore()[0]);
```

```
        else {
            PrintWriter out = response.getWriter();
            /* trying to record game with different
             * opponent than scheduled. We're not
             * gonna take it. */
            out.println("\nERROR: not posted because " +
            "there is already a game recorded for this " +
            "week against a different opponent!<br>" +
            "Home team " + g.getHome() + "<br>" +
            "Previously entered opponent " +
                prev.getVisitor() + "<br>" +
            "Attempted to add opponent " +
                g.getVisitor() + "<br>");
        }
    }

    // Update team statistics (also adds g to gamelist)
    standings.postGameData(g);
    }
}
```

Now we'll take a look at the various pages to which we forward requests from ServletThree. The simplest of these is the main page; it is merely a static HTML page, as shown in Listing 7.4.

Listing 7.4 `MainPage.html`

```
<HTML>
<HEAD>
<TITLE>NFL Standings Main Page</TITLE>
</HEAD>

<BODY>
<H1>Select a Function</H1>
<a href="/nfl/servlet3/ShowStandings">
    Show Current Standings</a>
<br>
<a href="/nfl/servlet3/GameResult">
    Post Game Results</a>
<br>
</BODY>
</HTML>
```

The `PostGameResult` JSP is shown in Listing 7.5. We're seeing these pages somewhat out of order, because we need to introduce a new feature before we can examine the page where game results are entered. `EnterGameResult.jsp`, the page we haven't yet shown, will produce exactly the same form that our `ServletTwoImpl` servlet produced (see Figure 5.4). Once

that form is submitted, all of the form's fields will be available as attributes of the
`HttpServletRequest` object. We could access these fields within the servlet, as we did in the
servlets chapter. Instead, the same `HttpServletRequest` object is being passed to the `Post-
GameResult` page by the `RequestDispatcher`'s `forward()` method. In the JSP, we use the
`<jsp:useBean>` action to instantiate a `Game` object, and then populate all of its fields by nest-
ing a `<jsp:setProperty>` action between the start and end tags of the `<jsp:useBean>`
action. You may recall from Chapter 6 that this causes the `<jsp:setProperty>` to only be executed conditionally when there is not already a `game` bean found at the appropriate scope.

Listing 7.5 `PostGameResult.jsp`

```
<HTML>
<HEAD>
<TITLE>Game Result Posted</TITLE>
<HEAD>

<BODY>

<jsp:useBean id="game" scope="request"
           type="nfl.application.Game"
           class="nfl.application.BeansGameImpl">
  <jsp:setProperty name="game" property="*"/>
</jsp:useBean>

<H1>Posting the following result</H1>

Week <jsp:getProperty name="game" property="week"/><br>
<jsp:getProperty name="game" property="visitor"/>
<jsp:getProperty name="game" property="vscore"/><br>
<jsp:getProperty name="game" property="home"/>
<jsp:getProperty name="game" property="hscore"/><br>

<A href="./GameResult">Post results for another game</a><br>
<A href="./Main">Return to the main page</a><br>

</FORM>
</BODY>
</HTML>
```

Our current implementation of the `Game` interface (`BasicGameImpl`) isn't going to work
with this JSP, for two important reasons. The `BasicGameImpl` class violates one of the rules of
JavaBeans: It doesn't provide a zero-element constructor. We've been able to get away with this
in some of the previous examples where we always ensured that a bean would be found at the
appropriate scope, so that the `<jsp:useBean>` action never had to actually instantiate a bean.
But in this case, we do want the creation of the bean to happen for us. The second problem is
that the `<jsp:setProperty>` and `<jsp:getProperty>` actions are too brain-dead to handle

indexed properties, even though they are a completely legal and supported feature of JavaBeans. To get around these problems, we've created a new class, BeansGameImpl, which is shown in Listing 7.6. This class provides a zero-argument constructor so that the <jsp:useBean> tag can successfully create beans of this class. The class also adds new methods to get and set the home team and visiting team scores individually, rather than as an array, to work around the limitation of using indexed properties within the standard bean tags.

Listing 7.6 The BeansGameImpl Class

```
// BeansGameImpl.java

package nfl.application;

public class BeansGameImpl extends BasicGameImpl
                      implements java.io.Serializable {

    /** Creates new BeansGameImpl */
    public BeansGameImpl() {
        super(0, "Home", 0, "Visitor", 0);
    }

    // JSPs are brain-dead about indexed properties.
    public int  getVscore() {
        return getScore()[0];
    }
    public void setVscore(int s) {
        int[] score = getScore();
        setScore(s, score[1]);
    }
    public int  getHscore() {
        return getScore()[1];
    }
    public void setHscore(int s) {
        int[] score = getScore();
        setScore(score[0], s);
    }
}
```

The BeansGameImpl class could have been made just slightly shorter by making the score array in the BasicGameImpl class protected, rather than private, so that we could update the fields directly. But using the public accessor methods is cleaner, and has the advantage of being an approach that can be used to wrapper any class, even if you don't have access to the source.

The other two pages that complete ServletThree's set of target pages aren't being shown. The EnterGameResult page needs a capability we haven't introduced yet, and the Show-Standings page is being left as an exercise for the reader.

7.4   Custom Tag Libraries

We've seen that JSP comes with a number of action tags that are predefined for our use, but if we try to avoid the use of scriptlets and do everything with action tags, we quickly find that they haven't enough capability to support many of the things we want to do.

JavaServer Pages actions are extensible through custom tag libraries. If there are additional actions you need to use, you can simply implement them yourself and make them accessible to your JSP. Many such libraries have already been created; an excellent source of them is the Apache Taglibs project (`http://jakarta.apache.org/taglibs`). At this site, you can find tag libraries for working with JDBC, regular expressions, XML, and many other capabilities that would be very useful to add to your JSP pages.

There is also an effort underway to create a standard tag library, which will likely become a part of the JSP specification in a future release. Development of the standard tag library, called JSPTL,[1] is being done under the Java Community Process (JCP) (see sidebar below). The specification request is JSR-052, and you can download the latest version of the work-in-progress specification at `http://jcp.org/jsr/detail/052.jsp`.

You can also download working copies of JSPTL from the Apache Taglibs page. Note that because the specification is still under development, the exact implementation is quite likely to change. Because this library is early in its development cycle, we aren't going to cover it in any detail, but we will use one tag to show how the library is used.

Where Do Java APIs Come From?

The Java Community Process (JCP)

Despite what you might have been told in your youth, new Java APIs are not brought by storks nor left under cabbage leaves. Instead, there is a process through which a group of parents-to-be known as an Expert Group define the specification. After a gestation period of several months to as much as a few years, an API specification is born, along with a reference implementation and compatibility tests. If the specification describes a part of the core JDK—for example, the new assertion capability, or logging APIs—then it is incorporated into a future JDK. If it describes APIs for non-core features, such as servlets or Enterprise JavaBeans, then the vendors who supply those software components will incorporate the specification into future versions of their products.

The JCP moves much faster than the typical standards body, but still provides for some level of industry and community participation in the process. Information about the Java Community Process can be found at `http://jcp.org`.

---

1. Although the version of the standard tag library used in this chapter was indeed called JSPTL, later versions of the same library have been rechristened JSTL.

Java Specification Requests (JSRs)

The product of a JCP Expert Group is a Java Specification Request. Each JSR goes through a life cycle that starts as a description of what the API is intended to do. It evolves through a private (Expert-Group only) draft, then a community draft in which feedback on the proposed API is solicited from the community. If everything goes well, the JSR becomes a finalized specification. Information about a particular JSR can be found by using the URL `http://jcp.org/jsr/detail/<JSR-NUM>.jsp`.

Visiting the JCP Web site and looking at the JSRs under development is like having a crystal ball to look into Java's potential future. If you're curious about what new features might find their way into Java, this is your best source for the latest information.

JSRs Relevant to This Book

Many JSRs currently in various stages of development cover APIs of interest to us in this book. What follows is an extensive, but not exhaustive, list. Many of the JSRs will be mentioned again in the text of the book, but some are provided here purely as reference links for readers who might want to explore particular topics that go beyond what this book covers.

JSR-005 XML Parsing Specification (JAXP 1.0)
JSR-031 XML Data Binding Specification (JAXB)
JSR-052 Java Standard Tag Library
JSR-053 Java Servlet 2.3 and JavaServer Pages 1.2
JSR-058 J2EE 1.3
JSR-063 JAXP 1.1
JSR-067 Java APIs for XML Messaging (JAXM) 1.0
JSR-093 Java API for XML Registries (JAXR) 1.0
JSR-101 Java APIs for XML based RPC (JAX-RPC)
JSR-102 JDOM 1.0
JSR-104 XML Trust Services API
JSR-105 XML Digital Signature APIs
JSR-106 XML Digital Encryption APIs
JSR-109 Implementing Enterprise Web Services
JSR-110 Java APIs for WSDL
JSR-151 J2EE 1.4
JSR-152 JavaServer Pages 1.3
JSR-153 Enterprise JavaBeans 2.1
JSR-154 Java Servlet 2.4
JSR-155 Web Services Security Assertions
JSR-156 XML Transactioning API for Java (JAXTX)
JSR-157 ebXML CPP/A APIs for Java
JSR-181 Web Services Metadata for the Java Platform

7.4.1 Using a Custom Tag Library

There are two primary components you'll need for any tag library you wish to use. The first component is the tag library descriptor (TLD) file, which contains XML-format descriptions of each tag available in the library. The second component is the JAR file that contains the actual implementation of the tags. To use the tag library, both of these components must be installed as part of your servlet context. The JAR file with the implementation should be placed in the `WEB-INF/lib` directory of your servlet context. The location of the TLD is more flexible; you can decide on any location for it, but must let the servlet container know where to find it via the `taglib` directive within the JSP. There are three scenarios for how the `taglib` directive can reference the `.tld` file:

1. The `taglib` directive provides either an absolute or a relative path to the location of the `.tld` file. Typically, the file is in `WEB-INF/`, but it could be elsewhere.
2. The `taglib` directive provides either an absolute or a relative path to the location of the `.jar` file containing the `taglib` implementation classes. Within this `.jar` file, the `.tld` file is included in the `META-INF/` directory, and is named `taglib.tld`.
3. The `taglib` directive provides a symbolic name for the TLD file (which, just to make things confusing, looks exactly like a relative or absolute URL path). In the `web.xml` file for the application, this symbolic name is mapped to a real absolute or relative path in a `<taglib>` element.

We use the first approach in our JSPTL example, and the second approach when we develop our own library. Once you've installed the required components (at least the `.jar` file, and the `.tld` file and `web.xml` entry if required), the tag library is ready for use within your JSPs. Each page that uses any tag from the library must have a `<taglib>` directive giving the library name and prefix, as described in the earlier section on JSP directives.

7.4.2 The Standard Tag Library: JSPTL

JSPTL is the open-source reference implementation of the standard tag library. The specification is still evolving and far from complete, under control of JSR-052. We've chosen to use this prerelease software because it will become part of the standard JSP functionality in the future. If you prefer, there are many other tag libraries available that provide the same functionality and are compatible with the earlier JSP 1.1 and Servlet 2.2 standards, and thus can be deployed in older servlet containers (such as Tomcat 3.x).

The standard tag library will provide features in a number of areas, such as iteration, conditional logic, and an expression language. For our purposes, we're just going to use an iteration tag in one of our examples, because this is functionality that has at least a reasonable chance of remaining stable until the 1.0 release of the library.

Listing 7.7 shows the `EnterGameResult` JSP. At the very top, you'll see the directive that allows us to use the JSPTL library within this page. We provide a pointer to the TLD file, and specify that action tags from this library within our page will all be prefixed by `jr`. We pick up the `teamList` bean that was passed to us by the servlet, and then use the `<jr:forEach>` tag to iterate over this list, making each team an option within the selection box. We do this twice, once for the home team and once for the visitor.

Listing 7.7 `EnterGameResult.jsp` (Using JSPTL Library)

```
<%@ taglib prefix="jr" uri="WEB-INF/jsptl-jr.tld" %>

<jsp:useBean id="teamList" scope="application"
             class="java.util.List"/>
<jsp:useBean id="game" scope="request"
             class="nfl.application.BeansGameImpl"
             type="nfl.application.Game"/>
<HTML>
<HEAD>
<TITLE>Post results of a game</TITLE>
<HEAD>
<BODY>
<FORM method=post action=GameResult>
<H1>Enter Game Results</H1>

Week Number <INPUT name='week' type=text size=3/><br/>

Visiting Team
<SELECT name=visitor>
    <jr:forEach var="team" items="<%= teamList %>">
       <OPTION><jsp:getProperty name="team"
                                 property="fullName"/>
       </OPTION>
    </jr:forEach>
</SELECT>
Score <INPUT name='vscore' type=text size=3/><br/>

Home Team
<SELECT name='home'>
    <jr:forEach var="team" items="<%= teamList %>">
       <OPTION><jsp:getProperty name="team"
                                 property="fullName"/>
       </OPTION>
    </jr:forEach>
</SELECT>
Score  <INPUT name='hscore' type=text size=3/><br/>
<INPUT type=submit value='Post Results'/>

</FORM>
</BODY>
</HTML>
```

JSPs: Write Once, Run . . . Once?

Having worked with Java since the 1.0 release, I've come to take the write-once, run-anywhere capability promised by Java for granted. I've had great success in writing Java classes and moving them freely around platforms without having to think too much about it.

So I was caught by surprise when I took the example JSPs that were developed for this and the following chapter and found they could not be redeployed successfully in different containers.

Here are some of the portability problems I encountered. Because the redeployment of the JSPs was tested very late in the development of the manuscript, these issues remain unresolved:

- Both HP-AS and WebLogic had problems with the `<jr:forEach>` tag used from the JSPTL library. In both containers, the JSP failed to compile with an error indicating that an instance of the "team" bean (which is created by the `forEach` tag) cannot be found on the page. The version of JSPTL used in the example is very early; chances are quite good that later versions of JSPTL will interoperate as expected among all the containers.

- WebLogic complained about a bean that was given a class of `java.util.List[]` (an array of `List`s); HP-AS and Tomcat both allowed the syntax. A close reading of the JSP 1.2 specification indicates that this is not defined as a legal type for a bean, so WebLogic cannot be faulted. The specification is silent as to what containers should do with data types not specifically covered by the specification, so the fact that Tomcat and HP-AS allow this syntax can be viewed as an added feature.

- In the custom tag library example, the `EnterGameResult.jsp` page did not compile in HP-AS, with an error indicating that an unexpected exception was thrown by the `taglib` validator. HP-AS also complained about the tag library TLD file on the `FavoriteTeamTaglib.jsp` page, reporting that "the markup in the document preceding the root element must be well-formed." The errors may in fact be related; and both look like they might be rooted in XML parsing difficulties.

Help on the Way?

The is a new tool coming that can help developers ensure that their J2EE components are portable. It is called the Application Verification Kit (AVK). Information can be found at `http://java.sun.com/j2ee/avk`. It is hoped that the AVK will help identify interoperability problems of the types outlined here, making it easier for a developer to feel confident that an application can be deployed in a wide variety of containers.

7.4.3   Building, Installing, and Running the Servlet/JSP Example

This example involves building a new servlet, and not just additional JSPs, so a full-blown Ant buildfile is in order. We'll just add it as a new target to the existing `build.xml` file in the servlet directory. First of all, we need to update our `web.xml` file to add ServletThree. As before, we continue to bring forward the entries for ServletOne and ServletTwo, so when this servlet is deployed, we can access any of our three example servlets.

Listing 7.8 `web.xml` File for ServletThree (`servlet3.xml`)

```
<?xml version="1.0" encoding="ISO-8859-1"?>

<!DOCTYPE web-app PUBLIC
  "-//Sun Microsystems, Inc.//DTD Web application 2.2//EN"
  "http://java.sun.com/j2ee/dtds/web-app_2.2.dtd">

<web-app>
  <servlet>
    <servlet-name>NFLStandings</servlet-name>
    <servlet-class>
       nfl.application.servlet.ServletOneImpl
    </servlet-class>
  </servlet>

  <servlet>
    <servlet-name>NFLServlet2</servlet-name>
    <servlet-class>
       nfl.application.servlet.ServletTwoImpl
    </servlet-class>
    <load-on-startup>1</load-on-startup>
  </servlet>

  <servlet>
    <servlet-name>NFLServlet3</servlet-name>
    <servlet-class>
       nfl.application.servlet.ServletThreeImpl
    </servlet-class>
    <load-on-startup>1</load-on-startup>
  </servlet>

  <servlet-mapping>
     <servlet-name>NFLStandings</servlet-name>
     <url-pattern>/servlet/*</url-pattern>
  </servlet-mapping>
```

```
<servlet-mapping>
  <servlet-name>NFLServlet2</servlet-name>
  <url-pattern>/servlet2/*</url-pattern>
</servlet-mapping>

<servlet-mapping>
  <servlet-name>NFLServlet3</servlet-name>
  <url-pattern>/servlet3/*</url-pattern>
</servlet-mapping>
</web-app>
```

In the `build.xml` file, we need to build our `ServletThreeImpl` class and the `Beans-GameImpl` class. Then we just copy the various class and JSP files to the appropriate locations in the `WEB-INF` directory, and create a WAR file of the entire hierarchy. The `servlet3` target must be specified when invoking the buildfile, otherwise `servlet1`, the default for the buildfile, will be constructed.

Deployment is as with previous servlets; the WAR file needs to be copied into the appropriate directory of the servlet container (`/webapps` for Tomcat) and the next time the container is restarted, you should be able to access the servlet.

Listing 7.9 Build Targets for ServletThree (in `application/servlet/build.xml`)

```
<target name="compile-servlet3">
    <javac srcdir="." classpath="${servlet.jar}">
        <include name="ServletThreeImpl.java" />
        <include name="ServletThreeVersionInfo.java" />
        <src path=".." />
        <include name="DynamicStandings.java" />
        <include name="DynamicStandingsImpl.java" />
        <include name="AsyncMessagingImpl.java" />
        <include name="BeansGameImpl.java" />
        <src path="../../presentation" />
        <include name="HTML.java" />
    </javac>
</target>

<target name="servlet3" depends="compile-servlet3">
    <delete file="nfl.war" />
    <copy file="../../presentation/jsp/S3MainPage.html"
        tofile="../../presentation/jsp/MainPage.html"
        overwrite="yes" />
    <war warfile="nfl.war" webxml="servlet3.xml">
        <fileset dir="../../presentation/jsp"
            includes="MainPage.html,EnterGameResult.jsp,
                    PostGameResult.jsp,ShowStandings.jsp" />
```

```
      <lib dir="../.." includes="layered.jar" />
      <lib dir="../../presentation/jsp"
             includes="jsptl.jar" />
      <classes dir="."
          includes="ServletTwo*.class,
                     ServletThree*.class"
           prefix="WEB-INF/classes/nfl/application/servlet"
          />
      <classes dir=".."
          includes="DynamicStandings*.class,
                     AsyncMessagingImpl.class,
                     BeansGameImpl.class"
           prefix="WEB-INF/classes/nfl/application" />
      <classes dir="../../presentation"
          includes="HTML.class"
            prefix="WEB-INF/classes/nfl/presentation" />
      <webinf dir="../../presentation/jsp"
             includes="jsptl-jr.tld" />
  </war>
</target>

<target name="clean-servlet3">
  <delete>
    <fileset dir="."
        includes="ServletThree*.class,nfl.war" />
    <fileset dir=".." includes="DynamicStandings*.class,
                                AsyncMessagingImpl.class,
                                BeansGameImpl.class" />
    <fileset dir="../../presentation"
        includes="HTML.class" />
  </delete>
</target>
```

To access this version of the example, point your browser to:

```
http://localhost:8080/nfl/servlet3/Main
```

7.4.4   Creating a Custom Tag Library

Our final example in this chapter will be to create our own custom tag library. In the previous example, we used an existing tag library (JSPTL), so the main thing we're emphasizing in this example is the implementation of the tag library, rather than its usage. Our tag library will be called the `nfl-taglib`, and will have three custom tags.

Table 7.3   Components in the Custom Tag Library Example

New Components		
Name	**Component Type**	**Comment**
FavoriteTeamTaglib.jsp	JSP	JSP that delegates business logic to servlet, and uses standard tag library for iteration.
DivisionRankTag.java	Class	Implementation of the `<getDivisionRank>` tag.
ConferenceRankTag.java	Class	Implementation of the `<getConferenceRank>` tag.
RecentGameTag.java	Class	Implementation of the `<getGamesSince>` tag.
EnterGameResult.jsp	JSP	JSP to enter game result.
Existing Components		
Component	**Description**	
laycrcd.jar	All classes and interfaces of the layered version of the application (as presented in Chapter 2).	
ServletThree	This example is deployed on top of ServletThree.	

The first component we'll look at is the tag library descriptor file for the new library. Here, we specify the three tags that we plan to implement, along with information about the attributes that are part of each tag. Two of the tags are very similar: the `<getDivisionRank>` and `<getConferenceRank>` tags are used to return the numerical value representing a particular team's position within a division. The `<getGamesSince>` tag is used to print information about games that have been played by a particular team since the specified week.

In Listing 7.10, you can see the complete TLD file. First, we specify some global information about the tag library—the version of the library, the version of JavaServer Pages that it requires as a minimum, and then a name and description. After this, we define each of the three tags that comprise the library. Each tag is defined by a `<name>` and implementing `<tagclass>`. The `<bodycontent>` describes what we expect to find within this tag, if it allows embedded text or elements. All of our tags are EMPTY, because the information needed by the tag is passed in attributes rather than elements. An `<info>` item allows us to describe the tag's purpose. We then have `<attribute>` elements for each legal attribute of the tag. Each `<attribute>` has a `<name>` element, a `<required>` boolean element, and optionally a `<rtexprvalue>` element. The last element, if true, indicates that the attribute value might contain a JSP expression, rather than just textual data.

That's all we need to define the tags in our library; next we'll look at a JSP that uses the tags.

Listing 7.10 Tag Library Descriptor File (`taglib.tld`)

```xml
<?xml version="1.0" ?>

<!DOCTYPE taglib PUBLIC
  "-//Sun Microsystems, Inc.//DTD JSP Tag Library 1.1//EN"
  "http://java.sun.com/j2ee/dtds/web-jsptaglibrary_1_1.dtd">

<taglib>
  <tlibversion>1.0</tlibversion>
  <jspversion>1.1</jspversion>
  <shortname>nfl</shortname>
  <info>Example custom tag library</info>

  <tag>
    <name>getDivisionRank</name>
    <tagclass>
        nfl.presentation.jsp.DivisionRankTag
    </tagclass>
    <bodycontent>EMPTY</bodycontent>
    <info>Return rank of team in division standings</info>
    <attribute>
      <name>team</name>
      <required>true</required>
      <rtexprvalue>true</rtexprvalue>
    </attribute>
    <attribute>
      <name>ordinal</name>
      <required>false</required>
    </attribute>
  </tag>

  <tag>
    <name>getConferenceRank</name>
    <tagclass>
        nfl.presentation.jsp.ConferenceRankTag
    </tagclass>
    <bodycontent>EMPTY</bodycontent>
    <info>
        Return rank of team in conference standings
    </info>
    <attribute>
      <name>team</name>
      <required>true</required>
```

```
        <rtexprvalue>true</rtexprvalue>
     </attribute>
     <attribute>
        <name>ordinal</name>
        <required>false</required>
     </attribute>
  </tag>

  <tag>
     <name>getGamesSince</name>
     <tagclass>
        nfl.presentation.jsp.RecentGamesTag
     </tagclass>
     <bodycontent>EMPTY</bodycontent>
     <info>Return games played by team since date</info>
     <attribute>
        <name>team</name>
        <required>false</required>
        <rtexprvalue>true</rtexprvalue>
     </attribute>
     <attribute>
        <name>week</name>
        <required>false</required>
        <rtexprvalue>true</rtexprvalue>
     </attribute>
  </tag>

</taglib>
```

In Listing 7.11, we've reworked the latter part of our Favorite Team JSP yet again, this time to use the new tags in our tag library. In each case, the parameter being passed to the tag attributes is specified in the form of a JSP expression. Note that by default, expressions are not allowed in attribute values; to allow this we needed to specify the `<rtexprvalue>` element on each attribute with a value of `true` (see Listing 7.10).

Listing 7.11 FavoriteTeamTaglib.jsp

```
<!-- HTML output using Custom Tags -->

<jsp:useBean id="team" class="nfl.application.Team"/>

<head>
<title>NFL Standings for
   <jsp:getProperty name="team" property="fullName"/>
</title>
</head>
```

```
<body>

<H1>Recent Results for
   <jsp:getProperty name="team" property="fullName"/>
</H1>

<!-- no longer able to print counter here -->

<nfl:getGamesSince team="<%= team.getFullName() %>"
                    week="<%= sVisit %>"/>


<H2>Division Standing</H2>

<jsp:getProperty name="team" property="name"/>
  are ranked
<nfl:getDivisionRank team="<%= team.getFullName() %>"
                     ordinal="true"/>
  in the <jsp:getProperty name="team" property="division"/>
<br>
<%= divisionStatus() %>

<H2>Conference Standing</H2>
<jsp:getProperty name="team" property="name"/>
  are ranked
<nfl:getConferenceRank team="<%= team.getFullName() %>"
                       ordinal="true"/>
  in the <jsp:getProperty name="team" property="conference"/>
<br>
<%= conferenceStatus() %>

</body>
</html>
```

Now let's see how we implement these tags. The division and conference rank tags are nearly identical, so we'll just look at one of them. In Listing 7.12, we see the implementation of the `<getDivisionRank>` tag. Within the TLD file, we specified that the implementation would be in a class named `DivisionRankTag`. Our class extends `TagSupport`, which is one of two classes used for custom tags. The other class is `BodyTagSupport`, which we would use if the tag we were defining contained any body content (that is, something other than attributes, which would appear between a start and an end tag). None of our tags have any body content, so `TagSupport` is the appropriate superclass.

Our tag is essentially a JavaBean, where each attribute that can be specified on the tag corresponds to a property in the handler class. So the first step in creating our tag handler is to define the properties and the accessor methods. From the TLD file, we can see that our properties are `team` and `ordinal`. For a tag with no body, such as ours, the only other method we need is the doStartTag() method, which will be called after the accessor methods are called to set property values based on the tag attributes. (If we had a body in the tag, we might also need to implement getBodyContent(), doAfterBody(), and doEndTag() methods.)

Listing 7.12 DivisionRankTag.java

```
// DivisionRankTag.java

package nfl.presentation.jsp;

import javax.servlet.jsp.*;
import javax.servlet.jsp.tagext.*;

import java.util.List;

import nfl.ObjectFactory;
import nfl.application.Team;
import nfl.application.Teams;
import nfl.application.DynamicStandings;

public class DivisionRankTag extends TagSupport {

    private Team team;
    private boolean ordinal = false;
    private Teams teams= (Teams)
        ObjectFactory.getHandle().getInstance("Teams");
    private DynamicStandings standings = (DynamicStandings)
        ObjectFactory.getHandle().getInstance(
                                    "DynamicStandings");

    //Attribute Handling
    public void setTeam(String team) {
        this.team = teams.getTeam(team);
    }

    public void setOrdinal(String ord) {
        // Default is false, and any invalid value will
        // just be treated as false
        if (ord.equals("true")) ordinal = true;
    }


    // Tag handling
    public int doStartTag() {
        JspWriter out = pageContext.getOut();
        int divisionRank = 0;
```

```
    List divStandings = standings.
        getDivisionStandings(team.getDivision());
    for (int i=0;i<divStandings.size(); i++) {
       Team rankedTeam = (Team) divStandings.get(i);
       if (rankedTeam.getFullName().equals(
                      team.getFullName())) {
          divisionRank = i+1;
          break;
       }
    }
    try {
       if (ordinal)
          out.print(intToOrdinal(divisionRank));
       else
          out.print(divisionRank);
    } catch (java.io.IOException e) {
       e.printStackTrace();
    }

    return SKIP_BODY;
  }

  // Utility functions
  public String intToOrdinal(int rank) {
     switch(rank) {
        case 1: return "1st";
        case 2: return "2nd";
        case 3: return "3rd";
        default: return (rank+"th");
     }
  }
}
```

7.5 Tag Library API Reference

The following API listings show the methods available to custom tag developers in the TagSupport and BodyTagSupport classes.

API 7.1 javax.servlet.jsp.tagext.**TagSupport** class

```
public class TagSupport implements Tag, Serializable
    // Constructor
    public TagSupport();
    // Constants from Tag interface
    public static final int EVAL_BODY_INCLUDE;
    public static final int EVAL_PAGE;
    public static final int SKIP_BODY;
    public static final int SKIP_PAGE;
    // Methods of Tag interface
    public int doEndTag() throws JspException;
    public int doStartTag() throws JspException;
    public Tag getParent();
    public void release();
    public void setPageContext(PageContext pc);
    public void setParent(Tag t)
    // Instance methods
    public static final Tag findAncestorWithClass(Tag from, Class klass);
    public String getId();
    public Object getValue(String attribute);
    public java.util.Enumeration getValues();
    public void removeValue(String attribute);
    public void setId(String id);
    public void setValue(String attribute, Object obj);
```

API 7.2 javax.servlet.jsp.tagext.**BodyTagSupport** class

```
public class BodyTagSupport  extends TagSupport implements BodyTag
    // Methods inherited from TagSupport NOT SHOWN; see API 7-1
    public int doAfterBody() throws JspException;
    public void doInitBody();
    public BodyContent getBodyContent();
    public JspWriter getPreviousOut();
    public void setBodyContent(BodyContent body)
```

The RecentGamesTag class is shown in Listing 7.13. No new tag capabilities are being introduced in this class, so we just show it for comparison with previous ways of implementing this functionality (via scriptlets or beans).

Listing 7.13 `RecentGamesTag.java`

```java
// RecentGamesTag.java

package nfl.presentation.jsp;

import javax.servlet.jsp.*;
import javax.servlet.jsp.tagext.*;

import java.util.List;
import java.util.Iterator;

import nfl.ObjectFactory;
import nfl.application.Team;
import nfl.application.Teams;
import nfl.application.Game;
import nfl.application.Games;

public class RecentGamesTag extends TagSupport {

   private Team team;
   private int  week = 0;
   private Teams teams= (Teams)
      ObjectFactory.getHandle().getInstance("Teams");
   private Games games = (Games)
      ObjectFactory.getHandle().getInstance("Games");

   //Attribute Handling
   public void setTeam(String team) {
      this.team = teams.getTeam(team);
      if (this.team == null)
         this.team = teams.getTeam("49ers");
   }

   public void setWeek(String week) {
      try {
        this.week = Integer.parseInt(week);
      } catch (NumberFormatException e) {
        this.week = 0;
      }
   }


   // Tag handling
   public int doStartTag() {
      JspWriter out = pageContext.getOut();
      List allGames = games.getAllGamesFor(
                             team.getFullName());
```

```
        // loop over games, finding those > week
        Iterator gi = allGames.iterator();
        while (gi.hasNext()) {
            Game g = (Game) gi.next();
            if (g.getWeek() <= week) continue;
            try {
                out.println("Week " + g.getWeek() + " "
                    + g.getVisitor() + " "
                    + g.getScore()[0] + " "
                    + g.getHome() + " "
                    + g.getScore()[1] + "<br>");
            } catch (java.io.IOException e) {
                e.printStackTrace();
            }
        }
        return SKIP_BODY;
    }
}
```

7.5.1 Building, Installing, and Running the Custom Tags Example

To build this example, we are assembling two separate packages. First, the tag library itself is a potentially reusable component that should be separately packaged in its own JAR file. The `<taglib>` target in the `build.xml` file (Listing 7.14) builds this `taglib`'s JAR file. All of the example classes are compiled, and then the `taglib` classes and the TLD file are assembled into a JAR file that we'll name `nfl-taglib.jar`. Next, we assemble the example application that uses the `taglib` into a WAR file. We're calling this one `nfljsp.war`; this means that `/nfljsp` becomes the context directory for the application. The `taglib` JAR we've just assembled goes into the `WEB-INF/lib` subdirectory, and our Favorite Team JSP page goes into the context (root) directory.

To install, we deploy the `nfljsp.war` file in our servlet container of choice. To access the new JSP, we point our browser to:

```
http://localhost:8080/nfljsp/FavoriteTeamTaglib.jsp
```

Listing 7.14 Ant Buildfile for JSP with Custom Tags

```
<project name="nfl-taglib" default="war" basedir=".">

<!-- this is an extended version of servlet3, with a
     few additional pieces added -->

<property name="servlet.jar" value="../../../servlet.jar" />
```

```
<target name="compile">
    <javac srcdir="." classpath="${servlet.jar}">
        <include name="DivisionRankTag.java" />
        <include name="ConferenceRankTag.java" />
        <include name="GamesPlayedTag.java" />
        <src path=".." />
        <include name="HTML.java" />
        <src path="../../application/servlet" />
        <include name="ServletThreeImpl.java" />
        <include name="ServletThreeVersionInfo.java" />
        <src path="../../application" />
        <include name="DynamicStandings.java" />
        <include name="DynamicStandingsImpl.java" />
        <include name="AsyncMessagingImpl.java" />
        <include name="BeansGameImpl.java" />
        <src path=".." />
        <include name="HTML.java" />
    </javac>
</target>

<target name="taglib" depends="compile">
    <jar jarfile="nfl-taglib.jar" >
        <zipfileset dir="." includes="*.class"
            prefix="nfl/presentation/jsp" />
        <metainf dir="." includes="taglib.*" />
    </jar>
</target>

<target name="war" depends="taglib">
    <delete file="nfljsp.war" />
    <copy file="JSPMainPage.html" tofile="MainPage.html"
        overwrite="yes" />
    <war warfile="nfljsp.war" webxml="web.xml">
        <fileset dir="." includes=
            "MainPage.html,EnterGameResult.jsp,
             PostGameResult.jsp,ShowStandings.jsp,
             FavoriteTeamTaglib.jsp" />
        <lib dir="../.." includes="layered.jar" />
        <lib dir="." includes="nfl-taglib.jar" />
        <lib dir="." includes="jsptl.jar" />
        <classes dir="../../application/servlet"
            includes="ServletTwo*.class,
                      ServletThree*.class"
               prefix=
                  "WEB-INF/classes/nfl/application/servlet" />
        <classes dir="../../application"
            includes="DynamicStandings*.class,
                      AsyncMessagingImpl.class,
                      BeansGameImpl.class"
```

```
            prefix="WEB-INF/classes/nfl/application" />
      <classes dir=".."
          includes="HTML.class"
              prefix="WEB-INF/classes/nfl/presentation" />
      <webinf  dir="." includes="jsptl-jr.tld" />
    </war>
</target>

<target name="clean">
  <delete>
    <fileset dir="." includes="nfl-taglib.jar" />
    <fileset dir="." includes="nfljsp.war" />
    <fileset dir="." includes="*.class" />
  </delete>
</target>

</project>
```

7.6   Exercises

7.1 Add a login page: Create a login page; allow the user to specify team and week to pass to favorite team page.

7.2 Add a user JavaBean: Introduce a JavaBean to hold user information (favorite team, last visit) to work along with the existing scriptlet.

7.3 Standings output JSP: Implement a JSP version of the standings output page.

7.7   Further Reading

The Jakarta project at Apache is working on numerous tag libraries; see `http://jakarta.apache.org/taglibs` for details.

The standard tag library (originally JSPTL, recently JSTL) is described at `http://java.sun.com/products/jsp/taglibraries.html`. The reference implementation is done by the Apache Taglibs project, and can be reached at `http://jakarta.apache.org/taglibs/doc/standard-doc/index.html`.

Struts

O ver the course of the last three chapters, we've examined servlets and JavaServer Pages (JSPs) and seen several ways that they can be used together. If we were to write enough applications this way, we'd start to see patterns emerge, and would start coming up with our own design patterns for using these technologies. We would also no doubt develop a handy collection of custom tags that we find to be generally applicable to problems we encounter repeatedly in our development process.

Fortunately, somebody has already done this, and the result of that effort is freely available to anyone who cares to use it. The project is called Struts, and it is a Web publishing framework from the Apache group. A look at Struts is the ideal way to bring together the topics we've talked about over the past few chapters, because it uses every component that we have introduced.

Software Used in This Chapter
Servlets
Servlet 2.2, from `http://java.sun.com/products/servlet`, is sufficient for all examples in this chapter. The examples have also been tested using the newer Servlet 2.3 standard APIs.
JavaServer Pages
Version 1.1. There are no development-time components needed, because JSPs are compiled dynamically by the container when they are deployed or accessed. All JSPs shown here are also compatible with the newer JSP 1.2 standard.
Tomcat Servlet Container
Version 3.2.3, from `jakarta.apache.org`. Tomcat 4.0.1 was also used to test the example program.
Struts
From the Apache Jakarta project. Software is included on the CD, or you can download it from `http://jakarta.apache.org/struts`. Version 1.0 was used.

8.1   What Is a Framework, Anyway?

I referred to Struts as a "framework," rather than just calling it a set of APIs and tag libraries. Frameworks generally are centered on a particular design philosophy, and everything else that comes along is to assist you in developing code that follows the philosophy. If you agree with the basic design concepts in the framework, then the framework components are great time savers. If you have a different idea about how best to structure things, then you'll be fighting the framework every step of the way. We're covering Struts at this point because it's very much in sync with the design philosophy we were already using in our code.

For our Struts example, we'll revisit the Favorite Team capability we added to our application in Chapter 5. This time, we'll do a more complete implementation that includes a logon page, a registration page for new users, and a page for the users to set their preferences.

8.2   Struts Components

The Struts framework provides:

- A servlet, known as the `ActionServlet`, to serve as the controller for the application, invoking actions as required and passing control to and from JavaServer Pages that make up the visible portion of the presentation layer.
- Four custom tag libraries that provide powerful capabilities for creating JavaServer Pages:
  — The `struts-html` tag library provides tags useful in generating HTML.

— The `struts-bean` tag library provides tags to create and access JavaBeans. Struts-bean tags can handle indexed properties, and properties that are themselves beans (nested beans). They are a superior alternative to the `<jsp:useBean>`, `<jsp:setProperty>`, and `<jsp:getProperty>` JSP action tags.

— The `struts-logic` tag library provides logic tags, such as iterators, switch tags, and if tags.

— The `struts-template` tag library provides tags that are useful in creating and using JSP templates; for example, include tags to allow the inclusion of standard components onto every JSP.

The first thing we must do in order to use Struts in our application is configure the `web.xml` file to include the `ActionServlet` servlet. Listing 8.1 shows the `web.xml` file we'll use. It's stripped down to just the single servlet in this file, although we could just as easily add this new servlet into the `web.xml` file we used in previous examples. We also add for the first time a `<welcome-file-list>` element. This isn't unique to Struts; it is a standard element that can be used in any `web.xml` file to specify what file under the context directory should be served to any user who surfs into the directory without specifying a specific page as a target.

Listing 8.1 Configuring the Struts Servlet (`web.xml`)

```
<?xml version="1.0" encoding="ISO-8859-1"?>

<!DOCTYPE web-app PUBLIC
  "-//Sun Microsystems, Inc.//DTD Web application 2.2//EN"
  "http://java.sun.com/j2ee/dtds/web-app_2_2.dtd">

<web-app>

  <servlet>
    <servlet-name>action</servlet-name>
    <servlet-class>
      org.apache.struts.action.ActionServlet
    </servlet-class>
    <init-param>
      <param-name>application</param-name>
      <param-value>nfl</param-value>
    </init-param>
    <init-param>
      <param-name>config</param-name>
      <param-value>/WEB-INF/struts-config.xml</param-value>
    </init-param>
    <load-on-startup>1</load-on-startup>
  </servlet>
```

```
<servlet-mapping>
   <servlet-name>action</servlet-name>
   <url-pattern>/struts/*</url-pattern>
</servlet-mapping>

<welcome-file-list>
   <welcome-file>logon.jsp</welcome-file>
</welcome-file-list>

</web-app>
```

In setting up a servlet mapping for the `ActionServlet`, we can choose to match based on path or on file extensions. When matching based on file extension, the Struts convention is to use a `.do` extension. For purposes of the example, I've chosen to match based on path, and require `/struts/` in the path of any actions we want to be handled by the Struts `ActionServlet`. The Struts `ActionServlet` provides a number of initialization parameters that can be used. In our example, we use two of them. The `application` parameter points to a resources file. The resources file must exist somewhere under the `WEB-INF/classes` directory, and will have the extension `.properties`. Because we haven't used any package name for our resources, and have given the filename `nfl`, the actual file searched for will be `WEB-INF/classes/nfl.properties` in the context directory of the `ActionServlet` (which, as we'll see shortly, is going to be `/nfl-struts`.)

The only other parameter we're setting in this example is the `config` parameter. All Struts applications are required to provide a configuration file, which is typically named `struts-config.xml` and located in the `WEB-INF/` directory. Table 8.1 shows other initialization parameters you can configure for the `ActionServlet`.

Table 8.1 ActionServlet Initialization Parameters

<param-name>	<param-value>	Comment
application	Class name	Name of resources file for application.
bufferSize	Integer	Input buffer size for uploads; default 4096.
config	File path	Default /WEB-INF/struts-config.xml.
content	MIME type	Default is text/html.
debug	Integer	Debugging detail level for servlet; higher number is more verbose.
detail	Integer	Debugging detail level for XML Digester utility.

Table 8.1 ActionServlet Initialization Parameters (Continued)

\<param-name\>	\<param-value\>	Comment
factory	Class name	Class used to generate messages. Default is `org.apache.struts.util.Property-MessageResourcesFactory`
formBean	Class name	Class used for `ActionFormBean`. Default is `org.apache.struts.action.ActionFormBean`
forward	Class name	Class used for `ActionForward`. Default is `org.apache.struts.action.ActionForward`
locale	true | false	
mapping	Class name	Class used for `ActionMapping`. Default is `org.apache.struts.ApplicationMapping`
maxFileSize	Size in bytes	Maximum size of file accepted in an upload. May use K, M, G suffix characters
multipart-Class	Class Name	Class to use for processing uploads. Default is `org.apache.struts.upload.Disk-MultipartRequestHandler`
nocache	true | false	(Default false)
null	true | false	If true, return null if we attempt to retrieve message by an invalid key. If false, generate an error message (default true)
tempDir	Directory path	Temporary working directory to use for file uploads
validate	true | false	If true, use new configuration file format (default true)
validating	true | false	If true, use validating XML parser to process config file (default true)

8.2.1   Finding the Actions

When we first introduced the example application in Chapter 2, we went through an exercise of "finding the objects." With a Struts application, there is a similar exercise of "finding the actions." Actions are the processing steps that need to be performed in Java code; in some cases, there are actions to be performed before a JSP is displayed; in other cases, there will be actions to be performed after a JSP page. Because this can be confusing, let's start thinking about our application flow without any actions, and then see where the actions fit in. Figure 8.1 shows the JSPs that we intend to develop for this version of that application, and how control is expected to flow between them.

Figure 8.1   Application flow showing only JSPs.

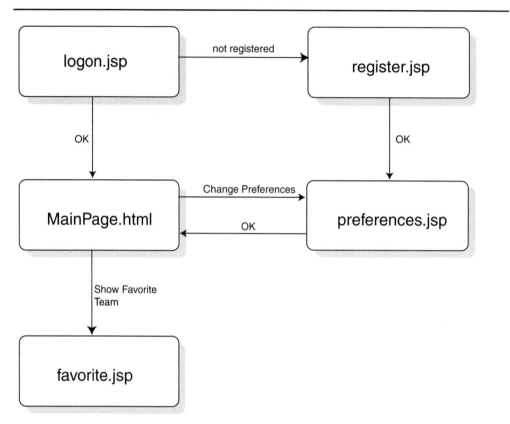

The flow is fairly straightforward; we begin at a logon page. Unregistered users are sent to a separate registration page, where they will register (providing a username and password) and then proceed on to set their preferences (which is just a single item, the favorite team). Both the logon and registration paths converge on the main page. From here, users can choose to change their preferences, or go on to the Favorite Team page and get recent results and status for their favorite team. That's the entire application flow in a nutshell.

Now, for each of those pages, we must ask whether there is preprocessing to be done before the JSP displays, or postprocessing to be done after leaving the JSP. From the answers to these questions we develop a diagram such as the one shown in Figure 8.2.

Figure 8.2 Application flow showing JSPs and actions.

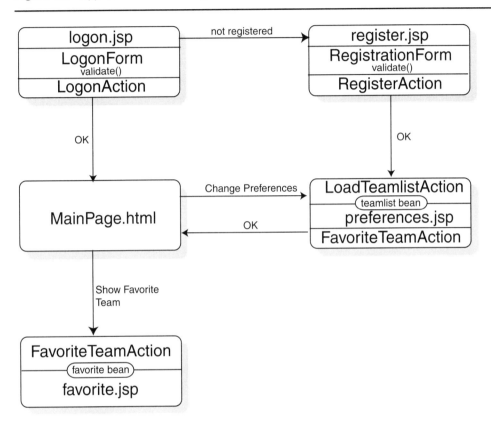

Our `logon.jsp` and `register.jsp` pages are forms; there is nothing needed before the forms are displayed, but afterward we must process the entered data. In addition to actions, Struts provides form beans, which are classes that simply provide properties to represent the field data from a JSP form. Form beans can be used to validate the data entered, so we've shown the form validation step in Figure 8.2 along with the action to perform. The `preferences.jsp` page is also a form, but it requires some pre-processing. As in earlier versions of the preferences page, the user selects their favorite team from a list; and we must load the list into a bean that is accessible to the JSP before processing the JSP. We create a `LoadTeamListAction` to handle this task (it could also have been done by embedding a declaration for a `jspInit()` method in the JSP, but this doesn't follow the Struts framework design). We don't really need any validation of this form because it's impossible for the user to make an invalid selection. The `MainPage.html` screen is just plain HTML, so there are no actions associated with that page. Finally, results are displayed on the `favorite.jsp` page. There are several pieces of data needed by this page; we create a new class called `FavoriteTeamBean` to package all the required fields conveniently together. The `FavoriteTeamAction` class is responsible for setting the fields of the bean, then making the bean available to the JSP. The `favorite.jsp` page simply displays the results.

Having gone through the design exercise, here's what we have: three forms, each of which will be implemented on a JSP and have an `ActionForm` bean associated with it to hold the form data; and five actions, each of which will be implemented in an `Action` class. This is enough information to create the `struts-config.xml` file, which is the configuration file required for all Struts applications.

The only elements we're using in our simple configuration are `form-beans` and `action-mappings`. The tables following Listing 8.2 show the various elements that can be specified within the `struts-config.xml` file, and what attributes may be set for each.

Listing 8.2 Configuring Struts: The `struts-config.xml` File

```xml
<?xml version="1.0" ?>

<!DOCTYPE struts-config PUBLIC
  "-//Apache Software Foundation//DTD Struts Configuration 1.0//EN"
  "http://jakarta.apache.org/struts/dtds/struts-config_1_0.dtd">

<struts-config>

  <form-beans>
    <form-bean name="logonForm"
        type="nfl.presentation.struts.LogonForm"/>
    <form-bean name="registrationForm"
        type="nfl.presentation.struts.RegistrationForm"/>
    <form-bean name="preferencesForm"
        type="nfl.presentation.struts.PreferencesForm" />
  </form-beans>

  <action-mappings>
    <action path="/Logon"
        type="nfl.presentation.struts.LogonAction"
        name="logonForm"
        scope="request"
        input="/logon.jsp"
        validate="true" >
        <forward name="pass" path="/MainPage.html" />
        <forward name="fail" path="/logon.jsp" />
    </action>
    <action path="/Register"
        type="nfl.presentation.struts.RegisterAction"
        name="registrationForm"
        scope="request"
```

```
            input="/register.jsp"
            validate="true" >
            <forward name="pass" path="/LoadTeamList" />
            <forward name="fail" path="/register.jsp" />
        </action>
        <action path="/Preferences"
            type="nfl.presentation.struts.PreferencesAction"
            name="preferencesForm"
            scope="request"
            input="/preferences.jsp" />
        <action path="/LoadTeamList"
            type="nfl.presentation.struts.LoadTeamListAction">
            <forward name="next" path="/preferences.jsp: />
        </action>
        <action path="/FavoriteTeam"
            type="nfl.presentation.struts.FavoriteTeamAction" />
    </action-mappings>

</struts-config>
```

Figure 8.3 Structure of the `struts-config.xml` document.

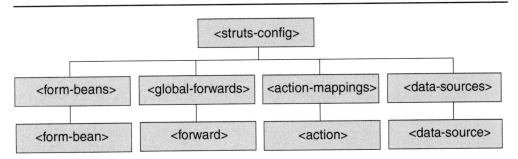

In Table 8.2, we explore further the configuration elements. The top-level elements—`<form-beans>`, `<global-forwards>`, `<action-mappings>`, and `<data-sources>`—are simple containers, so we won't delve any deeper into those. The attributes associated with each of the other configuration elements are shown in the table.

Table 8.2   `Struts-config` Elements and Attributes

Element Name	Attribute Name	Attribute Value
`<form-bean>`	`name`	Name of `form-bean`; ties bean to an action via the `action` name attribute.
	`type`	Class that implements bean.
`<forward>*`	`name`	Name by which forward is looked up.
	`path`	Actual URI path of target.
	`redirect`	
`<action>`	`type`	Class that implements `action`.
	`name`	The name of the `form-bean`.
	`path`	The URI that is matched to select this mapping.
	`unknown`	If true, this `action` becomes the default for any unmatched URI.
	`validate`	If true, invoke `validate()` method of `action`.
`<data-source>`	`autoCommit`	True if transactions should be committed automatically.
	`description`	Description of data source.
	`driverClass`	JDBC driver class.
	`maxCount`	Maximum size of database connection pool.
	`minCount`	Minimum size of database connection pool.
	`password`	Password used to access database.
	`url`	URL of jdbc-accessible database.
	`user`	User identity to use for JDBC calls.

* May be subelement of `<global-forwards>` or of `<action>`.

8.2.2   Building the Logon Screen

In reality, it's far more likely that you would build individual components first, and then develop the `struts-config.xml` file that described them. For instructional purposes, however, I felt it was better to start with the big-picture overview and then drill down to the individual components. The first component is the logon screen and its accompanying `ActionForm` and `Action` classes. The JSP to present the logon screen is shown in Listing 8.3, and the form itself is shown in Figure 8.4.

Listing 8.3 The Logon Screen (`logon.jsp`)

```
<!-- logon.jsp, Struts version -->

<%@ taglib prefix="html" uri="/WEB-INF/struts-html.tld" %>

<html:html>
 <head>
  <title>Logon for NFL Standings Application</title>
 </head>
 <body>
  <H1>Logon</H1>
  <html:errors/>

  If you aren't yet a registered user,
  <html:link href="/nfl-struts/register.jsp">
     Click here to register
  </html:link>

  <html:form action="/Logon">
   User Name
    <html:text property="username" size="20" /><br>

   Password
    <html:password property="password" size="20" /><br>

   <html:submit value="Logon"/>
   <html:reset />

  </html:form>
 </body>
</html:html>
```

Figure 8.4   Screenshot of the Logon form (`logon.jsp`).

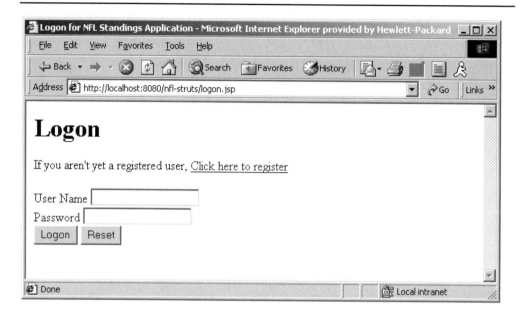

In Listing 8.3, we see that much of our HTML is actually being rendered by the use of specialized tags. From the `taglib` directive at the beginning of the file, we see that all of these tags are coming from the `struts-html` tag library. This library provides many useful tags; they are summarized in API 8.1. Because of the large number of attributes available on these tags, I haven't reproduced the attributes in the brief documentation; see the Struts documentation for full descriptions. The function of most tags can be easily guessed from their name or by examining the output shown in Figure 8.4. The `<html:errors>` tag is the only tag with no obvious tie to the output form. We'll come back and revisit how this tag works after we've finished all the components of our Logon screen.

API 8.1   Struts HTML tags

`<base>`	Defines base from which relative URLs in page will be located
`<button>`	Renders an HTML button
`<cancel>`	Renders an HTML Cancel button
`<checkbox>`	Renders an HTML checkbox input field
`<errors>`	Displays errors
`<file>`	Renders a file selection input field
`<form>`	Defines an HTML input form
`<hidden>`	Adds a hidden field to the form
`<html>`	Renders the `<html>` tag

`<image>`	Renders an image map input field
`<img>`	Renders an image
`<link>`	Renders an HTML link or anchor
`<messages>`	Displays messages
`<multibox>`	Renders a set of checkboxes that map to elements of an array
`<option>`	Renders an option for a selection field
`<options>`	Renders a collection of selection options
`<password>`	Renders a password input field
`<radio>`	Renders a radio-button input field
`<reset>`	Renders an HTML 'reset' button
`<rewrite>`	Renders the specified URL
`<select>`	Renders a Selection field
`<submit>`	Renders an HTML Submit button
`<text>`	Renders an HTML text input field
`<textarea>`	Renders an HTML multi-line text input field

One of the things that the Struts framework does on our behalf is to map all of the fields on our form onto properties of a JavaBean we provide.[1] In Listing 8.4, we see a class we created specifically to hold the input from the `logon.jsp` form. The two fields on the JSP form, username and password, are mirrored by identically named properties in our class, and each property is given both a `getter` and a `setter` method according to standard JavaBean naming conventions. We also provide an optional (but highly recommended) `validate()` method to perform validation of the form data.

Tying our JSP to this class is actually a two-step process. If you look back at our `struts-config.xml` file in Listing 8.2, you'll see that the `Logon` action associates the `logon.jsp` page with the `logonForm` form bean. We then have to find the `form-bean` entry within the file to see that the class that represents the `logonForm` bean is `nfl.presentation.struts.LogonForm`, which brings us to the code in Listing 8.4. Setting the `validate` attribute of the `/Logon` action mapping to `true` indicates to the `ActionServlet` that the `validate()` method should be called. (The `ActionForm` class that all form beans extend includes an empty `validate()` method that returns no errors, so there is no harm in setting `validate=true` for an action where you have no `validate()` method defined in the form bean.)

The `validate()` method can perform as much or as little validation as you like. One suggested design, which I have followed, is to have the form bean provide any validation that can be done using just the form contents, but to defer any complex validation (such as comparing against database lookups) to the `Action` class. The `validate()` method returns an `Action-Errors` instance, which is a collection made up of `ActionError` elements. We'll look at error handling in more detail following the `LogonAction` class.

---

1. In Struts 1.1, you'll be able to use a new `DynaActionForm` class to represent forms, rather than needing to hand-craft an `ActionForm` subclass for each form.

Listing 8.4 Logon Screen Form Bean (`LogonForm.java`)

```java
// LogonForm.java

package nfl.presentation.struts;

import javax.servlet.http.HttpServletRequest;
import javax.servlet.http.HttpServletResponse;

import org.apache.struts.action.ActionForm;
import org.apache.struts.action.ActionMapping;
import org.apache.struts.action.ActionError;
import org.apache.struts.action.ActionErrors;


/** Struts ActionForm for Logging on*/
public class LogonForm extends ActionForm {

    private String username;
    private String password;

    public void setUsername(String name) {
        this.username = name;
    }
    public String getUsername() { return username; }

    public void setPassword(String password){
        this.password = password;
    }
    public String getPassword() { return password; }

    public ActionErrors validate(ActionMapping mapping,
                        HttpServletRequest request) {
        ActionErrors errors = new ActionErrors();
        if (username.trim().equals("")) {
            errors.add("username",
                new ActionError("edit.required", "username"));
        }
        if (password.trim().equals("")) {
            errors.add("password",
                new ActionError("edit.required", "password"));
        } else if (password.length() < 6) {
            errors.add("password", new ActionError(
                "edit.minlength", "password", "6"));
        }
        return errors;
    }
}
```

Once the form has been validated, the Struts `ActionServlet` will pass control to our `Action` class, which in this case is the `LogonAction` class shown in Listing 8.5. Only a single method, `perform()`, is needed in an `Action` class. The `perform()` method will be passed the `ActionMapping` element that configures the action (this is essentially a class that mirrors the information in the `action` element within `struts-config.xml`), plus the form bean, plus the servlet `request` and `response` objects.

In our `Action` class, we provide further validation of the input we received. Namely, we verify that the user name we received is really a user in our users database, and that the password is the correct password for the user. If all is okay, we want to pass control along to the main menu for the application; if there is any problem, we return the user to the logon screen. We could have hard-coded the URL paths for these two destinations into our `Action` class, but a much more flexible alternative is to specify target pages as part of the `ActionMapping` back in `struts-config.xml`. If you look at the `/Logon` mapping again (in Listing 8.2), you'll see that we have defined two `forward` targets, one named `pass` and the other named `fail`, each with a URL path. Our `Action` class can retrieve these paths from the `ActionMapping` class that is passed into our `perform()` method, using the `mapping.findForward(String name)` method. Note that the `perform()` method returns an `ActionForward` instance, so it is always the responsibility of the method to return as its result the next `Action` or page that should be executed. If we had not specified paths in our action mapping, we could write:

```
return new ActionForward("/url/of/next/page");
```

to return the desired page from our `perform()` method.

Listing 8.5 Logon Screen Action (`LogonAction.java`)

```
// LogonAction.java

package nfl.presentation.struts;

import nfl.ObjectFactory;
import nfl.application.Teams;

import java.io.IOException;
import java.util.List;

import javax.servlet.ServletException;
import javax.servlet.http.HttpServletRequest;
import javax.servlet.http.HttpServletResponse;
import javax.servlet.http.HttpSession;

import org.apache.struts.action.Action;
import org.apache.struts.action.ActionError;
import org.apache.struts.action.ActionErrors;
```

```
import org.apache.struts.action.ActionForm;
import org.apache.struts.action.ActionForward;
import org.apache.struts.action.ActionMapping;

public class LogonAction extends Action {

    private ActionErrors errors = new ActionErrors();

    public ActionForward perform(ActionMapping mapping,
                                 ActionForm     formin,
                                 HttpServletRequest request,
                                 HttpServletResponse response)
            throws IOException, ServletException {

        // Validate user
        LogonForm form = (LogonForm) formin;
        Users users = Users.getHandle();
        User  user  = users.getUser(form.getUsername());
        if (user == null) {
            errors.add("username", new ActionError(
                                "edit.nosuchuser"));
            saveErrors(request, errors);
            return mapping.findForward("fail");
        }
        if (!form.getPassword().equals(user.getPassword())) {
            errors.add("password", new ActionError(
                                "edit.badpassword"));
            saveErrors(request, errors);
            return mapping.findForward("fail");
        }
        HttpSession session = request.getSession();
        session.setAttribute("user", user);

        return mapping.findForward("pass");
    }
}
```

8.2.3   Keeping Track of Users

None of our previous examples have had any provision for a user logon, so we need to introduce some new classes at this point to help us keep track of them. A full-blown design following the pattern of our layered application would actually introduce six new classes at this point: A `User` interface and `UserImpl` class to represent the user; a `Users` interface and `UsersImpl` class to provide a collection of users, and then a `UserData` interface and `UserDataImpl` class to handle persistence. In the interest of brevity, I did not separate out the interfaces of these classes, nor has the persistence code been separated from the `Users` class. We can get by with just two classes: a `User` class shown in Listing 8.6, and a `Users` class shown in

Listing 8.7. These have been made part of the `nfl.presentation.struts` package for now, but should probably get refactored higher into the hierarchy (`nfl.application`) so they can be leveraged by other parts of the application. The operation of these is straightforward enough that I won't provide any additional explanation.

Listing 8.6 `User.java`

```
// User.java

package nfl.presentation.struts;

import java.io.Serializable;

/** An application user */
public class User implements Serializable {

    private String name;
    private String password;
    private String favTeam;
    private int    lastVisit; // week #
    // possibly add preferred output format

    public void setName(String name) { this.name = name; }
    public String getName() { return name; }

    public void setPassword(String password) {
        this.password = password;
    }
    public String getPassword() { return password; }

    public void setFavTeam(String favTeam) {
        this.favTeam = favTeam;
    }
    public String getFavTeam() { return favTeam; }

    public void setLastVisit(int lastVisit) {
        this.lastVisit = lastVisit;
    }
    public int getLastVisit() { return lastVisit; }
}
```

Listing 8.7 `Users.java`

```java
// Users.java

package nfl.presentation.struts;

import java.io.*;
import java.util.Map;
import java.util.HashMap;

/** An application user */
public class Users {

   // Apply the Singleton pattern
   private static Users users = new Users();
   public  static Users getHandle() { return users; }

   private Users() {
      load();
   }

   // Class content is a Map
   private Map userMap;
   public void setUserMap(Map l) { userMap = l; }
   public Map getUserMap() { return userMap; }

   public void addUser(User u) {
      userMap.put(u.getName(), u);
      save();
   }

   public User getUser(String name) {
      if (userMap == null) {
         return null;
      }
      return (User) userMap.get(name);
   }

   public void update() {
      save();
   }

   // Add some very primitive persistence
   private String filename = "user.list";
   private void load() {
      try {
      File data = new File(filename);
      if (data.exists()) {
```

```
            FileInputStream fis = new FileInputStream(data);
            ObjectInputStream ois = new ObjectInputStream(fis);
            setUserMap((Map) ois.readObject());
        } else {
            // Create new empty Map
            setUserMap(new HashMap());
        }
        } catch (IOException e1) { e1.printStackTrace();
        } catch (ClassNotFoundException e2) {
            e2.printStackTrace();
        }
    }

    private void save() {
        try {
        File data = new File(filename);
        if (!data.exists()) {
            data.createNewFile();
        }
        FileOutputStream fos = new FileOutputStream(data);
        ObjectOutputStream oos = new ObjectOutputStream(fos);
        oos.writeObject((Object) getUserMap());
        } catch (IOException e1) { e1.printStackTrace();
        }
    }
}
```

8.2.4   Handling Errors

We've seen in both the form bean and the action classes that there is a provision for generating errors during our processing. If we go back to our first JSP, in Listing 8.3, we see the `<html:errors />` tag that we didn't explain at the time. That tag will cause the `ActionErrors` object to be examined, and any errors contained there to be printed. So the first time the form is displayed, the `ActionErrors` object should be empty. But if we encounter problems in processing the form, we'll create `ActionError` objects for each error, add them to the `ActionErrors` collection, and then redisplay the form, this time with the errors shown. Figure 8.5 shows the result of trying to submit a blank form.

Let's go back to some earlier listings to examine how errors are generated. The `ActionErrors.add()` method takes two parameters: a field name and an `ActionError` object. In this way, we can associate our error messages with particular fields on the input form. In Listings 8.4 and 8.5, you'll see that we pass as the first parameter to the `add()` method either "username" or "password," depending on which field was in error. For the second parameter, we construct an `ActionError` object. `ActionErrors` are intended to be localizable, so rather than hard-coding the error messages, we use a resource name, and then the corresponding message is retrieved from the application resource file. We named our resource file `nfl.properties` (and informed

Struts of our choice through the web.xml file entry for the ActionServlet). This file is shown in Listing 8.8; we have defined seven different error messages that might be returned. Some error messages also have parameters in them, which are shown as numbers in curly braces. Struts allows up to four parameter replacements in a generated message; replacement values for the placeholders are passed to the ActionError constructor following the resource name.

Localized versions of the resource file can be produced for every locale in which you need the application to operate. These files will be given the same name as the default file, plus the locale name appended to the filename.

The validate() method in our form-bean returns an ActionErrors collection, so returning errors from this method is very straightforward. Returning errors from the perform() method of the action is only slightly more complicated; we must save the errors by invoking the saveErrors() method, specifying the HttpServletRequest and ActionErrors objects as parameters.

There is a final bit of housekeeping. The <html:errors> tag won't display anything at all unless it successfully locates errors.header and errors.footer resources in the resources file. We create entries for these two resources, providing some text for each and creating the start and stop tags for an unnumbered list. Each error found in the ActionErrors collection will automatically be formatted by Struts as an HTML list item (<LI>).

Listing 8.8 nfl.properties

```
# NFL Application Resources

# MessageResources
errors.header=<b>The logon could not be processed due \
              to the following errors:</b><ul>
errors.footer=</ul>Please correct these and re-submit.

# Field edit errors
edit.minlength=Minimum length of {0} is {1} characters<br>
edit.required=Field {0} is required<br>
edit.nomatch=Password fields must match
edit.nosuchuser=User not found
edit.duplicateuser=Username already in use, choose another
edit.badpassword=Password incorrect
edit.notloggedon=Hey, no fair bypassing the logon screen
```

Figure 8.5 A failed logon attempt.

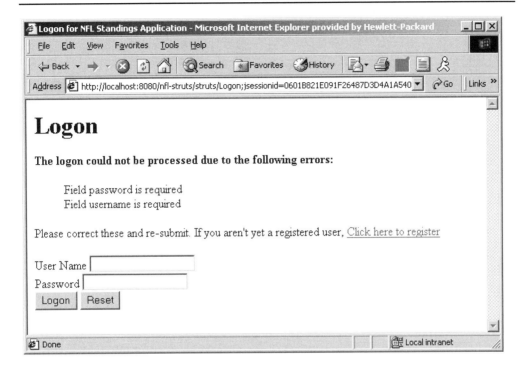

8.2.5   Adding a Registration Form

The logic of the `Logon` action expects to find a user already registered with our application. For users visiting our site for the first time, there needs to be a process to create a new user in the user list. The `Register` action takes care of this. The `Register` JSP page, form bean, and action are very similar to the `Logon` versions of the same elements, so I'll just present them here without further comment.

Listing 8.9 `register.jsp`

```
<!-- register.jsp, Struts version -->

<%@ taglib prefix="html" uri="/WEB-INF/struts-html.tld" %>

<html:html>
 <head>
  <title>Register for NFL Standings Application</title>
 </head>
 <body>
  <H1>Logon</H1>
```

```
<html:errors/>
<html:form action="/Register">
 User Name
  <html:text property="username" size="20" /><br>

 Password
  <html:password property="password" size="20" /><br>

 Repeat Password
  <html:password property="verify" size="20" /><br>

 <html:submit value="Register"/>
 <html:reset />

</html:form>
</body>
</html:html>
```

Listing 8.10 RegistrationForm.java

```
// RegistrationForm.java

package nfl.presentation.struts;

import javax.servlet.http.HttpServletRequest;
import javax.servlet.http.HttpServletResponse;

import org.apache.struts.action.ActionForm;
import org.apache.struts.action.ActionMapping;
import org.apache.struts.action.ActionError;
import org.apache.struts.action.ActionErrors;


/** Struts ActionForm for Registering */
public class RegistrationForm extends ActionForm {

    private String username;
    private String password;
    private String verify;

    public void setUsername(String name) {
        this.username = name;
    }
    public String getUsername() { return username; }

    public void setPassword(String password){
        this.password = password;
    }
```

```
   public String getPassword() { return password; }

   public void setVerify(String verify){
      this.verify = verify;
   }
   public String getVerify() { return verify; }

   public ActionErrors validate(ActionMapping mapping,
                        HttpServletRequest request) {
      ActionErrors errors = new ActionErrors();

      if (username.trim().equals("")) {
         errors.add("username",
            new ActionError("edit.required", "username"));
      }
      // Action is responsible for further tests - namely
      // that username isn't already in use.
      if (password.trim().equals("")) {
         errors.add("password",
            new ActionError("edit.required", "password"));
      } else if (password.length() < 6) {
         errors.add("password", new ActionError(
            "edit.minlength", "password", "6"));
      } else if (!password.equals(verify)) {
         errors.add("verify", new ActionError(
            "edit.nomatch"));
      }
      return errors;
   }
}
```

Listing 8.11 RegisterAction.java

```
// RegisterAction.java

package nfl.presentation.struts;

import nfl.ObjectFactory;
import nfl.application.Teams;

import java.io.IOException;
import java.util.List;

import javax.servlet.ServletException;
import javax.servlet.http.HttpServletRequest;
import javax.servlet.http.HttpServletResponse;
import javax.servlet.http.HttpSession;
```

```java
import org.apache.struts.action.Action;
import org.apache.struts.action.ActionError;
import org.apache.struts.action.ActionErrors;
import org.apache.struts.action.ActionForm;
import org.apache.struts.action.ActionForward;
import org.apache.struts.action.ActionMapping;

public class RegisterAction extends Action {

    public ActionForward perform(ActionMapping mapping,
                                 ActionForm    formin,
                                 HttpServletRequest request,
                                 HttpServletResponse response)
            throws IOException, ServletException {

        RegistrationForm form = (RegistrationForm) formin;
        Users users = Users.getHandle();
        User  user  = users.getUser(form.getUsername());

        ActionErrors errors = new ActionErrors();

        // Does username already exist?  If so, error.
        if (user != null) {
            errors.add("name", new ActionError(
                                 "edit.duplicateuser"));
            saveErrors(request, errors);
            return mapping.findForward("fail");
        }

        // Create new user and add.
        user = new User();
        user.setName(form.getUsername());
        user.setPassword(form.getPassword());
        users.addUser(user);

        HttpSession session = request.getSession();
        session.setAttribute("user", user);

        return mapping.findForward("pass");
    }
}
```

8.3   Handling User Preferences

For each user, we want to record their favorite team to be used in producing the output of the Favorite Team page. In earlier versions of the application, we didn't save this information and instead required the user to specify it as part of the page request each time they visited. The preferences.jsp page is used to set the team. A favorite team is selected from a list of all valid teams, which means we must prepare such a list before we can display the page. In Listing 8.12, we see the LoadTeamlistAction class that obtains a list of teams and places the list as a bean at application scope. (The same list of teams would be presented to any user who visited, so there is no need to restrict this to page or request scope.) The LoadTeamlistAction then forwards processing to the preferences.jsp page.

Listing 8.12 LoadTeamlistAction.java

```
// LoadTeamlistAction.java

package nfl.presentation.struts;

import nfl.ObjectFactory;
import nfl.application.Teams;
import nfl.application.Team;
import nfl.application.Game;
import nfl.application.Games;
import nfl.application.DynamicStandings;

import java.io.IOException;
import java.util.ArrayList;
import java.util.List;

import javax.servlet.ServletException;
import javax.servlet.http.HttpServletRequest;
import javax.servlet.http.HttpServletResponse;
import javax.servlet.http.HttpSession;

import org.apache.struts.action.Action;
import org.apache.struts.action.ActionForm;
import org.apache.struts.action.ActionForward;
import org.apache.struts.action.ActionMapping;

public class LoadTeamlistAction extends Action {

    private static Teams teams = null;
    private static List  teamList = null;
```

```
public ActionForward perform(ActionMapping mapping,
                             ActionForm     form,
                             HttpServletRequest request,
                             HttpServletResponse response)
        throws IOException, ServletException {

    if (teams == null) {
       teams = (Teams) ObjectFactory.getHandle().
                       getInstance("Teams");
       teamList = teams.getTeamList();
    }

    HttpSession session = request.getSession();
    session.setAttribute("teamList", teamList);

    // Return ActionForward for next page
    return mapping.findForward("next");
  }
}
```

Listing 8.13 shows the `preferences.jsp` page. As with the logon and registration pages, this page includes a form. The form on this page consists of just a single selection box, from which the user selects their favorite team (see Figure 8.6). The Struts tags make this a much cleaner operation than in our previous examples. Rather than having to write our own iteration code in an embedded scriptlet, or using a tag such as the JSPTL `forEach` tag, we can just use a single `<html:options>` tag. We provide the name of the collection we wish to iterate (`teamList`) and the property field to be used from each element in the iteration (`fullName`). The `<options>` tag must be enclosed within a `select` element. I used the `size=1` attribute on the `<select>` tag to force Struts to render the choice as a drop-down list; otherwise, it chose to display the selections in a scrollable text area, which I just didn't like as much. It's a purely cosmetic choice and you might prefer the Struts default.

Listing 8.13 `preferences.jsp`

```
<!-- preferences.jsp, Struts version -->

<%@ taglib prefix="html" uri="/WEB-INF/struts-html.tld" %>

<html:html>
 <head>
  <title>Preferences for Standings Application</title>
 </head>
 <body>
  <html:errors/>
  <H1>User Preferences</H1>
```

```
<html:form action="/Preferences">

  Favorite Team
   <html:select property="favorite" size="1" >
    <html:options collection="teamList"
                  property="fullName" />
   </html:select>

  <html:submit />
  <html:reset  />

 </html:form>
 </body>
</html:html>
```

Figure 8.6 The `preferences.jsp` form.

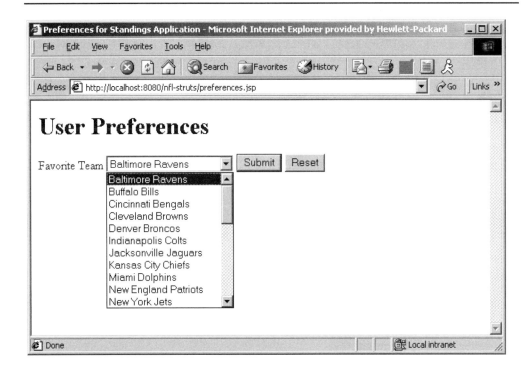

The code that handles this form shouldn't contain any surprises by this point. The `Pref-erencesForm` form bean contains only a single property. The `PreferencesAction` action class retrieves the `User` bean from session scope (where it will have been placed by either the `Register` or `Logon` action) and updates it with the preference information. Also, we invoke the update() method of the Users collection to make the choice persistent (this will force the User element to be rewritten to disk). Control is then passed to the MainPage HTML page.

Listing 8.14 PreferencesForm.java

```java
// PreferencesForm.java

package nfl.presentation.struts;

import javax.servlet.http.HttpServletRequest;
import javax.servlet.http.HttpServletResponse;

import org.apache.struts.action.ActionForm;
import org.apache.struts.action.ActionMapping;
import org.apache.struts.action.ActionError;
import org.apache.struts.action.ActionErrors;


/** Struts ActionForm for setting user prefs */
public class PreferencesForm extends ActionForm {

    private String favorite;
    public void setFavorite(String favorite){
        this.favorite = favorite;
    }
    public String getFavorite() { return favorite; }
}
```

Listing 8.15 PreferencesAction.java

```java
// PreferencesAction.java

package nfl.presentation.struts;

import java.io.IOException;

import javax.servlet.ServletException;
import javax.servlet.http.HttpServletRequest;
import javax.servlet.http.HttpServletResponse;
import javax.servlet.http.HttpSession;

import org.apache.struts.action.Action;
import org.apache.struts.action.ActionForm;
import org.apache.struts.action.ActionForward;
import org.apache.struts.action.ActionMapping;
```

```
public class PreferencesAction extends Action {

   public ActionForward perform(ActionMapping mapping,
                                ActionForm     formin,
                                HttpServletRequest request,
                                HttpServletResponse response)
          throws IOException, ServletException {

      PreferencesForm form = (PreferencesForm) formin;

      // Make preferences available for duration of session
      HttpSession session = request.getSession();
      User user = (User) session.getAttribute("user");
      user.setFavTeam(form.getFavorite());
      user.setLastVisit(0);
      Users.getHandle().update();

      // Return ActionForward for next page
      return new ActionForward("/MainPage.html");
   }

}
```

8.4   Getting Favorite Team Information from Struts

Our `MainPage` form is rendered as HTML, rather than a JSP, just to show that it is possible to mix and match. By doing so, we eliminate the possibility of using any tag libraries, so we must revert to "vanilla" HTML syntax.

Listing 8.16 `MainPage.html`

```
<HTML>
<HEAD>
<TITLE>NFL Standings Main Page</TITLE>
</HEAD>

<BODY>
<H1>Select a Function</H1>
<a href="/nfl-struts/struts/FavoriteTeam">
        Show Favorite Team Status</a><br>
<a href="/nfl-struts/struts/LoadTeamlist">
        Change User Preference Settings</a><br>
</BODY>
</HTML>
```

The `FavoriteTeamAction` class is a little different than the `Actions` we've seen so far. Here, we are preparing output, rather than processing input. We could attach several individual fields to the appropriate context to be picked up by our JSP, but Struts is designed around the concept of passing beans between the forms and the actions, so we'll follow that design. We create a new bean, the `FavoriteTeamBean`, to transfer data between the action and the JSP, and the `FavoriteTeamAction` is responsible for populating the fields of this bean.

The `FavoriteTeamAction` retrieves the `User` bean for our session, and then interacts with various classes of the `Standings` application to get the values needed for the `Favorite-TeamBean`. Once the fields are populated, we update the `User` bean to reflect their latest visit to the page, since part of the displayed output is games played since the last visit.

When all the `FavoriteTeamBean` properties are set, we add the bean to the session context using the name "favorite," and then pass control to the JSP.

Listing 8.17 `FavoriteTeamAction.java`

```
// FavoriteTeamAction.java

package nfl.presentation.struts;

import nfl.ObjectFactory;
import nfl.application.Teams;
import nfl.application.Team;
import nfl.application.Game;
import nfl.application.Games;
import nfl.application.DynamicStandings;

import java.io.IOException;
import java.util.ArrayList;
import java.util.List;

import javax.servlet.ServletException;
import javax.servlet.http.HttpServletRequest;
import javax.servlet.http.HttpServletResponse;
import javax.servlet.http.HttpSession;

import org.apache.struts.action.Action;
import org.apache.struts.action.ActionForm;
import org.apache.struts.action.ActionForward;
import org.apache.struts.action.ActionMapping;

public class FavoriteTeamAction extends Action {

    private static Teams teams = null;
    private static Games games = null;
    private static DynamicStandings standings = null;
```

```
public ActionForward perform(ActionMapping mapping,
                             ActionForm    form,
                             HttpServletRequest request,
                             HttpServletResponse response)
    throws IOException, ServletException {

  if (teams == null) {
     teams = (Teams) ObjectFactory.getHandle().
                  getInstance("Teams");
     games = (Games) ObjectFactory.getHandle().
                  getInstance("Games");
     standings = (DynamicStandings) ObjectFactory.
         getHandle().getInstance("DynamicStandings");
     standings.init();
  }

  // Where favorite.jsp will look for data
  FavoriteTeamBean bean = new FavoriteTeamBean();

  HttpSession session = request.getSession();
  User  user       = (User) session.getAttribute("user");
  String teamname  = user.getFavTeam();
  int lastVisit    = user.getLastVisit();
  Team team        = teams.getTeam(teamname);
  List allGames    = games.getAllGamesFor(teamname);

  bean.setTeam(team);
  int newLastVisit = lastVisit;
  List newGames =  new ArrayList();
  for (int i=0; i<allGames.size(); i++) {
     Game g = (Game) allGames.get(i);
     if (g.getWeek() > lastVisit)
        newGames.add(g);
     if (g.getWeek() > newLastVisit)
        newLastVisit = g.getWeek();
  }
  bean.setGames(newGames);
  user.setLastVisit(newLastVisit);
  Users.getHandle().update();

  List divStandings = standings.getDivisionStandings(
                            team.getDivision());
  List confStandings = standings.getConferenceStandings(
                            team.getConference());

  for (int i=0; i<divStandings.size(); i++) {
     Team rankedTeam = (Team) divStandings.get(i);
     if (rankedTeam.getFullName().equals(
                            team.getFullName())) {
```

```
            bean.setDivRank(i+1);
            break;
        }
    }

    for (int i=0; i<confStandings.size(); i++) {
        Team rankedTeam = (Team) confStandings.get(i);
        if (rankedTeam.getFullName().equals(
                               team.getFullName())) {
            bean.setConfRank(i+1);
            break;
        }
    }

    bean.setDivStatus(
        team.getDivisionChampStatus().toString() +
            " division championship");
    bean.setWildcardStatus(
        team.getWildcardStatus().toString() +
            " wildcard berth");
    bean.setHomefieldStatus(
        team.getHomeFieldStatus().toString() +
            " home field advantage");

    session.setAttribute("favorite", bean);

    // Return ActionForward for next page
    return new ActionForward("/favorite.jsp");
    }
}
```

Listing 8.18 FavoriteTeamBean.java

```
// FavoriteTeamBean.java

package nfl.presentation.struts;

import nfl.application.Team;

import java.util.List;

public class FavoriteTeamBean {

    private Team team;
    private List games;
    private int divRank;
    private int confRank;
    private String divStatus;
```

```
    private String wildcardStatus;
    private String homefieldStatus;

    public void setTeam(Team team) { this.team = team; }
    public Team getTeam() { return team; }

    public void setGames(List games) {
        this.games = games;
    }
    public List getGames() { return games; }

    public void setDivRank(int rank) { divRank = rank; }
    public int getDivRank() { return divRank; }

    public void setConfRank(int rank) { confRank = rank; }
    public int getConfRank() { return confRank; }

    public void setDivStatus(String status) {
        divStatus = status;
    }
    public String getDivStatus() { return divStatus; }

    public void setWildcardStatus(String status) {
        wildcardStatus = status;
    }
    public String getWildcardStatus() {
        return wildcardStatus;
    }

    public void setHomefieldStatus(String status) {
        homefieldStatus = status;
    }
    public String getHomefieldStatus() {
        return homefieldStatus;
    }
}
```

Listing 8.19 shows the final piece of the Struts application, the Favorite Team JSP. Unlike our other JSPs, which have used only the Struts HTML tags, this page uses tags from the bean and logic libraries as well. From the bean tag library, we use the `<write>` tag, which allows us to display as output properties of a bean. The `<bean:write>` tag allows us to specify a bean name and a property name in a syntax that is more straightforward than the combination of `<jsp:useBean>` and `<jsp:getProperty>` tags from the JSP standard.

From the struts-logic library, we use the `<iterate>` tag to iterate over the games that have been played. This one is rather tricky; we're selecting the `property` named `games` from the bean named `favorite`; that much is straightforward. But the games element is itself a class, so we specify its `type` as `nfl.application.Game`. Finally, we need to give an `id` by which members of the collection can be accessed in any tags that we nest between the `<iterate>` and `</iterate>` tags; so we'll give the `id` of `game` to each member of the collection.

Inside the iteration, we display the fields of each `game` element, with very little added formatting. One notable feature is that the Struts designers apparently have read the JavaBeans specification and acknowledged the existence of indexed properties, so we no longer have to jump through hoops to retrieve the values of our score property.

Listing 8.19 `favorite.jsp`

```
<!-- favorite.jsp, Struts version -->

<%@ taglib prefix="html" uri="/WEB-INF/struts-html.tld" %>
<%@ taglib prefix="bean" uri="/WEB-INF/struts-bean.tld" %>
<%@ taglib prefix="logic" uri="/WEB-INF/struts-logic.tld" %>

<html:html>
 <head>
  <title>Favorite Team Status</title>
 </head>
 <body>
  <html:errors/>
  <H1>Recent Results for
    <bean:write name="favorite" property="team.fullName" />
  </H1>

  <H2>Games played since your last visit</H2>
    <logic:iterate name="favorite" property="games"
                   id="game" type="nfl.application.Game">
      Week
      <bean:write name="game" property="week"/>
      <bean:write name="game" property="visitor"/>
      <bean:write name="game" property="score[0]"/> ,
      <bean:write name="game" property="home"/>
      <bean:write name="game" property="score[1]"/><br>
    </logic:iterate>

  <H2>Division Standing</H2>
    <bean:write name="favorite" property="team.name" />
    are ranked
    <bean:write name="favorite" property="divRank" />
    in the
    <bean:write name="favorite" property="team.division" />
    <br>
    <bean:write name="favorite" property="divStatus" />

  <H2>Conference Standing</H2>
    <bean:write name="favorite" property="team.name" />
    are ranked
```

```
    <bean:write name="favorite" property="confRank" />
    in the
    <bean:write name="favorite" property="team.conference"/>
    <br>
    <bean:write name="favorite" property="homefieldStatus"/>
    <br>
    <bean:write name="favorite" property="wildcardStatus" />
    <br>

  <html:link href="/nfl-struts/MainPage.html">
    Return to main page
  </html:link>
 </body>
</html:html>
```

Figure 8.7 Output for `favorite.jsp`.

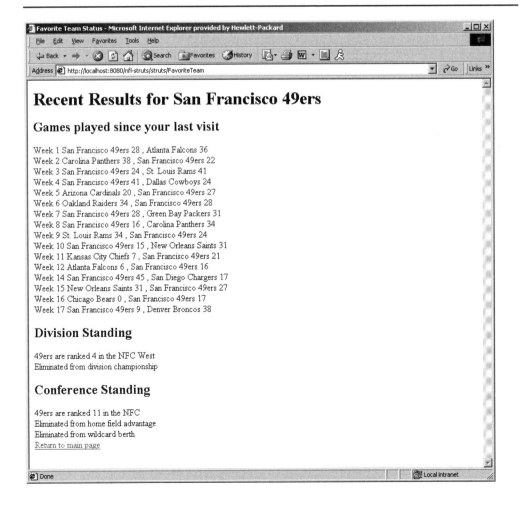

API 8.2 Struts Bean tags

`<cookie>`	Defines a variable based on contents of the cookie
`<define>`	Defines a variable based on contents of the specified bean property
`<header>`	Defines a variable based on contents of the request header
`<include>`	Makes a dynamic request and captures the output as a bean
`<message>`	Generates a localized message
`<page>`	Makes an item from the page context visible as a bean
`<parameter>`	Defines a variable based on a request parameter
`<resource>`	Loads a Web application resource and makes it visible as a bean
`<size>`	Defines a variable representing the number of entries in a Collection
`<struts>`	Makes struts configuration object accessible as a bean
`<write>`	Writes the value of the bean property to the JspWriter

API 8.3 Struts Logic tags

`<empty>`	Evaluates tag body if specified variable is null or empty
`<equal>`	Evaluates tag body if specified variable is equal to specified constant
`<forward>`	Forwards control to specified page
`<greaterEqual>`	Evaluates tag body if specified variable is >= specified constant
`<greaterThan>`	Evaluates tag body if specified variable is > specified constant
`<iterate>`	Evaluates tag body for each member of a collection
`<lessEqual>`	Evaluates tag body if specified variable is <= specified constant
`<lessThan>`	Evaluates tag body if specified variable is < specified constant
`<match>`	Evaluates tag body if specified value is appropriate substring of variable
`<messagesNotPresent>`	Evaluates tag body if no messages have been attached to the specified context object
`<messagesPresent>`	Evaluates tag body if messages are attached to the specified context object
`<notEmpty>`	Evaluates tag body if the specified variable is not null or empty
`<notEqual>`	Evaluates tag body if specified variable is not equal to specified constant
`<notMatch>`	Evaluates tag body if specified value is not an appropriate substring of specified variable
`<notPresent>`	Evaluates tag body if specified value is not present in this request
`<present>`	Evaluates tag body if specified value is present in this request
`<redirect>`	Redirects the request to the specified URL

API 8.4 Struts Template tags

`<insert>`	Includes a JSP template file
`<put>`	Puts specified content into request scope
`<get>`	Gets content from request scope that was placed there by <put>

8.5   Building, Installing, and Running the Struts Application

Listing 8.20 presents the Ant buildfile for this version of the application. There isn't anything really new here; I'll just point out as reminders that we need `struts.jar` on the CLASSPATH as we compile, and also need it deployed as part of the application. We also copy three of the four struts tag library descriptor files into `WEB-INF/` directory (we didn't use anything from `struts-template.tld`). The implementations of these tags are all in `struts.jar`, so no need to install anything else for the tag libraries.

Listing 8.20 Ant Buildfile for Struts Version of Example Application

```
<project name="nfl-struts" default="war" basedir=".">

<property name="servlet.jar" value="../../../servlet.jar" />
<property name="struts.jar"  value="struts.jar" />

<target name="compile">
   <javac srcdir="."
      classpath="${struts.jar}:${servlet.jar}">
      <include name="*.java" />
   </javac>
</target>

<target name="nfl-struts-jar" depends="compile" >
   <delete file="nfl-struts.jar" />
   <jar jarfile="nfl-struts.jar" >
      <fileset dir="." includes="nfl.properties" />
      <zipfileset dir="." includes="*.class"
         prefix="nfl/presentation/struts" />
   </jar>
</target>

<target name="war" depends="nfl-struts-jar">
   <delete file="nfl-struts.war" />
   <war warfile="nfl-struts.war" webxml="web.xml" >
      <webinf dir="." includes="struts-config.xml" />
      <webinf dir="." includes="struts-*.tld" />
      <fileset dir="."
         includes="MainPage.html,*.jsp" />
      <lib dir="../.." includes="layered.jar" />
      <lib dir="."     includes="struts.jar" />
      <lib dir="."     includes="nfl-struts.jar" />
      <classes dir="../../application/servlet"
         includes="ServletTwo*.class,
                   ServletThree*.class"
            prefix="WEB-INF/classes/nfl/application/servlet" />
```

```
        <classes dir="../../application"
            includes="DynamicStandings*.class,
                      AsyncMessagingImpl.class,
                      BeansGameImpl.class"
            prefix="WEB-INF/classes/nfl/application" />
        <classes dir=".."
            includes="HTML.class"
                prefix="WEB-INF/classes/nfl/presentation" />
    </war>
</target>

<target name="clean">
  <delete>
    <fileset dir="." includes="nfl-struts.jar" />
    <fileset dir="." includes="*.war" />
    <fileset dir="." includes="*.class" />
  </delete>
</target>

</project>
```

8.6   Other Frameworks

Struts is far from being the only such framework product available. However, it seems to be by far the most popular, so if you only have time to learn one, this is probably a good choice. The Apache Jakarta project also has, for example, the Turbine framework (which looks to provide a number of reusable components useful in building Web sites). From the XML side of Apache (http://xml.apache.org), there is the Cocoon framework, which is built around a concept of processing "pipelines" where various components can be strung together to build up complex processes out of small reusable parts.

8.7   Exercises

8.1 Use struts-logic tags: Incorporate one or more struts-logic tags into some of the JSP pages, perhaps printing different messages for teams meeting particular criteria (undefeated teams, winless teams, and so forth).

8.8   Further Reading

The home page for the Struts framework is http://jakarta.apache.org/struts. In addition to software downloads and documentation, you'll find mailing lists and links to many other references.

The HP Application Server (HP-AS) includes trail maps that provide an introductory-level tutorial to Struts.

CHAPTER 9

Web Presentation with XML and XSLT

XML shows up in every section of this book, just as it seems to be showing up in every imaginable place in information technology. In this chapter, we'll see how XML can be used to create a user interface that can support multiple types of devices. In later chapters, we'll see how it can be used to provide messaging and remote procedure call capabilities in distributed applications. We've already seen XML used for deployment descriptors and Ant buildfiles. It is truly becoming the universal format for portable data representation.

Whether XML will continue to expand into every aspect of computing remains to be seen. Perhaps we're just going through a cycle of XML hype and in a few years it will be relegated to a few uses for which it's particularly well-suited. Or it could go the other direction, and continue to be used in increasingly inappropriate roles. We provide an opportunity for you to push XML in the latter direction in the exercises at the end of this chapter.

In Chapter 4 we took a very brief look at XML, but without any regard to how an XML document is created or how it is parsed and used by programs. One nice thing about XML is that it is human-readable, and many XML documents (such as our `web.xml` deployment descriptors and Ant buildfiles) are simply created using text editors rather than any XML-generation software. But because this book isn't about teaching you to use a text editor, we're going to introduce some other tools now.

Software Used in This Chapter

Xerces XML Processor

From the Apache group. Downloadable from `http://xml.apache.org`. Includes support for DOM, SAX, and JAXP. Version 2.0 was used for the examples in this chapter and is included on the enclosed CD.

Xalan XSLT Engine

From the Apache group. Downloadable from `http://xml.apache.org`. Includes support for XSLT transformations. Version 2.2 was used for the examples in this chapter and is included on the enclosed CD.

JAXP

The Java API for XML Parsing. Included with the Xerces software from Apache, or can be downloaded separately from `http://java.sun.com/xml/`.

JDOM

Version 1.0 Beta 7, downloaded from `http://www.jdom.org`.

9.1 XML Acronyms FYI: An XML Glossary with References

Every area of information technology is replete with its set of acronyms, but perhaps in no other area has it been carried to the ridiculous extremes seen in the arena of XML processing. Before we can get into any serious discussion of XML, you'll need to consult the secret decoder ring, which has been transformed into a printed glossary for your convenience.

DOM   The Document Object Model. This is a specification provided by the World Wide Web Consortium (W3C) that specifies the in-memory representation of an XML document. Specification and additional information are at `http://www.w3.org/DOM`.

JAXB   The Java Architecture for XML Binding. This still-under-development specification will provide an API for mapping XML documents to Java objects. The specification is being developed under JSR-031. Further details can be found at `http://java.sun.com/xml/jaxb/index.html`.

JAXM   The Java API for XML Messaging. JAXM is intended to provide APIs for applications to use to send and receive XML-formatted messages. The JAXM APIs are built on the SOAP messaging protocol. The JAXM specification is currently in proposed final-draft status. The specification is being developed under JSR-067. Additional information is available at `http://java.sun.com/xml/jaxm/index.html`.

JAXP   The Java API for XML Processing. A specification from Sun to provide Java access to DOM, SAX, and XSLT. The original 1.0 version of the API provided support from DOM Level 1 and SAX-1. The current 1.1 version of the API supports DOM level 2 and SAX-2. Further details can be found at `http://java.sun.com/xml/jaxp/index.html`.

JAXR   The Java API for XML Registries. Currently there are several competing technologies for publishing XML information in registries. Being able to access a registry to find information about services offered is a key component of making Web Services available. Technologies in use for XML registries include UDDI, ebXML, and several others. JAXR provides an abstraction to permit Java applications to access data in registries regardless of the underlying technology used. The specification is being developed under JSR-093. Further information can be found at `http://java.sun.com/xml/jaxr/index.html`.

JAX-RPC   The Java API for XML-based Remote Procedure Calls. This set of APIs is also built on top of the SOAP protocol. JAX-RPC can be used to implement Web Services that are described via WSDL (go ahead and look, I'll wait). The specification is being developed under JSR-101. Further information is at `http://java.sun.com/xml/jaxrpc/index.html`.

JAX*   The name given to the various Java XML APIs, when taken as a group. See Table 9.1 for details of the APIs included in this designation.

JDOM   A DOM-like API for parsing API documents, specifically created for Java. An independent effort to make processing XML from Java easier. Originally started by Jason Hunter and Brett McLaughlin. Now under control of JSR-102. See `http://www.jdom.org`. At the insistence of Sun's trademark attorneys, the "J" in JDOM doesn't stand for anything.

SAX   Simple API for XML Processing. An event-driven way of parsing an XML document. The project Web site is `http://www.saxproject.org`.

SOAP   Simple Object Access Protocol. A mechanism for using XML across the network, including messaging and remote procedure call flavors. Additional information is at `http://www.w3.org/2000/xp/`.

UDDI   Uniform Description, Discovery, and Integration. Essentially, a dating service for Web applications. Provides mechanisms to register Web Services, and to search the registered services for ones meeting your requirements. See `http://www.uddi.org`.

WSDL   Web Services Description Language. An XML language used to describe a Web Service. This will be covered in Chapter 17.

XML   The eXtensible Markup Language. See `http://www.w3.org/XML`.

XPath   Not an acronym. XML Path language, A W3C standard for an expression language used in XSL stylesheets. See `http://www.w3.org/TR/xpath`.

XSL   eXtensible Stylesheet Language. A W3C standard for presenting XML. XSL consists of three parts: XSLT (XSL Transformations), XPath (an expression language), and XSL-FO (XSL Formatting Objects). XSL-FO is more print-oriented (for example, converting XML to PDF or PostScript) and won't be covered in this book, but both XSLT and XPath will be shown in examples in this chapter. More information is at `http://www.w3.org/Style/XSL/`.

XSLT   XSL Transformations. A W3C standard for transforming XML documents. Information is included on the XSL page listed just above, or go directly to the specification at `http://www.w3.org/TR/xslt`.

Table 9.1 shows the various Java APIs that are currently available or under development for processing XML documents.

Table 9.1   JAX* at a Glance

API Package	Subject Area	JSR	Status
JAXP 1.1	Processing	JSR-063	In SDK 1.4, J2EE 1.3.
JAXB	Binding	JSR-031	Pre-1.0. Will be an optional add-on to the Java SDK.
JAXR	Registries	JSR-093	Pre-1.0. May be standard in a future J2SE or J2EE release, optional until then.
JAX-RPC	Remote Procedure Calls	JSR-101	Pre-1.0. Will be an optional add-on to the Java SDK.
JAXM	Messaging	JSR-067	Pre-1.0. Will be an optional add-on to the Java SDK.

9.2   XML Processors and JAXP

There were a number of XML processors for Java before Sun jumped in and developed the Java API for XML Parsing (JAXP). The different processors were even mostly interchangeable, because they adhered to the standards for DOM and SAX. But there was one significant area in which you would need to change your code depending upon the processor you used. The import statements and creation of the processor itself tended to be vendor-specific.

For example, let's look at the code for creating a DOM parser with and without JAXP:

```
//Creating a DOM Parser prior to JAXP
import org.apache.xerces.parsers.DOMParser;

public class myClass {
      public static void main(String[] args) {
          DOMParser parser = new DOMParser();
          // use it . . .
```

This is simple and straightforward, but completely locks us in to the Apache Xerces parser. If we want to use a different parser, we'll need to change at least our import statement and recompile. Now let's see how we would do this with JAXP:

```
//Creating a DOM Parser using JAXP APIs
import javax.xml.parsers.DocumentBuilder;
import javax.xml.parsers.DocumentBuilderFactory;
import javax.xml.parsers.ParserConfigurationException;

public class myClass {
      public static void main(String[] args) {
          DocumentBuilder parser;
          DocumentBuilderFactory factory =
              DocumentBuilderFactory.newInstance();
          try {
              parser = factory.newDocumentBuilder();
          } catch (ParserConfigurationException pce) {
              // handle errors
          }
          // continue processing . . .
```

Obviously, this required a bit more code, but the operation is very straightforward. All JAXP-conforming processors will use exactly the same imports and the same APIs for getting an instance of the parser. A few other things, such as return types for some methods, are also standardized with JAXP-conforming processors. Each processor will provide a default parser that will get instantiated by default. There is also a property that can be set to cause a different factory to be used (and thereby most likely causing a different parser to be instantiated). The property name is `javax.xml.parsers.DocumentBuilderFactory`. The property can be set on the Java command line using the –D option, or programmatically using `setProperty`. (If you aren't familiar with `setProperty()`, see any of the servlet classes from Chapter 5 for examples of setting a system property programmatically.)

We haven't covered the Simple API for XML (SAX) yet, but because JAXP provides a nearly identical facility for creating a SAX processor, we'll go ahead and cover it here. Further details about using SAX are in Chapter 14.

The pre-JAXP method of getting a SAX processor is as follows:

```
//SAX processing, pre-JAXP
import org.xml.sax.XMLReader;   // this much is portable
import org.apache.xerces.parsers.SAXParser; // this isn't

public class MyClass {
      public static void main(String[] args) {
         XMLReader parser = new SAXParser();
         // and so it goes . . .
```

One nice thing about the JAXP syntax is that it brings the method of getting a DOM and SAX processor much closer together. This code should look quite familiar:

```
//JAX does SAX
import javax.xml.parsers.SAXParser;
import javax.xml.parsers.SAXParserFactory;
import javax.xml.parsers.ParserConfigurationException;

public class MyClass {
      public static void main(String[] args) {
         SAXParser parser;
         SAXParserFactory factory =
            SAXParserFactory.newInstance();
         try {
            parser = factory.newSAXParser();
         } catch (ParserConfigurationException pce) {
            // handle errors
         }
         // continue . . .
```

As you might expect, you can set the property `javax.xml.parsers.SAXParser-Factory` to cause a different factory than the default to be returned.

9.3   Creating an XML Document with DOM

We've already generated both plain text and HTML output from our Standings application. Now, we'd like to generate XML as output. In order to do so, we must design our XML format. What will be the elements and attributes included in the document?

With our previous output formats, we were generating exactly what we wanted the user to see. With XML, the situation is somewhat different. Although it is possible to view the XML directly in a browser, we really expect the XML to be transformed to another form, such as HTML or WML (Wireless Markup Language), before the user sees it. In our earlier designs, we chose to show some fields and not show others. In the XML output, we want to include everything, and defer the decision of what's important to the later step of transforming the XML. Table 9.2 shows the components that will be used in this version of the application.

Table 9.2   Components in the DOM Output Formatter

New Components			
Name	**Package**	**Class or Interface**	**Comment**
XML	nfl.presentation.xml	Class	Produces Standings in XML format using DOM APIs.

Existing Components	
Component	**Description**
layered.jar	All classes and interfaces of the layered version of the application (as presented in Chapter 2).

Our earlier output had a set of division standings, with lots of detail, and then a set of conference standings, with very little detail. In our XML document, we'll still have both a division and a conference standing list, but all detail will be placed in a third area, named teams. Figure 9.1 shows the basic structure of our document: a single root element (as required) named standings, under which there are three elements named divisionStandings, conferenceStandings, and teams.

Listing 9.1 shows an abbreviated version of the standings XML document that we'll be generating. You can look back and forth between Figure 9.1 and Listing 9.1 to verify that the structure is the same. The divisionStandings element is made up of divisions, and the conferenceStandings element is made up of conferences. The division or conference elements each have a single attribute, their name, and then have child elements that are teams. Each team element has a rank attribute and a child element containing the name.

The teams element is made up of teamDetails subelements. Unlike the team elements in the division or conference standings, these are detailed, containing as elements all of the class properties needed to produce either the division or the conference standings. This way we avoid duplicating any information between the conference and division standings other than the team name. Thinking ahead, it's obvious that when we produce user-readable output, we'll be using the team name elements in the rankings to pull details from the teams area of the document.

Figure 9.1   The element hierarchy of the Standings XML document.

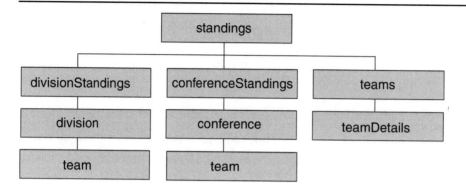

Listing 9.1   Standings Formatted as an XML Document

```xml
<?xml version="1.0" encoding="UTF-8"?>
<standings>
   <divisionStandings>
      <division name="AFC East">
         <team rank="1">
            <name>Miami Dolphins</name>
         </team>
         <team rank="2">
            <name>Indianapolis Colts</name>
         </team>
         <!-- other teams deleted -->
      </division>
      <!-- other divisions deleted -->
   </divisionStandings>
   <conferenceStandings>
      <conference name="AFC">
         <team rank="1">
            <name>Tennessee Titans</name>
         </team>
         <team rank="2">
            <name>Oakland Raiders</name>
         </team>
         <!-- other teams deleted -->
      </conference>
      <!-- NFC conference standings deleted -->
   </conferenceStandings>
   <teams>
      <teamDetails>
         <name>Baltimore Ravens</name>
         <wins>12</wins>
```

```
                    <losses>4</losses>
                    <ties>0</ties>
                    <divisionWins>8</divisionWins>
                    <divisionLosses>2</divisionLosses>
                    <DivisionTies>0</DivisionTies>
                    <conferenceWins>10</conferenceWins>
                    <conferenceLosses>3</conferenceLosses>
                    <conferenceTies>0</conferenceTies>
                    <points>333</points>
                    <pointsAllowed>165</pointsAllowed>
                    <winLossPct>0.75</winLossPct>
                    <divWinLossPct>-1.0</divWinLossPct>
                    <confWinLossPct>-1.0</confWinLossPct>
                    <netPoints>-1</netPoints>
                    <divNetPoints>-1</divNetPoints>
                    <confNetPoints>-1</confNetPoints>
                    <streak>7</streak>
                    <divChampStatus>Eliminated</divChampStatus>
                    <homeFieldStatus>Eliminated</homeFieldStatus>
                    <wildcardStatus>Clinched</wildcardStatus>
            </teamDetails>
            <!-- other teams deleted -->
        </teams>
</standings>
```

So let's jump right in and see how we create this document. In Listing 9.2, we have the first portion of the new XML class that we'll add to the application. Our single program will take care of both generating the XML seen earlier, as well as transforming that XML to a format that we select. Initially, our transformation is basically a no-op in terms of changing any formatting, but the step is required nonetheless. The Document Object Model only standardizes the in-memory representation of an XML document; if we want to read a document from, or write it to, an external source, then we have to do a XSL transformation of the document to a streamable representation.

In Listing 9.2, we include the `javax.xml.parsers` classes we'll need to create our document, and the `javax.xml.transform` classes we'll need to output it. These are all JAXP classes that make our code portable; we could have also used vendor-specific imports of classes that function identically but at the loss of portability.

After grabbing a standings class to generate results for us, and initializing its data, we only have two method calls to make from our `main()` method. `generateXMLDocument()` generates the XML document that conforms to the layout shown in Listing 9.1. Then `transform-XMLDocument()` transforms it to the selected output format. The `transformXMLDocument()` method takes three arguments: an XML source (typically either a `DOMSource` or a `SAXSource`), an XSL stylesheet which guides the transformation, and an XML result (`DOMResult`, `SAXResult`, or `StreamResult`). At this point, we'll just pass a null for the stylesheet. But you'll notice that we've built in the capability to pass in a stylesheet argument on the command line, and we'll use this later on to do more interesting transformations of the document. The default transformation provides a version of the document that we can write to an output stream, which is System.out wrapped in a StreamResult in this case.

Listing 9.2 XML.java (Part 1 of 4)

```
// XML.java

package nfl.presentation.xml;

import nfl.ObjectFactory;
import nfl.application.*;

// J2SE imports
import java.io.PrintWriter;
import java.util.List;
import java.util.Properties;

// W3C DOM imports
import org.w3c.dom.Document;
import org.w3c.dom.Element;

// JAXP imports
import javax.xml.parsers.DocumentBuilder;
import javax.xml.parsers.DocumentBuilderFactory;
import javax.xml.parsers.ParserConfigurationException;
import javax.xml.transform.Result;
import javax.xml.transform.Source;
import javax.xml.transform.TransformerFactory;
import javax.xml.transform.Transformer;
import javax.xml.transform.TransformerException;
import javax.xml.transform.TransformerConfigurationException;
import javax.xml.transform.dom.DOMSource;
import javax.xml.transform.stream.StreamSource;
import javax.xml.transform.stream.StreamResult;

/** Produces XML document of standings. Supports
  * plug-in transformers for rendering XML
  * into various formats
  */
public class XML
{
    private DynamicStandings standings;
    private Document   doc = null;
```

```
public static void main(String[] args) {

    XML xml = new XML();
    String stylesheet = null;

    Properties p = System.getProperties();
    if (p.getProperty("nfl.versioninfo") == null) {
      p.setProperty("nfl.versioninfo",
        "nfl.presentation.xml.XMLVersionInfo");
    }

    for (int i=0; i<args.length; i++) {
        if (args[i].equals("-xsl"))  {
           stylesheet = args[++i];
        } else {
           System.err.println("Usage: " +
           "java nfl.presentation.xml.XML [options]\n\n" +
           "where options include\n" +
           " -xsl <stylesheet>");
           System.exit(-1);
        }
    }

    xml.init();

    Source standingsdoc = xml.generateXMLDocument();
    xml.transformXMLDocument(standingsdoc, stylesheet,
        new StreamResult(new PrintWriter(System.out)));
 }

public void init() {
    standings =  (DynamicStandings)
      ObjectFactory.getHandle().getInstance(
                             "DynamicStandings");
    standings.init();
}

// Only used when invoking XML class from another
// source (i.e., not via main()), to allow an
// externally created & initialized Standings object
// to be used as basis for generating XML document.
public void setStandings(DynamicStandings s) {
    standings = s;
}

public Source generateXMLDocument() {
    DocumentBuilderFactory df      = null;
    DocumentBuilder        builder = null;
```

```
df = DocumentBuilderFactory.newInstance();
try {
    builder = df.newDocumentBuilder();
} catch (ParserConfigurationException pce) {
    pce.printStackTrace();
    return null;
}

doc = builder.newDocument();

Element stElement = doc.createElement("standings");
doc.appendChild(stElement);

Element dsElement = getDivisionStandings();
Element csElement = getConferenceStandings();
Element teamsElement = getTeams();

stElement.appendChild(dsElement);
stElement.appendChild(csElement);
stElement.appendChild(teamsElement);

return new DOMSource(doc);
}
```

The other method that is shown in Listing 9.2 is the `generateXMLDocument()` method. Here we instantiate a `DocumentBuilder`, as we've already shown earlier in this chapter. We ask the builder to create a new document for us, which we call `doc`. Then we begin working our way down the hierarchy. At the topmost level, we create a single element called <standings>, and then append that element to the document. There can only be a single root element in any XML document; attempting to attach another child at this level would result in an exception. We then call other methods to generate the <divisionStandings>, <conferenceStandings>, and <teams> elements, and attach each of these elements as children of the <standings> element.

The basic top-level structure of our document is clear from the layout of the method above. Although you're free to write your XML generation methods any way you choose, I find that the code is much more readable when laid out in this fashion, where there is a method that corresponds to the root element of the document, and additional method calls to create different elements within the document. (Strictly speaking, to adhere to this design fully, the method above should have done nothing more than call a `getStandings()` method and attach it to the document, and then you'd have to go to the `getStandings()` method to see the three subelements created. I preferred to put the "major structure" of the document in one place, and then the "minor structure" of those elements in other methods.)

In Listing 9.3, we continue building the next level of the document structure. We create the main element, and then have our familiar loop-the-divisions code. There is an outer loop that goes through the divisions, and then an inner loop that goes through teams in each division. In the outer loop, we create a `<division>` element, putting the division name in an attribute. In the inner loop, we create `<team>` elements. Each team element has an attribute representing the team `rank` within the division, and a `name` element for the team name.

Logic for the conference standings is virtually identical, so it isn't shown here. The final method at this level is the `getTeams()` method. We create the `teams` element, then loop through all the teams calling `getTeamDetails()` for each one.

Listing 9.3 `XML.java` (Part 2 of 4)

```
public Element getDivisionStandings() {
   Element dsElement =
      doc.createElement("divisionStandings");

   // Loop through divisions
   List divList = Division.DIVISIONS;
   for (int i=0; i<divList.size(); i++) {
      Division d = (Division) divList.get(i);
      List l = standings.computeDivisionStandings(d);
      Element divElement =
         doc.createElement("division");
      divElement.setAttribute("name", d.toString());
      dsElement.appendChild(divElement);
      // Loop through teams
      for (int j=0; j<l.size(); j++) {
         Team team = (Team) l.get(j);
         Element teamElement = doc.createElement("team");
         teamElement.setAttribute("rank",
                     Integer.toString(j+1));
         Element teamNameElement =
            doc.createElement("name");
         teamNameElement.appendChild(
            doc.createTextNode(team.getFullName()));
         teamElement.appendChild(teamNameElement);
         divElement.appendChild(teamElement);
      }
   }
   return dsElement;
}

public Element getConferenceStandings() {
   Element csElement =
      doc.createElement("conferenceStandings");
... logic follows same pattern as division
   return csElement;
}
```

```
public Element getTeams() {
    Element teamsElement =
        doc.createElement("teams");
    List teamList = standings.getTeamList();
    for (int i=0; i<teamList.size(); i++) {
        Team team = (Team) teamList.get(i);
        Element teamElement = getTeamDetails(team);
        teamsElement.appendChild(teamElement);
    }
    return teamsElement;
}
```

Listing 9.4 shows the method that populates the team details. For each team, we're passed in a `Team` class, and just need to create a corresponding `<teamDetails>` element in our document. Each property of the team becomes a subelement. Because of the sheer number of properties on the team, we haven't shown the code for each property in detail, but the full list can be discerned by examining the output shown in Listing 9.1.

As we build the document, there are essentially two types of nodes that we use. Element nodes are used for anything that has further structure, and text nodes are the "leaf" nodes. Even when the data is thought of as a numeric value, the XML representation will be as a text node, as XML is a text processing language that doesn't provide integers, floats, or other types.

Using the team name as an example, you can see in Listing 9.4 that we must create an `Element` node for the team name, and then attach a text node to it to contain the value for the team name.

Listing 9.4 `XML.java` (Part 3 of 4)

```
public Element getTeamDetails(Team t) {
    Element teamElement = doc.createElement("team");

    Element name = doc.createElement("name");
    name.appendChild(doc.createTextNode(t.getFullName()));
    Element wins = doc.createElement("wins");
    wins.appendChild(doc.createTextNode(
            Integer.toString(t.getWins())));
... repetitive details omitted

    teamElement.appendChild(name);
    teamElement.appendChild(wins);
    teamElement.appendChild(losses);
... more repetitive details omitted

    return teamElement;
}
```

Listing 9.5 shows how we write out the document. DOM doesn't actually provide a mechanism to do this, so we peek ahead slightly at the XSL transformation capabilities. The code for getting a `Transformer` is very similar to what we've already seen for getting DOM and SAX processors, so it should be familiar by now. If we are passed a `stylesheet` parameter, we use that to initialize the transformer; otherwise, we create a default transformer that just serializes the document. I found the default transformation difficult to read because it included no indentation. I've added the setting of a property to provide indentation, but this is done in a nonportable manner, so if you wish to use this code with something other than the Xerces processor, you'll need to modify the code accordingly. (Setting the property for other processors would not cause any compilation or runtime errors, it would simply have no effect on the output.)

Listing 9.5 XML.java (Part 4 of 4)

```
public void transformXMLDocument(Source source,
                                 String stylesheet,
                                 Result result) {
   // will read javax.xml.transform.TransformerFactory
   // property, if set. We just accept default.
   TransformerFactory tf = null;
   Transformer        t  = null;

   tf = TransformerFactory.newInstance();
   try {
      if (stylesheet == null)
        t = tf.newTransformer();
      else
        t = tf.newTransformer(
            new StreamSource(stylesheet));
   } catch (TransformerConfigurationException tce) {
      tce.printStackTrace();
      return;
   }

   // Use some indentation to improve readability
   Properties p = t.getOutputProperties();
   p.setProperty("indent", "yes");
   p.setProperty("{http://xml.apache.org/xslt}indent-amount", "3");
   t.setOutputProperties(p);

   try {
      t.transform(source, result);
   } catch (TransformerException te) {
      te.printStackTrace();
   }
   }
}
```

The API documentation for DOM can be found in Chapter 14, where we will revisit DOM in order to parse the document we've created here.

9.4   Creating an XML Document with JDOM

JDOM is a Java-specific API for processing XML documents. Its capabilities are very similar to DOM, but because it is language-specific it takes better advantage of Java language capabilities. It also strives to simplify XML processing by focusing on commonly used capabilities rather than going for 100 percent coverage of every possible operation that might conceivably be attempted.

Table 9.3   Components in the JDOM Output Formatter

New Components			
Name	**Package**	**Class or Interface**	**Comment**
JDOM	nfl.presentation.xml	Class	Produces Standings in XML format using JDOM APIs.
Existing Components			
Component	**Description**		
layered.jar	All classes and interfaces of the layered version of the application (as presented in Chapter 2).		

In Listing 9.6, the `main()` method is virtually identical to the same method in `XML.java`. The only appreciable change is that there are now separate methods used to output a serialized version of the document versus transforming the document via a stylesheet.

The `generateXMLDocument()` method is somewhat streamlined compared to the same method in the DOM version, but the flow is still the same. An abbreviated syntax of chaining together operations on the same document or element is shown, which is very commonly used with JDOM and can make the code quite compact. It can also make for a real challenge if you miscount your parentheses at some point, as the compiler will just point you to the first line of the block with the error.

One nice feature of JDOM is that you don't need to create a separate text node, but rather can just call the `setText()` method on an element instead. So a DOM `appendChild()`/ `createTextNode()` pair is replaced by just a single `setText()` method call.

In case you're using other books that are based on an older version of JDOM, it's worth noting that the `addContent()` method call shown in our code here was called `addChild()` in earlier versions of JDOM, and the `setAttribute()` method call replaces the deprecated `add-Attribute()` call.

Listing 9.6 Creating XML Code via JDOM (JDOM.java)

```
// JDOM.java

package nfl.presentation.xml;

import nfl.ObjectFactory;
import nfl.application.*;

// J2SE imports
import java.util.List;
import java.util.Properties;

// JDOM imports
import org.jdom.Document;
import org.jdom.Element;
import org.jdom.output.XMLOutputter;
import org.jdom.transform.JDOMResult;
import org.jdom.transform.JDOMSource;

// JAXP imports
import javax.xml.transform.Transformer;
import javax.xml.transform.TransformerFactory;
import javax.xml.transform.TransformerException;
import javax.xml.transform.stream.StreamSource;
import javax.xml.transform.stream.StreamResult;

/** Produces XML document of standings. Supports
  * plug-in transformers for rendering XML
  * into various formats
  */
public class JDOM
{
    private DynamicStandings standings;
    private Document  doc = null;

    public static void main(String[] args) {

        JDOM   jdom = new JDOM();
        String stylesheet = null;

        Properties p = System.getProperties();
        if (p.getProperty("nfl.versioninfo") == null) {
          p.setProperty("nfl.versioninfo",
            "nfl.presentation.xml.XMLVersionInfo");
        }

        for (int i=0; i<args.length; i++) {
```

```
         if (args[i].equals("-xsl"))  {
            stylesheet = args[++i];
         } else {
            System.err.println("Usage: " +
            "java nfl.presentation.xml.JDOM [options]\n" +
            "\nwhere options include\n" +
            " -xsl <stylesheet>");
            System.exit(-1);
         }
      }

      jdom.standings =  (DynamicStandings)
         ObjectFactory.getHandle().getInstance(
                              "DynamicStandings");
      jdom.standings.init();

      Document standingsdoc = jdom.generateXMLDocument();
      if (stylesheet == null)
         jdom.outputXMLDocument(standingsdoc);
      else
         jdom.transformXMLDocument(standingsdoc,
                              stylesheet);
   }

   public Document generateXMLDocument() {

      Document doc = new Document(new Element("standings"));

      doc.getRootElement()
         .addContent(getDivisionStandings())
         .addContent(getConferenceStandings())
         .addContent(getTeams());

      return doc;
   }

   public Element getDivisionStandings() {
      Element dsElement = new Element("divisionStandings");

      // Loop through divisions
      List divList = Division.DIVISIONS;
      for (int i=0; i<divList.size(); i++) {
         Division d = (Division) divList.get(i);
         List l = standings.computeDivisionStandings(d);
         Element divElement = new Element("division")
            .setAttribute("name", d.toString());
         dsElement.addContent(divElement);
```

```java
        // Loop through teams
        for (int j=0; j<l.size(); j++) {
           Team team = (Team) l.get(j);
           divElement.addContent(new Element("team")
              .setAttribute("rank", Integer.toString(j+1))
              .addContent(new Element("name")
                 .setText(team.getFullName())));
        }
     }
     return dsElement;
  }

  public Element getConferenceStandings() {
//... logic follows same pattern as division
  }

  public Element getTeams() {
     Element teamsElement = new Element("teams");
     List teamList = standings.getTeamList();
     for (int i=0; i<teamList.size(); i++) {
        Team team = (Team) teamList.get(i);
        teamsElement.addContent(getTeamDetails(team));
     }
     return teamsElement;
  }

  public Element getTeamDetails(Team t) {
     Element teamElement = new Element("team")
        .addContent(new Element("name")
           .setText(t.getFullName()))
        .addContent(new Element("wins")
           .setText(Integer.toString(t.getWins())))
        .addContent(new Element("losses")
           .setText(Integer.toString(t.getLosses())))
other properties set as expected . . .
     return teamElement;
  }

  public void outputXMLDocument(Document doc) {
     // parameters are indent string, newlines
     XMLOutputter out = new XMLOutputter("  ", true);
     try {
        out.output(doc, System.out);
     } catch (java.io.IOException e) {
       e.printStackTrace();
     }
  }
```

```
public void transformXMLDocument(Document doc,
                                 String stylesheet) {

    try {
        TransformerFactory factory = TransformerFactory.
                                         newInstance();
        Transformer t = factory.newTransformer(
            new StreamSource(stylesheet));
        Properties p = t.getOutputProperties();
        p.setProperty("indent", "yes");
        p.setProperty(
          "{http://xml.apache.org/xslt}indent-amount","3");
        t.setOutputProperties(p);
        t.transform(new JDOMSource(doc),
                    new StreamResult(System.out));
    } catch (TransformerException te) {
        te.printStackTrace();
    }
  }
}
```

Another advantage to using JDOM is that it appears to be faster than DOM, at least for this specific application. The output of the serialized document was roughly 25 percent faster using JDOM than with the Apache Xerces DOM parser. For transformations (discussed in the following section), the difference was much smaller—on the order of 2 to 3 percent—but JDOM still had a slight edge.

JDOM API documentation will be included in Chapter 14, along with API documentation for the DOM and SAX parsers.

9.5   Transforming XML to HTML via XSLT

Now that we've taken our application, which used to generate perfectly good HTML output, and changed it to output XML instead, what's our next step? Converting the XML back to HTML, of course. This isn't as futile as it sounds. If our only target had been HTML browsers, then we'd never have gone to XML in the first place. But starting from XML, we can target many different types of clients; just one of them happens to be the HTML browsers.

Converting from one XML-based format to another is known as a transformation. The transformation to be done is described in a document known as a stylesheet, which is itself written in an XML language known as XSL (eXtensible Stylesheet Language).

XSL is a declarative language, rather than a procedural one. An XSL stylesheet is made up of a number of templates, each of which is used to control the processing of particular nodes of the XML document. Selecting nodes is a very important part of stylesheet processing, and an expression language called XPath is the language used to do this. We'll need to understand a little about XPath before we'll be able to follow the processing flow of our stylesheet.

9.5.1   XPath

XPath is a W3C standard expression language. XPath expressions can be used in several contexts, but for our purposes we're just interested in the use of XPath expressions within XSL. XPath expressions can be used to select a subset of a document that matches the given expression. In this way, you might think of XPath as a regular-expression language for XML documents. However, unlike regular expressions, XPath expressions are very context-dependent, so the result of an expression will be quite different depending upon where you are in the document when the expression is evaluated. The "path" part of the name indicates this; XPath expressions are also much like navigating around a file system by using the parent directory, current directory, and directory names to construct a relative path to a target. Just like in a file system, XPath location paths can provide either a relative or absolute path to the target node(s).

An XPath location path takes the following form:

```
axis::node[predicate-list]
```

The axis specifies the relationship between the nodes to be selected by the expression and the current (context) node. For example, an axis of `child` specifies that the selected nodes are child nodes of the context node. Other common axis values include `attribute`, `descendent`, or `ancestor`; you can also use more esoteric axis values such as `preceding-sibling` or `third-cousin-twice-removed`. Okay, that last one isn't valid, at least in the current version. There are abbreviations that you can use for the most common axis values: a double slash (`//`) for descendent, a dot (`.`) for self, two dots (`..`) for the parent, an at-sign (`@`) for attribute, and blank for child. Note that when using abbreviated syntax, the abbreviation replaces both the axis name and the separating colons; so the abbreviated form of `attribute::foo` is simply `@foo`, not `@::foo`. Because the abbreviation for child nodes is blank, you essentially omit the axis declaration altogether.

The node portion of the location path is typically just a node name, although node type and namespace information may also be included. So `child::bubba` would select any children of the context node where the child's element name was `bubba`. Commonly used values for the node are a node name, an asterisk (`*`) to select all nodes, an at-sign followed by an attribute name to select a specific attribute, or an at-sign followed by an asterisk (`@*`) to select all attributes.

The predicate list allows further filtering of the node set. There is a set of functions available in XPath (see Table 9.4) that can be used to construct the predicates. Predicates can also be used to construct new nodes that didn't exist in the original document, but that are based on the document contents—for example, the `sum()` function can be used to create a node containing as its value the sum of values in the selected node-set.

9.5.2   An XSL Stylesheet

The stylesheet we'll use to convert our XML Standings document to HTML output is shown over the next several listings. We'll look at these in detail to understand the capabilities of XSL transformations.

In the first listing, Listing 9.7, we start with the `<stylesheet>` element. This declares the version of XSL we're using (1.0), and defines a namespace for the tags we'll use in our document. The XML namespace attribute can be read as follows: For any tag with a prefix of `xsl:` in this document, the tag that follows belongs to the namespace at the given URL. The use of URLs to delimit namespaces is merely a convention to avoid name collisions, just as the recommended construction of Java package names uses the domain name of the organization creating the code. If you were to go look at the URL given by the XSL namespace, it's simply a page that declares "This is the XSL namespace." There isn't any magical document there, and the XSL engine performing transformations on your code isn't going to go read anything from the URL. We also aren't required to use the prefix `xsl:`, it could be anything you like. But `xsl` is traditional for XSL tags, so to do otherwise is to make your code less understandable to the general reader. Next, we declare that the output of our transformation will be in HTML format (we could also have specified `method="xml"`). This simply tells the XSLT processor how we would like the document to be output, although there is no requirement for processors to support any specific set of formats.

The remainder of the stylesheet is made up of templates. A template is a transformation that will be applied to a particular piece of the input document. Each template has a `match` attribute that tells what portion of the document it will be applied to. Template matching is a recursive process; when you apply a transformation to an input document, the only thing that happens automatically on your behalf is the matching of the root element of the document. If you want to match anything else in the document, you'll need to ask the processor to look for additional templates.

The first template in our document has a `match` attribute of "/", which is the pattern used to match the document root. When the transformation is performed, everything between the `<xsl:template>` start tag and `</xsl:template>` end tag will be evaluated. The majority of the content between these two tags is simple HTML markup; this will be copied to the output document. Only one tag within the template is not standard HTML: the `<xsl:apply-templates>` tag. This tag is required in order to invoke other templates found in the stylesheet. Without `<apply-templates>`, the processor only matches and executes the template matching the root element.

Our `<apply-templates>` tag begins the next level of processing. The `select` attribute tells the processor to select from the input document any nodes that have a path of `standings/divisionStandings/division/`. Knowing the contents of our XML file, this will cause six nodes to be selected for further processing, because there are six divisions. We then scan the stylesheet looking for templates that can be applied to these nodes. The processor will use a "best match" algorithm to decide what template to use to transform these nodes.

The template that will be selected is the second one in the file, which has a match pattern of `"division"`. That template is shown in Listing 9.8. Note that although we specify a full path in our `<xsl:apply-templates>` tag (`standings/divisionStandings/division/`), within the `match` attribute of the `template` tag we specify only `division`. Division elements may exist at multiple levels within our XML document. In the first case, we are selecting nodes to be processed, and wish to be very specific that we select only the appropriate nodes. In the second case (the `<xsl:template>` tag), we could have specified the same full path. But by specifying only the division portion, we could conceivably reuse this same template on other division elements elsewhere in the document. We won't need to do so here, but this is frequently a useful option to leave yourself.

Listing 9.7 `XMLStandingsToHTML.xsl` (Part 1 of 3)

```
<xsl:stylesheet
     version="1.0"
     xmlns:xsl="http://www.w3.org/1999/XSL/Transform">

  <xsl:output method="html"/>
<!-- works OK, but no whitespace at all so not very readable
  <xsl:output method="xml"
    doctype-public="-//W3C//DTD XHTML 1.0  Transitional//EN"
    doctype-system=
       "http://www.w3.org/TR/xhtml1/DTD/xhtml1-transitional.dtd"/>
-->

<!-- Template to match root element -->
  <xsl:template match="/">
    <html>
      <head>
        <title>NFL Standings (via XML and XSLT)</title>
      </head>
      <body>
        <h1>NFL Standings</h1>
        <table>
          <xsl:apply-templates
             select="standings/divisionStandings/division"/>
        </table>
      </body>
    </html>
  </xsl:template>
```

The second template is similar to the first, in that it consists mainly of HTML code, with an `<apply-templates>` tag used to drive processing one level deeper. In this case, the HTML code creates a table, filling in the heading. The heading includes both constant information—the column names—and a single piece of variable information, which is the division name. The

division name needs to be extracted from the XML input document, and we do that with the
`<xsl:value-of>` tag. The `select` attribute identifies the piece we want to take from the current node, using XPath syntax. The `@` identifies that we are taking an attribute value, rather than
a subelement. So `@name` takes the `name` attribute from the current node, which we know from
the `match` attribute of the template is a `division` element. (We could have also used the more
verbose `attribute::name` syntax for the XPath expression.) You can verify that this matches
the actual document structure by examining Listing 9.1.

   The body of our table is empty at this level; we've delegated the responsibility of creating the contents to the template at the next level. We select all children of the current node that
match `team`, causing the processor to examine our stylesheet again looking for template
matches. (Again, we could have used more verbose `child::team` syntax for the `select`
expression.)

Listing 9.8 `XMLStandingsToHTML.xsl` (Part 2 of 3)

```
<!-- Template to match division -->
  <xsl:template match="division">
    <table border="1">
      <thead>
        <tr>
          <th colspan="10">
            <h2>
              <xsl:value-of select="@name"/>
            </h2>
          </th>
        </tr>
        <tr>
          <th><xsl:text>Team</xsl:text></th>
          <th><xsl:text>Wins</xsl:text></th>
          <th><xsl:text>Losses</xsl:text></th>
          <th><xsl:text>Ties</xsl:text></th>
          <th><xsl:text>PCT</xsl:text></th>
          <th><xsl:text>PF</xsl:text></th>
          <th><xsl:text>PA</xsl:text></th>
          <th><xsl:text>Div</xsl:text></th>
          <th><xsl:text>Conf</xsl:text></th>
          <th><xsl:text>Streak</xsl:text></th>
        </tr>
      </thead>
      <tbody>
        <xsl:apply-templates select="team"/>
      </tbody>
    </table>
  </xsl:template>
```

We need two templates to get to our team details. The element name `team` appears in two different locations within our input document: as a child element of a `<division>` in the `<divisionStandings>`, and as a child element of a `<conference>` in the `<conference-Standings>`. When encountering either of these, we want to be able to take the `<name>` subelement, and match it to the corresponding `<name>` subelement of a `<teamDetails>` element in the `<teams>` part of the document.

The first of the two templates, shown in Listing 9.9, is invoked by the division template while processing each of the teams in the division. Unlike the division name, which was an attribute, the team name is a child element of the division, so the `<xsl:value-of>` tag has a `select` attribute of `name` (without the @ prefix that would indicate an attribute). The entire contents of this template are going to be one row in our table, so the first and last elements within the template are HTML `<tr>` and `</tr>` tags to delimit the table row. The `name` element is likewise delimited by HTML `<td>` and `</td>` tags delimiting the table data cell.

The remaining two lines of the template are to drive processing to the final level. Because we are formatting just one line in the table at this point, we don't want to apply the next template to all teams, but rather to just the single team we are currently processing. To do this, we need to create a variable. The `<xsl:variable>` tag allows us to do this, giving it a name of `currentTeam` and a value that is the name of the team we are processing. Then, we have the `<apply-templates>` tag. Here, we select nodes whose path matches `/standings/teams/teamDetails`, but use an XPath predicate to place a further restriction that selects only nodes where the `name` element matches the value of the `currentTeam` variable.

In the final template, we format each column of the table. Each is delimited by HTML `<td>` and `</td>` tags. Most are just string values, so they can be retrieved by using the `<xsl:value-of>` tag with the element name. A few have special processing attached.

The `winLossPct` field is a float value represented as a string. To get the formatting we desire, we use the built-in `format-number` method. The `format` string passed to this method follows the same rules as the `java.lang.DecimalFormat` class.

Our conference and division record fields are actually built up from two elements, with the values separated by a dash. You can see in the template that the `wins` and `losses` elements are selected, with an `<xsl:text>` element placed between them to provide the dash.

Finally, our `streak` field is represented in the input document as an integer value, positive for a winning streak or negative for a losing streak. To print the "Wins" or "Losses" text for this field, we use an `<xsl:choose>` tag, which behaves just like a `switch` statement. Each case within the switch is represented by an `<xsl:when>` element; the `test` attribute of the element supplies the condition. We have three conditions: `streak > 0`, `streak < 0`, and `streak = 0`. But the less-than and greater-than signs are illegal for use within XML tags, because they are tag delimiters. The solution is to use the form `&gt;` for greater than, and `&lt;` for less than. (The ampersand also requires this syntax; use `&amp;` instead. If needed, you can also use `&quot;` and `&apos;` as stand-ins for double and single quotes, respectively. Because XML allows either single or double quotes, you usually won't need to resort to this syntax unless you need to include both styles of quote in an element.)

Listing 9.9   XMLStandingsToHTML.xsl (Part 3 of 3)

```
<!-- Template to match team in division -->
  <xsl:template match="division/team">
    <tr>
      <td><xsl:value-of select="name"/></td>
      <xsl:variable name="currentTeam" select="name"/>
      <xsl:apply-templates
          select="teamDetails[name=$currentTeam]"/>
    </tr>
  </xsl:template>

<!-- Template to match teamDetail in teams -->
  <xsl:template match="teams/teamDetails">
    <td><xsl:value-of select="wins"/></td>
    <td><xsl:value-of select="losses"/></td>
    <td><xsl:value-of select="ties"/></td>
    <xsl:variable name="pct" select="winLossPct"/>
    <td><xsl:value-of
        select="format-number($pct, '#.000')"/></td>
    <td><xsl:value-of select="points"/></td>
    <td><xsl:value-of select="pointsAllowed"/></td>
    <td><xsl:value-of select="divisionWins"/>
        <xsl:text>-</xsl:text>
        <xsl:value-of select="divisionLosses"/></td>
    <td><xsl:value-of select="conferenceWins"/>
        <xsl:text>-</xsl:text>
        <xsl:value-of select="conferenceLosses"/></td>
    <xsl:variable name="streak" select="streak"/>
    <xsl:choose>
        <xsl:when test="streak &gt; 0">
          <td><xsl:text>Won </xsl:text>
              <xsl:value-of select="$streak"/></td>
        </xsl:when>
        <xsl:when test="streak &lt; 0">
          <td><xsl:text>Lost </xsl:text>
              <xsl:value-of select="$streak * -1"/></td>
        </xsl:when>
        <xsl:when test="streak = 0">
            <td></td>
        </xsl:when>
    </xsl:choose>
  </xsl:template>
</xsl:stylesheet>
```

9.5.3   XSL Tags Quick Reference

The following list includes all of the legal XSL tags. The descriptions given are very rudimentary, and are intended to serve only as an idea of the capabilities provided by the tags. For full information, refer to the full specification at `http://www.w3.org/TR/xslt`.

```
<xsl:apply-imports />
```

Directs processor to find the matching template rule in an imported stylesheet and apply it to the current nodeset.

```
<xsl:apply-templates
    select= node-set
    mode= mode-name  >
    body may include xsl:sort element
    body may include xsl:with-param elements
</xsl:apply-templates>
```

Directs processor to select nodes indicated by `select` attribute, and then find and apply matching templates. By default, `select` operates on immediate child nodes of the current node, but XPath expression syntax in the selection value can alter this behavior.

```
<xsl:attribute
    name= attribute-name
    namespace= namespace-uri />
```

Adds an attribute to the current node.

```
<xsl:attribute-set
    name= attribute-set-name />
    body contains xsl:attribute elements
</xsl:attribute-set>
```

Creates a set of attributes that can then be referenced by the `use-attribute-sets` attribute of the `xsl:element`, `xsl:copy`, or `xsl:attribute-set` tags.

```
<xsl:call-template
    name= template-name>
    body may include xsl:with-param elements
</xsl:call-template>
```

Invokes the specified template. Unlike `apply-templates`, using `call-template` does not cause any change to the current node-set, and none of the selection/matching attributes of the called node will be applied.

```
<xsl:choose>
    body must contain one or more xsl:when elements
    body may include an xsl:otherwise element
</xsl:choose>
```

Implements a `switch` statement.

```
<xsl:comment>
    body contains comment text
</xsl:comment>
```

Inserts comments.

```
<xsl:copy
    use-attribute-sets = attribute-sets>
```

Creates a copy of the current node.

```
<xsl:copy-of
    select= expression />
```

Inserts the result of the expression into the result tree at the current location. The result is not converted to a string as would happen with `xsl:value-of`.

```
<xsl:decimal-format
    name= fieldname
    decimal-separator= character
    grouping-separator= character
    infinity= string
    minus-sign= char
    NaN = string
    percent = char
    per-mille= char
    digit= char
    pattern-separator= char />
```

Formats a number.

```
<xsl:element
    name= name
    namespace= uri
    use-attribute-sets= attribute-sets>
    body contains element template
</xsl:element>
```

Defines an element.

```
<xsl:fallback>
    body contains template
</xsl:fallback>
```

Specifies a template to be executed if a fallback is executed. Sort of an XSL equivalent of `try-catch`. This would allow the attempted invocation of a nonstandard XSL extension; if the code for the extension were not present in the processor, the fallback template would be executed instead.

```
<xsl:for-each
    select= node-set-expression>
    body may contain xsl:sort elements
    body contains template
</xsl:for-each>
```

Creates a loop, iterating over the elements specified by the `select` attribute.

```
<xsl:if
    test= boolean-expression>
    body contains template
</xsl:if>
```

Executes the body conditionally if the expression in the test element evaluates to true.

```
<xsl:import
    href= uri/>
```

Imports the document specified by the URI.

```
<xsl:include
    href= uri/>
```

Includes the document specified by the URI. The only difference between `import` and `include` is that with `import`, the importing ("outer") stylesheets definitions and templates will take precedence; with an `include`, the included ("inner") stylesheet takes precedence.

```
<xsl:key
    name= keyname
    match= pattern
    use= expression>
```

Declares keys. I haven't used this, and don't pretend to understand how it would be used. The specification indicates it is used to enable implicit cross-references within a document (contrasted to explicit cross-references supported by the `id` functions).

```
<xsl:message
    terminate= "yes" | "no">
    body contains template
</xsl:message>
```

Generates a message during processing. What happens is implementation-dependent; processor may log the message, or display it on `stderr`, or pop up a window.

```
<xsl:namespace-alias
    stylesheet-prefix= prefix | "#default"
    result-prefix= prefix | "#default"/>
```

Allows specification of a namespace URI as an alias for a different namespace URI.

```
<xsl:number
    level= "single" | "multiple" | "any"
    count= pattern
    from= pattern
    format= { string }
    lang= { nmtoken }
    letter-value= { "alphabetic" | "traditional" }
    grouping-separator= { char }
    grouping-size= { number } />
```

Inserts a formatted number into the result tree.

```
<xsl:otherwise>
    body contains template
</xsl:otherwise
```

Only legal within body of `xsl:choose` element. Provides default case for content which does not match any `xsl:when` choice.

```
<xsl:output
    method= "xml" | "html" | "text" | method-name
    version= nmtoken
    encoding= string
    omit-xml-declaration= "yes" | "no"
    standalone= "yes" | "no"
    doctype-public= string
    doctype-system= string
    cdata-section-elements= names
    indent= "yes" | "no"
    media-type= string/>
```

Allows specifications controlling how the result tree will be output when written to a stream.

```
<xsl:param
    name= name
    select= expression>
    body contains template
</xsl:param>
```

Similar to `xsl:variable`, but the value specified with `param` is simply a default that may be overridden when the template is invoked.

```
<xsl:preserve-space
    elements= tokens/>
```

Instructs processor to preserve whitespace in the elements named. By default, all nodes are part of the `preserve-space` set, and none are in the `strip-space` set.

```
<xsl:processing-instruction
    name= { name }>
    body contains template
</xsl:processing-instruction>
```

Creates a processing instruction node within the document.

```
<xsl:sort
    select= string-expression
    lang= { nmtoken }
    data-type = { "text" | "number" | name }
    order= { "ascending" | "descending" }
    case-order= { "upper-first" | "lower-first" }/>
```

When xsl:sort elements appear as children of an xsl:apply-templates or an xsl:for-each element, the selected nodes will be sorted as specified by the xsl:sort tag rather than processing them in document order. There may be multiple xsl:sort tags, in which case the first encountered becomes the major sort, the second specifies the secondary key, and so on.

```
<xsl:strip-space
    elements= tokens/>
```

Specifies that whitespace should be stripped from the indicated elements.

```
<xsl:stylesheet
    id= id
    extension-element-prefixes= tokens
    exclude-result-prefixes= tokens
    version= number>
    body may contain xsl:import statements
    body may contain any top-level elements
</xsl:stylesheet>
```

The outermost element of a stylesheet. xsl:transform is a synonym. The version attribute is required; all others are optional.

```
<xsl:template
    match= pattern
    name= name
    priority= number
    mode= name>
    body may contain xsl:param elements
    body may contain template
<xsl:template>
```

Specifies processing to be applied to a node. Invoked by xsl:call-template or xsl:apply-templates. In the former case, the name attribute is used to identify the template to invoke; in the later case, templates are selected by the match attribute.

```
<xsl:text>
    disable-output-escaping= "yes" | "no">
    body may contain #PCDATA text
</xsl:text>
```

Inserts a text node into the document.

```
<xsl:transform
    id= id
    extension-element-prefixes= tokens
    exclude-result-prefixes= tokens
    version= number>
    body may contain xsl:import statements
    body may contain any top-level elements
</xsl:transform>
```

A synonym for xsl:stylesheet.

```
<xsl:value-of
    select= string-expression
    disable-output-escaping= "yes" | "no" />
```

Creates a text node in the output tree. The value of the text is taken from the object specified by the select attribute.

```
<xsl:variable
    name= name
    select= expression>
    body may contain template
</xsl:variable>
```

Declares a variable. The name attribute provides the variable name; the select attribute identifies the object that contains the variable value.

```
<xsl:when
    text= Boolean-expression>
    body contains template
</xsl:when>
```

Delineates a possible value of the choice within an xsl:choose tag, and a template to be executed for matching nodes.

```
<xsl:with-param
   name= name
   select= expression>
   body contains template
</xsl:with-param>
```

Passes parameter values to templates. Allowed within `call-template` and `apply-tem-plates` tags; the name must match the name of an `xsl:param` element.

Table 9.4   XPath Functions Available in XSL

Return Type	Function and Parameters	Operation
NodeSet Functions		
number	last()	Returns context node size.
number	position()	Returns context node position.
number	count(node-set)	Returns number of nodes in node-set.
node-set	id(object)	Returns unique ID of object.
string	local-name(node-set)	Returns local name of first node in node-set.
string	namespace-uri(node-set)	Returns namespace URI of first node in node-set.
string	name(node-set)	Returns expanded name of first node in node-set.
string	string(object?)	Converts object to string.
string	concat(string, string, string*)	Concatenates strings.
Boolean Functions		
boolean	starts-with(string, string)	Returns true if first string begins with second string.
boolean	contains(string, string)	Returns true if first string contains second string.
string	substring-before(string, string)	Returns portion of first string that precedes second string (empty if first string does not contain second string).
string	substring-after(string, string)	Returns portion of first string that follows second string (empty if first string does not contain second string).

Table 9.4   XPath Functions Available in XSL (Continued)

Boolean Functions (Continued)		
string	substring(string, number, number?)	Returns substring of string beginning at position identified by first number, for length specified by second number. If length is omitted, substring is to end of string.
number	string-length(string?)	Length of string. If no string argument is passed, length of current node expressed as a string.
string	normalize-space(string?)	Returns string with whitespace normalized (leading and trailing whitespace removed, interior whitespace repetition eliminated). If no string is provided, operates on current (context) node.
string	translate(string, string, string)	Performs translation of first string by replacing each character that appears in second string by character in same position in third string.
boolean	boolean(object)	Returns object as a boolean.
boolean	not(boolean)	Logical not function on a boolean.
boolean	true()	Returns true.
boolean	false()	Returns false.
boolean	lang(string)	True if context node's language (specified by `xml:lang` attribute) is same as language named in the string.
Number Functions		
number	number(object?)	Returns object as number.
number	sum(node-set)	Returns sum of the numeric values of nodes in node-set.
number	floor(number)	Returns largest integer less than argument.
number	ceiling(number)	Returns smallest integer greater than argument.
number	round(number)	Returns nearest integer to argument.

Table 9.4   XPath Functions Available in XSL (Continued)

XSLT Additions to XPath Functions		
node-set	document(object, node-set)	Provides access to another XML document.
node-set	key(string, object)	Declares keys. See XSLT specification.
string	format-number(string, string, string?)	Converts number in first argument to string. Second argument is format string; third (optional) argument is decimal format.
node-set	current()	Returns node-set containing only current node.
string	unparsed-entity-uri(string)	Returns URI of unparsed entity named by argument string.
object	system-property(string)	Returns value of system property named by argument string.

Either the client or the server can do the transformation of an XML document using XSLT. In our examples, we are doing the conversion on the server side, by invoking the transformer and sending the resulting document as output. To use client-side transformation, we would simply send the original XML document, and include within the document an `xml-stylesheet` processing instruction. While you may have a situation where client-side transformation makes sense, generally the XML market is not mature enough to assume the presence of stylesheet processors on all clients. Also, with increasing emphasis on thin clients such as cellphones or PDAs, the offloading of heavyweight processing is not necessarily a good design choice.

Now that we have a stylesheet to perform the transformation of our XML standings, we'd like to see it in operation. The easiest way to do this is to invoke the transformation manually, from the command line. The syntax for this will vary between processors; here's how to do it using Xalan:

```
java org.apache.xalan.xslt.Process \
        -IN out.xml \
        -XSL XMLStandingsToHTML.xsl \
        -OUT out.html
```

We invoke the class `org.apache.xalan.xslt.Process`, giving it parameters for the input file, output file, and stylesheet (`-XSL`). If the output file is omitted, output is written to `stdout`. Many additional parameters are also supported; invoke the class with no parameters to get usage information.

This is a great way to test our stylesheet, but obviously not how we would perform transformations in a production environment. We need to be able to invoke the transformation programmatically. The steps to do so are quite simple; if fact, it's so similar to the process for just outputting straight HTML that we have already built the capability into our classes. If you go back and reexamine both `XML.java` and `JDOM.java`, you'll see that we accept an –XSL parameter on the command line. If such a parameter is provided, then we use the name that follows as a stylesheet name, and initialize the `Transformer` instance with this name. Once the `Transformer` is thus initialized, invoking its `transform()` method performs the transformation described by the stylesheet. In the next chapter, after we introduce some wireless capabilities, we'll put this programmatic transformation capability into a new servlet.

9.6 Building, Installing, and Running the XML Presentation Classes

The Ant `build.xml` file for this chapter, shown in Listing 9.10, is located in the `nfl/presentation/xml` directory, and builds our XML outputters (`XML.java` and `JDOM.java`) along with their version_info file. The only notable requirement about this buildfile is the JAR files that need to be provided. `xerces.jar` is needed to create or parse the XML file using DOM; `jdom.jar` is needed to create or parse an XML file using JDOM. In both cases, `xalan.jar` is needed to provide the XSL transformer classes for output or transformation.

The three property values at the beginning of the file will need to be updated to reflect your system's directory structure. The first property indicates where you have installed the Java XML Pack. The second property points to the JAXP directory within the Java XML Pack; this needs to be updated only if the version of JAXP included with the Java XML Pack you download is different than the one indicated here. Finally, the third variable indicates the directory where you have downloaded and installed JDOM.

Listing 9.10 Ant Buildfile for XML Presentation Classes

```
<project name="xml" default="dom" basedir=".">

<property name="JAVA_XML_PACK_HOME"
        value="/home/myawn/webservices/java_xml_pack-winter-01-dev" />
<property name="JAXP_HOME"
        value="${JAVA_XML_PACK_HOME}/jaxp-1.2-ea1" />
<property name="JDOM_HOME"
        value="/home/myawn/webservices" />

<path id="dom-classpath">
   <pathelement path="${java.class.path}" />
   <pathelement location="${JAXP_HOME}/xerces.jar" />
   <pathelement location="${JAXP_HOME}/xalan.jar" />
</path>
```

```
<path id="jdom-classpath">
    <pathelement path="${java.class.path}" />
    <pathelement location="${JDOM_HOME}/jdom.jar" />
</path>

<target name="dom">
    <javac srcdir="." classpathref="dom-classpath" >
        <include name="XML.java" />
        <include name="XMLVersionInfo.java" />
    </javac>
</target>

<target name="jdom">
    <javac srcdir="." classpathref="jdom-classpath">
        <include name="JDOM.java" />
    </javac>
</target>

<target name="test-dom" depends="dom" >
    <java classname="nfl.presentation.xml.XML" fork="true"
        classpathref="dom-classpath" />
</target>

<target name="test-jdom" depends="jdom" >
    <java classname="nfl.presentation.xml.JDOM" fork="true"
        classpathref="jdom-classpath" />
</target>

<target name="test-xslt" depends="dom" >
    <java classname="nfl.presentation.xml.XML" fork="true"
        classpathref="dom-classpath" >
        <arg value="-xsl" />
        <arg value="XMLStandingsToHTML.xsl" />
    </java>
</target>

<target name="clean">
    <delete>
        <fileset dir="." includes="*.class" />
    </delete>
</target>

</project>
```

9.7   Exercises

9.1 XML syntax for programming language: Develop an XML language for writing programs (perhaps we'll call it Xperanto). To get you started, here's a possible syntax for a variable declaration:

```
<variable>
    <name>i</name>
    <type>integer</type>
    <initialvalue>0</initialvalue>
</variable>
```

9.2 XML conversion to program code: Write a simple program using this format, and then use XSLT to convert the program to a variety of languages (such as Java and COBOL). Is the program you just wrote code, or data? If all programs were written this way, could all the world's software be replaced with just a single XML processor? For extra credit, write an operating system in this XML language. Does it boot faster or slower than Windows?

9.3 Conference standings: Add another template to the `XMLStandingsToHTML.xsl` stylesheet. Make this template format the conference standings, as previous versions of standings output have included. You can use either a table or an item list as you prefer. Modify the root template to invoke your new template.

9.4 Add conference information to division standings: A more popular way of presenting the conference information is as an additional column before the team name in the division standings. Alter the division template to add this additional column. For each team, place an X in this column if the team has clinched their division, a Y if the team has clinched a wild-card berth, and a Z if the team has clinched home-field advantage. (You can use alternate notation to provide greater detail if you wish.)

9.8   Further Reading

The Bibliography lists several XML related books, including Brett McLaughlin's *Java and XML* and Eric Burke's *Java and XSLT*.

The Document Object Model (DOM) is a W3C standard; you can access the standard and related documents at `http://www.w3.org/DOM`.

The Java API for XML Parsing (JAXP) home page is `http://java.sun.com/xml/jaxp/index.html`. Other XML-related APIs (most of which are covered in Chapter 14) are also at this site; just truncate the URI after `xml/` to see the others.

The JDOM home page is at `http://www.jdom.org`.

The Apache site `http://xml.apache.org` has the Xalan and Xerces processors plus many other free tools and utilities.

The Web sites `http://www.xml.com` and `http://www.xml.org` both have a lot of good XML-related content. The first tends to be more instructional in nature, with the latter being more of a news site.

## CHAPTER 10

Using XML with Wireless Clients

O ur efforts to convert our HTML output into XML are all going to seem rather silly if the only thing we do with the XML is convert it back to HTML. The purpose of generating XML was to enable us to defer the decision of what our output format would be, and allow the output formats to be easily extended in the future to support new types of devices.

One area where many different device types are encountered is in support for wireless clients. By taking a brief look at the two most popular wireless markup protocols, we can begin to see the real value in having our application generate XML rather than a specific markup language.

Most wireless devices in the U.S. operate using the Wireless Application Protocol, or WAP. (Different standards are in use in Europe and Japan, so WAP is far from universal.) The original versions of WAP (WAP 1.0 through 1.3) required the use of a markup language known as WML, or Wireless Markup Language. Beginning with WAP 2.0, the markup language for WAP is XHTML Basic, which brings wireless devices into greater conformance with browsers and other types of clients.

Software Used in This Chapter

Xerces XML Processor

From the Apache group. Downloadable from `http://xml.apache.org`. Includes support for DOM, SAX, and JAXP. Version 2.0.0.beta2 was used for the examples in this chapter.

Xalan XSLT Engine

From the Apache group. Downloadable from `http://xml.apache.org`. Includes support for XSLT transformations. Version 2.2-D11 was used for the examples in this chapter.

JAXP

The Java API for XML Parsing. Included with the Xerces software from Apache, or can be downloaded separately from `http://java.sun.com/xml/`.

Nokia Mobile Internet Toolkit

Version 3.0, downloaded from `http://forum.nokia.com`, was used to display the WML- and XHTML-formatted output. The User's Guide, WAP Overview, and XHTML Guidelines documents included with the toolkit are good references for development of WML and XHTML presentation code.

HP mBuilder

Version 1.5, downloaded from `http://www.hp.com/go/mbuilder`, can be used to create XSL stylesheets to support mobile devices, rather than creating stylesheets by hand.

10.1 WML and XHTML Markup Languages

Our task in this chapter will be to examine the process for taking our XML Standings output and transforming it into both WML and XHTML formats. The solution will not be fully developed, leaving some of the interesting parts as an exercise for you. But the full framework and methodology for accomplishing this will be presented.

Before getting into specifics of the code, I want to talk briefly about the development process. If you were writing a program to produce as output a tabular report, you'd probably make at least some effort to sketch out the output by hand before starting to code. Similarly, it would be difficult to write an XSL transformation to a new markup language without having a pretty good idea of what the code you were trying to produce looked like. So the first step is not to do an XSL transformation, but rather to prototype the result by hand-coding a subset of the output.

Listing 10.1 shows the hand-coded WML markup for the Standings application. WML can be thought of in concept as a "deck" made up of "cards." Because screens on wireless devices are typically much smaller than browser windows, the ability to break a screen into multiple parts and page through them was desired. A WML deck can be thought of as roughly equivalent to an HTML page, with each card being whatever portion of the page can be displayed at once. This is only an approximation, for a WML designer is in no way constrained to mirror any part of the HTML presentation of similar pages.

Our WML deck has a `<template>`, which is an item that will be repeated on each card (unless the card element overrides it). Our template adds a `Prev` function to each card. Then we have a main menu card, which allows the user to select which division to display results for. The hyperlinks are all to cards within the same WML deck, although they could also be full URLs that caused a new deck to be downloaded from the server. Each link has an `accesskey` associated with it, which allows for access through a cellphone or PDA keyboard. Clients are not required to support the `accesskey` syntax, and neither of the cellphone simulators I experimented with enabled the access keys.

Only one of the six detail cards was actually hand-coded, because that is enough to verify the presentation works as expected. Each detail card contains a table, in which a subset of the Standings data is reproduced. Figure 10.1 shows the output of the menu and detail cards when accessed via a cellphone simulator.

Listing 10.1 `nflstandings.wml`

```
<?xml version="1.0"?>
<!DOCTYPE wml PUBLIC "-//WAPFORUM//DTD WML 1.3//EN"
          "http://www.wapforum.org/DTD/wml13.dtd">


<wml>
  <template>
    <do type="prev"><prev/></do>
  </template>

  <card id="mainMenu" title="NFL Main">
    <p>
    <a href="#afce" accesskey="1">AFC East</a><br/>
    <a href="#afcc" accesskey="2">AFC Central</a><br/>
    <a href="#afcw" accesskey="3">AFC West</a><br/>
    <a href="#nfce" accesskey="4">NFC East</a><br/>
    <a href="#nfcc" accesskey="5">NFC Central</a><br/>
    <a href="#nfcw" accesskey="6">NFC West</a><br/>
    </p>

  </card>

  <card id="afce" title="AFC East">
    <p>
    <table columns="4">
      <tr><td>Dolphins</td><td>11</td><td>5</td>
                          <td>.668</td></tr>
```

```
            <tr><td>Colts</td>      <td>10</td><td>6</td>
                                    <td>.625</td></tr>
            <tr><td>Jets</td>       <td>9</td> <td>7</td>
                                    <td>.562</td></tr>
            <tr><td>Bills</td>      <td>8</td> <td>8</td>
                                    <td>.500</td></tr>
            <tr><td>Patriots</td><td>5</td> <td>11</td>
                                    <td>.312</td></tr>
      </table>
      </p>
  </card>

  <card id="afcc" title="AFC Central"></card>
  <card id="afcw" title="AFC West"></card>
  <card id="nfce" title="NFC East"></card>
  <card id="nfcc" title="NFC Central"></card>
  <card id="nfcw" title="NFC West"></card>
</wml>
```

Figure 10.1 WML output displayed on simulator.

The alternative to WML is to use XHTML Basic, which is the latest incarnation of the HTML syntax. XHTML is an XML language, so markup rules are stricter than the HTML we used previously. For example, all XHTML tags are case-sensitive, and all elements must have matching start and end tags, or else be standalone tags that include the closing slash (for example, <br/>).

The deck concept is dropped, so we are back to specifying separate pages rather than cards within a deck. Listing 10.2 shows the menu page, and Listing 10.3 the detail page, of the hand-coded markup for the standings. Figure 10.2 shows how the menu page looks when displayed on a XHTML-capable cellphone.

Listing 10.2 `menu.xhtml`

```
<?xml version="1.0"?>
<!DOCTYPE html PUBLIC "-//W3C//DTD XHTML Basic 1.0//EN"
        "http://www.w3.org/TR/xhtml-basic/xhtml-basic10.dtd">

<html xmlns="http://www.w3.org/1999/xhtml">
  <head>
    <title>NFL Main</title>
    <link rel="stylesheet" href="style.css"
        type="text/css"/>
  </head>
  <body>
    <p>
    <a href="afce.xhtml" accesskey="1">AFC East</a><br/>
    <a href="afcc.xhtml" accesskey="2">AFC Central</a><br/>
    <a href="afcw.xhtml" accesskey="3">AFC West</a><br/>
    <a href="nfce.xhmtl" accesskey="4">NFC East</a><br/>
    <a href="nfcc.xhtml" accesskey="5">NFC Central</a><br/>
    <a href="nfcw.xhtml" accesskey="6">NFL West</a><br/>
    </p>
  </body>
</html>
```

Listing 10.3 Detailed XHTML Markup for AFC East (`afce.xhtml`)

```
<?xml version="1.0"?>
<!DOCTYPE html PUBLIC "-//W3C//DTD XHTML Basic 1.0//EN"
        "http://www.w3.org/TR/xhtml-basic/xhtml-basic10.dtd">

<html xmlns="http://www.w3.org/1999/xhtml">
    <head>
        <title>AFC East</title>
        <link rel="stylesheet" href="style.css"
            type="text/css"/>
    </head>
    <body>
        <table>
            <tr><td>Dolphins</td><td>11</td><td>5</td>
                            <td>.668</td></tr>
```

```
        <tr><td>Colts</td>    <td>10</td><td>6</td>
                              <td>.625</td></tr>
        <tr><td>Jets</td>     <td>9</td><td>7</td>
                              <td>.562</td></tr>
        <tr><td>Bills</td>    <td>8</td><td>8</td>
                              <td>.500</td></tr>
        <tr><td>Patriots</td><td>5</td><td>11</td>
                              <td>.312</td></tr>
      </table>
    </body>
</html>
```

Figure 10.2 XHTML menu page displayed in cellphone emulator.

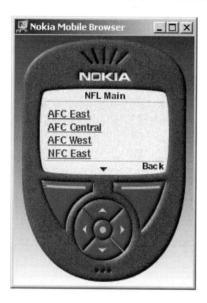

Once the required markup is understood, it is then necessary to write XSL transformations that can take the XML output produced by one of our XML classes (XML.java or JDOM.java) and transform it into either the WML or XHTML format. The creation of the XMLStandings-ToWML.xsl and XMLStandingsToXHTML.xsl stylesheets has been left as an exercise for you.

10.1.1 Creating XSL Stylesheets with HP mBuilder

Based on the information in the previous section, you should be able to create XSL stylesheets by hand if you desire. However, there are a number of tools available that can help you generate the stylesheets much more quickly and with fewer errors. One such tool is HP mBuilder, which enables you to design your output just once, and then create multiple XSL stylesheets to target different devices and markup languages.

Figure 10.3 shows a partially developed mobile interface for the Standings application. There are a number of device simulators included with HP mBuilder; you can also plug in additional simulators from other vendors. The general process is to select elements from the palette and add them to the work area, which then causes the display to be updated accordingly. For dynamic content, you can import an XML document and drag and drop elements from the XML document into the Dynamic Data Source box; this will then cause the stylesheet to include proper code to retrieve the dynamic content at runtime. I found that only XML elements could be dragged and dropped this way; if you need to use an XML attribute, you can instead type the proper XPath selector into the Dynamic Data Source box.

When you're satisfied with the appearance of the user interface, you can select the menu option or toolbar button to Generate XSL, and the stylesheets will be created.

Figure 10.3 Using HP mBuilder to design a mobile user interface.

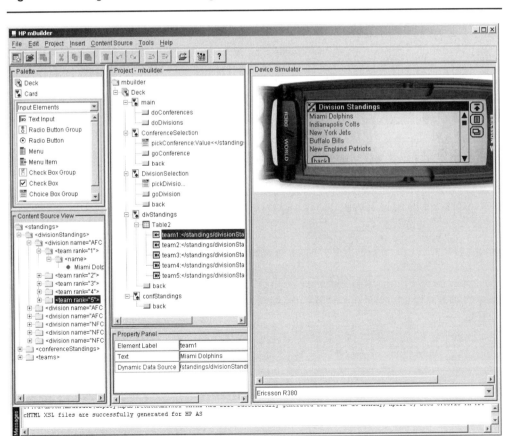

10.1.2 Generating and Transforming XML from a Servlet

Assuming, with a little hand waving, that we have XSL stylesheets that can transform our XML standings into HTML, WML, or XHTML, we still have an important component missing. We need to be able to detect the type of client we are dealing with and select the appropriate transformation for that client.

For this, we'll create a new servlet that we'll call XMLServlet. It is very similar to the previous servlets we've developed. Components of the new servlet are shown in Table 10.1; the full servlet is shown in Listing 10.4. During servlet initialization, we generate the XML Standings document. Then for each client request, we call the new method identifyClient() to determine the device type, set the stylesheet appropriately, and transform the document to the markup language appropriate for the client.

Table 10.1 Components in the XML Servlet Application

New Components			
Name	**Package**	**Class or Interface**	**Comment**
XMLServlet	nfl.application.wireless	Class	Detects client type; transforms XML output appropriately and sends result.
Existing Components			
Component	**Description**		
layered.jar	All classes and interfaces of the layered version of the application (as presented in Chapter 2).		
DynamicStandingsImpl	The Dynamic version of the Standings implementation.		
XML	The XML output formatter from Chapter 9.		

In order to determine the appropriate markup, we're reading the Accept: string from the HttpServletRequest object. In this header, the client identifies all the various types of formatting that it is prepared to handle. Quite simply, we just search this string for MIME types corresponding to WML and XHTML, and set the content-type appropriately. The identifyClient() method also queries the User-Agent string from the request object, but doesn't currently use the information. In a more sophisticated servlet, this more precise identity of the client device could be used to decide how much detail to return based on the screen size of the device, for example.

Listing 10.4 XMLServlet.java

```
// XMLServlet.java
package nfl.application.wireless;

import java.io.*;
import java.text.DecimalFormat;
import java.util.*;

import javax.servlet.*;
import javax.servlet.http.*;

//import org.w3c.dom.Document;
import javax.xml.transform.Source;
import javax.xml.transform.stream.StreamResult;

import nfl.ObjectFactory;
import nfl.application.*;
import nfl.presentation.xml.XML;

public class XMLServlet extends HttpServlet
                        implements SingleThreadModel
{
   // Client capability flags.
   boolean wmlCapable   = false;
   boolean xhtmlCapable = false;

   private DynamicStandings standings = null;
   private Teams      teams      = null;
   private Games      games      = null;
   private List       teamList   = null;

   private XML        xml        = null;
   private Source     doc        = null;

   public void init() throws ServletException {
      Properties p = System.getProperties();
      // note: other apps in same servlet container can set this
      // value and we see it! So don't make set conditional.
      p.setProperty("nfl.versioninfo",
           "nfl.application.DynamicVersionInfo");

      standings = (DynamicStandings)
         ObjectFactory.getHandle().getInstance("DynamicStandings");
      standings.init();

      xml = new XML();
      xml.init();
```

```
      doc = xml.generateXMLDocument();
  }

  public void doGet(HttpServletRequest request,
                    HttpServletResponse response)
              throws ServletException, IOException {

      identifyClient(request, response);

      String uri = request.getRequestURI();
      String url = null;
      StreamResult out = new StreamResult(response.getWriter());
      //PrintWriter out = response.getWriter();
      String stylesheet = null;

      // Stylesheet is searched for relative to
      // CATALINA-HOME/bin. This may not be portable
      // across servlet containers!
      String path = "../webapps/nfl-xml/";

      if (uri.equals("/nfl-xml/servlet/Main")) {
         if (xhtmlCapable)
            stylesheet = path + "XMLStandingsToCHTML.xsl";
         else if (wmlCapable)
            stylesheet = path + "XMLStandingsToWML.xsl";
         else
            stylesheet = path + "XMLStandingsToHTML.xsl";

         System.out.println("Using stylesheet " +
                            stylesheet);
         xml.transformXMLDocument(doc, stylesheet, out);

      } else if (uri.endsWith("/.xhtml")){
         // HTML and WML clients get just a single response;
         // only XHTML is 'paged'.
         // TODO: get the appropriate doc and transform it.
         stylesheet = null;
         xml.transformXMLDocument(doc, stylesheet, out);
      } else {
         response.setStatus(response.SC_NOT_FOUND); /*404*/
      }
  }

  public void doPost(HttpServletRequest request,
                     HttpServletResponse response)
              throws ServletException, IOException {

      doGet(request, response);
  }
```

```
public void identifyClient(HttpServletRequest req,
                           HttpServletResponse res) {
   String userAgent =  req.getHeader("User-Agent");
   String accept    =  req.getHeader("Accept");

   if (accept.indexOf("text/vnd.wap.wml") > -1)
      wmlCapable = true;
   if (accept.indexOf("text/xhmtl") > -1)
      xhtmlCapable = true;

   // Arbitrarily, we will use XHTML for any device
   // that supports both XHTML and WML. We use HTML
   // for devices that support neither.

   if (xhtmlCapable) {
      res.setContentType("text/xhtml");
   } else if (wmlCapable) {
      res.setContentType("text/vnd.wap.wml");
   } else {
      res.setContentType("text/html");
   }
  }
}
```

A new servlet will need a new web.xml file, so we've created one and show it in Listing 10.5.

Listing 10.5 web.xml for XML Servlet

```
<?xml version="1.0" encoding="ISO-8859-1"?>

<!DOCTYPE web-app PUBLIC
   "-//Sun Microsystems, Inc.//DTD Web application 2.2//EN"
   "http://java.sun.com/j2ee/dtds/web-app_2.2.dtd">

<web-app>
  <servlet>
    <servlet-name>XMLStandings</servlet-name>
    <servlet-class>
       nfl.application.wireless.XMLServlet
    </servlet-class>
  </servlet>

  <servlet-mapping>
     <servlet-name>XMLStandings</servlet-name>
     <url-pattern>/servlet/*</url-pattern>
  </servlet-mapping>
</web-app>
```

10.2 Building, Installing, and Running the Wireless Presentation and Servlet Classes

The Ant buildfile shown in Listing 10.6 is used to build the XML servlet. This file is located in `nfl/application/wireless`. The `XMLServlet` file is the only new source to be compiled, but several previously used classes need to be made available within the WAR file for the servlet to function. The WAR file also will include our hand-coded `.wml` and `.xhtml` files, although these were used only in testing and wouldn't be required in production. You can surf directly to them to test their output from a cellphone simulator. The servlet also references nonexistent stylesheets for the WML and XHTML transformations. You could provide these by hand-coding them or creating them using a tool such as HP mBuilder.

You'll need to update the buildfile to reflect the correct location for the `servlet.jar` file on your development system. The default target for this buildfile is the `<servlet>` target, which will create the WAR file `nfl-xml.war`. This WAR file can then be deployed in a servlet container in the usual manner.

One packaging note: I had problems with trying to incorporate `xalan.jar` into the `WEB-INF/lib` directory; when I did so, I received errors saying that "`class org/w3c/dom/Document violates loader constraints`." It appears that this class is being loaded by Tomcat itself via another classloader, and Java security does not permit the same class to be loaded through two different classloaders. To resolve this problem, I instead installed `xalan.jar` in `$CATALINA_HOME/lib`, which has the effect of making it available to all servlets and not just this one.

Listing 10.6 Ant `build.xml` File for XML Servlet Classes

```
<project name="wireless" default="servlet" basedir=".">

<property name="servlet.jar" value="../../../servlet.jar" />

<target name="compile">
   <javac srcdir="." classpath="${servlet.jar}">
      <include name="XMLServlet.java" />
      <src path="../../presentation/xml" />
      <include name="XML.java" />
      <src path=".." />
      <include name="DynamicStandings.java" />
      <include name="DynamicStandingsImpl.java" />
      <include name="DynamicVersionInfo.java" />
   </javac>
</target>

<target name="servlet" depends="compile">
   <delete file="nfl-xml.war" />
   <war warfile="nfl-xml.war" webxml="web.xml" >
```

```
      <!-- wml & xhtml files are the hand-coded examples,
           no longer being served by the servlet, but
           can still be reached by direct URL -->
      <fileset dir="." includes="*.wml,*.xhtml" />
      <fileset dir="." includes="*.xsl" />
      <lib dir="../.." includes="layered.jar" />
      <classes dir="."
          includes="XMLServlet.class"
            prefix=
              "WEB-INF/classes/nfl/application/wireless" />
      <classes dir=".."
          includes="DynamicStandings*.class,
                    DynamicVersionInfo.class"
            prefix="WEB-INF/classes/nfl/application" />
      <classes dir="../../presentation/xml"
          includes="XML.class"
            prefix="WEB-INF/classes/nfl/presentation/xml" />
  </war>
</target>

<target name="clean">
  <delete>
    <fileset dir="." includes="*.class,nfl-xml.war" />
    <fileset dir="../../presentation/xml"
        includes="XML.class" />
  </delete>
</target>

</project>
```

If you have hand-coded WML or XHTML files, you can place them in the build directory and they will get picked up by the packaging step. You can then browse to them at `http://localhost:<port>/nfl-xml/<filename>`. You can access the XMLServlet at `http://localhost:<port>/nfl-xml/servlet/Main`.

10.3 Presentation Architecture Wrap-Up and Review

This concludes our look at presentation options for Web applications. The technologies we've looked at can be broadly categorized into two groups: structural and formatting. The structural technologies, such as servlets, address the issues of how the client and servers communicate. The formatting technologies, such as JSPs and XML, address how the presentation will be formatted.

On the structural side, servlets are the clear winners of those technologies we've examined so far. We'll need to wait until we've looked at Enterprise JavaBeans (EJBs) before we understand the whole story, but anyone starting out with new Web applications would be in good shape if they started out with a servlet architecture, and then moved to EJB if and when dictated by business requirements.

On the formatting side, HTML is still the dominant technology, but XML is the direction nearly everything is moving. For Web Services, XML is already the *lingua franca*, and it will become more pervasive in other applications as well.

10.4 Exercises

10.1 XSLT stylesheets for WML and XHTML: Create stylesheets to transform the Standings XML output to WML and/or XHTML, as described in chapter text. You can do this either by hand or with a tool such as HP mBuilder.

10.5 Further Reading

More information about the Wireless Access Protocol and related markup languages is at `http://www.wapforum.org`.

XHTML Basic is another World Wide Web Consortium (W3C) specification. You can find the specification and related documents at `http://www.w3.org/MarkUp`.

HP mBuilder information and downloads are available at `http://www.hp.com/go/mbuilder`.

## PART III

Distributed Objects
and Web Services

In servlets and JSPs, our clients are very lightweight—just a browser is required. The examples in this section move on to true distributed applications, where an appreciable part of the processing load may be handled by the client. We'll look at distributed objects within Web applications, as enabled by the Java RMI and JMS technologies. And we'll look at the emerging Web-Service technologies that are changing how people think about using the Internet for business-to-business applications.

Introduction to Distributed Objects and Web Services

Web Services is a main theme of this book, and yet so far we haven't really seen a true Web Service. All of the examples we've built up to this point are really Web applications. But these applications have been gradually converging on the fuzzy barrier that separates Web Services from Web applications, and in the next several chapters we'll cross that barrier and enter Web-Services territory. What all of the technologies in this part of the book have in common is the requirement for more work on the part of the client. Most of the technologies we've looked at so far assume a browser at the client side. In the upcoming examples, we move into the realm of distributed objects, where we expect more of the processing to be done on the client side. So instead of passing back a fully formatted HTML screen, we might pass back an XML document that the client can parse and process as required. Or we might pass Java objects, with the client responsible for invoking methods on the objects rather than just passively displaying results.

Web Services are just an evolutionary step, and much of what we've covered so far is the foundation upon which Web Services are built. Most of the underlying technologies of Web Services—such as HTTP and XML—are also part of the foundation of many Web applications. In the next few chapters, we'll look at a few technologies that are important to both Web applications and Web Services, but that are handled differently between the two. These technologies are messaging (Java Message Service (JMS) for Web applications; Java API for XML Messaging (JAXM) for Web Services) and remote procedure calls (Remote Method Invocation (RMI) for Web applications; Java API for XML Remote Procedure Calls (JAX-RPC) for Web Services). We'll also revisit XML, to look at alternatives for parsing and manipulating XML documents.

By the time we've covered these topics, you will be able to create your own Web Services. We'll then look at some of the consumer-side issues of locating Web Services and designing clients to talk to existing Web Services.

11.1 Web Services Defined

There are many definitions of Web Services floating around. Here's one from HP's middleware organization: "Web Services are self-contained, modular business applications that have open, Internet-oriented, standards-based interfaces."

Definitions from other sources frequently get more specific, mentioning for example the use of XML in Web Services. I like HP's definition because it focuses more on what a Web Service is, rather than how it's implemented. When it comes to the implementation, there are many things that are frequently true of Web Services. They frequently use HTTP as the transport, although other standard protocols such as Simple Mail Transport Protocol (SMTP) are also allowed. They frequently use servlets for the runtime component on the server side. They are nearly always based on the SOAP standards for transporting XML documents. But it's possible to find exceptions to nearly all of these, so it's best to think of a Web Service in terms separate from how it is implemented.

There are a few important attributes of Web Services that many of the definitions pick up on. One is that they are *coarse-grained*. A JavaBean's interface is fine-grained; each property has its own accessor methods. To update the internal state of a JavaBean whose interface was exported as a Web Service could take a dozen or more calls across the network, with each call also involving the overhead of encoding and decoding XML. A better interface would transport the entire bean, update it on the client, and then send the updated bean back. The best design, in keeping with the Web-Services philosophy, would be to take any related beans or objects that might be part of the same transaction, send an entire XML document including each such object as an element within the document, and process the entire document as one operation.

Another important attribute of Web Services is that they are *loosely coupled*. In building our Web application examples, the client and server portions together constituted a single application. With a Web Service, it's more correct to think of the client and server pieces as different applications altogether. A client of a Web Service can conceivably be changed to utilize a different Web Service that provides the same information. Or, a client might be used to aggregate information from many Web Services. For example, think of a portal that provides stock quotes, sports scores, news headlines, and weather information. All of these could be coming from different Web Services, and the portal should be easily extensible to plug in other Web Services as needed.

Because of this need for flexibility—flexibility to change out one Web Service for another, or to extend a client to use additional Web Services—there is a need to define Web Services in terms of the service provided, rather than in terms of a specific interface (which is an implementation detail that can change between services, or even in the same service over time). To meet this need, Web Services are described at a high level in terms of the service provided. Typically, this is done via the Web Services Description Language (WSDL). The description of a Web Service, written in WSDL, can then be placed in a registry so that clients can locate it. Clients can search registries using protocols such as Uniform Description, Discovery and Integration (UDDI) and/or Electronic Business XML (ebXML). These topics will be covered in detail in the registries chapter (Chapter 17); I introduce them here just to scope out the boundaries of what Web Services include.

Web Services are immature; the standards, APIs, and implementations are all evolving together and many details will no doubt change over time. The vision of the future goes something like this: An application requiring a service will be able to search registries on the Internet to locate various providers of the service required. The registries will contain enough information that the application can choose which service is best-suited—perhaps based on price, but maybe on the amount or accuracy of data provided, or the timeliness of updates, or any other criteria that are important for the specific application. An application can locate the services it requires and then dynamically assemble itself on the fly to interact with these services.

The reality today is something more like this: There are not many Web Services operating today, and the registry mechanisms for finding a suitable service will probably require a human to evaluate the services and pick the most appropriate. After locating a service, the WSDL description of the service can be downloaded, and client code will probably be written specifically to interact with that service. Adapting code to use another service is not a complete rewrite of the application, but requires enough changes that the creation of a "universal client" that can adapt to any service it finds is not yet a reality.

The evolution from today's reality to tomorrow's vision will proceed at different rates within different industries. Some industry groups will no doubt do an excellent job of defining those attributes that will be common across services; standard terminology in the WSDL will make it easier to locate the right service, and agreements on part or all of the XML structures that will be passed around will make the creation of flexible clients possible. In other industries, competitors will not be able to agree on these things, and client programs will continue to be hand-crafted to match up with specific services.

11.2 Web-Service Models

There are two main models used in the development of Web Services; each of these models can then be further subdivided. The first model is a messaging model. In this model, messages or documents are being exchanged between the server and one or more clients. Messaging is inherently asynchronous, although you can write an application that sends a message and then waits for a message in response, causing synchronous behavior.

The second model is based on Remote Procedure Calls (RPC). RPC systems are generally synchronous, with calls expected to return some value just as in local procedure calls. Again, this is not an absolute. RPC models might be implemented synchronously (wait for a response), asynchronously (response will come at some future point), or one-way (no response is expected).

For the messaging model, we'll look at the JMS first, and then at JAXM. For the RPC model, we'll start with Java RMI, and then move on to JAX-RPC. For both models, the technologies we're examining first are more generally used for Web applications, while the latter ones are more typically used in Web Services. However, I expect to see convergence in these as more Web-Services features find their way into JMS and RMI, and as JAXM and JAX-RPC become more widely adopted, they'll no doubt grow into additional roles as well.

11.3 Web-Service Security

Almost all of the standards relating to Web Services are still evolving, and the security standards are no exception. The lack of maturity in the Web-Service security standards is the biggest barrier to adopting Web-Services technology today. If the security models were complete, we could cover them in the following chapters as an integrated part of our Web Services. Instead, we'll briefly cover them here as a future step in Web-Services evolution.

Starting at the lowest level in the stack, Web Services will require a secure transport mechanism. This is largely in place; Secure Sockets Layer (SSL) and various ways of encrypting information as it is passed over the Internet are well understood. The XML Digital Encryption APIs (JSR-106) will provide a standard for encoding and decoding content that is in XML format. Limited encryption will be allowed—for example, encrypting just a credit-card number in a purchase document. One issue is that encryption can cause validity to break; an XML schema might impose requirements on fields within the document that are no longer true if the fields are encrypted. Several approaches to resolve this are under consideration.

Encryption mechanisms generally operate using a Public Key Infrastructure (PKI) system, and XML Encryption is no different. There is also an XML Key Management Specification (XKMS) that addresses protocols for distributing, registering, and managing the public keys that are used with XML digital encryption and XML digital signatures.

XML Digital Signatures (JSR-105) is the one Web-Service security specification that has actually been completed. An XML document can be digitally signed to authenticate that it was indeed generated by the party from which it claims to come. The digital signature is built up from the sender's private key and a hash code of the data being signed; the hash code helps to ensure that the data being signed is not altered after signing. A variant or extension of an XML signature is a SOAP signature, in which the body of a SOAP document is signed with the signature being placed in a SOAP Header element.

The final area needing to be addressed for Web-Services security is authorization. The emerging standard here is the Security Assertion Markup Language (SAML), which grew out of the AuthXML project at OASIS. SAML can be used to make various types of assertions, including Authentication assertions (the identity of the party is confirmed), Attribute assertions (the account number is valid), Decision assertions (credit is approved), and Authorization assertions (access to a resource is permitted).

Exercises and further reading links for distributed objects and Web Services can be found in the more detailed chapters in the remainder of the part of the book (see Chapters 12 through 18).

The Java Message Service

T he Java Message Service (JMS) belongs to a category of middleware commonly referred to as MOM, or Message-Oriented Middleware. MOM is most commonly used for cross-application messaging, rather than for passing messages within an application. For example, messaging products are frequently used in the area of Enterprise Application Integration (EAI), for tying together different applications provided by different vendors (or perhaps written in-house) that might be in different languages, running on different operating systems and platforms.

The original purpose of JMS was to allow Java to play nicely with the existing messaging products, rather than to suggest an all-Java messaging solution. So not surprisingly, the first products to support JMS were the existing MOM vendors, such as IBM's MQSeries, because JMS provided them a foothold into the rapidly expanding Java market. JMS was added to the J2EE specification as of J2EE version 1.3, so now JMS services are provided by all J2EE-compliant application servers.

JMS still is more commonly encountered in application integration and Java-to-legacy integration roles, but it provides a good introduction to the whole concept of MOM. In the next chapter, we'll look at the JAXM specification, which brings an XML flavor to messaging. It is JAXM that will be more commonly used in Web Services, but JMS has a role to play there as well.

Also in this chapter, we'll take our first look at the Java Naming and Directory Interface (JNDI). JNDI is an interface to several types of directory services, such as LDAP or DNS. Several Java APIs, including JMS and EJB, require the use of JNDI as the naming service interface that allows clients to locate the servers they need to connect to. We'll cover the basics on JNDI as needed to support our JMS examples.

Software Used in This Chapter

Java Message Service

Version 1.0.2. The examples in this chapter use the Java Message Service API. You will need JMS provider software, which is available as either a standalone product (for example, IBM MQSeries, Progress SonicMQ) or integrated into an application server product.

Java Naming and Directory Services (JNDI)

JMS implementations include a messaging provider. Clients of the messaging provider connect to it in order to send and receive messages. The messaging provider is located by clients by looking it up in a JNDI directory.

BEA WebLogic Application Server

Version 6.1 with Service Pack 2. The included implementation of JMS was used to test the example programs. WebLogic also includes a JNDI provider that is also used by the example programs.

12.1 JMS Features

JMS is a set of APIs that supports two different modes of messaging operation. In the first mode, point-to-point, messages are sent from a single source to a single destination. In the second mode, publish-subscribe, a single source can send messages that are replicated to any number of recipients.

The ability to send messages, either to a single recipient or to multiple recipients, can be written fairly easily just using sockets. So what are the benefits provided by using MOM software such as a JMS provider?

The sender and receiver of a JMS message are frequently described as being loosely coupled. In a sockets application, the sender and receiver are tightly coupled—they are generally designed as a unit. For a message to be delivered, a sockets application expects both the sender and the receiver to be up and running simultaneously, and often one cannot operate without the other. JMS senders and receivers are less interdependent; for example, if there is no receiver for a particular JMS message, it can simply be stored until a receiver becomes ready. Some of the features of JMS that make it more flexible than a generic sockets program are outlined in the next few paragraphs.

Asynchronous delivery. In a sockets application, client and server run concurrently. If either side is not running initially, the connection cannot be established. If either side stops running after the connection is made, the connection will fail, frequently causing the program at the other side of the connection to terminate abnormally. In a JMS application, the sender needs only to be able to communicate with the messaging provider, which will then be responsible for delivery to the receiver.

Guaranteed delivery. When a connection is interrupted in a sockets connection, it is frequently unclear whether the last message was delivered successfully or not. With a messaging product conforming to the JMS specification, delivery is guaranteed. When a send operation returns to the caller, it indicates that the messaging service has responsibility for that message. If the message is not successfully delivered upon the first try, the message server will retry until it is successful. Guaranteed delivery also ensures that each message is delivered only once (unless configured to allow duplicates).

Durable subscriptions. In publish/subscribe mode, durable subscriptions cause the message server to store messages so that any subscribers who aren't currently connected will receive any unexpired messages when they reconnect.

Message selectors. These allow a JMS client to filter the messages being received. There is a robust expression syntax allowing complex filters to be constructed.

Integration with Enterprise JavaBeans (EJB). The EJB 2.0 specification introduced a new bean type, the `MessageDrivenBean`, which is an EJB that consumes JMS messages.

12.1.1 Messaging Scenarios

These various capabilities can be better understood if we think of some common messaging scenarios that help illustrate various features of messaging software.

E-mail scenario. An e-mail message is to be delivered to one or more recipients. If the recipients aren't currently available, the message should be stored until it can be delivered to them. This could be implemented using the point-to-point model, and guaranteed delivery, or in a publish-subscribe model if multiple recipients are targeted.

Stock ticker scenario. Stock quotes are published out to any currently active subscribers. If for any reason delivery fails, there is no need to store the results or to retry. This would be implemented using the publish-subscribe model.

Task broker scenario. Clients needing work done add task descriptions to a message queue. A pool of worker processes or threads take messages from the queue and complete the task.

12.1.2 Limitations of JMS

The most important limitation to understand about JMS is that it is not intended to provide interoperability between heterogeneous messaging providers. That is, JMS software from vendor A cannot be expected to receive and properly understand messages from vendor B, as JMS specifications do not specify the on-the-wire protocol used in passing messages between producers and consumers. This is perhaps the biggest reason why, while JMS plays an important role in the integration of legacy applications, it is less suitable for the Web Services arena where interoperability with many different clients is of prime importance. For that level of interoperability, the SOAP messaging protocol was created, and we'll look at that in the next chapter.

12.2 JMS Pieces and Parts

The Java Message Service introduces us to some new terminology. Here are some of the important terms to know to make sense of the APIs and documentation.

Connections. In our application, we talk of a client portion and a server portion, but in JMS terms both of these entities are clients of the JMS messaging provider. The JMS clients connect to the messaging provider by creating a `Connection`, which is done via a `ConnectionFactory` object. In the publish-subscribe model, the specific classes used are `TopicConnection` and `TopicConnectionFactory`; for point-to-point messages, `QueueConnection` and `QueueConnectionFactory` are used.

Sessions. Once a connection is obtained with the messaging provider, one or more sessions are then created. The session object is itself another type of factory; this one is used for creating `Message`, `Publisher`, and `Subscriber` objects. As with `Connections`, there are `TopicSessions` for publish/subscribe operations and `QueueSessions` for point-to-point operations.

Topics. In the publish-subscribe model, a `Topic` is a channel to which messages are published. Subscribers to a topic will receive each message published to the topic. If a message is made durable, then the message is delivered not only to currently connected subscribers, but also to any subscribers who connect later. A stock ticker, for example, would not use durable messages; a client is typically only interested in seeing quotations during the time the connection is live, and doesn't need to catch up on quotes missed while offline. If messages instead contained bid information, going from a customer to potential vendors, then a durable message should be used so that all vendors would receive the material whether they are currently connected or not.

Publishers. A publisher writes messages to a specific `Topic`.

Subscribers. A subscriber receives messages from a `Topic`.

Messages. `Messages` are what the JMS server is passing around. Every message consists of a header (which specifies attributes of the message) and a payload (the application data). There are several types of messages; they differ based on the type of data carried as the payload.

  • The `Message` type has no payload; it can be used as a simple event. It is also the superclass of all the other message types.

- The `TextMessage` type carries a text message (`java.lang.String`). It might contain just a simple text string, or something as complex as a full XML document. Some JMS providers provide a specific `XMLMessage` type, and it's possible that this will become a standard part of a later version of the JMS specification.
- The `ObjectMessage` carries a serialized Java `Object` as its payload.
- The `BytesMessage` carries a byte array payload.
- The `StreamMessage` carries a stream that comprises primitive types (such as `int`, `long`, `float`, `double`) for its payload.
- The `MapMessage` carries an associative array (name-value pairs) as its payload.

Queues. Queues in the point-to-point model are analogous to topics in the publish-subscribe model. Messages are written to a `Queue` and then received by clients reading from that queue. Reading a message deletes it from the queue; so while there can be multiple readers of the `Queue`, each message will only be received by a single reader. There may also be multiple writers to the queue. As implied by the name, the queue is kept in order; messages will be taken from the queue in the same order they were added.

Senders. `Senders` write messages to `Queues` (analogous to `Publishers`).

Receivers. `Receivers` read messages from `Queues` (analogous to `Subscribers`).

12.3 A JMS-Based Game Server

In all the versions of the example application we've developed so far, the results of games have been received from sources inside the application. For the purposes of illustrating Web Services, we're going to start thinking about our application as two independent components. The application we've developed up until now is the Standings application. Now we'll look at a new application, a Game Server, which provides the results of games played. Our Standings application will be a client of the `GameServer` application. The relationship is depicted graphically in Figure 12.1.

In this chapter, we'll develop a `GameServer` using JMS, and then we'll revisit the application in the next chapter using the JAXM messaging APIs. The `GameServer` application consists of just a single class, shown in Listing 12.1.[1]

The logic flow is very straightforward. We read in the `Games` list of games played, and then loop through the entire list, sending a message for each game result. A `sleep()` command in the loop spaces out the messages; in a real application, the game results would be spaced out over the length of the season, and not just a span of minutes.

---

1. If we were going to make `GameServer` truly a separate application, it would be in a different package and share no classes with the existing application. However, for ease of illustration, I've left it in the `nfl` package so that we can reuse the same `ObjectFactory`, `Games`, and `Game` classes rather than creating new classes with the same functionality.

Figure 12.1 Flow diagram for the JMS version of the application.

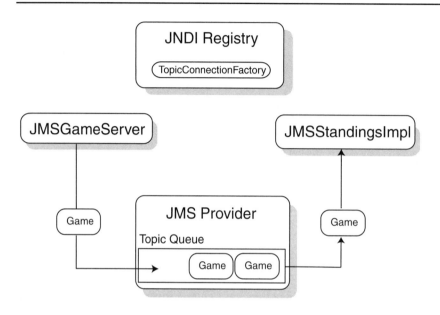

Table 12.1   Components in the JMS Client Applications

New Components			
Name	**Package**	**Class or Interface**	**Comment**
JMSGameServer	nfl.application.jms	Class	Sends a message representing each game played.
JMSStandingsImpl	nfl.application.jms	Class	Extends `DynamicStandings-Impl` and implements `Message-Listener`. Receives messages sent by `JMSGameServer` and updates standings accordingly.
EmptyGameDataImpl	nfl.persistence	Class	Creates an empty `GameList`.
Existing Components			
Component	**Description**		
layered.jar	All classes and interfaces of the layered version of the application (as presented in Chapter 2).		
DynamicStandingsImpl	Version of Standings developed originally for servlet chapter.		

As you look at the program listing, there are a number of statements dealing with the JNDI service used to locate and connect to the messaging provider. We'll defer looking at those until the next section. Here are the steps that we go through in the code to handle creating and delivering messages:

- *(in method init())* Look up the `TopicConnectionFactory` object that is registered with JNDI.
- Use the `TopicConnectionFactory` to create a topic connection, which is the connection type used for publish-subscribe messaging. (If we were doing point-to-point messaging, we would instead have obtained a `QueueConnectionFactory` to create a `QueueConnection`.)
- Using the `connection` object, we create a session (`TopicSession` in this example, `QueueSession` for point-to-point).
- Using the session object, we look up a topic. The API name `createTopic()` is misleading; the topic must be pre-created using the JMS administration tools. (Exception: Temporary topics, which do not outlive the session, can be created programmatically on the fly; but we want a long-lived topic that we can reconnect to in later sessions.)
- In order to write messages to the topic, we create a `Publisher`. (For point-to-point messages, we would instead create a `Sender`.)
- We can optionally set attributes for all messages created by the publisher by calling APIs of the `Publisher` object, or attributes for individual messages by calling similar APIs of the `Message` object. We set our messages to be persistent, without expiration, and at the default priority.
- We call the `start()` method on the connection, which must be called before any messages can be sent or received.
- This completes the initialization of the connection. In the `run()` method, we loop through the list of game results, sending messages for each. We've chosen to send object messages, so the `createObjectMessage()` method is used. If we were concerned about interoperating with non-Java subscribers, a text message would be more appropriate.
- The created message is then sent using the `publish()` method of the `Publisher`.

Listing 12.1 A Messaging-Based Game Server

```
// JMSGameServer.java

package nfl.application.jms;

import nfl.ObjectFactory;
import nfl.application.*;
```

```java
import java.util.List;
import javax.jms.*;
import javax.naming.InitialContext;
import javax.naming.NamingException;

public class JMSGameServer {

    private Games games;
    private List  gameList;

    // command-line configurable args. Default values are
    // for WebLogic 6.1
    private static String jndiUrl = "t3://localhost:7001";
    private static String tcfName = "weblogic.jms.ConnectionFactory";

    private int msgInterval = 60000; /* millisecs */

    private TopicSession   session;
    private TopicPublisher publisher;
    private Topic          nflGames;

    public JMSGameServer() {
        ObjectFactory of = ObjectFactory.getHandle();
        games = (Games) of.getInstance("Games");
        gameList = games.getGameList();
    }

    public void init() {
        TopicConnectionFactory tcFactory;
        TopicConnection        connection;
        String                 user, pass;

        try {
            InitialContext jndiContext = new InitialContext();

            tcFactory = (TopicConnectionFactory)
                        jndiContext.lookup(tcfName);

            user = "guest";
            pass = "guest";
            connection = tcFactory.createTopicConnection(user,
                                                         pass);

            session = connection.createTopicSession(
                        false,                /* not transacted */
                        Session.AUTO_ACKNOWLEDGE /* ack mode */
                    );
```

```
        nflGames   = session.createTopic(
                              "MyJMSServer/NFL Game Results");
        publisher = session.createPublisher(nflGames);
        // Following 3 lines are just setting the default
        // values; they're included to allow playing with
        // settings.
        publisher.setDeliveryMode(DeliveryMode.PERSISTENT);
        publisher.setPriority(Message.DEFAULT_PRIORITY);
        publisher.setTimeToLive(0); /* never expire */
        connection.start();
    } catch (JMSException e) {
        e.printStackTrace();
        System.exit(-1);
    } catch (NamingException e) {
        e.printStackTrace();
        System.exit(-1);
    }
}

public void run() {
    ObjectMessage gameResult = null;
    Game            game;

    for (int i=0; i<gameList.size(); i++) {
        game = (Game) gameList.get(i);
        try {
            System.out.println("creating message");
            // Must be Serializable, so (Game) doesn't work.
            gameResult = session.createObjectMessage(
                                  (BasicGameImpl)game);
            // TimeToLive, DeliveryMode, Priority could
            // also be set at the Message level.
            System.out.println("publishing message");
            publisher.publish(gameResult);
            Thread.sleep(msgInterval);
        } catch (JMSException e) {
            e.printStackTrace();
        } catch (InterruptedException e) {
            /* ignore */
        }
    }
}

public static void main(String [] args) {
    java.util.Properties p = System.getProperties();
    p.setProperty("nfl.versioninfo",
                        "nfl.application.jms.JMSServerVInfo");
    JMSGameServer gameServer = new JMSGameServer();
```

```
        for (int i=0; i<args.length; i++) {
            if (args[i].equals("-jndiURL"))
                jndiUrl = args[++i];
            if (args[i].equals("-tcfName"))
                tcfName = args[++i];
        }

        gameServer.init();
        gameServer.run();
    }
}
```

If you are familiar with event handling as implemented in JavaBeans or the Java AWT classes, you'll probably find the messaging model familiar. Sending a message to a target is very similar to firing an event on that target, but the messaging model has broader flexibility in being able to have targets on other systems and the message delivered at some future time.

12.4 JMS API Reference

The following API reference is not exhaustive, but rather covers the most frequently used APIs, or those that best give a feel of the capabilities available in JMS. The various JMS message sub-types are not shown.

API 12.1 javax.jms.**QueueConnectionFactory**

```
public interface QueueConnectionFactory extends ConnectionFactory
    // No methods in ConnectionFactory superclass
    public QueueConnection createQueueConnection() throws JMSException;
    public QueueConnection createQueueConnection(String user, String pass)
        throws JMSException;
```

API 12.2 javax.jms.**TopicConnectionFactory**

```
public interface TopicConnectionFactory extends ConnectionFactory
    public TopicConnection createTopicConnection() throws JMSException;
    public TopicConnection createTopicConnection(String user, String pass)
        throws JMSException;
```

API 12.3 javax.jms.**Connection**

```
public interface Connection
    public void close() throws JMSException;
    public ExceptionListener getExceptionListener() throws JMSException;
    public ConnectionMetaData getMetaData() throws JMSException;
    public void setClientID(java.lang.String clientID) throws JMSException;
    public void setExceptionListener(ExceptionListener l) throws JMSException;
    public void start() throws JMSException;
    public void stop() throws JMSException;
```

API 12.4   javax.jms.**QueueConnection**

```
public interface QueueConnection extends Connection
    public QueueSession createQueueSession(boolean transacted,
        int acknowledgeMode) throws JMSException;
    public ConnectionConsumer createConnectionConsumer(Queue name,
        String messageSelector, ServerSessionPool sessionPool,
        int maxMessages) throws JMSException;
```

API 12.5   javax.jms.**TopicConnection**

```
public interface TopicConnection extends Connection
    public TopicSession createTopicSession(boolean transacted, int acknowledgeMode)
        throws JMSException;
    public ConnectionConsumer createConnectionConsumer(Topic topic,
        String messageSelector, ServerSessionPool sessionPool,
        int maxMessages) throws JMSException;
    public ConnectionConsumer createDurableConnectionConsumer(Topic topic,
        String subscriptionName, String messageSelector,
        ServerSessionPool sessionPool,  int maxMessages)
        throws JMSException;
```

API 12.6   javax.jms.**Session**

```
public interface Session extends java.lang.Runnable
    public static final int AUTO_ACKNOWLEDGE = 1;
    public static final int CLIENT_ACKNOWLEDGE = 2;
    public static final int DUPS_OK_ACKNOWLEDGE = 3;

    public BytesMessage createBytesMessage() throws JMSException;
    public MapMessage createMapMessage() throws JMSException;
    public Message createMessage() throws JMSException;
    public ObjectMessage createObjectMessage() throws JMSException;
    public ObjectMessage createObjectMessage(Serializable object)
                throws JMSException;
    public StreamMessage createStreamMessage() throws JMSException;
    public TextMessage createTextMessage() throws JMSException;
    public TextMessage createTextMessage(String text) throws JMSException;
    public boolean getTransacted() throws JMSException;
    public void commit() throws JMSException;
    public void rollback() throws JMSException;
    public void close() throws JMSException;
    public void recover() throws JMSException;
    public MessageListener getMessageListener() throws JMSException;
    public void setMessageListener(MessageListener listener) throws JMSException;
    public void run();
```

API 12.7 javax.jms.**QueueSession**

```
public interface QueueSession extends Session
    public Queue createQueue(String queueName) throws JMSException;
    public QueueReceiver createReceiver(Queue queue) throws JMSException;
    public QueueReceiver createReceiver(Queue queue, String messageSelector)
        throws JMSException;
    public QueueSender createSender(Queue queue) throws JMSException;
    public QueueBrowser createBrowser(Queue queue) throws JMSException;
    public QueueBrowser createBrowser(Queue queue, String messageSelector)
        throws JMSException;
    public TemporaryQueue createTemporaryQueue() throws JMSException;
```

API 12.8 javax.jms.**TopicSession**

```
public interface TopicSession extends Session
    public Topic createTopic(String topicName) throws JMSException;
    public TopicSubscriber createSubscriber(Topic topic) throws JMSException;
    public TopicSubscriber createSubscriber(Topic topic, String messageSelector,
        boolean noLocal) throws JMSException;
    public TopicSubscriber createDurableSubscriber(Topic topic, String name)
        throws JMSException;
    public TopicSubscriber createDurableSubscriber(Topic topic, String name,
        String messageSelector, boolean noLocal) throws JMSException;
    public TopicPublisher createPublisher(Topic topic) throws JMSException;
    public TemporaryTopic createTemporaryTopic() throws JMSException;
    public void unsubscribe(String name) throws JMSException;
```

API 12.9 javax.jms.**MessageProducer**

```
public interface MessageProducer
    public void setDisableMessageID(boolean value) throws JMSException;
    public boolean getDisableMessageID() throws JMSException;
    public void setDisableMessageTimestamp(boolean value) throws JMSException;
    public boolean getDisableMessageTimestamp() throws JMSException;
    public void setDeliveryMode(int mode) throws JMSException;
    public int getDeliveryMode() throws JMSException;
    public void setPriority(int priority) throws JMSException;
    public int getPriority() throws JMSException;
    public void setTimeToLive(long ttl) throws JMSException;
    public long getTimeToLive() throws JMSException;
    public void close() throws JMSException;
```

API 12.10 javax.jms.**QueueSender**

```
public interface QueueSender extends MessageProducer
    public Queue getQueue() throws JMSException;
    public void send(Message message) throws JMSException;
    public void send(Message message, int deliveryMode, int priority, long timeToLive)
        throws JMSException;
    public void send(Queue queue, Message message) throws JMSException;
    public void send(Queue queue, Message message, int deliveryMode, int priority,
        long timeToLive) throws JMSException;
```

API 12.11 javax.jms.**TopicPublisher**

```
public interface TopicPublisher extends MessageProducer
    public Topic getTopic() throws JMSException;
    public void publish(Message message) throws JMSException;
    public void publish(Message message, int deliveryMode, int priority,
        long timeToLive) throws JMSException;
    public void publish(Topic topic, Message message) throws JMSException;
    public void publish(Topic topic, Message message, int deliveryMode, int priority,
        long timeToLive) throws JMSException;
```

API 12.12 javax.jms.**MessageListener**

```
public interface MessageListener
    public void onMessage(Message message);
```

API 12.13 javax.jms.**MessageConsumer**

```
public interface MessageConsumer
    public void close() throws JMSException
    public MessageListener getMessageListener() throws JMSException
    public String getMessageSelector() throws JMSException;
    public Message receive() throws JMSException;
    public Message receive(long timeout) throws JMSException;
    public Message receiveNoWait() throws JMSException;
    public void setMessageListener(MessageListener) throws JMSException;
```

API 12.14 javax.jms.**QueueReceiver**

```
public interface QueueReceiver extends MessageConsumer
    public Queue getQueue() throws JMSException;
```

API 12.15 javax.jms.**TopicSubscriber**

```
public interface TopicSubscriber extends MessageConsumer
    public Topic getTopic() throws JMSException;
    public boolean getNoLocal() throws JMSException;
```

API 12.16 javax.jms.**Message**

```
public interface Message
    public void acknowledge() throws JMSException;
    public void clearBody() throws JMSException;
    public void clearProperties() throws JMSException;
    public Enumeration getPropertyNames() throws JMSException;
    public boolean propertyExists(String name) throws JMSException;
```

Not shown: property getter/setter methods for the following properties:
   Destination **JMSDestination**; int **JMSDeliveryMode**; String **JMSMessageID**;
   long **JMSTimestamp**; long **JMSExpiration**; boolean **JMSRedelivered**;
   int **JMSPriority**; Destination **JMSReplyTo**; String **JMSCorrelationID**;
   StringJMSType.

Also not shown; a series of getter/setter methods for message properties,
   of the form
      <type> **get**<Type>**Property**(String name)
   and
      void **set**<Type>**Property**(String name, <type> value)
   where type is each of `String`, `int`, `boolean`, `double`, `float`, `byte`, `long`,
   `short`, and `Object`

12.5 Java Naming and Directory Interface

We skipped over some of the setup code in the previous example so that we could concentrate on the messaging functionality. Whenever clients and servers need to communicate, there must be a way for the side initiating the connection to locate the other side. With a typical sockets application, this is done via a well-known port number. For JMS, as well as several other J2EE APIs, the Java Naming and Directory Interface (JNDI) is used to facilitate this location. A service can register itself in a JNDI registry; clients can then look up the service by name. The process of using JNDI is straightforward:

- The server obtains a connection to the JNDI registry via the call `getInitialContext()`.
- Using the `initialContext`, the server registers itself with a `bind()` or `rebind()` call that registers the name by which the server can be accessed. (The `bind()` call will throw an exception if the name is already bound in the registry; a `rebind()` call will replace any existing name binding, or create a new one if none exists.)

- A client then connects to the JNDI registry, also using the `getInitialContext()` call.
- The client then does a `lookup()` call with the service name. It will return an object through which the service can be accessed.

Note that JNDI doesn't care what interface is supported by the objects that it hands around; there is no particular interface that a `TopicConnectionFactory`, for example, must implement in order for JNDI to store the object in its registry. Because the client looking up the object is very frequently on a different system than the server that registered the object, the object is likely to implement a remote protocol such as RMI, but this is not a requirement imposed by JNDI.

There are many different implementations of JNDI. Any J2EE-compliant application server is required to support JNDI, so such calls as `getInitialContext()` and `lookup()` can be expected to work with any J2EE application server. However, there are certain configuration tasks for JNDI that tend to be implementation-specific. To avoid putting implementation-specific code in the application source, JNDI will look for and read a file named `jndi.properties` to find values for these implementation-specific properties. Listing 12.2 shows the `jndi.properties` file that is included with the example code; it is configured for the BEA WebLogic application server.

Listing 12.2 `jndi.properties` File

```
#
# jndi.properties for BEA WebLogic 6.1, 7.0
#
java.naming.provider.url=t3://localhost:7001
java.naming.factory.initial=weblogic.jndi.WLInitialContextFactory
```

JNDI is designed to work with different directory types that use different naming conventions. For example, within the Internet namespace we have such names as `myserver.mydomain.com`, where the highest-level element is the rightmost, and name components are separated by periods. Within the UNIX file system namespace, we have names such as `/mydirectory/mysubdirectory/myfile`, where the highest-level element is the leftmost, and components are separated by slashes. JNDI can also work with composite names, which are those that cross namespaces; a URL is perhaps the most common example of this, because it usually contains both an Internet-style name combined with a filespace-style name.

The only JNDI object we interact with is the `InitialContext` object, which implements the `Context` interface. A `Context` is defined as "an object whose state is a set of bindings with distinct atomic names."[2] It's easier to think of a `Context` as a location within the "directory

---

2. From the API documentation.

tree" of the namespace. So if your `Context` was the root of the Internet namespace, the bindings accessible to you would be top-level domains such as `com`, `org`, `net`, and `edu`. If you moved to the `com` context, you could access the next set of bindings, and so on, building a directory path until you reach the desired entry.

Because our usage is very simple, we just operate in a flat namespace where any object we need to register and access is directly under the `InitialContext`.

12.6 JNDI API Reference

There are many classes within the JNDI API set, but for our very basic usage we use only one, the `InitialContext` class. Only a small selection of the methods are shown in the following API summary.

API 12.17 javax.naming.**InitialContext**

```
public class InitialContext implements Context
    // All methods are defined in interface Context
    public void bind(Name name, Object obj);
    public void bind(String name, Object obj);
    public NamingEnumeration list(Name name);
    public NamingEnumeration list(String name);
    public Object lookup(Name name);
    public Object lookup(String name);
    public void rebind(Name name, Object obj);
    public void rebind(String name, Object obj);
    public void rename(Name old, Name new);
    public void rename(String old, String new);
    public void unbind(Name name);
    public void unbind(String name);
```

12.7 A JMS Subscriber

Our `JMSGameServer` is a JMS publisher; now we need to see what the subscriber for this service would look like. Listing 12.3 shows the `JMSStandingsImpl` class. In this class, we extend the `DynamicStandingsImpl` class that provides the application behavior we need. We also implement the `javax.jms.MessageListener` interface, which requires that we implement a single method, `onMessage()`, which will be invoked by the JMS messaging provider whenever a message is ready to be delivered to us.

Much of the code in this class is the same as in the `GameServer`. We follow the same procedure to find the messaging provider using the JNDI. We also use the same code to create `TopicConnectionFactory`, `TopicConnection`, and `TopicSession` objects. The difference comes at the next step: While the `GameServer` created a `Publisher`, in this class we instead create a `Subscriber`. Specifically, we create a `DurableSubscriber`, which means we want the JMS middleware to remember us when we're gone; once we are registered as a subscriber, if we disconnect from the messaging software, it will save messages for us until we reconnect (or the messages expire, if they are given expiration times). We use the setMessageListener() method of the subscriber object to indicate what class should receive the messages; we pass the this pointer because this is the target class.

All of this setup is done in the constructor method. In main(), after we create the object and thus execute the constructor, we simply call Thread.sleep() to wait for messages. Each message received will cause the onMessage() method to execute. Within this method, we simply extract the Game object from the object and call the postGameData() method inherited from DynamicStandings to update our results.

Our DynamicStandingsImpl class was designed to load any completed games when the class is loaded, and then it can receive new game results while it is running. We created a trivial EmptyGameDataImpl class that returns an empty list to the DynamicStandings class when it starts up. Our system as currently implemented is flawed in that it has no facility to persist game results it receives while it is running; so if the application is terminated before all games have been processed, results will be lost.

Our implementation uses an asynchronous messaging model. This means that our application is free to be doing other useful work rather than just waiting on a message to be received. (Okay, Thread.sleep() isn't exactly useful work, but we could have done something more interesting.) Asynchronous messaging can also be thought of as a "push" messaging model; the messaging provider will push messages to use as they become available. JMS also allows us to us a synchronous messaging model, in which we pull messages from the messaging provider by calling an explicit receive() method, typically blocking until a message is available. Although not in use as the application currently stands, the JMSStandingsImpl class also includes a run() method that implements synchronous messaging by calling the receive() method.

Listing 12.3 JMSStandingsImpl Class

```
// JMSStandingsImpl.java

package nfl.application.jms;

import nfl.ObjectFactory;
import nfl.application.*;
import nfl.application.jndi.*;

import java.util.Properties;
import javax.jms.*;
import javax.naming.*;

public class JMSStandingsImpl
            extends DynamicStandingsImpl
            implements javax.jms.MessageListener {
```

```
private TopicSubscriber subscriber = null;
private static ObjectFactory   of  = null;

// Command-line configurable args
private static String user = "guest";
private static String pass = "guest";
private static String jndiUrl =
                  "t3://localhost:7001";
private static String tcfName =
                  "weblogic.jms.ConnectionFactory";
private static String clientID = "Client-1";
private static String topicName = "NFL Game Results";
private static String subName = "Subscription-1";

// doing in constructor would be too late
static {
   Properties env = System.getProperties();
   env.put("nfl.versioninfo",
           "nfl.application.jms.JMSClientVInfo");
}

// Constructor
public JMSStandingsImpl() {
   super.init();

   TopicConnectionFactory tcFactory = null;
   TopicConnection        connection = null;
   TopicSession           session   = null;
   Topic                  results   = null;

   try {
      Context jndiContext = new InitialContext();
      tcFactory = (TopicConnectionFactory)
                  jndiContext.lookup(tcfName);
      connection = tcFactory.createTopicConnection(user,
                                               pass);
      connection.setClientID(clientID);
      session = connection.createTopicSession(false,
                     Session.AUTO_ACKNOWLEDGE);

      results = (Topic) jndiContext.lookup(topicName);
      subscriber = session.createDurableSubscriber(
                          results, subName);
      subscriber.setMessageListener(this);
      connection.start();
      System.out.println("Connection started");
   } catch (JMSException e) {
      e.printStackTrace();
```

```java
      } catch (NamingException e) {
         e.printStackTrace();
      }
   }

   // Receive a message
   public void onMessage(Message message) {
      System.out.println("Received async message: " + message);
      Game g = null;
      try {
         g = (Game)((ObjectMessage)message).getObject();
         postGameData(g);
         System.out.println("Game has been posted.");
      } catch (JMSException e) {
         e.printStackTrace();
      }
   }

   // This method for synchronous operation; not in use.
   public void run() {
      Message m = null;
      while(true) {
         try {
            m = subscriber.receive();
         } catch (JMSException e) {
            e.printStackTrace();
         }
         System.out.println("Received sync message: " + m);
         //todo: process, perhaps via onMessage
      }
   }

   public static void main(String[] args) {
      of = ObjectFactory.getHandle();

      // Parse command line args.
      for (int i=0; i<args.length; i++) {
         if (args[i].equals("-user"))
            user = args[++i];
         if (args[i].equals("-pass"))
            pass = args[++i];
         if (args[i].equals("-jndiUrl"))
            jndiUrl = args[++i];
         if (args[i].equals("-tcfName"))
            tcfName = args[++i];
         if (args[i].equals("-client"))
            clientID = args[++i];
         if (args[i].equals("-topic"))
            topicName = args[++i];
```

```
        if (args[i].equals("-sub"))
           subName = args[++i];
     }

     JMSStandingsImpl standings = new JMSStandingsImpl();

     //For synchronous operation, remove setMessageListener
     //call in constructor, remove sleep, and call this:
     //standings.run();

     try {
        Thread.sleep(Long.MAX_VALUE);
     } catch (InterruptedException e) {
        System.out.println("interrupted while sleeping");
     }
   }
}
```

12.8 Building, Deploying, and Running the JMS Examples

The Ant `build.xml` file for the JMS examples is located in the `nfl/application/jms` directory, and shown in Listing 12.4. There are properties set at the beginning of the file that should be changed if you are using a different JMS provider than the BEA WebLogic server. The properties specify the class name of the `TopiConnectionFactory` implementation class, and the URL at which the JNDI provider is located. You should also have your system CLASSPATH set so that the JNDI and JMS providers will be found (the `weblogic.jar` file in this case of BEA).

In order to run the examples, you must configure your JMS provider, including creating the topic. Instructions for doing so in WebLogic follow the buildfile listing. Once JMS is configured, you can invoke the `<test-server>` target in one window, and the `<test-client>` target in another, to see the messaging application in operation.

Listing 12.4 `build.xml` for JMS Examples

```xml
<project name="nfl-jms" default="both" basedir=".">

<!-- Set this property to the classname of the
     ConnectionFactory object in your JNDI provider -->
<property name="jms.tcfName"
        value="weblogic.jms.ConnectionFactory" />
<!-- Set this property to the URL of the JNDI provider -->
<property name="jndi.url"
        value="t3://localhost:7001" />

<!-- You must also ensure that CLASSPATH setting includes
     JNDI provider and JMS provider -->
```

```
<target name="compile">
  <javac srcdir="..">
    <include name="DynamicStandings.java"/>
    <include name="DynamicStandingsImpl.java"/>
  </javac>
  <javac srcdir=".">
    <include name="JMSGameServer.java"/>
    <include name="JMSStandingsImpl.java"/>
    <include name="JMSClientVInfo.java"/>
    <include name="JMSServerVInfo.java"/>
  </javac>
  <javac srcdir="../../persistence">
    <include name="EmptyGameDataImpl.java"/>
  </javac>
</target>

<target name="both">
   <antcall target="server" />
   <antcall target="client" />
</target>

<target name="server" depends="compile">
   <jar jarfile="jmsserver.jar">
      <zipfileset dir="." includes="jndi.properties" />
      <zipfileset dir="." prefix="nfl/application/jms" >
         <include name="JMSGameServer.class" />
         <include name="JMSServerVInfo.class" />
      </zipfileset>
   </jar>
</target>

<target name="client" depends="compile">
   <jar jarfile="jmsclient.jar">
      <zipfileset dir="." includes="jndi.properties" />
      <zipfileset dir=".." prefix="nfl/application"
         includes="DynamicStandings*.class" />
      <zipfileset dir="." prefix="nfl/application/jms" >
         <include name="JMSStandingsImpl.class" />
         <include name="JMSClientVInfo.class" />
      </zipfileset>
   </jar>
</target>

<target name="test-server">
   <java classname="nfl.application.jms.JMSGameServer"
            fork="true" >
      <classpath>
          <pathelement location="jmsserver.jar" />
```

```
            <pathelement location="layered.jar" />
            <pathelement path="${java.class.path}" />
        </classpath>
        <arg value="-jndiURL ${jndi.url}" />
        <arg value="-tcfName ${jms.tcfName}" />
    </java>
</target>

<target name="test-client">
    <java classname="nfl.application.jms.JMSStandingsImpl"
             fork="true" >
        <classpath>
            <pathelement location="jmsclient.jar" />
            <pathelement location="layered.jar" />
            <pathelement path="${java.class.path}" />
        </classpath>
        <arg value="-jndiURL ${jndi.url}" />
    </java>
</target>

<target name="clean">
  <delete includeEmptyDirs="true">
    <fileset dir="." includes="*.class" />
    <fileset dir="." includes="*.jar" />
  </delete>
</target>

</project>
```

12.8.1 Configuring BEA WebLogic 6.1 as a JMS Provider

Use the following steps to configure the BEA WebLogic application server for use with the examples in this chapter.

- Install WebLogic (if not already installed) following the vendor's instructions.
- If already installed, obtain the administrator login and password. If installing, you'll have the opportunity to set these.
- Start WebLogic. This is typically done by running the script `startWebLogic.sh` in the directory `$WLS_HOME/config/mydomain`.
- Start the Web console; surf to `http://systemname:7001/console`. (Port 7001 is the default, but it may be different in your configuration.)
- From the tree list at the left side of the Web console, select the Services node and expand it if not already expanded.
- Select the JMS node under Services.
- Select the Servers item under the JMS node.
- Click Configure a new JMSServer. All defaults are okay, so just click Create.

- Select the newly created server (MyJMSServer) from the left-hand pane, and then the Targets tab in the right-hand pane. Assign the server a target of "myserver," and click Apply.
- A JMS messaging provider is now running!

Now we need to create the topic. Because we want messages in this topic to be kept around, even when there is no active server or client, we must first create a store to hold the messages:

- Under servers/jms/stores, select Configure a new JMSFile store activity.
- A directory path is required.
- If you are creating a new store, you must shut down and restart the server for this to take effect.
- Go back to the JMSServer config screen. Select MyJMSServer, and change the Store drop-down from None to MyJMSFile store, or whatever name you have given your store.
- Now you can create the topic. Under servers/jms/servers/MyJMSServer/Destinations, select Configure a new JMSTopic.
- Enter "NFL Game Results" for both Name and JNDI Name.
- Set Enable store to true. Click Create. Topic is now created.

12.8.2 User IDs

You'll need a user ID and password for connecting to the JMS server. By default, the user "guest" and password "guest" should work. If this user isn't present on your system, you can create a new user under the Web console by going to the Security item, selecting Users, and then filling in the username and password and clicking the Create button. There will be a message (link) stating: "The changes you have made must be saved to the realm implementation." Click the message to persist the change.

12.9 Exercises

12.1 Synchronous messaging: Enable the synchronous messaging code in the `JMSStandingsImpl` class by following the instructions within the code.

12.2 Client access: The example as shown includes no client, so there is no way to observe changes to the standings as messages are received. Connect an existing client to the `JMSStandingsImpl` class and view standings at various times while messages are being sent.

12.10 Further Reading

The Java Message Service home page is `http://java.sun.com/products/jms/index.html`.

The book *Java Message Service*, by Richard Monson-Haefel and David A. Chappell, provides a more detailed look at the Java Message Service.

The Java Naming and Directory Interface home page is `http://java.sun.com/products/jndi/index.html`. Tutorials and API documentation are available from this page.

CHAPTER 13

XML Messaging:
SOAP and JAXM

The Java Message Service (JMS) introduced us to the concept of Message Oriented Middleware (MOM). The messages created by one JMS implementer are not necessarily compatible with messages from other providers, so pure JMS doesn't give us a great interoperability solution. With what we now know about XML and its role as a portable data format, the use of XML as the format for messages certainly seems like a step in the right direction. Some MOM vendors have already extended their JMS products to deal with XML-formatted messages, but this alone isn't sufficient to ensure complete interoperability. The on-the-wire format between different JMS vendors will still be different. For a Web Service, we want to be as unrestrictive as possible—allowing programs on different platforms, written in different languages, and using different MOM middleware, to interoperate with each other. Simple Object Access Protocol (SOAP) provides a MOM format that meets these requirements. The Java API for XML Messaging (JAXM) provides a set of Java APIs for creating and sending SOAP messages.

JAXM also provides the ability to work without messaging middleware at all, with the two message endpoints connected directly to one another. This approach obviously takes away many of the features provided by the middleware, such as asynchronous messaging and guaranteed delivery, but might be appropriate in some simple applications.

Software Used in This Chapter

SOAP 1.1 with Attachments

Not software per se, but a specification. There are several software packages, for Java and other languages, that can produce messages conforming to the SOAP specification. The examples in this chapter use JAXM, but you could produce functionally equivalent programs using any software conforming to the specification.

JAXM

Version 1.0, Early Access 2 release. The Java API for XML Messaging (JAXM) is also a specification rather than a product. We used an early access download of the reference implementation. In the future, expect all the application server providers to provide their own implementations of the JAXM specification.

There are two options for downloading the JAXM reference implementation. The Java XML Pack includes early-access releases of all the JAX* APIs; JAX Packs, as they are called, are released quarterly. Examples for this book were originally developed using the Winter 2001 JAX Pack, and then updated to work with the Spring 2002 JAX Pack when it was released.

Another option is the Java Web Services Developer's Pack (JWSDP). This is a bundle that includes the JAX Pack plus Tomcat, Ant, and other utilities. You can download either the JAX pack or the JWSDP from `http://java.sun.com/xml`.

Java Naming and Directory Services (JNDI)

If you are using JAXM with a messaging provider, then you will also need to use JNDI to lookup and obtain a reference to the messaging provider. JMS implementations include a messaging provider. Clients of the messaging provider connect to it in order to send and receive messages. The messaging provider is located by clients by looking it up in a JNDI directory.

13.1 SOAP

Nothing prevents us from passing XML messages in middleware such as JMS, or even across a simple socket connection we manage ourselves. But in these cases, it is only the message content itself—the payload—that is formatted in XML. Information used to get the message to its destination—such as routing information, priority, and any other message options—is specified in a different manner, typically as parameters to API calls.

The standard for XML messaging is something known as SOAP, for Simple Object Access Protocol. It is yet another W3C standard, which originated from Microsoft. In a SOAP message, not just the payload but everything about the message is in XML. SOAP messages comprise an envelope part and a body part, both of which are XML (see Figure 13.1). SOAP 1.1 also allows for non-XML attachments, which are typically used to attach a file type such as a .JPG that is not sensible to render as an XML document.

Figure 13.1 SOAP message structure.

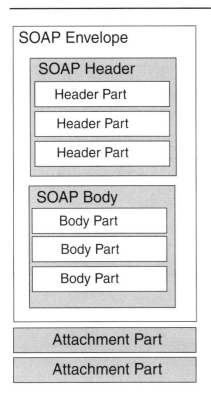

By using a pure XML messaging protocol, we can achieve interoperability between .NET, CORBA, and J2EE applications. SOAP provides two primary models: messaging and Remote Procedure Call (RPC). The messaging mode of SOAP can be thought of as analogous to JMS; that is the model we'll be examining in this chapter. The RPC model is analogous to Java Remote Method Invocation (RMI), so we'll wait until we've examined RMI before looking at SOAP-based RPC.

13.2 Creating SOAP Messages with JAXM

SOAP is a language- and platform-independent protocol. To be able to use SOAP from Java, we'll need some Java classes that can create and manipulate messages conforming to the SOAP protocol. JAXM is not the first set of Java APIs for dealing with SOAP; earlier software from Apache and IBM provided SOAP capabilities for Java. In this book, we'll focus on JAXM because, although it is still in an early access release, it will become the baseline for future SOAP messaging products in Java. There is still quite a bit of room for vendors to add innovative features or improve ease-of-use, so JAXM will likely become the starting point, rather than the final word, in SOAP support for Java applications.

Table 13.1 Components in the JAXM SOAP Messaging Application

New Components			
Name	**Package**	**Class or Interface**	**Comment**
JaxmGameServer	nfl.application.jaxm	Class	Sends a message representing each game played.
JaxmStandingsImpl	nfl.application.jaxm	Class	Extends `DynamicStand-ingsImpl` and implements `ReqRespListener`. Receives messages sent by `JaxmGameServer` and updates standings accordingly.

Existing Components	
Component	**Description**
layered.jar	All classes and interfaces of the layered version of the application (as presented in Chapter 2).
DynamicStandingsImpl	Version of Standings developed originally for Chapter 5, "Servlets."

The application in this chapter is nearly identical to the one developed in the previous chapter using JMS. One difference was that here we have chosen to connect the endpoints directly, rather than using a messaging provider. JAXM can work either in this direct point-to-point configuration, or through a messaging provider; JMS requires the use of a messaging provider.

The `JaxmGameServer` class is shown in Listing 13.1. Although it makes the listing quite a bit longer, we've imported individual classes separately rather than using the more common (and sensible) whole-package import syntax. We did this primarily to document which classes are coming from which packages. Also, had we implemented both the `javax.naming.*` package and `javax.xml.soap.*`, then the use of the `Name` class would become ambiguous in the code, because both of these packages have classes called `Name`. (It's the one in the `soap` package we actually want.)

Just as we did in the JMS example, the class has code in place to support a messaging model we chose not to use. In this case, it's the code to connect to a messaging provider rather than directly to the client.

The basic logic flow of the `JaxmGameServer` is this: Loop through the list of `Games` played; at regular intervals (configurable), create a message and send it; we don't need a response, but get one anyway—this is an artifact of the messaging model we have chosen. When going through a messaging provider, both synchronous (wait for response) and asynchronous (send it and forget it) messaging models are supported. When connecting directly, only the synchronous model is supported. Because there is nothing we need back from the recipient, the message receiver (which we'll examine later) just sends back a null, and we throw away the response object when we receive it back in the server code.

In JMS, we took advantage of the `ObjectMessage` message type to simply attach our `Game` object as the content of the message. In JAXM, we can't assume that the recipient is a Java class, so sending objects would not be portable. We must instead create a SOAP message piece by piece. It is particularly egregious that JAXM doesn't provide any facility to attach well-formed XML into the message, so if your application already has access to the desired content in XML format, you'll need to parse your way through it attaching the elements individually.[1]

Here are the detailed steps involved in setting up the connection:

- Get an instance of the `SOAPConnectionFactory`.
- Create a connection using the `SOAPConnectionFactory`. Connection seems an odd term to use here, given that it isn't until much later that we will provide the URI of the thing we're connecting to. What we are really creating is a local endpoint, and we'll specify the remote endpoint when we are ready to send a message.

A detailed examination of the steps in creating and sending the message will be provided after the code listing.

There is one difference worth noting between the `SOAPConnection` (point-to-point) and `ProviderConnection` (messaging provider) modes of operation. With a `SOAPConnection`, you create a `MessageFactory` using the `MessageFactory.newInstance()` call. With a `ProviderConnection`, you can use this same mechanism, or you can create a specialized message factory by calling `ProviderConnection.createMessageFactory(String profile)`. A message factory created in this way will dispense messages that conform to the named profile. Given a profile name of "ebXML," the message factory will create messages that have SOAP header entries that conform to the Electronic Business XML messaging specification. Other profiles may become standard in the future, or may appear in specific vendors' implementations of JAXM.

---

1. There is a `SOAPPart.setContent()` method that takes a `DOMSource` element, allowing you to attach a DOM element as the `SOAPPart` of the message. However, this requires that your `DOMSource` be a legal SOAP body, including `<soap-env:body>` markup tags. It's not likely that XML documents you might want to import from will just happen to be marked up in this way. After the next chapter, however, you should be able to manipulate XML documents programmatically in such a fashion that you could attach the SOAP body markup to an existing document and use this as the `DOMSource` for the `setContent()` call.

Listing 13.1 JAXM Version of the Game Server

```java
// JaxmGameServer.java

package nfl.application.jaxm;

import nfl.ObjectFactory;
import nfl.application.*;

import java.io.IOException;
import java.util.List;
import java.util.Properties;

import javax.naming.Context;
import javax.naming.InitialContext;
import javax.naming.NamingException;
import javax.xml.soap.MessageFactory;
import javax.xml.soap.Name;
import javax.xml.soap.SOAPBody;
import javax.xml.soap.SOAPBodyElement;
import javax.xml.soap.SOAPConnection;
import javax.xml.soap.SOAPConnectionFactory;
import javax.xml.soap.SOAPElement;
import javax.xml.soap.SOAPElementFactory;
import javax.xml.soap.SOAPEnvelope;
import javax.xml.soap.SOAPException;
import javax.xml.soap.SOAPHeader;
import javax.xml.soap.SOAPMessage;
import javax.xml.soap.SOAPPart;
import javax.xml.messaging.JAXMException;
import javax.xml.messaging.ProviderConnection;
import javax.xml.messaging.ProviderConnectionFactory;
import javax.xml.messaging.URLEndpoint;

/* This should be set up to work either with or without
 * a provider. Default without,
 * pass -provider <uri> on command line to use.
 */

public class JaxmGameServer {

    private ObjectFactory of;
    private Games games;
    private List   gameList;
    private int    msgInterval = 15000; /* millisecs */

    private static boolean   usingProvider = false;
    private static String    directURI = null;
```

```
private static String      providerURI = null;
private SOAPConnection     directConnection;
private ProviderConnection providerConnection;
private static String      jndiUrl =
                           "t3://localhost:7001";


public JaxmGameServer() {
   Properties env = System.getProperties();
   // don't use JaxmVersionInfo here; empty gamelist!
   env.setProperty("nfl.versioninfo",
             "nfl.application.DynamicVersionInfo");
   of = ObjectFactory.getHandle();
   games = (Games) of.getInstance("Games");
   gameList = games.getGameList();
}

/** Used to create a connection when no messaging
  * provider is being used. Connection is created
  * directly to client.
  */
public void createConnection() {
   try {
      SOAPConnectionFactory scf =
         SOAPConnectionFactory.newInstance();
      directConnection = scf.createConnection();
   } catch (SOAPException e) {
      e.printStackTrace();
   }
}

/** Used to create a connection via a messaging provider.
  * All messages are routed through the provider.
  */
public void createConnection(String provider) {
   try {
      Context context = new InitialContext();
      ProviderConnectionFactory pcf =
         (ProviderConnectionFactory)
         context.lookup(provider);
      providerConnection = pcf.createConnection();
   } catch (SOAPException e) {
      e.printStackTrace();
   } catch (NamingException e) {
      e.printStackTrace();
   }
}
```

```java
public void sendMessage(SOAPMessage message) {
    if (usingProvider) {
        try {
            providerConnection.send(message);
        } catch (JAXMException e) {
            e.printStackTrace();
            System.exit(-1);
        }
    } else {
        URLEndpoint dest = new URLEndpoint(directURI);
        try {
            SOAPMessage reply =
                directConnection.call(message, dest);
        } catch (SOAPException e) {
            e.printStackTrace();
            System.exit(-1);
        }
    }
}

public void closeConnection() {
    if (usingProvider) {
        try {
            providerConnection.close();
        } catch (SOAPException e) {
            e.printStackTrace();
        }
    } else {
        try {
            directConnection.close();
        } catch (SOAPException e) {
            e.printStackTrace();
        }
    }
}

public void run() {
    Game game;

    if (usingProvider)
        createConnection(providerURI);
    else
        createConnection();

    SOAPMessage  message  = null;
    SOAPHeader   header   = null;
    SOAPBody     body     = null;
    SOAPEnvelope envelope = null;
    SOAPElementFactory sef = null;
```

```
try {
   MessageFactory mf = MessageFactory.newInstance();
   message  = mf.createMessage();
   SOAPPart sp = message.getSOAPPart();
   envelope = sp.getEnvelope();
   header   = envelope.getHeader();
   body     = envelope.getBody();
   sef      = SOAPElementFactory.newInstance();
} catch (SOAPException e) {
   e.printStackTrace();
}

//Here we could populate the header.
//Default empty header works fine for us; we could
//detach it if desired.

// XML PROTOTYPE:
// <game week="#" >
//     <home team="?" score="?" />
//     <visitor team="?" score="?" />
// </game>

// Creating names was originally inside loop;
// moved out here for efficiency.
Name bodyName = null, weekName = null,
     homeName = null, teamName = null,
     scoreName = null, visName = null;
try {
   bodyName = envelope.createName(
      "game", "nfl", "http://nfl.mydomain.com");
   weekName = envelope.createName("week");
   homeName = envelope.createName("home");
   teamName = envelope.createName("team");
   scoreName = envelope.createName("score");
   visName = envelope.createName("visitor");
} catch (SOAPException e) {
   e.printStackTrace();
}

for (int i=0; i<gameList.size(); i++) {
   game = (Game) gameList.get(i);

   try {
      SOAPBodyElement soapGame =
         body.addBodyElement(bodyName);
      soapGame.addAttribute(weekName,
         Integer.toString(game.getWeek()));
```

```java
            SOAPElement soapHome = sef.create(homeName);
            soapHome.addAttribute(teamName, game.getHome());
            soapHome.addAttribute(scoreName,
               Integer.toString(game.getScore()[1]));
            soapGame.addChildElement(soapHome);

            SOAPElement soapVis = sef.create(visName);
            soapVis.addAttribute(teamName,
               game.getVisitor());
            soapVis.addAttribute(scoreName,
               Integer.toString(game.getScore()[0]));
            soapGame.addChildElement(soapVis);

            //Optional; allow visual inspection
            try {
               message.writeTo(System.out);
               System.out.flush();
            } catch (IOException e) {
               e.printStackTrace();
            }

            sendMessage(message);

            // We reuse same message, just swapping out the
            // contents.
            soapGame.detachNode();
            soapGame.recycleNode();

            Thread.sleep(msgInterval);
         } catch (SOAPException e) {
            e.printStackTrace();
         } catch (InterruptedException e) {
            // Only possible source is Thread.sleep()
            e.printStackTrace();
         }
      }
      closeConnection();
   }

   public static void main(String[] args) {
      JaxmGameServer gameServer = new JaxmGameServer();

      for (int i=0; i<args.length; i++) {
         if (args[i].equals("-jndiUrl"))
            jndiUrl = args[++i];
         if (args[i].equals("-host")) {
            directURI = args[++i];
            usingProvider = false;
```

```
      }
      if (args[i].equals("-provider")) {
         providerURI = args[++i];
         usingProvider = true;
      }
   }
   gameServer.run();
}
}
```

Let's examine the code in this class that actually deals with messages. Messages are created by a `MessageFactory`, so we instantiate one and then call its `createMessage()` method to create our message. We then dissect this message into its constituent parts. The `Message` itself will contain a `SOAPPart` and, optionally, attachments. We aren't dealing with any attachments in this example, so we just retrieve the `SOAPPart` of the message. From the `SOAPPart` we get the `SOAPEnvelope`. From the envelope, we get the `SOAPHeader` (which we don't actually use, so that's a wasted call—it just seemed clearer to show it than to omit it) and the `SOAP-Body`. Although we don't use the `SOAPHeader` in our example code, there are two types of entries you might commonly find there. A `SOAPAction` entry in the header can be used to include information intended for the SOAP processing middleware, rather than the final message recipient. Information about how a message should be routed is a good example. `SOAPAction` elements could thus be used to implement a workflow system based on SOAP messages. Another common `SOAPHeader` element is a `SOAPFault`. If the recipient of the message cannot process it, a `SOAPFault` element could be created and placed in the `SOAPHeader` of the return message to indicate the problem encountered.

To populate our SOAP message, we'll have to create `SOAPElements`. This is done by a `SOAPElementFactory`, so we get an instance of that class. Also, every element we add to the message must have a SOAP `Name` attached. For our highest-level element, we create a name using both a namespace and a localname; for everything below that element, just a local name is sufficient. Creation of names is a function of the `SOAPEnvelope` object; we go ahead and pre-create all the names we need before entering the main processing loop, because there's no point in repeatedly creating the same `Name` objects.

Within the main processing loop (executed once per `Game`), we build up the `SOAPMes-sage`. The first thing we attach is the main element, which has been given the name `bodyName`. This is the element `<game />`, although with a namespace attached it becomes `<nfl:game xmlns:nfl="http://nfl.mydomain.com" />`. Note that we show this as an empty element, because if we stopped at this point, that's what we would have. But we'll be hanging some subelements off of this very shortly.

The next step is to add an attribute to the game element, with the name `weekName` we created earlier, and a value taken directly from the `Game` object.

Next, we add the home and visiting team subelements. Each one is given two attributes—the `name` and the `score`—and then attached as children of the `soapGame` (main body) element. This completes the SOAP representation of the played game.

Just to facilitate debugging and understanding, we call the `writeTo()` method of the message to write its contents to `System.out`. The resulting output is shown below. Then, we send the message using the `sendMessage()` call. Rather than create a new message, we reuse the same `Message` object in our next iteration through the loop. To prepare the message for reuse, we detach the `soapGame` node and mark it recyclable.

Here's the output from the `message.writeto()` call. Line breaks and indentation have been added manually for readability:

```
<soap-env:Envelope
    xmlns:soap-env=
        "http://schemas.xmlsoap.org/soap/envelope/">
    <soap-env:Header/>
    <soap-env:Body>
        <nfl:game
                xmlns:nfl="http://nfl.mydomain.com"
                week="1">
            <home team="Atlanta Falcons" score="36"/>
            <visitor team="San Francisco 49ers" score="28"/>
        </nfl:game>
    </soap-env:Body>
</soap-env:Envelope>
```

13.3 Consuming the Web Service

Now we want to flip over and see the other side, the receiver of the message. Messages are always targeted at a URL. When using a messaging provider, the URL is the location of the messaging middleware. In a direct (providerless) model, the URL is the location of the intended recipient. The fact that we are communicating with software listening at a particular URL suggests that a servlet implementation would be appropriate for our listener, and indeed JAXM includes a `JAXMServlet` that is a good starting point for creating our own endpoint. We create a `JaxmStandingsServlet` that extends the `JaxmServlet` and holds an instance of `Dynamic-Standings` that we'll update each time we receive a message.

There are two listener interfaces we might choose to implement. In what I feel was a poor choice, they were both given the same name and arguments, differing only in return type. This means it is impossible for a single receiver to implement both interfaces, although there is a workaround that we'll see shortly.

The `OneWayListener` interface is used for asynchronous messages; the interface requires that we implement a single method called `onMessage()`, with a void return type. This would actually be the most appropriate interface to use for the example we have created thus far, because the `JaxmGameServer` requires no reply from us. However, we will extend this example in the next chapter to handle additional messages that are synchronous messages requiring replies. This means our class must implement `ReqRespListener`, the Request-Response (synchronous) messaging interface. `ReqRespListener` requires that we implement a single method called `onMessage()`, with a `SOAPMessage` return type. You see where this creates a problem: Java does not allow overloaded methods to differ only in their return type.

Fortunately, there is a workaround. If you implement the `ReqRespListener` and return a null, the behavior is the same as the `OneWayListener`. So that is what we do in the `JaxmStandingsServlet` class.

Within the `onMessage()` method, we pull apart the message until we get at the body part. We then iterate over the body parts (there should just be one in every case), testing the name of the top-level element. The only type we've seen so far is the `<game>` element. If we see this, we call the `processGame()` method. Our class is also set up to process `<division>` and `<conference>` messages—these are requests for standing results that will be sent to us from an as-yet-unseen client program. The processing methods for these message types aren't shown in the listing below; we'll come back to them in Chapter 14. These hidden methods use the `javax.xml.Transform` package, so the imports you see for classes in that package aren't actually required by any code shown in Listing 13.2.

Within `processGame()`, we further dissect the `SOAPMessage` body, until we finally have enough pieces to invoke a `Game` constructor and reconstitute a replica of the object we started with. Then, we call `postGameData()` with this object to update the standings. This has obviously been far more work than we had to go through with JMS; the point is that either (or both) of the components we've examined might have been a non-Java program, requiring the representation of every element in a portable fashion.

It would certainly be nice if there were classes or utilities to facilitate this mapping between `SOAPMessages` and Java classes. Not surprisingly, there are such things, as we will see when we look at JAX-RPC in Chapter 16.

Listing 13.2 Standings Servlet

```
// JaxmStandingsServlet.java

package nfl.application.jaxm;

import nfl.ObjectFactory;
import nfl.application.*;
import nfl.presentation.xml.XML;

import java.util.Iterator;
import java.util.Properties;

// DOM imports (for Division message)
import org.w3c.dom.CharacterData;
```

```java
import org.w3c.dom.Document;
import org.w3c.dom.Element;
import org.w3c.dom.Node;
import org.w3c.dom.NodeList;

// JAXP Transformer imports
import javax.xml.transform.Source;
import javax.xml.transform.dom.DOMResult;
import javax.xml.transform.sax.SAXResult;
import javax.xml.transform.stream.StreamResult;

// JAXM imports
import javax.xml.soap.*;
import javax.xml.messaging.JAXMServlet;
//import javax.xml.messaging.OnewayListener;
import javax.xml.messaging.ReqRespListener;

public class JaxmStandingsServlet
            extends JAXMServlet
            implements ReqRespListener {

   private DynamicStandings standings;
   private XML             xmlGenerator;
   private SOAPEnvelope    envelope;

   // Constructor
   public JaxmStandingsServlet() {
      Properties env = System.getProperties();
      env.setProperty("nfl.versioninfo" ,
          "nfl.application.jaxm.JaxmVersionInfo");
      ObjectFactory of = ObjectFactory.getHandle();
      standings = (DynamicStandings)
                of.getInstance("DynamicStandings");
      standings.init();
      xmlGenerator = new XML();
      xmlGenerator.setStandings(standings);
   }

   // the single method of the ReqRespListener interface
   public SOAPMessage onMessage(SOAPMessage message) {
      SOAPPart sp   = null;
      SOAPBody body = null;
      Name nameAttr = null;
      // SOAPEnvelope env is now at file scope

      try {
         sp      = message.getSOAPPart();
         envelope = sp.getEnvelope();
```

```
      body       = envelope.getBody();
      // don't care about SOAPHeader
      nameAttr = envelope.createName("name");
   } catch (SOAPException e) {
      e.printStackTrace();
      return null;
   }

   Iterator iter = body.getChildElements();
   while (iter.hasNext()) {
      SOAPElement elem = (SOAPElement) iter.next();
      Name name = elem.getElementName();
      String lName = name.getLocalName();
      if (lName.equals("game")) {
         processGame(elem);
         return null;
      } else if (lName.equals("conference")) {
         String conf = elem.getAttributeValue(nameAttr);
         return processConference(conf);
      } else if (lName.equals("division"))  {
         String div = elem.getAttributeValue(nameAttr);
         return processDivision(div);
      } else {
         System.out.println("unknown msg type"
             + lName);
         return null;
      }
   }
   return null;
}

private void processGame(SOAPElement gameElem) {
   Name nWeek = null, nTeam = null, nScore = null;
   try {
      nWeek = envelope.createName("week");
      nTeam = envelope.createName("team");
      nScore = envelope.createName("score");
   } catch (SOAPException e) {
      e.printStackTrace();
      return;
   }
   int week = Integer.parseInt(
      gameElem.getAttributeValue(nWeek));
   String home = null, visitor = null;
   int hScore = 0, vScore = 0;
   Iterator tIter = gameElem.getChildElements();
   while (tIter.hasNext()) {
```

```
        SOAPElement tElem = (SOAPElement) tIter.next();
        String tName =
          tElem.getElementName().getLocalName();
        if (tName.equals("home")) {
          home = tElem.getAttributeValue(nTeam);
          hScore = Integer.parseInt(
            tElem.getAttributeValue(nScore));
        } else if (tName.equals("visitor")) {
          visitor = tElem.getAttributeValue(nTeam);
          vScore = Integer.parseInt(
            tElem.getAttributeValue(nScore));
        } else {
          System.out.println("bad name: " + tName);
          return;
        }
      }
      Game g = new BasicGameImpl(week, visitor, vScore,
                                     home, hScore);
      standings.postGameData(g);
      System.out.println("Game " + g + " posted.");
    }
}
```

13.4 JAXM API Docs

The following API documentation covers the most frequently used classes, and the most useful or informative methods within those classes.

API 13.1 javax.xml.soap.**SOAPConnectionFactory**

```
public abstract class SOAPConnectionFactory
    public SOAPConnection createConnection() throws SOAPException;
    public static SOAPConnectionFactory newInstance() throws SOAPException;
```

API 13.2 javax.xml.soap.**SOAPConnection**

```
public abstract class SOAPConnection
    public abstract SOAPMessage call(SOAPMessage request, Endpoint endpoint)
        throws SOAPException;
    public abstract void close() throws SOAPException;
```

API 13.3 javax.xml.messaging.**ProviderConnectionFactory**

```
public abstract class ProviderConnectionFactory
    public abstract ProviderConnection createConnection() throws JAXMException;
    public static ProviderConnectionFactory newInstance() throws JAXMException;
```

API 13.4 javax.xml.messaging.**ProviderConnection**

```
public interface ProviderConnection
    public ProviderMetaData getMetaData() throws JAXMException;
    public void close() throws JAXMException;
    public MessageFactory createMessageFactory(String profile) throws JAXMException;
    public void send(SOAPMessage message) throws JAXMException;
```

API 13.5 javax.xml.soap.**MessageFactory**

```
public abstract class MessageFactory
    public static MessageFactory newInstance() throws SOAPException;
    public abstract SOAPMessage createMessage() throws SOAPException;
    public abstract SOAPMessage createMessage(MimeHeaders headers,
        InputStream in) throws IOException, SOAPException;
```

API 13.6 javax.xml.soap.**SOAPMessage**

```
public abstract class SOAPMessage
    public abstract String getContentDescription();
    public abstract void setContentDescription(String description);
    public abstract SOAPPart getSOAPPart();
    public abstract void removeAllAttachments();
    public abstract int countAttachments();
    public abstract Iterator getAttachments();
    public abstract Iterator getAttachments(MimeHeaders headers);
    public abstract void addAttachmentPart(AttachmentPart attachmentPart);
    public abstract AttachmentPart createAttachmentPart();
    public AttachmentPart createAttachmentPart(
        javax.activiation.DataHandler dataHandler);
    public abstract MimeHeaders getMimeHeaders();
    public AttachmentPart createAttachmentPart(Object content, String contentType);
    public abstract void saveChanges() throws SOAPException;
    public abstract boolean saveRequired();
    public abstract void writeTo(OutputStream out) throws SOAPException, IOException;
```

API 13.7   javax.xml.soap.**SOAPPart**

```
public abstract class SOAPPart
    public abstract SOAPEnvelope getEnvelope() throws SOAPException;
    public String getContentId();
    public String getContentLocation();
    public void setContentId(String contentId);
    public void setContentLocation(String contentLocation);
    public abstract void removeMimeHeader(String header);
    public abstract void removeAllMimeHeaders();
    public abstract String[] getMimeHeader(String name);
    public abstract void setMimeHeader(String name, String value);
    public abstract void addMimeHeader(String name, String value);
    public abstract Iterator getAllMimeHeaders();
    public abstract Iterator getMatchingMimeHeaders(String[] names);
    public abstract Iterator getNonMatchingMimeHeaders(String[] names);
    public abstract void setContent(Source source) throws SOAPException;
    public abstract Source getContent() throws SOAPException;
```

API 13.8   javax.xml.soap.**SOAPEnvelope**

```
public interface SOAPEnvelope extends SOAPElement
    public Name createName(String localName, String prefix, String uri)
        throws SOAPException;
    public Name createName(String localName) throws SOAPException;
    public SOAPHeader getHeader() throws SOAPException;
    public SOAPBody getBody() throws SOAPException;
    public SOAPHeader addHeader() throws SOAPException;
    public SOAPBody addBody() throws SOAPException;
```

API 13.9   javax.xml.soap.**SOAPHeader**

```
public interface SOAPHeader extends SOAPElement
    public SOAPHeaderElement addHeaderElement(Name name)
        throws SOAPException;
    public Iterator examineHeaderElements(String actor);
    public Iterator extractHeaderElements(String actor);
```

API 13.10   javax.xml.soap.**SOAPBody**

```
public interface SOAPBody extends SOAPElement
    public SOAPFault addFault() throws SOAPException;
    public boolean hasFault();
    public SOAPFault getFault();
    public SOAPBodyElement addBodyElement(Name name) throws SOAPException;
```

API 13.11 javax.xml.soap.**SOAPElementFactory**

---

public abstract class SOAPElementFactory
    public abstract SOAPElement **create**(Name name) throws SOAPException;
    public abstract SOAPElement **create**(String localName) throws SOAPException;
    public abstract SOAPElement **create**(String localName, String prefix, String uri)
        throws SOAPException;
    public static SOAPElementFactory **newInstance**() throws SOAPException;

API 13.12 javax.xml.soap.**SOAPElement**

---

public interface SOAPElement extends Node
    // Methods inherited from Node
    public String **getValue**();
    public void **setParentElement**(SOAPElement parent) throws SOAPException;
    public SOAPElement **getParentElement**();
    public void **detachNode**();
    public void **recycleNode**();
    // Methods of SOAPElement
    public SOAPElement **addChildElement**(Name name) throws SOAPException;
    public SOAPElement **addChildElement**(String localName) throws SOAPException;
    public SOAPElement **addChildElement**(String localName, String prefix)
        throws SOAPException;
    public SOAPElement **addChildElement**(String localName, String prefix, String uri)
        throws SOAPException;
    public SOAPElement **addChildElement**(SOAPElement element)
        throws SOAPException
    public SOAPElement **addTextNode**(String text) throws SOAPException;
    public SOAPElement **addAttribute**(Name name, String value)
        throws SOAPException;
    public SOAPElement **addNamespaceDeclaration**(String prefix, String uri)
        throws SOAPException;
    public String **getAttributeValue**(Name name);
    public Iterator **getAllAttributes**();
    public String **getNamespaceURI**(String prefix);
    public Iterator **getNamespacePrefixes**();
    public Name **getElementName**();
    public boolean **removeAttribute**(Name name);
    public boolean **removeNamespaceDeclaration**(String prefix);
    public Iterator **getChildElements**();
    public Iterator **getChildElements**(Name name);
    public void **setEncodingStyle**(String encodingStyle) throws SOAPException;
    public String **getEncodingStyle**();

API 13.13   javax.xml.soap.**SOAPBodyElement**

```
public interface SOAPBodyElement extends SOAPElement
    // no added methods
```

API 13.14   javax.xml.soap.**SOAPFault**

```
public inteface SOAPFault extends SOAPBodyElement
    public void setFaultCode(String faultCode) throws SOAPException;
    public String getFaultCode();
    public void setFaultActor(String faultActor) throws SOAPException;
    public String getFaultActor();
    public void setFaultString(String faultString) throws SOAPException;
    public String getFaultString();
    public Detail getDetail();
    public Detail addDetail() throws SOAPException;
```

API 13.15   javax.xml.soap.**Name**

```
public interface Name
    public String getLocalName();
    public String getQualifiedName();
    public String getPrefix();
    public String getURI();
```

API 13.16   javax.xml.messaging.**JAXMServlet**

```
public class JAXMServlet extends HttpServlet
    // Fields
    protected MessageFactory msgFactory;
    // Methods
    public void init(ServletConfig servletConfig) throws ServletException;
    public void setMessageFactory(MessageFactory msgFactory);
    protected static MimeHeaders getHeaders(HttpServletRequest req);
    protected static void putHeaders(MimeHeaders headers, HttpServletResponse res);
    public void doPost(HttpServletRequest req, HttpServletResponse resp)
        throws ServletException, IOException;
```

API 13.17   javax.xml.messaging.**OneWayListener**

```
public interface OneWayListener
    public void onMessage(SOAPMessage message);
```

```
public interface ReqRespListener
    public SOAPMessage onMessage(SOAPMessage message);
```

13.5 Building, Deploying, and Running the Application

Listing 13.3 shows the buildfile for the JAXM version of the application. This single buildfile creates the examples shown in this chapter, but also several targets that aren't used until Chapter 14. So for now you can ignore the `<client>` target (and its associated `<clean>` and `<test>` targets.)

To use this buildfile on your own system, you'll need to adjust the properties near the top of the file to point to locations where you have installed the `servlet.jar` file and the Java XML Pack (which contains JAXM). If you look at the example buildfiles included with the JAXM, they refer to quite a few jar files; we've duplicated the list in our own `build.xml` file. You'll need to make sure all these files are available both at compile and at deployment time. (Exception: If you deploy in the version of Tomcat included with the Java Web Services developers pack, all of the required JAR files have already been made accessible, by placing them in Tomcat's `common/lib` directory).

There are three primary elements in this buildfile: the server (`JaxmGameServer`), the servlet (`JaxmStandingsServlet`), and the client, which will be shown in the next chapter (`Jaxm-Client`). The `JaxmGameServer` has two related targets: `<server>` builds the class, and `<test-server>` invokes the class, with a reference to a target URI. You'll need to update the URI to point to where you have installed the second component, the servlet, on your own system.

The servlet has a `<compile-servlet>` target that compiles the servlet and dependent classes, and a `<servlet>` target that packages the classes in a WAR file. There isn't a separate test target for the servlet, because testing the server will essentially cause the servlet to be tested as well.

Listing 13.3 `build.xml` File for JAXM Version of Application

```
<project name="nfl-jaxm" default="all" basedir=".">

<!-- set these as appropriate for your installation -->
<property name="servlet.home" value="/home/myawn/webservices"/>
<property name="jdom.home" value="/home/myawn/webservices"/>
<property name="JAVA_XML_PACK_HOME"
        value="/home/myawn/webservices/java_xml_pack-spring-02-dev" />
<property name="JAXM_HOME"
        value="${JAVA_XML_PACK_HOME}/jaxm-1.0.1-ea2/" />

<path id="classpath">
   <pathelement path="${java.class.path}" />
```

```xml
      <pathelement location="${servlet.home}/servlet.jar" />
      <pathelement location="${jdom.home}/jdom.jar" />
      <pathelement location="${JAXM_HOME}/lib/jaxm-api.jar" />
      <pathelement location="${JAXM_HOME}/lib/commons-logging.jar" />
      <pathelement location="${JAXM_HOME}/lib/dom4j.jar" />
      <pathelement location="${JAXM_HOME}/lib/mail.jar" />
      <pathelement location="${JAXM_HOME}/lib/activation.jar" />
      <pathelement location="${JAXM_HOME}/jaxm/jaxm-client.jar" />
</path>

<target name="all">
   <antcall target="server" />
   <antcall target="servlet" />
   <antcall target="client" />
</target>

<target name="server">
  <javac srcdir="." >
    <classpath refid="classpath"/>
    <include name="JaxmGameServer.java"/>
  </javac>
</target>

<target name="client">
   <javac srcdir="." >
     <classpath refid="classpath"/>
     <include name="JaxmClient.java"/>
   </javac>
</target>

<target name="compile-servlet">
  <javac srcdir="..">
    <include name="DynamicStandings.java"/>
    <include name="DynamicStandingsImpl.java"/>
    <include name="NullMessagingImpl.java"/>
  </javac>
  <javac srcdir="../../persistence">
    <include name="EmptyGameDataImpl.java"/>
  </javac>
  <javac srcdir="../../presentation/xml">
    <include name="XML.java"/>
  </javac>
  <javac srcdir=".">
    <classpath refid="classpath"/>
    <include name="MySAXParser.java"/>
    <include name="JaxmStandingsServlet.java"/>
    <include name="JaxmVersionInfo.java"/>
  </javac>
</target>
```

```
<target name="servlet" depends="compile-servlet">
   <war warfile="nfl-jaxm.war" webxml="web.xml">
      <lib dir="../.." includes="layered.jar" />
      <lib dir="${JAXM_HOME}/lib">
         <include name="jaxm-api.jar" />
         <include name="activation.jar" />
         <include name="mail.jar" />
         <include name="commons-logging.jar" />
         <include name="dom4j.jar" />
      </lib>
      <lib dir="${JAXM_HOME}/jaxm">
         <include name="jaxm-client.jar" />
      </lib>
      <lib dir=".">
         <include name="jndi.properties" />
      </lib>
      <classes dir="../../..">
         <include name="nfl/application/jaxm/*.class" />
         <include name="nfl/application/Dynamic*.class" />
         <include name="nfl/application/NullMess*.class" />
         <include name="nfl/persistence/Empty*.class" />
         <include name="nfl/presentation/xml/XML.class" />
      </classes>
   </war>
</target>

<target name="test-server" depends="server" >
   <java classname="nfl.application.jaxm.JaxmGameServer"
            fork="true" >
      <classpath refid="classpath" />
      <arg value="-host" />
      <arg value="http://ros8365miy.rose:8080/nfl-jaxm/" />
   </java>
</target>

<target name="test-client" depends="client" >
   <java classname="nfl.application.jaxm.JaxmClient"
            fork="true" >
      <classpath refid="classpath" />
      <arg value="-host" />
      <arg value="http://ros8365miy.rose:8080/nfl-jaxm/" />
      <arg value="-division" />
      <arg value="NFC West" />
   </java>
   <java classname="nfl.application.jaxm.JaxmClient"
            fork="true" >
      <classpath refid="classpath" />
```

```
        <arg value="-host" />
        <arg value="http://ros8365miy.rose:8080/nfl-jaxm/" />
        <arg value="-conference" />
        <arg value="NFC" />
    </java>
</target>

<target name="clean">
  <delete>
    <fileset dir="." includes="*.class,*.war" />
  </delete>
</target>

</project>
```

13.6 Exercises

13.1 JAXM using a messaging provider: Alter the example to use a messaging provider. A messaging provider that runs as a servlet is included with the JAXM early access implementation.

13.2 JaxmGameServer processing game requests: The current design of the `Jaxm-GameServer` has it initiating messages to the client. This might be seen in an Enterprise Application Integration use of JAXM, but not in a typical Web Service. Because JAXM has no publish-subscribe mode, a "push" distribution of game results does not really work if we consider multiple clients. After the JAXM client code is introduced in Chapter 14, rework the example so that the client requests game results, rather than having the servlet push results to the client.

13.7 Further Reading

The SOAP specification can be found from links on the World Wide Web Consortium's (W3C) Web Services page, at `http://www.w3.org/2002/ws`.

JAXM specification and reference implementation can be found at the site `http://java.sun.com/xml/jaxm/index.html`.

Parsing and Manipulating XML

Web Services are highly dependent on XML as the underlying data representation, and Web applications are increasingly adopting XML for their data as well. Because of this, it would seem logical that parsing and manipulating XML documents would be one of the most basic skills needed to author Web applications and Web Services. But as I went through one example after another in creating this book, the topic kept getting pushed away time after time. It seems that the parsing of XML documents is so basic that nobody needs to do it anymore. It's all been taken over by the tools.

As nice as the tools are, using a tool always involves some trade-off of convenience for control. Most of the time, you probably won't have to manipulate an XML document directly; you'll be able to transform it using XSL or one of the many other tools that create or interpret XML documents. But there will always be times when you want to disengage the autopilot and take control yourself. In this chapter, we'll look at the most popular APIs for manipulating XML documents, and incorporate them into the example program from Chapter 13.

Software Used in This Chapter
DOM
The Document Object Model. The Apache Xerces processor was used as a DOM parser.
SAX
The Simple API for XML processing. The Apache Xerces processor also provides a SAX processor.
JDOM
Version 1.0, Beta 7. A DOM-like API that is designed to incorporate Java concepts. Downloadable from `http://www.jdom.org`.

Our example code for most of this chapter will be built directly on the JAXM example code from the previous chapter. As you may recall, in that chapter we created a `Jaxm-GameServer` that created messages for each game result, and a `JaxmStandingsServlet` that updated the standings results as each game result was received. However, these two classes only provided functions to get data into the system and update it, but no way to get data out of the system.

In this chapter, we'll create a `JaxmClient` that also sends messages to the `JaxmStandingsServlet`. These messages will be very simple; they will contain either a conference element, requesting standings for that conference, or a division element, requesting standings for that division. Each invocation of the client only handles one message, so to get the full standings you would need to run the client program repeatedly.

We'll follow the code flow through the application as we look at the listings in this chapter. We'll start with the `JaxmClient` creating and sending a message; then we'll look at the code in `JaxmStandingsServlet` that receives the message and creates a reply using either DOM or SAX; we'll then finish by coming back to the `JaxmClient` to see how the response message is handled. After we've followed this entire flow, we'll introduce a new API package, JAXB, and show how it can be used to turn an XML document into a set of Java classes.

Listing 14.1 shows the `JaxmClient` class. We won't examine this code in detail, because the process of creating and sending a JAXM message was covered in detail in Chapter 13. The only things I'll point out are that in the previous chapter, we sent messages to the servlet but did not do anything with the response object; they were essentially one-way (notification) messages. The messages we send here are requests for information, so the reply is very important (although processing the reply isn't shown until Listing 14.8).

The other thing you might want to observe in the following code is the comments that show the format for the XML messages we are creating; this will help in following the flow of disassembling the message content when it reaches the `JaxmStandingsServlet`.

Listing 14.1 JaxmClient Class

```java
// JaxmClient.java

package nfl.application.jaxm;

import nfl.ObjectFactory;
import nfl.application.*;

import java.io.IOException;
import java.util.Properties;
import java.util.List;

// JAXM imports to create & send message
import javax.xml.soap.*;
import javax.xml.messaging.*;

// JAXP input needed by JDOM
import javax.xml.transform.stream.StreamSource;

// JDOM imports to parser reply message
import org.jdom.Document;
import org.jdom.Element;
import org.jdom.Attribute;
import org.jdom.JDOMException;
import org.jdom.Namespace;
import org.jdom.input.DOMBuilder;

public class JaxmClient {

    private ObjectFactory of;

    private static String       directURI = null;
    private SOAPConnection      connection;

    // from command line arguments
    private static boolean doConf   = true;
    private static String  confName = null;
    private static String  divName  = null;

    public JaxmClient() {
        Properties env = System.getProperties();
        // don't use JaxmVersionInfo here; empty gamelist!
        env.setProperty("nfl.versioninfo",
                    "nfl.application.DynamicVersionInfo");
        of = ObjectFactory.getHandle();
    }
```

```
  public void createConnection() {
... see JaxmGameServer for details
  }

  public void closeConnection() {
... see JaxmGameServer for details
  }

  public void run() {

     createConnection();

     SOAPMessage  message  = null;
     SOAPHeader   header   = null;
     SOAPBody     body     = null;
     SOAPEnvelope envelope = null;
     //SOAPElementFactory sef = null;

     try {
        MessageFactory mf = MessageFactory.newInstance();
        message  = mf.createMessage();
        SOAPPart sp = message.getSOAPPart();
        envelope = sp.getEnvelope();
        header   = envelope.getHeader();
        body     = envelope.getBody();
        //sef      = SOAPElementFactory.newInstance();
     } catch (SOAPException e) {
        e.printStackTrace();
     }

     // XML PROTOTYPES
     // <conference name="#" />
     // <division name="#" />

     Name conference = null;
     Name division = null;
     Name name = null;
     try {
        conference = envelope.createName(
           "conference","nfl","http://nfl.mydomain.com");
        division = envelope.createName(
           "division","nfl","http://nfl.mydomain.com");
        name = envelope.createName("name");
     } catch (SOAPException e) {
        e.printStackTrace();
     }
```

```
    try {
        SOAPBodyElement bodyElement;
        if (doConf) {
            bodyElement = body.addBodyElement(conference);
            bodyElement.addAttribute(name, confName);
        } else {
            bodyElement = body.addBodyElement(division);
            bodyElement.addAttribute(name, divName);
        }

        //Optional; allow visual inspection
        try {
            message.writeTo(System.out);
            System.out.println();
            System.out.flush();
        } catch (IOException e) {
            e.printStackTrace();
        }

        URLEndpoint dest = new URLEndpoint(directURI);
        SOAPMessage reply = connection.call(message, dest);

        // code to parse reply to be shown later ...

    } catch (SOAPException e) {
        e.printStackTrace();
    }
    closeConnection();
}

public static void main(String[] args) {
    JaxmClient client = new JaxmClient();

    for (int i=0; i<args.length; i++) {
        if (args[i].equals("-host")) {
            directURI = args[++i];
        }
        if (args[i].equals("-conference")) {
            confName = args[++i];
            doConf = true;
        }
        if (args[i].equals("-division")) {
            divName = args[++i];
            doConf = false;
        }
    }
    client.run();
}
}
```

The whole point of the `JaxmClient` is to create a simple SOAP message that contains either a conference or a division element. Here is what the SOAP message looks like when it contains a division (whitespace added manually for readability):

Listing 14.2 SOAP Message Requesting Division Standings

```
<soap-env:Envelope
     xmlns:soap-env=
        "http://schemas.xmlsoap.org/soap/envelope/">
    <soap-env:Header/>
    <soap-env:Body>
      <nfl:division xmlns:nfl="http://nfl.mydomain.com"
                    name="NFC East"/>
    </soap-env:Body>
</soap-env:Envelope>
```

And here is what the SOAP message looks like when it contains a conference:

Listing 14.3 SOAP Message Requesting Conference Standings

```
<soap-env:Envelope
     xmlns:soap-env=
          "http://schemas.xmlsoap.org/soap/envelope/">
    <soap-env:Header/>
    <soap-env:Body>
      <nfl:conference xmlns:nfl="http://nfl.mydomain.com"
                    name="AFC"/>
    </soap-env:Body>
</soap-env:Envelope>
```

Because the messages are so similar, any sane programmer would leverage the code for handling these two message types to the greatest degree possible. Because I don't fit the profile, I've implemented the handler for the division message using DOM, and the handler for the conference message using SAX. This allows us to see both APIs in use for a very similar task. Listing 14.4 shows the `processDivision()` method; the division name has already been extracted from the SOAP message by the `onMessage()` method before invoking `processDivision()`.

14.1 Using DOM

We'll leverage the code from Chapter 9 that represents the standings as an XML document. Because that example code produced a single document for the entire standings, our main task is to navigate our way through the XML document until we find the specific division requested, and return just that fragment of the document in a SOAP message.

Because there are multiple ways of processing XML documents (DOM, SAX, JDOM), we need a common format that can be understood by all of the software, or they will never be able to interoperate. The `javax.xml.tranform` package provides this capability with the `Source` interface. Each XML API set has a class that implements this interface—`DOMSource`, `SAX-Source`, and `JDOMSource`. There is also a `StreamSource`, which represents a streamed version of the document (for example, if you are reading an XML document directly in from a file). The `Transformer` class can take any `Source` object and convert it to a `Result` object. The classes implementing the `Result` interface are `DOMResult`, `SAXResult`, `JDOMResult`, and `StreamResult`. By using the `Transformer`, we can freely pass around `Source` objects without regard to what APIs are being used in particular areas of processing. For this reason, any code you develop that returns an XML document should do so as a `Source` object, rather than an API-specific class such as `org.w3c.dom.Document`.

You can see how this works in Listing 14.4. We start by calling the `generateXML-Document()` method of our `XML` class from Chapter 9. This returns us a `Source` object, which we then transform to a `DOMResult`. We use the `XML` class' `transformXMLDocument()` method for this, rather than providing our own transformer. In this case, it happens that we're transforming DOM to DOM, so the transformation is technically unnecessary; but we preserve encapsulation by pretending ignorance of the actual type of `Source` object we're being returned. From the `DOMResult` object resulting from the transformation, we can get the DOM `Document` object by a call to `getNode()`.

Next, we build the framework of our SOAP message, using the same code as in the JAXM examples from the previous chapter. We start (Step 1) by getting the document root with a `getDocumentElement()` call. We then (Step 2) use the `getElementsByTagName()` method call to find all the `<division>` elements within the document. Note that these elements are not directly attached to root, so the method call works through the entire document finding matches. We also go ahead and use the same method to find the `<teamDatails>` element, knowing that we will need it later.

In Step 3, we loop through the `<division>` elements that were found, doing a `get-Attribute()` call for the attribute called `name`. Once we find a match, we break out of the loop and go to Step 4. Here, we use `getElementsByTagName()` again, here to find `<team>` elements. We make the method call on the `<division>` node we matched earlier; had we made the same call on the root element, we would have found all teams, not just the ones we want in this division.

We know that in the document structure there is only one element in the `<team>`, which is the `<name>` element. We thus can use `getFirstChild()` instead of `getElementsByTag-Name()`. However, doing so makes our program more fragile: If the XML document structure changed and added a new sub-element to the `<team>`, prior to `<name>`, then we would break this code. Using tag names is therefore preferable; I did something different here purely to avoid monotony. The actual text of the name node is a child of the `<name>` element, so we use `get-FirstChild()` again on the name node, and cast the result to a `CharacterData` object. The

CharacterData object supports a getData() call, which finally gives us the name in a String. We attach the name to our SOAPMessage reply, and then (Step 4B) set off in search of the team details.

There are no new calls involved in finding the team details; we just loop through the nodes, getting elements called name, pulling out the CharacterData value of the name, and checking it against the team name we just found in the previous step. When we find a match, we jump to Step 4C to pull interesting detail fields. Since we're already at the appropriate "level" in the document, we now want to look not for child elements, but for siblings of the <name> element in the <teamDetails>. For this, we just loop through the sibling nodes using the get-NextSibling() method, until we find the one named <winLossPct>. We add this value as an attribute to the team in our response message. Certainly, a production version of this application would probably return more than just the single detail field, but one is sufficient to illustrate the process.

Listing 14.4 Using DOM to Return Division Standings

```
// Use DOM to create an XML response
private SOAPMessage processDivision(String div) {

    // Get the XML-formatted data
    Source xmlsource = xmlGenerator.generateXMLDocument();
    DOMResult xmlresult = new DOMResult();
    xmlGenerator.transformXMLDocument(xmlsource, null,
                                      xmlresult);
    Document xmldoc = (Document) xmlresult.getNode();

    // Build and send the reply
    try {
        MessageFactory mf = MessageFactory.newInstance();
        SOAPMessage reply = mf.createMessage();
        SOAPPart       sp = reply.getSOAPPart();
        SOAPEnvelope  env = sp.getEnvelope();
        SOAPBody     body = env.getBody();

        // Create a 'reply' element
        Name nameReply = env.createName(
            "reply", "nfl", "http://nfl.mydomain.com");
        SOAPBodyElement replyElement =
            body.addBodyElement(nameReply);

        // Build content for the replyElement
        // Step 1: Get document root
        Element root = xmldoc.getDocumentElement();
        // Step 2: Find division and teamDetail elements
        NodeList list =
            root.getElementsByTagName("division");
```

```
         NodeList teamDetails =
            root.getElementsByTagName("teamDetails");
         // Step 3: Find the divison match
         Element match = null;
         for (int i=0; i<list.getLength(); i++) {
            Element node = (Element) list.item(i);
            String name = node.getAttribute("name");
            if (name.equals(div)) {
               match = node;
               break;
            }
         }
         // Step 4: Add team items to reply
         // start another loop here to get teams. . .
         NodeList teams =
            match.getElementsByTagName("team");
         Name teamName = env.createName("team");
         Name nameName = env.createName("name");
         Name pctName  = env.createName("winLossPct");
         // Step 4A: get team name in division part
         for (int i=0; i<teams.getLength(); i++) {
            Element team = (Element) teams.item(i);
            // Only child is the text node
            Element name = (Element) team.getFirstChild();
            // Only child is the data string
            CharacterData text =
               (CharacterData) name.getFirstChild();
            String chars = text.getData();

            SOAPElement teamElement =
               replyElement.addChildElement(teamName);
            teamElement.addAttribute(nameName, chars);

            // Step 4B: find matching team in teamDetails
            // Now loop through teamDetails to find match
            Element detail=null, ePct=null, dName=null;
            for (int j=0; j<teamDetails.getLength(); j++) {
               detail = (Element) teamDetails.item(j);
               NodeList dNames =
                  detail.getElementsByTagName("name");
               dName = (Element) dNames.item(0);
               CharacterData dText = (CharacterData)
                  dName.getFirstChild();
               if (dText.getData().equals(chars)) break;
            }
            // Step 4C: get other detail field[s]
            //  find sibling node named winLossPct
            Element sib = dName;
```

```
        while (true) {
            sib = (Element) sib.getNextSibling();
            if (sib == null) break; // no more
            if (sib.getNodeName().equals("winLossPct")) {
                text = (CharacterData)
                        sib.getFirstChild();
                chars = text.getData();
                teamElement.addAttribute(pctName, chars);
                break; // done with siblings
            }
        }
    }
    // Step 5: return
    return reply;
} catch (SOAPException e) {
    e.printStackTrace();
    return null;
}
}
```

In Listing 14.5, we see what the response message we have built looks like. Output has been formatted for better readability.

Listing 14.5 SOAP Message Containing Division Standings Reply

```
<soap-env:Envelope
    xmlns:soap-env=
        "http://schemas.xmlsoap.org/soap/envelope/">
    <soap-env:Header/>
    <soap-env:Body>
        <nfl:reply xmlns:nfl="http://nfl.mydomain.com">
            <team name="Arizona Cardinals" winLossPct="0.75"/>
            <team name="Dallas Cowboys" winLossPct="0.6875"/>
            <team name="New York Giants" winLossPct="0.5"/>
            <team name="Philadelphia Eagles"
                                        winLossPct="0.3125"/>
            <team name="Washington Redskins"
                                        winLossPct="0.1875"/>
        </nfl:reply>
    </soap-env:Body>
</soap-env:Envelope>
```

Handling Whitespace in XML Documents

Whenever we show a fragment of XML, such as in Listing 14.5, it has been formatted with newlines and indentation to improve readability. But the actual XML content, if we displayed it raw, is just one continuous string with no whitespace added. This makes our parsing simpler, since we don't have to account for the whitespace.

In production applications, you should always allow for the fact that XML documents might include whitespace. To a human reader, once we've learned a little basic XML, we have no problem viewing the following two bits of markup as being equivalent:

```
<team>Miami Dolphins</team>
```

```
<team>
   Miami Dolphins
</team>
```

To an XML parser, these are not equivalent. In the first case, the content of the team element is simply the team name. But in the second case, the content is a newline, the team name, and then another newline. For most XML processing, you can simply discard whitespace; but there are times when you need to preserve formatting, and therefore must handle the whitespace

Handling Whitespace in DOM

In a DOM tree, you will find nodes that consist of only whitespace (the previous markup would likely be represented as three text nodes: newline, "Miami Dolphins," newline. You may also encounter additional spaces or even a newline in the middle of the text string, so you may need to assemble a text string by appending multiple nodes together. DOM provides less assistance in this area than the other parsing alternatives.

Handling Whitespace in SAX

SAX has a `characters()` event that is used to return meaningful text, and an `ignorableWhitespace()` event that returns ignorable whitespace. (In the previous example, the newlines before and after the team name are ignorable; the space between "Miami" and "Dolphins" is not.) This makes it a simple matter for the programmer to decide whether to process the whitespace or not. However, determining whether whitespace is ignorable can only be done if the document is described by a DTD, and some SAX parsers will only distinguish ignorable whitespace when they are validating.

Handling Whitespace in JDOM

The JDOM APIs provide several methods for controlling how much, if any, whitespace is returned. When getting the value of a node, you can use the `get-Text()` method to retrieve the content with whitespace, as you would see with DOM. Or you can use the `getTextTrim()` method, which removes any leading or trailing whitespace characters. Finally, you can use the `getTextNormalized()` method to return the element text with any leading or trailing whitespace trimmed, and with any internal whitespace normalized to a single space per occurrence.

Handling Whitespace in XSLT

When performing XSLT transformations, by default any whitespace will be preserved by the transformation. You can use an `<xsl:strip-space>` function to instead have whitespace removed. There is also an `<xsl:preserve-space>` directive. Because `preserve` is the default, this is only needed if you want to return to default behavior after `strip-space` has been used.

14.2 DOM API Reference

The following API sections show only a small sampling of the classes that are included in the DOM package. For those classes that have been shown, all methods of the class are included.

API 14.1 org.w3c.dom.**Node**

```
public interface Node
    public String getNodeName();
    public String getNodeValue() throws DOMException;
    public void setNodeValue(String nodeValue) throws DOMException;
    public short getNodeType();
    public Node getParentNode();
    public NodeList getChildNodes();
    public Node getFirstChild();
    public Node getLastChild();
    public Node getPreviousSibling();
    public Node getNextSibling();
    public NamedNodeMap getAttributes();
    public Document getOwnerDocument();
    public Node insertBefore(Node newChild, Node refChild) throws DOMException;
    public Node replaceChild(Node newChild, Node oldChild) throws DOMException;
    public Node removeChild(Node oldChild) throws DOMException;
    public Node appendChild(Node newChild) throws DOMException;
    public boolean hasChildNodes();
    public Node cloneNode(boolean deep);
```

```
    public void normalize();
    public boolean isSupported(String feature, String version);
    public String getNamespaceURI();
    public String getPrefix();
    public void setPrefix(String prefix) throws DOMException;
    public String getLocalName();
    public boolean hasAttributes();
```

API 14.2   org.w3c.dom.**Document**

```
public interface Document extends Node
    // Experimental (DOM Level 3) methods not shown
    public DocumentType getDocType();
    public DOMImplementation getImplementation();
    public Element getDocumentElement();
    public Element createElement(String tagName) throws DOMException;
    public DocumentFragment createDocumentFragment();
    public Text createTextNode(String data);
    public Comment createComment(String data);
    public CDATASection createCDATASection(String data) throws DOMException;
    public ProcessingInstruction createProcessingInstruction(String target, String data)
        throws DOMException;
    public Attr createAttribute(String name) throws DOMException;
    public EntityReference createEntityReference(String name) throws DOMException;
    public NodeList getElementsByTagName(String tagName);
    public Node importNode(Node importedNode, boolean deep) throws DOMException;
    public Element createElementNS(String namespaceURI, String qualifiedName)
        throws DOMException;
    public Attr createAttributeNS(String namespaceURI, String qualifiedName)
        throws DOMException;
    public NodeList getElementsByTagNameNS(String namespaceURI,
        String localName) throws DOMException;
    public Element getElementById(String elementId);
```

API 14.3   org.w3c.dom.**NodeList**

```
public interface NodeList
    public Node item(int index);
    public int getLength();
```

API 14.4   org.w3c.dom.**Element**

```
public interface Element extends Node
    public String getTagName();
    public String getAttribute(String name);
    public void setAttribute(String name, String value) throws DOMException;
    public void removeAttribute(String name) throws DOMException;
    public Attr getAttributeNode(String name);
    public Attr setAttributeNode(Attr newAttr) throws DOMException;
    public Attr removeAttributeNode(Attr oldAttr) throws DOMException;
    public NodeList getElementsByTagName(String name);
    public String getAttributeNS(String namespaceURI, String localName);
    public void setAttributeNS(String namespaceURI, String qualifiedName,
        String value) throws DOMException;
    public void removeAttributeNS(String namespaceURI, String localName)
        throws DOMException;
    public Attr getAttributeNodeNS(String namespaceURI, String localName);
    public Attr setAttributeNodeNS(Attr newAttr) throws DOMException;
    public NodeList getElementsByTagNameNS(String namespaceURI,
        String localName);
    public boolean hasAttribute(String name);
    public boolean hasAttributeNS(String namespaceURI, String localName);
```

API 14.5   org.w3c.dom.**Attr**

```
public interface Attr extends Node
    public String getName();
    public boolean getSpecified();
    public String getValue();
    public void setValue(String value) throws DOMException;
    public Element getOwnerElement();
```

API 14.6   org.w3c.dom.**CharacterData**

```
public interface CharacterData extends Node
    public String getData() throws DOMException;
    public void setData(String data) throws DOMException;
    public int getLength();
    public String substringData(int offset, int count) throws DOMException;
    public void appendData(String arg) throws DOMException;
    public void insertData(int offset, String arg) throws DOMException;
    public void deleteData(int offset, int count) throws DOMException;
    public void replaceData(int offset, int count, String arg) throws DOMException;
```

Classes not shown:

CDATASection	DOMImplementation	Notation
Comment	Entity	ProcessingInstruction
DocumentFragment	EntityReference	Text
DocumentType	NamedNodeMap	

14.3 Using SAX

Now we'll look at using SAX to process a request for the Conference standings. The task to be performed is nearly identical to what must be done to process a request for the Division standings, but the implementation is quite different.

While DOM is based on having an in-memory representation of the entire document, and navigating around the tree, SAX is event-based, and deals with the document as it is being parsed. This has both advantages and drawbacks. One advantage is less memory use; DOM requires that the document fit in memory, and will fail if the entire document tree cannot be built in memory. However, once the DOM tree is built, you can navigate around it freely, moving back and forth, revisiting nodes, and so forth. With SAX, you get one shot at the data as it's being parsed; if you need to revisit it later, you had better save it.

In Listing 14.6, we start by creating an instance of a class called MySAXParser. We'll look at this class in Listing 14.7; for now, it's enough to say that this is a class we will provide that handles a set of events triggered during the parsing of an XML document. We then see familiar code to transform an XML document: getting the Source class, and invoking the transformation given a Source and a Result. The result in this case is a SAXResult, and the SAXResult class is being initialized with a reference to our parser. The MySAXParser class is designed to store the information we're interested in as two String arrays—one with team names, the other with the win-loss percentages. The act of doing the transformation will cause the entire document to be parsed, so once the transformation is complete, the result fields can be picked up and used to create the SOAP reply message.

Listing 14.6 Using SAX to Return Conference Standings

```
// Use SAX to create an XML response
private SOAPMessage processConference(String conf) {

    MySAXParser myParser = new MySAXParser();
    // Configure the parser for the result we want
    myParser.setConfName(conf);

    Source xmlsource = xmlGenerator.generateXMLDocument();
    xmlGenerator.transformXMLDocument(xmlsource, null,
            new SAXResult(myParser));

    String[] teams = myParser.getTeamNames();
    String[] pcts  = myParser.getTeamPcts();
```

```
      // Build and send the reply
      try {
         MessageFactory mf = MessageFactory.newInstance();
         SOAPMessage reply = mf.createMessage();
         SOAPPart       sp = reply.getSOAPPart();
         SOAPEnvelope  env = sp.getEnvelope();
         SOAPBody     body = env.getBody();

         // Create a 'reply' element
         Name nameReply = env.createName(
            "reply", "nfl", "http://nfl.mydomain.com");
         SOAPBodyElement replyElement = body.addBodyElement(nameReply);

         Name teamName = env.createName("team");
         Name nameName = env.createName("name");
         Name pctName  = env.createName("winLossPct");

         for (int i=0; i<teams.length; i++) {
            // Array contains empty entries at end
            if (teams[i] == null) break;
            SOAPElement teamElement =
               replyElement.addChildElement(teamName);
            teamElement.addAttribute(nameName, teams[i]);
            teamElement.addAttribute(pctName, pcts[i]);
         }
         return reply;
      } catch (SOAPException e) {
         e.printStackTrace();
         return null;
      }
   }
```

Listing 14.7 shows our SAX parser. SAX parsers should implement the `ContentHandler` interface. Rather than implement the interface directly, we instead are subclassing the `Default-Handler` class. The `DefaultHandler` implements `ContentHandler` and provides default (mostly no-op) implementations of each event. By using `DefaultHandler`, we can safely ignore XML constructs we aren't interested in, such as the DOCTYPE declaration.

The methods from `ContentHandler` that our parser implements are `startDocument()`, `endDocument()`, `startElement()`, `endElement()`, and `characters()`. The point at which these will each be called should be obvious for the most part; `characters()` is called whenever a text node is processed. Each event call carries no context information, so it is the responsibility of the implementer to construct a state machine that carries any needed contextual information. Our `startDocument()` and `endDocument()` calls are no-ops that could easily have been left to the `DefaultHandler`.

The `startElement()` event calls receive as parameters the namespace of the element (if any), and both the localname and qualified name. They also get an `Attributes` object that contains any attributes for the element. The text part of the element must be processed by the `characters()` call.

SAX makes no guarantee of how much data will be returned in any particular invocation of the `characters()` call. It is therefore the responsibility of the implementer to allow the possibility that the text might be received in multiple chunks, and not as a single unit. For this reason, we initialize a `StringBuffer` in the `startElement()` call, append to it in each `characters()` call, and do not consider the string completed until we receive the `endElement()` call.

Listing 14.7 `MySAXParser` Class

```
// MySAXParser.java

package nfl.application.jaxm;

import org.xml.sax.Attributes;
import org.xml.sax.helpers.DefaultHandler;

public class MySAXParser extends DefaultHandler {

    private static final int MAX_ENTRIES = 30;

    private String confName;
    private String[] teamNames = new String[MAX_ENTRIES];
    private String[] teamPcts  = new String[MAX_ENTRIES];

    private int teamsFound = 0;

    // State tracking.
    boolean inConfPart = false;
    boolean inTeamsPart = false;

    boolean interestingConference = false;
    boolean interestingTeam = false;

    boolean inNameElement = false;
    private StringBuffer nameSB = null;
    boolean inPctElement = false;
    private StringBuffer pctSB = null;
    int      teamIndex;

// Methods from the ContentHandler interface
    public void startDocument() {
       //System.out.println("Start of document.");
    }
```

```java
public void endDocument() {
    //System.out.println("End of document.");
}

public void startElement(String namespace,
                         String localname,
                         String qname,
                         Attributes attrs) {
    //System.out.println("Start of element " + localname)
    if (localname.equals("conference")) {
        inConfPart = true;
        // Check name attribute; match?
        if (attrs.getValue("name").equals(confName))
            interestingConference = true;
        else
            interestingConference = false;
    }
    if (localname.equals("teams")) {
        inTeamsPart = true;
    }
    if (localname.equals("team")) {
        if (interestingConference)
            interestingTeam = true;
    }
    if (localname.equals("teamDetails")) {
        // must defer decision until name parsed
        interestingTeam = true;
    }
    if (localname.equals("name")) {
        if (interestingTeam) {
            inNameElement = true;
            nameSB = new StringBuffer();
        }
    }
    if (localname.equals("winLossPct")) {
        if (interestingTeam) {
            inPctElement = true;
            pctSB = new StringBuffer();
        }
    }
}
public void endElement(String namespace,
                       String localname,
                       String qname) {
    //System.out.println("End of element " + qName);
    if (localname.equals("conference")) {
        inConfPart = false;
        interestingConference = false;
    }
```

```
      if (localname.equals("teams")) {
         inTeamsPart = false;
      }
      if (localname.equals("team")) {
         interestingTeam = false;
      }
      if (localname.equals("name")) {
         if (inNameElement) {
            // Only true if name was 'interesting'.
            if (inConfPart) {
               // Preserve the StringBuffer.
               teamNames[teamsFound++] = nameSB.toString();
            }
            if (inTeamsPart) {
               // did we save this team earlier?
               String name = nameSB.toString();
               teamIndex = -1;
               for (int i=0; i<MAX_ENTRIES; i++) {
                  if (teamNames[i] == null)
                     break; // past used slots
                  if (teamNames[i].equals(name)) {
                     teamIndex = i;
                  }
               }
               if (teamIndex == -1) {
                  interestingTeam = false;
               }
            }
            nameSB = null;
            inNameElement = false;
         }
      }
      if (localname.equals("winLossPct")) {
         if (inPctElement) {
            // Only true for interesting teams
            teamPcts[teamIndex] = pctSB.toString();
            inPctElement = false;
         }
      }
   }

   public void characters(char[] ch, int start, int length) {
      // non-interesting fields will not have booleans on
      if (inNameElement) {
         nameSB.append(ch);
      }
      if (inPctElement) {
         pctSB.append(ch);
      }
   }
```

```
// Methods to pass data to/from servlet
   public void setConfName(String conf) {
      this.confName = conf;
   }

   public String[] getTeamNames() {
      return teamNames;
   }

   public String[] getTeamPcts() {
      return teamPcts;
   }
}
```

14.4 SAX API Reference

API 14.7   org.xml.sax.**ContentHandler**

```
public interface ContentHandler
    public void characters(char[] ch, int start, int length);
    public void endDocument();
    public void endElement(String uri, String localname, String qname);
    public void endPrefixMapping(String uri);
    public void ignoreableWhitespace(char[] ch, int start, int length);
    public void processingInstruction(String target, String data);
    public void setDocumentLocator(Locator locator);
    public void skippedEntity(String name);
    public void startDocument();
    public void startElement(String uri, String localname, String qname, Attributes attrs);
    public void startPrefixMapping(String prefix, String uri);
```

API 14.8   API 14.8: org.xml.sax.**Attributes**

```
public interface Attributes
    public int getIndex(String qName);
    public int getIndex(String uri, String localname);
    public int getLength();
    public String getLocalName(int index);
    public String getQName(int index);
    public String getType(int index);
    public String getType(String qName);
    public String getType(String uri, String localname);
    public String getURI(int index);
    public String getValue(int index);
    public String getValue(String qName);
    public String getValue(String uri, String qName);
```

14.5 Using JDOM

After our `JaxmClient` requests either conference or division standings, and the `Jaxm-StandingsServlet` has built a reply using either SAX or DOM, the reply is received back in the `JaxmClient`. The `JaxmClient` will now use yet a third XML API, JDOM, to parse the result. JDOM, as the name implies, has far more in common with DOM than with SAX. We pick up the code in Listing 14.8 at the point immediately following our message passing, to which we receive a `SOAPMessage` called `reply` in return.

Listing 14.8 JDOM Code to Parse SOAP Reply

```
//Optional; allow visual inspection
try {
   reply.writeTo(System.out);
   System.out.println();
   System.out.flush();
} catch (IOException e) {
   e.printStackTrace();
}
SOAPPart soap = reply.getSOAPPart();
StreamSource xmlStream = (StreamSource)
                       soap.getContent();
DOMBuilder builder = new DOMBuilder();
Document   doc     = null;
try {
   doc = builder.build(
              xmlStream.getInputStream());
} catch (JDOMException e) {
   e.printStackTrace();
}
Namespace ns = Namespace.getNamespace(
   "nfl", "http://nfl.mydomain.com");
Namespace ns2 = Namespace.getNamespace(
   "soap-env",
   "http://schemas.xmlsoap.org/soap/envelope/");

// replyroot is the <soap-env:Envelope> element
Element replyRoot = doc.getRootElement();

// replyBody is <soap-env:Body> element
Element replyBody = replyRoot.getChild("Body",ns2);

// replyElem = <nfl:reply> element
Element replyElem = replyBody.getChild("reply",ns);
```

```
        // get all children
        List teams = replyElem.getChildren();
        for (int i=0; i<teams.size(); i++) {
            // each replyTeam is a <team>
            Element replyTeam = (Element) teams.get(i);
            Attribute teamName =
                    replyTeam.getAttribute("name");
            Attribute wlPct =
                    replyTeam.getAttribute("winLossPct");
            System.out.println(teamName.getValue() + "   " +
                            wlPct.getValue());
        }
```

14.6 JDOM API Reference

API 14.9   org.jdom.input.**DOMBuilder**

```
public class DOMBuilder
    // Constructors
    public DOMBuilder();
    public DOMBuilder(boolean validate);
    public DOMBuilder(String adapterClass);
    public DOMBuilder(String adapterClass, boolean validate);
    // Methods
    public Document build(org.w3c.dom.Document domDocument);
    public Element build(org.w3c.dom.Element domElement);
    // deprecated build methods not shown
    public void setFactory(JDOMFactory factory);
    public void setValidation(boolean validate);
```

API 14.10   org.jdom.**Document**

```
public class Document
    // Constructors
    public Document();
    public Document(Element rootElement);
    public Document(Element rootElement, DocType docType);
    public Document(java.util.List content);
    public Document(java.util.List newContent, DocType docType);
    // Methods
    public Document addContent(Comment comment);
    public Document addContent(ProcessingInstruction pi);
    public Element detachRootElement();
    public List getContent();
    public List getContent(Filter filter);
```

```
    public DocType getDocType();
    public Element getRootElement();
    public boolean hasRootElement();
    public boolean removeContent(Comment comment);
    public boolean removeContent(ProcessingInstruction pi);
    public Document setContent(java.util.List newContent);
    public Document setDocType(DocType docType);
    public Document setRootElement(Element rootElement);
```

API 14.11   org.jdom.**Namespace**

```
public class Namespace
    public static Namespace getNamespace(String uri);
    public static Namespace getNamespace(String prefix, String uri);
    public String getPrefix();
    public String getURI();
```

API 14.12   org.jdom.**Element**

```
public class Element
    // Constructors
    protected Element();
    public Element(String name);
    public Element(String name, Namespace namespace);
    public Element(String name, String uri);
    public Element(String name, String prefix, String uri);
    // Methods
    public Element addContent(CDATA cdata);
    public Element addContent(Comment comment);
    public Element addContent(Element element);
    public Element addContent(EntityRef entity);
    public Element addContent(ProcessingInstruction pi);
    public Element addContent(String str);
    public Element addContent(Text text);
    public void addNamespaceDeclaration(Namespace additional);
    public Element detach();
    public List getAdditionalNamespaces();
    public Attribute getAttribute(String name);
    public Attribute getAttribute(String name, Namespace ns);
    public List getAttributes();
    public String getAttributeValue(String name);
    public String getAttributeValue(String name, Namespace ns);
    public String getAttributeValue(String name, Namespace ns, String defaultValue);
    public String getAttributeValue(String name, String defaultValue);
    public Element getChild(String name);
```

```
public Element getChild(String name, Namespace ns);
public List getChildren();
public List getChildren(String name);
public List getChildren(String name, Namespace ns);
public String getChildText(String name);
public String getChildText(String name, Namespace ns);
public String getChildTextNormalize(String name);
public String getChildTextNormalize(String name, Namespace ns);
public String getChildTextTrim(String name);
public String getChildTextTrim(String name, Namespace ns);
public List getContent();
public List getContent(Filter filter);
public Document getDocument();
public String getName();
public Namespace getNamespace();
public Namespace getNamespace(String prefix);
public String getNamespacePreflx();
public String getNamespaceURI();
public Element getParent();
public String getQualifiedName();
public String getText();
public String getTextNormalize();
public String getTextTrim();
public boolean hasChildren();
public boolean isAncestor(Element element);
public boolean isRootElement();
public boolean removeAttribute(Attribute attribute);
public boolean removeAttribute(String name);
public boolean removeAttribute(String name, Namespace ns);
public boolean removeChild(String name);
public boolean removeChild(String name, Namespace ns);
public boolean removeChildren();
public boolean removeChildren(String name);
public boolean removeChildren(String name, Namespace ns);
public boolean removeContent(CDATA cdata);
public boolean removeContent(Comment comment);
public boolean removeContent(Element element);
public boolean removeContent(EntityRef entity);
public boolean removeContent(ProcessingInstruction pi);
public boolean removeContent(Text text);
public void removeNamespaceDeclaration(Namespace additionalNamespace);
public Element setAttribute(Attribute attribute);
public Element setAttribute(String name, String value);
public Element setAttribute(String name, String value, Namespace ns);
public Element setAttributes(List newAttributes);
```

```
public Element setChildren(List children);
public Element setContent(List newContent);
protected Element setDocument(Document document);
public Element setName(String name);
public Element setNamespace(Namespace namespace);
protected Element setParent(Element parent);
public Element setText(String text);
```

API 14.13 org.jdom.**Attribute**

```
public class Attribute
    // Constructors
    protected Attribute();
    public Attribute(String name, String value);
    public Attribute(String name, String value, int type);
    public Attribute(String name, String value, int type, Namespace namespace);
    public Attribute(String name, String value, Namespace namespace);
    // Methods
    public Attribute detach();
    public int getAttributeType();
    public boolean getBooleanValue();
    public Document getDocument();
    public double getDoubleValue();
    public float getFloatValue();
    public int getIntValue();
    public long getLongValue();
    public String getName();
    public Namespace getNamespace();
    public String getNamespacePrefix();
    public String getNamespaceURI();
    public Element getParent();
    public String getQualifiedName();
    public String getValue();
    public Attribute setAttributeType(int type);
    public Attribute setName(String name);
    public Attribute setNamespace(Namespace namespace);
    protected Attribute setParent(Element parent);
    public Attribute setValue(String value);
```

Design Center: DOM, SAX, or JDOM?

Many people have a strong preference for either the DOM/JDOM or the SAX style of programming, so many times the decision is made purely on the basis of what the programmer prefers. However, there are some real functional differences that also have to be considered.

- JDOM and DOM require that the document tree fit into memory; this makes them more resource-intensive than SAX.
- A DOM or JDOM tree can be freely navigated—forward, backward, revisiting nodes, etc. SAX events are seen once and only once; if you miss it, it's gone. SAX may be better for processing just a small part of a large document, while DOM and JDOM would be favored for processing that required repetitive access to part or all of the document.
- JDOM has (in my opinion) the best handling of whitespace, DOM the worst, with SAX falling in the middle.
- JDOM makes use of Java capabilities such as method overloading and Java's data types (such as Lists).
- DOM and SAX are language-independent APIs; if you have the need to work in multiple languages, knowing these APIs will allow you to parse XML from any language that supports them.
- SAX is a read-only API. If you need to create or manipulate documents, then you must use either DOM or JDOM.
- Given a DOM or JDOM node, you can find anything about its context by querying the APIs—what is the parent element, the child elements, siblings, and so forth. With SAX, you must determine this information by tracking events as they are seen.

14.7 Building and Running the JaxmClient Example

Rather than split out a separate Ant buildfile for the `JaxmClient` program, it was integrated into the buildfile created in Chapter 13; see the listing in that chapter if you are interested in the specifics. A command of `ant client` will build the client program.

To run the client, the `JaxmStandingsServlet` must first be running. Again, details are in Chapter 13; if you haven't done anything to uninstall the code then the servlet should be available whenever your application server is up and running.

Optionally, you can run the `JaxmGameServer` process as well. If the game server is not running, then the client will essentially report data as of the start of the season, with no games played. You can run the server in one window and periodically run the client in another to see the standings change as additional games are posted.

The `<test-client>` task in the buildfile runs the client program twice—once to get results for a division, then again to get results for a conference. You can edit the buildfile to have it return standings for a different conference or division. You also might need to adjust the `host` argument on the client invocation to reflect the hostname and port where your servlet is running.

14.8 Using JAXB

The Java API for XML Binding (JAXB) is potentially the most interesting of the JAX* family of APIs. It is also, unfortunately, the least ready for use. An early-access implementation has been made available through the Java Developer Connection Web site. The JAXB early-access release is not included in the current (Spring 2002) releases of the Java XML Pack or the Java Web Services Developer's Pack.

Based on feedback to this early JAXB release, the designers decided not to move forward with the current implementation, but to do a radical redesign and start over. Therefore, you should realize that the code in this section is merely to give an indication of how JAXB works and can be used. The actual code examples will not work with the released version of JAXB when it comes available. Where possible, I'll note changes between the reference implementation and the redesigned version, but full information about the new design has not been released.

The purpose of JAXB is to map XML objects into Java classes. For example, JAXB could take our `standings.xml` document and from it create a set of Java classes such as `Conference`, `Division`, and `Team`. One of the reasons for the redesign of JAXB is to use an architecture that can be extended in the future to also support mapping in the other direction, from an arbitrary set of Java classes to an XML document. This will not be a feature of the first release of JAXB.

If you don't want to wait for JAXB, the open-source Castor project (`http://castor.exolab.org`) provides a similar XML-to-Java mapping capability.

The early-access version of JAXB works from a Document Type Definition (DTD) file. As it turns out, XML schema files provide a much better basis for describing XML in the amount of detail that JAXB needs, so the released version will work from XML schemas rather than DTDs. But for now, we must settle for a DTD. Listing 14.9 shows the DTD file that was created to describe our `standings.xml` document.

Listing 14.9 `standings.dtd` File

```
<!ELEMENT standings (divisionStandings,
                     conferenceStandings,
                     teams)>
<!ELEMENT divisionStandings (division+)>
<!ELEMENT division (team+)>
<!ATTLIST division
    name CDATA #REQUIRED >
<!ELEMENT team (name)>
<!ATTLIST team
    rank CDATA #REQUIRED >
```

```
<!ELEMENT name (#PCDATA)>
<!ELEMENT conferenceStandings (conference+)>
<!ELEMENT conference (team+)>
<!ATTLIST conference
     name CDATA #REQUIRED >
<!ELEMENT teams (teamDetails+)>
<!ELEMENT teamDetails (name, wins, losses, ties,
     divisionWins, divisionLosses, divisionTies,
     conferenceWins, conferenceLosses, conferenceTies,
     points, pointsAllowed, winLossPct, divWinLossPct,
     confWinLossPct, netPoints, divNetPoints,
     confNetPoints, streak, divChampStatus,
     homeFieldStatus, wildcardStatus)>
<!ELEMENT wins            (#PCDATA)>
<!ELEMENT losses          (#PCDATA)>
<!ELEMENT ties            (#PCDATA)>
<!ELEMENT divisionWins    (#PCDATA)>
<!ELEMENT divisionLosses  (#PCDATA)>
<!ELEMENT divisionTies    (#PCDATA)>
<!ELEMENT conferenceWins  (#PCDATA)>
<!ELEMENT conferenceLosses (#PCDATA)>
<!ELEMENT conferenceTies  (#PCDATA)>
<!ELEMENT points          (#PCDATA)>
<!ELEMENT pointsAllowed   (#PCDATA)>
<!ELEMENT winLossPct      (#PCDATA)>
<!ELEMENT divWinLossPct   (#PCDATA)>
<!ELEMENT confWinLossPct  (#PCDATA)>
<!ELEMENT netPoints       (#PCDATA)>
<!ELEMENT divNetPoints    (#PCDATA)>
<!ELEMENT confNetPoints   (#PCDATA)>
<!ELEMENT streak          (#PCDATA)>
<!ELEMENT divChampStatus  (#PCDATA)>
<!ELEMENT homeFieldStatus (#PCDATA)>
<!ELEMENT wildcardStatus  (#PCDATA)>
```

The JAXB reference implementation includes a program called xjc, which is the XML to Java compiler. The compiler requires two files as input: the DTD file and something called a binding schema. The binding schema in the early access release is essentially a workaround for some of the limitations of DTD files. In the released version, binding schemas will probably be optional, and in fact may just be particular notations that can be made in an XML schema file, rather than a separate file as they are today.

The early-access version provides a number of options that can be specified in the binding schema. Because these are all likely to change, I've gone with the simplest schema allowed. Listing 14.10 shows the minimum required binding schema. The <element> identifies that we want to build an object tree whose root will be the standings element in the file, and that standings will become a Java class (as opposed to an interface).

Listing 14.10 `JaxbApp.xjs` Binding Schema

```
<xml-java-binding-schema>
   <element name="standings" type="class" root="true" />
</xml-java-binding-schema>
```

When we run `xjc` giving it the DTD and binding schema files as shown, it produces a series of Java source files as a result. The full set of classes produced was `Standings`, `Confer-ence`, `ConferenceStandings`, `Division`, `DivisionStandings`, `Team`, and `TeamDetails`. Several of these had nested or inner classes generated as well. We'll just look at one of these, the `Standings` class, which is shown in Listing 14.11. There are several things about this class that will certainly change in the final release; we'll cover at least some of the changes below. The listing has been reformatted (for width), and certain of the method's contents have been omitted.

Listing 14.11 `Standings.java`

```
import java.io.IOException;
import java.io.InputStream;
import javax.xml.bind.Dispatcher;
import javax.xml.bind.InvalidAttributeException;
import javax.xml.bind.LocalValidationException;
import javax.xml.bind.MarshallableRootElement;
import javax.xml.bind.Marshaller;
import javax.xml.bind.MissingContentException;
import javax.xml.bind.RootElement;
import javax.xml.bind.StructureValidationException;
import javax.xml.bind.UnmarshalException;
import javax.xml.bind.Unmarshaller;
import javax.xml.bind.Validator;
import javax.xml.marshal.XMLScanner;
import javax.xml.marshal.XMLWriter;


public class Standings
    extends MarshallableRootElement
    implements RootElement
{

    private DivisionStandings _DivisionStandings;
    private ConferenceStandings _ConferenceStandings;
    private Teams _Teams;

    public DivisionStandings getDivisionStandings() {
        return _DivisionStandings;
    }
```

```java
public void setDivisionStandings(
            DivisionStandings _DivisionStandings) {
    this._DivisionStandings = _DivisionStandings;
    if (_DivisionStandings == null) {
        invalidate();
    }
}

public ConferenceStandings getConferenceStandings() {
    return _ConferenceStandings;
}

public void setConferenceStandings(
        ConferenceStandings _ConferenceStandings) {
    this._ConferenceStandings = _ConferenceStandings;
    if (_ConferenceStandings == null) {
        invalidate();
    }
}

public Teams getTeams() {
    return _Teams;
}

public void setTeams(Teams _Teams) {
    this._Teams = _Teams;
    if (_Teams == null) {
        invalidate();
    }
}

public void validateThis()
    throws LocalValidationException
{
    if (_DivisionStandings == null) {
        throw new MissingContentException(
                    "divisionStandings");
    }
    if (_ConferenceStandings == null) {
        throw new MissingContentException(
                    "conferenceStandings");
    }
    if (_Teams == null) {
        throw new MissingContentException("teams");
    }
}
```

```
public void validate(Validator v)
    throws StructureValidationException
{
    v.validate(_DivisionStandings);
    v.validate(_ConferenceStandings);
    v.validate(_Teams);
}

public void marshal(Marshaller m)
    throws IOException
{
    XMLWriter w = m.writer();
    w.start("standings");
    m.marshal(_DivisionStandings);
    m.marshal(_ConferenceStandings);
    m.marshal(_Teams);
    w.end("standings");
}

public void unmarshal(Unmarshaller u)
    throws UnmarshalException
{
    XMLScanner xs = u.scanner();
    Validator v = u.validator();
    xs.takeStart("standings");
    while (xs.atAttribute()) {
        String an = xs.takeAttributeName();
        throw new InvalidAttributeException(an);
    }
    _DivisionStandings = ((DivisionStandings)
                          u.unmarshal());
    _ConferenceStandings = ((ConferenceStandings)
                            u.unmarshal());
    _Teams = ((Teams) u.unmarshal());
    xs.takeEnd("standings");
}

public static Standings unmarshal(InputStream in)
    throws UnmarshalException
{
    return unmarshal(XMLScanner.open(in));
}

public static Standings unmarshal(XMLScanner xs)
    throws UnmarshalException
{
    return unmarshal(xs, newDispatcher());
}
```

```
    public static Standings unmarshal(XMLScanner xs,
                                      Dispatcher d)
        throws UnmarshalException
    {
        return ((Standings) d.unmarshal(xs,
                            (Standings.class)));
    }

    public boolean equals(Object ob) {
        // Details omitted
    }

    public int hashCode() {
        // Details omitted
    }

    public String toString() {
        // Details omitted
    }

    public static Dispatcher newDispatcher() {
        return Conference.newDispatcher();
    }


}
```

Now that we have generated a set of classes that correspond to elements within the XML document, we can build a simple application to show how these JAXB-generated classes can be used. In Listing 14.12, we show a very simple JAXB application.

The key functionality here is the ability to unmarshal an XML document into a set of classes. This is shown in Listing 14.12 as an `unmarshal()` call on the `Standings` object. In the final release, this design has been changed to instead have separate `Marshaller` and `Unmarshaller` objects, rather than embedding this functionality into the generated classes. Among other things, this change is required to allow JAXB to work in the Java-to-XML direction.

Once we've unmarshalled the document, we can navigate around the document somewhat like a DOM tree. Because the standings element in our original XML document had three sub-elements (`conferences`, `divisions`, and `teams`), our `Standings` object has three property fields with accessor methods that provide both read and write capabilities.

In this simple example, we get the `Teams` object, from that retrieve the `List` of `Team-Details`, and then loop through the details looking for a particular team. When we find the team, we print the win-loss record, merely to verify that the data from the XML document has in fact been properly represented in our Java classes.

Listing 14.12 `JaxbApp.java`

```java
// MinimalJaxbApp.java

import java.io.*;
//import java.util.*;
import javax.xml.bind.UnmarshalException;
//import javax.xml.marshal.UnmarshalException;

public class MinimalJaxbApp {

    public static Standings standings = new Standings();

    public static void main(String[] args) {
        Standings standings = new Standings();

        // Build object tree from XML document
        FileInputStream fis = null;
        try {
            File stand = new File(
                    "../../presentation/xml/standings.xml");
            fis = new FileInputStream(stand);
            standings = standings.unmarshal(fis);
        } catch (FileNotFoundException e) {
            e.printStackTrace();
        } catch (IOException e) {
            e.printStackTrace();
        } catch (UnmarshalException e) {
            e.printStackTrace();
        } finally {
            try {
                fis.close();
            } catch (IOException e) {
                // give me a break!
            }
        }

        // Traverse tree to find some data
        // - W/L/T record for Denver Broncos
        Teams teams = standings.getTeams();
        java.util.List details = teams.getTeamDetails();
        for (int i=0; i<details.size(); i++) {
            TeamDetails team = (TeamDetails) details.get(i);
            if (team.getName().equals("Denver Broncos")) {
                String wins = team.getWins();
                String ties = team.getTies();
                String losses = team.getLosses();
```

```
            System.out.println("Denver's record is " +
                wins + "-" + losses + "-" + ties + ".");
            break;
        }
    }
}
}
```

14.9　Building and Running the JAXB Example

Listing 14.13 shows the `build.xml` file for the JAXB example. In order to build the JAXB example, you'll need to alter the `JAXB_HOME` property to the location where you've installed the early-access release. Because of changes being made to the JAXB implementation, the example code here will not work as written with future releases of JAXB.

The default `<build>` target will run the `xjc` compiler to generate classes from the `standings.dtd` file, and then compile those classes as well as the source for our example program. The `<test>` target will invoke our example, which utilizes the `xjc`-generated classes.

Listing 14.13 `build.xml` From `jaxb` Directory

```xml
<project name="jaxb" default="build" basedir=".">

<property name="JAXB_HOME"
        value="/home/myawn/webservices/jaxb-1.0-ea" />

<property name="jaxb.path"
        value="${JAXB_HOME}/lib/jaxb-rt-1.0-ea.jar" />

<target name="build">
    <exec executable="${JAXB_HOME}/bin/xjc">
        <arg line="-d" />
        <arg line="build" />
        <arg line="standings.dtd" />
        <arg line="JaxbApp.xjs" />
    </exec>
    <javac srcdir="build" includes="*.java"
        classpath="${jaxb.path}" />
    <javac srcdir="." includes="JaxbApp.java"
        classpath="${jaxb.path}:build" />
</target>

<target name="test">
    <java classpath="${jaxb.path}:.:build"
        classname="JaxbApp" />
</target>
```

```
<target name="clean">
   <delete>
      <fileset dir="." includes="*.class" />
      <fileset dir="build" includes="*" />
   </delete>
</target>

</project>
```

14.10 Exercises

14.1 Add fields to JAXM result messages: Extend both the SAX and DOM examples (the Conference and Division result messages) to add more team statistics, then have JDOM (the JAXMClient) parse the additional fields.

14.2 JAXM client output: Add the proper numeric formatting (using the DecimalFormat class) to the output of the JaxmClient program.

14.11 Further Reading

The home page for the DOM standard is `http://www.w3.org/DOM`.

The SAX Project home page is `http://www.saxproject.org`.

The home page for the JDOM project is `http://www.jdom.org`.

The JAXB (XML Binding) and JAXP (XML Parsing) APIs are located at `http://java.sun.com/xml/jaxb/index.html` and `http://java.sun.com/xml/jaxp/index.html`, respectively.

The Xerces and Xalan XML parsers are from the Apache group and can be downloaded at `http://xml.apache.org`.

Additional XML references are listed at the end of Chapter 9.

## CHAPTER 15

Remote Method Invocation (RMI)

Y ou don't need to see this chapter. These aren't the APIs you're looking for. You can go about your business. Move along.

I'll state it right up front: I'm not a fan of RMI. Every time I've used it in a project, it has had me tearing my hair out over simple problems made maddeningly complex by useless error messages and design choices that seem punitive at best.

I could well be in the minority on this, and that's fine. You may decide you love RMI, and I hope to give you enough information here for you to decide that yourself. It certainly provides you a greater degree of control over the distribution of your objects than using an API set such as JSP/Servlets (where only the presentation is on the client) or JDBC (where only the database is on the server). With RMI, you can put every object exactly where you want (or need) it to be.

It could be that my lack of enthusiasm is due to how I've tried to use RMI. I very rarely set out to write an RMI program, because I like to follow a rapid prototyping process where I try to get the basic code running as quickly as possible. Then I go back to enhance and extend as necessary. But RMI stubbornly refuses to be compatible with any classes you might write, even if future extensibility to RMI is one of your design goals going in. You'll see what I mean as we go through the examples.

RMI is actually part of Java 2 Standard Edition (J2SE), so a JDK is the only software required to use the examples in this chapter. This J2SE technology is being covered in a book that mainly focuses on J2EE because the concepts of distributed objects will be seen again in several technologies yet to come, and RMI forms the basis for technologies such as JAX-RPC and Enterprise JavaBeans (EJB).

15.1   Basic RMI Concepts

So, you have an object on System A, and would like to call some method in another object on System B. Obviously, there's going to be some network calls involved in this process. Without RMI, you'd be making those network calls yourself. With RMI, the actual network code is provided for you. In a RMI application, the remotely accessible object is shadowed by two new objects that provide this networking code. On the server side, the code is called a skeleton; on the client side, it is called a stub. The stubs and skeletons are theoretically there to isolate your code from the network, yet in a completely unsatisfying way that forces you to nevertheless remain constantly aware of when an object is local and when it is remote, and be prepared in your code to deal with any problems that may arise as a result.

Figure 15.1 Remote procedure call process flow.

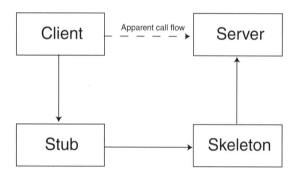

The idea is that to the client, it appears that a method call is being made directly on the remote object. In reality, the method call is being made to the stub object. The stub object then sends the method parameters across the network to the skeleton object. The skeleton makes the actual procedure call on behalf of the client, and receives back any return value. This return value is then sent back over the network to the stub, who then returns it to the original caller.

The process of preparing parameters or return values to be passed across the network is called *marshalling*. You'll see this word a lot in the error messages you'll see each time you try to write an RMI program. The key to marshalling parameters is serialization—turning an object into a stream of bytes that can be squirted across the network. Because any parameters to a method, and any return value from a method, must be sent across the network, it is necessary that any object type you use as a parameter or as a return value be marked `Serializable`.

15.2   Creating a Remotely Accessible Standings Object

The best way to gain an understanding of RMI is to write some code. Let's say that for some reason, we'd like a client program to be able to access a `Standings` object residing on a remote system, but without the use of servlets. The first requirement of RMI is that there must be a remote interface that enumerates the methods that are remotely callable.

Now, because we separated interface from implementation in our application way back in Chapter 2, you might think we would be well set for this. But RMI places some unique requirements on the remote interface. First, the interface itself must extend `java.rmi.Remote`; then, each method within the interface must throw `java.rmi.RemoteException`. While I can understand the need for these, I cannot believe that RMI could not have been designed in such a way as to be more transparent. This ensures that we cannot use `Standings` as our interface (because it does not extend `Remote`), nor can we create a new interface that extends `Standings` to be our remote interface (because adding `RemoteException` changes the signature of each method, which is not a legal thing to do in a subclass). So our remote interface (and its implementation to come) create sort of a parallel universe version of the `Standings` class.

Table 15.1   Components in the RMI Application

New Components			
Name	**Package**	**Class or Interface**	**Comment**
RemoteStandings	nfl.application.rmi	Interface	Mimics the `DynamicStandings` interface.
RemoteStandingsAdapter	nfl.application.rmi	Class	An Adapter that implements `RemoteStandings` and forwards to a `DynamicStandings`.
RemoteConsole	nfl.presentation	Class	A RMI client.
Existing Components			
Component	**Description**		
layered.jar	All classes and interfaces of the layered version of the application (as presented in Chapter 2).		
DynamicStandings	The interface and implementation of dynamic standings are also used in the RMI application.		

Listing 15.1 shows the interface that we'll use. It incorporates methods from both the `Standings` and `DynamicStandings` interfaces. As required, it extends `Remote` and every method throws `RemoteException`.

Listing 15.1 Remote Interface for `Standings` Class (`RemoteStandings.java`)

```java
// RemoteStandings.java

package nfl.application.rmi;

import nfl.application.*;

import java.rmi.RemoteException;
import java.util.List;

import nfl.ObjectFactory;

/* Calculates and prints standings for all NFL conferences
 * and divisions */
public interface RemoteStandings extends java.rmi.Remote
{
// Methods from Standings
    public void loadData() throws RemoteException;

    public List computeDivisionStandings(Division div)
        throws RemoteException;
    public List computeConferenceStandings(Conference conf)
        throws RemoteException;

// Methods from DynamicStandings
    public void init() throws RemoteException;

    public List getDivisionStandings(int i)
        throws RemoteException;
    public List getDivisionStandings(Division d)
        throws RemoteException;
    public List[] getDivisionStandings()
        throws RemoteException;

    public List getConferenceStandings(int i)
        throws RemoteException;
    public List getConferenceStandings(Conference c)
        throws RemoteException;
    public List[] getConferenceStandings()
        throws RemoteException;

    public void postGameData(Game g)
        throws RemoteException;
}
```

Now we need a class that implements the interface. As with the interface, RMI places restrictions on the implementing class that seem designed to thwart any attempt at code reuse. Our implementing class must extend `java.rmi.server.UnicastRemoteObject`; because Java has no multiple inheritance, this means our class cannot be a subclass of anything in the current `Standings` hierarchy. Fortunately, there is a design pattern to come to our rescue here; the Adapter pattern can be used to make our new remote class forward requests to an underlying `Standings` object, essentially replacing inheritance with composition.

The Adapter Design Pattern

The idea behind the Adapter pattern is to convert one interface into another. Adapters can be dropped in between classes that originally weren't designed to be used together, if the basic data needed is present but there is simply a disagreement about method names, data types, or parameter ordering. Adapters can also be used for interface versioning, allowing an implementation to change but continuing to provide the older interface via an adapter.

For our purposes, in both the RMI example and in later EJB examples, we are forced by the APIs to make an incompatible change to method signatures—the introduction of the `throws RemoteException` clause to our interfaces. We can create Adapters that provide the interface expected by clients—the methods without `RemoteException`—while our Adapter implementation calls the "real" implementation, and catches and handles and `RemoteExceptions` that might be thrown.

Our Adapters don't do very much; the interface supported by the Adapter differs from the implementing class' interface only by the `RemoteException`. Adapters can be used to make far greater changes; a single interface might invoke multiple operations on the implementing class, or might translate between data types for parameters and return values.

Listing 15.2 shows the `RemoteStandingsAdapter` class, which implements the `Remote-Standings` interface. Its job is to instantiate a `Standings` object (actually a `Dynamic-Standings`), and then forward any method calls to this object. This code also exposes a new concept: the registry.

15.3 The RMI Registry

In all client-server applications, there must be a way for the client to locate the server to which it will connect. In a typical sockets-based application, this is done by having the server listen on a well-known TCP port number, and the client connects to that port. For many Java architectures, such as JMS or EJB, JNDI is used. With RMI applications, there is an intermediary process known as the `rmiregistry`. The server object registers itself in the registry using a name, rather than a numeric port number. Clients contact the registry and ask for a server by name.

Behind the scenes, all of this is still getting mapped down to port numbers, but it makes it a little easier on the programmer to think in terms of service names, such as RemoteStandings, rather than port numbers.

How, you may be wondering, does the client find the registry? Oh, that's simple. It's listening on a well-known port number, 1099. Didn't that simplify your life? Seriously, as long as you keep the default RMI registry port, you are relieved of the responsibility of having to remember the port number. And if you have a large number of Java RMI applications, there is still just one registry to connect to, rather than having to remember a different well-known port for each server process.)

In the main method shown in Listing 15.2, you can see that the RemoteStandings-Adapter instantiates itself, and then registers itself in the registry using the Naming.rebind() call. The name used for the binding can be anything you choose; we used the interface name, which I think adds clarity. Naming.bind() is a call that registers a particular name in the registry, but a bind() call will fail if there is already such a name in the registry. In this case, we choose to register our object, and if there is already one registered by the same name, we just replace that binding with the new one.

Listing 15.2 Remote Adapter Class for Standings

```
// RemoteStandingsAdapter.java

package nfl.application.rmi;

import nfl.ObjectFactory;
import nfl.application.*;

import java.net.MalformedURLException;
import java.rmi.RemoteException;
import java.rmi.Naming;
import java.rmi.server.UnicastRemoteObject;

import java.util.List;

public class RemoteStandingsAdapter
            extends UnicastRemoteObject
            implements RemoteStandings
{
    public static void main(String[] args) {
        // Register self in registry
        RemoteStandings remote = null;
        java.util.Properties p = System.getProperties();
        p.setProperty("nfl.versioninfo",
                    "nfl.application.DynamicVersionInfo");
```

```
   try {
      remote = new RemoteStandingsAdapter();
      Naming.rebind("RemoteStandings", remote);
      System.out.println("RemoteStandings registered");
   } catch (RemoteException e) {
      e.printStackTrace(); System.exit(-1);
   } catch (MalformedURLException e) {
      e.printStackTrace(); System.exit(-2);
   }
}

private DynamicStandings standings;

// Constructor
public RemoteStandingsAdapter() throws RemoteException {
   java.util.Properties p = System.getProperties();
   p.put("nfl.versioninfo",
         "nfl.application.DynamicVersionInfo");
   standings = (DynamicStandings)
      ObjectFactory.getHandle().getInstance(
                                 "DynamicStandings");
}

// Methods from Standings
public void loadData() throws RemoteException {
   standings.loadData();
}

public List computeDivisionStandings(Division div)
                  throws RemoteException {
   return standings.computeDivisionStandings(div);
}

public List computeConferenceStandings(Conference conf)
                  throws RemoteException {
   return standings.computeConferenceStandings(conf);
}

// Methods from DynamicStandings
public void init() throws RemoteException {
   standings.init();
}

public List[] getDivisionStandings()
                  throws RemoteException {
   return standings.getDivisionStandings();
}
```

```java
    public List getDivisionStandings(int i)
                  throws RemoteException {
       return standings.getDivisionStandings(i);
    }

    public List getDivisionStandings(Division d)
                  throws RemoteException {
       return standings.getDivisionStandings(d);
    }

    public List[] getConferenceStandings()
                     throws RemoteException {
       return standings.getConferenceStandings();
    }

    public List getConferenceStandings(int i)
                  throws RemoteException {
       return standings.getConferenceStandings(i);
    }

    public List getConferenceStandings(Conference c)
                  throws RemoteException {
       return standings.getConferenceStandings(c);
    }

    public void postGameData(Game g)
                   throws RemoteException {
       standings.postGameData(g);
    }
}
```

15.4 An RMI Client

Now we need a client that can talk to our remote object. For simplicity, we'll go back to our original `Console` class. The first change you'll notice is how we get a reference to the `Standings` object. Rather than invoking an object constructor via `new()`, we look up the object in the registry via a call to `Naming.lookup()`, using the same name string that was passed to the `bind()` or `rebind()` call. We then need to modify all of our calls to the remote class to account for the possibility that they will throw a `RemoteException`.

Listing 15.3 RemoteConsole.java

```java
// RemoteConsole.java

package nfl.presentation;

import java.rmi.Naming;
import java.rmi.RemoteException;
import java.util.List;
import java.util.Properties;
import nfl.ObjectFactory;
import nfl.application.Division;
import nfl.application.Conference;
import nfl.application.rmi.RemoteStandings;

public class RemoteConsole extends nfl.presentation.Console
{
    public static void main(String[] args) {
        Properties p = System.getProperties();
        p.setProperty("nfl.versioninfo",
                    "nfl.application.DynamicVersionInfo");
        System.setProperties(p);
        RemoteConsole con = new RemoteConsole();
        con.run();
    }

    public void run() {
        RemoteStandings s = null;
        try {
           s = (RemoteStandings) Naming.lookup(
                                    "RemoteStandings");
        } catch (java.rmi.RemoteException e) {
           e.printStackTrace(); System.exit(-1);
        } catch (java.net.MalformedURLException e) {
           e.printStackTrace(); System.exit(-2);
        } catch (java.rmi.NotBoundException e) {
           e.printStackTrace(); System.exit(-3);
        }

        try {
            s.init();
        } catch (RemoteException e) {
           e.printStackTrace(); System.exit(-1);
        }

        // Loop through divisions
        for (int i=0; i<Division.DIVISIONS.size(); i++) {
           Division d = (Division) Division.DIVISIONS.get(i);
           List l = null;
```

```
            try {
                l = s.getDivisionStandings(d);
            } catch (RemoteException e) {
                e.printStackTrace(); System.exit(-1);
            }
            printDivisionStandings(d, l);
        }

        if (!getPrintConferenceStandings()) return;
        // Loop through conferences
        for (int i=0; i<Conference.CONFERENCES.size(); i++) {
            Conference c = (Conference)
                            Conference.CONFERENCES.get(i);
            List l = null;
            try {
                l = s.getConferenceStandings(c);
            } catch (RemoteException e) {
                e.printStackTrace(); System.exit(-1);
            }
            printConferenceStandings(c, l);
        }
    }
}
```

15.5 RMI APIs

API 15.1 java.rmi.**Naming**

public class Naming
    public static void **bind**(String name, Remote obj);
    public static String[] **list**(String name);
    public static Remote **lookup**(String name);
    public static void **rebind**(String name, Remote obj);
    public static void **unbind**(String name)

API 15.2 java.rmi.registry.**LocateRegistry**

public class LocateRegistry
    public static Registry **createRegistry**(int port);
    public static Registry **createRegistry**(int port, RMIClientSocketFactory csf,
             RMIServerSocketFactory rsf);
    public static Registry **getRegistry**();
    public static Registry **getRegistry**(int port);
    public static Registry **getRegistry**(String host);
    public static Registry **getRegistry**(String host, int port);
    public static Registry **getRegistry**(String host, int port, RMIClientSocketFactory csf);

API 15.3 java.rmi.server.**UnicastRemoteObject**

```
public class UnicastRemoteObject
    // Constructors
    protected UnicastRemoteObject();
    protected UnicastRemoteObject(int port);
    protected UnicastRemoteObject(int port, RMIClientSocketFactory csf,
                RMIServerSocketFactory rsf);
    // Methods
    public Object clone();
    public static RemoteStub exportObject(Remote obj);
    public static Remote exportObject(Remote obj, int port);
    public static Remote exportObject(Remote obj, int port, RMIClientSocketFactory csf,
                RMIServerSocketFactory rsf);
    public static boolean unexportObject(Remote obj, boolean force);
```

15.6 A Remote Object Factory

There is a different design approach that we could take to this problem. Within RMI, you can imagine there being two types of remote objects: those that are accessed remotely, through stubs and skeletons, and those that are actually mobile and move between the client and server systems.

We've already seen the requirements for remotely accessible objects: They must have an interface that extends `Remote`, and an implementation that extends `UnicastRemoteObject`. But the only requirement for a mobile object is that it implement `Serializable`, which puts far less of a burden on the class designer to rework the class to be RMI compatible.

Table 15.2 Components in the RMI "Mobile Objects" Application

New Components			
Name	Package	Class or Interface	Comment
RemoteServer	nfl.application.rmi	Interface	A remotely accessible Object Factory.
RemoteServerImpl	nfl.application.rmi	Class	The implementation class for `RemoteServer`.
RemoteDSI	nfl.application.rmi	Class	Extends `DynamicStandingsImpl`.
RemoteConsole2	nfl.presentation	Class	An RMI client.

Table 15.2 Components in the RMI "Mobile Objects" Application (Continued)

Existing Components	
Component	**Description**
layered.jar	All classes and interfaces of the layered version of the application (as presented in Chapter 2).
DynamicStandings	The interface and implementation of dynamic standings are also used in the RMI application.

In this scenario, rather than making Standings a remotely accessible object, we would instead make it a mobile object. To do this, we create a new server class that contains a method, getStandings(), which returns a Standings object. Once the Standings object is returned, it will then be a local, client-side object easily usable by client code, without the need to worry about RemoteExceptions or other RMI-specific behavior. The net effect is another way of implementing an object factory. Although not as flexible as our original object factory, we can call methods on the RemoteServer to return to us instances of the classes we specify. We can't just call our existing ObjectFactory remotely, as it is required that each method throw RemoteException. The RemoteServer could be seen as an Adapter for accessing our ObjectFactory, just as RemoteStandings was an Adapter for accessing the DynamicStandings.

This re-implementation is somewhat complicated in that Standings itself creates other objects—the Games and Teams container objects—and so we need to modify the creation of these objects to go through the remote interface as well. So we end up with an interface supporting the creation of three remote objects, as shown in Listings 15.4 (interface) and 15.5 (implementation).

Listing 15.4 RemoteServer.java

```java
// RemoteServer.java

package nfl.application.rmi;

import nfl.application.*;

import java.rmi.RemoteException;

public interface RemoteServer extends java.rmi.Remote
{
   public DynamicStandings getStandings()
      throws RemoteException;
   public Teams getTeams() throws RemoteException;
   public Games getGames() throws RemoteException;
}
```

Listing 15.5 `RemoteServerImpl.java`

```java
// RemoteServerImpl.java

package nfl.application.rmi;

import nfl.ObjectFactory;
import nfl.application.*;

import java.rmi.Naming;
import java.rmi.RemoteException;
import java.rmi.registry.LocateRegistry;
import java.rmi.server.UnicastRemoteObject;

public class RemoteServerImpl extends UnicastRemoteObject
                            implements RemoteServer
{
    private static RemoteServerImpl server;
    private ObjectFactory factory;

    public RemoteServerImpl() throws RemoteException {}

    public static void main(String[] argv) {
        boolean startRegistry = false;
        int     registryPort  = 1099;

        for(int i=0; i<argv.length; i++) {
            if (argv[i].equals("-startregistry")) {
                startRegistry = true;
                continue;
            }
            if (argv[i].equals("-registryport")) {
                registryPort = Integer.parseInt(argv[++i]);
                continue;
            }
        }
        if (startRegistry)
            startregistry(registryPort);

        try {
            server = new RemoteServerImpl();
            Naming.rebind("RemoteServer", server);
        } catch (RemoteException e) {
            e.printStackTrace();
        } catch (java.net.MalformedURLException e) {
            e.printStackTrace();
        }
    }
```

```
public static void startregistry(int port) {
   try {
      LocateRegistry.createRegistry(port);
   } catch (RemoteException e) {
      System.err.println("Start of registry failed");
      e.printStackTrace();
   }
}

public DynamicStandings getStandings()
                        throws RemoteException {
   DynamicStandings standings = null;
   java.util.Properties p = System.getProperties();
   p.put("nfl.versioninfo",
         "nfl.application.rmi.RemoteVersionInfo");
   factory = ObjectFactory.getHandle();
   standings = (DynamicStandings)
      factory.getInstance("DynamicStandings");
   return standings;
}

public Teams getTeams() throws RemoteException {
   return (Teams) factory.getInstance("Teams");
}

public Games getGames() throws RemoteException {
   return (Games) factory.getInstance("Games");
}
}
```

In our earlier example, we had a separate `rmiregistry` process running. It's also possible for a server to create its own `rmiregistry` running as a thread; this is helpful if you don't expect there to be other users needing an `rmiregistry` in your deployed environment. Our previous example does so, using the static `createRegistry()` method of the `LocateRegistry` class to start up our own registry.

Now, we must modify the `DynamicStandingsImpl` class to use the remote interface when creating the `Teams` and `Games` objects. We do this by creating a new subclass, which is given the abbreviated name `RemoteDSI`.

Listing 15.6 `RemoteDSI.java`

```
// RemoteDSI.java

package nfl.application.rmi;

import nfl.application.DynamicStandingsImpl;
```

```
import nfl.application.rmi.RemoteServer;

import java.rmi.Naming;

public class RemoteDSI extends DynamicStandingsImpl
{
    // Constructor. Replace handles to local Teams and
    // Games objects with handles to remote objects
    public RemoteDSI() {
        java.util.Properties p = System.getProperties();
        p.setProperty("nfl.versioninfo",
                      "nfl.application.rmi.RemoteVersionInfo");

        try {
            RemoteServer server = (RemoteServer)
                    Naming.lookup("RemoteServer");
            setTeams(server.getTeams());
            setGames(server.getGames());
        } catch (java.rmi.RemoteException e) {
            e.printStackTrace();
        } catch (java.net.MalformedURLException e) {
            e.printStackTrace();
        } catch (java.rmi.NotBoundException e) {
            e.printStackTrace();
        }
    }
}
```

Finally, we need a new client program to connect to the server and get the ball rolling. This is shown in Listing 15.7.

Listing 15.7 RemoteClient2.java

```
// RemoteConsole2.java

package nfl.presentation;

import java.rmi.Naming;
import java.rmi.RemoteException;
import java.util.List;
import java.util.Properties;
import nfl.ObjectFactory;
import nfl.application.Division;
import nfl.application.Conference;
import nfl.application.DynamicStandings;
import nfl.application.rmi.RemoteServer;
```

```
public class RemoteConsole2 extends nfl.presentation.Console
{
    public static void main(String[] args) {
        Properties p = System.getProperties();
        p.setProperty("nfl.versioninfo",
                      "nfl.application.rmi.RemoteVersionInfo");
        RemoteConsole2 con = new RemoteConsole2();
        con.run();
    }

    public void run() {
        RemoteServer server = null;
        DynamicStandings s = null;
        try {
            server = (RemoteServer)
                     Naming.lookup("RemoteServer");
            s = (DynamicStandings) server.getStandings();
        } catch (java.rmi.RemoteException e) {
            e.printStackTrace(); System.exit(-1);
        } catch (java.net.MalformedURLException e) {
            e.printStackTrace(); System.exit(-2);
        } catch (java.rmi.NotBoundException e) {
            e.printStackTrace(); System.exit(-3);
        }

        s.init();

        // Loop through divisions
        for (int i=0; i<Division.DIVISIONS.size(); i++) {
            Division d = (Division) Division.DIVISIONS.get(i);
            List l = null;
            l = s.getDivisionStandings(d);
            printDivisionStandings(d, l);
        }

        if (!getPrintConferenceStandings()) return;
        // Loop through conferences
        for (int i=0; i<Conference.CONFERENCES.size(); i++) {
            Conference c = (Conference)
                          Conference.CONFERENCES.get(i);
            List l = null;
            l = s.getConferenceStandings(c);
            printConferenceStandings(c, l);
        }
    }
}
```

With the mobile objects, we can now make calls on the `Standings` object without having to wrap them in a `try/catch`, since `RemoteExceptions` aren't thrown by anything other than the factory methods used to instantiate the objects.

15.7 RMI Troubleshooting

RMI seems to frequently take common problems and obfuscate their cause with unusual error methods. This may become greatly improved in the JDK 1.4 release, where the stack trace for RMI failures will include both server-side and client-side method calls. With JDK 1.3.1 and prior, only the client's stack trace is seen, and frequently it's difficult to discern what problem on the server could have resulted in the error seen on the client. Table 15.3 lists just a few of these problems that I encountered during development of these examples.

Table 15.3 Troubleshooting RMI Server Problems

Problem	Cause
Null pointer exception	A class could not be created, perhaps due to leaving something out of a distribution JAR file. Perhaps in SDK 1.4, the server-side `ClassNotFoundException` or `NoClassDefFoundError` will be seen in the stack trace, making this much simpler to resolve.
Error unmarshalling a class	Object is not serializable. Note that serialization works through the entire object graph; so even if a particular object is marked `Serializable`, it will fail to serialize properly if it contains references to other objects that are not serializable.
Server exits immediately after binding itself in registry	Server class does not extend `UnicastRemoteObject`.

15.8 Building and Running the RMI Examples

The buildfile shown in Listing 15.8 builds components for all of the examples shown in this chapter. The buildfile introduces a new Ant task, `<rmic>`. This task invokes the `rmic` compiler on the indicated class (not `.java` source) files to produce the stubs and skeletons needed for the application.

Listing 15.8 Ant Buildfile for RMI Examples

```
<project name="rmi" default="stubs" basedir=".">

<target name="compile">
   <javac srcdir="." classpath="../../.." >
      <include name="RemoteStandings.java" />
      <include name="RemoteStandingsAdapter.java" />
      <include name="RemoteServer.java" />
      <include name="RemoteServerImpl.java" />
      <include name="RemoteDSI.java" />
      <include name="RemoteVersionInfo.java" />
      <src path=".." />
      <include name="DynamicStandings.java" />
      <include name="DynamicStandingsImpl.java" />
      <include name="DynamicVersionInfo.java" />
      <src path="../../presentation" />
      <include name="RemoteConsole.java" />
      <include name="RemoteConsole2.java" />
   </javac>
</target>

<target name="stubs" depends="compile">
   <rmic base="../../..">
      <include name=
        "nfl/application/rmi/RemoteStandingsAdapter.class" />
      <include name=
        "nfl/application/rmi/RemoteServerImpl.class" />
   </rmic>
</target>

<target name="clean">
   <delete>
      <fileset dir="." includes="*.class" />
   </delete>
</target>

<target name="test-server1">
   <java classpath="../../.." classname=
             "nfl.application.rmi.RemoteStandingsAdapter"
         fork="yes" />
</target>

<target name="test-server2">
   <java classpath="../../.." fork="yes" classname=
             "nfl.application.rmi.RemoteServerImpl" >
      <arg value="-startregistry" />
   </java>
</target>
```

```
<target name="test-client1">
    <java classpath="../../.." classname=
                "nfl.presentation.RemoteConsole"
          fork="yes" />
</target>

<target name="test-client2">
    <java classpath="../../.." classname=
                "nfl.presentation.RemoteConsole2"
          fork="yes" />
</target>

</project>
```

All of our RMI examples simply run from the command line, so there is no packaging or deployment to worry about. The first example has three components that must be run; so you can do each of the following in a separate window:

    1. On server: `rmiregistry`

    2. On server: `java nfl.application.rmi.RemoteStandingsAdapter`

    3. On client: `java nfl.presentation.RemoteConsole`

You can use the provided Ant tasks to make this a little easier; there is a task named `<test-server1>` to start the server process, and one named `<test-client1>` to start the client process. There isn't an Ant task for the registry, because it wouldn't save any effort. However, you do need to have the `rmiregistry` CLASSPATH include the root of the `nfl` hierarchy.

For the second example, we gave our server the capability of starting a registry itself, therefore we don't need to start one independently. The second example can be tested as follows:

    1. On server: `java nfl.application.rmi.RemoteServerImpl -startregistry`

    2. On client: `java nfl.presentation.RemoteConsole2`

There are also Ant tasks in the buildfile to automate these tests; use `<test-server2>` and `<test-client2>` to invoke the server and client portions, respectively.

15.9 Exercises

15.1 Make an application class remotely accessible: Take an existing application and make it accessible via RMI by exposing its methods as remote interfaces.

15.2 Make an application class mobile: Take an existing application and make one or more of its classes mobile by creating a remotely accessible object factory that will return serializable instances of the class.

15.10 Further Reading

Because RMI is part of the Java 2 Standard Edition, information about RMI can be found in many standard Java references. The home page for RMI is `http://java.sun.com/products/jdk/rmi/index.html`.

There are also release-specific pages for RMI, from which you can find links to the specification, Javadoc API documentation, and tutorials. For SDK 1.3, the link is `http://java.sun.com/j2se/1.3/docs/guide/rmi/index.html`; for SDK 1.4, the link is `http://java.sun.com/j2se/1.4/docs/guide/rmi/index.html`.

## CHAPTER 16

Building a Web Service with JAX-RPC

J ava Remote Method Invocation (RMI) is most commonly used for making calls between Java Virtual Machines (JVMs). Although there is an RMI over Internet Inter-Orb Protocol (IIOP) capability that permits interoperability with CORBA, interoperability with CORBA is hardly the key to providing universal access. For Web Services to succeed, we need to be able to interoperate not only with CORBA and other Java users, but with .NET as well.

We've seen how the concepts of MOM were combined with XML-formatted data and SOAP protocols to create a completely interoperable messaging solution in JAXM. Now we'd like to do something similar for creating an RPC solution. Our data will still be in the form of XML; SOAP will still be the basic transport mechanism. In this chapter, we'll update our RMI example by replacing the RMI calls with JAX-RPC calls, and this will change our application into a Web Service.

SOAP messages are primarily one-way communications, whereas SOAP RPC is a request-response protocol. On the surface, it seems that adjusting for this behavior difference might be the only thing separating JAXM from JAX-RPC, as this seems to be the only difference in the underlying technology that needs to be carried upward to the application layer.

Although this might have happened, the JAXM and JAX-RPC specifications diverged far more than the underlying protocols suggest. JAXM is focused on giving developers low-level access to the underlying SOAP message components. JAXM clients and servers need to be proficient at assembling and parsing SOAP messages, as we have seen in our examples. JAX-RPC instead hides these details, allowing the developer to deal with Java objects rather than SOAP.

> **Software Used in This Chapter**
>
> **JAX-RPC**
>
> Version 1.0, Early-Access 1 release. This was downloaded as part of the JAX Pack, Winter 2001 edition, which also includes early-access versions of JAXP, JAXM, and JAXR. Early-Access 2 release was also tested, and is required for the dynamic examples in Chapter 18, so you might want to just start with Early-Access 2 or later if you're downloading the software.
>
> **Tomcat Servlet Container**
>
> Version 4.0.1. The JAX-RPC runtime is provided in the form of a servlet.

16.1 The Basics of JAX-RPC

Beneath the surface, JAX-RPC clients and servers are exchanging SOAP messages, each of which contains XML representations of the parameters and return values of the methods being called. But as a JAX-RPC programmer, you only need to think in terms of Java objects; the fact that SOAP is being used underneath is completely transparent. In fact, JAX-RPC is designed to be fully compatible with other underlying transports. At the first release of JAX-RPC, SOAP 1.1 and HTTP are required, but future releases may allow different low-level implementations.

Because of this focus on objects, using JAX-RPC is very similar to using Java RMI; it feels much more familiar to a Java programmer than JAXM does. But some surprises are in store because the need for interoperability will tie our hands when designing the interfaces we choose to export for our Web Service.

16.1.1 Legal JAX-RPC Data Types

To ensure interoperability between various platforms and languages, the interfaces you create to be exported as a Web Service can only use a restricted set of data types for parameters and return types. The legal types are:

- Java primitive types (for example, `int`, `short`, `long`, `float`, `double`)
- Object wrappers of primitive types (for example, `Integer`, `Boolean`, and so forth)
- Instances of the following Java classes:
    ```
    java.lang.String
    java.util.Date
    java.util.Calendar
    java.math.BigInteger
    java.math.BigDecimal
    ```
- Arrays (single or multidimensional) of legal JAX-RPC data types
- JAX-RPC value types

The JAX-RPC value type requires elaboration. Essentially, a JAX-RPC value type is a class whose state can be captured on the client and reproduced on the server (or the reverse). Classes that represent structures are the basic idea; although a JAX-RPC value type can contain code, the code will not be moved across the network (unlike Java RMI), just the data. The following are all required of a JAX-RPC value type:

- All data fields are of legal JAX-RPC types.
- All data fields are `public`, or have `public` JavaBean-style accessor methods.
- Data fields are not `final` or `transient`.
- The class does not extend (directly or indirectly) `java.rmi.Remote`.
- The class implements `java.rmi.Serializable`.

Other data types can be used with JAX-RPC, but require the creation of customized serializers and deserializers that can handle the mapping between the class and the SOAP representation.

16.2 Publishing a Web Service with JAX-RPC

As with RMI, JAX-RPC services use a Java interface to describe the interface available to remote callers. The first step in creating our JAX-RPC Web Service is to create this interface. Like RMI interfaces, JAX-RPC interfaces extend `java.rmi.Remote`, and methods within the interface can each throw `java.rmi.RemoteException`. Because of these common requirements, and just a general desire for code reuse, we'd like to use the same interface we created for the RMI version of the application (see Chapter 15). As it turns out, there are a few things that prevent us from doing this. Although it would be possible to design an interface that worked equally well with either RMI or JAX-RPC, our current interface falls short of this.

Several of the data types we used in the RMI version of the application are not legal JAX-RPC types. In particular, our `Team` object is not a legal type, for reasons we'll go into shortly. To address this, we will create another Adapter-type class called `SoapTeamImpl`. Depending on the amount of functionality we want to expose via the Web Service, we might choose to replicate every field available in the `Team` object within the `SoapTeamImpl` adapter. For brevity, we've only represented a few of the fields within the example class.

Another change is based on the fact that we're trying to make our service available to external clients. Within our application, we have `Conference` and `Division` types, but we can't expect an external user to have compatible types defined within their application. So instead of requesting division and conference standings based on `Conference` and `Division` objects, we instead create interfaces that allow us to ask for standings by providing a string of the conference or division name. This, however, is also error prone: Although there aren't too many ways to represent the names, it's guaranteed that some user will send us a string we didn't expect. We try to minimize this by providing additional interfaces that return arrays of the division and conference names; at least this way, a client willing to make the effort can pass us a correct string. We also define exception types to be thrown when an invalid string is passed; these exceptions will be mapped onto SOAP faults.

Table 16.1 Components in the JAX-RPC Application

New Components			
Name	**Package**	**Class or Interface**	**Comment**
JaxRpcStandingsIF	nfl.application.jaxrpc	Interface	Subset of the Dynamic-Standings interface with JAX-RPC data types.
JaxRpcStandingsAdapter	nfl.application.jaxrpc	Class	An Adapter that implements JaxRpcStandingsIF and forwards to a Dynamic-Standings.
SOAPTeamImpl	nfl.application.jaxrpc	Class	A subset of Team that conforms to the JAX-RPC value type restrictions.
Client	nfl.application.jaxrpc	Class	A client that uses stubs to access the service.

Existing Components	
Component	**Description**
layered.jar	All classes and interfaces of the layered version of the application (as presented in Chapter 2).
DynamicStandings	The interface and implementation of dynamic standings are also used in the RMI application.

Listing 16.1 shows the remote interface for our JAX-RPC Web Service.

Listing 16.1 The Remote Interface of the Web Service

```
// JaxRpcStandingsIF.java

package nfl.application.jaxrpc;

import java.rmi.Remote;
import java.rmi.RemoteException;

public interface JaxRpcStandingsIF extends Remote
{
    public void init() throws RemoteException;
```

```
public String[] getDivisionNames()
    throws RemoteException;

public String[] getConferenceNames()
    throws RemoteException;

public SoapTeamImpl[] getDivisionStandings(String s)
    throws RemoteException, NoSuchDivisionException;

public SoapTeamImpl[] getConferenceStandings(String s)
    throws RemoteException, NoSuchConferenceException;

}
```

Listing 16.2 shows the SoapTeamImpl class that is used for Team objects. The class has a constructor that takes a Team as an argument. Strictly speaking, this isn't an Adapter, because it replaces the Team object with its own methods and attributes rather than forwarding requests along to the underlying team, but it plays a very similar role to an Adapter. It's important that this class implement Serializable, as it will be passed over the wire to clients. The process of serialization and deserialization is different in the JAX-RPC runtime than in RMI or other code that uses the Serializable interface. In fact, there is some mention in the JAX-RPC specification that a different marker interface might be used in the future to prevent confusion between the types of serialization. As long as you don't ever attempt to mix-and-match—for example, to use a readObject() call to deserialize an object that has been serialized by the JAX-RPC runtime—you'll have no problems. You'd actually have to work fairly hard to create a situation where things did not behave as you would expect.

Listing 16.2 SoapTeamImpl.java

```
// SoapTeamImpl.java

package nfl.application.jaxrpc;

import nfl.application.*;

/* A simplified version of the Team object. Uses only
 * JAXRPC-supported datatypes. Just properties, no
 * methods (other than accessors). Has been stripped
 * down for brevity, but could be extended to shadow
 * every field in the Team object if desired.
 */

public class SoapTeamImpl implements java.io.Serializable {
```

```
/* JavaBean-standard no arg constructor */
public SoapTeamImpl() {}

/* Transmogrify a Team object to a SoapTeamImpl */
public SoapTeamImpl(Team team) {
    setName(team.getFullName());
    setRecord(team.getOverallRecord());
    setWinLossPct(team.getOverallWinLossPct());
}

// Now the properties, getters and setters
private String name;
public String getName() { return name; }
public void setName(String n) { name = n; }

private int[] record;
public int[] getRecord() { return record; }
public void setRecord(int[] r) { record = r; }

private float winLossPct;
public float getWinLossPct() { return winLossPct; }
public void setWinLossPct(float p) { winLossPct = p; }
}
```

Now we need to create yet another Adapter, for the Standings class. We call this one JaxRpcStandingsAdapter; the code is shown in Listing 16.3. Note that in the implementation, parameter types and return types must be classes, not interfaces. The automatically-generated serializers and deserializers operate on classes; interfaces cannot be serialized. This Adapter wraps an instance of the DynamicStandingsImpl class. It has utility functions to allow us to convert the Strings of conference and division names into the Conference and Division objects that the underlying implementation class expects. It then takes the Array-List results, made up of BasicTeamImpl objects, and loops through the results converting each Team object to a SoapTeamImpl. The return type is a Java array, because the collection types (such as ArrayList) aren't supported directly by JAX-RPC.[1]

---

1. These classes could be serialized by providing customized Serializer and Deserializer classes, which are permitted by the JAX-RPC specification. However, doing so would break interoperability with non-Java clients. Some Collection types will be supported by the standard serialization process by the time the general release version of JAX-RPC ships (only early-access releases were available during the time this code was written and tested.)

Listing 16.3 `JaxRpcStandingsAdapter.java`

```java
// JaxRpcStandingsAdapter.java

package nfl.application.jaxrpc;

import nfl.ObjectFactory;
import nfl.application.*;

import java.rmi.RemoteException;
import java.util.List;

public class JaxRpcStandingsAdapter
            implements JaxRpcStandingsIF
{
   private DynamicStandings standings;

   // Constructor
   public JaxRpcStandingsAdapter() throws RemoteException {
      java.util.Properties p = System.getProperties();
      p.put("nfl.versioninfo",
            "nfl.application.DynamicVersionInfo");
      standings = (DynamicStandings)
         ObjectFactory.getHandle().getInstance("DynamicStandings");
   }

   public void init() throws RemoteException {
      standings.init();
   }

   public String[] getDivisionNames()
                  throws RemoteException {
      List divisions = Division.DIVISIONS;
      String[] names = new String[divisions.size()];
      for (int i=0; i<divisions.size(); i++) {
         names[i] = divisions.get(i).toString();
      }
      return names;
   }

   public String[] getConferenceNames()
                  throws RemoteException {
      List conferences = Conference.CONFERENCES;
      String[] names = new String[conferences.size()];
      for (int i=0; i<conferences.size(); i++) {
         names[i] = conferences.get(i).toString();
      }
      return names;
   }
```

```java
    public SoapTeamImpl[] getDivisionStandings(String name)
            throws RemoteException, NoSuchDivisionException {
        SoapTeamImpl[] retval;
        Division d = getDivisionNamed(name);
        if (d == null)
            throw new NoSuchDivisionException(name);
        List results = standings.getDivisionStandings(d);
        int resultSize = results.size();
        retval = new SoapTeamImpl[resultSize];
        for (int i=0; i<resultSize; i++) {
            retval[i] = new SoapTeamImpl((Team)results.get(i));
        }
        return retval;
    }

    public SoapTeamImpl[] getConferenceStandings(String name)
            throws RemoteException, NoSuchConferenceException {
        SoapTeamImpl[] retval;
        Conference c = getConferenceNamed(name);
        if (c == null)
            throw new NoSuchConferenceException(name);
        List results = standings.getConferenceStandings(c);
        int resultSize = results.size();
        retval = new SoapTeamImpl[resultSize];
        for (int i=0; i<resultSize; i++) {
            retval[i] = new SoapTeamImpl((Team)results.get(i));
        }
        return retval;
    }

    private Division getDivisionNamed(String name) {
        List candidates = Division.DIVISIONS;
        for (int i=0; i<candidates.size(); i++) {
            if (candidates.get(i).toString().equalsIgnoreCase(name))
                return (Division) candidates.get(i);
        }
        return null;  // bad name passed
    }

    private Conference getConferenceNamed(String name) {
        List candidates = Conference.CONFERENCES;
        for (int i=0; i<candidates.size(); i++) {
            if (candidates.get(i).toString().equalsIgnoreCase(name))
                return (Conference) candidates.get(i);
        }
        return null;  // bad name passed
    }
}
```

Our `JaxRpcStandingsAdapter` will throw an exception if a conference or division name is passed that doesn't exist. Because the exception classes are nearly identical, we'll just look at one of them in Listing 16.4. The JAX-RPC reference implementation imposes some specific requirements on exception classes, in order for them to be correctly mapped to SOAP faults. The exception must have a constructor that takes a single argument, and the type of that argument must match the return type of a property `get()` method implemented in the exception class. Our exception class takes a `String` parameter in the constructor, and has the `getName()` method that returns a `String`, thus satisfying the requirement. Exceptions that fail to meet the requirement will be rejected when `xrpcc` compiles the class whose methods throw the exception. (This is an early-access restriction; the requirements on exceptions are expected to be relaxed in JAX-RPC version 1.0 and later.)

Listing 16.4 `NoSuchDivisionException.java`

```
// NoSuchDivisionException.java

package nfl.application.jaxrpc;

public class NoSuchDivisionException
               extends java.lang.Exception
            implements java.io.Serializable {

    private String name;

    public NoSuchDivisionException(String name) {
        this.name = name;
    }

    public String getName() {
        return name;
    }
}
```

16.3 Creating Stubs and Ties with XRPCC

At this point, the user-written code for our Web Service is complete. There is also a good bit of machine-generated code that is going to be part of the Web Service. The utility that generates this code in the reference implementation is `xrpcc`.

The `xrpcc` tool comes with a `.sh` script (for UNIX) and a `.bat` file (for Windows). The script expects certain environment variables to be set; in particular, `JAVA_HOME` should point to the location where Java is installed on your system (for example, `C:\jdk1.3.1`, `/usr/local/java/jdk1.3.1`, `/opt/java1.3`) and `JAVA_XML_PACK_HOME` should point to the location where the XML pack was installed. When installing on UNIX systems, I found it necessary to `chmod` the `xrpcc.sh` file to permit execute access.

The `xrpcc` utility takes as input an XML configuration file. The configuration file for this example is shown in Listing 16.5. The root element for the XML document is the `<con-figuration>` element. For describing a service beginning from a Java interface, we use an `<rmi>` element. (In Chapter 18, we'll show a `config.xml` file that describes a service using a Web Services Description Language (WSDL) document via a `<wsdl>` element.) The `<rmi>` element has two attributes, both of which designate namespaces. The `targetNamespace` attribute designates the namespace that will contain the interfaces and operations of the service. The `typeNamespace` attribute designates the namespace where schema definitions will be created for the data types used by the defined interfaces. Within the `<rmi>` element, we can define one or more `<service>` elements; each service exports at least one `<interface>`. For the `<service>` element, we simply provide a name for our service and the Java package in which the `xrpcc`-generated classes will be placed. For each interface, we provide the name of an interface class and of a class implementing the interface.

Listing 16.5 `config.xml`

```
<?xml version="1.0" encoding="UTF-8"?>

<configuration
        xmlns="http://java.sun.com/jax-rpc-ri/xrpcc-config">
 <rmi name="NFLStandingsService"
        targetNamespace="http://hp.com/wsdl"
        typeNamespace="http://hp.com/types">
  <service name="NFLStandings"
        packageName="nfl.application.jaxrpc">
   <interface
      name= "nfl.application.jaxrpc.JaxRpcStandingsIF"
      servantName=
        "nfl.application.jaxrpc.JaxRpcStandingsAdapter"/>
  </service>
 </rmi>
</configuration>
```

Once the configuration file has been created, we run it through `xrpcc`. The command needed to build the server-side artifacts is:

```
xrpcc -server config.xml
```

The –server option says we want to generate server-side components for this application. We could also have specified –client, to generate the client-side artifacts, or –both, to generate components for both sides. (The exact command used by the example code is slightly different because of the need to get things into the proper directories; see the `<xrpcc>` target in the `build.xml` file for the exact syntax.) A –verbose option is also available; this is useful if the generation is failing in ways that aren't immediately obvious.

The `xrpcc` utility generates quite a few files for us. It generates a description of our service in WSDL format; we'll defer looking at this until Chapter 17. It will generate a properties file that will be read by the JAXRPC runtime (servlet) when our service is started; this file is shown in Listing 16.6. It also generates quite a number of class files, according to the following pattern: each method in our interface class has a request part (the method call) and a response part (the return value). For the request part for a method named `aMethod`, there will be classes generated named *aMethod*`_RequestStruct` and *aMethod*`_RequestStruct_SOAPSerializer`. For the response part for the same method, there will be classes created named *aMethod*`_ResponseStruct`, *aMethod*`_ResponseStruct_SOAPBuilder`, and *aMethod*`_Re-sponseStruct_SOAPSerializer`. There is also a *servicename*`_SerializerRegistry` class generated. If you are curious, you can pass the `–keep` option to `xrpcc` to have the source code for all of these classes left in place, so that you can study their inner workings.

Listing 16.6 The Generated Properties File

```
# This file is generated by xrpcc.

port0.tie=nfl.application.jaxrpc.JaxRpcStandingsIF_Tie
port0.servant=nfl.application.jaxrpc.JaxRpcStandingsAdapter
port0.name=JaxRpcStandingsIF
port0.wsdl.targetNamespace=http://hp.com/wsdl
port0.wsdl.serviceName=NFLStandings
port0.wsdl.portName=JaxRpcStandingsIFPort
portcount=1
```

16.4 Consuming a JAX-RPC Web Service

There are actually several ways in which a client can connect to and utilize a JAX-RPC Web Service. We'll look at the dynamic possibilities in Chapter 18. Here, we'll look at the static case, in which we use an `xrpcc`-generated `Stub` class.

If you're providing a Web Service, you'll want to create at least one client to ensure that the service actually works; a static client is ideal for this use. Static clients are also a good choice if you are redistributing client software, rather than having service users develop their own clients.

Once you get to the case where users are finding your service dynamically, it's really up to them whether to use static or dynamic clients. Static clients are easier to develop, but are more closely tied to a specific service. Most users will probably create static clients, unless they are specifically trying to build flexible clients that will be able to access multiple services.

Listing 16.7 shows the client program created for our Web Service. It utilizes two classes that were generated by the `xrpcc` program. The `NFLStandings_Impl` class gives us access to the service endpoint, where we can request an instance of a `Stub` object through which we can access the service. The class name is composed of the `name` attribute from the `<service>` element in our `config.xml` file, plus the standard `_Impl` suffix. Our service defined only a single interface, but if others had been defined, then there would be additional `get` calls defined to

obtain stubs for the other interfaces. The `Stub` class (`JaxRpcStandingsIF_Stub`) is a class
that implements the interface we defined for our service, with all of the implementation details
needed to handle remote access to the service, encoding of SOAP procedure calls, and so forth.
The name of this class is the name of our original Java interface with the suffix `_Stub`.

We build up a URL through which to access the service based on command-line parameters. In a more dynamic environment, we might extract this information from the WSDL instead.

Listing 16.7 `Client.java`

```
// Client.java

package nfl.application.jaxrpc;

import java.io.*;
import java.rmi.RemoteException;
import java.text.DecimalFormat;

import javax.xml.rpc.JAXRPCException;

public class Client {

    private static JaxRpcStandingsIF_Stub stub;

    public static void main(String[] args) {

        String hostname = "localhost";
        String port     = "8080";
        String context  = "nfl-jaxrpc";
        String pattern  = "jaxrpc";
        String ifname   = "JaxRpcStandingsIF";

        for (int i=0; i<args.length; i++) {
            String parm = args[i];
            if (parm.equals("-help") ||
                parm.equals("-usage"))
                usage();
            if (parm.equals("-host") ||
                parm.equals("-hostname")) {
                hostname = args[++i];
            }
            if (parm.equals("-port"))
                port = args[++i];

        }

        try {
            stub = (JaxRpcStandingsIF_Stub)
```

```
                (new NFLStandings_Impl().
                    getJaxRpcStandingsIF());
    } catch (JAXRPCException e) { e.printStackTrace(); }

    String url = "http://" + hostname + ":" + port +
                        "/" + context + "/" + pattern +
                        "/" + ifname;

    //EA1 syntax:
    //stub._setTargetEndpoint(url);
    //EA2 syntax:
    //Note: spec has
    //  javax.xml.rpc.service.endpoint.address
    //as property name; so this may change in FCS
    stub._setProperty(
        javax.xml.rpc.Stub.ENDPOINT_ADDRESS_PROPERTY,
        url);

    Client client = new Client();
    client.run();
}

public static void usage() {
    System.out.println("Usage: " +
        "java nfl.application.jaxrpc.Client <options>\n" +
        "where <options> include:\n" +
        "-hostname <name>   host name\n" +
        "-port      <number> port number (default 8080)\n"
    );
    System.exit(0);
}

public void run() {

    SoapTeamImpl[] teams = null;
    String[]       divnames = null;

    try {
        stub.init();
        divnames = stub.getDivisionNames();
    } catch (RemoteException e) {
        e.printStackTrace();  System.exit(-1);
    }

    for (int i=0; i<divnames.length; i++)
        System.out.println(i + ". " + divnames[i]);
    System.out.print("Get results for which division?");

    BufferedReader in = new BufferedReader(
                new InputStreamReader(System.in));
```

```
      int a = 0;
      try {
         String input = in.readLine();
         a = Integer.parseInt(input);
      } catch (IOException e) {
           e.printStackTrace();
      } catch (NumberFormatException e) {
           e.printStackTrace();
      }

      try {
         teams = stub.getDivisionStandings(divnames[a]);
      } catch (RemoteException e) {
         e.printStackTrace();  System.exit(-1);
      } catch (NoSuchDivisionException e) {
         e.printStackTrace();  System.exit(-1);
      }

      System.out.println();
      for (int i=0; i<teams.length; i++) {
         System.out.print(i+1 + ". ");
         printDetail(teams[i]);
      }
   }

   public void printDetail(SoapTeamImpl team) {

      System.out.print(team.getName());
      for (int pad=team.getName().length(); pad<23; pad++)
         System.out.print(" "); /* pad name */

      int wins   = team.getRecord()[0];
      int losses = team.getRecord()[1];
      int ties   = team.getRecord()[2];
      if (wins < 10) System.out.print(" "); /* pad */
      System.out.print(wins + " ");

      if (losses < 10) System.out.print(" ");
      System.out.print(losses + " ");

      if (ties < 10) System.out.print(" ");
      System.out.print(ties + " ");

      if (team.getWinLossPct() < 1) System.out.print(" ");
      DecimalFormat nf = new DecimalFormat("#.000");
      System.out.print(nf.format(team.getWinLossPct()));
      System.out.println();

   }
}
```

API documentation for the `Stub` class is included in Chapter 18, where we'll introduce additional client-side classes and alternate means of accessing a JAX-RPC service.

Design Center: JAXM or JAX-RPC?

JAXM and JAX-RPC both provide the capability of developing a Web Service. What determines which one should be used when?

If you are exposing an existing application as a Web Service, the existing interface is likely to determine your best choice. Generally, applications have procedure-call interfaces, and thus it is easier to expose the application by making its methods callable via JAX-RPC. There are some applications, however, that are more document-oriented. Workflow applications may be designed to accept and generate documents, for example taking as input a purchase order and generating documents such as inventory picklists, shipping notifications, and invoices.

If you aren't trying to fit around an existing interface, then your choice may be based on which you would rather work with. JAXM appeals more to programmers who are very comfortable with XML. If you are an experienced XML jockey, you might find JAXM is the more natural style for you. However, the majority of Java programmers will find JAX-RPCs style of working with Java interfaces more familiar and will probably be more productive using JAX-RPC.

At least in the reference implementations, the tools provided with JAX-RPC to generate WSDL from the interfaces save a lot of work in describing a Web Service, which the JAXM programmer will have to do manually. As vendors implement JAXM and JAX-RPC products, this may change; tools for generating WSDL from XML schemas will no doubt be part of the toolbox used by JAXM programmers.

16.5 Building, Deploying, and Running the JAX-RPC Examples

The JAX-RPC reference implementation includes a servlet named `JAXRPCServlet` that can accept requests and route them to the appropriate service implementations. Like all servlets, we'll need a `web.xml` deployment descriptor to configure the servlet. The `web.xml` is shown in Listing 16.8. Note that the `.properties` file generated by `xrpcc` is passed in via an initialization parameter. We've also set the servlet to catch requests having `/jaxrpc/` in their URLs, so we'll need to include this in our access URL.

As mentioned earlier, I found that I needed to `chmod` the `xrpcc` program to have execute access with both the EA1 and EA2 distributions (`chmod a+x xrpcc.sh`.) in order for the build to succeed.

Listing 16.8 web.xml Deployment Descriptor

```
<?xml version="1.0" encoding="UTF-8"?>

<!DOCTYPE web-app PUBLIC
    "-//Sun Microsystems, Inc.//DTD Web application 2.3//EN"
    "http://java.sun.com/dtd/web-app_2_3.dtd">

<web-app>
    <servlet>
        <servlet-name>JAXRPCEndpoint</servlet-name>
        <servlet-class>
            com.sun.xml.rpc.server.http.JAXRPCServlet
        </servlet-class>
        <init-param>
            <param-name>configuration.file</param-name>
            <param-value>
                /WEB-INF/NFLStandings_Config.properties
            </param-value>
        </init-param>
    </servlet>
    <servlet-mapping>
        <servlet-name>JAXRPCEndpoint</servlet-name>
        <url-pattern>/jaxrpc/*</url-pattern>
    </servlet-mapping>
</web-app>
```

Listing 16.9 shows the Ant buildfile for the service. The two main targets are <server>, which builds our service and packages it in file nfl-jaxrpc.war, and <client>, which builds our Client class. Although there is a <test> target in the buildfile, it doesn't work properly; our service requires user input at one point, and Ant has control of terminal input and doesn't pass it along to the Client class. Instead, a test.sh script is included for testing the Client program.

There is quite a list of JAR files required for the client to operate, and a smaller set required for compilation of the server and client components. Many of these are part of JAXM, which JAX-RPC leverages for the actual transport of messages. Our JAX-RPC implementation here is an early-access version of the reference implementation; future implementers will probably redo the packaging to reduce the number of required components.

Once the server has been built and the WAR file deployed in a servlet container, the JAX-RPCEndpoint has a convenience feature in which you can point a browser at it and it will report on all installed services. If we deployed in Tomcat, this URL would be something like:

```
http://localhost:8080/nfl-jaxrpc/jaxrpc
```

If you deployed successfully, you'll see a message that shows the name of the service. If there was any problem deploying, you'll most likely see something like error 500, Internal Server Error. In this case, the `stdout` of the servlet container and the logfiles should contain information that indicates the problem.

Listing 16.9 `build.xml`

```
<project name="nfl-jaxrpc" default="server" basedir=".">

<!-- Adjust first 2 properties for your installation -->
<!-- set this to where XML pack installed -->
<property name="JAVA_XML_PACK_HOME"
   value="/home/myawn/webservices/java_xml_pack-spring-02-dev" />
<!-- set this to where /nfl is rooted -->
<property name="nfl.classpath"
    value="../../.." />

<property name="JAXRPC_HOME"
   value="${JAVA_XML_PACK_HOME}/jaxrpc-1.0-ea2" />
<property name="JAXM_HOME"
   value="${JAVA_XML_PACK_HOME}/jaxm-1.0.1-ea2" />
<property name="JAXP_HOME"
   value="${JAVA_XML_PACK_HOME}/jaxp-1.2-ea2" />

<property name="jaxrpc.api.jar"
    value="${JAXRPC_HOME}/lib/jaxrpc-api.jar"/>
<property name="jaxrpc.ri.jar"
    value="${JAXRPC_HOME}/lib/jaxrpc-ri.jar"/>
<!-- changed from jaxm (EA1) to jaxm-api (EA2) -->
<property name="jaxm.jar"
    value="${JAXM_HOME}/lib/jaxm-api.jar"/>
<property name="mail.jar"
    value="${JAXM_HOME}/lib/mail.jar"/>
<property name="activation.jar"
    value="${JAXM_HOME}/lib/activation.jar"/>
<property name="dom4j.jar"
    value="${JAXM_HOME}/lib/dom4j.jar"/>
<!-- log4j replaced by commons logging in EA2 -->
<property name="jaxm-client.jar"
    value="${JAXM_HOME}/jaxm/jaxm-client.jar"/>
<property name="xalan.jar"
    value="${JAXP_HOME}/xalan.jar"/>
<!-- changed from xerces (EA1) to xercesImpl (EA2) -->
<property name="xerces.jar"
    value="${JAXP_HOME}/xercesImpl.jar"/>
<!-- new requirements in EA2 -->
```

```
<property name="jaxp.jar"
    value="${JAXP_HOME}/jaxp-api.jar"/>
<property name="sax.jar"
    value="${JAXP_HOME}/sax.jar"/>
<property name="dom.jar"
    value="${JAXP_HOME}/dom.jar"/>
<property name="logging.jar"
    value="${JAXM_HOME}/lib/commons-logging.jar" />


<path id="server.compile.path" >
   <pathelement location="${nfl.classpath}" />
</path>

<path id="client.compile.path" >
   <pathelement location="${nfl.classpath}" />
   <pathelement location="${jaxrpc.api.jar}" />
   <pathelement location="${jaxrpc.ri.jar}" />
</path>

<path id="client.test.path">
   <pathelement path="${nfl.classpath}" />
   <pathelement location="${jaxrpc.api.jar}" />
   <pathelement location="${jaxrpc.ri.jar}" />
   <pathelement location="${jaxm-client.jar}" />
   <pathelement location="${jaxm.jar}" />
   <pathelement location="${mail.jar}" />
   <pathelement location="${activation.jar}" />
   <pathelement location="${xalan.jar}" />
   <pathelement location="${xerces.jar}" />
</path>

<target name="all" depends="server,client"/>

<target name="server" depends="xrpcc">
  <war warfile="nfl-jaxrpc.war"
      webxml="web.xml" >
    <lib dir="../.." includes="layered.jar" />
    <lib dir="${JAXRPC_HOME}/lib"
         includes="jaxrpc-api.jar,jaxrpc-ri.jar" />
    <lib dir="${JAXM_HOME}/lib"
         includes="jaxm-api.jar,mail.jar,activation.jar,
                   dom4j.jar,commons-logging.jar" />
    <lib dir="${JAXM_HOME}/jaxm"
         includes="jaxm-client.jar" />
    <lib dir="${JAXP_HOME}"
         includes="jaxp-api.jar,sax.jar,dom.jar,
                   xalan.jar,xercesImpl.jar" />
```

```
        <classes dir="../../..">
           <include name="nfl/application/jaxrpc/*.class" />
           <include name=
                 "nfl/application/Dynamic*.class" />
        </classes>
        <webinf dir="../../..">
           <include name="NFLStandings_Config.properties" />
        </webinf>
      </war>
</target>

<target name="xrpcc" depends="server-compile">
    <!-- for windows platform, change extension to .bat -->
    <exec executable="${JAXRPC_HOME}/bin/xrpcc.sh"
                   dir="../../..">
        <env key="JAVA_XML_PACK_HOME"
           value="${JAVA_XML_PACK_HOME}" />
        <env key="CLASSPATH" value="${server.compile.path}" />
        <arg line="-both" />
        <!-- arg line="-verbose" / -->
        <!-- arg line="-keep" / -->
        <arg line="nfl/application/jaxrpc/config.xml"/>
    </exec>
</target>

<target name="server-compile">
   <javac srcdir=".." classpathref="server.compile.path">
     <include name="DynamicStandings.java"/>
     <include name="DynamicStandingsImpl.java"/>
     <include name="DynamicVersionInfo.java"/>
   </javac>
   <javac srcdir="." classpathref="server.compile.path}">
     <include name="SoapTeamImpl.java"/>
     <include name="NoSuchConferenceException.java"/>
     <include name="NoSuchDivisionException.java"/>
     <include name="JaxRpcStandingsIF.java"/>
     <include name="JaxRpcStandingsAdapter.java"/>
   </javac>
</target>

<target name="client" depends="xrpcc">
   <javac srcdir="." classpathref="client.compile.path">
     <include name="Client.java"/>
   </javac>
   <jar jarfile="./client.jar">
     <fileset dir=".">
        <include name="nfl/application/jaxrpc/*.class"/>
     </fileset>
```

```
      <fileset dir="../../..">
        <include name=
          "nfl.application.jaxrpc.Client.class"/>
        <include name=
          "nfl.application.jaxrpc.JaxRpcStandingsIF.class"/>
        <include name=
          "nfl.application.jaxrpc.SoapTeamImpl.class"/>
    </fileset>
  </jar>
</target>

<target name="test" >
  <!-- not functional. Use test.sh instead -->
  <java classname="nfl.application.jaxrpc.Client"
            fork="true">
      <classpath refid="client.test.path" />
      <arg value="-host" />
      <arg value="localhost" />
  </java>
</target>

<target name="clean">
  <delete includeEmptyDirs="true" quiet="true" >
    <fileset dir="." includes="*.class, *.war, *.jar"/>
    <fileset dir="." includes="*.properties, *.wsdl"/>
  </delete>
</target>

</project>
```

Although the buildfile includes a `<test>` target, it is not functional. Because our `Client` tries to read from `stdin`, Ant isn't an appropriate way to invoke the client because Ant will intercept all terminal I/O and it will never be seen by our client program. Instead, you'll need to run the client by hand. A simple test script is provided for use on UNIX systems, as shown in Listing 16.10.

Listing 16.10 `test.sh` Test Script

```
# Script to test JAXRPC Client
#
# used because ANT eats terminal input
#
export NFL_HOME=/home/myawn/webservices
export JAVA_XML_PACK_HOME=/home/myawn/webservices/
  java_xml_pack-spring-02-dev
export JAXRPC_HOME=$JAVA_XML_PACK_HOME/jaxrpc-1.0-ea2
```

```
export JAXM_HOME=$JAVA_XML_PACK_HOME/jaxm-1.0.1-ea2
export JAXP_HOME=$JAVA_XML_PACK_HOME/jaxp-1.2-ea2

export CLASSPATH=$NFL_HOME
export CLASSPATH=$CLASSPATH:$JAXRPC_HOME/lib/jaxrpc-ri.jar
export CLASSPATH=$CLASSPATH:$JAXRPC_HOME/lib/jaxrpc-api.jar
export CLASSPATH=$CLASSPATH:$JAXM_HOME/jaxm/jaxm-client.jar
export CLASSPATH=$CLASSPATH:$JAXM_HOME/lib/jaxm-api.jar
export CLASSPATH=$CLASSPATH:$JAXM_HOME/lib/mail.jar
export CLASSPATH=$CLASSPATH:$JAXM_HOME/lib/activation.jar
export CLASSPATH=$CLASSPATH:$JAXP_HOME/jaxp-api.jar
export CLASSPATH=$CLASSPATH:$JAXP_HOME/sax.jar
export CLASSPATH=$CLASSPATH:$JAXP_HOME/dom.jar

java nfl.application.jaxrpc.Client -host localhost
```

16.6 Exercises

16.1 Create a Web Service: Expose one or more methods of an existing application as a Web Service via JAX-RPC. Issues you may have to deal with include changing method signatures to conform to JAX-RPC types (thereby requiring adapter classes) and defining exceptions for the methods.

16.7 Further Reading

The home page for JAX-RPC is `http://java.sun.com/xml/jaxrpc/index.html`. JAX-RPC can be downloaded as part of the Java XML Pack at `http://java.sun.com/xml/javaxmlpack.html` or as part of the Java Web Services Developer's Pack at `http://java.sun.com/webservices/downloads/webservicespack.html`.

The JAXRPC-INTEREST mailing list is a good source for up-to-date information on JAX-RPC. To subscribe to this and other Java mailing lists, go to `http://archives.java.sun.com`.

The Java Web Services tutorial provides coverage of JAX-RPC. The EA1 version of the tutorial is available in printed form, but this version does not include coverage of dynamic invocation (which is covered in Chapter 18). The EA2 version of the tutorial is available online at `http://java.sun.com/webservices/docs/ea2/tutorial/index.html`.

Describing, Publishing, and Finding Web Services

W e have created Web Services and clients (consumers) for those Web Services. However, up until this point, we've ignored how potential clients of a service locate the service. The process of describing a Web Service, publishing that description to a registry, and searching for Web Services within registries is the topic of this chapter.

In all of our examples so far, the side initiating a connection knew something about how to find the other component; either a URL was known, or at the very least we knew a name that could be used to look up the service via the Java Naming and Directory Interface (JNDI). In real Web Services, we very often won't have any such information; we will know only the characteristics of the service we are looking for. For example, our Standings application would like to connect to a Web Service that reports sports scores. A travel agent client would like Web Services that provide reservation services for airlines, rental cars, and hotels. A purchasing client wants Web Services of those suppliers whose products the purchaser is looking to buy. This means we need to describe our Web Service in two distinct ways: technically, in terms of the interfaces, data types, and protocols used to access the service; but also a business description—what the service offers, and under what business terms it is being offered.

We'll start with the technical description of the service. This is done using the Web Services Description Language (WSDL). Later, we'll look at two different schemes for describing the business aspects of our service: UDDI, the Uniform Description, Discovery, and Integration (UDDI) service, and Electronic Business XML (ebXML).

Software Used in This Chapter

HP Service Composer

HP Service Composer can be used to construct or modify WSDL documents. It is part of the Web Services Platform from HP. Evaluation copies can be downloaded at no charge from `http://www.middleware.hp.com`.

HP Registry Composer

HP Registry Composer can be used to query or publish to public or private UDDI registries. It is part of the HP Web Services Platform, and also included with the HP Web Services Registry.

BEA WebLogic UDDI Directory Explorer

The 7.0 version of BEA's WebLogic server includes the UDDI Directory Explorer, which can be used to query public or private UDDI registries and publish to private UDDI registries. Evaluation copics of the WebLogic server can be downloaded from `http://www.bea.com`.

17.1 Describing Web Services with WSDL

The Web Services Description Language is an XML language for producing documents that describe Web Services. It is not particularly easy to read; like many XML languages, it is primarily intended for processing electronically. We won't attempt to create WSDL by hand; instead, we'll look at some tools that can do this for us.

One tool is the `xrpcc` utility we already used for our JAX-RPC example. At the same time that we were creating server-side artifacts for the JAX-RPC server, a WSDL document was created for us. Figure 17.1 shows graphically the components that make up a WSDL document; in our description of the document format, we'll provide specific examples from the `xrpcc`-generated WSDL document for the service we developed in Chapter 16. The actual WSDL document generated for us is included in Listings 17.1 through 17.6; each listing corresponds to one of the major elements described in the following paragraphs.

As Figure 17.1 shows, a WSDL document has a single root element, called the **<definitions>** element, with five element types that appear as subelements. Listing 17.1 shows the `<definitions>` element for our service; this is a convenient place for the definition of the several namespaces that are used throughout the WSDL document. The document content begins with a single **<types>** element, containing a `<schema>` element, which holds definitions for all of the data types that are needed to support the services described within the WSDL. This is shown in Listing 17.2. The `<schema>` element is itself an embedded XML schema document (see Chapter 4). Any legal XML schema elements might appear in the `<schema>` section, but in our simple examples the child elements will be either `<simpleType>` or `<complexType>` elements. WSDL also allows for other methods of providing type information, although these appear to be as yet undefined. If something else were to come along and gain widespread acceptance as a way of describing XML documents, then the new typing system could be easily fitted into WSDL as a new subelement of the `<types>` element.

Figure 17.1 WSDL document structure.

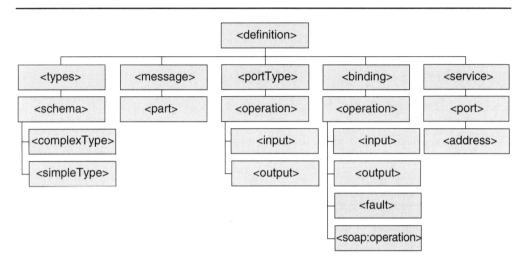

As a concrete illustration of the `<types>` element, the WSDL for our JAX-RPC service from Chapter 16 defines four `<complexType>` types: an `ArrayOfstring`, an `ArrayOfSoap-TeamImpl`, a `SoapTeamImpl`, and an `ArrayOfint`. See Listing 17.2.

Moving on through our WSDL document, we next encounter a series of **`<message>`** elements. Each `<message>` represents a document (for a document-centric service) or, for RPC-style services, either an RPC call or the response to the RPC call. Each parameter or result item is represented by a `<part>` element within the `<message>`; the `<part>` elements have a `type` attribute, which ties back to the types defined in the first part of the WSDL. Listing 17.3 shows the messages that are defined for our example service.

The third subelement type for the WSDL document is the **`<portType>`** element, as shown in Listing 17.4. The `<portType>` provides an abstract description of our service. The `<port-Type>` is the element that most closely resembles a Java interface, and is thus probably the element that most closely matches what we originally started with when we defined the interface to our service. The `<portType>` is a set of `<operation>`s; each operation corresponds to a single procedure call. The `<operation>` consists of `<input>` and `<output>` elements; each of these simply names a message from the `<message>` part of the WSDL document. If any exceptions are defined as being thrown by our interfaces, then `<fault>` elements are seen here, as JAX-RPC will map Java exceptions onto SOAP faults. While the names of the messages make it pretty obvious to a human reader that, for example, `getDivisionNames` and `getDivisionNames-Response` are probably related, the `<operation>` will make this explicit by naming them as the `<input>` and `<output>` components of the `<operation>` named `getDivisionNames`.

While the `<portType>` element defines our interface in abstract terms, the **`<binding>`** element (Listing 17.5) describes it concretely. The structure of the `<binding>` element mirrors the `<portType>`, containing the same `<operation>`s with the same `<input>` and `<output>` subelements. There may also be `<fault>` elements if the operation has defined fault conditions For each `<operation>` in the `<binding>` section, our sample WSDL specifies that the encoding of each `<input>` and `<output>` element will be as a `<soap:body>` element. In the `<soap:operation>` element (the namespace prefix is required so as not to clash with the WSDL element also named `<operation>`), we can specify a SOAP action. SOAP actions, if specified, are attached to the SOAP Header part of the message, and can be used to help route messages to the proper location. For example, in our `JaxmStandingsServlet` in Chapter 13, we have to parse the message body to determine what message type we have received and process it. Because the same servlet handles all message types, this is not particularly inefficient. But if our design used different servlets or Enterprise JavaBeans to process different types of messages, then without a SOAP action we would have to create a new front-end processor that read enough of the message to determine where it should be processed, and then route the message to that recipient where it would be parsed again. The SOAP action replaces this front-end processor by allowing the SOAP processor to route the message directly to the proper location.

For the port we are describing, we specify that the `transport` is HTTP, and the `style` is RPC. Although WSDL can describe Web Services that bind to protocols other than SOAP over HTTP, these are rare at this point, and in particular, the JAX-RPC reference implementation used for the examples supports no other binding options.

The final element in the WSDL document is the **`<service>`** definition, which associates the `<portType>` and `<binding>` elements with each other, and provides a `<soap:address>` (URL) where the service can be reached. This is shown in Listing 17.6.

In the next chapter, we'll show how a client of a Web Service can use this WSDL document to generate everything needed to connect to and consume the Web Service.

Listing 17.1 WSDL `<definitions>` Element

```
<?xml version="1.0" encoding="UTF-8"?>

<definitions
    name="NFLStandingsService"
    targetNamespace="http://hp.com/wsdl"
    xmlns:tns="http://hp.com/wsdl"
    xmlns="http://schemas.xmlsoap.org/wsdl/"
    xmlns:ns2="http://hp.com/types"
    xmlns:xsd="http://www.w3.org/2001/XMLSchema"
    xmlns:soap="http://schemas.xmlsoap.org/wsdl/soap/">
```

Listing 17.2 WSDL `<types>` Element

```
<types>
    <schema targetNamespace="http://hp.com/types"
            xmlns:wsdl="http://schemas.xmlsoap.org/wsdl/"
            xmlns:tns="http://hp.com/types"
            xmlns:xsi=
                "http://www.w3.org/2001/XMLSchema-instance"
            xmlns:soap-enc=
                "http://schemas.xmlsoap.org/soap/encoding/"
            xmlns="http://www.w3.org/2001/XMLSchema">
        <complexType name="ArrayOfstring">
          <complexContent>
            <restriction base="soap-enc:Array">
              <attribute ref="soap-enc:arrayType"
                    wsdl:arrayType="string[]"/>
            </restriction>
          </complexContent>
        </complexType>
        <complexType name="ArrayOfSoapTeamImpl">
          <complexContent>
            <restriction base="soap-enc:Array">
              <attribute ref="soap-enc:arrayType"
                    wsdl:arrayType="tns:SoapTeamImpl[]"/>
            </restriction>
          </complexContent>
        </complexType>
        <complexType name="SoapTeamImpl">
          <sequence>
            <element name="record" type="tns:ArrayOfint"/>
            <element name="name" type="string"/>
            <element name="winLossPct" type="float"/>
          </sequence>
        </complexType>
        <complexType name="ArrayOfint">
          <complexContent>
            <restriction base="soap-enc:Array">
              <attribute ref="soap-enc:arrayType"
                    wsdl:arrayType="int[]"/>
            </restriction>
          </complexContent>
        </complexType>
    </schema>
</types>
```

Listing 17.3 WSDL `<message>` Elements

```
<message name="getConferenceNames"/>
<message name="getConferenceNamesResponse">
  <part name="result" type="ns2:ArrayOfstring"/></message>
<message name="getConferenceStandings">
  <part name="String_1" type="xsd:string"/></message>
<message name="getConferenceStandingsResponse">
  <part name="result" type="ns2:ArrayOfSoapTeamImpl"/>
</message>
<message name="getDivisionNames"/>
<message name="getDivisionNamesResponse">
  <part name="result" type="ns2:ArrayOfstring"/></message>
<message name="getDivisionStandings">
  <part name="String_1" type="xsd:string"/></message>
<message name="getDivisionStandingsResponse">
  <part name="result" type="ns2:ArrayOfSoapTeamImpl"/>
</message>
<message name="init"/>
<message name="initResponse"/>
```

Listing 17.4 WSDL `<portType>` Element

```
<portType name="JaxRpcStandingsIFPortType">
  <operation name="getConferenceNames">
    <input message="tns:getConferenceNames"/>
    <output message="tns:getConferenceNamesResponse"/>
  </operation>
  <operation name="getConferenceStandings">
    <input message="tns:getConferenceStandings"/>
    <output message="tns:getConferenceStandingsResponse"/>
  </operation>
  <operation name="getDivisionNames">
    <input message="tns:getDivisionNames"/>
    <output message="tns:getDivisionNamesResponse"/>
  </operation>
  <operation name="getDivisionStandings">
    <input message="tns:getDivisionStandings"/>
    <output message="tns:getDivisionStandingsResponse"/>
  </operation>
  <operation name="init">
    <input message="tns:init"/>
    <output message="tns:initResponse"/>
  </operation>
</portType>
```

Listing 17.5 WSDL `<binding>` Element

```
<binding name="JaxRpcStandingsIFBinding"
        type="tns:JaxRpcStandingsIFPortType">
  <operation name="getConferenceNames">
    <input>
      <soap:body encodingStyle=
            "http://schemas.xmlsoap.org/soap/encoding/"
            use="encoded" namespace="http://hp.com/wsdl"/>
    </input>
    <output>
      <soap:body encodingStyle=
            "http://schemas.xmlsoap.org/soap/encoding/"
            use="encoded" namespace="http://hp.com/wsdl"/>
    </output>
    <soap:operation soapAction=""/>
  </operation>
  <operation name="getConferenceStandings">
    <input>
      <soap:body encodingStyle=
            "http://schemas.xmlsoap.org/soap/encoding/"
            use="encoded" namespace="http://hp.com/wsdl"/>
    </input>
    <output>
      <soap:body encodingStyle=
            "http://schemas.xmlsoap.org/soap/encoding/"
            use="encoded" namespace="http://hp.com/wsdl"/>
    </output>
      <fault name="NoSuchConferenceException">
      <soap:fault encodingStyle=
            "http://schemas.xmlsoap.org/soap/encoding/"
            use="encoded" namespace="http://hp.com/wsdl"/>
    </fault>
    <soap:operation soapAction=""/>
  </operation>
  <operation name="getDivisionNames">
    <input>
      <soap:body encodingStyle=
            "http://schemas.xmlsoap.org/soap/encoding/"
            use="encoded" namespace="http://hp.com/wsdl"/>
    </input>
    <output>
      <soap:body encodingStyle=
            "http://schemas.xmlsoap.org/soap/encoding/"
            use="encoded" namespace="http://hp.com/wsdl"/>
    </output>
    <soap:operation soapAction=""/>
  </operation>
```

```
    <operation name="getDivisionStandings">
      <input>
        <soap:body encodingStyle=
             "http://schemas.xmlsoap.org/soap/encoding/"
             use="encoded" namespace="http://hp.com/wsdl"/>
      </input>
      <output>
        <soap:body encodingStyle=
             "http://schemas.xmlsoap.org/soap/encoding/"
             use="encoded" namespace="http://hp.com/wsdl"/>
      </output>
        <fault name="NoSuchDivisionException">
        <soap:fault encodingStyle=
             "http://schemas.xmlsoap.org/soap/encoding/"
             use="encoded" namespace="http://hp.com/wsdl"/>
      </fault>
      <soap:operation soapAction=""/>
    </operation>
    <operation name="init">
      <input>
        <soap:body encodingStyle=
             "http://schemas.xmlsoap.org/soap/encoding/"
             use="encoded" namespace="http://hp.com/wsdl"/>
      </input>
      <output>
        <soap:body encodingStyle=
             "http://schemas.xmlsoap.org/soap/encoding/"
             use="encoded" namespace="http://hp.com/wsdl"/>
       </output>
      <soap:operation soapAction=""/></operation>
    <soap:binding
         transport="http://schemas.xmlsoap.org/soap/http"
         style="rpc"/>
  </binding>
```

Listing 17.6 WSDL `<service>` Element

```
  <service name="NFLStandings">
    <port name="JaxRpcStandingsIFPort"
      binding="tns:JaxRpcStandingsIFBinding">
      <soap:address location="REPLACE_WITH_ACTUAL_URL"/>
    </port>
  </service>
</definitions>
```

Although we generated our WSDL using the `xrpcc` tool, this tool is unique to the reference implementation of JAX-RPC. As the JAX-RPC standard finalizes and is implemented by vendors, expect each vendor to come up with their own tools for generating and manipulating WSDL. For example, the HP Web Services Platform includes a tool called HP Service Composer. HP Service Composer can import WSDL, XSD (XML Schema Definition), or a Java class or EJB. It provides a graphical tree-like representation of the data, which you can manipulate as required, and then use this schema to provide the `<types>` portion of a WSDL document. You can then create the remainder of the WSDL through a straightforward interface that allows you to define messages, operations, and other attributes of the service. Figure 17.2 shows the above WSDL document after importing into HP Service Composer. I also tried using the Java Import Wizard to import our JAX-RPC classes. At this point, the set of data types supported by HP-SC is more restricted than those of the JAX-RPC reference implementation, so our methods that returned arrays or JAX-RPC value types (for example, `SoapTeamImpl`) were grayed out in the wizard, not allowing them to be part of our exported interface. The command-line tools that can be used in place of the wizard actually do provide access to a wider selection of data types

Figure 17.2 HP Service Composer with WSDL imported.

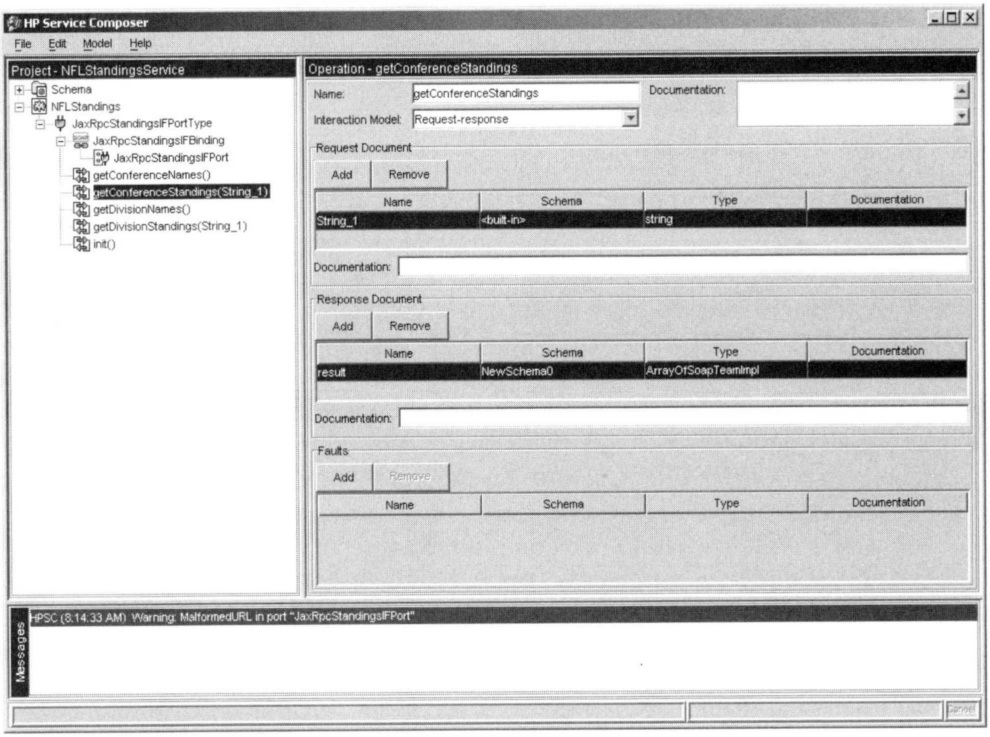

than those available through the wizard. I expect that after the JAX-RPC specification is finalized, future versions of this and other tools will provide complete support for all data types
required by the specification.

For a document-style Web Service, you might want to generate WSDL based on an XML
schema rather than a Java interface. You might remember that we previewed HP Service Composer in Chapter 4, when we used it to examine the XML schema for the `Game` class (see Figure
4.5 on page 95). You can use HP Service Composer to develop an XML schema from scratch if
none exists for your documents. Once your XML schema is satisfactory, you can then export it
as part of a WSDL document.

17.2 Standardized Web Services

We expect that our Web Service is unique, and there aren't any standards from which we can
take guidance about how to develop our interfaces and implementation. If you are trying to
implement a fairly standard business procedure like purchasing, however, it would be beneficial
to see what other purchasing Web Services look like. Over time, standards should emerge that
make it possible to have a universal client for common functions such as purchasing, rather than
have to create a specialized client for each vendor.

One of the organizations working in this area today is RosettaNet (`http://
www.rosettanet.org`). They are a non-profit organization seeking to create standards for
business processes and message schemas. This would be a good starting place to get ideas for
how an XML purchase order should be constructed, as an example, so that it would stand a
greater chance of being understood by a large number of services.

17.3 Publishing Web Services

There are various levels of complexity we can tackle when publishing our Web Service. At the
simplest end, we may have a service that we just want to use inside our own organization, or perhaps between business partners that we have already identified and have business relationships
with. In this case, we might not even need a registry at all; we can just email someone our
WSDL document (or for that matter, ignore the WSDL altogether and mail them the client software). At the opposite end of the spectrum, we can imagine needing a service, but having no
idea what companies might offer the service, so we would need an ability to search a registry
based only on descriptive information about the service desired.

Another axis of complexity comes from the business relationship required to use the service. At the simplest end, our service might be free; anyone who locates it is free to use it. At the
other end, there might be costs involved, and the need for contractual agreements about business
terms before anyone is permitted access.

We'll explore various ways of publishing and finding services that match up to various
points in the complexity model. For starters, let's go with a very simple service. Perhaps we'd
like to offer our standings service as a free service. We'll publish our WSDL document to a registry, and allow anyone to connect to the service once they've located the WSDL.

17.3.1 A Simple Use of a UDDI Registry

UDDI stands for Universal Description, Discovery, and Integration. The UDDI project (whose home is `http://www.uddi.org`) seeks to provide a common method of describing, publishing, and finding Web Services. There are public UDDI registries, in which you can search for existing Web Services and publish services that you want to make widely available. You can also run private registries, which allows you to test services before deploying them to a public registry, and also to publish services that are available only to a limited group that has access to your private registry (for example, you might be making a service available via a virtual marketplace or private ecosystem, or just internally on a corporate intranet). HP is one of four companies cooperating to provide a Universal Business Registry (UBR) that is accessible at `http://uddi.hp.com`; HP also offers a Web Services Registry product for hosting private registries.

Information in a UDDI registry can be thought of as being accessible in three ways. You can use a UDDI registry as a "white pages" service, looking up a business by a full or partial name. You can use it as a "yellow pages," finding businesses or services based on standard industry classification schemes. Or you can use it as a "green pages" service, specifying technical aspects of the desired service. While our examples access UDDI registries directly, no doubt new index and search services will emerge over time to provide even more flexible mechanisms for accessing UDDI registries.

There are several options for working programmatically with registries. JAXR, the Java API for XML Registries, provides a set of APIs that is designed to be compatible with any current or future Web-Service registries, including UDDI and ebXML. If you know that you're going to be using a UDDI registry, the UDDI4j APIs provide a closer mapping of UDDI concepts to the APIs, and tend to support new features earlier (UDDI4j supports UDDI 2.0, whereas JAXR supports only UDDI version 1.0). UDDI4j is an open-source project that began at IBM, with the UDDI 2.0 version being co-developed by IBM and HP. The anticipated audience for these registry-access APIs is not people writing Web Services, but rather the tools providers who create tools used by Web-Service developers. Because of this, we won't delve into API code examples in this chapter; instead, we'll look at some of the tools that allow you to access registries.

Let's start with a very simple usage of a UDDI registry. We have created a Web Service, which is described by a WSDL document (our JAX-RPC example from Chapter 16). Now we'd like to publish the WSDL document in a registry, so that potential clients can find it. For simplicity, let's assume that we are at least initially making the service available only to our internal network, so we'll publish to a private registry.

In the BEA WebLogic 7.0 release, a UDDI tool called UDDI Directory Explorer is introduced. The tool can be accessed simply by pointing a browser to `http://localhost:7001/uddiexplorer` (assuming that localhost is running an instance of WebLogic 7.0 on port 7001). The initial screen of the UDDI explorer is shown in Figure 17.3.

Figure 17.3 UDDI Explorer main screen.

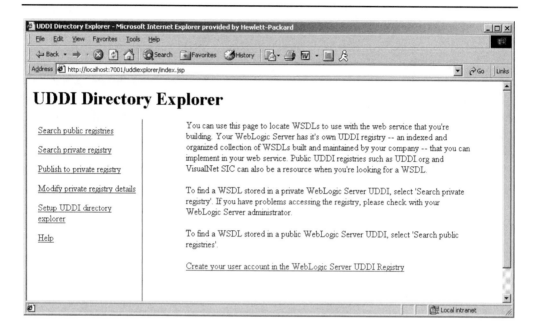

Because UDDI is a registry, not a repository, it does not contain WSDL directly, but rather has references to WSDL documents that are stored externally. These references are held in a *tModel* structure, which can be used to hold references to WSDL or other document types that might be used to fully describe a service. The UDDI Directory Explorer, however, hides this from us and allows us to treat a UDDI directory as if it were a simple repository for WSDL documents. In Figure 17.4, we have selected the "Publish to a private registry" option from the main screen, and filled in information about our service. Most important is the URL at which the WSDL for our service can be found.

Once we click on Add Service on this screen, we'll get a confirmation screen; if we confirm our desire to publish, we'll get a success screen indicating that our service has now been published to the registry. Just that simply, we've published our Web Service.

Now let's switch hats and play the role of a potential client. We want to find what Web Services are available on our intranet. So we connect to the UDDI Explorer, and select the "Search private registry" option from the main menu. This takes us to a search screen on which we can enter search criteria. In this case, I just asked for all services; but a search by department name, project name, or service name could also be used. In Figure 17.5, the search results are shown. There is only one service available.

Figure 17.4 Publishing to the private UDDI registry.

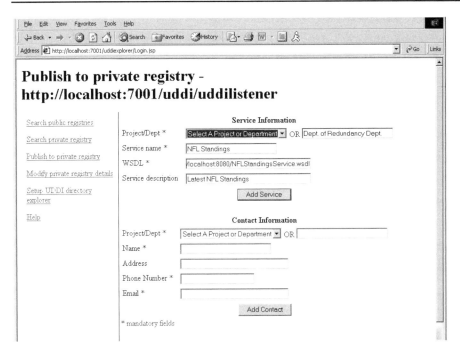

Figure 17.5 Searching the UDDI registry.

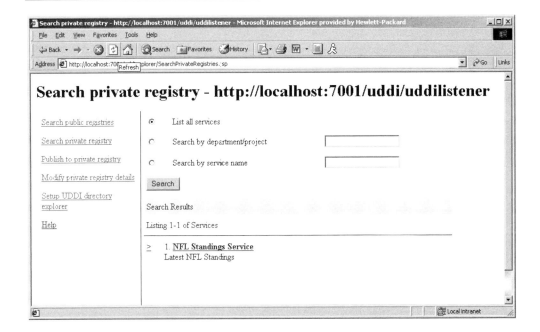

If we click on the link to the service, we're taken to a detailed information screen as shown in Figure 17.6. The Overview URL link is our WSDL document. By right-clicking on this and selecting Save Link as or Save Target as, we can save a copy of the WSDL document on our local system. We can then use this WSDL to generate a client for the service, as will be shown in the next chapter.

Figure 17.6 Service details from the UDDI registry.

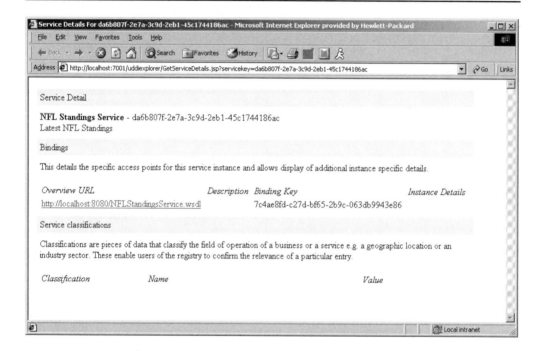

All we've really shown at this point is how we can reference a WSDL document in a UDDI registry, and then retrieve the referenced document. For many Web Services, especially simple ones like ours, that may in fact be all you need from UDDI. Not all uses will be so straightforward, as we're about to see.

17.3.2 A More Complex Use of UDDI

It's important for our understanding of UDDI for us to once again separate the interface of a service from the implementation of that service. For our example service, this isn't particularly relevant; we created our service independently, without regard for any industry standards that might pertain to the reporting of sports information. If someone is going to be a client of our particular service, chances are they're going to have to write code specifically to access our service.

Consider instead if our service had arisen from an industry effort to standardize on a service design, as is in fact happening in many industries. In such a case, there would be a standardized interface that would be agreed upon industry-wide, and then each service implementer would develop Web Services that conformed to the agreed-upon interface. This separation was visible in the WSDL: the `<message>` and `<portType>` elements described an interface that could potentially be implemented by several services. The `<binding>` and `<service>` elements described a specific implementation of the service.

The UDDI concepts reflecting this separation are the `<tModel>` and the `<businessSer-vice>`. A tModel (technical model) is an overloaded concept within UDDI; but for our present purpose it represents the specification (interface) of a Web Service. The `<businessService>` represents the service offered by a company. A `<businessService>` element within a UDDI registry is contained within a `<businessEntity>` element, which is the "white pages" information about the business—such as company name, contact information, and industry classification. The business service is what we need to find in order to use the service; we can find it in a number of ways. First, we could search for the `<businessEntity>` by name if we knew the name of the company we want to deal with. We can search for a `<businessEntity>` based on several industry classification or company identity codes, such as DUNS (Dun & Bradstreet) number, Thomas Register, or UNSPSC codes. Or, we could search based on the tModel identifier, if we had a specific service definition we were looking for. A business service is associated with a tModel by a `<bindingTemplate>` entry within the UDDI entry.

In Figure 17.7, we've searched the public UDDI registry at `http://uddi.hp.com` by Company Name, using a wildcard to find all companies listed in the registry. By clicking on a company, we can see the specific services published by that company.

Searching by codes is a better approach if you know the industry you're interested in, but not the specific company. The UNSPSC industry codes list is quite exhaustive (you can scroll through the full list in the HP Registry Composer). Unfortunately, not all industries have yet jumped on the Web Services bandwagon, so I could not find any services in categories such as Witch Doctors, Mercenaries, or Skywriting Services.

The UDDI registries are themselves Web Services, so behind the scenes it is SOAP messages going back and forth between tools such as UDDI Explorer and HP Registry Composer and the underlying registries. In fact, if you squint just right, you can see HP's UDDI registry inquiry service listed as one of the Web Services shown in Figure 17.7.

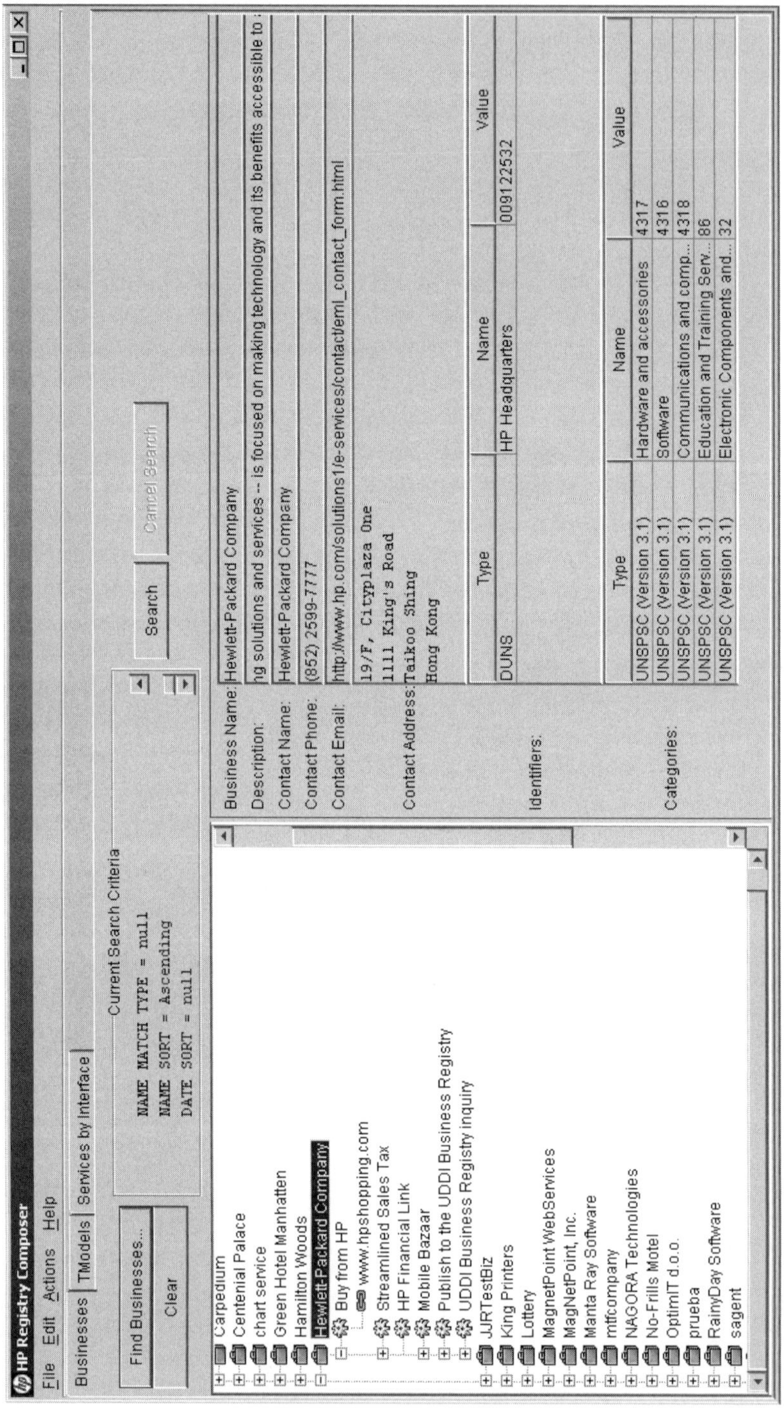

Figure 17.7 Public registry search (using HP Registry Composer).

17.4 Describing Complex Business Relationships

UDDI deals primarily with the need to find a business that provides a Web Service. Many Web Services, such as our Standings service, are appropriate to think of as being accessible on an ad-hoc basis without the need for a comprehensive set of business agreements between the provider of the service and users of the service. However, for Web Services to replace existing complex business models such major purchasing activities currently done via EDI, we need a more robust set of capabilities.

As an example, if I am going to manufacture computers and want to find a supplier of cases, I probably want something more than just who is selling cases today (I could do that on eBay). I instead want to get a commitment that a supplier can handle my projected volumes over a long period; I don't want to have to retool in the middle of a production run because the cases I started using are no longer available.

Electronic Business XML (ebXML) is a series of specifications and services that help provide the business infrastructure required to do serious business via Web Services. These types of Web Services are going to be far more complex; they will define business processes that involve many steps, such as requesting product information, obtaining price quotes, entering purchase orders, getting shipment acknowledgements, canceling or changing orders, and so forth.

17.4.1 An ebXML Scenario

An example scenario will help illustrate ebXML usage and also introduce the various components that make up ebXML.

ebXML defines a *Registry/Repository* (REGREP) that, like a UDDI registry, serves as a point for various document types to be cataloged for search and retrieval. Because ebXML is a repository as well as a registry, the documents are stored directly in the ebXML registry/repository, rather than just references to an external source.

To begin a business collaboration, someone models a business process that can be conducted via a Web Service. This is likely to be done via some type of industry consortium, because ebXML business processes are complex enough that they won't be thrown together in an ad-hoc fashion. The business process is described in a *Business Process Specification Schema* (BPSS). The BPSS specifies the documents and signals that will be exchanged by parties taking place in the collaboration; for example, a purchase order and a shipping notification.

Businesses that wish to conduct business via ebXML describe themselves in a document known as a *Collaboration Protocol Profile* (CPP), and place their CPPs in an ebXML registry. The CPP contains both the company information similar to a UDDI `<businessEntity>`, as well as the descriptions of services (the BPSSes) that the business is willing to participate in (analogous to the UDDI `<businessService>` and `<bindingTemplate>` information). Note that while in UDDI, it is only the service supplier that needs to be listed in the registry; for ebXML, all participants need to have collaboration profiles.

When two businesses decide to become trading partners, then a *Collaboration Protocol Agreement* (CPA) is produced. The CPA can be thought of as the intersection of two CPPs; both trading partners must agree to the CPA. While a CPP might suggest several different messaging protocols, for example, that a service can be offered through, the CPA will indicate a specific service that both parties agree to use. The CPA may itself be recorded in the ebXML registry, but this is not required.

ebXML also defines a *Messaging Service* (ebMS). ebXML ebMS is based on SOAP 1.1 with attachments, but adds additional features. For example, while SOAP doesn't define any required usage of the SOAP headers, ebXML specifies certain SOAP headers that participants are required to use. The ebXML messaging protocol provides for reliable, secure delivery of messages. The JAXM APIs provide support for ebXML messaging through a profile; by specifying this profile when creating a `MessageFactory`, you can generate JAXM messages that have the appropriate SOAP headers as required by ebXML.

The same Java API can be used for accessing both UDDI and ebXML registries; JAXR was designed to be flexible enough to support both of these, plus extensible to allow for support of additional registries in the future.

ebXML has some really powerful concepts at its core, seemingly providing a framework for doing large-scale e-business on the Web. However, the tools, vendor support, and general infrastructure for ebXML do not appear to be nearly as pervasive as UDDI. While things may change rapidly, today it seems like UDDI is where you should probably be planning to deploy Web Services, while ebXML is a technology to be watching for in the future.

17.5 Exercises

17.1 Programmatic access: Use either UDDI4j or JAXR to access information from a UDDI or ebXML registry.

17.2 SOAP faults: Add exceptions to the JAX-RPC example interface and see what changes are made to the WSDL document.

17.3 SOAP actions: Add SOAP action headers to the JAX-RPC example code and see how these are reflected in the generated WSDL.

17.4 ebXML profile: Specify the ebXML profile when creating a message factory for the JAXM example, and see what header information is added to the messages.

17.6 Further Reading

The Web Services Description Language is a W3C specification and can be accessed at `http://www.w3.org/TR/wsdl`.

The home page for UDDI is `http://www.uddi.org`.

The UDDI4J software and documentation is available at `http://uddi4j.org`.

The HP Web Services Registry contains a UDDI private registry, with client tools like UDDI4j and Registry Composer. Free evaluation copies can be downloaded from `http://www.hpmiddleware.com`.

The BEA WebLogic server includes UDDI Directory Explorer in the 7.0 release. Evaluation copies can be downloaded from `http://www.bea.com`.

ebXML is a joint effort of UN/CEFACT and OASIS. The OASIS group home page is `http://www.oasis-open.org`; the home page for ebXML is `http://www.ebxml.org`.

The HP Registry Composer and HP Service Composer products are part of the HP Web Services Platform; evaluation copies can be downloaded at no charge from `http://www.hpmiddleware.com`.

Information on JAXR can be found at `http://java.sun.com/xml/jaxr/index.html`.

## CHAPTER 18

Clients for JAX-RPC Web Services

When we created our JAX-RPC Web Service in Chapter 16, we created a client for the service as well. It would be impossible to create a Web Service and convince oneself that it was functioning properly without creating such a client to test out the service. However, for the most part, Web-Service clients will not be getting code from the service provider to access the service, but instead will be developing their own clients based solely on the information contained in the WSDL description of the service. In this chapter, we'll see how such clients can be created for our example Web Service.

18.1 JAX-RPC Clients

The JAX-RPC specification describes three ways in which clients can access the service: via stubs, via a dynamic proxy, and via the dynamic invocation interface (DII). The dynamic proxy access is not yet supported by the reference implementation, so we won't develop an example using that method. But we will create examples for the other two methods.

Software Used in This Chapter
JAX-RPC EA2 (Early-Access 2) version, from the Java XML Pack, spring 2002 release.

18.1.1 Static Access via Stubs

We've already shown this method of access in Chapter 16. In that chapter, the `xrpcc` tool was using our Java interfaces as a starting point from which to create the stubs. For a remote Web-Service client, we would instead start with the WSDL file, but `xrpcc` in fact generates nearly identical stubs for us when starting with WSDL.

Recall that the `xrpcc` utility takes as input a configuration file. In Chapter 16, our configuration file (see Listing 16.5 on page 412) specified the Java interface and implementation classes. In Listing 18.1, we show an `xrpcc` configuration file that we can use as a Web-Service client. Instead of an `<rmi>` element that describes the class and interface, we have a `<wsdl>` element that points to a WSDL document.

Listing 18.1 `xrpcc config.xml` File for the Client

```
<?xml version="1.0" encoding="UTF-8"?>

<configuration
        xmlns="http://java.sun.com/jax-rpc-ri/xrpcc-config">
    <wsdl name="NFLStandingsService"
          location="NFLStandingsService.wsdl"
          packageName="nfl.application.jaxrpc_clients">
      <!-- optional typeMappingRegistry -->
    </wsdl>
</configuration>
```

The stubs and classes generated by `xrpcc` when starting with the WSDL document are virtually identical to those generated from the Java interfaces, so we won't repeat the entire exercise of building a static client here. The CD includes everything you need to build the client in the `jaxrpc_clients` directory, if you want to go through the exercise and compare the results to those obtained when starting from the interfaces.

18.1.2 Access via Dynamic Proxy

Access via a proxy is very similar to access via a stub. The difference is that the stub is created ahead of time, via a program such as `xrpcc`. The proxy is generated on the fly, using the capabilities of Java's reflection APIs to find the methods available for the remote service. Proxy objects are not unique to JAX-RPC; look at the `Proxy` and `InvocationHandler` objects in the `java.lang.reflect` package to get an idea of how proxies work.

Because the latest early-access release of JAX-RPC available at the time this book was written does not include support for dynamic proxies, no code example was created. The code snippet, adapted slightly from the Web-Services tutorial included with the early-access release, shows how the code should work. A `Service` object is created from a `ServiceFactory`; this same process is used in the dynamic invocation interface so you can see a complete code example in Listing 18.2. Then, the `getPort()` method of the `Service` object is invoked, using as parameters the port name (interface name) and implementation class name. The call returns an instance of the class passed in as the second parameter. The returned object then functions just like a pre-generated stub object, and can be used to call the various methods of the Web Service's interface.

```
service = factory.createService(…)
JaxRpcStandingsIF endpoint = service.getPort(portName,
                    JaxRpcStandingsIF.class);
// Now, can make calls just as with pre-generated stub
endpoint.getDivisionNames();
```

18.1.3 Dynamic Invocation Interface

The dynamic invocation interface (DII) capability of JAX-RPC is quite different from the stub and proxy methods of interface. In dynamic invocation, we painstakingly build up method calls by describing each parameter. For any parameter types that are not built-in types that JAX-RPC supports, we must construct serializer and deserializer classes for those types, because we are operating without the benefit of xrpcc-generated classes. In the example that follows, we go through the process of doing all this, even though our application is no more flexible as a result of doing so.

A typical use-case for DII would be where we need the flexibility of connecting to multiple Web Services, or to a Web Service that might change its published API. A dynamic client would thus normally have logic to check the interface, most likely by parsing the WSDL document, and then building the method calls based on what is discovered this way. Our example application doesn't have this intelligence; we in fact are going to build the exact same method calls every time, because they are hard-coded into the program's logic. If the program is never going to change how it makes calls, then it should just use a stub or proxy; but doing the example this way allows us to show the mechanisms of dynamic invocation without the added code required to parse a WSDL document and the complex logic to decide what to do with the result.

A final and important note about this example: The JAX-RPC specification provides for the TypeMapping and TypeMappingRegistry classes shown in the next example, as well as the SerializerFactory and DeserializerFactory classes. All of these are part of the javax.xml.rpc.encoding package. All of the com.sun.xml.rpc.encoding classes that are used, however, are not part of the specification. These are specific to the reference implementation. When you develop code to do dynamic invocation of JAX-RPC services using a vendor implementation of JAX-RPC, you will need to use that vendor's implementation classes for creating serializers and deserializers, which may be completely different. A future version of JAX-RPC is expected to support portable serializers and deserializers, but for now any implementation that you do will be specific to the vendor's product for which it is developed.

The first part of our dynamic client is shown in Listing 18.2. The main() method is very similar to its counterpart in the stub-based client and won't be re-examined here. In the run() method, we start by getting a reference to the service() object, which is a connection to the endpoint of the Web Service we want to communicate with. We then create three `Call` objects, one for each of the methods we plan to call during our use of the service. Listing 18.2 shows the usage of the first of these `Call` objects, which will be used to invoke the `init()` method of the service. The `init()` method has no parameters and no return, so it is the simplest possible procedure call. The next five procedure calls—`setPortTypeName()`, `setTargetEndpoint-Address()`, and three `setProperty()` calls—will be common for any dynamic calls. They identify the interface we are using (the port), the URL location of the service we are talking to, and then (in the `setProperty()` calls) we establish that we are communicating via SOAP and set up default header actions.

Now we come to the calls that will be unique to each method call. We need to set the name of the method we want to invoke, via the `Call.setOperationName()` call. There are no parameters in the `init()` method we are invoking, so no calls to set parameter types or values are required for this call. We do still have to specify a return type, which in this case is null. Finally, we invoke the call using the `Call.invokeOneWay()` call that is used to invoke methods which have no return (or return void, if you prefer to think of it that way). Although there are no parameters in the `init()` call we are targeting, `invokeOneWay()` still expects an object array for the parameters, so we create an empty object array to satisfy this requirement.

Listing 18.2 `DynamicClient.java` (Part 1 of 4): A Simple One-Way Call

```
// DynamicClient.java

package nfl.application.jaxrpc_clients;

import java.io.*;
import java.rmi.RemoteException;
import java.text.DecimalFormat;

// General DII Imports
import javax.xml.rpc.Call;
import javax.xml.rpc.Service;
import javax.xml.rpc.JAXRPCException;
import javax.xml.rpc.namespace.QName;
import javax.xml.rpc.ServiceFactory;
import javax.xml.rpc.ParameterMode;
import javax.xml.rpc.ServiceException;

// Imports for [de]serialization of complex types, arrays
import javax.xml.rpc.encoding.TypeMapping;
import javax.xml.rpc.encoding.TypeMappingRegistry;
import javax.xml.rpc.encoding.SerializerFactory;
import javax.xml.rpc.encoding.DeserializerFactory;
import javax.xml.soap.SOAPConstants;
```

```java
import com.sun.xml.rpc.encoding.AttachmentSerializer;
import com.sun.xml.rpc.encoding.CombinedSerializer;
import com.sun.xml.rpc.encoding.ObjectArraySerializer;
import com.sun.xml.rpc.encoding.ReferenceableSerializerImpl;
import com.sun.xml.rpc.encoding.SerializerConstants;
import com.sun.xml.rpc.encoding.SimpleTypeArraySerializer;
import com.sun.xml.rpc.encoding.SimpleTypeSerializer;
import com.sun.xml.rpc.encoding.SingletonSerializerFactory;
import com.sun.xml.rpc.encoding.SingletonDeserializerFactory;
import com.sun.xml.rpc.encoding.simpletype.XSDIntEncoder;
import com.sun.xml.rpc.encoding.simpletype.XSDStringEncoder;
import com.sun.xml.rpc.wsdl.document.schema.SchemaConstants;

public class DynamicClient
        implements SerializerConstants, SchemaConstants {

    private static String ENCODING_STYLE_PROPERTY =
            "javax.xml.rpc.encodingstyle.namespace.uri";
    private static String TYPE_NAMESPACE =
            "http://hp.com/types";
    private static String WSDL_NAMESPACE =
            "http://hp.com/wsdl";

    private static String svcname = null;
    private static String ifname  = null;

    public static void main(String[] args) {

        String hostname = "localhost";
        String port     = "8080";
        String context  = "nfl-jaxrpc";
        String pattern  = "jaxrpc";

        svcname = "NFLStandings";  /* NEW */
        ifname  = "JaxRpcStandingsIF";

        for (int i=0; i<args.length; i++) {
            String parm = args[i];
            if (parm.equals("-help") ||
                parm.equals("-usage"))
                usage();
            if (parm.equals("-host") ||
                parm.equals("-hostname")) {
                hostname = args[++i];
            }
            if (parm.equals("-port"))
                port = args[++i];
        }
```

```
    String URL = "http://" + hostname + ":" + port +
                         "/" + context + "/" + pattern +
                         "/" + ifname;

    DynamicClient client = new DynamicClient();
    client.run(URL);
}

public static void usage() {
    System.out.println("Usage: " +
       "java nfl.application.jaxrpc_clients.DynamicClient"
          + " <options>\n" +
       "where <options> include:\n" +
       "-hostname <name>   host name\n" +
       "-port      <number> port number (default 8080)\n"
    );
    System.exit(0);
}

public void run(String endpointAddress) {

    ServiceFactory factory            = null;
    Service        service            = null;
    Call           initCall           = null;
    Call           getNamesCall       = null;
    Call           getStandingsCall = null;
    try {
       factory = ServiceFactory.newInstance();
       service = factory.createService(
                          new QName(svcname));
       initCall = service.createCall();
       getNamesCall = service.createCall();
       getStandingsCall = service.createCall();
    } catch (ServiceException e) {
       e.printStackTrace(); System.exit(-1);
    }

    // Call init().
    QName port = new QName(ifname);
    initCall.setPortTypeName(port);
    initCall.setTargetEndpointAddress(endpointAddress);
    initCall.setProperty(Call.SOAPACTION_USE_PROPERTY,
              new Boolean(true));
    initCall.setProperty(
              Call.SOAPACTION_URI_PROPERTY, "");
    initCall.setProperty(ENCODING_STYLE_PROPERTY,
              SOAPConstants.URI_NS_SOAP_ENCODING);
```

```
// init call has no params and no return value.
initCall.setOperationName(
    new QName(WSDL_NAMESPACE, "init"));
initCall.setReturnType(null);
initCall.invokeOneWay(new Object[0]);
```

The second call we make is slightly more complex, because it has a return value. Because the return value is not a simple type (it is an array of Strings), we must create serializers and deserializers for it. Any time we create serializers and deserializers, we must register them in the `TypeMappingRegistry`. So our first step in Listing 18.3 is to gain access to the `TypeMappingRegistry` for our service, and then get the `TypeMappings` that are already defined for SOAP messages.

The process for creating these objects is unique to the reference implementation, so we won't examine it at any length because you will need to create serializers and deserializers in accordance with the process for the implementation of JAX-RPC you are using. In simple terms, we create a serializer for type `String`, and then use this as a parameter to the constructor for the creation of an array serializer. With the serializer constructed, we then instantiate both a `SerializerFactory` and a `DeserializerFactory` for our type (`String[]`), and register these two objects in the `TypeMappingRegistry`.

With serialization taken care of, we can now actually make the call. We set the standard properties, then set the return type and operation name before invoking the call.

Listing 18.3 `DynamicClient` (Part 2 of 4): A Call Returning a Simple Array Type

```
// Must register serializers for String[]
TypeMappingRegistry registry =
    service.getTypeMappingRegistry();
TypeMapping mapping = registry.getTypeMapping(
    SOAPConstants.URI_NS_SOAP_ENCODING);

// Create [de]serializers for String[]
QName stringArrayTypeQname =
    new QName(TYPE_NAMESPACE, "ArrayOfstring");
QName stringArrayElementQname =
    new QName("", "string");
CombinedSerializer stringSerializer =
    new SimpleTypeSerializer(
        SchemaConstants.QNAME_TYPE_STRING,
        DONT_ENCODE_TYPE,
        NULLABLE,
        SOAPConstants.URI_NS_SOAP_ENCODING,
        XSDStringEncoder.getInstance());
CombinedSerializer stringArraySerializer =
    new SimpleTypeArraySerializer(
```

```
            stringArrayTypeQname,
            ENCODE_TYPE,
            NULLABLE,
            SOAPConstants.URI_NS_SOAP_ENCODING,
            null,
            SchemaConstants.QNAME_TYPE_STRING,
            String.class,
            1,
            null,
            (SimpleTypeSerializer) stringSerializer);
stringArraySerializer=
    new ReferenceableSerializerImpl(
            SERIALIZE_AS_REF, stringArraySerializer);
SerializerFactory stringArraySerializerFactory =
    new SingletonSerializerFactory(
            stringArraySerializer);
DeserializerFactory stringArrayDeserializerFactory =
    new SingletonDeserializerFactory(
            stringArraySerializer);
mapping.register(String[].class,
                  stringArrayTypeQname,
                  stringArraySerializerFactory,
                  stringArrayDeserializerFactory);

// call getDivisionNames()
getNamesCall.setProperty(Call.SOAPACTION_USE_PROPERTY,
            new Boolean(true));
getNamesCall.setProperty(
            Call.SOAPACTION_URI_PROPERTY, "");
getNamesCall.setProperty(ENCODING_STYLE_PROPERTY,
            SOAPConstants.URI_NS_SOAP_ENCODING);
getNamesCall.setPortTypeName(port);
getNamesCall.setTargetEndpointAddress(
                            endpointAddress);
getNamesCall.setReturnType(stringArrayTypeQname);
getNamesCall.setOperationName(
    new QName(WSDL_NAMESPACE, "getDivisionNames"));

String[] divnames = null;
try {
    divnames = (String[])
            getNamesCall.invoke(new Object[0]);
} catch (RemoteException e) {
    e.printStackTrace(); System.exit(-1);
}
```

For the final call in our example, we have both an input parameter (a `String`) and another array as a return type—although this array is of a user-defined type (`SoapTeamImpl`) rather than a well-known system type (`String`). In the code shown in Listing 18.4, you can see that we first create and register serializers for the `SoapTeamImpl` class, and then for the Array of `SoapTeamImpl` objects.

Listing 18.4 `DynamicClient` (Part 3 of 4): Creating Serializers for a Complex Array Type

```
QName soapteamTypeQname =
   new QName(TYPE_NAMESPACE, "SoapTeamImpl");
CombinedSerializer soapteamSerializer =
   new SoapTeamImpl_SOAPSerializer(
        soapteamTypeQname,
        ENCODE_TYPE,
        NULLABLE,
        SOAPConstants.URI_NS_SOAP_ENCODING);
soapteamSerializer =
   new ReferenceableSerializerImpl(
        SERIALIZE_AS_REF, soapteamSerializer);
SerializerFactory soapteamSerializerFactory =
   new SingletonSerializerFactory(
        soapteamSerializer);
DeserializerFactory soapteamDeserializerFactory =
   new SingletonDeserializerFactory(
        soapteamSerializer);
mapping.register(SoapTeamImpl.class,
                 soapteamTypeQname,
                 soapteamSerializerFactory,
                 soapteamDeserializerFactory);

// Create [de]serializers for SoapTeamImpl[]
QName soapteamArrayTypeQname =
   new QName(TYPE_NAMESPACE, "ArrayOfSoapTeamImpl");
QName soapteamArrayElementQname =
   new QName("", "SoapTeamImpl");
CombinedSerializer soapteamArraySerializer =
   new ObjectArraySerializer(
        soapteamArrayTypeQname,
        ENCODE_TYPE,
        NULLABLE,
        SOAPConstants.URI_NS_SOAP_ENCODING,
        soapteamArrayElementQname,
        soapteamTypeQname,
        SoapTeamImpl.class,
        1,
        null);
```

```
soapteamArraySerializer=
    new ReferenceableSerializerImpl(
            SERIALIZE_AS_REF, soapteamArraySerializer);
SerializerFactory soapteamArraySerializerFactory =
    new SingletonSerializerFactory(
            soapteamArraySerializer);
DeserializerFactory soapteamArrayDeserializerFactory =
    new SingletonDeserializerFactory(
            soapteamArraySerializer);
mapping.register(SoapTeamImpl[].class,
                 soapteamArrayTypeQname,
                 soapteamArraySerializerFactory,
                 soapteamArrayDeserializerFactory);
```

With the serializers registered, we can now make our final call. This is the first time we've had an input parameter as well as a return type, so the code to add the parameter has been highlighted in addition to the code setting the return type of the call.

Listing 18.5 DynamicClient (Part 4 of 4): Making a Call Using Complex Types and Arrays

```
// Call getDivisionStandings(divnames[a])
SoapTeamImpl[] teams = null;
getStandingsCall.setProperty(
            Call.SOAPACTION_USE_PROPERTY,
            new Boolean(true));
getStandingsCall.setProperty(
            Call.SOAPACTION_URI_PROPERTY, "");
getStandingsCall.setProperty(ENCODING_STYLE_PROPERTY,
            SOAPConstants.URI_NS_SOAP_ENCODING);
getStandingsCall.setPortTypeName(port);
getStandingsCall.setTargetEndpointAddress(
                    endpointAddress);
getStandingsCall.setReturnType(
                    soapteamArrayTypeQname);
getStandingsCall.setOperationName(
        new QName(WSDL_NAMESPACE,
                "getDivisionStandings"));
getStandingsCall.addParameter("String_1",
        SchemaConstants.QNAME_TYPE_STRING,
        //NOTE: spec says IN rather than PARAM_MODE_IN,
        //   so this may change in FCS
        ParameterMode.PARAM_MODE_IN);
Object[] parms = new Object[] { divnames[a] };
try {
    teams = (SoapTeamImpl[])
            getStandingsCall.invoke(parms);
} catch (RemoteException e) { e.printStackTrace(); }
```

18.2 JAX-RPC API Documentation

These first four APIs are the basic classes that participate in making a JAX-RPC call. For access via stubs, you will have an endpoint class that provides a call that returns an instance of the Stub class. (In Listing 16.7 on page 414, for example, we called the getJaxRpcStandingsIF() method of the NFLStandings_Impl class.)

If you are using dynamic proxies, you first obtain a reference to the service via the ServiceFactory. Then, you obtain a reference to the remote object by calling one of the getPort() variants. To use dynamic proxies, your client must already know specifics about the interfaces being called.

To use dynamic invocation, you create Call objects on the fly, build parameter lists for the Calls, then invoke them via their invoke() method. If all of your parameters and return types are simple types, these are the only four classes you'll need.

API 18.1 javax.xml.rpc.**ServiceFactory**

```
public class ServiceFactory
    public abstract Service createService(QName serviceName);
    public abstract Service createService(java.net.URL wsdlLocation,
        QName serviceName);
    public static ServiceFactory newInstance();
```

API 18.2 javax.xml.rpc.**Service**

```
public interface Service
    public Call createCall();
    public Call createCall(QName portName);
    public Call createCall(QName portName, QName operationName);
    public Call createCall(QName portName, String operationName);
    public HandlerRegistry getHandlerRegistry();
    public java.rmi.Remote getPort(Class serviceDefinitionInterface);
    public java.rmi.Remote getPort(QName portName, Class serviceDefinitionInterface);
    public Iterator getPorts();
    public QName getServiceName();
    public TypeMappingRegistry getTypeMappingRegistry();
    public java.net.URL getWSDLDocumentLocation();
```

API 18.3 javax.xml.rpc.**Stub**

```
public interface Stub
    public Object _getProperty(String name);
    public Iterator _getPropertyNames();
    public void _setProperty(String name, Object value);
```

API 18.4   javax.xml.rpc.**Call**

```
public interface Call
    public void addParameter(String paramName, QName xmlType, Class javaType,
        ParameterNode paramNode);
    public void addParameter(String paramName, QName xmlType,
        ParameterNode paramNode);
    public QName getOperationName();
    public Map getOutputParams();
    public QName getParameterTypeByName(String paramName);
    public QName getPortTypeName();
    public Object getProperty(String name);
    public Iterator getPropertyNames();
    public QName getReturnType();
    public String getTargetEndpointAddress();
    public Object invoke(Object[] inputParams);
    public void invokeOneWay(Object[] inputParams);
    public boolean isParameterAndReturnSpecRequired(QName operationName);
    public void removeAllParameters();
    public void removeProperty(String propertyName);
    public void setOperationName(QName operationName);
    public void setPortTypeName(QName portType);
    public void setProperty(String name, Object value);
    public void setReturnType(QName xmlType);
    public void setReturnType(QName xmlType, Class javaType);
    public void setTargetEndpointAddress(String address);
```

These remaining APIs are for dealing with complex data types. The APIs shown are standard, and will be utilized with any JAX-RPC implementation. The com.sun.xml.rpc classes that were heavily utilized in the dynamic example are undocumented, and will most likely remain so. Therefore, developing with the reference implementation requires a good deal of reverse-engineering; you will almost certainly need to use xrpcc to generate stubs for the targeted interface, and then use the generated code as a basis for your dynamic clients. Or, simply use vendor implementations that have documented methods for generating serializers and deserializers, rather than developing with the reference implementation.

API 18.5 javax.xml.rpc.encoding.**TypeMappingRegistry**

```
public interface TypeMappingRegistry
    public void clear()
    public TypeMapping createTypeMapping();
    public TypeMapping getDefaultTypeMapping();
    public String[] getRegisteredNamespaces();
    public TypeMapping getTypeMapping(String namespaceURI);
    public TypeMapping register(String namespaceURI, TypeMapping mapping);
    public void registerDefault(TypeMapping mapping);
    public boolean removeTypeMapping(TypeMapping mapping);
    public TypeMapping unregisterTypeMapping(String namespaceURI);
```

API 18.6 javax.xml.rpc.encoding.**TypeMapping**

```
public interface TypeMapping
    public DeserializerFactory getDeserializer(Class javaType, QName xmlType);
    public SerializerFactory getSerializer(Class javaType, QName xmlType);
    public String[] getSupportedNamespaces();
    public boolean isRegistered(Class javaType, QName xmlType);
    public boolean register(Class javaType, QName xmlType, SerializerFactory sf,
        DeserializerFactory dsf);
    public void removeDeserializer(Class javaType, QName xmlType);
    public void removeSerializer(Class javaType, QName xmlType);
    public void setSupportedNamespaces(String[] namespaceURIs);
```

API 18.7 javax.xml.rpc.encoding.**SerializerFactory**

```
public interface SerializerFactory
    public Serializer getSerializerAs(String mechanismType) throws JAXRPCException;
    public Iterator getSupportedMechanismTypes();
```

API 18.8 javax.xml.rpc.encoding.**DeserializerFactory**

```
public interface DeserializerFactory
    public Deserializer getDeserializerAs(String mechanismType)
        throws JAXRPCException;
    public Iterator getSupportedMechanismTypes();
```

18.3 Building and Running the Examples

The Ant buildfile for the JAX-RPC clients is shown in Listing 18.6. The two main targets are `<static>` and `<dynamic>`. `<static>` builds essentially the same client we used in Chapter 16, while `<dynamic>` builds the client we've been examining in this chapter. As with the example in Chapter 16, the client cannot be tested from within Ant because it needs to accept input from the terminal. There are two scripts, `test-static.sh` and `test-dynamic.sh`, which can be used to test the client classes.

Listing 18.6 `build.xml`

```
<project name="jaxrpc-clients" default="dynamic" basedir=".">

<!-- Adjust these for your installation -->
<property name="JAVA_XML_PACK_HOME"
   value="/home/myawn/webservices/java_xml_pack-spring-02-dev" />
<property name="JAXRPC_HOME"
   value="${JAVA_XML_PACK_HOME}/jaxrpc-1.0-ea2" />
<property name="JAXM_HOME"
   value="${JAVA_XML_PACK_HOME}/jaxm-1.0.1-ea2" />
<!-- CLASSPATH is set to where nfl is rooted -->
<property name="CLASSPATH"
   value="/home/myawn/webservices:
         ${JAXRPC_HOME}/lib/jaxrpc-api.jar:
         ${JAXRPC_HOME}/lib/jaxrpc-ri.jar:
         ${JAXM_HOME}/lib/jaxm-api.jar" />

<target name="xrpcc" >
   <!-- for windows platform, change extension to .bat -->
   <exec executable="${JAXRPC_HOME}/bin/xrpcc.sh"
              dir="../../..">
     <env key="JAVA_XML_PACK_HOME"
        value="${JAVA_XML_PACK_HOME}" />
     <env key="CLASSPATH" value="${CLASSPATH}" />
     <arg line="-client" />
     <!-- arg line="-keep" / -->
     <arg line="nfl/application/jaxrpc_clients/config.xml"/>
   </exec>
</target>

<target name="static" depends="xrpcc">
  <javac srcdir="." classpath="${CLASSPATH}" >
    <include name="StaticClient.java"/>
  </javac>
</target>
```

```
<target name="dynamic">
  <javac srcdir="." classpath="${CLASSPATH}" >
    <include name="DynamicClient.java"/>
  </javac>
</target>

<!-- shouldn't use any server-side artifacts! -->
<!-- do we really need to be packaging this? -->
<target name="package-static" depends="static">
  <jar jarfile="./static-client.jar">
    <fileset dir="../../..">
        <include name="nfl/application/jaxrpc_clients/*.class"/>
    </fileset>
  </jar>
</target>


<target name="clean">
  <delete includeEmptyDirs="true" quiet="true" >
    <fileset dir="." includes="*.class, *.war, *.jar"/>
  </delete>
</target>

</project>
```

18.4 Exercises

18.1 Re-implement dynamic client: Re-implement the `DynamicClient` using an implementation of JAX-RPC other than the reference implementation.

18.5 Further Reading

See the further reading links at the end of Chapter 16.

Enterprise
JavaBeans

In this final part, we'll look at the technology that is at the heart of J2EE: Enterprise Java-Beans (EJB). Web Services today are almost always constructed on top of servlets, although the Enterprise JavaBeans 2.1 standard (a part of the J2EE 1.4 specification) will make Enterprise JavaBeans a player in Web Services. But as of today, the primary uses for Enterprise Java-Beans are in the development of Web applications, so that is the model we'll examine.

CHAPTER 19

Session Beans

No discussion of J2EE can be complete without a look at Enterprise JavaBeans (EJBs). Enterprise JavaBeans are at the heart of J2EE, and I've heard many people use the terms interchangeably. For example, someone recently told me that he had "a pretty good understanding of servlets, but don't know anything about J2EE." That's quite a contradictory statement, given that servlets are a major component of J2EE. But the equivalence between EJB and J2EE is strong in many people's minds, perhaps unfortunately leading them to think that any "serious" enterprise application must be developed around EJB.

For this last part of the book, we'll be leaving Web Services behind and returning to more traditional Web applications. This is because the Web-Service technologies we've examined, such as JAXM and JAX-RPC, are currently focused on the servlet model of deployment. Work is underway, in particular through JSR-109, to define the deployment model for Web Services as Enterprise JavaBeans. When J2EE 1.4 is introduced, you can expect to see support for Web Services deployed as either servlets or as Enterprise JavaBeans. But for now, our introduction to EJBs must focus on Web applications.

Software Used in the EJB Chapters

The following software was used for developing and deploying the Enterprise Java-Bean examples in the next three chapters.

Enterprise JavaBeans

Version 2.0, as part of J2EE 1.3. Included as part of the two application servers (HP-AS and WebLogic) that were used in testing the examples.

HP Application Server (HP-AS)

Version 8.0. Downloaded from `http://www.hpmiddleware.com`.

HP RadPak

Version 1.0. Packaging and Deployment utility for Enterprise JavaBeans and other J2EE software components. Separately downloadable from the same site as HP-AS.

BEA WebLogic Application Server

Version 6.1. Evaluation copy downloaded from `http://www.bea.com`.

19.1 Introduction to Enterprise JavaBeans

If we were to move from a simple Java application, such as the one we began with in Chapter 2, and try to redesign it directly as an Enterprise JavaBean, the amount of new material we would have to absorb would probably seem overwhelming. Over the course of this book, however, we have introduced many of the changes needed to evolve our simple example application into an EJB. For example, we introduced the concept of a container in which application code is deployed beginning with servlets in Chapter 5. We introduced the separation of interface from implementation in Chapter 3, and specifically the use of remote interfaces in Chapter 15 (RMI). We've already made many of our classes `Serializable`, to facilitate moving them across the network, and we've been exposed to using deployment descriptors (`web.xml` files for servlets) to describe our application to the container in which it will be deployed. The Java Message Service (see Chapter 12) prepared us for a discussion of message-driven beans, and several of the APIs we've used (JAX-RPC, JAXB, and RMI) have included helper classes that are generated as part of the packaging and deployment of the application.

Even given this very good start, the final step from the application we've developed so far to an Enterprise JavaBean-based application is still a large one. The role of the container is greatly expanded compared to the Web containers within which we deployed our servlets and JSPs. The deployment descriptors for EJBs are far more complex than those we've used so far. The separation of interface from implementation was a small separation in all our previous examples—the connection between the interface and the class that implemented the interface was a simple one-to-one mapping of methods in the interface to methods in the implementing class. For EJBs, the connections will frequently be far less obvious.

The expanded role of the container deserves elaboration because the services provided by the container are the reason developers choose Enterprise JavaBeans over the simpler architectures we've already examined. An EJB container provides some of the services we've already seen—such as naming services through JNDI, and messaging services through JMS—but also additional services that may not be available in non-EJB containers. These include transaction management, life-cycle management, resource pooling, and security. If these capabilities are needed by your application, then an EJB implementation may be your best design choice. If you don't need these capabilities, an EJB implementation is almost certainly overkill for your requirements.

There are three types of Enterprise JavaBeans, and we'll take one type as the main topic of each of the next three chapters. In this chapter, we'll look at session beans, which perform operations on behalf of users (clients). In the next chapter, we'll look at message-driven beans, which are new in EJB 2.0. Message-driven beans allow Enterprise JavaBeans to be used with messaging providers such as JMS and, in the future, JAXM. Finally, we'll look at entity beans, which provide access to persistent data such as tables in a relational database.

19.1.1 Session Beans

Session beans can be thought of as the "process" beans, while entity beans are the "data" beans. Thought of another way, session beans are the verbs, and entity beans the nouns, of an application implementation. Within our example application, `Team` objects and `Game` objects are natural candidates for implementation as entity beans. The process of calculating the standings based on these data objects is a candidate for a session bean.

Within a shopping application (perhaps one of the most common examples used for introducing EJBs), the various items for sale are entity beans, and so is the customer data. But the shopping cart is a session bean—although it contains data, that data is there to facilitate the process of purchasing an item. The shopping cart is not itself a permanent entity; once the purchase is complete, the object will cease to exist.

These two examples illustrate the two subcategories of session beans: *stateless* and *stateful*. A stateless session bean contains no client-specific state. Our Standings application is a good example of this. Although the bean does have internal state—the standings will change as new data is received—this data is completely independent of the client. Therefore, a single instance of the bean can be reused over and over for requests coming from different clients. The shopping cart, on the other hand, is stateful—once a customer has put an item into the cart, the cart is then uniquely tied to that customer, and we really don't want to be sharing the cart with any other customers who are shopping at the same time.

Stateless session beans are more scaleable, because any instance of the bean can be used to handle any client request that comes in.

19.1.2 Message-Driven Beans

Both session beans and entity beans provide only synchronous access mechanisms, and therefore aren't suitable for many of the situations in which we'd like to use message-driven behavior. In EJB 2.0, a new message-driven bean (MDB) type was introduced specifically to provide a bean that could consume JMS messages. In EJB 2.1, message-driven beans will be further enhanced to provide support for JAXM messages as well. We'll look at message-driven beans in Chapter 20.

19.1.3 Entity Beans

Entity beans can be thought of as data beans, or database beans. They represent persistent data. There are two major subcategories of entity beans. Beans that use Bean-Managed Persistence (BMP) are responsible for their own persistence, typically through embedded JDBC code. Beans that use Container-Managed Persistence (CMP) instead delegate this responsibility to the container, which will manage the load and store of data for the bean at appropriate times in the bean's life cycle. Container-managed persistence was radically changed going from EJB 1.1 to EJB 2.0; in this book, we will examine only the EJB 2.0 CMP implementation. Entity beans will be covered in Chapter 21.

19.2 Creating a Session Bean for the Standings

Converting our `Standings` class to a session bean involves many of the same steps we went through in preparing the class to be accessed via RMI. This is no surprise, because Enterprise JavaBeans use RMI as the communication mechanism between the client and server portions, and even between beans running in the same container.

For RMI, we needed to create a remote interface to our class. With EJB, we will need to create two (and optionally, as many as four) interfaces. The first interface is the familiar remote interface, just as we created for RMI. The `Remote` interface describes the methods that are callable from the clients of the EJB, and like the RMI interface, each method in the interface must be declared to throw `java.rmi.RemoteException`. The second interface is the `Home` interface, which is a new concept in EJB. The `Home` interface contains life-cycle methods for the bean, such as `create()` to instantiate a bean, and `remove()` to remove a bean from the container.

Prior to EJB 2.0, these were the only interfaces supported or required. If two beans were deployed into the same EJB container, they would communicate with each other via the same remote interface exposed to non-local clients. Beginning with EJB 2.0, there are optional `Local` and `LocalHome` interfaces that can be used to define interfaces for use only by other beans that might be deployed with the target bean. A `Local` interface provides some optimization over the `Remote` interface; most notably, methods do not have to be declared to throw `RemoteException`. It is expected that accessing a bean through a `Local` interface can be a more lightweight call, although it is really up to the container provider to determine what, if any, optimizations will be done in the case of a local call.

Table 19.1 Components in the Session EJB Example

New Components			
Name	**Package**	**Class or Interface**	**Comment**
StandingsHome	nfl.application.ejb	Interface	The `Remote Home` interface
StandingsRemote	nfl.application.ejb	Interface	The `Remote` interface
StandingsLocalHome	nfl.application.ejb	Interface	The `LocalHome` interface
StandingsLocal	nfl.application.ejb	Interface	The `Local` interface
StandingsSessionBean	nfl.application.ejb	Class	The session bean
EJBClient	nfl.presentation	Class	A client

Existing Components	
Component	**Description**
layered.jar	All classes and interfaces of the layered version of the application (as presented in Chapter 2). Classes are actually included individually, rather than as part of the JAR file.
DynamicStandings	The interface and implementation of dynamic behavior for the `Standings` class.

In Listing 19.1, we show the first of the four interfaces for our `Standings` session bean: the `Home` interface. There is only one life-cycle method we need to provide, which is the `create()` method. The create method needs to be declared to throw both `java.rmi.RemoteException` and `javax.ejb.CreateException`.

At this point, let's talk about how EJB interfaces get mapped on to EJB implementations. Although we've only seen one of the four interfaces, we probably believe that we can tell something about the eventual bean class—namely, that it will implement `StandingsHome` and have the implementation for a method called `create()`. In fact, neither of these is true. The class that `implements StandingsHome` will actually be a class that is generated on our behalf by the container where we deploy the bean (or perhaps by a separate utility program provided by the container vendor). That generated class will take care of the implementation of the `create()` method. Our implementation class, rather than implementing `create()`, must instead implement a method called `ejbCreate()`, which will be invoked by the container-generated class after it has completed its work. The `ejbCreate()` method gives us a chance to do any initialization we might want to do at creation time, but it is not responsible for creating the EJB—the container is responsible for that, and for all other stages of the EJB's life cycle.

Listing 19.1 `StandingsHome` Interface

```
// StandingsHome.java

package nfl.application.ejb;

import javax.ejb.*;
import java.rmi.RemoteException;

public interface StandingsHome extends EJBHome {

    public StandingsRemote create() throws RemoteException,
                                            CreateException;

}
```

In Listing 19.2, we see the second of our four interfaces. Given the opportunity to separate our calls into those intended for use by clients, and those intended for use by other beans within our application, we find that there are really only a few methods we need to expose to the client. In fact, we really only need to expose the `getDivisionStandings()` and `getConference-Standings()` methods. When we get to the implementation of our EJB, we'll see that bean initialization is being handled automatically, and we are not depending on the client to call an `init()` method on the bean. However, because many earlier versions of the application depended on the client performing this initialization step, we decided to carry the method forward so that the EJB could be accessed from various clients we've developed along the way (although in each case, some modifications to the client would be required).

It is a requirement that the remote interface extends `javax.ejb.EJBObject`, and like the `Home` interface, methods must throw `RemoteException`.

Listing 19.2 `StandingsRemote` Interface

```
// StandingsRemote.java

package nfl.application.ejb;

import java.util.List;
import java.rmi.RemoteException;
import nfl.ObjectFactory;
import nfl.application.*;

public interface StandingsRemote extends javax.ejb.EJBObject
{
    public void loadData() throws RemoteException;
```

```
    public List getDivisionStandings(Division div)
                throws RemoteException;
    public List getConferenceStandings(Conference conf)
                throws RemoteException;
}
```

The interfaces that follow are not required, but can be added to any session or entity bean in EJB 2.0 and later. The StandingsLocalHome interface is shown in Listing 19.3. It provides the same single method call, create(), with two differences: The local variant returns a StandingsLocal, rather than a StandingsRemote, and the local variant does not include RemoteException in its throws clause. The interface extends EJBLocalHome rather than EJBHome as in the remote Home interface.

Listing 19.3 StandingsLocalHome Interface

```
// StandingsLocalHome.java

package nfl.application.ejb;

import javax.ejb.*;

public interface StandingsLocalHome extends EJBLocalHome {

    public StandingsLocal create() throws CreateException;
}
```

Our final interface, the StandingsLocal interface, is shown in Listing 19.4. This interface extends javax.ejb.EJBLocalObject, and contains a larger set of the functionality of the original Standings object. Note that we could have included the exact same set of methods in both the Local and Remote interfaces, if we had preferred to do so.

Listing 19.4 StandingsLocal Interface

```
// StandingsLocal.java

package nfl.application.ejb;

import java.util.List;
import nfl.ObjectFactory;
import nfl.application.*;

public interface StandingsLocal
                extends javax.ejb.EJBLocalObject
{
```

```
// Holds all teams
public Teams getTeams();
public void   setTeams(Teams t);

public List getTeamList();
public void setTeamList(List t);

// Holds all games
public Games getGames();
public void   setGames(Games g);

public List getGameList();
public void setGameList(List g);

public boolean getVerbose();
public void       setVerbose(boolean b)  ;

public boolean getPrintTimings();
public void       setPrintTimings(boolean b);

public int  findTeam(String name);
public void loadData();

public void postGameData(Game game);

public List getDivisionStandings(Division div);
public List getConferenceStandings(Conference conf);
}
```

In Listing 19.5, we finally reach the bean itself. The bean implements `javax.ejb.Ses-sionBean`, but none of the four interfaces declared for it. The business methods are there, and match the signatures given in the interfaces, but the connection is indirect, and will be made through a container-provided intermediary. There are a set of life-cycle methods that any session bean is required to implement: These are the `ejbCreate()`, `ejbRemove()`, `ejbActivate()`, `ejbPassivate()`, and `setSessionContext()` methods. These methods are notification or callback methods that will be invoked by the container at the corresponding points in the bean's life cycle. Many beans, like ours, won't need to take any action when these events happen, but they are nevertheless required to implement the methods.

If resources such as memory are tight in the server container, or an EJB is inactive, it might be passivated by the container. Passivating a bean frees resources for use by other beans; if the passivated bean needs to run again, the container is responsible for reactivating it. The container will be responsible for resources it has obtained on your behalf, but if your application code is holding other resources such as locks, you should release them in the `ejbPassivate()` callback method, and reacquire them in the `ejbActivate()` method.

The session bean has initialization code to set different values for the `nfl.VersionInfo` object. When the bean is deployed by itself, no setting is required. When deployed with the message-driven bean from Chapter 20, the `MDBVInfo` class should be used; and when deployed with both the message-driven bean and the entity bean from Chapter 21, the `EBVInfo` class should be used. It is necessary to modify the source of the bean and recompile to change the `Version-Info` variant being used in each case.

Listing 19.5 `StandingsSessionBean` Implementation

```
// StandingsSessionBean.java

package nfl.application.ejb;

import nfl.ObjectFactory;
import nfl.application.*;
import java.util.List;

import javax.ejb.SessionContext;

public class StandingsSessionBean
    implements javax.ejb.SessionBean {

   // SessionBean callback methods
   public void ejbCreate() {}
   public void ejbRemove() {}
   public void ejbActivate() {}
   public void ejbPassivate() {}
   public void setSessionContext(SessionContext cntx) {
      ObjectFactory o = ObjectFactory.getHandle();
      standings = (DynamicStandings)
            o.getInstance("DynamicStandings");
      standings.init();
   }

   private static DynamicStandings standings = null;

   // Waiting until setSessionContext or ejbCreate will
   // be too late to initialize ObjectFactory object
   static {
      java.util.Properties env = System.getProperties();
      // Use default version info when the session
      // bean is the only bean deployed.

      // Use the MDB version info when running with
      // message-driven bean
      env.put("nfl.versioninfo",
            "nfl.application.ejb.MDBVInfo");
```

```
        // Use the EB version info when running with all three beans
        env.put("nfl.versioninfo",
                "nfl.application.ejb.EBVInfo");

    }

    // Interface methods
    public Teams getTeams() {
        return standings.getTeams();
    }

    public void setTeams(Teams t) {
        standings.setTeams(t);
    }

    public List getTeamList() {
        return standings.getTeamList();
    }
    public void setTeamList(List t) {
        standings.setTeamList(t);
    }

    public Games getGames() {
        return standings.getGames();
    }

    public void setGames(Games g) {
        standings.setGames(g);
    }

    public List getGameList() {
        return standings.getGameList();
    }

    public void setGameList(List g) {
        standings.setGameList(g);
    }

    public boolean getVerbose() {
        return standings.getVerbose();
    }

    public void setVerbose(boolean b) {
        standings.setVerbose(b);
    }

    public boolean getPrintTimings() {
        return standings.getPrintTimings();
    }
```

```
public void setPrintTimings(boolean b) {
    standings.setPrintTimings(b);
}

public int findTeam(String name) {
    return standings.findTeam(name);
}

public void loadData() {
    standings.loadData();
}

public void postGameData(Game game) {
    standings.postGameData(game);
}

public List getDivisionStandings(Division div) {
    return standings.getDivisionStandings(div);
}

public List getConferenceStandings(Conference conf) {
    return standings.getConferenceStandings(conf);
}
}
```

Here's a quick checklist of requirements for implementing a session bean:

- The bean must implement the `javax.ejb.SessionBean` interface.
- The bean class must be defined `public`, and cannot be declared either `abstract` or `final`.
- The bean class must implement one or more `ejbCreate()` methods. Each `ejbCreate()` method should correspond to a `create()` method of the `Home` or `LocalHome` interface.
- The bean class must provide a public no-argument constructor.
- The bean class must not define a `finalize()` method.

Note that for the `ejbCreate()`/`create()` methods, the arguments passed to the `create()` method should match those received by `ejbCreate()`. However, the `create()` method will have a return type of either the `Remote` or `Local` interface (depending on which of the `Home` interfaces it is defined within), while `ejbCreate()` is defined to return `void`. This is because `ejbCreate()` doesn't actually create the object, but is merely given the opportunity to perform some initialization before it is returned to the caller.

19.3 Session Bean APIs

The APIs used by all of the Enterprise JavaBean classes are very simple and straightforward, consisting primarily of the life-cycle methods that EJBs are required to implement (even though the implementations will frequently be empty).

API 19.1 javax.ejb.**EnterpriseBean**

```
public interface EnterpriseBean
    // defines no methods; simply common base class for 3 EJB subclasses
```

API 19.2 javax.ejb.**SessionBean**

```
public interface SessionBean extends EnterpriseBean
    public void ejbActivate();
    public void ejbPassivate();
    public void ejbRemove();
    public void setSessionContext(SessionContext context);
```

19.4 Building, Deploying, and Running the Examples

Coding an EJB is only half the fun. Deploying it introduces several new concepts and complexities. We've already used JAR and WAR files; for EJBs, we introduce two new variations on the theme. An EJB-JAR file is a JAR file that contains one or more Enterprise JavaBeans. An EAR (Enterprise ARchive) file is a file that can contain multiple components, which are themselves archive files—so, an EAR might contain several EJB-JARs, plus a WAR file that contains the user interface (servlet and JSP) components of the application.

We'll begin by packaging our bean in an EJB-JAR file. Each EJB-JAR file requires a deployment descriptor. The deployment descriptor for an EJB-JAR file is named `ejb-jar.xml` (whereas WAR files had a `web.xml` file instead). The `ejb-jar.xml` for our session bean is shown in Listing 19.6. The first part of the file, the `<enterprise-beans>` element, could probably be largely deduced from the code we have written; it serves mainly to associate together the five files we have created (four interfaces plus the implementation). The second part of the file, the `<assembly-descriptor>`, represents a different approach for EJBs. Because EJBs are intended to be reusable components, efforts have been made to separate out the code of the bean from the attributes that describe how it will be used by a particular bean user. Security, for example, is one of those aspects to which different users will likely have very different approaches. If all of the security code was embedded within the bean, then the user would be forced to implement security in the way the bean's developer thought best. In the EJB model, the deployer of the bean, rather than the developer, gets to determine what methods will be generally accessible, and which will be restricted. In our sample deployment, we create two security roles—`<everyone>` and `<administrator>`—but have granted each full access to all methods. For a more realistic deployment, you can alter the `<everyone>` identity to have access to a more limited set of methods.

Another decision left up to the deployer is how the bean will participate in transactions. Our bean is set up to not participate (the `NotSupported` value is set for the `<trans-attribute>` element of all methods). There are six possible values for the transaction attribute; here are their meanings:

`Required`	Methods of the bean must be invoked as part of a transaction. If a transaction is not active when the method is called, the container will start a new transaction before invoking any method of the bean.
`RequiresNew`	A new transaction must be started before invoking the bean's methods. If a transaction is already active, the container will suspend that transaction and start a new transaction. After the method call completes, the previously active transaction will be resumed.
`Supports`	If a transaction is active when the bean's methods are called, the method executes as part of that transaction. If no transaction is active, no new transaction will be started.
`NotSupported`	The methods of the bean do not need transactional support. If a transaction is already active, it will be suspended for the duration of the execution of this bean's methods.
`Mandatory`	This indicates that a transaction must be active when the bean's methods are called. If no transaction is active, the container will throw a `TransactionRequiredException`.
`Never`	This indicates that a transaction must not be active when the bean's methods are called. If a transaction is active, the container will throw a `RemoteException`.

Listing 19.6 `ejb-jar.xml` File for Session Bean

```
<?xml version="1.0" encoding="UTF-8"?>

<!DOCTYPE ejb-jar PUBLIC
    "-//Sun Microsystems, Inc.//DTD Enterprise JavaBeans 2.0//EN"
    "http://java.sun.com/dtd/ejb-jar_2_0.dtd">

<ejb-jar>
  <enterprise-beans>
    <session>
      <description>
        The Standings session bean calculates NFL standings
      </description>
```

```xml
    <ejb-name>StandingsSessionBean</ejb-name>
    <home>nfl.application.ejb.StandingsHome</home>
    <remote>nfl.application.ejb.StandingsRemote</remote>
    <local-home>
        nfl.application.ejb.StandingsLocalHome
    </local-home>
    <local>nfl.application.ejb.StandingsLocal</local>
    <ejb-class>
        nfl.application.ejb.StandingsSessionBean
    </ejb-class>
    <session-type>Stateless</session-type>
    <transaction-type>Container</transaction-type>
    <ejb-ref>
        <!-- unused in first two deployments -->
        <ejb-ref-name>ejb/GameEntityBean</ejb-ref-name>
        <ejb-ref-type>Entity</ejb-ref-type>
        <home>nfl.application.ejb.GameHome</home>
        <remote>nfl.application.ejb.GameRemote</remote>
    </ejb-ref>
  </session>
</enterprise-beans>

<assembly-descriptor>
  <security-role>
    <description>Any user</description>
    <role-name>everyone</role-name>
  </security-role>
  <security-role>
    <description>The boss. The big cheese.</description>
    <role-name>administrator</role-name>
  </security-role>
  <method-permission>
    <role-name>everyone</role-name>
    <method>
      <ejb-name>StandingsSessionBean</ejb-name>
      <method-name>*</method-name>
    </method>
  </method-permission>
  <method-permission>
    <role-name>administrator</role-name>
    <method>
      <ejb-name>StandingsSessionBean</ejb-name>
      <method-name>*</method-name>
    </method>
  </method-permission>
  <container-transaction>
    <method>
      <ejb-name>StandingsSessionBean</ejb-name>
```

```
            <method-name>*</method-name>
          </method>
          <trans-attribute>NotSupported</trans-attribute>
        </container-transaction>
      </assembly-descriptor>

</ejb-jar>
```

Listing 19.7 shows a portion of the EJB buildfile. The single `build.xml` file in the `application/ejb` directory handles all three example beans (in this chapter and the two that follow); Listing 19.7 includes only the session bean targets.

Because we have three different beans built in the same directory, we have to do some file renaming to allow us to keep different versions of the deployment descriptors around. The `ejb-jar.xml` file for the session bean is named `sessionbean.xml` in the directory, and renamed to the proper name only when we build the session bean EJB-JAR file. The `ejb-jar.xml` file must be placed in the `META-INF` directory of the JAR. We are also including a WebLogic-specific file named `weblogic-ejb-jar.xml`; this file is also renamed, being kept as `weblogic-ejb-jar.session` when the build isn't looking.

Later on, we'll deploy our bean in an EAR file, and the code to build the EAR is also shown in this listing. An EAR has a deployment descriptor called `application.xml`; this file is also versioned based on which bean we are building, with the session bean version called `sessionapp.xml`. The build of the EAR file is straightforward, and Ant provides an `<ear>` task to simplify it. We simply specify the `application.xml` file and include the EJB-JAR for our bean, and the EAR is done.

Listing 19.7 `build.xml`

```
<project name="ejbs" default="entityear" basedir=".">

<property name="j2ee.home"
        value="/home/myawn/webservices" />
<property name="j2ee.jar"
        value="${j2ee.home}/j2ee.jar" />

<target name="compile-session">
    <javac srcdir=".." classpath="../../.." >
        <include name="DynamicStandings.java" />
        <include name="DynamicStandingsImpl.java" />
    </javac>
    <javac srcdir="." classpath="${j2ee.jar}:../../.." >
        <include name="StandingsRemote.java" />
        <include name="StandingsHome.java" />
        <include name="StandingsLocal.java" />
        <include name="StandingsLocalHome.java" />
        <include name="StandingsSessionBean.java" />
```

```
        </javac>
</target>

<target name="sessionbean" depends="compile-session">
    <copy file="sessionbean.xml"
        tofile="ejb-jar.xml" overwrite="yes" />
    <copy file="weblogic-ejb-jar.session"
        tofile="weblogic-ejb-jar.xml" overwrite="yes" />
    <jar jarfile="sessionbean.jar" >
        <metainf dir="."
            includes="ejb-jar.xml,
                      weblogic-ejb-jar.xml" />
        <zipfileset dir="../.." prefix="nfl">
            <include name="ObjectFactory.class" />
            <include name="VersionInfo.class" />
            <include name="LayeredVersionInfo.class" />
        </zipfileset>
        <zipfileset dir=".." prefix="nfl/application">
            <include name="*.class" />
        </zipfileset>
        <zipfileset dir="." prefix="nfl/application/ejb" >
            <include name="StandingsRemote.class" />
            <include name="StandingsHome.class" />
            <include name="StandingsLocal.class" />
            <include name="StandingsLocalHome.class" />
            <include name="StandingsSessionBean.class" />
            <!-- only used when deployed with MDB -->
            <include name="MDBVInfo.class" />
            <!-- only used when deployed with EntityBean -->
            <include name="EBVInfo.class" />
        </zipfileset>
        <zipfileset dir="../../persistence"
                prefix="nfl/persistence">
            <include name="*.class" />
        </zipfileset>
    </jar>
</target>

<target name="sessionear" depends="sessionbean" >
    <copy file="sessionapp.xml"
        tofile="application.xml" overwrite="yes" />
    <ear earfile="nflstandings.ear"
          appxml="application.xml">
        <fileset dir=".">
            <include name="sessionbean.jar" />
        </fileset>
    </ear>
</target>
```

The Ant buildfile will create an EJB-JAR file, but this EJB-JAR file is incomplete. In order for the bean to be successfully deployed, we must generate container-specific classes that implement the interfaces we have defined. Those generated classes will then invoke our bean class to perform the business methods we have written.

How this happens is container-specific, and can change even between releases of a particular container. The session bean example was deployed in both the HP Application Server (HP-AS) and the BEA WebLogic server. Each of these servers provided both command-line tools and graphical deployment tools. We'll cover the various deployment options here, but recommend you refer to the vendor documentation of whatever J2EE application server you are deploying into for full information about how to package and deploy EJBs in that server.

19.4.1 Deploying an EJB in HP-AS

HP recommends using the HP RadPak tool to package and deploy EJB-JAR or EAR files. If you prefer to use command-line tools, there are several options available. There is an `hpejbc` command-line utility program that generates the container-specific classes. Rather than having to invoke this by hand, there are also defined Ant tasks that you can use, including the `<j2eec>` task and the `<ejbjar>` task. To use these tasks, you'll need the Ant optional tasks bundle (downloadable from `jakarta.apache.org`) and also the Ant tasks bundle distributed with HP-AS.

Although I did experiment with these tools, I eventually decided that RadPak was a much easier way to go. I did two different deployments; in the first case, I had already built an EJB-JAR file using the Ant buildfile presented previously. In the second case, I let RadPak handle the entire packaging process.

Deployment Option 1: Deploying an Existing EJB-JAR File with HP Radpak 1.0

1. Run HP Radpak. On Windows, select Start → HP Middleware → HP RadPak → Start RadPak. (Optional: If you are behind a firewall, configure a proxy so that DTDs can be read successfully. Select File → Options, the Connections tab, and fill in values for the HTTP proxy and HTTP port.)
2. Open a new RadPak file browser (File → New Browser).
3. In the left-hand pane, navigate the directory tree to your EJB-JAR file (`session-bean.jar` in our example). (Optional, but recommended: Right-click on the EJB-JAR file and select J2EE Verifier. This will verify the EJB-JAR file is correct (has a valid deployment descriptor). On the dialog that pops up, just click Run Verification.)
4. Right-click on the EJB-JAR file and select Deploy to Server. At the warning about using default options, click OK. Next is a dialog with three options: generate and deploy, generate only, or deploy only. Choose the generate and deploy option. The necessary helper classes are generated and added to the EJB-JAR file, and then the EJB-JAR file is deployed. (Note: You need to have HP-AS running for this step.)

Deployment Option 2: Building and Deploying with HP RadPak 1.0

I'm normally resistant to the lure of point-and-drool interfaces, preferring to build things by hand. If it you can't do it in vi (insert your preferred editor), you don't understand it. I've always felt that the more a tool does for me—especially when it does it silently behind my back—the less I'll understand where to look when something invariably goes wrong.

In the process of building an EJB by hand, I ended up with an EJB-JAR file that failed to deploy. The failures looked different on HP-AS and BEA, but neither gave me a real feel for where the problem was. In talking with HP-AS support, they suspected that classes weren't being packaged properly, and convinced me to try building the entire project via HP RadPak.

Here's the process I followed to do so:

1. Start HP RadPak.
2. Select File → New from the menu. In the dialog box that appears, choose New EJB Project Wizard and click OK.
3. On the first screen of the wizard, simply click Next.
4. On the second screen, provide a project name and click Next. I called my project NFLSessionBean.
5. On the third screen, provide a directory path for the project. You'll have the option of copying source files into the hierarchy later, so it's probably best to just go with a new directory here rather than trying to map the project onto your existing directory structure. After clicking Next, respond OK to the dialog asking if it is OK to create a new directory.
6. The fourth screen will show the build of the directories; once it is complete (green check marks by each task), click Next to continue.
7. The fifth screen of the wizard gives side-by-side directory views. You can pick source directories from the left panel and copy them to the right panel. However, this can only be done for entire directories, not selected files. RadPak expects source directories separate from build (where the class files go) directories. To accommodate this, I created a stripped-down directory structure containing only .java source files, and only for the packages required by the EJB.[1] I then copied this slimmed-down directory into the project source tree.
8. On the sixth screen, any imported sources are compiled.
9. On the seventh screen, the wizard searches for EJBs. As expected, it found exactly one, in the application/ejb subdirectory. If there are multiple beans, you can select only some of them to be included in the deployment descriptor; by default, all beans are selected (checked). The multicolumn display includes columns for the names of the

---

1. What the EJB requires is the application directory and the application/ejb subdirectory (all other subdirectories under application can be removed); the persistence directory; and an empty presentation directory (no files are required, but if the directory itself is purged, the build will fail). Within each directory, only .java source files were retained; all .class, .jar, .war, and .xml files were removed.

Home, LocalHome, Remote, and Local interfaces. You can use the drop-down list to select from interfaces that are considered likely, based on their names, or just type in the name of the appropriate interface. Click Next to go to the completion screen, and then Finish to exit the wizard. A file browser opens showing the new EJB project.

10. In the file browser, right-click the EJB project (for example, NFLSessionBean) and select Build. This recompiles the sources and packages them in a JAR file.

11. When the compilation is completed, the resulting JAR is named `<projectname>/dist/lib/<projectname>-generic.jar`.

12. Select the JAR in the file browser and right-click it. Optionally, select the J2EE verifier option to verify the JAR file. Then, select the Deploy to Server option to generate the container-specific files and deploy the project to HP-AS.

19.4.2 Deploying an EJB in BEA WebLogic

WebLogic also provides both command-line utilities and the graphical administration console. For the command-line aficionados, you can create the container-specific classes using the ejbc utility, as follows:

```
java weblogic.ejbc \
c:\tmp\sessionbean.jar c:\tmp\wlssessionbean.jar
```

The resulting JAR file (`wlssessionbean.jar`) can then be deployed by copying it into the `applications` directory.

For those who prefer to use a graphical approach, the deployment of EJB-JAR files in WebLogic is thankfully nearly identical to deploying WAR files. The additional step of generating the container-specific files is hidden from the user; you can go through the same process of uploading a file, deploying it, and assigning it to server instances just as you did with the servlet WAR files.

While this step is simple, WebLogic does require that you supplement the standard deployment descriptor with a WebLogic-specific descriptor called `weblogic-ejb-jar.xml`. (HP-AS also has a container-specific descriptor, but it is not generally required if you aren't using any non-portable features. The WebLogic descriptor is always required.)

There are several things done in the WebLogic descriptor, shown in Listing 19.8:

- The EJB name (`StandingsSessionBean`) is equated to a JNDI name (also `StandingsSessionBean`) that will be used by clients to look up the bean. It is also associated with another JNDI name (`LocalStandingsEJB`) that will be used by other beans to access the local interface.

- Any other beans or resources referenced by this bean are also given JNDI names. We are defining the `GameEntityBean` here, because this bean needs to access it for the example in Chapter 21. The reference is unused until that time.

• We also implement security for the bean, mapping the role names from the generic deployment descriptor to specific user names known to WebLogic.

The association of JNDI names is required; other elements are optional.

Listing 19.8 `weblogic-ejb-jar.xml` for Session Bean

```xml
<?xml version="1.0"?>

<!DOCTYPE weblogic-ejb-jar PUBLIC
  "-//BEA Systems, Inc.//DTD WebLogic 6.0.0 EJB//EN"
  "http://www.bea.com/servers/wls600/dtd/weblogic-ejb-jar.dtd">

<weblogic-ejb-jar>
  <weblogic-enterprise-bean>
    <ejb-name>StandingsSessionBean</ejb-name>
    <!-- following only used in 3rd deployment -->
    <reference-descriptor>
      <ejb-reference-description>
        <ejb-ref-name>ejb/GameEntityBean</ejb-ref-name>
        <jndi-name>GameEntityBean</jndi-name>
      </ejb-reference-description>
    </reference-descriptor>
    <jndi-name>StandingsSessionBean</jndi-name>
    <local-jndi-name>LocalStandingsEJB</local-jndi-name>
  </weblogic-enterprise-bean>

  <security-role-assignment>
    <role-name>administrator</role-name>
    <principal-name>admin</principal-name>
  </security-role-assignment>

  <security-role-assignment>
    <role-name>everyone</role-name>
    <principal-name>guest</principal-name>
  </security-role-assignment>
</weblogic-ejb-jar>
```

19.4.3 Deploying via an Enterprise Archive (EAR) File

An EJB-JAR file can only contain Enterprise JavaBeans. Many times, in fact probably most times, an application that contains EJBs will also have Web components such as servlets and JSPs. An EAR file is an "archive of archives"; you can bundle EJB-JAR files containing EJBs and WAR files containing JSPs and servlets into a single file for easier distribution and deployment. Our EJB examples do not involve any Web components, but we'll show the use of EAR files as a way of bundling our separate EJB-JAR files together in a single unit.

Each EAR file has a deployment descriptor, which simply identifies the included components. Each included file is a `<module>`; the module can be of type `<ejb>` or `<web>`. Refer back to the `<sessionear>` task in the `build.xml` file (Listing 19.7) to see how the EAR file is built.

Listing 19.9 `application.xml` Deployment Descriptor for Session Bean

```xml
<?xml version="1.0" encoding="UTF-8"?>
<!DOCTYPE application PUBLIC
  "-//Sun Microsystems, Inc.//DTD J2EE Application 1.3//EN"
  "http://java.sun.com/dtd/application_1_3.dtd">

<application>
   <display-name>NFL Standings Application</display-name>

   <module>
      <ejb>sessionbean.jar</ejb>
   </module>

</application>
```

19.5 Developing an EJB Client

With the bean created and deployed, we need a client in order to test it. Normally, a sophisticated EJB component such as the one we've developed would deserve a nice, meaty client like a JSP/servlet combination. But to keep the code size simple and not introduce any extraneous features, we'll actually go back to our very first example client—the `Console` class—and modify it to work with our Enterprise JavaBean.

The main difference is in gaining access to the `Standings` EJB. In the original client, we obtained a reference from the `ObjectFactory`. For the EJB client, we instead need to look up the bean in the JNDI service.

When we've looked up objects previously in the JNDI or RMI registries, we've simply used the Java language cast to allow us to assign the resulting `Object` to an instance of our application-specific class. Because casting is not supported by all languages, CORBA provides a method, `PortableRemoteObject.narrow()`, to perform any necessary conversion of the object. Enterprise JavaBeans are designed to interoperate with CORBA objects, so the CORBA convention is followed when looking up EJBs.

The object returned to us is a container-generated class that implements the bean's `Home` interface. We then use the `create()` method defined in the `Home` interface to get an instance of the session bean. On this bean, we then make the business method calls such as `getConferenceStandings()` and `getDivisionStandings()`. These calls have to be wrapped in a `try/catch` block that catches `java.rmi.RemoteException`, since any `Remote` methods on a bean may throw this exception. (In the next two chapters, we'll use adapters to allow us to access EJBs without having to wrap our access in `try/catch` blocks.)

Listing 19.10 EJBClient

```
// EJBClient.java

package nfl.presentation.ejb;

import java.rmi.RemoteException;
import java.util.List;
import javax.ejb.*;
import javax.naming.*;
import javax.rmi.PortableRemoteObject;
import nfl.application.*;
import nfl.application.ejb.*;

/** Displays standings on the stdout device */
public class EJBClient extends nfl.presentation.Console
{
    public static void main(String[] args) {

        StandingsRemote standings = null;
        StandingsHome   sHome     = null;

        try {
            InitialContext context = new InitialContext();

            // Lookup by <ejb-name> specified in ejb-jar.xml
            // Although this name matches the implementation
            // class, what we actually get back is the
            // remote home interface
            Object obj =
                context.lookup("StandingsSessionBean");

            sHome = (StandingsHome)
                    PortableRemoteObject.narrow(obj,
                            StandingsHome.class);

            standings = sHome.create();
        } catch (Exception e) {
            // Possibilities here are NamingException from
            // lookup, ClassCastException from narrow, or
            // RemoteException from create
            e.printStackTrace();
            System.exit(0);
        }

        EJBClient client = new EJBClient();
```

```
        try {
            // non-EJB clients invoke loadData here. For
            // the EJB, we made it part of constructor

            // Loop through divisions
            List divList = Division.DIVISIONS;
            for (int i=0; i<divList.size(); i++) {
                Division d = (Division) divList.get(i);
                List    l = standings.getDivisionStandings(d);
                client.printDivisionStandings(d, l);
            }

            if (!client.getPrintConferenceStandings()) return;
            // Loop through conferences

            List confList = Conference.CONFERENCES;
            for (int i=0; i<confList.size(); i++) {
                Conference c = (Conference) confList.get(i);
                List l = standings.getConferenceStandings(c);
                client.printConferenceStandings(c, l);
            }
        } catch (RemoteException e) {
            e.printStackTrace();
        }
    }
}
```

In Listing 19.11, we see the buildfile for the EJBClient. Most of the space is taken up by setting up the required CLASSPATH settings for the compilation and execution of the examples. For testing, we provide two targets: <test-hp> and <test-bea>. The only difference is that each causes a vendor-specific version of the jndi.properties file to be used, thus setting the proper values for that vendor's implementation of JNDI.

Listing 19.11 build.xml for EJBClient

```
<project name="ejbclient" default="compile" basedir=".">

<!-- j2ee.jar has APIs, needed to compile -->
<property name="j2ee.jar"
          value="/home/myawn/webservices/j2ee.jar" />

<property name="j2ee-weblogic"
    value="/proj/jcs/bea/wls61/wlserver6.1/lib/weblogic.jar" />

<path id="j2ee-hp">
    <pathelement path="C:\hpmw\hpas\lib" />
```

```
        <pathelement location="c:\hpmw\hpas\lib\baseservices.jar" />
        <pathelement location="c:\hpmw\hpas\lib\orbservice.jar" />
        <pathelement location="c:\hpmw\hpas\lib\csf_tet_2_2_0_orbix.jar" />
        <pathelement location="c:\hpmw\hpas\lib\extendedservices.jar" />
        <pathelement location="c:\hpmw\hpas\lib\hpas.jar" />
        <pathelement location="c:\hpmw\hpas\lib\ejbservice.jar" />
        <pathelement location=
            "c:\hpmw\hpas\orbix\orbix_art\1.2\classes\58209_2.jar" />
        <pathelement location=
            "c:\hpmw\hpas\orbix\orbix_art\1.2\classes\omg.jar" />
        <pathelement location=
            "c:\hpmw\hpas\orbix\orbix_art\1.2\classes\orbix2000.jar" />
        <pathelement path=
            "c:\hpmw\hpas\orbix\orbix_art\1.2\localhost" />
        <pathelement path="c:\hpmw\hpas\orbix\etc" />
        <!-- not listed in HPAS developer guide, but required -->
        <pathelement location="c:\hpmw\hpas\lib\common.jar" />
        <pathelement location="c:\hpmw\hpas\lib\ext\ejb.jar" />
        <pathelement path="../../.." />
        <pathelement path="." />
    </path>

    <target name="compile">
        <javac srcdir="." includes="*.java"
            classpath="${j2ee.jar}:../../.." />
    </target>

    <target name="test-hp">
        <copy file="jndi.properties.hp"
            tofile="jndi.properties" overwrite="yes"/>
        <java classname="nfl.presentation.ejb.EJBClient"
            classpathref="j2ee-hp" fork="yes" />
    </target>

    <target name="test-bea">
        <copy file="jndi.properties.bea"
            tofile="jndi.properties" overwrite="yes"/>
        <java classname="nfl.presentation.ejb.EJBClient"
            classpath="../../..::.:${j2ee-weblogic}"
            fork="yes" />
    </target>

</project>
```

19.6 Exercises

19.1 Stateful session bean: Create a stateful session bean.

19.7 Further Reading

See references at the end of Chapter 21.

## CHAPTER 20

Message-Driven
Beans

Message-driven beans are not a big leap from where we have been before. In Chapter 12, "The Java Message Service," we introduced the JMS, and the idea of a message consumer that is activated by receipt of messages. Message-driven beans simply extend this capability to the EJB world, without changing very much else about the nature of the message consumer.

Where we will see a similarity to other EJB types is in the use of deployment descriptors, rather than embedded code, to configure aspects of our bean's behavior. With the earlier JMS examples, we coded directly into our classes the name of the Topic to which we wanted to connect. With the MDB, this will be configured as part of the deployment descriptor, giving greater flexibility to the deployer to configure the messaging system as needed without having to change and recompile code.

20.1 Writing a Message-Driven Bean

When we introduced JMS in Chapter 12, we made a version of the `Standings` class the recipient of the messages. Because we've already reworked the `Standings` class as a session bean, I decided to focus on the `Games` class for the message-driven bean example. The net effect is identical: Games can be added to the game list by either object, but the `Standings` object is always just passing these updates through to the `Games` object anyway, so having the `Games` object receive updates directly is actually a small optimization.

Our `GamesMessageBean` includes both familiar and unfamiliar pieces. What is familiar is the implementation of the `javax.jms.MessageListener` interface, and the inclusion of an `onMessage()` call that processes the messages we receive. What is different is the addition of the EJB life-cycle methods: `setMessageDrivenContext()`, `ejbCreate()`, and `ejbRemove()`.

There is also a familiar-yet-different access to the `InitialContext` to obtain a JNDI reference. In our original JMS example, we used JNDI to access the `TopicConnectionFactory`. With a message-driven bean, the container will be responsible for connecting us to the messaging provider, so we do not control this explicitly from code. Instead, we'll provide information in our deployment descriptor that helps guide the container to the right location.

What we are using JNDI for instead is to get a reference to another EJB. We mentioned in the previous chapter that when EJBs are deployed together, they communicate with each other via either `Local` (if present) or `Remote` interfaces. These interfaces ensure that even an intra-container call will be passed through the container's helper classes, so that such container services as transactions can be provided.

With Enterprise JavaBeans, there is a special naming context provided in JNDI to allow beans to find references to each other and to other container-managed resources. The context is the *Environment Naming Context (ENC)*. When looking up items in the ENC, a special URL format is used, which looks like:

```
java:comp/env/<subcontext>/<uniquename>
```

The `java:comp/env` portion of the URL identifies the ENC context, and is therefore constant. The next element is a subcontext, which is optional but highly recommended. The subcontext can identify the type of resource that is being sought. For example, a subcontext of `ejb` is used when looking up references to other EJBs; `jms` is used for looking up Java Message Service resources, and `jdbc` is used when looking up database resources. Finally, the last part of the URL identifies the specific resource we seek, such as a bean name or database name.

Our message-driven bean needs access to the `StandingsSessionBean`, so we obtain a reference to it by looking up the local home interface in the ENC, and then calling the `create()` method to obtain an instance of the standings bean. Because the container is responsible for bean life cycles, we don't know how many different instances of the `StandingsSession-Bean` might exist. We don't care, however; the Singleton property of our `Standings` object is still intact, because every `StandingsSessionBean` obtains a reference to the underlying `DynamicStandingsImpl` object via the `ObjectFactory`. There could be many instances of the `StandingsSessionBean`, but they would all have references to the single instance of `DynamicStandingsImpl`.

You might have noticed that although our enterprise beans look things up in the JNDI registry, we never seem to put anything there. Binding objects into the registry is another service the container handles for us. We need to provide information in the deployment descriptor that identifies any objects that we'll be accessing via the registry, but we don't write any actual code to perform the insertion.(See the `<ejb-local-ref>` element in Listing 20.2 for how we notify the container of our need to access the session bean.)

Recall that our messages are of type `ObjectMessage`, which means that each message contains a `Game` object that could, in many cases, just be passed directly into the `postGame-Data()` method of the `Standings` object. In fact, when this example was originally written,

Table 20.1   Components in the Message-Driven EJB Application

New Components			
Name	**Package**	**Class or Interface**	**Comment**
GamesMessageBean	nfl.application.ejb	Class	A message-driven bean.
Existing Components			
Component	**Description**		
layered.jar	All classes and interfaces of the layered version of the application (as presented in Chapter 2). Classes are actually included individually, rather than as part of the JAR file.		
StandingsSessionBean	Our message-driven bean is deployed alongside the session bean developed in the previous chapter.		

that was exactly the way the code worked. In the next chapter, however, we're going to introduce an entity bean to represent the Game objects in the application. Once we do that, we need to make sure any time we introduce a Game into the system, it is a GameEntityBean[1]; otherwise, the Game will not get properly persisted to the database. We don't really know what subclass of Game might be passed into us by the JMS middleware, and we don't know (although we could find out) what subclass of Game we've been directed to use by the VersionInfo class in this version of the application. The simplest and most flexible solution is to take whatever Game object we're passed, and use it to instantiate a new Game object via the ObjectFactory. As the application stands right now, we'll be creating an object that is identical to the one passed to us, and so the effort is somewhat wasted. But in the next chapter this will be key to making things work properly, and it also gives our class the flexibility to be reconfigured to operate with any other Game subclass simply by providing a different VersionInfo to the ObjectFactory.

Listing 20.1 GamesMessageBean

```
// GamesMessageBean.java

package nfl.application.ejb;

import nfl.ObjectFactory;
import nfl.application.Game;
```

---

1. It's actually a GameEJBAdapter, which is an adapter class for the GameEntityBean, but I'd rather not dive too deeply into the details at this point or there will be nothing left to discuss in Chapter 21.

```java
import java.io.Serializable;
import javax.ejb.CreateException;
import javax.ejb.MessageDrivenBean;
import javax.ejb.MessageDrivenContext;
import javax.jms.MessageListener;
import javax.jms.Message;
import javax.jms.ObjectMessage;
import javax.jms.JMSException;
import javax.naming.Context;
import javax.naming.InitialContext;
import javax.naming.NamingException;

public class GamesMessageBean
            implements MessageDrivenBean,
                       MessageListener,
                       Serializable {

   private MessageDrivenContext ourEjbContext;
   private Context              jndiContext;
   private StandingsLocalHome   standingsLH;
   private StandingsLocal       standings;
   private ObjectFactory        of;

   // EJB MessageDrivenBean methods

   // Called by the container to cause us to store
   // some info it wants us to hold
   public void setMessageDrivenContext(
               MessageDrivenContext mdc) {
      ourEjbContext = mdc;
      of = ObjectFactory.getHandle();
   }

   // Life-cycle methods
   public void ejbCreate() {
      try {
         // Get a handle to the JNDI context
         jndiContext = new InitialContext();
         // Lookup local interface to session bean
         standingsLH = (StandingsLocalHome)
            jndiContext.lookup(
               "java:comp/env/ejb/StandingsSessionBean");
         standings = standingsLH.create();
      } catch (NamingException e) {
         e.printStackTrace();
      } catch (CreateException e) {
         e.printStackTrace();
      }
```

```
   }
   public void ejbRemove() {
      ourEjbContext = null;
      jndiContext = null;
   }

   //JMS MessageListener methods
   public void onMessage(Message message) {
      try {
         ObjectMessage gameMsg = (ObjectMessage) message;
         Game game = (Game) gameMsg.getObject();

         // When using EntityBean, we want to use a
         // different Game implementation than the one
         // sent to us by JMS. To keep this code
         // flexible, we'll always create a new Game
         // via the ObjectFactory; in some cases it
         // will be identical to the one passed us.
         int week = game.getWeek();
         int[] score    = game.getScore();
         String home    = game.getHome();
         String visitor = game.getVisitor();
         Game newGame = (Game) of.getInstance("Game", week,
            visitor, score[0], home, score[1]);

         standings.postGameData(newGame);
      } catch (JMSException e) {
         e.printStackTrace();
      }
   }
}
```

20.2 Message-Driven Bean API Reference

API 20.1 javax.ejb.**MessageDrivenBean**

```
public interface MessageDrivenBean extends EnterpriseBean
    public void ejbRemove();
    public void setMessageDrivenContext(MessageDrivenContext context);
```

20.3 Building, Deploying, and Running the Message-Driven Bean Example

Like the session bean we saw previously, and the entity bean we'll examine next, the message-driven bean needs to be described via a deployment descriptor that is named `ejb-jar.xml`. We'll also once again need a WebLogic-specific deployment descriptor to further describe the bean.

The `ejb-jar.xml` file is shown in Listing 20.2. We provide an `<ejb-name>` and `<ejb-class>` as with the other bean types, but a message-driven bean has no interfaces so that part of the deployment descriptor is omitted.

We then have a number of MDB-specific configuration settings. The settings of `<acknowledge-mode>`, `<destination-type>`, and `<subscription-durability>` allow us to set values that in the non-EJB JMS implementation we provided as parameters to various method calls (for example, we set acknowledge-mode on the `createTopicSession()` call in our `JMSGameServer` example). Note that our MDB-related settings have been segregated to two places within the deployment descriptor. The settings we just saw are those that the application programmer would provide—by the very nature of the code, we expect to be connected to a Topic as a durable subscriber. The remaining settings, such as the topic name and what connection factory to use, are described further down in the file. These settings might be changed by the person deploying the bean or administering the J2EE application server.

Roughly the second half of the deployment descriptor is made up of reference entries. This is where we make connections between our EJB and other EJBs or services provided by the container. We have four different types of references in this particular descriptor.

1. An `<ejb-ref>` is used to reference another EJB that we are deployed alongside. In EJB 1.1, all references to other beans were done this way. In EJB 2.0 and later, we also have the ability to use `<ejb-local-refs>`, and access other beans through their `Local`, rather than `Remote`, interfaces. We have an `<ejb-ref>` that refers to the `GameEntityBean`. When we first deploy this bean, this reference will be unused. When we redeploy this bean in Chapter 21 along with the `GameEntityBean`, this reference allows us to find the other bean. (If the `GameEntityBean` provided a `Local` interface, it would be preferable to use it. Because it does not, we use the `Remote` interface.)

2. An `<ejb-local-ref>` is provided for the `StandingsSessionBean`.

3. A `<resource-ref>` is provided for the JMS `TopicConnectionFactory`.

4. A `<resource-env-ref>` is provided for the specific topic to which we want to connect. This element is used to refer to a specific administered resource (the NFL Game Results topic, not just any instance of Topic) whereas the `<resource-ref>` reference can be satisfied by connecting us to any `TopicConnectionFactory`.

Listing 20.2 `ejb-jar.xml` for Message-Driven Bean

```xml
<?xml version="1.0" encoding="UTF-8"?>

<!DOCTYPE ejb-jar PUBLIC
   "-//Sun Microsystems, Inc.//DTD Enterprise JavaBeans 2.0//EN"
   "http://java.sun.com/dtd/ejb-jar_2_0.dtd">

<ejb-jar>
  <enterprise-beans>
    <message-driven>
      <ejb-name>GamesMessageBean</ejb-name>
      <ejb-class>
         nfl.application.ejb.GamesMessageBean
      </ejb-class>
      <transaction-type>Container</transaction-type>
      <!-- optional message-selector omitted -->
      <acknowledge-mode>Auto-acknowledge</acknowledge-mode>
      <message-driven-destination>
        <destination-type>
           javax.jms.Topic
        </destination-type>
        <subscription-durability>
           Durable
        </subscription-durability>
      </message-driven-destination>
      <ejb-ref>
         <!-- used only when deployed with entitybean -->
         <ejb-ref-name>ejb/GameEntityBean</ejb-ref-name>
         <ejb-ref-type>Entity</ejb-ref-type>
         <home>nfl.application.ejb.GameHome</home>
         <remote>nfl.application.ejb.GameRemote</remote>
      </ejb-ref>
      <ejb-local-ref>
         <ejb-ref-name>
            ejb/StandingsSessionBean
         </ejb-ref-name>
         <ejb-ref-type>Session</ejb-ref-type>
         <local-home>
            nfl.application.ejb.StandingsLocalHome
         </local-home>
         <local>nfl.application.ejb.StandingsLocal</local>
      </ejb-local-ref>
      <!-- optional security-identity omitted -->
      <resource-ref>
        <res-ref-name>jms/TopicFactory</res-ref-name>
        <res-type>
           javax.jms.TopicConnectionFactory
```

```
            </res-type>
            <res-auth>Container</res-auth>
        </resource-ref>
        <resource-env-ref>
            <resource-env-ref-name>
                NFL Game Results
            </resource-env-ref-name>
            <resource-env-ref-type>
                javax.jms.Topic
            </resource-env-ref-type>
        </resource-env-ref>
    </message-driven>
  </enterprise-beans>
</ejb-jar>
```

In the WebLogic deployment descriptor, we're given the opportunity—no, actually we're required—to go through every named resource and specify for it a JNDI name. This creates a real opportunity for confusion. The more different names you assign to what is essentially the same resource, the greater the likelihood that somewhere along the way something will fail to match up correctly and your application will fail to deploy. I would have much preferred a design where assigning JNDI names was optional, and if not specified they would have the same value as the EJB name. This would have made most of our beans deployable in WebLogic without any WebLogic-specific descriptors.

Listing 20.3 `weblogic-ejb-jar.xml` for Message-Driven Bean

```
<?xml version="1.0"?>

<!DOCTYPE weblogic-ejb-jar PUBLIC
    "-//BEA Systems, Inc.//DTD WebLogic 6.0.0 EJB//EN"
    "http://www.bea.com/servers/wls600/dtd/weblogic-ejb-jar.dtd">

<weblogic-ejb-jar>
  <weblogic-enterprise-bean>
    <ejb-name>StandingsSessionBean</ejb-name>
    <jndi-name>StandingsSessionBean</jndi-name>
    <local-jndi-name>LocalStandingsEJB</local-jndi-name>
  </weblogic-enterprise-bean>

  <weblogic-enterprise-bean>
    <ejb-name>GamesMessageBean</ejb-name>
    <message-driven-descriptor>
        <destination-jndi-name>
            NFL Game Results
        </destination-jndi-name>
    </message-driven-descriptor>
```

```
        <reference-descriptor>
            <resource-description>
                <res-ref-name>jms/TopicFactory</res-ref-name>
                <jndi-name>jms/TopicFactory</jndi-name>
            </resource-description>
            <resource-env-description>
                <res-env-ref-name>
                    NFL Game Results
                </res-env-ref-name>
                <jndi-name>NFL Game Results</jndi-name>
            </resource-env-description>
            <ejb-reference-description>
                <!-- used only when deployed with entitybean -->
                <ejb-ref-name>ejb/GameEntityBean</ejb-ref-name>
                <jndi-name>GameEntityBean</jndi-name>
            </ejb-reference-description>
            <ejb-local-reference-description>
                <ejb-ref-name>
                    ejb/StandingsSessionBean
                </ejb-ref-name>
                <jndi-name>LocalStandingsEJB</jndi-name>
            </ejb-local-reference-description>
        </reference-descriptor>
    </weblogic-enterprise-bean>

    <security-role-assignment>
        <role-name>administrator</role-name>
        <principal-name>admin</principal-name>
    </security-role-assignment>

    <security-role-assignment>
        <role-name>everyone</role-name>
        <principal-name>guest</principal-name>
    </security-role-assignment>
</weblogic-ejb-jar>
```

With the deployment descriptors created, we can now create and package our bean. There is only the single source file for the bean, plus a `VersionInfo` subclass that is used to deploy the message-driven bean along with the session bean. We also have a `<messageear>` target that creates an EAR file with the two beans we've developed so far.

Listing 20.4 `build.xml` (Fragment)

```
<target name="compile-message" depends="compile-session">
   <javac srcdir="." classpath="${j2ee.jar}:../../.." >
      <include name="GamesMessageBean.java" />
      <include name="MDBVInfo.java" />
   </javac>
</target>

<target name="messagebean" depends="compile-message">
   <copy file="messagebean.xml"
      tofile="ejb-jar.xml" overwrite="yes" />
   <copy file="weblogic-ejb-jar.message"
      tofile="weblogic-ejb-jar.xml" overwrite="yes" />
   <jar jarfile="messagebean.jar">
      <metainf dir="." includes="ejb-jar.xml,
                     weblogic-ejb-jar.xml" />
      <zipfileset dir="." prefix="nfl/application/ejb" >
         <include name="GamesMessageBean.class" />
      </zipfileset>
   </jar>
</target>

<target name="messageear"
      depends="sessionbean,messagebean" >
   <copy file="messageapp.xml"
      tofile="application.xml" overwrite="yes" />
   <ear earfile="nflstandings.ear"
         appxml="application.xml">
      <fileset dir=".">
         <include name="sessionbean.jar" />
         <include name="messagebean.jar" />
      </fileset>
   </ear>
</target>
```

The EAR file target requires an updated version of the `application.xml` file, which is shown in Listing 20.5.

Listing 20.5 `application.xml` for Message-Driven Bean

```xml
<?xml version="1.0" encoding="UTF-8"?>
<!DOCTYPE application PUBLIC
    "-//Sun Microsystems, Inc.//DTD J2EE Application 1.3//EN"
    "http://java.sun.com/dtd/application_1_3.dtd">

<application>
    <display-name>NFL Standings Application</display-name>

    <module>
        <ejb>sessionbean.jar</ejb>
    </module>
    <module>
        <ejb>messagebean.jar</ejb>
    </module>

</application>
```

20.4 Exercises

20.1 JAXM and message-driven beans: When EJB 2.1 becomes available, modify the `GamesMessageBean` to handle JAXM messages, and modify the `JAXMGameServer` to scnd a message to an MDB.

20.5 Further Reading

See references at the end of Chapter 21.

## CHAPTER 21

Entity Beans

Our final topic in the book is the use of entity beans. Entity EJBs represent persistent data, which most commonly resides in an SQL database that will be accessed via JDBC. This is not a requirement by any means—the data could reside in any file structure the developer chooses—but most EJB container providers provide tools and utilities that greatly simplify the use of the most common data sources, while supporting something more esoteric is left completely to the developer.

In our example application, we have two candidates for making entity beans; the `Team` class and the `Game` class. We don't dynamically create new teams during the year, and although the data for a team changes, the changes do not really need to be persisted—as long as we have access to the game data, we can always recreate the `Team` state at any point during the season. Games, on the other hand, are created as the application runs, and in the dynamic versions of the application, the creation of new `Game` objects drives the application processing. For this reason, we've chosen to use the `Game` object as our example for creating an entity bean.

21.1 Bean-Managed versus Container-Managed Persistence

There are two options in handling persistence for an entity bean. With bean-managed persistence (BMP), the bean developer is responsible for writing all of the code needed to handle the bean's persistence. This means, for example, that when an `ejbCreate()` operation is invoked, the bean developer will write the code to do a JDBC table insert (if a JDBC data source is being used), and likewise the code to do a delete operation if the `remove()` operation is invoked.

With container-managed persistence (CMP), the developer leaves it to the container to handle the persistence of the bean. CMP is thus easier for the developer to write, although the deployment descriptor becomes more complex with the need to map bean fields onto database columns. In earlier versions of J2EE, many developers believed that well-written BMP code could outperform CMP. This is no longer the case; especially in the EJB 2.0 model, the container has much more information about what objects are being actively accessed, and can implement caching, pre-fetching, and synchronization strategies that an individual entity bean, with a much more limited view of the environment in which it operates, could not possibly accomplish.

CMP was significantly changed between the EJB 1.1 (J2EE 1.2) and EJB 2.0 (J2EE 1.3) releases; we'll only cover the newer EJB 2.0 CMP syntax and behavior. Our examples won't cover bean-managed persistence at all; if you are familiar with JDBC programming, then implementing bean-managed persistence will be straightforward. But even if you are an experienced JDBC programmer, CMP is the recommended approach unless you have specific requirements for persistence behavior that can't be handled by CMP.

21.2 Writing an Entity Bean

Session beans introduced the idea that the interface was actually implemented in a generated code layer, rather than in our implementation class. But we could draw a direct line from each interface method to our implementing method. In entity beans, the relationships become fuzzier; we're relying on the container more than in any other architecture we've seen.

Table 21.1   Components in the Entity EJB Application

New Components			
Name	**Package**	**Class or Interface**	**Comment**
GameHome	nfl.application.ejb	Interface	The `Remote Home` interface.
GameRemote	nfl.application.ejb	Interface	The `Remote` interface.
GameEntityBean	nfl.application.ejb	Interface	The bean implementation.
GamePK	nfl.application.ejb	Interface	Primary key for the entity bean.
GameEJBAdapter	nfl.application.ejb	Class	An adapter class that implements Game and forwards calls to the `GameEntityBean`.
EJBGameDataImpl	nfl.presentation	Class	An implementation of `Game-Data` that loads persistent `Game` data.

Table 21.1 Components in the Entity EJB Application (Continued)

Existing Components	
Component	**Description**
layered.jar	All classes and interfaces of the layered version of the application (as presented in Chapter 2). Classes are actually included individually, rather than as part of the JAR file.
DynamicStandings	The interface and implementation of dynamic behavior for the `Standings` class.
StandingsSessionBean	The session bean developed in Chapter 19.
GamesMessageBean	The message-driven bean developed in Chapter 20.

Like our session bean, we can have up to four interfaces for our entity bean. In this case, just to reduce the amount of code, only the remote interfaces are being provided. The `EJBHome` interface is shown in Listing 21.1. The two required methods are `create()` and `findByPrimaryKey()`. We've given the `create()` method the same signature as we used in the other implementations of the `Game` class. Entity beans can have a number of finder methods, which are used to return individual beans or collections of beans. One such method is required—the `findByPrimaryKey()` method. Any others are optional. We've chosen to implement just one other, the `findAll()` method, which returns a `Collection` of all `Games` in the database. We've listed as comments several other finder methods that we could implement, if we wanted the `Games` class to delegate the responsibility of finding various subsets of the game list to our bean.

All entity beans are required to designate a primary key, and the primary key is required to be unique. There is no field within our `Game` object that is unique. This gives us two alternatives: We can create a compound key, or we can create an id-type key (for example, just use a sequence number that we increment each time a new bean is created). I've chosen to use a compound key: The combination of home team and week number will give us a unique key. (The visiting team name would have worked just as well; it's an arbitrary choice.) In order to use a compound key, we must create a class for it. We'll call the class `GamePK` (for Game Primary Key), and will come to it later (in Listing 21.4). I mention it here just because it is shown in the method signature for `findByPrimaryKey()`.

Listing 21.1 `GameHome.java`

```
// GameHome.java

package nfl.application.ejb;

import java.rmi.RemoteException;
import java.util.Collection;
import javax.ejb.EJBHome;
import javax.ejb.CreateException;
import javax.ejb.FinderException;

public interface GameHome extends EJBHome {

    public GameRemote create(int week, String home,
            int hscore, String visitor, int vscore)
        throws CreateException, RemoteException;

    public GameRemote findByPrimaryKey(GamePK key)
        throws FinderException, RemoteException;

    public Collection findAll()
        throws FinderException, RemoteException;

/* method ideas for future implementation. These
 * would need to throw FinderException, RemoteException
 *
 * -- Helper methods for use by the Games class --
 * public GameRemote findGame(int week, String team);
 * public Collection getAllGamesFor(String team);
 * public Collection getDivisionGamesFor(String team);
 * public Collection getConferenceGamesFor(String team);
 * public Collection getGamesBetween(String team1,
                                      String team2);
 * public Collection getCommonGamesFor(String team1,
 *                                     String team2);
 */
}
```

Listing 21.2 shows the `Remote` interface for the `Game` entity bean. This consists primarily of the same methods that are exposed by the `Game` interface itself. Not all SQL databases support array types; in particular, the Cloudscape database I used for deploying this example in WebLogic didn't allow me to create an array for the score. To make the transition transparent, the `GameRemote` interface supports access to the score as either an array of integers or as two separate integer fields. As we progress through the other classes and interfaces, we'll see where each style of access is being used.

Listing 21.2 GameRemote.java

```java
// GameRemote.java

package nfl.application.ejb;

import nfl.application.Game;
import java.rmi.RemoteException;
import javax.ejb.EJBObject;

public interface GameRemote extends EJBObject {

    public String getHome() throws RemoteException;
    // part of primary key, setter not allowed

    public String getVisitor() throws RemoteException;
    public void setVisitor(String visitor)
                            throws RemoteException;

    // Score methods from Game interface
    public int[] getScore() throws RemoteException;
    public void setScore(int[] score)
                            throws RemoteException;
    public void setScore(int vscore, int hscore)
                            throws RemoteException;

    // New score methods, used only by Adapter class
    public void setHScore(int h) throws RemoteException;
    public void setVScore(int v) throws RemoteException;
    public int getHScore() throws RemoteException;
    public int getVScore() throws RemoteException;

    public int getWeek() throws RemoteException;
    // part of primary key, setter not allowed
}
```

Now we get to the implementation of the bean, which is the GameEntityBean class shown in Listing 21.3. GameEntityBean is an abstract class, and all of the property accessor methods are declared abstract. This seems an unusual design at first, until you understand the reason. If a CMP entity bean were defined with properties, rather than with accessor methods for the properties, a developer might not resist the temptation to just access a property directly, rather than via its accessors. And once a developer does this, the container can no longer guarantee the integrity of the data. If a developer updates a data field directly, the container does not know the value has been changed, and may not persist the change to the database. Even read access is unsafe; other beans may have changed the data value, and any attempt to read a value from the bean should trigger a check to see whether the cached value is the most current.

The entity bean has a larger set of life-cycle methods than the beans we've looked at so far: they are `ejbCreate()`, `ejbPostCreate()`, `setEntityContext()`, `unsetEntityContext()`, `ejbActivate()`, `ejbPassivate()`, `ejbLoad()`, `ejbStore()` and `ejbRemove()`. We only need an implementation for one of these, the `ejbCreate()` method. We use the parameters passed in to set the bean's properties. Note that our implementation is not responsible for creating or setting any values of the `GamePK` primary key field; the container manages this for us.

Given the very application-specific signature of the `ejbCreate()` method, it stands to reason that we aren't overriding a method in `EntityBean` that has this particular calling sequence. While all the other life-cycle methods are explicitly declared in the `EntityBean` interface, there is no `ejbCreate()` call defined, allowing developers the freedom to use whatever parameters and return types are required by the application. There could be multiple `ejbCreate()` methods defined, just as a class can have multiple constructors; they just need to match up with `create()` methods defined in the `Home` (and/or `LocalHome`) interface.

Listing 21.3 GameEntityBean.java

```
// GameEntityBean.java

package nfl.application.ejb;

import nfl.application.Game;

import java.rmi.RemoteException;
import javax.ejb.EntityBean;
import javax.ejb.EntityContext;

public abstract class GameEntityBean
               implements EntityBean {

   // Life-cycle methods from EntityBean
   public GamePK ejbCreate(int week, String visitor,
      int vscore, String home, int hscore)
                     throws RemoteException {
      setWeek(week);
      setVisitor(visitor);
      setHome(home);
      setVScore(vscore);
      setHScore(hscore);
      // BMP returns instance; CMP returns null
      return null;
   }

   public void ejbPostCreate(int week, String visitor,
      int vscore, String home, int hscore) {}
```

```
public void setEntityContext(EntityContext context) {}
public void unsetEntityContext() {}
public void ejbActivate() {}
public void ejbPassivate() {}
public void ejbLoad() {}
public void ejbStore() {}
public void ejbRemove() {}

public abstract String getHome() throws RemoteException;
public abstract void setHome(String home)
   throws RemoteException;

public abstract void setVisitor(String home)
   throws RemoteException;
public abstract String getVisitor()
   throws RemoteException;

public abstract int getWeek() throws RemoteException;
public abstract void setWeek(int week)
   throws RemoteException;

// These are the score methods that are needed
// to set up CMP in a manner that maps cleanly
// to the underlying database
public abstract void setHScore(int h)
                  throws RemoteException;
public abstract void setVScore(int v)
                  throws RemoteException;
public abstract int getHScore()
                  throws RemoteException;
public abstract int getVScore()
                  throws RemoteException;

public int[] getScore()
              throws RemoteException {
   return new int[] {
      getVScore(), getHScore() };
}

public void setScore(int v, int h)
              throws RemoteException {
   setVScore(v);
   setHScore(h);
}
```

```
public void setScore(int[] score)
              throws RemoteException {
   setVScore(score[0]);
   setHScore(score[1]);
}
}
```

The last bit of code for our entity bean is the primary key class. The primary key class needs to implement `Serializable`, and have properties (including accessor methods) for each element of the compound key. The class is required to provide a no-argument constructor, and should implement `equals()` and `hashCode()`. There are common idioms for implementing both of these methods, which have been followed in the code shown in Listing 21.4.

For the `hashCode()` method, we create a hash code by combining (via an exclusive OR) the hash codes of each field that comprises the key. For the `equals()` method, we first check for identity (with `==`), to shortcut the more expensive comparisons where possible. Then we check whether the classes of the objects match, and whether each of the attributes of the objects are identical.

Listing 21.4 GamePK.java

```
// GamePK.java

package nfl.application.ejb;

import java.io.Serializable;

// Primary Key field for Game entity bean
public final class GamePK implements Serializable {

   public String home;
   public int    week;

   // No-arg constructor required for CMP beans
   public GamePK() {}

   public GamePK(int week, String home) {
      this.week = week;
      this.home = home;
   }

   private int hashcode = -1;

   public int hashCode() {
      if (hashcode == -1)
         hashcode = home.hashCode() ^ week;
```

```
        return hashcode;
    }

    public boolean equals(Object o) {
        if (o == this)
            return true;
        if (! (o instanceof GamePK))
            return false;
        GamePK obj = (GamePK) o;
        if (this.hashcode == obj.hashcode &&
            this.week == obj.week &&
            this.home.equals(obj.home))
            return true;
        return false;
    }

}
```

21.3 Entity Bean API Reference

API 21.1 javax.ejb.**EntityBean**

```
public interface EntityBean extends EnterpriseBean
    public void ejbActivate();
    public void ejbLoad();
    public void ejbPassivate();
    public void ejbRemove();
    public void ejbStore();
    public void setEntityContext(EntityContext context);
    public void unsetEntityContext();
```

21.4 Building and Deploying the Entity Bean

The compilation and packaging of the bean doesn't introduce anything new. Listing 21.5 shows excerpts from the `nfl/application/ejb/build.xml` file that build the targets related to our entity bean. There is one more WebLogic-specific file we now have to include in the `META-INF` directory of our EJB-JAR; we'll look at that in detail shortly.

Listing 21.5 `build.xml`

```
<target name="compile-entity">
    <javac srcdir="." classpath="${j2ee.jar}:../../.." >
        <include name="GameHome.java" />
        <include name="GameRemote.java" />
        <include name="GameEntityBean.java" />
```

```
            <include name="GamePK.java" />
            <include name="EBVInfo.java" />
            <include name="GameEJBAdapter.java" />
        </javac>
        <javac srcdir="../../persistence"
                        classpath="${j2ee.jar}:../../.." >
            <include name="EJBGameDataImpl.java" />
        </javac>
    </target>

    <target name="entitybean" depends="compile-entity">
        <copy file="entitybean.xml"
            tofile="ejb-jar.xml" overwrite="yes" />
        <copy file="weblogic-ejb-jar.entity"
            tofile="weblogic-ejb-jar.xml" overwrite="yes" />
        <jar jarfile="entitybean.jar">
            <metainf dir-"." includes="ejb-jar.xml,
                weblogic-ejb-jar.xml,weblogic-cmp-rdbms-jar.xml"/>
            <zipfileset dir="." prefix="nfl/application/ejb" >
                <include name="GameEntityBean.class" />
                <include name="GameHome.class" />
                <include name="GameRemote.class" />
                <include name="GamePK.class" />
                <include name="GameEJBAdapter.class" />
            </zipfileset>
            <zipfileset dir="../../persistence"
                    prefix="nfl/persistence" >
                <include name="EJBGameDataImpl.class" />
            </zipfileset>
        </jar>
    </target>

    <target name="entityear"
        depends="sessionbean,messagebean,entitybean" >
        <copy file="entityapp.xml"
            tofile="application.xml" overwrite="yes" />
        <ear earfile="nflstandings.ear"
            appxml="application.xml">
            <fileset dir=".">
                <include name="sessionbean.jar" />
                <include name="messagebean.jar" />
                <include name="entitybean.jar" />
            </fileset>
        </ear>
    </target>
```

Listing 21.6 is the `ejb-jar.xml` file for our entity bean. The declaration of the bean's name, class, and interfaces is just the same as it was for a session bean. Then, we get into attributes that are specific to entity beans, mostly relating to container-managed persistence.

We indicate a `<persistence-type>` of `Container`; the alternative would be `Bean` for bean-managed persistence. We then declare that the primary key for the bean will be of class `GamePK`, and the bean is not reentrant. Because CMP changed radically between EJB 1.1 and EJB 2.0, we have to indicate which flavor we are using by specifying a `<cmp-version>` attribute of either `2.x` (which we use) or `1.x`.

We also provide an `<abstract-schema-name>` for this bean, choosing the name `GameCMPBean`. This is used in the EJB Query Language (EJB QL) to allow queries to be performed against beans of this type. An example query is shown at the bottom of the deployment descriptor, but we won't be covering it until later in the chapter.

Next, we define the data fields (or columns, if you're thinking from the relational side) of our entity bean. Each `<cmp-field>` defines a single data element that is managed. We're only providing `<field-names>`; you could also provide an optional `<description>` for each field. The `<field-name>` values must match the names of accessor methods provided in the bean's interface, when each field name has its initial character upshifted and the prefix `get` or `set` added.

If our primary key for this bean were a single field within the bean, rather than a compound key, we would need to have a `<primkey-field>` element next, and the `<prim-key-class>` declared earlier would need to specify the type of the named field.

If our entity bean referred to any other beans or resources, then we would declare resource references at this point in the deployment descriptor. Our entity bean is the target of such references for both the session and message-driven beans developed earlier, but does not itself reference any other resources, so this can be omitted.

Finally, we have a `<query>` element. The query name matches the name of a finder method declared in the bean's `Home` (or `LocalHome`) interface. The finder method has no implementation in the bean class itself; the container will use the information provided here in the deployment descriptor to generate the implementation code for the method. There is a section on finder methods later in this chapter.

Listing 21.6 `ejb-jar.xml` for Entity Bean

```
<?xml version="1.0"?>

<!DOCTYPE ejb-jar PUBLIC
  "-//Sun Microsystems, Inc.//DTD Enterprise JavaBeans 2.0//EN"
  "http://java.sun.com/dtd/ejb-jar_2_0.dtd">

<ejb-jar>
  <enterprise-beans>
```

```
<entity>
  <description>
    The Game entity bean represents a game
  </description>
  <ejb-name>GameEntityBean</ejb-name>
  <home>nfl.application.ejb.GameHome</home>
  <remote>nfl.application.ejb.GameRemote</remote>
  <!-- could also have local, local-home interfaces -->
  <ejb-class>
      nfl.application.ejb.GameEntityBean
  </ejb-class>
  <persistence-type>Container</persistence-type>
  <prim-key-class>
      nfl.application.ejb.GamePK
  </prim-key-class>
  <reentrant>False</reentrant>
  <cmp-version>2.x</cmp-version>
  <abstract-schema-name>
      GameCMPBean
  </abstract-schema-name>
  <cmp-field><field-name>home</field-name></cmp-field>
  <cmp-field>
      <field-name>visitor</field-name>
  </cmp-field>
  <cmp-field><field-name>week</field-name></cmp-field>
  <cmp-field><field-name>vScore</field-name></cmp-field>
  <cmp-field><field-name>hScore</field-name></cmp-field>
  <!-- primkey-field here when CMP & not compound -->
  <query>
      <description>Return all games</description>
      <query-method>
        <method-name>findAll</method-name>
        <method-params><!-- none --></method-params>
      </query-method>
      <ejb-ql>
        SELECT OBJECT(g) FROM GameCMPBean AS g
      </ejb-ql>
  </query>
  </entity>
  </enterprise-beans>
</ejb-jar>
```

If this bean is being deployed in WebLogic, two additional deployment descriptor files are required. The first is a `weblogic-ejb-jar.xml` file similar to those provided with our session and message-driven beans. The other is unique to CMP entity beans.

The first and last elements, the `<ejb-name>` and `<jndi-name>`, are the same elements used in all bean types. In between, we have the `<entity-descriptor>`, which is unique to entity beans. WebLogic is designed to provide a pluggable CMP implementation, so that it is possible to substitute another vendor's CMP implementation (for example, a specific database provider) in place of the default. The deployment descriptor in Listing 21.7 is set to use the WebLogic-provided CMP; there are no application-specific fields, so any application using WebLogic's CMP implementation would use exactly these values. If you are using another vendor's CMP, that vendor should provide documentation of the required settings.

Listing 21.7 `weblogic-ejb-jar.xml` for Entity Bean

```
<?xml version="1.0"?>

<!DOCTYPE weblogic-ejb-jar PUBLIC
  "-//BEA Systems, Inc.//DTD WebLogic 6.0.0 EJB//EN"
  "http://www.bea.com/servers/wls600/dtd/weblogic-ejb-jar.dtd">

<weblogic-ejb-jar>
  <weblogic-enterprise-bean>
     <ejb-name>GameEntityBean</ejb-name>
     <entity-descriptor>
        <persistence>
           <persistence-type>
              <type-identifier>
                 WebLogic_CMP_RDBMS
              </type-identifier>
              <type-version>6.0</type-version>
              <type-storage>
                 META-INF/weblogic-cmp-rdbms-jar.xml
              </type-storage>
           </persistence-type>
           <persistence-use>
              <type-identifier>
                 WebLogic_CMP_RDBMS
              </type-identifier>
              <type-version>6.0</type-version>
           </persistence-use>
        </persistence>
     </entity-descriptor>
     <jndi-name>GameEntityBean</jndi-name>
  </weblogic-enterprise-bean>

  <security-role-assignment>
    <role-name>administrator</role-name>
    <principal-name>admin</principal-name>
  </security-role-assignment>
```

```
<security-role-assignment>
  <role-name>everyone</role-name>
  <principal-name>guest</principal-name>
</security-role-assignment>
</weblogic-ejb-jar>
```

The next file, in Listing 21.8, provides the specific configuration details for the WebLogic CMP we selected as our CMP provider. For the given `<ejb-name>`, we provide a `<data-source-name>` (the database), a `<table-name>` within the database, and then `<field-map>` entries for each database column.

Listing 21.8 `weblogic-cmp-rdbms-jar.xml` for Entity Bean

```
<?xml version="1.0"?>

<!DOCTYPE weblogic-rdbms-jar PUBLIC
  "-//BEA Systems, Inc.//DTD WebLogic 6.0.0 EJB RDBMS Persistence//EN"
  "http://www.bea.com/servers/wls600/dtd/weblogic-rdbms20-persistence-
600.dtd">

<weblogic-rdbms-jar>
  <weblogic-rdbms-bean>
    <ejb-name>GameEntityBean</ejb-name>
    <data-source-name>nfldb</data-source-name>
    <table-name>games</table-name>
    <field-map>
      <cmp-field>home</cmp-field>
      <dbms-column>home</dbms-column>
    </field-map>
    <field-map>
      <cmp-field>visitor</cmp-field>
      <dbms-column>visitor</dbms-column>
    </field-map>
    <field-map>
      <cmp-field>week</cmp-field>
      <dbms-column>week</dbms-column>
    </field-map>
    <field-map>
      <cmp-field>vScore</cmp-field>
      <dbms-column>vscore</dbms-column>
    </field-map>
    <field-map>
      <cmp-field>hScore</cmp-field>
      <dbms-column>hscore</dbms-column>
    </field-map>
  </weblogic-rdbms-bean>
```

```
<create-default-dbms-tables>
    True
</create-default-dbms-tables>
</weblogic-rdbms-jar>
```

Our final server-side, in Listing, 21.9, shows the `application.xml` deployment descriptor used to create an EAR file with all three of our beans.

Listing 21.9 `application.xml` for Entity Bean

```
<?xml version="1.0" encoding="UTF-8"?>

<!DOCTYPE application PUBLIC
 "-//Sun Microsystems, Inc.//DTD J2EE Application 1.3//EN"
 "http://java.sun.com/dtd/application_1_3.dtd">

<application>
    <display-name>NFL Standings EJB</display-name>
    <module>
        <ejb>sessionbean.jar</ejb>
    </module>
    <module>
        <ejb>messagebean.jar</ejb>
    </module>
    <module>
        <ejb>entitybean.jar</ejb>
    </module>
</application>
```

21.5 Bean Relationships

An added wrinkle to container-managed persistence is the idea of container-managed relationships (CMR). Because we are modeling only a single entity bean, there aren't any relationships to be considered. If we were to convert other classes to entity beans, however, it would then be necessary to describe how these entity beans are related to one another. Relationships may be characterized as one-to-one, one-to-many, many-to-one, or many-to-many; they can also be further categorized as unidirectional or bi-directional.

For example, if we were to create a `Team` entity bean, then we would want to describe the relationship between the `Team` and `Game` objects using CMR. What is being described is a physical relationship—what data fields in a table can be used as key values to access another table—and not logical relationships. An example can help clarify the distinction.

If we think about the relationship between the `Team` and `Game` objects, it can logically be thought of as a many-to-many, bi-directional relationship: A `Team` plays in many `Games`; each `Game` involves more than one `Team`. But if we examine our classes, the physically implemented direction of the relationship is only one way: The `Game` includes the `Team` names that can be used to directly access the appropriate teams, but the `Team` objects have no field that is a reference to any `Game` object. Also, because relationships are attached to a particular field, we do not have a one-to-many relationship wherein a `Game` involves two teams, but rather two separate one-to-one relationships: The `home` property references one `Team` object, and the `visitor` property references one `Team` object.

In order for the relationship to be `Many`, we would instead have needed to implement the two `Teams` as a `Collection` type. Given this, our calculated fields of Division and Conference standings participate in one-to-many relationships with the `Teams`. For example, the standings for each division are represented as a `List`; each element in the list references a specific `Team`.

If we created `Conference` and `Division` entity beans, these would likely be modeled as many-to-one, unidirectional. Several `Team` instances have fields that reference back to a particular `Conference` or `Division`, but there is no reference within the `Conference` and `Division` objects to provide access to the set of `Teams` that belong. (We've coded helper methods in our `Teams` container class that allows us to obtain such a list, but in order for the relationship to exist in the CMR sense there must be a property field that provides the linkage.)

We are creating only one bean in our examples, and therefore don't have any "live" code example showing CMR. When CMR is implemented, it is specified entirely in the deployment descriptor; there is no code provided by the bean developer. Here's a brief example of how the relationship between our `Game` entity bean and a theoretical `Team` entity bean could be modeled:

```
<ejb-jar>
   <enterprise-beans>
      <entity>
         <ejb-name>GameEntityBean</ejb-name>
         ...
      </entity>
      <entity>
         <ejb-name>TeamEntityBean</ejb-name>
         ...
      </entity>
   </enterprise-beans>

   <relationships>
      <ejb-relation>
         <ejb-relationship-name>
            Game-HomeTeam
         </ejb-relationship-name>
         <ejb-relationship-role>
            <ejb-relationship-role-name>
               Game-has-a-home-Team
            </ejb-relationship-role-name>
            <multiplicity>One</multiplicity>
            <relationship-role-source>
               GameEntityBean
```

```
            </relationship-role-source>
            <cmr-field>
               <cmr-field-name>home</cmr-field-name>
            </cmr-field>
         </ejb-relationship-role>
            <ejb-relationship-role-name>
               Team-hosts-Game
            </ejb-relationship-role-name>
            <multiplicity>One</multiplicity>
            <relationship-role-source>
               TeamEntityBean
            </relationship-role-source>
            <!-- no cmr-field, since unidirectional.
                 You can't get there from here. -->
         <ejb-relationship-role>
         </ejb-relationship-role>
      </ejb-relation>
      <!-- also needs a Game-VisitingTeam relationship -->
   </relationships>
</ejb-jar>
```

Whenever you define a CMR relationship, there will always be exactly two `<ejb-rela-tionship-role>` entities contained within it. The `<multiplicity>` element, required in both halves of the relationship, and the `<cmr-field>`, which will occur in one side for unidirectional relationships and in both sides for bi-directional relationships, serve to determine the type of the relationship.

21.6 Finder Methods and the EJB Query Language

Entity beans are required to provide at least a `findByPrimaryKey()` method, and may include additional finder methods as well. If you are using bean-managed persistence, then it is the responsibility of the bean developer to code the implementation of these methods. Like the life-cycle methods, the implementation will be prefixed by `ejb`—so if our `GameEntityBean` used BMP, we would be responsible for implementing `ejbFindByPrimaryKey()` and `ejbFind-All()` methods for it.

With container-managed persistence, the container will generate these methods. We've already given the container enough information to generate the `findByPrimaryKey()` method. For any additional finder methods, we have to give the container some idea of what set of objects we want returned when the method is called. We do this by writing statements in the EJB Query Language (EJB-QL).

There are also select methods that can be defined much like finder methods. The difference is that where a finder will return an object or collection of objects, the select method can return just fields (either an individual field or a `Collection` of fields) from an object. Select methods are not exposed via the bean's interfaces; they are for the internal use of the bean's business methods. It is always the responsibility of the bean developer to implement select methods; the container doesn't do these for you even in a CMP entity bean. We won't provide any further coverage of select methods, but you should be aware that the capability exists, in case your application has a need for it.

We've implemented only one query so far, the `findAll` query. This was introduced in Listing 21.6, but we'll reproduce just the query here for convenience:

```
SELECT OBJECT(g) FROM GameCMPBean AS g
```

An EJB-QL query consists of a `SELECT` clause, a `FROM` clause, and an optional `WHERE` clause. The `SELECT` clause identifies what we are to return; the `FROM` clause identifies where it comes from; and the `WHERE` clause filters the results based on various conditions. Because there is no `WHERE` clause in the example query, we will essentially select all elements identified in the `FROM` clause. The `FROM` clause identifies the `GameCMPBean` abstract schema, which is the persistent representation of our `GameEntityBean` objects, so we select all beans of this type. The word `AS` is optional, so we could have written "`FROM GameCMPBean g`" as an alternative. EJB-QL requires the use of the `OBJECT` keyword when used with a standalone identifier; this would not be required if we were returning just a field (for example, `SELECT g.score`). But finder methods can only return objects, not fields, so we must use it here.

This is the only query method implemented in our example. More complete coverage of EJB-QL can be found in the J2EE tutorial or the EJB reference books listed at the end of the chapter. To give just a little better flavor of EJB-QL, I've dummied up a few possible queries below, but these have not actually been implemented or tested.

A finder method `findTeamsInConference(Conference conf)` would, given our hypothetical `TeamEntityBean`, return those `Team` beans that belong to the specified conference. The `?1` will be replaced by the first parameter passed into the finder method.

```
SELECT OBJECT(t) FROM TeamCMPBean t
    WHERE t.conference = ?1
```

Another finder method `getAllGamesFor(String team)` could be used on our `Game` bean to find all games in which the specified `Team` was a participant. Because the team may be either the home or the visiting team in the game, we must check both possibilities in the `WHERE` clause.

```
SELECT OBJECT(g) FROM GameCMPBean g
WHERE g.home = ?1 OR
    g.visitor = ?1
```

Also, finder methods can navigate from one table to another, if the tables are associated via CMR relationships. For example, we'd like to implement a finder method corresponding to the `getDivisionGamesFor(String team)` method in the `Games` interface. In order to do this, we must take the team names found in the GAMES table, and look up those teams in the TEAMS table in order to retrieve their division. Such a query could be implemented as:

```
SELECT OBJECT(g) FROM GameCMPBean g
    WHERE (g.home = ?1 OR g.visitor = ?1)
      AND (g.home.division = g.visitor.division)
```

This finds games for which one of the opponents matches the team name passed as a parameter, and where both the home and visiting teams have the same division.

21.7 Creating the Database

In order to run our examples, there has to be a database matching the description provided in the preceding deployment descriptors. Our database schema is very simple, containing only a single table (GAMES) with five fields. The score array from our Game class has been split into two separate fields, because not all databases handle array types. This change has already been reflected in the interface and implementation code for our entity bean.

Listing 21.10 shows the Data Description Language (DDL) schema for an SQL implementation of our database.

Listing 21.10 entitybean.ddl

```
drop table GAMES;
create table GAMES (
   HOME     varchar(30),
   VISITOR varchar(30),
   WEEK     integer,
   VSCORE   integer,
   HSCORE   integer
);
```

WebLogic provides a Schema utility that can be used to build the database from the DDL file. You can also use vendor-specific database tools for this purpose. The command format for the Schema utility is:

```
java utils.Schema <url> <driver> [options] <sql file>
```

To construct our database using the Cloudscape database included with WebLogic, this would result in the following command sequence:

```
cd $WLS_HOME/config/mydomain
setEnv.sh
cd $WLS_HOME/samples/eval/cloudscape/data
java utils.Schema jdbc:cloudscape:nfldb\;create=true \
   COM.cloudscape.core.JDBCDriver \
   -verbose entitybean.ddl
```

The first two lines are simply to set up our environment (in particular, it gets the `weblogic.jar` file on our `CLASSPATH`). You could do this manually if you prefer. On the invocation of the Schema utility, the backslash before `;create` is not part of the URL, but is required in UNIX shells to escape the semicolon that would otherwise be a command separator. By changing into the Cloudscape data directory before executing the command, we create a database in the default location. If we wanted the database elsewhere, or wanted to refer to an existing database rather than build a new one, we could expand the URL reference to include a path to the database, as in any of the following:

```
jdbc:cloudscape:/home/myawn/nfldb
jdbc:cloudscape:C:/j2ee/nfldb
jdbc:cloudscape:../../nfldb
```

21.8 Deploying An Entity Bean in BEA WLS 6.1

After the database is created, we must make sure that the application server can find both the database and the JDBC driver software needed to access it. The first step we must take in enabling the database is to place the database software on the application server classpath. To accomplish this, we modified the `startWebLogic.sh` script file and added the following to the end of the `CLASSPATH` variable:

```
$WL_HOME/samples/eval/cloudscape/lib/cloudscape.jar
```

If you're using a different database or application server, you'll need to alter the `CLASSPATH` as appropriate for your situation. For Cloudscape, we also need to pass an environment variable to the Java Virtual Machine (JVM). Find the invocation of Java in the `startWebLogic.sh` script file, and add the following:

```
-Dcloudscape.system.home=./samples/eval/cloudscape/data
```

Next, we need to make the database available as a resource to the application server. This can be done through the administration console. We start by configuring a JDBC connection pool with the appropriate database driver. Connection pools help improve the performance of JDBC applications because establishing JDBC connections can be very expensive, and clients frequently only use a connection for a single query. Therefore, rather than create a JDBC connection each time a client accesses a database, we create a pool of connections that can be used to satisfy client requests.

Expand the node Services/JDBC, and select the Connection Pools item. In the right-hand panel, click on the link to Configure a New JDBC Connection Pool. You can give the pool any name you like; I kept the default value of MyJDBC Connection Pool. The remaining fields will depend on the database software you are using. For Cloudscape, the URL was the same value passed to the Schema creation utility (minus the `;create` option), `jdbc:cloudscape:nfldb`. For the Driver Classname, `COM.cloudscape.core.JDBCDriver` is the required value. All other fields can be left blank; click the Create button to create the connection pool. Now click on the Deployment tab to deploy the pool. Select the server on which the pool should be deployed (for example, myserver) in the left-hand (available) box, and click the right-facing arrow to move it into the right-hand (selected) box. Then click Apply to complete the deployment.

Next, we need to create a JDBC data source. Expand the node Services/JDBC, and select the Data Sources item. In the right-hand panel, select Configure a New JDBC Data Source. I again went with the default name, in this case MyJDBC Data Source. I provided a value for the JNDI Name of `nfldb`; this is how clients and other beans will refer to the data source. For the Pool Name, enter the name of the connection pool just configured (MyJDBC Connection Pool). All other fields can be left at default settings; click Create to create the data source. Deploy the data source in the same way the connection pool was deployed.

21.9 Using the Entity Bean

With the entity bean completed and deployed, we need to figure out how to get our application to use it. We can't just change our `VersionInfo` object to tell the `ObjectFactory` to create `GameEntityBean` objects every time we want a new `Game` for two reasons. One is that we've changed the interface, by adding `throws RemoteException` to every method, in a fashion that makes our class incompatible as a subclass for `Game`. Secondly, the container is responsible for the life cycle of EJBs, so even if we didn't have the first problem, we cannot create new EJBs simply by calling `new GameEntityBean()`—we must instead look up the home interface, and call the `create()` method it provides.

The solution to both of these problems is the creation of a new Adapter object, which we'll call `GameEJBAdapter`. The class is shown in Listing 21.11. The `GameEJBAdapter` implements the `Game` interface, and for each method in the interface calls the corresponding method on the entity bean and handles any resulting `RemoteException`. There are several interesting details in the `GameEJBAdapter` class.

It is a rule of entity beans that the primary key cannot be changed once a bean is created. Recall that we are using a compound primary key made up of the home team and week number. Our original `Game` interface provided set methods for both of these fields, even though they are never called within the application. Our `GameEJBAdapter` class must implement these calls in order to satisfy the requirements of the `Game` interface, but they have been coded to return an error if invoked. The `UnsupportedOperationException` was chosen because it is a runtime (or unchecked) exception. Using an unchecked exception means that we do not have to add a `throws` clause to our method signature, which would violate the interface.

There are two constructors included in the Adapter. (Actually three, but the no-argument constructor will just return an error if invoked.) The first is the constructor we would expect—one that has the same method signature as the `BasicGameImpl` class, and thus makes our Adapter a simple drop-in replacement for the existing implementation. The second constructor takes as an argument an instance of the `GameEntityBean` class. The need for this constructor will be revealed when we examine the next listing.

Listing 21.11 GameEJBAdapter

```
// GameEJBAdapter.java

package nfl.application.ejb;

import nfl.application.*;
import java.rmi.RemoteException;
import javax.ejb.CreateException;
import javax.naming.Context;
import javax.naming.InitialContext;
import javax.naming.NamingException;

/** Wraps a GameEntityBean so that it can function as a Game
  */
public class GameEJBAdapter implements Game {

    private GameRemote gameEJB;
    private static GameHome    gameHome = null;
    private static Context     jndiContext;

    // Methods of Game interface
    public String getHome() {
        try {
            return gameEJB.getHome();
        } catch (RemoteException e) {
            e.printStackTrace();
            return null;
        }
    }
    public void setHome(String home) {
        throw new UnsupportedOperationException (
          "Home is part of primary key, cannot set!");
    }

    public String getVisitor() {
        try {
            return gameEJB.getVisitor();
        } catch (RemoteException e) {
            e.printStackTrace();
            return null;
        }
    }
    public void setVisitor(String visitor) {
        try {
            gameEJB.setVisitor(visitor);
        } catch (RemoteException e) {
            e.printStackTrace();
        }
```

```
   }

   public int[] getScore() {
      try {
         return gameEJB.getScore();
      } catch (RemoteException e) {
         e.printStackTrace();
         return null;
      }
   }
   public void setScore(int v, int h) {
      try {
         gameEJB.setScore(v, h);
      } catch (RemoteException e) {
         e.printStackTrace();
      }
   }

   public void setWeek(int week) {
      throw new UnsupportedOperationException (
         "week is part of primary key, cannot set!");
   }

   public int getWeek() {
      try {
         return gameEJB.getWeek();
      } catch (RemoteException e) {
         e.printStackTrace();
         return -1;
      }
   }


   //Constructors
   public GameEJBAdapter() {
      throw new UnsupportedOperationException(
         "didn't expect call to Game no-arg constructor");
   }

   // This constructor is called to re-create adapters
   // to wrap beans as they are loaded from database
   public GameEJBAdapter(GameRemote bean) {
      gameEJB = bean;
   }

   public GameEJBAdapter(int week, String home, int hscore,
                         String visitor, int vscore)  {
      if (gameHome == null) {
         try {
            Context jndiContext = new InitialContext();
```

```
        gameHome = (GameHome) jndiContext.lookup(
            "java:comp/env/ejb/GameEntityBean");
    } catch (NamingException e) {
        e.printStackTrace();
    }
}
try {
    gameEJB = gameHome.create(week, home, hscore,
                                 visitor, vscore);
    } catch (CreateException e) {
        e.printStackTrace();
    } catch (RemoteException e) {
        e.printStackTrace();
    }
}
}
```

Because entity beans are all about implementing persistence, it should come as no surprise that we'll need to replace the class that has been handling persistence for Game objects in earlier versions of the application. The BasicGameDataImpl class simply had hard-coded data for all of the games, which it used to construct a List of game results. Now we need an implementation that instead accesses the entity beans, which handle their own persistence.

We'll follow the same basic design model as BasicGameDataImpl: The class is implemented as a singleton, and when the single instance is instantiated, it reads all available Game results and builds a List of the objects. This List is then available to clients (the Games class) via the getGameList() method.

The only change between BasicGameDataImpl and EJBGameDataImpl is the constructor. In the following constructor, we use JNDI to obtain a reference to the GameEntityBean Home method, and then call the finder method which we added to the Home interface specifically for this purpose: the findAll() method. The lookup via JNDI uses the Environment Naming Context (ENC) syntax, which means that we must have defined the bean we're looking for in our deployment descriptor. Since the GameData classes are accessed from Standings, it is the deployment descriptor for the StandingsSessionBean that needs to have a reference to the GameEntity-Bean; if you refer back to Listing 19.6, you'll see that there is indeed such a reference.

A similar reference is also needed for the GamesMessageBean. Each time a message is received by the MDB, it instantiates a new Game class with the received message. When the MDB was deployed only with the Standings bean, the VersionInfo file caused a Basic-GameImpl object to be used for this purpose. But once we deploy all three beans together, the VersionInfo file we provide will cause a GameEJBAdapter to be used instead. This requires that the GamesMessageBean be able to find the GameEntityBean home interface in the JNDI registry. If you refer back to Listing 20.2, you'll see that we've provided for this by including a reference that was unused in previous deployments, but now comes into play.

The Collection returned by findAll() must be expressed as a List, because that is what we'll be returning to any users of the class. But there's another step we must perform.

When data was persisted to the database, only the GameEntityBean objects were stored. Recall that we had wrapped each GameEntityBean with a GameEJBAdapter so that the bean could provide the interface defined by the Game interface. We need to recreate these Adapters. So we iterate over the collection, wrapping each GameEntityBean with a GameEJBAdapter. This is done by invoking the constructor of the GameEJBAdapter which takes a GameEntityBean argument (see Listing 21.11).

Listing 21.12 EJBGameDataImpl

```
// EJBGameDataImpl.java

package nfl.persistence;

import nfl.application.ejb.GameHome;
import nfl.application.ejb.GameRemote;
import nfl.application.ejb.GameEJBAdapter;

import java.rmi.RemoteException;
import java.util.ArrayList;
import java.util.Collection;
import java.util.List;
import javax.ejb.FinderException;
import javax.naming.Context;
import javax.naming.InitialContext;
import javax.naming.NamingException;

public class EJBGameDataImpl implements GameData {

    // Make class a Singleton
    private static GameData gamedata = new EJBGameDataImpl();
    public static GameData getHandle() { return gamedata; }

    private List gameList = new ArrayList();

    // The only method of the GameData interface
    public  List getGameList() { return gameList; }

    // private Constructor
    private EJBGameDataImpl() {
        try {
            Context jndiContext = new InitialContext();
            GameHome gameHome = (GameHome) jndiContext.lookup(
                "java:comp/env/ejb/GameEntityBean");
            Collection c = gameHome.findAll();
            java.util.Iterator i = c.iterator();
            while (i.hasNext()) {
```

```
      gameList.add(new GameEJBAdapter(
                            (GameRemote)i.next()));
    }
  } catch (NamingException e) {
      e.printStackTrace();
  } catch (FinderException e) {
      e.printStackTrace();
  } catch (RemoteException e) {
      e.printStackTrace();
  }
 }
}
```

When all three beans are deployed, the same `EJBClient` program developed for the session bean example can be used for testing. You'll need to modify the client so that the `EBVInfo` class is passed to the `ObjectFactory`, which will cause the appropriate adapter classes to be used. These adapters will then find the appropriate EJBs via the JNDI registry.

21.10 Exercises

21.1 Local interfaces: Add `Local` and `LocalHome` interfaces to the `GameEntity-Bean`. Update deployment descriptors accordingly, and have the other beans (`Standings-SessionBean` and `GamesMessageBean`) utilize the `Local`, rather than `Remote`, interfaces.

21.2 Team entity bean: Create a `Team` entity bean. This provides an opportunity to work through every aspect of creating and deploying an entity bean. You should use CMR to define the relationships between the `Game` and `Team` beans.

21.3 Bean-managed persistence: Make a version of the `GameEntityBean` (or the `TeamEntityBean`, if you did Exercise 21.2) that uses BMP.

21.4 Finder methods and EJB-QL: Implement the various finder methods listed as comments in the `GameEntityBean` Home interface. Each will require implementation via EJB-QL. For extra credit, create an implementation of the `Games` class that uses these queries rather than its own sequential searches of the game list.

21.11 Further Reading

Richard Monson-Haefel's *Enterprise JavaBeans* and Girdley/Woollen/Emerson's *J2EE Applications and BEA WebLogic Server* are both good introductory-level EJB texts that will go beyond the brief introduction provided in the last three chapters.

The J2EE tutorial at `http://java.sun.com/j2ee/tutorial` includes coverage of various EJB-related topics.

## CHAPTER 22

A Look Back,
A Look Ahead

As I look back over the material that I've developed for this book over the past 16 months, in a very real sense it is like coming to the end of a journey. I started with some specific ideas about what I would like to accomplish, but many of the details of exactly what topics would be covered, what examples would be developed, and how everything might fit together were very unclear at the beginning.

Given the nature of publishing, at some point a book has to be "done." What you have in your hands is a static view of a dynamic, rapidly changing area of technology. By the time this book actually reaches your bookshelf, many of the products or APIs covered here will have had at least one version roll, and some of them will have had even more.

I hope I've succeeded in communicating some ideas that have lasting value; ideas about software architecture and concepts that will be valuable in your work long after the specific pieces of software described have been supplanted by the new and improved versions.

22.1 Where We've Been, What We've Learned

We've covered nearly all the technologies that make up J2EE, as of the 1.3 version of the specification. JDBC wasn't explicitly covered, although it was working behind the scenes on our behalf in our entity bean implementation.

When we separated out the interface and implementation of our example application, I suspected at that point that all of the application components would be undergoing several iterations of change during the course of the book. I was surprised at how little change was required to adapt the application to one architecture after another. If I were to start the project over again, I could incorporate additional features up front (like putting dynamic behavior in from the very beginning) that would make the application even more adaptable to different architectural designs with minimal effort.

Some of this is just general object-oriented goodness, and some is specifically creditable to Java. I don't think any of it lies with the application itself, as the application was originally developed just as a fun exercise without any intention of making it particularly suitable for architectural rework.

It seems appropriate to offer some kind of summarization, a reflection on what came out of the effort of doing all of these program examples. Depending on what you already knew coming into this book, you may have come away with very different ideas, but here are some that occur to me:

- Although most people associate J2EE with EJB, I think I'll never start a J2EE project without thinking about it in terms of servlets. Where specific services like transaction management or resource pooling may be required, I might end up with an EJB, but I'd probably prototype the function as a servlet first.
- The Adapter pattern seemed to be the one I reached for most often in trying to evolve my application. I don't feel it's the most useful pattern for new application development, where you can make all the pieces fit right the first time, but when trying to retrofit classes into existing frameworks, the Adapter is a real lifesaver.
- "Write once, run anywhere" didn't come easily to some of the J2EE components, in particular the JSPs. Testing on multiple platforms appears to be a necessity to ensure true portability. The J2EE Application Verification Kit (AVK), which is being piloted at the time I write this, may provide at least a partial solution.
- While the task of programming EJBs can be done in a very platform-independent way, packaging and deployment is today very container-specific. There is a JSR that has recently reached final draft stage, JSR-88, which deals with J2EE application deployment. This technology should arrive with J2EE 1.4, and appears to make it possible for a single tool to target any compliant J2EE platform for deployment. I eagerly look forward to this capability.

22.2 What's Ahead for XML and Web Services

We were able to take a look at XML namespaces and XML schemas, but at this time not all of the tools offer full support for these features. The movement to support these is well underway, so I don't expect these limitations to be an issue for much longer.

Of the JAX* APIs we used, only JAXP was a general release; everything else was an early-access version. JAXB will show the most radical change, and any future revisions to this book should be able to dive more deeply into the uses and features of JAXB. JAXM and JAX-RPC appear to be reasonably stable; by the release of these products, there may be additional capabilities introduced, but I don't believe any of our example code will cease to work. I've seen recent communication on the JAXRPC-INTEREST mailing list indicating that Collection types will be supported by the first general release of JAX-RPC. This means we could have avoided some of the hoops we jumped through to rework methods that returned `Lists` to instead return arrays. Of course, how quickly this capability makes it into vendor implementations of JAX-RPC remains to be seen, so the arrays may be with us for a while yet.

22.3 What's Ahead for Enterprise JavaBeans

By J2EE 1.4, Web-Services support should be pervasive in J2EE. The message-driven bean type will be extended to allow consumption of JAXM messages in addition to the JMS messages. JSR-109 will specify the changes made to deployment descriptors to allow EJBs access to the various resources needed by beans providing a Web Service. The J2EE application deployment JSR mentioned previously should make the deployment process more consistent across different J2EE platforms.

22.4 What's Ahead for This Book

All of the changes happening with Web Services and J2EE present opportunities for follow-up work, such as a second edition of the book. No definitive plans have been made for what form any follow-up will take, but I encourage you to visit my Web site, `http://www.theYawns.com`, to see what might be underway. If I have any corrections, updates to material, or news to share, that's where it will appear. Once I complete the screenplay adaptation, I'll post some information about J2EE and JAX: The Movie.

I also welcome your feedback; the next edition of this book will be shaped not only by the technology changes happening to the software, but by your responses to this first effort. What topics do you feel needed further coverage? What questions specifically were left unanswered?

Every one of the topics covered could easily have been expanded, but there is only a limited amount of time and space available—I've gone about 20 percent over the specified length for this manuscript, and by the time the last chapters were being written, the software used in the earlier chapters was out-of-date, requiring updates and retesting of the programs. If you'd like to see deeper coverage of something, I'd also like to hear your ideas about how to reorganize the material to accommodate it. Are there topics that should be dropped or significantly reduced? Should the book become two volumes, and if so, what is the logical separation between parts?

Program Listings for the Original Application

This appendix contains all the program listings for classes of the original version of the example program, which is covered in Chapter 2. Listings are presented in alphabetical order.

A.1 The Conference Class

```java
// Conference.java

package nfl.original;

/** This class provides numeric constants to represent the
  * NFL Conferences, and Strings associated with each
  * conference.
  */
public class Conference
{
    public final static int AFC = 0;
    public final static int NFC = 1;

    public static String getName(int i) {
        if (i == NFC) return "NFC";
        else if (i == AFC) return "AFC";
        else return "INVALID";
    }
}
```

A.2   The Division Class

```
// Division.java

package nfl.original;

/** This class provides numeric constants for the NFL
  * divisions, and strings for each division name.
  */
public class Division
{
   public static final int AFC_EAST    = 0;
   public static final int AFC_CENTRAL = 1;
   public static final int AFC_WEST    = 2;

   public static final int NFC_EAST    = 3;
   public static final int NFC_CENTRAL = 4;
   public static final int NFC_WEST    = 5;

   /** Return the name associated with a numeric constant.
     */
   public static String getName(int i) {
      if (i == AFC_EAST) return "AFC East";
      else if (i == AFC_CENTRAL) return "AFC Central";
      else if (i == AFC_WEST)    return "AFC West";
      else if (i == NFC_EAST)    return "NFC East";
      else if (i == NFC_CENTRAL) return "NFC Central";
      else if (i == NFC_WEST)    return "NFC West";
      else return "INVALID";
   }
}
```

A.3   The Game Class

```
// Game.java

package nfl.original;

/** This class represents a game that has been played. */
public class Game
{
   private static Teams teams = Teams.getHandle();

   // Home team for this game
   private String home;
   /** Returns the full name of the home team for this game
     */
   public  String getHome()                { return home; }
```

```
/** Sets the name of the Home team for the game. If only
 * a partial name is provided, the full name is looked
 * up and set */
public  void    setHome(String home) {
   // Validate & get full name if partial was provided
   this.home = (String) teams.findName(home);
}

// Visiting team for this game
private String visitor;
/** Returns the full name of the visiting team for this
 * game
 */
public  String getVisitor()          { return visitor; }
/** Sets the name of the visiting team for the game. If
 * only a partial name is provided, the full name is
 * looked up and set */
public  void    setVisitor(String visitor) {
   this.visitor = (String) teams.findName(visitor);
}

// Score of game (score[0] = visitor, score[1] = home)
private int[] score = new int[2];
/** Returns the final score of the game.
 * @return an array of two integers;
 *       first value is home team score, second value is
 *       visiting team score
 */
public  int[] getScore()             { return score; }
/** Records the score of the game
 * @param h  home team score
 * @param v  visiting team score
 */
public void setScore(int v, int h) {
   score[0] = v;
   score[1] = h;
}

private int  weekNumber;
/** Sets the week number during the season when the game
 * was played
 * @param week  an integer value from 1 to
 *              length of season
 */
public  void setWeek(int week)    { weekNumber = week; }
/** Returns the week number during the season when the
 * game was played.
 */
public  int  getWeek()               { return weekNumber; }
```

```
/** Constructs a Game object.
  * @param week    Week number during season when game
  *                was played.
  * @param visitor Full or partial name of visiting team
  * @param vscore  Final score of the visiting team
  * @param home    Full or partial name of home team
  * @param hscore  Final score of the home team
  */
public Game(int week, String visitor, int vscore,
                      String home, int hscore) {
   setWeek(week);
   setHome(home);
   setVisitor(visitor);
   setScore(vscore, hscore);
}

/** Convenience method to print game result */
public String toString() {
   return new String(getVisitor() + " " + getScore()[0]
            + ", " + getHome() + " " + getScore()[1]);
}
}
```

A.4 The Games Class

```
// Games.java

package nfl.original;

import java.io.*;
import java.util.*;

/** All games that have been played, and summary
  * information about them
  */
public class Games
{
   public static final int GAMES_IN_SEASON = 16;

   private List gameList = new ArrayList(250);
   /** Returns all games played as a List */
   public  List getGameList()        { return gameList; }
   /** Sets the list of played games */
   public  void setGameList(List g)  { gameList = g; }

   /** A handle to the Teams object is used for determining
     * conference & division membership.
     */
```

```
private Teams teams = Teams.getHandle();

private static Games games = new Games();
public  static Games getHandle() { return games; }

/** Constructor for the Games object. */
private Games() {
   // Week 1
   // format is week, visiting team & score,
   //                  home team & score
   gameList.add(new Game(1, "San Francisco", 28,
                            "Atlanta", 36));
   gameList.add(new Game(1, "Jacksonville", 27,
                            "Cleveland", 7));
   gameList.add(new Game(1, "Colts", 27,
                            "Kansas City", 14));
   gameList.add(new Game(1, "Chicago", 27,
                            "Minnesota", 30));
   gameList.add(new Game(1, "Tampa Bay", 21,
                            "New England", 16));
   gameList.add(new Game(1, "Detroit", 14,
                            "New Orleans", 10));
   gameList.add(new Game(1, "Arizona", 16,
                            "Giants", 21));
   gameList.add(new Game(1, "Baltimore", 16,
                            "Pittsburgh", 0));
   gameList.add(new Game(1, "Carolina", 17,
                            "Washington", 20));
   gameList.add(new Game(1, "Philadelphia", 41,
                            "Dallas", 14));
   gameList.add(new Game(1, "Jets", 20,
                            "Green Bay", 16));
   gameList.add(new Game(1, "San Diego", 6,
                            "Oakland", 9));
   gameList.add(new Game(1, "Seattle", 0,
                            "Miami", 23));
   gameList.add(new Game(1, "Tennessee", 13,
                            "Buffalo", 16));
   gameList.add(new Game(1, "Denver", 36,
                            "St. Louis", 41));

   /* Data for weeks 2-17 omitted */
}

/** Returns a List of all games for the indicated team
 * @param team  String containing full name of team
 */
public List getAllGamesFor(String team) {
```

```
      List matches = new ArrayList();
      Iterator i = gameList.iterator();
      while (i.hasNext()) {
         Game g = (Game) i.next();
         if (g.getHome().equals(team) ||
             g.getVisitor().equals(team))
            matches.add(g);
      }
      return matches;
   }


   /** Returns a list of games played by the team against
    * opponents in the team's own division
    * @param team  String containing full name of team
    */
   public List getDivisionGamesFor(String team) {
      List matches = getAllGamesFor(team);
      Iterator i = matches.iterator();
      while (i.hasNext()) {
         Game g = (Game) i.next();
         if (teams.getDivisionOf(g.getHome()) !=
             teams.getDivisionOf(g.getVisitor())) {
            i.remove();
         }
      }
      return matches;
   }


   /** Returns a list of games played by the team against
    * opponents in the team's own conference.
    * @param team  String containing full name of team.
    */
   public List getConferenceGamesFor(String team) {
      List matches = getAllGamesFor(team);
      Iterator i = matches.iterator();
      while (i.hasNext()) {
         Game g = (Game) i.next();
         if (teams.getConferenceOf(g.getHome()) !=
             teams.getConferenceOf(g.getVisitor())) {
            i.remove();
         }
      }
      return matches;
   }


   /** Returns a list of games played head-to-head between
    * the two teams indicated.
    * @param team1 String with full name of either team.
```

```
   * @param team2 String with full.name of opposing team.
   */
public List getGamesBetween(String team1, String team2) {
   List matches = getAllGamesFor(team1);
   Iterator i = matches.iterator();
   while (i.hasNext()) {
      Game g = (Game) i.next();
      if (g.getHome().equals(team2) ||
         g.getVisitor().equals(team2))
        continue;
      i.remove();
   }
   return matches;
}

/** Returns a list of games played against common
  * opponents for the two teams indicated.
  * @param team1  String with full name of one team.
  * @param team2  String with full name of other team.
  */
public List getCommonGamesFor(String team1,
                              String team2) {
   List games1 = getAllGamesFor(team1);
   List games2 = getAllGamesFor(team2);
   // Build a HashMap of team1's games, keyed by opponent
   Map candidates = new HashMap();
   Iterator i = games1.iterator();
   while (i.hasNext()) {
      Game g = (Game) i.next();
      if (g.getHome().equals(team1))
         candidates.put(g.getVisitor(), g);
      else
         candidates.put(g.getHome(), g);
   }
   // Now transfer to results any that are also opponents
   // of team2
   List results = new ArrayList();
   i = games2.iterator();
   while (i.hasNext()) {
      Game g = (Game) i.next();
      if (g.getHome().equals(team2)) {
         if (candidates.containsKey(g.getVisitor())) {
            results.add(candidates.get(g.getVisitor()));
         }
      } else if (g.getVisitor().equals(team2)) {
         if (candidates.containsKey(g.getHome())) {
            results.add(candidates.get(g.getHome()));
         }
```

```
            }
        }
        return results;
    }

    /** Returns the win-loss percentage for the team for
      * only those games passed in the games parameter
      * @param team  String containing full name of team.
      * @param games List containing the games of interest.
      * @return a float indicating the Win/Loss percentage.
      */
    public static float computeWinLossPctFor(String team,
                                            List games) {
        int[] record = new int[] { 0,0,0 };
        for (int i=0; i<games.size(); i++) {
            Game g = (Game) games.get(i);
            int score[] = g.getScore();
            if (team.equals(g.getHome())) {
                if (score[0] > score[1])
                    record[1]++; /* home loss */
                else if (score[0] < score[1])
                        record[0]++; /* home win */
                else record[2]++; /* home tie */
            } else if (team.equals(g.getVisitor())) {
                if (score[0] > score[1])
                    record[0]++; /* away win */
                else if (score[0] < score[1])
                        record[1]++; /* away loss */
                else record[2]++; /* home tie */
            } /* else we didn't play, why were we passed this game? */
        }
        return (float) (record[0] + record[2]/2) /
            (record[0] + record[1] + record[2]);
    }
}
```

A.5 The Standings Class

```
// Standings.java

package nfl.original;

import java.io.*;
import java.text.DecimalFormat;
import java.util.*;
```

```
/* Calculates and prints standings for all NFL conferences
 * and divisions */
public class Standings
{
    // Hold all teams
    private Teams teams = Teams.getHandle();
    public  Teams getTeams()          { return teams; }
    public  void  setTeams(Teams t) { teams = t; }

    private List teamList;
    public  List getTeamList()            { return teamList; }
    public  void setTeamList(List t)      { teamList = t; }

    // Holds all games
    private static Games games = Games.getHandle();
    public  static Games getGames()          { return games; }
    public  static void  setGames(Games g) { games = g; }

    private List gameList;
    public  List getGameList()        { return gameList; }
    public void  setGameList(List g) { gameList = g; }

    // Variables which control what we print.
    private boolean verbose = false;
    public  boolean getVerbose()         { return verbose; }
    public  void    setVerbose(boolean b) { verbose = b; }

    private boolean printConferenceStandings = true;
    public  boolean getPrintConferenceStandings() {
        return printConferenceStandings; }
    public  void    setPrintConferenceStandings(boolean b) {
        printConferenceStandings = b; }

    private boolean printTimings = false;
    public  boolean getPrintTimings() {
            return printTimings; }
    public  void    setPrintTimings(boolean b) {
            printTimings = b; }

    // only used by Conference standings
    private boolean printEliminatedTeams = false;
    public  boolean getPrintEliminatedTeams() {
        return printEliminatedTeams; }
    public  void    setPrintEliminatedTeams(boolean b) {
        printEliminatedTeams = b; }

    // Implementation of Singleton pattern for Standings
    private static Standings standings = new Standings();
```

```java
public  static Standings getHandle() {
        return standings; }

// Constructor
private Standings() {}

public static void main(String[] args) {
    List l;
    getHandle().loadData();
    // Loop through divisions
    for (int i=0; i<6; i++) {
       l = getHandle().computeDivisionStandings(i);
       getHandle().printDivisionStandings(i, l);
    }

    if (!getHandle().getPrintConferenceStandings())
       return;

    // Loop through conferences
    for (int i=0; i<2; i++) {
       l = getHandle().computeConferenceStandings(i);
       getHandle().printConferenceStandings(i, l);
    }
}

public int findTeam(String name) {
    for (int t=0; t<teamList.size(); t++) {
       Team team = (Team) teamList.get(t);
       if (team.getFullName().startsWith(name)) return t;
       if (team.getName().startsWith(name)) return t;
       if (team.getCity().startsWith(name)) return t;
    }
    System.out.println("no match " + name);
    return -1;
}

public void loadData() {
    teamList = teams.getTeamList();
    gameList = games.getGameList();

    long starttime = 0;
    if (printTimings) {
       starttime = System.currentTimeMillis();
    }
    for (int g=0; g<gameList.size(); g++) {
       boolean confgame = false, divgame = false;
       int thindex, tvindex;
       int[] score;
```

```
Game game = (Game) gameList.get(g);
if (verbose)
   System.out.println("Posting results: " + game);
thindex = findTeam(game.getHome());
tvindex = findTeam(game.getVisitor());
Team th = (Team) teamList.get(thindex);
Team tv = (Team) teamList.get(tvindex);
if (th.getConference() == tv.getConference())
   confgame = true;
if (th.getDivision() == tv.getDivision())
   divgame = true;
score = game.getScore();
th.addPoints(score[1]);
th.addPointsAllowed(score[0]);
tv.addPoints(score[0]);
tv.addPointsAllowed(score[1]);
teamList.set(thindex, th);
teamList.set(tvindex, tv);
if (score[0] > score[1]) {
   // Visiting team won
   th.addLoss(); tv.addWin();
   if (confgame) {
      th.addConferenceLoss();
      tv.addConferenceWin();
   }
   if (divgame) {
      th.addDivisionLoss();
      tv.addDivisionWin();
   }
} else if (score[0] < score[1]) {
   // Home team won
   th.addWin(); tv.addLoss();
   if (confgame) {
      th.addConferenceWin();
      tv.addConferenceLoss();
   }
   if (divgame) {
      th.addDivisionWin();
      tv.addDivisionLoss();
   }
} else {
   // Tie
   th.addTie(); tv.addTie();
   if (confgame) {
      th.addConferenceTie();
      tv.addConferenceTie();
   }
   if (divgame) {
```

```
                    th.addDivisionTie();
                    tv.addDivisionTie();
                }
            }
        }
        if (printTimings) {
            System.out.println(System.currentTimeMillis() -
                starttime + " millisecs loading game data");
        }

    public List computeDivisionStandings(int div) {

        long starttime = 0;
        if (printTimings) {
            starttime = System.currentTimeMillis();
        }

        // Sort the division into order, using tiebreakers
        Comparator comp = new Team.DivisionComparator();
        List divisionList = teams.getDivisionTeams(div);
        if (verbose)
            System.out.println("\nComparing teams in " +
                               Division.getName(div));

        Collections.sort(divisionList, comp);
        if (printTimings) {
            System.out.println(System.currentTimeMillis() -
                starttime + " millisecs in division sort");
        }

        // Get division leader
        Team leader = (Team) divisionList.get(0);

        // Special case: if no games played, don't make any
        // changes to team status fields and just return the
        // sorted array
        if (leader.getGamesRemaining() ==
                Games.GAMES_IN_SEASON)
            return divisionList;

        // Mark leader, clinches and eliminated teams
        leader.setDivisionChampStatus(Team.LEADING);
        boolean leaderCouldLose = false;
        boolean leaderCouldTie = false;
        for (int i=1; i<divisionList.size(); i++) {
            Team contender = (Team) divisionList.get(i);
            int leftToPlay = contender.getGamesRemaining();
            int trailingBy = leader.getWins() -
                        contender.getWins();
```

```
        if ((leftToPlay == 0) ||
            (trailingBy > leftToPlay)) {
          contender.setDivisionChampStatus(
                            Team.ELIMINATED);
          // Team might appear in homefield contention
          // judging just by by Win-Loss %, but if you
          // can't win division it just won't happen.
          contender.setHomeFieldStatus(Team.ELIMINATED);
        } else if (i == 1) {
            if (trailingBy == leftToPlay) {
              // team in 2nd could catch leader
              leaderCouldTie = true;
            } else {
              // team in 2nd could overtake leader
              leaderCouldLose = true;
            }
        }
    }
    if (!leaderCouldLose)
        leader.setDivisionChampStatus(Team.CLINCHED);
    if (leaderCouldTie)
        leader.setDivisionChampStatus(Team.CLINCHED_TIE);

    return divisionList;
}

public List computeConferenceStandings(int conf) {
    long starttime = 0;

    // Sort into conference-standing order
    if (printTimings)
        starttime = System.currentTimeMillis();
    List conferenceList = teams.getConferenceTeams(conf);
    Comparator comp = new Team.ConferenceComparator();
    if (verbose)
        System.out.println("\nComparing teams in " +
                        Conference.getName(conf));

    Collections.sort(conferenceList, comp);
    if (printTimings)
        System.out.println(System.currentTimeMillis() -
        starttime + " milliseconds in conference sort");

    // Get leader, 6th seed (lowest seeded wildcard),
    // 7th seed (1st team to miss cut for playoffs)
    Team leader = (Team) conferenceList.get(0);
    Team seed6  = (Team) conferenceList.get(5);
    Team seed7  = (Team) conferenceList.get(6);
```

```
// Special case: if no games have been played, we
// have a simple alpha sort, and shouldn't use that
// to mark anything.
if (leader.getGamesRemaining() ==
    Games.GAMES_IN_SEASON)
    return conferenceList;

// We do comparision loop starting at first
// contender, since we don't need to compare the
// division leader to itself.  But that means we
// need to do a special check of the division leader
// to see if (at least) a wildcard berth is clinched
int leftToPlay = seed7.getGamesRemaining();
int leadingBy  = leader.getWins() - seed7.getWins();
int wildcardsClinched = 0;
if ((leftToPlay == 0) || (leadingBy > leftToPlay)) {
    leader.setWildcardStatus(Team.CLINCHED);
    wildcardsClinched++;
} else if (leadingBy == leftToPlay) {
    leader.setWildcardStatus(Team.CLINCHED_TIE);
    wildcardsClinched++;
}

// Loop through teams 2-n, marking clinches &
// eliminations
leader.setHomeFieldStatus(Team.LEADING);
boolean leaderCouldTieForHomeField = false;
boolean leaderCouldLoseHomeField = false;
for(int i=1; i<conferenceList.size(); i++) {
    Team contender = (Team) conferenceList.get(i);
    leftToPlay = contender.getGamesRemaining();
    // in contention for home field advantage?
    int trailingBy = leader.getWins() -
                contender.getWins();
    if ((leftToPlay == 0) ||
        (trailingBy > leftToPlay)) {
      contender.setHomeFieldStatus(Team.ELIMINATED);
    } else if (trailingBy == leftToPlay) {
      leaderCouldTieForHomeField = true;
    } else {
      leaderCouldLoseHomeField = true;
    }

    // Currently leading wildcard race (4th-6th seeds)
    if (i<=5) {
      // for teams in position, set lead true,
      // check for clinch
      if (i<=5)
        contender.setWildcardStatus(Team.LEADING);
```

```
                leftToPlay = seed7.getGamesRemaining();
                leadingBy = contender.getWins() -
                            seed7.getWins();
                if ((leftToPlay == 0) ||
                    (leadingBy > leftToPlay)) {
                  contender.setWildcardStatus(Team.CLINCHED);
                  wildcardsClinched++;
                } else if (leadingBy == leftToPlay) {
                  contender.setWildcardStatus(
                            Team.CLINCHED_TIE);
                  // not incrementing # clinched for ties
                }
            } else  /* i>5 */ {
                // For teams seeded >=7, is wildcard berth 6
                // reachable?
                if (wildcardsClinched == 6) {
                  contender.setWildcardStatus(
                            Team.ELIMINATED);
                } else {
                  leftToPlay = contender.getGamesRemaining();
                  trailingBy = seed6.getWins() -
                            contender.getWins();
                  if ((leftToPlay == 0) ||
                      (trailingBy > leftToPlay)) {
                    contender.setWildcardStatus(
                            Team.ELIMINATED);
                  } else if (leadingBy == leftToPlay) {
                    contender.setWildcardStatus(
                            Team.CLINCHED_TIE);
                  }
                }
            }
        }
    }

    if (!leaderCouldLoseHomeField)
        leader.setHomeFieldStatus(Team.CLINCHED);
    if (leaderCouldTieForHomeField)
        leader.setHomeFieldStatus(Team.CLINCHED_TIE);

    return conferenceList;
}

public void printDivisionStandings(int div, List list) {
    // Print details
    /* need team object to pull division name from */
    Team team = (Team) list.get(0);
```

```
System.out.println(" ----- " + Division.getName(div)
                 + " ---- ");
System.out.println("    Team                    " +
    "  W  L  T   PCT  PF  PA  Div  Conf Streak");
/*  9  9  9  .999   0   0   0-0   0-0 xxxx nn */
/* 99 99 99 1.999 999 999 15-15 15-15 xxxx nn */

for (int i=0; i<list.size(); i++) {
   team = (Team) list.get(i);

   System.out.print("     " + team.getFullName());
   for (int pad=team.getFullName().length();
           pad<23; pad++)
     System.out.print(" "); /* padding */

   if (team.getWins() < 10) System.out.print(" ");
   System.out.print(team.getWins() + " ");

   if (team.getLosses() < 10) System.out.print(" ");
   System.out.print(team.getLosses() + " ");

   if (team.getTies() < 10) System.out.print(" ");
   System.out.print(team.getTies() + " ");

   if (team.getOverallWinLossPct() < 1)
      System.out.print(" ");
   DecimalFormat nf = new DecimalFormat("#.000");
   System.out.print(nf.format(
              team.getOverallWinLossPct()) + " ");

   if (team.getPoints() < 100) System.out.print(" ");
   if (team.getPoints() <  10) System.out.print(" ");
   System.out.print( team.getPoints() + "  " );

   if (team.getPointsAllowed() < 100)
      System.out.print(" ");
   if (team.getPointsAllowed() <  10)
      System.out.print(" ");
   System.out.print( team.getPointsAllowed() + "  " );

   if (team.getDivisionWins() < 10)
      System.out.print(" ");
   if (team.getDivisionLosses() < 10)
      System.out.print(" ");
   System.out.print( team.getDivisionWins() + "-" +
      team.getDivisionLosses() + "  " );
```

```
      if (team.getConferenceWins() < 10)
         System.out.print(" ");
      if (team.getConferenceLosses() < 10)
         System.out.print(" ");
      System.out.print( team.getConferenceWins() + "-" +
         team.getConferenceLosses() + " ");

      if (team.getStreak() > 0) {
         System.out.println("Won " + team.getStreak());
      } else if (team.getStreak() < 0) {
         System.out.println("Lost " +
                         (-1 * team.getStreak()));
      } else System.out.println();
   }
   System.out.println();
}

public void printConferenceStandings(int conf,
                               List list) {
   Team t = null;

   System.out.println("\n" + Conference.getName(conf) +
                   " Playoff Seedings\n");

   for (int i=0; i<list.size(); i++) {
      t = (Team) list.get(i);

      if (!printEliminatedTeams)
         // Don't print teams that are eliminated from
         // playoff contention
         if (t.getWildcardStatus() == Team.ELIMINATED)
            break;

      System.out.print((i+1) + ". ");
      if (i<9) System.out.print(" "); /* padding */

      System.out.print(t.getFullName() );
      for (int pad=t.getFullName().length();
         pad<23; pad++)
         System.out.print(" "); /* pad name */

      // Home field advantage
      if (t.getHomeFieldStatus() == Team.CLINCHED) {
         System.out.print("Clinched homefield. ");
      } else if (t.getHomeFieldStatus() ==
               Team.CLINCHED_TIE) {
         System.out.print(
                  "Clinched tie for homefield. ");
```

```
    } else if (t.getHomeFieldStatus() ==
            Team.LEADING) {
        System.out.print("Leading in homefield. ");
    } else if (t.getHomeFieldStatus() ==
            Team.IN_CONTENTION) {
        System.out.print("Contender for homefield. ");
    } /* print nothing for eliminated teams */

    // Division leaders
    if (t.getDivisionChampStatus() == Team.CLINCHED) {
        System.out.print("Clinched " +
            Division.getName(t.getDivision()) + ". ");
    } else if (t.getDivisionChampStatus() ==
            Team.CLINCHED_TIE) {
        System.out.print("Clinched at least tie in " +
            Division.getName(t.getDivision()) + ". ");
    } else if (t.getDivisionChampStatus() ==
            Team.LEADING) {
        System.out.print("Leads " +
            Division.getName(t.getDivision()) + ". ");
    } else if (t.getDivisionChampStatus() ==
            Team.IN_CONTENTION) {
        System.out.print("Contender for " +
            Division.getName(t.getDivision()) + ". ");
    } /* print nothing for eliminated teams */

    // Wildcards
    if (t.getWildcardStatus() == Team.CLINCHED) {
        // If division clinched, don't print wildcard
        // clinched also.
        if (t.getDivisionChampStatus() !=
            Team.CLINCHED)
            System.out.print("Clinched wildcard");
    } else if (t.getWildcardStatus() ==
            Team.CLINCHED_TIE) {
        if (t.getDivisionChampStatus() !=
            Team.CLINCHED)
            System.out.print(
                "Clinched tie for wildcard");
    } else if (t.getWildcardStatus() ==
            Team.LEADING) {
        // We only print something here if not leading
        // a division
        if (t.getDivisionChampStatus() > Team.LEADING)
            System.out.print(
                "In position for wildcard berth");
    } else if (t.getWildcardStatus() ==
            Team.IN_CONTENTION) {
```

```
                // We only print something here if not in
                // division contention
                if (t.getDivisionChampStatus() ==
                    Team.ELIMINATED)
                   System.out.print("Contender for wildcard");
            } else
                System.out.print("Eliminated from playoffs");
            System.out.println();
        }
        System.out.println();
    }
}
```

A.6 The Team Class

```java
// Team.java

package nfl.original;

import java.io.*;
import java.util.*;

/** An NFL team.  Includes various statistics needed to
  * produce the standings.
  */
public class Team
{
    // Identity
    private String name;
    public  String getName()          { return name; }
    public  void   setName(String n) { name = n; }

    private String city;
    public  String getCity()          { return city; }
    public  void   setCity(String c) { city = c;  }
    public  String getFullName() {
        return new String(city + " " + name); }

    private int  conference;
    public  void setConference(int c) { conference = c; }
    public  int  getConference()      { return conference; }

    private int  division;
    public  void setDivision(int d)   { division  = d; }
    public  int  getDivision()        { return division; }

    // data for standings, updated as game results are posted
    private int[] overallRecord; // overall, W-L-T
```

```java
public  int[] getOverallRecord(){ return overallRecord; }
public  int    getWins()       { return overallRecord[0]; }
public  int    getLosses()     { return overallRecord[1]; }
public  int    getTies()       { return overallRecord[2]; }
public  void   addWin() {
   overallRecord[0]++;
   if (streak >= 0) streak++;
   else streak = 1;
   gamesRemaining--;
}

public void addLoss() {
   overallRecord[1]++;
   if (streak <= 0) streak--;
   else streak = -1;
   gamesRemaining--;
}

public void addTie() {
   overallRecord[2]++;
   streak = 0;
   gamesRemaining--;
}

/** Compute win-loss percentage given team record  */
public static float winLossPct(int[] record) {
   if (record[0] + record[1] + record[2] == 0) {
      return 0;
   } else {
      // Ties count as 1/2 win; % = wins / games played
      return (float) (record[0] + record[2]/2) /
          (record[0] + record[1] + record[2]);
   }
}

private int[] divisionRecord;
public  int[] getDivisionRecord() {
   return divisionRecord; }
public int getDivisionWins() {
   return divisionRecord[0]; }
public int getDivisionLosses() {
   return divisionRecord[1]; }
public int getDivisionTies() {
   return divisionRecord[2]; }
public void addDivisionWin()  { divisionRecord[0]++; }
public void addDivisionLoss() { divisionRecord[1]++; }
public void addDivisionTie()  { divisionRecord[2]++; }
```

```java
private int[] conferenceRecord;
public  int[] getConferenceRecord() {
   return conferenceRecord; }
public int getConferenceWins() {
   return conferenceRecord[0]; }
public int getConferenceLosses() {
   return conferenceRecord[1]; }
public int getConferenceTies() {
   return conferenceRecord[2]; }
public void addConferenceWin() { conferenceRecord[0]++; }
public void addConferenceLoss(){ conferenceRecord[1]++; }
public void addConferenceTie() { conferenceRecord[2]++; }

private int  points;
public  int  getPoints()       { return points; }
public  void addPoints(int p) { points += p; }

private int  pointsAllowed;
public  int  getPointsAllowed() { return pointsAllowed; }
public  void addPointsAllowed(int p) {
   pointsAllowed += p; }

// Tiebreaker 8, which is unimplemented, would require
// following 2 data fields:
private int   touchdowns;
private int   touchdownsAllowed;

private int gamesRemaining = Games.GAMES_IN_SEASON;
public int getGamesRemaining() { return gamesRemaining; }

// Fields calculated at time standings are computed
private float overallWinLossPct    = -1.0f;
public float getOverallWinLossPct() {
   return overallWinLossPct; }
public void setOverallWinLossPct(float p) {
   overallWinLossPct = p; }

private float divisionWinLossPct   = -1.0f;
public float getDivisionWinLossPct() {
   return divisionWinLossPct; }
public void setDivisionWinLossPct(float p) {
   divisionWinLossPct = p; }

private float conferenceWinLossPct = -1.0f;
public float getConferenceWinLossPct() {
   return conferenceWinLossPct; }
public void setConferenceWinLossPct(float p) {
   conferenceWinLossPct = p; }
```

```
private int netOverallPoints    = -1;
public int getNetOverallPoints() {
   return netOverallPoints; }
public void setNetOverallPoints(int p) {
   netOverallPoints = p; }

private int netDivisionPoints    = -1;
public int getNetDivisionPoints() {
   return netDivisionPoints; }
public void setNetDivisionPoints(int p) {
   netDivisionPoints = p; }

private int netConferencePoints = -1;
public int getNetConferencePoints() {
   return netConferencePoints; }
public void setNetConferencePoints(int p) {
   netConferencePoints = p; }

// Completely irrelevant for standings, but frequently
// reported along with standings.  Other interesting but
// irrelevant statistics could be home & away records.
private int streak;    // + for wins, - for losses
public  int getStreak() { return streak; }

public static final int CLINCHED      = 1;
public static final int CLINCHED_TIE  = 2;
public static final int LEADING       = 3;
public static final int IN_CONTENTION = 4;
public static final int ELIMINATED    = 5;

private int  divisionChampStatus = IN_CONTENTION;
public int getDivisionChampStatus() {
   return divisionChampStatus; }
public void setDivisionChampStatus(int s) {
   divisionChampStatus = s; }

private int homeFieldStatus = IN_CONTENTION;
public int getHomeFieldStatus() {
   return homeFieldStatus; }
public void setHomeFieldStatus(int s) {
   homeFieldStatus = s; }

private int wildcardStatus = IN_CONTENTION;
public int getWildcardStatus() { return wildcardStatus; }
public void setWildcardStatus(int s) {
   wildcardStatus = s; }
```

```
   // Constructor
   public Team(String city, String name) {
      this.city = city;
      this.name = name;
      overallRecord    = new int[] { 0,0,0 };
      divisionRecord   = new int[] { 0,0,0 };
      conferenceRecord = new int[] { 0,0,0 };
      points = 0; pointsAllowed = 0; streak = 0;
   }

   private static List    gameList;
   private static Games    games;

   public static void loadGames() {
      games =    Games.getHandle();
      gameList = games.getGameList();
   }

// Following methods are for use by division and
// conference comparators

   private static boolean verbose = true;

   private static int compareHeadToHead(Team t1, Team t2) {
      List head2head = games.getGamesBetween(
                     t1.getFullName(), t2.getFullName());
      float h2hpct;
      if (head2head.size() > 0) {
         h2hpct = Games.computeWinLossPctFor(
                 t1.getFullName(), head2head);
         if (h2hpct > .500) {
            if (verbose)
               System.out.println(t1.getName() + " over " +
                  t2.getName() + " based on head-to-head" +
                  " record (Tiebreaker 1)");
            return -1;
         } else if (h2hpct < .500) {
            if (verbose)
               System.out.println(t2.getName() + " over " +
                  t1.getName() + " based on head-to-head" +
                  " record (Tiebreaker 1)");
            return 1;
         }
      }
      return 0;
   }
```

```
private static int compareOverallRecords(Team t1,
                                         Team t2) {
   if (t1.getOverallWinLossPct() == -1.0f)
      t1.setOverallWinLossPct(
         winLossPct(t1.getOverallRecord()));
   if (t2.getOverallWinLossPct() == -1.0f)
      t2.setOverallWinLossPct(
         winLossPct(t2.getOverallRecord()));

   if (t1.getOverallWinLossPct() >
      t2.getOverallWinLossPct())
         return -1;
   else if (t2.getOverallWinLossPct() >
         t1.getOverallWinLossPct())
         return 1;
   else return 0;
}

private static int compareDivisionRecords(Team t1,
                                          Team t2) {
   if (t1.getDivisionWinLossPct() == -1.0f)
      t1.setDivisionWinLossPct(
         winLossPct(t1.getDivisionRecord()));
   if (t2.getDivisionWinLossPct() == -1.0f)
      t2.setDivisionWinLossPct(
         winLossPct(t2.getDivisionRecord()));

   if (t1.getDivisionWinLossPct() >
      t2.getDivisionWinLossPct())
         return -1;
   else if (t2.getDivisionWinLossPct() >
         t1.getDivisionWinLossPct())
         return 1;
   else return 0;
}

private static int compareConferenceRecords(Team t1,
                                            Team t2) {
   if (t1.getConferenceWinLossPct() == -1.0f)
      t1.setConferenceWinLossPct(
         winLossPct(t1.getConferenceRecord()));
   if (t2.getConferenceWinLossPct() == -1.0f)
      t2.setConferenceWinLossPct(
         winLossPct(t2.getConferenceRecord()));

   if (t1.getConferenceWinLossPct() >
      t2.getConferenceWinLossPct())
         return -1;
```

```
    else if (t2.getConferenceWinLossPct() >
            t1.getConferenceWinLossPct())
        return 1;
    else return 0;
}

private static int compareNetPointsDivisionGames(Team t1,
                                                 Team t2) {

    int t1NetPoints = t1.getNetDivisionPoints();
    int t2NetPoints = t2.getNetDivisionPoints();

    if (t1NetPoints == -1) {
        List t1DivGames = games.getDivisionGamesFor(
                            t1.getFullName());
        Iterator it = t1DivGames.iterator();
        t1NetPoints = 0;
        while (it.hasNext()) {
            Game g = (Game) it.next();
            int[] score = g.getScore();
            if (g.getHome().equals(t1.getFullName()))
                t1NetPoints += score[1] - score[0];
            else
                t1NetPoints += score[0] - score[1];
        }
        t1.setNetDivisionPoints(t1NetPoints);
    }

    if (t2NetPoints == -1) {
        List t2DivGames = games.getDivisionGamesFor(
                            t2.getFullName());
        Iterator it = t2DivGames.iterator();
        t2NetPoints = 0;
        while (it.hasNext()) {
            Game g = (Game) it.next();
            int[] score = g.getScore();
            if (g.getHome().equals(t2.getFullName()))
                t2NetPoints += score[1] - score[0];
            else
                t2NetPoints += score[0] - score[1];
        }
        t2.setNetDivisionPoints(t2NetPoints);
    }

    if (t1NetPoints > t2NetPoints) {
        if (verbose)
            System.out.println(t1.getName() + " over " +
                t2.getName() + " based on net points in " +
                "division games (Tiebreaker 6)");
```

```
            return -1;
        } else if (t1NetPoints < t2NetPoints) {
            if (verbose)
                System.out.println(t2.getName() + " over " +
                    t1.getName() + " based on net points in " +
                    "division games (Tiebreaker 6)");
            return 1;
        } else return 0;
    }


    private static int compareNetPointsConferenceGames(
                                    Team t1, Team t2) {

        int t1NetPoints = t1.getNetConferencePoints();
        int t2NetPoints = t2.getNetConferencePoints();

        if (t1NetPoints == -1) {
            List t1ConfGames = games.getConferenceGamesFor(
                                    t1.getFullName());
            Iterator it = t1ConfGames.iterator();
            t1NetPoints = 0;
            while (it.hasNext()) {
                Game g = (Game) it.next();
                int[] score = g.getScore();
                if (g.getHome().equals(t1.getFullName()))
                    t1NetPoints += score[1] - score[0];
                else
                    t1NetPoints += score[0] - score[1];
            }
            t1.setNetConferencePoints(t1NetPoints);
        }


        if (t2NetPoints == -1) {
            List t2ConfGames = games.getConferenceGamesFor(
                                    t2.getFullName());
            Iterator it = t2ConfGames.iterator();
            t2NetPoints = 0;
            while (it.hasNext()) {
                Game g = (Game) it.next();
                int[] score = g.getScore();
                if (g.getHome().equals(t2.getFullName()))
                    t2NetPoints += score[1] - score[0];
                else
                    t2NetPoints += score[0] - score[1];
            }
            t2.setNetConferencePoints(t2NetPoints);
        }
```

```
    if (t1NetPoints > t2NetPoints) {
       if (verbose)
          System.out.println(t1.getName() + " over " +
             t2.getName() + " based on net points in " +
             "conference games (Tiebreaker 5)");
       return -1;
    } else if (t1NetPoints < t2NetPoints) {
       if (verbose)
          System.out.println(t2.getName() + " over " +
             t1.getName() + " based on net points in " +
             "conference games (Tiebreaker 6)");
       return 1;
    } else return 0;
}

private static int compareNetPointsAllGames(Team t1,
                                            Team t2) {
    int t1NetPoints = t1.getNetOverallPoints();
    int t2NetPoints = t2.getNetOverallPoints();

    if (t1NetPoints == -1) {
       t1NetPoints = t1.getPoints() -
                     t1.getPointsAllowed();
       t1.setNetOverallPoints(t1NetPoints);
    }
    if (t2NetPoints == -1) {
       t2NetPoints = t2.getPoints() -
                     t2.getPointsAllowed();
       t2.setNetOverallPoints(t2NetPoints);
    }

    if (t1NetPoints > t2NetPoints) {
       if (verbose)
          System.out.println(t1.getName() + " over " +
             t2.getName() + " based on net points in " +
             "all games (Tiebreaker 7)");
       return -1;
    } else if (t1NetPoints < t2NetPoints) {
       if (verbose)
          System.out.println(t2.getName() + " over " +
             t1.getName() + " based on net points in " +
             "all games (Tiebreaker 7)");
       return 1;
    } else return 0;
}

// Comparator for Division Standings (inner class)
public static class DivisionComparator
                  implements Comparator {
```

```
public int compare(Object o1, Object o2) {
   Team t1 = (Team) o1;
   Team t2 = (Team) o2;

   if (games == null) loadGames();

   // Have any games been played?  If not, alpha sort
   if (gameList.size() == 0)
      return t1.getFullName().compareTo(
                              t2.getFullName());

   // Sort by overall win-loss-tied percentage
   int result = compareOverallRecords(t1, t2);
   if (result != 0) return result;

   // Begin tiebreakers

   // Tiebreaker 1: Head-to-Head record
   result = compareHeadToHead(t1, t2);
   if (result != 0) return result;

   // Tiebreaker 2: Division record
   result = compareDivisionRecords(t1, t2);
   if (result < 0) {
      if (verbose)
         System.out.println(t1.getName() + " over " +
         t2.getName() + " based on division record " +
         "(Tiebreaker 2)");
      return -1;
   } else if (result > 0) {
      if (verbose)
         System.out.println(t2.getName() + " over " +
         t1.getName() + " based on division record " +
         "(Tiebreaker 2)");
      return 1;
   }

   // Tiebreaker 3: Conference record
   result = compareConferenceRecords(t1, t2);
   if (result < 0) {
      if (verbose)
         System.out.println(t1.getName() + " over " +
         t2.getName() + " based on conference record" +
         " (Tiebreaker 3)");
      return -1;
   } else if (result > 0) {
      if (verbose)
```

```
            System.out.println(t2.getName() + " over " +
                t1.getName() + " based on conference " +
                "record (Tiebreaker 3)");
        return 1;
    }

    // Tiebreaker 4: Record in common games
    List common = games.getCommonGamesFor(
                    t1.getFullName(), t2.getFullName());
    if (common.size() == 0) { /* skip to next test */
    } else {
        float commonPct = Games.computeWinLossPctFor(
                            t1.getFullName(), common);
        if (commonPct > .500) {
            if (verbose)
                System.out.println(t1.getName() + " over "
                    + t2.getName() + " based on record " +
                    "against common opponents " +
                    "(Tiebreaker 4)");
            return -1;
        } else if (commonPct < .500) {
            if (verbose)
                System.out.println(t2.getName() + " over "
                    + t1.getName() + " based on record " +
                    "against common opponents " +
                    "(Tiebreaker 4)");
            return 1;
        }
    }

    // Tiebreaker 5: Net points in division games
    result = compareNetPointsDivisionGames(t1, t2);
    // note: printing done in called method if verbose
    if (result != 0) return result;

    // Tiebreaker 6: Net points in all games
    result = compareNetPointsAllGames(t1, t2);
    if (result != 0) return result;

    // Tiebreaker 7: Strength of Schedule
    System.out.println(
        "Need strength of schedule test (Tiebreaker 7)");

    // Tiebreaker 8: Net touchdowns
    //System.out.println(
    //   "Need net touchdowns test (Tiebreaker 8)");
```

```
        // Tiebreaker 9: Coin toss
        // System.out.println(
        //    "Need coin toss (Tiebreaker 9)");

        System.out.println("Unable to break tie between " +
                t1.getName() + " and " + t2.getName() );
          return 0;
      }
  }


  // Comparator for Conference standings (inner class)
  /** Class used to sort into conference standing order.
    * First 3 slots will be division winners, with #1 slot
    * having home-field advantage throughout the playoffs.
    * Slots 4-6 will be the wild cards.
    */
  public static class ConferenceComparator
                      implements Comparator {
    public int compare(Object o1, Object o2) {
      Team t1 = (Team) o1;
      Team t2 = (Team) o2;

        // Have any games been played?  If not, alpha sort
        if (gameList.size() == 0)
          return t1.getFullName().compareTo(
                                  t2.getFullName());

        // Division leaders sort first, even ahead of
        //   W-L-T % leaders
        boolean t1LeadsDivision =
          t1.getDivisionChampStatus() < Team.LEADING;
        boolean t2LeadsDivision =
          t2.getDivisionChampStatus() < Team.LEADING;

        if (t1LeadsDivision != t2LeadsDivision) {
          if (t1LeadsDivision) {
            if (verbose &&
              (t1.getOverallWinLossPct() <=
               t2.getOverallWinLossPct()))
              System.out.println(t1.getName() + " over "
                + t2.getName() + " because " +
                t1.getName() + " lead a division");
            return -1;
          } else /* t2 leads a division */ {
            if (verbose &&
              (t2.getOverallWinLossPct() <=
               t1.getOverallWinLossPct()))
```

```
            System.out.println(t2.getName() + " over "
                + t1.getName() + " because " +
                t2.getName() + " lead a division");
         return 1;
      }
   }

   // Sort by overall win-loss-tie percentage
   if (t1.getOverallWinLossPct() !=
       t2.getOverallWinLossPct())
      if (t1.getOverallWinLossPct() >
          t2.getOverallWinLossPct())
         return -1;
      else
         return 1;

   // if teams are in the same division,
   // we use division tiebreakers instead
   if (t1.getDivision() == t2.getDivision()) {
      Comparator comp = new Team.DivisionComparator();
      return comp.compare(t1, t2);
   }

   // Begin Conference tiebreakers:

   // Tiebreaker 1: Head-to-Head record
   int result = 0;
   result = compareHeadToHead(t1, t2);
   if (result != 0) return result;

   // Tiebreaker 2: Conference record
   result = compareConferenceRecords(t1, t2);
   if (result < 0) {
      if (verbose)
         System.out.println(t1.getName() + " over " +
            t2.getName() + " based on conference " +
            "record (Tiebreaker 2)");
      return -1;
   } else if (result > 0) {
      if (verbose)
         System.out.println(t2.getName() + " over " +
            t1.getName() + " based on conference " +
            "record (Tiebreaker 2)");
      return 1;
   }

   // Tiebreaker 3: Record in common games
   List common = games.getCommonGamesFor(
                 t1.getFullName(), t2.getFullName());
```

```
        if (common.size() == 0) { /* skip to next test */
        } else {
           float commonPct = Games.computeWinLossPctFor(
                              t1.getFullName(), common);
           if (commonPct > .500) {
              if (verbose)
                 System.out.println(t1.getName() + " over "
                    + t2.getName() + " based on record " +
                    "against common opponents " +
                    "(Tiebreaker 3)");
              return -1;
           } else if (commonPct < .500) {
              if (verbose)
                 System.out.println(t2.getName() + " over "
                    + t1.getName() + " based on record " +
                    "against common opponents " +
                    "(Tiebreaker 3)");
              return 1;
           }
        }

        // Tiebreaker 4: Net points in conference games
        result = compareNetPointsConferenceGames(t1, t2);
        /* note: verbose printing done by called method */
        if (result != 0) return result;

        // Tiebreaker 5: Net points in all games
        result = compareNetPointsAllGames(t1, t2);
        if (result != 0) return result;

        // Tiebreaker 6. strength of schedule
        System.out.println(
              "Need strength of schedule test!");

        // Tiebreaker 7. net touchdowns
        //System.out.println("Need net touchdowns test!");

        // Tiebreaker 8. coin toss
        //System.out.println("need coin toss!");

        System.out.println("Unable to break tie between "
           + t1.getName() + " and " + t2.getName() );
        return 0;
      }
   }
}
```

A.7 The Teams Class

```java
// Teams.java

package nfl.original;

import java.io.FileInputStream;
import java.io.ObjectInputStream;
import java.util.*;

public class Teams
{
   // This class is a Singleton
   private static Teams teams = new Teams();
   public  static Teams getHandle() { return teams; }

   // Two views of the same data
   private Map  teamMap   = new HashMap();
   private List teamList  = new ArrayList(32);
   public  List getTeamList() { return teamList; }

   // Constructor
   private Teams() {
      // Create AFC Teams
      Team bal = new Team("Baltimore", "Ravens");
      bal.setConference(Conference.AFC);
      bal.setDivision(Division.AFC_CENTRAL);
      teamList.add(bal);

      Team buf = new Team("Buffalo", "Bills");
      buf.setConference(Conference.AFC);
      buf.setDivision(Division.AFC_EAST);
      teamList.add(buf);

   /* Data for other teams omitted */

      // The serialized teamList is an ArrayList, but we also
      // require random access by name so we build a HashMap.
      for (int i=0; i<teamList.size(); i++) {
         Team t = (Team) teamList.get(i);
         teamMap.put(t.getFullName(), t);
      }
   }

   public List getConferenceTeams(int conf) {
      List result = new ArrayList();
      for (int i=0; i<teamList.size(); i++) {
         Team t = (Team) teamList.get(i);
```

```
            if (t.getConference() == conf) {
                result.add(t);
            }
        }
        return result;
    }

    public List getDivisionTeams(int div) {
        List result = new ArrayList();
        for (int i=0; i<teamList.size(); i++) {
            Team t = (Team) teamList.get(i);
            if (t.getDivision() == div) {
                result.add(t);
            }
        }
        return result;
    }

    // This is used when we only have the Team name; if we had a
    // Team object we'd just call Team.getConference() directly.
    public int getConferenceOf(String team) {
        return ((Team)teamMap.get(team)).getConference();
    }

    // This is used when we only have the Team name; if we had a
    // Team object we'd just call Team.getDivision() directly.
    public int getDivisionOf(String team) {
        return ((Team)teamMap.get(team)).getDivision();
    }

    public String findName(String partial) {
        Collection a = (Collection)teamMap.values();
        Iterator i = a.iterator();
        while (i.hasNext()) {
            Team t = (Team) i.next();
            if (t.getName().startsWith(partial) ||
                t.getCity().startsWith(partial) ||
                t.getFullName().startsWith(partial)) {
                return t.getFullName();
            }
            if (partial.equals("Home") ||
                partial.equals("Visitor")) {
                // these names used by zero-element constructor
                return partial;
            }
        }
        System.out.println("Invalid name lookup " + partial);
        return null;
    }
}
```

BIBLIOGRAPHY

Alur, Deepak; John Crupi; and Dan Malks. *Core J2EE Patterns: Best Practices and Design Strategies.* Prentice Hall, 2001.

Bergsten, Hans. *JavaServer Pages.* O'Reilly & Associates, 2001.

Bloch, Joshua. *Effective Java: Programming Language Guide.* Addison-Wesley, 2001.

Burke, Eric M. *Java and XSLT.* O'Reilly & Associates, 2001.

Eckel, Bruce. *Thinking in Java, Second Edition.* Prentice Hall, 2000.

Gamma, Eric; Richard Helm; Ralph Johnson; and John Vlissides. *Design Patterns: Elements of Reusable Object-Oriented Software.* Addison-Wesley, 1995.

Girdley, Michael; Rob Woollen; Sandra L. Emerson; *J2EE Applications and BEA WebLogic Server.* Prentice Hall PTR, 2002.

Hall, Marty. *Core Servlets and JavaServer Pages.* Prentice Hall PTR, 2000.

McLaughlin, Brett. *Java and XML, First Edition.* O'Reilly & Associates, 2000.

Monson-Haefel, Richard. *Enterprise JavaBeans, Third Edition.* O'Reilly & Associates, 2001.

Monson-Haefel, Richard, and David A. Chappel. *Java Message Service.* O'Reilly & Associates, 2001.

INDEX

HP's world-class education and training offers hands on education solutions including:

- Linux
- HP-UX System and Network Administration
- Advanced HP-UX System Administration
- IT Service Management using advanced Internet technologies
- Microsoft Windows NT/2000
- Internet/Intranet
- MPE/iX
- Database Administration
- Software Development

HP's new IT Professional Certification program provides rigorous technical qualification for specific IT job roles including HP-UX System Administration, Network Management, Unix/NT Servers and Applications Management, and IT Service Management.

become hp certified

http://education.hp.com

free
subscription

Want to know about new products, services and solutions from Hewlett-Packard Company — as soon as they're invented?

Need information about new HP services to help you implement new or existing products?

Looking for HP's newest solution to a specific challenge in your business?

inview features the latest from HP!

4 easy ways to subscribe, and it's FREE:

- **fax** complete and fax the form below to (651) 430-3388, or

- **online** sign up online at www.hp.com/go/inview, or

- **email** complete the information below and send to hporders@earthlink.net, or

- **mail** complete and mail the form below to:

Twin Cities Fulfillment Center
Hewlett-Packard Company
P.O. Box 408
Stillwater, MN 55082

hp
i n v e n t

reply now and don't miss an issue!

name _____ title _____

company _____ dept./mail stop _____

address _____

city _____ state _____ zip _____

email _____ signature _____ date _____

please indicate your industry below:

☐ accounting	☐ healthcare/medical	☐ online services	☐ telecommunications
☐ education	☐ legal	☐ real estate	☐ transport and travel
☐ financial services	☐ manufacturing	☐ retail/wholesale distrib	☐ utilities
☐ government	☐ publishing/printing	☐ technical	☐ other: _____

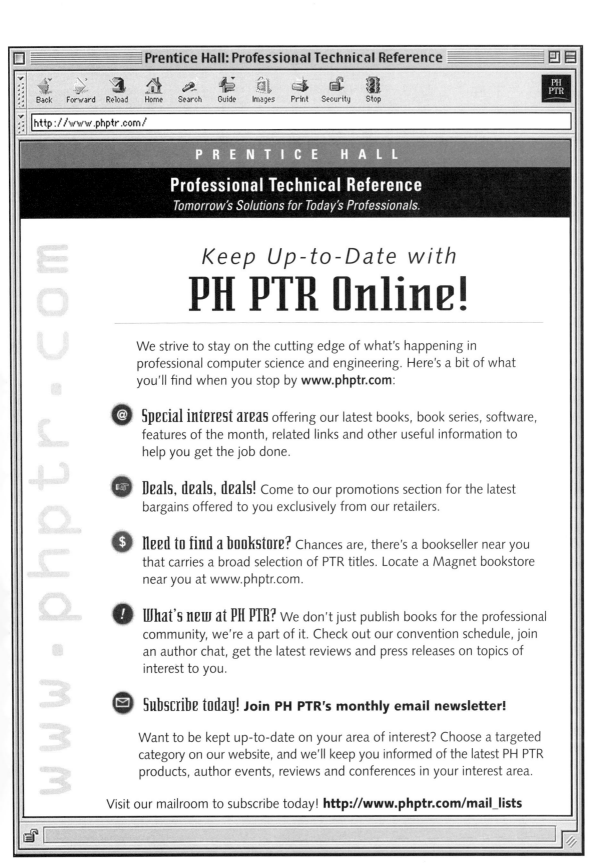

LICENSE AGREEMENT AND LIMITED WARRANTY

READ THE FOLLOWING TERMS AND CONDITIONS CAREFULLY BEFORE OPENING THIS SOFTWARE PACKAGE. THIS LEGAL DOCUMENT IS AN AGREEMENT BETWEEN YOU AND PRENTICE-HALL, INC. (THE "COMPANY"). BY OPENING THIS SEALED SOFTWARE PACKAGE, YOU ARE AGREEING TO BE BOUND BY THESE TERMS AND CONDITIONS. IF YOU DO NOT AGREE WITH THESE TERMS AND CONDITIONS, DO NOT OPEN THE SOFTWARE PACKAGE. PROMPTLY RETURN THE UNOPENED SOFTWARE PACKAGE AND ALL ACCOMPANYING ITEMS TO THE PLACE YOU OBTAINED THEM FOR A FULL REFUND OF ANY SUMS YOU HAVE PAID.

1.   **GRANT OF LICENSE:** In consideration of your payment of the license fee, which is part of the price you paid for this product, and your agreement to abide by the terms and conditions of this Agreement, the Company grants to you a nonexclusive right to use and display the copy of the enclosed software program (hereinafter the "software") on a single computer (i.e., with a single CPU) at a single location so long as you comply with the terms of this Agreement. The Company reserves all rights not expressly granted to you under this Agreement.

2.   **OWNERSHIP OF SOFTWARE:** You own only the magnetic or physical media (the enclosed software) on which the software is recorded or fixed, but the Company retains all the rights, title, and ownership to the software recorded on the original software copy(ies) and all subsequent copies of the software, regardless of the form or media on which the original or other copies may exist. This license is not a sale of the original software or any copy to you.

3.   **COPY RESTRICTIONS:** This software and the accompanying printed materials and user manual (the "Documentation") are the subject of copyright. You may not copy the Documentation or the software, except that you may make a single copy of the software for backup or archival purposes only. You may be held legally responsible for any copying or copyright infringement which is caused or encouraged by your failure to abide by the terms of this restriction.

4.   **USE RESTRICTIONS:** You may not network the software or otherwise use it on more than one computer or computer terminal at the same time. You may physically transfer the software from one computer to another provided that the software is used on only one computer at a time. You may not distribute copies of the software or Documentation to others. You may not reverse engineer, disassemble, decompile, modify, adapt, translate, or create derivative works based on the software or the Documentation without the prior written consent of the Company.

5.   **TRANSFER RESTRICTIONS:** The enclosed software is licensed only to you and may not be transferred to any one else without the prior written consent of the Company. Any unauthorized transfer of the software shall result in the immediate termination of this Agreement.

6.   **TERMINATION:** This license is effective until terminated. This license will terminate automatically without notice from the Company and become null and void if you fail to comply with any provisions or limitations of this license. Upon termination, you shall destroy the Documentation and all copies of the software. All provisions of this Agreement as to warranties, limitation of liability, remedies or damages, and our ownership rights shall survive termination.

7.   **MISCELLANEOUS:** This Agreement shall be construed in accordance with the laws of the United States of America and the State of New York and shall benefit the Company, its affiliates, and assignees.

8.   **LIMITED WARRANTY AND DISCLAIMER OF WARRANTY:** The Company warrants that the software, when properly used in accordance with the Documentation, will operate in substantial conformity with the description of the software set forth in the Documentation. The Company does not warrant that the software will meet your requirements or that the operation of the software will be uninterrupted or error-free. The Company warrants that the media on which the software is delivered shall be free from defects in materials and workmanship under normal use

for a period of thirty (30) days from the date of your purchase. Your only remedy and the Company's only obligation under these limited warranties is, at the Company's option, return of the warranted item for a refund of any amounts paid by you or replacement of the item. Any replacement of software or media under the warranties shall not extend the original warranty period. The limited warranty set forth above shall not apply to any software which the Company determines in good faith has been subject to misuse, neglect, improper installation, repair, alteration, or damage by you. EXCEPT FOR THE EXPRESSED WARRANTIES SET FORTH ABOVE, THE COMPANY DISCLAIMS ALL WARRANTIES, EXPRESS OR IMPLIED, INCLUDING WITHOUT LIMITATION, THE IMPLIED WARRANTIES OF MERCHANTABILITY AND FITNESS FOR A PARTICULAR PURPOSE. EXCEPT FOR THE EXPRESS WARRANTY SET FORTH ABOVE, THE COMPANY DOES NOT WARRANT, GUARANTEE, OR MAKE ANY REPRESENTATION REGARDING THE USE OR THE RESULTS OF THE USE OF THE SOFTWARE IN TERMS OF ITS CORRECTNESS, ACCURACY, RELIABILITY, CURRENTNESS, OR OTHERWISE.

IN NO EVENT, SHALL THE COMPANY OR ITS EMPLOYEES, AGENTS, SUPPLIERS, OR CONTRACTORS BE LIABLE FOR ANY INCIDENTAL, INDIRECT, SPECIAL, OR CONSEQUENTIAL DAMAGES ARISING OUT OF OR IN CONNECTION WITH THE LICENSE GRANTED UNDER THIS AGREEMENT, OR FOR LOSS OF USE, LOSS OF DATA, LOSS OF INCOME OR PROFIT, OR OTHER LOSSES, SUSTAINED AS A RESULT OF INJURY TO ANY PERSON, OR LOSS OF OR DAMAGE TO PROPERTY, OR CLAIMS OF THIRD PARTIES, EVEN IF THE COMPANY OR AN AUTHORIZED REPRESENTATIVE OF THE COMPANY HAS BEEN ADVISED OF THE POSSIBILITY OF SUCH DAMAGES. IN NO EVENT SHALL LIABILITY OF THE COMPANY FOR DAMAGES WITH RESPECT TO THE SOFTWARE EXCEED THE AMOUNTS ACTUALLY PAID BY YOU, IF ANY, FOR THE SOFTWARE.

SOME JURISDICTIONS DO NOT ALLOW THE LIMITATION OF IMPLIED WARRANTIES OR LIABILITY FOR INCIDENTAL, INDIRECT, SPECIAL, OR CONSEQUENTIAL DAMAGES, SO THE ABOVE LIMITATIONS MAY NOT ALWAYS APPLY. THE WARRANTIES IN THIS AGREEMENT GIVE YOU SPECIFIC LEGAL RIGHTS AND YOU MAY ALSO HAVE OTHER RIGHTS WHICH VARY IN ACCORDANCE WITH LOCAL LAW.

ACKNOWLEDGMENT

YOU ACKNOWLEDGE THAT YOU HAVE READ THIS AGREEMENT, UNDERSTAND IT, AND AGREE TO BE BOUND BY ITS TERMS AND CONDITIONS. YOU ALSO AGREE THAT THIS AGREEMENT IS THE COMPLETE AND EXCLUSIVE STATEMENT OF THE AGREEMENT BETWEEN YOU AND THE COMPANY AND SUPERSEDES ALL PROPOSALS OR PRIOR AGREEMENTS, ORAL, OR WRITTEN, AND ANY OTHER COMMUNICATIONS BETWEEN YOU AND THE COMPANY OR ANY REPRESENTATIVE OF THE COMPANY RELATING TO THE SUBJECT MATTER OF THIS AGREEMENT.

Should you have any questions concerning this Agreement or if you wish to contact the Company for any reason, please contact in writing at the address below.

Robin Short
Prentice Hall PTR
One Lake Street
Upper Saddle River, New Jersey 07458

ABOUT THE CD-ROM

The CD-ROM included with *J2EE and JAX: Designing Web Applications and Web Services* contains the following:
- Source code for all examples shown in the text of the book
- The following software from the Apache Software Foundation (http://www.apache.org):
  - Ant build utility, version 1.4.1
  - Tomcat server, version 4.0.4
  - Xerces XML parser, version 2.0.2
  - Xalan XML processor, version 2.0.0
  - Struts framework, version 1.0.2

The CD-ROM can be used on Microsoft Windows® 95/98/ME/NT/2000/XP®.

The UNIX versions of the Apache software are provided in gzipped tar format. Not all versions of tar are compatible with the Apache distributions. The HP-UX version of tar is compatible; the Solaris version is not.

If you encounter a checksum error when untarring the files, then you should use the GNU tar program (available at *http://www.gnu.org/software/tar*). Or, you can use a zip-compatible extract utility (including Java's jar utility) and unzip the Windows distribution instead; the contents are identical and only the packaging is different between the distributions.

License Agreement
Use of the software accompanying *J2EE and JAX: Designing Web Applications and Web Services* is subject to the terms of the License Agreement and Limited Warranty, found on the previous two pages.

Technical Support
Prentice Hall does not offer technical support for any of the programs on the CD-ROM. However, if the CD-ROM is damaged, you may obtain a replacement copy by sending an e-mail that describes the problem to: disc_exchange@prenhall.com.